D0071219

Contents

5

YOUTH EDUCATION
in the CHURCH

YOUTH EDUCATION in the CHURCH

Edited by

ROY B. ZUCK, Th.D.

and

WARREN S. BENSON, Ph.D.

MOODY PRESS
CHICAGO

All Scripture quotations are from the King James Version, unless otherwise noted. The use of selected references from various versions of the Bible in this publication does not necessarily imply publisher endorsement of the versions in their entirety.

All Scripture quotations taken from the New American Standard Bible, © 1960, 1962, 1963, 1968, 1971, 1972, 1973, and 1975 are used by permission of The Lockman Foundation.

All Scripture quotations from J. B. Phillips, *The New Testament in Modern English,* rev. ed., © J. B. Phillips, 1958, 1960, 1972, are used by permission of the Macmillan Company.

All Scripture quotations from *The New International Version, New Testament,* copyright © 1973 by The New York Bible Society International are used by permission of Zondervan Publishing House.

Table 1.1 (p. 21), the chart on pp. 23-24 and excerpts from *Five Cries of Youth* by Merton P. Strommen, copyright © 1974 by Merton P. Strommen. By permission of Harper & Row, Publishers, Inc.

Library of Congress Cataloging in Publication Data

Main entry under title:
Youth education in the church.

"A complete revision and a substantial expansion of Youth and the church . . . co-edited by Roy G. Irving and Roy B. Zuck . . . published in 1968."

Includes bibliographies.

1. Christian education of adolescents—Addresses, essays, lectures. 2. Christian education of young people—Addresses, essays, lectures. I. Zuck, Roy B. II. Benson, Warren S. III. Irving, Roy G. Youth and the church.

BV1475.9I7   1978   268'.433   77-18503

ISBN 0-8024-9844-2

Paperback Edition, 1984

5 6 7 Printing/BC/Year 87 86 85 84

Printed in the United States of America

Preface

AMERICAN SOCIETY is intensely competitive. From the main bunny in the nursery school play, to the retired person's place in the cafeteria line, competition is inescapable. It is a cultural value undergirded by position, power, and honor. These values have determined the middle school, high school, and college's educational form: a series of interlocking pyramids which allow only a select few to reach the apex. The grade pyramid, the athletic pyramid, the social pyramid—these and many others overlap and interlock in subtle ways. Some are encouraged by age, parental values, internal reference points, and peer pressure; but all of them shape the reality of youth's milieu. But is worth really determined by this kind of success?

Such questions must be faced by youth workers, pastors, and teachers as well as by youth themselves. It is crucial to know and understand our culture in order to minister authentically and creatively to youth. Desiring to work with the Holy Spirit forces us to create an interface between our biblical philosophy of ministry and the disciplines of philosophy, psychology, and sociology. A high view and thorough knowledge of Scripture enables one to build a well-integrated philosophy of ministry which can then approximate its greatest potential through the tandem thrusts of evangelism and edification.

Youth Education in the Church is an attempt to meet these needs. It is designed as a biblically oriented compendium of pertinent information for ministers of youth, pastors, college and seminary students, Sunday school teachers, and other youth leaders. The writers were chosen because of their direct involvement and experience with youth, in addition to their possession of a solid theoretical base. Though some of the authors are presently in academic teaching posts, almost without exception each has been an effective minister with youth in local church or parachurch ministries. Therefore the ring of reality reverberates throughout the volume. The book is a complete revision and a substantial expansion of *Youth and the Church,* which was co-edited by Roy G. Irving and Roy B. Zuck. The world of youth has changed dramatically since that volume was published in 1968.

7

While every effort was made to reduce omissions and overlapping to a minimum, a few are inevitable in such a work.

This is an unusual day for the acceleration of evangelical ministries. Such growth should humble us and cause us to be grateful. May this volume assist you in strategizing for maximum ministry with young people.

WARREN S. BENSON, Ph.D.
ROY B. ZUCK, Th.D.

1

Adolescents in an Age of Acceleration and Crisis

Warren S. Benson

THE ONLY CONSTANT in ministry with youth is the fact of change. In the late 1960s and early 1970s, rebels rocked the North American continent with violent protests and new life patterns attuned to rock music, drugs, sexual promiscuity, and mysticism. While all except the protests remain, a generation that is practical in its goals and cautious in its values is taking shape.

The bland acquiescence to adult authority for which the "silent generation" of the 1950s was remembered is gone. Yet in a way almost comparable with the World War II veterans who flocked to campuses under the GI Bill of Rights, the new generation of young people in both high school and college, think less about fun and "self-fulfillment" and more about careers and jobs.[1]

Idealism is on the rise again, not in the radical sense of yesterday's rebels, but in the candor and concern of their questions about politics, society, and religion. There is a new approval of firm discipline in the schools and at home. On the other hand, community leaders and teachers are alarmed by indications of increasing disorders among the young—alcoholism, vandalism, venereal disease, violence, and disruptive behavior in the schools.[2]

Just when Christian educators, psychologists, and sociologists think they have the youth culture characterized and postured, evidence of radical shifts emerges. And this is the challenge of reaching, teaching, and discipling young people. It is both frustrating and fulfilling. Within the

1. "A New Generation: Where It's Heading," *U.S. News and World Report*, September 6, 1976, p. 45.
2. Ibid.

WARREN S. BENSON, Ph.D., is Associate Dean of Academic Affairs and Professor of Christian Education, Trinity Evangelical Divinity School, Deerfield, Illinois, and formerly Minister of Education and Minister of Youth for twelve years in local churches.

last fifty years, in the judgment of this writer, the evangelical church and her parachurch organizations have never had a greater opportunity for touching the lives of youth both inside and outside the local expression of the body of Christ.

But why is ministry with youth so crucial? Young people are opinion-shapers. They represent a key market for business interests. Youth are the idealists who will give their lives away for Jesus Christ in ministries so diverse as missions and banking (all vocations are "sacred" for the committed Christian). Many Christian young people are hearing Aleksandr Solzhenitsyn's recent words, and desire to live strategically:

> We are approaching a major turning point in history. I can compare it only with the turning point from the Middle Ages to the modern era, a shift of civilizations. It is the sort of turning point at which the hierarchy of values to which we have been dedicated all our lives is starting to waver, and may collapse.[3]

And young people will respond to adults who consummately care enough about them to love and listen to them and who will take the time to understand their culture and problems. One has to earn the right to be heard. Young Life strategists and others have been saying this for almost forty years. The church has begun to get the message.

Yes, in the recent past the world was moving along at a reasonably slow pace. The task of growing from childhood into becoming an adult could be accomplished with relative ease and with temporal leisure. Children had time to be children, and adolescents faced few of the pressures they encounter today. But philosophical shifts in Western culture and science have abruptly changed this life-style. They have moved people forward so quickly that their ability to keep pace has left them feeling inadequate, sometimes guilty, and often frustrated.

EXISTENTIALISM AND CRISIS

Present-day American civilization is an existentialist culture. What was once an esoteric European philosophy based on the writings of Kierkegaard, Nietzsche, Heidegger, and Sartre is now a social reality in North America. To young people, who "tend to be precise indicators of what is going on within a culture,"[4] what is significant is the existential now.

Psychoanalyst Erik Erikson describes the rationale for this trend among contemporary youth:

3. Aleksandr Solzhenitsyn, "Wake Up! Wake Up!" *Reader's Digest*, December 1975, p. 72.
4. Allen J. Moore, *The Young Adult Generation* (Nashville: Abingdon, 1969), p. 16.

> First, the past grows increasingly distant from the present. . . . Social changes that would have taken a century now occur in less than a generation. As a result, the past grows progressively more different from the present in fact, and seems more remote and irrelevant psychologically. Second, the future, too, grows more remote and uncertain. Because the future directions of social change are virtually unpredictable, today's young men and women are growing into a world that is more unknowable than that confronted by any previous generation. The kind of society today's students will confront as mature adults is almost impossible for them or anyone else to anticipate. Third, the present assumes a new significance as the one time in which environment is relevant, immediate, and knowable. The past's solution to life's problems are not necessarily relevant to the here-and-now, and no one can know whether what is decided today will remain valid in tomorrow's world; hence, the present assumes an autonomy unknown in more static societies.[5]

The immediacy of the present tends to motivate young people to adopt an existential and hedonistic life-style. It encourages youth to live unexamined lives that traffic in pleasure-seeking on the path to meaninglessness. Existentialism is an empty message of despair that cultivates the use of drugs and alcohol in the hope of finding meaning in life.[6] To fail to understand the effect of existentialism is to misinterpret the present society and culture. Many adults, even parents and ministers to youth, fail to comprehend the dimensions of its impact, which in part is due to the fact that the majority of evangelical youth do not exhibit "Sunday evidence" of this pernicious philosophy.

The woeful lack of historical perspective—a continuity of meaning over time—is a direct result of existentialism. Young people do not possess the frame of reference for interpreting cultural change. If youth have little sense of history—and little motivation to acquire it—the answer does not lie simply in reminding them of the past. What is at stake, however, is a willingness to take responsibility for shaping the future. Anomie, or the prevalence of normlessness, produces people who function without goals and standards.[7] For Christian youth, this need not be! The Scriptures give purpose, goals, standards, and instruction concerning the ministry of the Holy Spirit and the church as the support system for living productive and meaningful lives (Gal 5:16, 22, 23; Eph 4:12-16; 5:18; Col 1:27-29).

5. Erik H. Erikson, *Youth, Change and Challenge* (New York: Basic Books, 1962), p. 168.
6. Lawrence O. Richards, *Youth Ministry: Its Renewal in the Local Church* (Grand Rapids: Zondervan, 1972), pp. 22-23.
7. James W. Maddock, "The Future without History: Youth's Crisis of Commitment," *Religious Education* 71 (January-February 1976):8.

SCIENCE AND ACCELERATION

Alvin Toffler has estimated that from the time a child is born today to the time he is graduated from college, the fund of the world's knowledge will have increased *fourfold*. When he is fifty years of age, the knowledge data bank will have increased thirty-two times, and 97 percent of everything known in the world will have been learned since he was born.[8]

In the field of psychology, 8,532 contributions were made to psychological literature in 1960. By 1970, the number of listings in *Psychological Abstracts* had increased to 21,722, and by the end of 1974 it reached 25,558. Psychologist James F. Adams estimates, "If I have some inkling of 20 percent of what is occurring in my profession, and an in-depth understanding of 5 percent, I should consider myself fortunate. It is just impossible for a scientist today to be broadly conversant within his chosen field of specialization."[9]

What is true for the scientist is also the experience of the industrialist, the businessman, the laborer, and the average citizen. Eminent economist and imaginative social thinker Kenneth Boulding said in 1966 that "the world of today . . . is as different from the world in which I was born as that world was from Julius Caesar's. I was born in the middle of human history, to date, roughly. Almost as much has happened since I was born as happened before."[10] Attempts to keep pace with the changes in society have created a state of myopia in one's concern for human values. This age of quick acceleration is the context in which the adolescents of today develop, a rapidly changing environment that brings a blinding bewilderment to many young people. Many adolescents, whirled in today's vortex of change, experience mental confusion, moral abandon, social estrangement, and spiritual decay.

THE ORIGINS OF ALIENATION

At the center of the adolescent context stands the home. Distinguished scholar on the family, Urie Bronfenbrenner, cites the following as evidence of the home's rapid and radical transformation: Today almost 45 percent of America's mothers work outside the home. The percent of children from divorced families is twice what it was ten years ago.[11]

The growing number of divorces is now accompanied by the phenome-

8. Alvin Toffler, *Future Shock* (New York: Random House, 1970), p. 141.
9. James F. Adams, ed., *Understanding Adolescence*, 3d ed. (Boston: Allyn & Bacon, 1975), p. 1.
10. Kenneth Boulding, "The Prospects of Economic Abundance," (Lecture at the Nobel Conference, Gustavus Adolphus College, St. Peter, Minn., 1966).
11. Urie Bronfenbrenner, "The Origins of Alienation," *Scientific American*, August 1974, pp. 53-59.

non of the unwillingness of either parent to take custody of the child. Women are fleeing without waiting for a formal separation. In addition, infanticide and child abuse are dramatically on the rise.

When children or teens are not in school, they spend increasing amounts of time in the company of only their age-mates. The vacuum created by the withdrawal of their parents and other adults has been filled by the informal peer group. Their attachment to their peers is influenced more by a lack of attention and love at home than by the positive attraction of the peer group itself. In fact, these children and youth have a negative view of their friends and of themselves. In discussing college youth, sociologist David Riesman has pointed out that as adult authority disintegrates, the young are more and more the captives of each other. When adult control disappears, the young's control of their peers intensifies.[12]

Over the last three decades thousands of investigations have been conducted to identify the developmental antecedents of behavioral disorders and social pathology. The results indicate one omnipresent, overriding factor: family disorganization. The forces of disorganization come primarily from the circumstances in which the family finds itself and from the way of life that is imposed on it by those circumstances.

> Specifically, when those circumstances and the way of life they generate undermine relationships of trust and emotional security between family members, when they make it difficult for parents to care for, educate, and enjoy their children, when there is no support or recognition from the outside world for one's role as a parent and when time spent with one's family means frustration of career, personal fulfillment, and peace of mind, then the development of the child is adversely affected.[13]

That may be a gross understatement. The situation in the home, whether Christian or not, is grim and grave. The secularist is not alone in his struggle for answers. The notable studies by James Colman[14] and Christopher Jencks[15] demonstrates rather conclusively that the panacea is not the public school, nor is this author convinced that it is necessarily only the Christian day school. The latter has flourished because of (1) the near collapse of the public schools and (2) the recognition on the part of Christian parents of the need for an additional spiritual support system. However, more analysis is in order.

12. David Riesman, "The Young Are Captives of Each Other: A Conversation with David Riesman and T. George Harris," *Psychology Today,* October 1969, pp. 28-31, 64-67.
13. Bronfenbrenner, "The Origins of Alienation," p. 56.
14. James S. Coleman, *The Adolescent Society* (New York: Free Press, 1963).
15. Christopher Jencks et al., *Inequality* (New York: Harper & Row, 1974).

THE IDENTITY CRISIS

In the midst of these dilemmas that stalk the adolescent, none looms as large as his task of self-definition. There are a number of opinions advanced by psychologists and psychoanalysts as to how the adolescent achieves self-identity. The basic concepts of a few of the representatives of the various schools and modes of thought are given.

It is with Erik Erikson that one generally associates the term "identity crisis." To the question of what constitutes identity, Erikson initially was purposefully vague. However, on close examination he refers to identity as "an unconscious striving for continuity of experience,"[16] or more significantly, as "a conscious sense of individual uniqueness."[17] He remarks,

> Individually speaking, identity includes, but is more than, the sum of all successive identifications of those earlier years when the child wanted to be, and often was forced to become, like the people he depended upon. Identity is a unique product, which meets a crisis to be solved only in new identifications with age-mates and with leader figures outside of the family.[18]

In adolescence the youngster's intellect has matured sufficiently for him to perceive himself differently from his childhood days and begin to determine his eventual choices in life. Only at adolescence, according to Erikson, has he encountered serious pressure that motivates him to start defining himself and ultimately settle on an identity. Erikson believes that each individual is unique, and that even within the same culture, no two people ever develop in quite the same manner for each resolves his problems somewhat differently. Therefore, adolescence may be turbulent and conflict-ridden or it may not. Erikson has said, "The task is to be performed here by the young person and his society is formidable. It necessitates in different individuals and in different societies, great variations in the duration, intensity, and ritualization of adolescence.[19]

Edgar Friedenberg, however, postulates that there must be conflict between the adolescent and society as a consequence of his task of self-definition.

> Adolescence is the period during which a young person learns who he is, and what he really feels. It is the time during which he differentiates himself from his culture, though on the culture's terms. It is the age at which, by becoming a person in his own right, he becomes capable of

16. Erik Erikson, *Identity: Youth and Crisis* (New York: Norton, 1968), p. 208.
17. Ibid.
18. Ibid., p. 87.
19. Ibid., p. 155.

deeply felt relationships to other individuals perceived clearly as such. . . . Must there be conflict between the adolescent and society? The point is that adolescence *is* conflict—protracted conflict—between the individual and society.[20]

By conflict, according to Friedenberg, an individual learns the complex, subtle, and precious difference between himself and his environment. But conflict is not war nor does it even necessarily involve hostile action. Delinquency and apathy are not aspects of this conflict but rather the consequences of the conflict gone terribly wrong. By wisdom and patience, the trauma encountered by adolescents through the task of self-definition may be understood and restored to a somewhat fruitful process.

Albert Bandura has questioned the stage theory assumption that adolescence is a turbulent decade inevitably characterized by "storm and stress, tension, rebellion, dependency conflicts, peer-group conformity, black leather jackets, and the like."[21] While he does not deny that some of these kinds of behavior occur in some individuals, such behaviors are viewed as being due to cultural conditioning and social experimentation rather than as inevitable developmental phenomena characteristic of the period of adolescence per se. Bandura suggests that aggressive behavior in adolescence—when it does occur—is viewed as the consequence of specific antecedent conditions in the child-rearing pattern and the parent-child relationship such as dependency training, socialization pressure, imitation and modeling, rather than as the result of adolescent adjustment problems.

Bandura is convinced that the prototypical adolescent with his turmoils and anxieties, sexual tensions, compulsive conformity, and acute identity crisis so frequently referred to in the literature fits only the "deviant 10 percent of the adolescent population."[22] The myth that such behavior is believed to be a normal aspect of adolescent development is more due to cultural expectations and the representation of youth in movies, literature, and other mass media than based on actual facts.

Daniel Offer states in his thorough ten-year study of adolescent boys, that responsible, happy, well-adjusted, parent-respecting youth are more common than had been assumed. He concludes his chapter on adolescent turmoil as follows:

> Studies of normal populations that exhibit little behavioral disequilibrium might eventually lead to the concept that adolescence as a period of

20. Edgar Z. Friedenberg, *The Vanishing Adolescent* (New York: Dell, 1959), pp. 29, 32.
21. Albert Bandura, "The Stormy Decade: Fact or Fiction?" *Psychology in the School* 1 (1964):224.
22. Ibid.

growth can be undergone without serious disruptions between the generations or between the adolescent and his former identity. The transition
to adulthood may be accomplished gradually, but accomplished all the
same. Our findings emphatically suggest that a state of inner turmoil need
not be the password of adolescence.[23]

William Glasser is of the opinion that young people achieve identity
only through personal fulfillment. His perspective came from this cata-
lytic statement by Marshall McLuhan, "From Tokyo to Paris to Colombia,
youth mindlessly acts its identity quest in the theatre of the streets searching not for goals, but for roles, striving for an identity that eludes them."[24]
From Glasser's vantage point, almost everyone aspires to live in a way that
can provide a happy, successful, pleasurable belief in himself. Role, or
identity, is now so important for the young that it must be achieved in
some degree before they will work hard for any goal. Glasser feels that
this new priority in human motivation cannot be ignored. In his judgment, schools and families that function as if this new motivational sequence did not exist are now in serious trouble.[25]

THE BIBLICAL POINT OF REFERENCE

From each of these educators, psychologists, and psychoanalysts profound and significant insights can be gained. However, each has a faulty
understanding of the nature of man. Following in the footsteps of Jean
Jacques Rousseau, John Dewey, and Sigmund Freud, they fail to discern
the sinfulness of the child and adolescent. To them, all behavior can be
explained in cultural, psychological, and sociological terms. However, a
biblical perspective enables a youth minister, a pastor, a psychologist, and
a lay leader to present the redemptive message in Jesus Christ and to see
genuine behavioral change take place. Understanding God's point of
view on the basis of the inerrant Scriptures opens vistas of thinking and
the development of a biblical philosophy of ministry to youth—to erratic
but exuberant junior highers, to searching yet enthusiastic high schoolers,
and to philosophical but practical collegians and young careerists.

Enabling one to build a biblical philosophy of youth ministry is the
objective of this book. But to close one's mind to the contributions of
scholars regarding the developmental patterns of persons, the milieu of
culture, and the philosophical movements of the times is simply evan-

23. Daniel Offer, *The Psychological World of the Teen-ager: A Study of Normal
    Adolescent Boys*, rev. ed. (New York: Basic Books, 1973), p. 192.
24. William Glasser, *The Identity Society*, rev. ed. (New York: Harper & Row, 1975),
    p. 2.
25. Ibid.; see also chapter 6, "Adolescents in Socio-Psychological Perspective," for
    conclusions regarding the identity crisis, and for an agenda for ministry that
    arises from it.

gelical provincialism and obscurantism. While discussing Christian education, which is what building a biblical philosophy of ministry is all about, Frank E. Gaebelein states,

> For Christian education, therefore, to adopt as its unifying principle Christ and the Bible means nothing short of the recognition that *all truth is God's truth*. It is no accident that St. Paul, setting before the Philippian church a charter for Christian thought, wrote: "Finally, brethren, whatsoever things are true . . . think on these things" (Phil 4:8). He knew that Christian truth embraces all truth, and that nothing true is outside the scope of Christianity. . . . But at the same time we have fallen into the error of failing to see as clearly as we should that there are areas of truth not fully explicated in Scripture and that these, too, are part of God's truth.[26]

The "center of certitude"[27] comes from God in His Book. One's understanding of man (anthropology), how his basic needs may be met (bibliology and methodology), and the place of the body of Christ particularly in its local church embodiment (ecclesiology) are exegeted from the Scriptures. The foundation and superstructure for ministry to youth must be biblical.[28] The contributions of developmental psychology, for example, enrich and sharpen one's understanding of young people in order to minister to them with greater skill and a more profound impact. Lawrence Richards has observed,

> It is vital in planning for ministry with youth that we understand the styles in which youth tend to think and feel, and shape our ministries to what they *are*, not to what we might think they ought to be. It is particularly important when we examine the values of youth that we understand the cultural forces that affect them.[29]

THE FIVE CRIES OF YOUTH

Scholarly research on youth in the church has never been the forte of the evangelical movement. Until Zuck and Getz's solid contribution, *Christian Youth: An In-Depth Study,* appeared in 1968, there was virtually little valid research except among Lutheran young people.* How-

---

26. Frank E. Gaebelein, *The Pattern of God's Truth* (Chicago: Moody, 1968), pp. 20-21 (italics in the original).
27. The phrase is D. Elton Trueblood's, *A Place to Stand* (New York: Harper & Row, 1974), p. 37.
28. See chapter 2, "The Biblical Basis of Youth Work."
29. Richards, *Youth Ministry,* p. 14.
   *Roy B. Zuck and Gene A. Getz, eds., *Christian Youth: An In-Depth Study* (Chicago: Moody, 1968), and the work of Merton P. Strommen are the exceptions. Zuck and Getz, with the support of the then active National Sunday School Association's Research Commission, studied three thousand evangelical teenagers. Merton P.

ever, it became obsolete quickly (as does any youth research) because of
the rapid historical and cultural changes that evolved. While his study
was completed several years ago (research done in 1970, published in
1974), Merton P. Strommen has given the religious community excep-
tionally precise and insightful data in his *Five Cries of Youth*.[30] He reported on his study of 7,050 high school students from more than a dozen
denominations, one parachurch organization (Young Life), and young
people from groups with no discernible religious affiliation. Twenty-five
clusters or characteristics (e.g., family unity, lack of self-confidence, moral
responsibility) were cross-referenced and five basic concerns of young
people emerged: self-esteem, family unity and well-being, welfare of people, achieving favor, and personal faith. Dissatisfaction with adult institutions was prominent. While some of that disenchantment can be explained by virtue of the study's having been done at the zenith of student
unrest and campus violence in 1970, the youth have potently poked holes
in the adult security blanket. In the next few pages of this chapter, the
first "cry" will be discussed at some length, but the other four will be
treated in brief fashion.

The *first cry*, self-hatred, rises out of feelings of low self-esteem, self-
criticism, and loneliness. Sometimes this concern is difficult to identify.
One may notice an individual who acts as though he is the most important person in the group. There is a phoniness in his behavior. His feelings of inadequacy prompt his look-at-me actions. The home and the
church should construct congenial atmospheres in which reaffirming and
empathetic adults may minister. Youth can then gain new outlooks on
life and change their self-perceptions while guilt and anxiety are dimin-
ished.

Strommen suggests that a philosophy of youth ministry should be an
extension of one's theology. Therefore, the major thrust should not be
on problem solving (e.g., overcoming fears, gaining confidence, and improving one's self-concept), "but on helping youth to become aware of the
possibilities found in a relationship with Jesus Christ."[31]

This means communicating to them that they are loved by God and the
people of God, that they are important, have potential, and can look forward to growth and positive change. Strommen observes that a change

---

Strommen has no peer in statistical research with church youth; but until the study
published in *Five Cries of Youth* (New York: Harper & Row, 1974), his subjects were
almost totally restricted to the Lutheran communions. See Robert J. Havighurst and
Barry Keating's chapter, "The Religion of Youth," in *Research on Religious Development*, edited by Merton P. Strommen (New York: Hawthorn, 1971), to sense the
frustration regarding the dearth of reliable data on religious youth.

30. Strommen, *Five Cries of Youth*.
31. Ibid., p. 30.

in their awareness will not come through indoctrination or the repetition of words and phrases, but through the "living words" of people who embody God's message. While it is important that those working with youth be knowledgeable concerning Scripture, the reality seen in their lives is inestimable. Modeling the message is still the greatest method.

Social learning theorist Albert Bandura has demonstrated that the effectiveness of the model in producing matching responses in the observer depends on a variey of factors, such as the model's attractiveness, prestige, competence, and his willingness to dispense rewards and praise. If the model has some characteristics in common with the observing subject, the young person is more inclined to imitate the model's behavior. The apostle Paul was far ahead of the learning theoreticians when he wrote to the Philippians, "The things you have learned and received and heard and seen in me, practice these things . . ." (Phil 4:9, NASB) , and to the Corinthians, "Be imitators of me, just as I also am of Christ" (1 Cor 11:1, NASB) .

The *second cry* of youth is that of being psychological orphans. Strommen comments on this in these stabbing words:

> The most poignant cry is the sob of despair or shriek of sheer frustration among youth living in atmospheres of parental hatred and distrust. Often it ends in running away from home, delinquent behavior, suicide, or other self-destructive behavior.[32]

Strommen presents the four major characteristics of such homes: family pressures, distress over relationships with parents, disappointment in family unity, and a negative perception of one's family social concerns. One aspect will be cited.

Emerging from the youth's self-reports are a number of psychological issues.

> The one that most strongly predicts family disunity is the simple statement "My father and mother do not get along. This bothers me." It is at least twenty times more powerful a predictor of family disunity than the fact of divorce. When parents are at odds with each other, youth are most likely to report a fractured or disunited home. This is far and away the most decisive variable in identifying a family that is bleeding and youth who are hurting.[33]

It is axiomatic that the most important thing a father can do for his children is love their mother.

The *third cry* is that of social protest. The high watermark in youth's unrest and rebellion came at Kent State University on May 4, 1970, when

---

32. Ibid., p. 33.
33. Ibid., p. 44.

four young people were killed and nine were wounded following an order for the National Guard to fire on anti-war demonstrators. In response, on May 10, 448 universities and colleges were either closed or on strike. The spirit of protest also permeated many high schools. The mid-1970s seem to have silenced or forgotten the memory of this source of national polarization. But as Strommen states:

> The voice of social conscience is not always loud and insistent. . . . The signals of social concern that high-school students send require a special alertness. They may come subtly, infrequently, or perhaps in such an exaggerated form that the impulse is to laugh and forget them, or, perhaps, to refuse to allow them to be put into action through the church.[34]

Some adults are almost relieved to know that this study indicates that many of the socially concerned are "solid humanists who do not believe in the gospel" and that they are some of the unbelieving critics of the church. However, those same people are chagrined to know that an equal proportion of youth who take this same stance "reflect a knowledge of the Christian faith and a love for their church."[35] Youth of both motivations are sufficiently bright, sophisticated, and mature to have observed their church's track record in the social area. The sensitive youth worker or parent will be alert to indications of concern and will provide avenues for expression of them. Youth are very critical of a lack of involvement.

The *fourth cry* is that of the prejudiced. This cry also has the distinct overtones of the days of campus unrest. Strommen summarizes their findings in this manner:

> About one in seven church youth embody the prejudice that haunts the Christian church. They differ from other church youth in their consistent belief that acceptance with God is earned by meritorious living. They are less reflective and thoughtful and hence prone to think in stereotypes and make prejudgments. They rank lower than other church youth in academic achievement and are somewhat more self-seeking in their values.[36]

This author is inclined to think that the researchers were unduly harsh on conservative evangelical youth in their comments concerning the fact that youth who speak of "being saved" believe that a successful Christian life consists of living by a set of rules and standards and their innuendo that these young people try "to pad their scores in their little Christian game" with God.

34. Ibid., p. 53.
35. Ibid.
36. Ibid., p. 82.

The *fifth cry* is that of the joyous, Christian youth who are deeply committed to Jesus Christ. "As a minority group (about one-third of all church youth), they exemplify in what they value, believe, perceive, and do the impact of identifying with a personal God and a believing community."[37] They have found a meaning and value system that brings order into their lives and gives answers to ultimate questions of existence. But they have not solved all their problems either. Those who profess a personal faith in Jesus Christ are as bothered by a lack of self-confidence, academic difficulties, classroom relationships, and national issues as those who do not. However, their faith profoundly affects not only their belief and value system but also their ethical behavior, concern for others, and

TABLE 1.1

WHAT HIGHLY COMMITTED YOUTH WANT MOST

(N = 918)

Activity	Percentage Declaring Much Interest
To experience a closer relationship with God.	93
Meetings where I experience the presence of God.	87
To learn to speak naturally and intelligently about my faith.	86
Guidance in finding out what God's will is for my life.	86
To learn how to make friends and be a friend.	81
To learn to know and understand the Bible better.	81
To find meaning and purpose in my life.	80
To experience acceptance in a group of people who really care about each other.	77
To learn to be more of the real me when I am with other people.	77
Group meetings where people feel free to say what they really think and are honest about what bothers them.	76
To learn how to be a friend to those who are lonely and rejected.	76
To learn what a Christian really is.	74
Recreation and social activities where youth get acquainted.	74
To find a good basis for deciding what is right and wrong.	72
To learn to get along better with members of the opposite sex.	72
To learn about Christian views of sex, dating, and marriage.	72
To develop greater ability to show a loving concern for others (both near and far away).	70

NOTE: Reprinted from Merton P. Strommen, *Five Cries of Youth* (New York: Harper & Row, 1974), p. 103. Used by permission of Harper & Row, Publishers, Inc.

37. Ibid., p. 92.

attitudes toward parents and toward their local church. Interestingly, the data indicates "that 'faith-is-important' youth and 'saved' youth rank much higher in self-regard. Because feelings of worth are a vital ingredient in the adolescent's experience, this is an important difference."[38] Unsurprisingly, youth who are active with God's people are willing to delay gratification of premarital sex and they are more mature and socially adequate than nonattenders. They are not "losers"—as some have supposed.[39] Their attitudes and desires, revealed effectively in table 1.1, should be given study by those involved in a ministry to church young people.

This writer is of the opinion that Strommen and his associates have made an unusually perceptive contribution to understanding what church youth are thinking and where they are.† The data must be analyzed with care for each youth ministry is different, and obviously any single group of young people are only reflected in part in this study.[40]

THE TRIO OF TORNADOES: ALCOHOL, DRUGS, AND SEX

Into the already difficult psychological period of storm and stress in adolescence come the devastating threats of alcohol, drugs, and sex. Because their powerful presence is constantly recognized by the popular press as well as by academia, only a brief discussion will be given here.

For a decade, hundreds of thousands of American youth made headlines with riots, open sex, free use of drugs, and hostility toward authority. To many adults, it seemed that older and firmer standards would disappear forever. Now young people in significant numbers are beginning to return to more traditional values. One national survey of hundreds of youth indicates that homes, churches, and schools again are the primary sources of education and morality.[41]

On the national scene, despite the furor over marijuana, LSD, heroin, and tranquilizers, alcohol remains the leading drug of American teenagers. Authorities on drinking believe that alcohol abuse has contributed to the fact that from 1960 to 1968 deaths from cirrhosis of the liver rose

38. Ibid., p. 98.
39. Ibid., pp. 99-101.

†Four questions were asked of successful church youth workers by Merton P. Strommen and his associates: "What ways of approaching youth have you found helpful? How do you get next to them? What are you doing to accomplish your purposes with youth? If you were to describe the secret of your effectiveness, what are some of the ways of working with people that you have found effective?" The insightful results are tabulated on pages 119-21 of *Five Cries of Youth*.

40. For further details on the findings in Strommen's work *Five Cries of Youth* the reader is referred to chapter 5, "Research on Adolescent Religiosity," by J. Roland Fleck. Fleck's chapter reports the research results, whereas the foregoing pages have attempted to summarize some of the implications of Strommen's book for present-day youth ministry.
41. "A New Generation: Where It's Heading," p. 48.

500 percent for males ages fifteen to twenty-four. Studies of alcohol consumption in Massachusetts and Mississippi indicate that teenagers with drinking problems make up between 2 percent and 5 percent of the adolescent population, or about the same as adults.[42] It seems likely that a major factor in the meteoric increase of youthful alcohol abuse is related to parental acceptance of alcohol. While parents strongly disapprove of illicit drugs, by contrast they have almost condoned alcoholic usage with a sigh of relief. For adolescents below legal drinking age, alcohol is the most frequently used illegal drug. With the destructiveness of alcohol amply documented, it seems particularly tragic that young people are turning to alcohol with parental approval![43]

As in the area of alcohol, no recent studies have been done exclusively with evangelical youth regarding drugs and premarital sex. However, using the broad church perspective of a study of eight hundred students by Donald Chipman and Clyde Parker in a midwestern liberal arts college will give perspective. The random sample was divided into four groups:

> (1) regular users of marijuana; (2) casual users; (3) experimental users (e.g., tried it once or twice); and (4) nonusers. They found that the four groups were distinctly different in some areas and quite alike in others.
>
> The most striking contrasts were between group one (regular users) and group four (nonusers). Group one members did not attend church frequently, if at all, and held a wide range of nontraditional as well as agnostic beliefs. Nonusers attended church regularly and espoused traditional beliefs about the supreme deity. Following are other controls.

Frequent Users of Marijuana	*Nonusers of Marijuana*
Highest use of strong and dangerous drugs.	Little use of drugs (except in diet pills).
Highest alcohol usage and for some a problem.	Least use of alcohol.
More active politically.	Least active politically.
Most critical of father's upbringing.	Least critical of father's upbringing.
Lowest grades.	Highest grades.
Most who feel estranged from their families.	Fewest who feel estranged from their families.
Most cynical about life.	Least cynical about life.

42. Strommen, *Five Cries of Youth*, p. 148.
43. Randall R. Kleinhesselink, Clarke St. Dennis, and Herbert J. Cross, "Contemporary Drug Issues Involving Youth," in *Understanding Adolescence*, ed. James F. Adams, p. 382.

The authors identify the nonusers as the most distinctive of the four groups. Members of this group appear well adjusted, show confidence in what they are doing, and are willing to deal with life as they find it. The high correlation between religiosity and nonusage confirms our finding on the probable impact of a personal faith on youth's life-style and world view.[44]

The close tie between the use of drugs and absence of faith suggests that religious commitment is, for many, the way of release from drug abuse. Using psychotherapy is obviously inferior to spiritual convictions as a means of reducing and eliminating drug abuse.

A MINISTRY TO WHOM?

On close examination a ministry to youth must inevitably include their parents as well. As Strommen summarized:

> It should not be assumed that adults have outgrown youth issues. On the contrary, the preceding analyses show how much adults are linked to youth needs.
> Low self-esteem is probably passed on from parents. Family disunity centers in parental conflict. Social concern is characterized by youth's sharp criticism of congregational adults' lack of manifest caring. Prejudice is found more readily among adults than among youth. Loss of faith is an issue that is no respecter of age.[45]

In short, while one's major thrust should be with young people, a concern for and a ministry to adults moves in tandem with that of youth. Why not a retreat for parents of teenagers? Or courses such as "Discipling Youth in the Home"? Or private sessions with the parents of a teenager? These are no longer optional but mandatory.[46]

As a minister of youth, one should be aware of the breadth of the teenagers' culture and pressures. They face ominous problems in alcohol, sex, satanism, and Eastern religions. Yet they possess the resilience and potential to rise above these menaces, particularly when they appropriate the power and meaningfulness that a relationship with Jesus Christ offers. That relationship begins by building bridges of friendship and concern that grow into a context for trusting Christ as Saviour and Lord. These words descriptive of Paul's ministry should characterize each youth worker's concern: "The ultimate aim of the Christian ministry, after all is to produce the love which springs from a pure heart, a good conscience and a genuine faith" (1 Tim 1:5, Phillips).

44. Strommen, *Five Cries of Youth*, p. 147.
45. Ibid., p. 125.
46. Also see chapter 33, "Working with Parents of Youth."

FOR FURTHER READING

Adams, James F. *Understanding Adolescence.* 3d ed. Boston: Allyn & Bacon, 1975.

Blum, Richard H. *The Dream Sellers: Perspectives on Drug Dealers.* San Francisco: Jossey-Bass, 1972.

Briscoe, Stuart. *Where Was the Church When the Youth Exploded?* Grand Rapids: Zondervan, 1972.

Carroll, John L., and Ignatius, Keith L. *Youth Ministry: Sunday, Monday, and Every Day.* Valley Forge, Pa.: Judson, 1972.

Clark, Ted. *The Oppression of Youth.* New York: Harper & Row, 1975.

Duska, Ronald, and Whelan, Mariellen. *Moral Development: A Guide to Piaget and Kohlberg.* New York: Paulist, 1975.

Elkind, David. *Children and Adolescents: Interpretive Essays on Jean Piaget.* New York: Oxford, 1970.

Erikson, Erik H. *The Challenge of Youth.* Garden City, N.Y.: Anchor, 1965.

———. *Identity: Youth and Crisis.* New York: Norton, 1968.

Gleason, John F., Jr. *Growing Up to God.* Nashville: Abingdon, 1975.

Goldman, Ronald. *Religious Thinking from Childhood to Adolescence.* New York: Seabury, 1968.

Guinness, Os. *The Dust of Death.* Downers Grove, Ill.: InterVarsity, 1973.

Hendin, Herbert. *The Age of Sensation.* New York: Norton, 1975.

Henry, Carl F. H. et al. *The Quest for Reality: Christianity and the Counter-Culture.* Downers Grove, Ill.: InterVarsity, 1973.

Hoge, Dean R. *Commitment on Campus: Changes in Religion and Values over Five Decades.* Philadelphia: Westminster, 1974.

Joy, Donald A. *Meaningful Learning in the Church.* Winona Lake, Ind.: Light & Life, 1969.

Keniston, Kenneth. *The Young Radicals.* New York: Harcourt, Brace, 1968.

Little, Sara. *Youth, World, and the Church.* Richmond: John Knox, 1972.

Mead, Margaret. *Culture and Commitment.* Garden City, N.Y.: Doubleday, 1970.

Offer, Daniel. *The Psychological World of the Teenager.* Rev. ed. New York: Basic Books, 1973.

Powell, John. *Why Am I Afraid to Tell You Who I Am?* Niles, Ill.: Argus, 1969.

Reich, Charles A. *The Greening of America.* New York: Random House, 1970.

Richards, Lawrence O. *A Theology of Christian Education.* Grand Rapids: Zondervan, 1975.

———. *Youth Ministry: Its Renewal in the Local Church.* Grand Rapids: Zondervan, 1972.

Schaeffer, Francis. *The Church at the End of the Twentieth Century.* Downers Grove, Ill.: InterVarsity, 1970.

———. *Escape from Reason.* Downers Grove, Ill.: InterVarsity, 1969.

———. *The God Who Is There.* Downers Grove, Ill.: InterVarsity, 1968.

Snyder, Ross A. *Young People and Their Culture.* Nashville: Abingdon, 1969.

Strommen, Merton P. *Bridging the Gap*. Minneapolis: Augsburg, 1973.

——. *Five Cries of Youth*. New York: Harper & Row, 1974.

——. *Profiles of Church Youth*. St. Louis: Concordia, 1963.

——. *Research on Religious Development*. New York: Hawthorn, 1971.

——. *A Study of Generations*. Minneapolis: Augsburg, 1972.

Talbot, Gordon. *The Breakdown of Authority*. Old Tappan, N.J.: Revell, 1976.

"The New Youth." Special report. *Life*, fall 1977.

Towns, Elmer. *Successful Biblical Youth Work*. Nashville: Impact, 1973.

Ward, Ted. *Memo for the Underground*. Wheaton, Ill.: Creation House, 1971.

Woods, C. Stacey. *Some Ways of God*. Downers Grove, Ill.: InterVarsity, 1975.

Yankelovich, Daniel. *The New Morality: a Profile of American Youth in the Seventies*. New York: McGraw-Hill, 1974.

Zuck, Roy B., and Clark, Robert E., eds. *Childhood Education in the Church*. Chicago: Moody, 1975.

Zuck, Roy B., and Getz, Gene A., eds. *Adult Education in the Church*. Chicago: Moody, 1970.

Zuck, Roy B., and Getz, Gene A. *Christian Youth: An In-Depth Study*. Chicago: Moody, 1968.

2

The Biblical Basis of Youth Work

Kenneth O. Gangel

SCRIPTURE REVEALS the truth about God, the truth about man, and the truth about the relationship between the two. The truth about God, of course, is that He is holy, infinite, eternal, and loving. The truth about man is that he is sinful, finite, temporal, and very much distant from real love in his natural state. The glorious crown of biblical truth is the story of redemption, telling us how the holy God can sustain a relationship with sinful man. Of course the whole plan of salvation with all of its wonderful aspects and eternal glories is God's pattern for this relationship.

But what does this have to do with working with young people? Our whole teaching and guiding ministry must be based on truth and must seek to lead teens into right relationships with God and others. Therefore because the Bible is the only Sourcebook of truth about God and about man's relation to Him, a solid foundation in God's written Word provides the proper framework for any Christian approach to working with young people. Certainly youth workers can gain much from psychology, education, and sociology. These can enhance one's knowledge of youth and youth work. But evangelicals seek to evaluate these principles in the light of God's Word.

But there are differing viewpoints in our day regarding the nature of the Bible. What in essence is the evangelical position on which youth work is to be based? Perhaps it can best be summarized by four words.

The first word is *revelation*. This pertains to the divine message itself. The self-communicating God chose to allow man to know something about His nature and His work. The Bible is God's written revelation to man.[1] The second word, *inspiration,* focuses our attention on the written

---

1. The Bible is more than an instrument of, witness to, or record of revelation. See James I. Packer, "Contemporary Views of Revelation," in *Revelation and the Bible,* ed. Carl F. H. Henry (Grand Rapids: Baker, 1958), pp. 89-104; and Robert Preus, "The Doctrine of Revelation in Contemporary Theology," *Bulletin of the Evangelical Theological Society* 9 (Summer 1966): 111-23.

KENNETH O. GANGEL, Ph.D., is President of Miami Christian College, Miami, Florida.

form of the revelation. Peter wrote, "No prophecy ever resulted from human design; instead, holy men from God spoke as they were carried along by the Holy Spirit" (2 Pet 1:21, Berkeley). God was concerned not only with the origin of the message but also with the way it was recorded. Paul wrote to young Timothy, "Every scripture is God-breathed, and is profitable for teaching, for conviction, for improvement, for training with respect to righteousness, in order that the man of God may be complete, fitted out for every good work" (2 Tim 3:16-17, *Expanded New Testament* by K. S. Wuest).

The third word which relates to our position on the Bible is the word *preservation.* A game sometimes played at parties is the one in which one person originates a story, whispers it to the person next to him, and so on around the room. By the time the story reaches the last person in the line, it is grossly perverted and the end result is nothing like the original version. This is exactly what could have happened to Scripture if God had not superintended the transmission of His written Word down through the ages. No book on earth has been more often translated, more abused and rejected, confiscated and burned, and yet exists today in a form which adequately gives the originally written message. God has preserved His Word.

The fourth word, *illumination,* is related to the reader of the message. As a believer studies the Word of God, the Holy Spirit works in his mind and heart to enable him to understand and live out God's truth. Apart from the ministry of the Holy Spirit, we would be unable by our natural minds to understand the Bible. God has not left Himself without a witness; in this confused world He has provided a solid foundation for our service for Jesus Christ. That foundation is the Bible, God's truth *revealed, inspired, preserved,* and *illuminated* by the Holy Spirit.

THE BIBLE AND THEOLOGY IN CHRISTIAN EDUCATION

A young pastor, candidating at a small rural church, met with the deacons to ask and answer questions. The conversation turned to a discussion of the type of preaching the young man would engage in if he were to come; and one of the brethren indicated his preference by saying, "Well, don't give us any theology; just preach the Bible!" Unfortunately many Christians share the view of this gentleman though they might not word it so bluntly.

Some people have the false notion that there is a "great gulf fixed" between the Bible and theology, and that the latter is relatively undesirable. However, one cannot give consideration to the things of God without dealing in the realm of theology. Theology simply has to do with the truth about God; and as soon as a person says, "Christ died for our sins" or "Ye must be born again," he is speaking theologically.

Christian education, if it is to be true *Christian* education, must have a solid theological basis. Actually, the two cannot be severed. What one believes about theology affects what he does in Christian education—including youth work. Therefore an adequate program of youth work in the church must be based on a solid foundation of biblical theology. Three reasons justify this statement.

THEOLOGY DETERMINES OBJECTIVES

Perhaps the most basic question that can be asked of any educational institution is whether or not it is fulfilling its stated objectives.[2] This question also has great importance for any church or for any part of its educational program. It is imperative that every youth group have objectives that are "brief enough to be remembered . . . clear enough to be written down . . . [and] specific enough to be achieved."[3] Such objectives can spell out what one expects to achieve in his group.

For the Christian, the determining factor in the formulation of objectives is his relationship to God through His eternal Word. For example, if a youth worker says, "We want our youth group to be evangelistic so that other teenagers will find Christ through the witness of our own young people," he is suggesting that evangelism is one of the objectives for which a youth group exists. He has verbalized a concept which has many theological ramifications: (1) people are in need of salvation; (2) this salvation is obtainable; (3) Christian young people should communicate these facts to others. Another church which is not evangelical in its theology might state its objectives in terms of social fitness or relationship to the church as an organization rather than in terms of regeneration and commitment to Jesus Christ. The most important factor, therefore, in determining objectives for youth work is one's view of theology and his relation to the Word of God.

THEOLOGY DETERMINES PHILOSOPHY

J. Oliver Buswell, Jr., wrote:

> Our generation needs an orderly system of thought related to the factual realities which surround us. It is my conviction that Christian philosophy has the answer, and that it will not be impossible to present this answer in terms of our current problems and in the language of our contemporaries.

2. See chapter 3, "Objectives and Standards for Youth Work" and chapter 14, "Discipling of Youth."
3. Findley B. Edge, *Teaching for Results* (Nashville: Broadman, 1956), pp. 92-93.

. . . The Christian philosophy of being begins with the Eternal Being of God. It then includes the objective reality of the created world and of created man in unique relationship with God. . . . It can be shown that every philosophy of ethics . . . which leaves God out of consideration, leads to a contradiction; and that the holy character of God, revealed by His will, is the only consistent criterion of good and evil, and right and wrong.[4]

These sentences make it plain that the Christian cannot divorce his theology from his philosophy of life. One's outlook on life will be determined by his understanding of God, His Word, and His world. But what does philosophy have to do with planning interesting lessons and meetings for youth?

In a very real sense it has everything to do with youth work—not only in the matter of planning activities but also in evaluating why the group exists, what it is doing, and what effect it is having on the lives of its members. The questions most commonly asked today by young people of high school and college age have to do with the matter of being. Many of these questions are philosophical in nature: "Who am I?" "Why am I here?" "What should I be doing with my life?"[5] It is to these philosophical questions that the Christian faith can speak with clarity. Indeed, only when young people see temporal life in the wider perspective of eternal life will the reality and meaning of their existence come into focus. Is not this focus exactly what leaders should seek to help youth achieve? The leaders' purpose is—or should be—to help young people lead lives that are in proper relationship to God, His Son Jesus Christ and the Holy Spirit.

One's approach to leadership development, program planning, selection of curriculum materials, social events, and service activities will be determined by his views of God's Word. When a youth group and its leaders begin to see the group's relationship to theology, they will test the songs and choruses they sing to see if these meet the standards of sound Bible doctrine.

THEOLOGY DETERMINES AUTHORITY

In all education someone or something is considered the ultimate source or authority for what is believed, taught and practiced. The question of authority is not unique to Christian education; it is faced by all educational organizations on all levels. Zuck has reminded us that "much of what happens in teaching situations is determined by the teacher's concept of the final authority in Christian education. Lesson aims or objectives, classroom atmosphere, student activities, teaching materials, les-

---

4. J. Oliver Buswell, Jr., "Why We Need a Christian Philosophy," *Eternity*, November 1961, p. 35.
5. Compare chapter 10, "Later Adolescence."

son approaches, and subject matter are influenced by the teacher's outlook on this problem."[6]

Some say that the church is the ultimate authority and that the counsels
and traditions which have been transmitted through the years of church
history must be the determining factor for what is believed and taught.
Others suggest teachers as their authority, or perhaps their or others'
religious experiences. (Many cults have set up extrabiblical revelation and
human prophets as the authority for their practices and beliefs.) Some
would argue that educational, not religious, experience is the authorita-
tive sun around which the solar system of education revolves.

In our day, absolutes are frowned on by many people, and those who
look to an immutable source for authority are considered old-fashioned,
narrowminded, and bigoted. Yet, since the days of the early church, evangelical Christians have accepted and insisted on the Bible as their authori-
tative Guide for faith and conduct. This is the testimony that Scripture
gives of itself (Matt 5:18; John 10:35; Acts 20:35; Rom 15:4; 1 Cor 10:11;
2 Tim 3:16; 2 Peter 3:2; 1 John 1:1-5; Rev 22:18-19). The Christian's absolute authority is that special written revelation which we call the Bible.

After examining a number of possible authorities for Christian education, Zuck concludes that "education that bypasses the central authority
of God's Word is not evangelical Christian education."[7] The implications
of this for the Christian education of youth are many, but they all boil
down to one simple statement: Biblical theology is the basis on which all
evangelical youth work must be founded. The written Word of God is the
authority for our educational work with young people.

THE BIBLE AND EDUCATION-RELATED DISCIPLINES

The preceding section is not meant to imply that information from education, psychology, sociology, and other related disciplines of study is not
beneficial. It certainly is! In fact, one of the failures of evangelical
Christianity at almost all levels of its educational ministry, has been to
neglect the holistic nature of God's truth and de-emphasize the value of
natural revelation when properly understood through the message of special revelation. Consequently, if we think of the Scriptures as special
revelation and related fields of study as natural revelation, we can say
that there is at least a twofold relationship between the biblical discipline
and other related disciplines.

First, the Bible provides a means of evaluating insights to be gained

6. Roy B. Zuck, "The Problem of Authority in Christian Education," *Bibliotheca
Sacra* 119 (January-March, 1962): 54.
7. Ibid., p. 63.

from other sources. If principles in other areas contradict Bible truth, then the evangelical youth worker feels obligated, because of his commitment to the final authority of Scripture, to accept the latter rather than the former. For example, some psychologists maintain man's nature is basically and inherently good, not evil. Because this is at variance with divine revelation, it is untenable for evangelicals. Or if psychology or education books teach that man is no more than animal, that he has no spiritual nature, this too is rejected by evangelicals because it does not corroborate scriptural authority. Or if sociology teaches that improving one's environment is the chief means of bettering the world, this does not correlate with the biblical teaching on man's sinful condition and his need of regeneration. Certain learning theories advocated in education and psychology should be analyzed in the light of a Christian theory of learning, based on a careful study of what scriptural statements and examples suggest with regard to the nature and process of learning.

Byrne summarizes this point by saying that "claims to truth from other areas should be tested and evaluated by the philosophical and theological truths of the Word of God."[8] And Zuck writes:

> Secular educational principles are often built on unscriptural philosophical bases such as pragmatism, empiricism, and naturalism. When there is conflict or variance in principles, Christian educators need to go back to their divine source to be sure that the principles they have formulated are drawn from or are consistent with Scripture.[9]

Second, the Bible provides the basis for a Christian perspective or frame of reference in which to view these other disciplines. In other words, the Scriptures enable one to see psychology, sociology, and education from a *Christian* point of view. The wise youth leader seeks to relate the insights from the psychology of adolescence, the sociology of adolescence, and the education of adolescence to the Bible, and to integrate the Bible to these areas of study. For example, he asks how the fact of puberty in adolescence affects the content and activities to be included in the *Christian* education of youth. Or he asks how the changes in today's society as faced by college-age youth relate to the *Christian* education of that age-group. What does the Bible suggest with regard to the ways and means whereby teachers may best teach and learners may best learn? The wise youth leader lets the Bible have a directing and formative influence on his approach to various subjects. Byrne also speaks on this point:

8. Herbert W. Byrne, *A Christian Approach to Education* (Grand Rapids: Zondervan, 1961), p. 67.
9. Roy B. Zuck, *Spiritual Power in Your Teaching* (Chicago: Moody, 1963), p. 100.

Through the Bible the interrelatedness of all other subjects and truths is made possible and clear. This means that all other subjects and truths have their first point of reference in the Word of God, draw their materials from the Bible wherever possible and return to the Bible with their accumulation of facts for interpretation and practical application.[10]

The following statements suggest some of the areas of correlation between Scripture and education-related disciplines. Perhaps they may serve as the basis for further thought and study in this area.

1. The Scriptures teach that every person is a sinner, depraved and distant from God, and therefore in need of regeneration; but psychology points up how this degeneracy may be revealed in adolescent behavior, and observes the growing awareness of personal guilt of sin in the early teen years.
2. The Scriptures challenge Christian youth to be committed to the Lord and to serve Him; but education and psychology may suggest ways in which teens' growing interest in service opportunities may be channeled.
3. The Scriptures indicate that Christian educators have Bible truths to transmit; but education can help us learn *how* to communicate that content.
4. The Bible stresses that an intellectual grasp of Christianity is insufficient; and psychology and education can help the youth worker see how to take young people beyond this mere mental assent into a personal life-transforming relationship to Christ.
5, The Scriptures indicate that Christianity is timeless and always relevant to peoples' needs; psychology and sociology can call to the attention of youth workers some of the needs teens face in today's society, thus helping youth workers point up the relevance of Scripture.
6. The Bible teaches that the illuminating, teaching ministry of the Holy Spirit is necessary if one is to apprehend and appropriate Bible truth; but education can point up essential principles of teaching and learning through which the Holy Spirit seeks to teach.[11]
7. The Bible indicates something of youth's "spiritual potential." According to the Scriptures, young people need God and are capable of knowing God. Psychology studies the specific expressions of this spiritual potential or religiosity among adolescents.[12]
8. The Bible challenges teens to a high standard of moral, Christ-honoring living (1 Tim 4:12). Christian adolescents are not excluded from

10. Byrne, *A Christian Approach to Education*, pp. 66-67.
11. Zuck, *Spiritual Power in Your Teaching*, chaps. 13-14.
12. For example, see chapter 5, "Research on Adolescent Religiosity."

the Lord's call to holy, Spirit-filled living. Sociology can acquaint the youth worker with some of the problems in today's society which make it difficult for Christian youth to maintain purity of mind and body.[13]

9. The Bible stresses the need for knowing, being concerned for, and fostering the welfare of other believers. Psychology and education can enable Christian leaders to grasp something of the nature and needs of adolescents,[14] and how to counsel personally with youth.[15]

THE BIBLE AND THE YOUTH LEADER

A youth program stands or falls depending to a great extent, on the adult leadership responsible for the group. It is the adult leader who can help promote enthusiasm, give guidance to the group, insure progress in the work, find and train other leaders, and, above all, be an example of Christian maturity. All these tasks (particularly the latter) demonstrate the necessity for competent Bible knowledge on the part of the youh leader.[16]

KNOWLEDGE OF THE SCRIPTURES

There are many ingredients of sound leadership. For the Christian, a proper attitude toward and understanding of God's Word is high on the list. Joshua, for example, was a man whom God called to a place of leadership. Joshua had been preparing for many years as "Moses' minister." He depended on Jehovah, and he was filled with courage for the task that lay ahead. These qualities were insufficient without the saturation in the Word which Jehovah demanded of His human leader: "This book of the law shall not depart out of thy mouth; but thou shalt meditate therein day and night, that thou mayest observe to do according to all that is written therein: for then thou shalt make thy way prosperous, and then thou shalt have good success" (Josh 1:8).

The Christian may be ignorant in many fields of knowledge and still render acceptable service to Jesus Christ. But a knowledge of the Bible is not one of those fields. Of course God never makes any demands on His servants which they cannot fulfill with His help. Therefore for one to say, "I cannot work with young people because I don't know the Bible well enough" is to state a self-indictment which should be promptly remedied. A Christian need not be a professional theologian to possess and use a working knowledge of Scripture.

13. See chapter 6, "Adolescents in Socio-Psychological Perspective."
14. See chaps. 8-10.
15. See chaps. 30-32.
16. Also see chapter 11, "Adult Leaders of Youth."

A knowledge of the Bible is important for several reasons. First, spiritual growth comes through the Word. Every Christian, especially one who holds a position of leadership, should be growing in the grace and knowledge of Jesus Christ (2 Pet 3:18). This growth depends entirely on the supernatural power of the Word applied to the life by the Holy Spirit. Jesus prayed that the disciples would be sanctified through the Father's truth. And then He added, "Thy word is truth" (John 17:17). The Christian life is a process of progress toward being like the Saviour Himself, and a necessary instrument or agent in this process is the Bible.

Second, a knowledge of the Scriptures helps the leader know his young people. Many of the desires and actions of young people strike adults as strange and unnatural. But actually many of those desires and actions fit perfectly into the pattern of natural, or carnal, living described in the Word of God. The Bible teaches what an unregenerate person is like and why he thinks and acts as he does. His condition is described as "lost," "blind," "ungodly," and "dead." A proper understanding of the biblical doctrines of anthropology (the doctrine of man) and hamartiology (the doctrine of sin) will enable the youth leader to understand and even anticipate behavior on the part of both Christian and non-Christian young people.

Third, a knowledge of God's Word equips youth leaders to help their young people. The process of guiding young people is not a ministry of solving their problems as much as it is giving them the tools and the techniques whereby they may solve their own problems through God's Word. If the youth leader has a growing knowledge of the Bible, he is better equipped to direct his young people to passages of Scripture which are needed in their lives. And he will be able to teach them principles of Bible study which they can then use in feeding themselves spiritually.

Fourth, the Scriptures give motivation to the youth leader. Working with young people can be discouraging at times, but the worker who is acquainted with the Scriptures will find encouragement. He will see that God rewards faithfulness (Matt 25:20-23; 1 Cor 4:2), that He encourages the worker to be steadfast in view of the fact that our work for Him is not in vain (1 Cor 15:58), that difficulties are to draw us to greater dependence on Him (Cor 9:8; 12:9-10), and that rewards will be given to faithful laborers (1 Pet 5:2-4).

Knowing a subject does not automatically mean that one can communicate that subject. Many people have known great scholars who had full knowledge and understanding of a certain subject but who, when standing before a class, could not communicate that knowledge. Likewise youth leader must not only *know* the Bible but be able to use it in teaching, counseling, and leading youth.[17]

One of the greatest problems in working with young people is knowing how to apply eternal truth to everyday living. It is foolish to think that simply referring a teen to a few selected passages will automatically cause him to realize that all the Bible is relevant to his life. Some teachers, preachers, and youth leaders in evangelical churches have the false idea that young people will automatically see how biblical truths relate to teen living.

Through the Scriptures youth leaders learn of the motivating forces of the love of Christ (2 Cor 5:14) and coming judgment (2 Cor 5:11). These urge them on to continue reaching and ministering to young people.

THE BIBLE AND THE YOUNG PERSON

In honesty it must be stated that the Bible is in no way a book written for or about young people. There are many stories about courageous young people in the Scriptures, but they are almost always within an adult context. Many youth leaders make the mistake of leading their teenagers to believe that God focused on teens when he gave the Scriptures or designed the plan of salvation. That simply is not the case and it leads to a perverted view of exaggerated self-importance on the part of the teenage segment of the evangelical community.

What we must have is a biblical recognition that teenagers in relation to Christ, the family, the church, and the world are to be viewed in the beautiful balance of Scripture.

The youth leader is responsible to help the young person understand the Word of God and how it relates to him. But the young person is responsible to act on that understanding and bring his life into conformity with eternal truth. In a real sense, the Christian life is the process of coming to see all of life in *divine* perspective. Christian growth is learning, and learning includes seeing relationships.

Every aspect of the Christian life is based on some kind of a relationship between the believer and the Son of God. The initial relationship is one of sinner to Saviour. The continuing relationship is one of disciple to Lord, or commissioned to Commissioner. It is the task of youth workers to help youth develop a biblical philosophy of life and to see their relationships to the Lord and others in a biblical frame of reference.

17. See chapter 15, "Guiding Youth in Bible Study." Also see Lois E. LeBar, *Education That Is Christian* (Westwood, N.J.: Revell, 1958), chapter 5, "The Use of the Bible in Teaching"; and Lawrence O. Richards, *Creative Bible Teaching* (Grand Rapids: Zondervan, 1970), chaps. 21-24.

THE YOUNG PERSON'S RELATIONSHIP TO THE LORD MUST BE BASED ON THE
WORD

The life of Peter presents a checkered but very informative lesson in relationships between disciple and Lord. John 6 records Christ's sermon on
the bread of life and the results which followed as many so-called disciples
left Him at that time. Jesus turned to the Twelve and said, "Will ye also
go away?" Simon Peter answered Him, "Lord, to whom shall we go? thou
hast the words of eternal life. And we believe and are sure that thou art
that Christ, the Son of the living God" (John 6:67-69).

Here Peter identified himself with the One whom he called "Lord,"
"Christ," and "the Son of the living God." Through this experience Peter
learned (and through him *we* learn) that discipleship is not merely an
outward form of following but rather that which demands absolute adherence to the truth. In other words, a young person's relationship to his
Lord, like that of Peter, must be based not on what he thinks about truth
but on what Jesus Christ Himself insists is God's truth.

Both verbs in the first part of verse 69 indicate, in the Greek, a past
event with a continuing condition or result. Peter's relationship was one
of faith and assurance which had its roots in a past commitment of his life
to this One to whom he spoke. The results of that commitment were continuing even to the time when he was speaking. This Lordship-disciple-
ship contact based on the assurance of eternal truth is the key to victorious
Christian living.

THE YOUNG PERSON'S RELATIONSHIP TO THE FAMILY MUST BE BASED ON THE
WORD

The family—not the youth group, weekday club, or teen evangelistic organization—is the primary unit of God's operation. We see the family
in focus from the second chapter of Genesis until the twenty-first chapter
of Revelation when the New Jerusalem comes down out of heaven "as a
bride beautifully dressed for her husband" (21:2, NIV). The teenager
who does not find his proper role in the family may have difficulty finding
his proper role in the church.

Of course the church youth director or sponsor is working on two levels
in relation to teens and their families.[18] There will be those, for example,
who come out of completely pagan backgrounds whose parents care nothing about their involvement with the church or Christian activities. For
these the youth leader and other church workers may almost become substitute parents as far as spiritual instruction is concerned. Nevertheless,

18. For more on this subject, see chapter 33, "Working with Parents of Youth."

obedience to parents, whether they are Christians or not, is essential if the Christian teenager wants to be in subjection to the Word of God.

But the family emphasis is even more important when working with children from Christian families. Here the youth leader must become a positive influence in teen-parent communication. The cardinal sin of a youth leader is to somehow insert himself as "father confessor," encouraging his young people to neglect or ignore their parents while regularly bringing their problems to him. If he sets himself up in the place of Christian parents, he is defying the central theme of the Word of God and contributing to communication breakdown in the families of his church.

The biblically oriented youth leader recognizes that there are three responses required of young people (or children) in Scripture: obedience, reverence or honor, and requiting.

Obedience is called for in such key passages as Ephesians 6:1 and Colossians 3:20. In both cases the Greek word rendered by the English word "children" is a word which has no relationship to age and is clearly intended in the context to refer to teenagers as well.

Reverence or honor is called for in Ephesians 6, verses 2 and 3 which, of course, refer back to the listing of the commandments in Exodus 20. Teenagers who honor their parents are promised long physical life by God. It is a most interesting phenomenon among the commandments, and Paul calls attention to the fact of the unique promise connected with this command to children and young people.

Requiting is an unusual idea dealt with in 1 Timothy 5:4. Greek scholars call this a *hapax legomenon,* which means that this is the only place in the New Testament this particular Greek word appears. The word "requite" might also be rendered "to return returns" or "to pay back for service." And in the context in which it appears, it is evident that young people must anticipate a biblical responsibility to care for their parents in economic matters during the old age of those parents if that caring becomes necessary.

Blessed is the youth leader who emphasizes these three basic commands even above such things as Bible study, witness, and faithfulness at church activities. God's priorities cannot be ignored and the witnessing teenager who is not obedient to his parents can never be acceptable to God.

THE YOUNG PERSON'S RELATIONSHIP TO THE CHURCH MUST BE BASED ON THE WORD

The word *church* has various meanings. It describes a building or a denomination; but neither of these uses is ever found in Scripture. The Greek word *ekklesia,* from which the word *church* is derived, meant one of two things in the New Testament: (1) the universal body of believers who belong to Christ through regeneration, or (2) any specific geographical representation of that body in any place at any time (a local church).

The Christian young person needs to realize that because he is a part of the church, the body of Christ, he has obligations and responsibilities to his local church. He is as much a part of the local church as any member of the official local church board. When the Christian teenager begins to see himself in this biblical perspective, his whole outlook on church attendance, support of and participation in church activities, and personal witness may be revolutionized.

In recent years churches have been giving much more serious responsibility to young people and in some cases, discovering that a willingness to share leadership with teens in the church has productive results. For example, many churches include a teenage representative on the board or committee of Christian education. He or she holds full voting membership and is, for all practical purposes, the "voice of youth" on that committee. Some churches even extend the committee responsibilities to most of the major committees in the church since teenagers need to get involved in service and leadership as well as attendance of church activities.

THE YOUNG PERSON'S RELATIONSHIP TO THE WORLD MUST BE BASED ON THE WORD

Probably most youth directors or pastors face at some time or other the problem of worldliness in their young people. There are a number of controversial ramifications of this whole issue, and youth groups spend hours every year discussing and debating what a Christian "should" or "should not" do. Yet when one puts these various issues under the scrutiny of God's Word, there surely is no uncertain sound to the trumpet on basic principles of godly living. Note again the words of John the apostle: "Do not love the world or anything in the world. If anyone loves the world, the love of the Father is not in him. For everything in the world—the cravings of sinful man, the lust of his eyes and his pride in possessions—comes not from the Father but from the world. The world and its desires pass away, but the man who does the will of God lives forever" (1 John 2:15-17, NIV).

This is not an isolated text but a permeating principle of the entire Bible regarding the Christian's behavior. One of the reasons we have difficulty instructing and convincing our young people in the matter of holy Christian living may be that we have not based our arguments for such living on a careful analysis and full understanding of the Word of God. Young people need to replace the shaky reasons such as "My church says I should do this" or "My pastor wouldn't like it" with solid, Bible-based convictions that God has spoken and that our duty as Christians is to obey.

But a young person's relationship to the world is broader than the matter of separation from questionable practices. It includes the positive aspects of Christlike living in all relationships—to one's parents, siblings, schoolmates, teachers, Christian and non-Christian friends, employers, neighbors, people in need in one's neighborhood, city, country, and to lost millions in foreign lands. Because the Bible provides specific directives for standards to be followed in each of these areas, it is important that youth workers seek to help youth know—and live out—the Word.

Of course, there are times when the Bible does not provide specific directives with respect to certain activities. Then it becomes important to develop a solid array of biblical principles which can be applied to specific situations. For example, there is no specific biblical directive against the use of drugs, but Paul's words in 1 Corinthians 6:12 are a profound principle which can be applied to drugs, alcohol, nicotine, rock music, and a number of other strong influences on the lives of people: "All things are lawful for me, but not all things are profitable. All things are lawful for me, but I will not be mastered by anything" (NASB).[19]

THE YOUNG PERSON'S RELATIONSHIP TO THE FUTURE MUST BE BASED ON THE WORD

In John 21, Peter's future as a disciple was at stake. He was the recipient of a question, a prophecy, and a command. The question "Lovest thou me more than these?" immediately removed Peter's decision of life vocation from the realm of the natural and placed it in the realm of the supernatural. His relation to God's will for his life was not to be based on the rationale of man but on his love for the Saviour.

Christ's prophecy regarding Peter's coming imprisonment and martyrdom showed the dynamic apostle that he was not entering a debatable situation but was like a soldier receiving marching orders from the general of the army. Peter was learning in this brief dialogue in John 21 the very things Thomas had learned just a few days earlier when he responded to the authority of Jesus Christ over his life with the form of address "my Lord and my God."

After positing a genuine love relationship for Peter's Christian service and warning him that the road ahead would not be an easy one, the Lord gave the simple but engaging command "Follow me." Christ was not

19. For more on this subject, see Kenneth O. Gangel, *The Family First* (Minneapolis: His International Service, 1972), chapter 8, "Teaching Convictions and Principles."

interested in Peter's comparing his life with God's plan for another. The relationship of the other disciple to the Lord was a matter between those two and was not to be the concern of Peter. His only task was to follow wherever the will of God and the lordship of Christ should lead him.

This is precisely the kind of future we wish for our young people. It might be a future in vocational Christian service or it might be an active lay witness, but in any case it is to be a genuine discipleship, a discipleship which tolerates no reservations or concern for one's own life. This kind of complete commitment should be the guideline for the future of every Christian young person; but until he sees his life in the light of the teaching of God's Word regarding discipleship, he probably will not make this kind of commitment.

Teenagers need to be taught an understanding of how to know the will of God for their lives. Involvement in such things as serious Bible study, a willingness to listen to the guidance of others, an understanding of and sensitivity to the Holy Spirit's leading, and an appreciation of the way God uses divine providence to steer events in the lives of His children must be taught by Sunday school teachers and youth leaders who work with teens in evangelical churches.[20]

THE BIBLE AND THE YOUTH PROGRAM

Any youth activity must have a *purpose;* it should include a maximum of *participation* on the part of the young people; there ought to be adequate *preparation* and effective *publicity;* and certainly the whole operation ought to be backed with fervent *prayer.* Stated in another way, every youth program and learning experience for teens must include at least three basic elements: objectives, content, and methods.

THE OBJECTIVES OF YOUTH PROGRAMS MUST BE BASED ON THE BIBLE

Earlier we discussed the relationship of theology to objectives in Christian education. However, here we are considering more specifically those goals or aims which the youth leader and his young people will set for a particular program or series of programs, or the aims of a Sunday school teacher for a unit of study or a single lesson. The Bible and the needs of young people are to be kept in mind as one considers such aims.

THE CONTENT OF YOUTH ACTIVITIES MUST BE PERMEATED WITH THE BIBLE

Lessons and youth programs must be dynamic in the sense that they relate to the life experiences of the young people, and they must also be biblical. Having a "biblical curriculum" means more than just attaching

20. Also see chapter 32, "Vocational Counseling"; and Kenneth O. Gangel, *Guiding Teens Regarding Their Future,* Christian Education Monographs: Youth Workers Series, no. 7 (Glen Ellyn, Ill.: Scripture Press Ministries, 1971).

some Scripture text to whatever lesson or program has been planned. Lois E. LeBar has stated:

> Experience with the Word cannot be left to chance. It will not automatically proceed from the written Word. Teachers must make definite provision for including experience in the curriculum. . . . As the divine and human teachers stimulate interaction between the Word and the pupil, both written and living Word gradually or suddenly penetrate to the interior of the pupil.[21]

A Bible-based theology indicates that education of youth includes the transmission of subject matter but goes beyond it toward the shaping of character.

THE METHODS USED IN YOUTH PROGRAMS MUST BE CONSISTENT WITH THE BIBLE

Methods in youth work are the ways by which leaders seek to help teens learn. Our choice of teaching methods is to be controlled by our educational objectives and by biblical content. Methods are not ends in themselves, but rather means to achieve the learning and the life-change which we hope to see in our young people. Edge reminds us that "method is concerned with the following questions which the teacher must answer in preparing to teach: (1) How can I help my class develop an interest in this study? (2) How can I help my class develop a purpose for this study? (3) How can I help my class to see meaning in this study?"[22]

Keeping methods consistent with Scripture may involve several things. It might, for example, cause us to study more carefully the life of Christ, noticing how He taught. This kind of study would immediately reveal the necessity for variety in methods and interaction on the part of those being taught. Another implication is that of avoiding those elements in our youth programming that are in poor taste when compared with the holiness of God reflected in His Word.

One of the very important aspects of method in working with teenagers is the process of their own use of Scripture. The Bible ought to be a constantly handled tool in class and in group activities as well as in home assignments. The Christian teenager must get familiar not only with the content of Scripture but also with the process of studying the Bible for himself. This can only happen when the methodology of youth programming includes a heavy dose of actual usage of the Bible "on location."

The principle of scriptural consistency when carried to its logical conclusions will affect the songs sung, the way the youth work is financed, the type of personnel used in the meetings, and the attitudes we seek to develop in young people regarding their programs.

21. LeBar, *Education That Is Christian*, pp. 205-6.
22. Findley B. Edge, *Helping the Teacher* (Nashville: Broadman, 1956), p. 72.

A church may have the finest study materials, the best-equipped plant, the most adequately trained leaders, and a group of intelligent, dynamic young people. But it can accomplish little of lasting, eternal value if its entire operation is not based solidly on the immutable, infallible Word of the living God.

FOR FURTHER READING

Briscoe, Stuart. *Where Was the Church When the Youth Exploded?* Grand Rapids: Zondervan, 1972.

Brunk, Ada Z., and Metzler, Ethel Y. *The Christian Nurture of Youth.* Scottdale, Pa.: Herald, 1960.

Coleman, Robert A. *The Master Plan of Evangelism.* Old Tappan, N.J.: Revell, 1963.

Gangel, Kenneth O. *Leadership for Church Education.* Chicago: Moody, 1970. Chaps. 1-3.

——. *So You Want to Be a Leader.* Harrisburg, Pa.: Christian Pubns., 1973.

——. *The Family First.* Minneapolis: His International Service, 1972. Chaps. 5-8.

Getz, Gene A. *Sharpening the Focus of the Church.* Chicago: Moody, 1974.

Hakes, J. Edward, ed. *An Introduction to Evangelical Christian Education.* Chicago: Moody, 1964.

Jenkins, Jerry B. *You Can Get Thru to Teens.* Wheaton, Ill.: Victor, 1973. Chapter 4.

Kuhne, Gary W. *The Dynamics of Personal Follow-Up.* Grand Rapids: Zondervan, 1976.

LeBar, Lois E. *Education That Is Christian.* Westwood, N.J.: Revell, 1958.

Miller, Chuck. *Now That I'm a Christian.* 2 vols. Glendale, Calif.: Regal, 1974, 1976.

Miller, Randolph Crump. *Education for Christian Living.* Englewood Cliffs, N.J.: Prentice-Hall, 1956. Chaps. 3-5.

Reed, Bobbie, and Johnson, Rex . *Bible Learning Activities: Youth.* Glendale, Calif.: Regal, 1974.

Richards, Lawrence O. *Creative Bible Teaching.* Grand Rapids: Zondervan, 1970.

——. *You and Youth.* Chicago: Moody, 1973. Chaps. 8-9.

——. *Youth Ministry: Its Renewal in the Local Church.* Grand Rapids: Zondervan, 1972. Chaps. 3, 10-11.

Strommen, Merton P. *Bridging the Gap.* Minneapolis, Augsburg, 1973. Chapter 7.

Strommen, Merton P., ed. *Research on Religious Development.* New York: Hawthorn, 1971. Chaps. 17-18.

Towns, Elmer. *Successful Biblical Youth Work.* Nashville: Impact, 1973.

Zuck, Roy B. *Spiritual Power in Your Teaching.* Chicago: Moody, 1963.

Zuck, Roy B., and Getz, Gene A. *Christian Youth: An In-Depth Study.* Chicago: Moody, 1968. Chaps. 4, 5, 11.

3

Objectives and Standards for Youth Work

William M. Pinson, Jr., and Edwin J. Potts

NATURE AND IMPORTANCE OF OBJECTIVES

WHAT ARE OBJECTIVES?

Objectives are goals or desired ends toward which some action is directed.[1] In addition to this simple and precise definition, it is important to distinguish between various types of objectives. In education the terms *aim, objective, goal,* and *purpose* are used interchangeably and distinguish between levels of objectives which lead into one another like links in a chain, and together achieve ultimate purposes. The following levels are generally accepted:

1. *lesson objectives* (for one class session)
2. *unit objectives* (for a quarter's work)
3. *course objectives* (for a year's work)
4. *departmental objectives* (for two or three years' work)
5. *divisional objectives* (for children, youth, and adults)
6. *overall objectives* (ultimate desired outcomes)

Age-level objectives, such as those for departments and divisions, are generally based on averages. Thus they gloss over important individual differences, and imply uniform starting points. But there is some question as to whether age-level objectives are genuinely useful categories. New people enter church programs at every age level without fulfilling any "prerequisite requirements," and after entering may advance at vastly different rates. This greatly magnifies existing individual differences.

---

1. For a helpful discussion of how to set and analyze goals, see Robert F. Mager, *Goal Analysis* (Belmont, Calif.: Fearson, 1972).

WILLIAM M. PINSON, Jr., Th.D., is President of Golden Gate Baptist Theological Seminary, Mill Valley, California.
EDWIN J. POTTS, Th.D., is Assistant to the President, Westmont College, Santa Barbara, California.

Small-group Bible studies, discipleship seminars, or retreats geared to the level of maturity of the participants may help ease the problem.[2]

One way of looking at objectives is to state them as means by which to involve youth in the nurturing process at each stage of overall development. Besides avoiding the dangers of overly close age grading, this broadens the perspective to include both divine and human tasks—and distinguishes between them. *Maturity* is perhaps the best word to describe the overall objective. C. W. Brister states, "In modifying the noun 'person,' *mature* implies a quality, state, or condition of full development." He adds that maturity means "the full development of all resources to capacity for a given age."[3] Maturity as an overarching objective lends a dynamic quality to a youth program.

In a church, maturity is linked to the standards of Christlikeness. The overall objective of becoming like Christ through a growing, experiential knowledge of God guides the entire nurturing process. Both God and man are involved in this goal.

God's part in bringing about spiritual maturity includes: (1) revelation, (2) spiritual illumination, and (3) transformation.* Christian leaders may formulate objectives which include these but must realize that these are not humanly attainable. The human instrument cooperates with God and is controlled by Him to accomplish His purposes, not vice versa. The difficulty of stating objectives as "desired behavioral changes" is that it puts the Christian leader in the position of attempting to use or control God to accomplish human purposes.

Man's part in spiritual maturity includes: (1) experiencing God's revelation, (2) preparing one's heart for spiritual illumination, and (3) responding to God in ways that lead toward spiritual transformation. This approach is age-related. Designed tasks must correspond to a person's abilities. His response to God will stem from his ability to relate God's truth to his experience, and will lead to a modification of that experience. People at the same age level tend to experience much in common. Spiritual development often parallels other areas in the growth of the total person.

2. For many different types of programs, see Helen May, *Impactivity: Youth Programs Resources* (Nashville: Broadman, 1974).

3. C. W. Brister, *It's Tough Growing Up* (Nashville: Broadman, 1971), pp. 112-13.

*Evangelicals view special revelation as the work of God by which He discloses Himself and truth about Himself. God reveals Himself today through the Scriptures which were recorded without error by human authors whose writings were inspired by the Holy Spirit. Illumination, on the other hand, is that supernatural work of the Holy Spirit whereby He enables man to apprehend and appropriate God's written Word. See Roy B. Zuck, *Spiritual Power in Your Teaching* (Chicago: Moody, 1963), pp. 23, 35-50. Transformation is the process through which God changes human lives and institutions through the ministry of the Holy Spirit.

In this chapter, youth objectives are viewed in relation to *experiences* youth should undergo as means of encouraging spiritual growth. Lesson, unit, and course aims must be developed in Bible study which will lead toward these "youth objectives." In addition to Bible study programs other aspects of church youth work should have carefully defined objectives—camps, fellowships, athletics, mission tours, and discussion groups, for example. Too often, careful attention is given to objectives for classroom work and little or none is given to other activities. This is unfortunate.

WHY HAVE OBJECTIVES?

The saying, "Aim at nothing and you are sure to hit it," wraps a kernel of truth in a husk of falsehood. People are constantly learning something—even if it is nothing more than that they don't like church!

1. *Good objectives help leaders and youth know how to submit cooperatively to God's work in and through them.*
2. *Objectives give direction for the entire nurturing process and provide a general basis for the development of programs and materials.*
3. *Objectives serve as guides to help young people and adult leaders take successive steps in the desired direction.* Learning is progressive and cumulative. Care must be taken that objectives are not stated or followed so strictly that they become straitjackets that restrict spiritual growth.
4. *Objectives serve as guards against slipping into inappropriate or meaningless activity.* Appropriate aims can help prevent a leader from becoming so involved in incidental details that he misses the main points. Aims must not be permitted, however, to limit individual freedom to search out and act on the truth.
5. *Objectives provide limitations to group experiences within bounds that a leader can handle.* Only frustration and failure will result from attempts to reach ultimate goals immediately. Aims must not limit so much that they hinder effort to meet the genuine needs of individuals.
6. *Objectives express purposes common to both leader and youth.* They are useful aids in stimulating motivation, cooperation, and participation. However, a leader must always avoid any tendency to force his aims on others or to manipulate rather than educate.
7. *Objectives provide good bases for evaluating how well a youth program is developing maturity.* They must therefore be broader than merely "content to be learned" but not so general that they provide little or no help in measuring spiritual growth.

DETERMINING YOUTH OBJECTIVES

OBJECTIVES AND DEVELOPMENT

Spiritual goals must be determined in relation to the total development and changing needs of persons.[4] Past physical, intellectual, social, emotional, and spiritual development determines one's readiness for further spiritual growth. Developmental sequence is involved in spiritual growth as well as in psychophysical maturation. Spiritual maturation is inevitably related to areas of development other than the spiritual. This is true because a person develops as a functional whole. Each new task builds on tasks previously completed and prepares for successful completion of future tasks.† Objectives for a youth group must not obscure the importance of ministering to individuals within the group with concern for their unique developmental needs.

OBJECTIVES, THE BIBLE, AND HUMAN EXPERIENCE

Christian nurture is a cooperative effort between God and man. When God uses man to accomplish His spiritual purposes, it is through His Word.[5] Objectives must be formulated to help a person interact with God's Word meaningfully.

The Old Testament prophets did not merely quote the law to God's erring people.[6] They pointed up how God's Word relates to human experience. Christ expounded Scripture in terms of current situations.[7] The variety of material in the epistles is due not only to different areas of divine truth but to varying situations and different needs of people. Thus, youth objectives must be stated in terms of the relevance of God's truth to

4. For a careful evaluation of who teenagers are, see Merton P. Strommen, *Five Cries of Youth* (New York: Harper & Row, 1974), and the Youth Forum Series published by Thomas Nelson.

†Gladys Gardner Jenkins, W. W. Bauer, and Helen S. Schacter, in *Teen-Agers* (New York: Scott, Foresman, 1954), identify seven developmental tasks for adolescents: (1) to acquire a set of values, (2) to learn social skills, (3) to accept oneself as boy or girl, (4) to understand and accept one's body and its changes, (5) to learn to get along with family members, (6) to decide on and prepare for lifework, and (7) to learn to become a responsible citizen.

Clarice Bowman, in *Ways Youth Learn* (New York: Harper & Row, 1953), pp. 49-50, summarizes these and adds spiritual tasks to the list. Robert J. Havighurst, in *Developmental Tasks and Education* (New York: McKay, 1952), pp. 33-71, lists ten tasks for adolescents. John J. Gleason, Jr., in *Growing Up to God* (Nashville: Abingdon, 1975), discusses Erik Erikson's eight developmental crises from the standpoint of religious development.

5. For instance, note the experiences of Moses and Aaron (Exod 4:28, 30; 19:7), Joshua (Josh 3:9; 8:34-35), Samuel (1 Sam 3:21—4:1), Ezra (Neh 8:5-8), various prophets (1 Kings 12:22; 18:1; 22:19; 2 Kings 19:21; 20:16), Christ (John 14:24), and the apostles (Acts 4:29, 31; 8:4, 25; 10:44; 11:1; 13:5, 34; 15:35).

6. See, e.g., Hosea 4; Amos 3-4; Malachi 1-3.

7. See Matthew 9:13; 12:7; 13:14-15; 15:7-9; 18:16; 19:4-8; 21:13, 16; 22:32.

the lives of youth. Each aspect of a young person's life—family, church, school, social activity, work, sex—calls for attention to the question: How does biblical truth relate here?

OBJECTIVES AND MENTAL PROCESSES

An indispensable but often missing link between hearing the Word of God and responding to it is *thinking* on it. The Scriptures often speak of thinking as meditation or remembering. When a Christian person truly thinks on God's Word, is open to its meanings, and exerts himself mentally with its implications to his life, this enables the Holy Spirit to do His work of illumination and transformation most fruitfully. Youth should be challenged to think and probe—in church activities as much as or more than in the schoolroom. The youth generation is question-oriented and desires to explore all points of view.[8]

The following considerations, then, must be involved in formulating youth objectives: (1) objectives must be formulated during youth years as steps of maturing which are consistent with youth ability, which build on preceding growth, which are related to present experience and needs, and which prepare for future growth; (2) objectives must include helping the young person relate God's truth to his present situation and experiences; and (3) youth objectives must include involvement in mental activity and meditation beyond merely recognizing, memorizing, or remembering facts and ideas. The Word of God must be contemplated in depth and in relation to life as it is.

OBJECTIVES OF YOUTH WORK

To lead youth to Christ for salvation and then into responsible spiritual maturity, and to help them retain and utilize their abundant youthful resources under the lordship of Christ is the primary challenge of youth workers. This overarching objective is expressed by Paul in Ephesians 4:13: "That the whole body might be built up until the time comes when, in the unity of common faith and common knowledge of the Son of God, we arrive at real maturity—that measure of development which is mean by 'the fulness of Christ' " (Phillips).

Overall objectives may be stated in various ways. The Baptist Sunday School Board of the Southern Baptist Convention has pinpointed seven broad areas for objectives for any age level:

8. See chaps. 2, 3 in Lawrence Richards, *Youth Ministry* (Grand Rapids: Zondervan, 1972), for a discussion of the necessity of youth thinking and questioning and establishing goals in youth ministry.

1. Christian conversion—to lead each person to a genuine experience of the saving grace of God through Jesus Christ
2. Church membership—to guide each Christian into intelligent, active, and devoted membership in a New Testament church
3. Christian worship—to help each person make Christian worship a vital and constant part of his expanding experience
4. Christian knowledge and conviction—to help each person grow toward mature Christian knowledge, understanding, and conviction
5. Christian attitude and appreciations—to assist each person in developing such Christian attitudes and appreciations that he will have a Christian approach to all of life
6. Christian living—to guide each person in developing habits and skills which promote spiritual growth and in applying Christian standards of conduct in every area of life
7. Christian service—to lead each person to invest his talents and skills in Christian service[9]

Sometimes overall objectives are stated in terms of relationships—the youth and his relationship to (1) God, (2) Christ, (3) the Holy Spirit, (4) the Bible, (5) the Church, (6) himself, (7) others, (8) culture, and (9) social institutions. Sometimes aims are stated in terms of age-groups—for junior highs, senior highs, and for older youth.[10] Another way to state the overall objectives of youth work is as follows:

A. To lead youth to
   1. Accept Christ as Saviour
   2. Commit their lives to Christ as their Lord and Master
   3. Be sensitive to the guidance and power of the Holy Spirit
   4. Become church members and loyal Christian disciples
   5. Participate in Christian ministries and world missions
   6. Witness for Christ, thus directing others to Him
   7. Be faithful stewards of their time, talents, and money
   8. Use their leisure time constructively

B. To help youth to
   1. Genuinely worship the Lord
   2. Grow in their knowledge and understanding of Bible truths
   3. Apply Christian principles in every area and relationship of life
   4. Develop habits of personal Bible study and devotions
   5. Recognize and respond to the will of God in all decisions

9. John T. Sisemore, ed., *Vital Principles in Religious Education* (Nashville: Broadman, 1966), pp. 20-21.
10. See George M. Schreyer, *Christian Education in Theological Focus* (Philadelphia: Christian Education, 1962), pp. 120-22.

The following aims are broader statements encompassing many of the above. They are objectives for which every teacher or leader of youth should strive.‡

TO LEAD YOUTH TO A PERSONAL RELATIONSHIP TO JESUS CHRIST BY THEIR RECEIVING HIM AS SAVIOUR

This is the first overall goal concern of evangelical educators. As Gaebelein has stated, "The first aim of Christian education must be defined in terms of evangelism."[11] Of course this is not the sole aim, but it is certainly the initial aim. Genuine spiritual nurture of young people is impossible unless they have first received spiritual life through regeneration. This suggests that the plan of salvation—including the fact of personal sin, God's gracious provision of Christ as Saviour, and the necessity of personal acknowledgment of sin and a by-faith acceptance of Christ as Saviour—be made explicitly clear to young people.

A young person's lack of interest in spiritual things may be due to several factors, and one of these factors in the case of some teens is lack of a genuine spiritual conversion experience. Being brought up in an evangelical church and a Christian home is no substitute for personal salvation. Nor is confirmation for young people completing junior high school, as practiced by some evangelical churches, to be considered a substitute for regeneration. Methods by which youth may be evangelized—and by which Christian youth may be engaged in evangelizing unsaved youth—are discussed in another chapter of this book.[12]

TO CONFRONT YOUTH WITH THE BIBLICAL MESSAGE IN MEANINGFUL RELATION TO THEIR OWN EXPERIENCE

Two approaches to youth work have predominated in the past as either-or alternatives: (1) the Bible could be the starting point and its truth expounded and applied to life, or (2) problems of youth could serve as starting points toward biblical answers. Both approaches have dangers and problems.

The first approach has the danger of possibly answering questions which youth are not asking. It also raises problems of establishing meaningful

‡Objectives listed here are "Youth Objectives" in the widest sense. They are not categorized into junior high, high school, and college-age levels. By the end of adolescence, some objectives should have been attained. Others are lifelong tasks. In general the junior higher is beginning, the high schooler is proceeding toward, and the college-age person is achieving these objectives. More specific objectives than these tend to be individual rather than departmental.

11. Frank E. Gaebelein, *Christian Education in a Democracy* (New York: Oxford, 1951), p. 30.
12. See chapter 13, "Evangelism of Youth."

contact and maintaining interest. The second approach has the danger of possibly hindering the Scriptures from speaking their genuine message by reducing the approach to a set of psychological gimmicks. Even though specific youth problems may be raised, this approach does little to overcome biblical illiteracy or to enable young people to use the Bible for themselves.

Some kind of synthesis of these two is desirable. Problems of twentieth-century youth grow out of cultural settings so diverse from those of the Bible that much biblical understanding is necessary before any genuine relationship between problem and answer can be established. While neither Scripture-dominating nor experience-dominating approaches provide the final answer, an experience-initiating approach is to be preferred. The teacher begins where the students are and moves to the biblical solutions to their deepest problems. Be aware of the superficial exigencies of the youth culture and environment. To understand—at ever deepening levels—God's love, His noncondemning acceptance, and His gifts which relate to youth's greatest needs and experiences are the most vital Christian insights youth can gain. Broader scriptural knowledge must build on these ever deepening understandings.

Ideas apart from biblical contexts are not enough. The understandings suggested above should result from group and personal study of the Scriptures. Young people must see how the Word relates to their present needs and experiences. Sufficient depth of meaning is usually attained through receiving the Word in a variety of ways, through many senses, and in differing contexts. For youth to understand how the Bible relates to life, it may be necessary to get out of the typical classroom or Bible study setting and confront human need on mission trips, in ministry programs, or in visitation efforts. When a young person is called on for answers, not by a teacher in a classroom but by a person needing help, he is more likely to search for answers and find them. We learn God's truth by doing it as well as by hearing it. Dietrich Bonhoeffer, the German martyr, wrote, "We shall never know what we do not do."[13]

TO HELP YOUTH THINK SERIOUSLY AND CONSTRUCTIVELY CONCERNING THE DEEP IMPLICATIONS OF THE WORD OF GOD

Learning at in-depth levels involves painful, mind-stretching thought. Christian thought should include not only critical thinking but also faith in action involving submission of the mind to Christ. A short time of concentrated thought can do more to cooperate with God's Spirit toward

13. Cited in John H. Westerhoff III, *Values for Tomorrow's Children* (Philadelphia: Pilgrim Press, 1970), p. 44.

change than many hours of skipping from pat answer to pat answer, or of skimming along the surface of biblical truth.

Questions such as the following would provide meaningful content for youth's meditation:

1. How does my love differ from God's love in kind rather than quantity? Where could I most likely begin to express God's kind of love?
2. Do I exercise and exhibit other Christ-honoring virtues such as patience, self-control, gentleness, peace, joy?
3. Have I ever accepted anyone completely without any condemnation, as God has accepted me? Could I? Am I willing, as God is, to pay the necessary price?
4. Which of God's gifts and blessings could I share with others? Could I forgive and forget? Could I help someone else feel important even if I lost some status in the process? Could I give my life to bring the gospel to a strange people?
5. Are my activities and rationalizations free from self-interest?
6. Am I a responsible person? Do my requests from God reflect a responsible attitude? Could all Christians reasonably expect as much as I request? If all Christians lived as I do, would God be magnified? What activities or attitudes in my life need to be omitted, added, or altered, to help me become more pleasing to the Lord?

TO EQUIP YOUTH TO STUDY THE BIBLE WITH ZEST AND TO INTERACT WITH ITS BASIC ISSUES INDEPENDENTLY

The young person, who is gaining more and more independence, must be prepared to be responsibly dependent on God and His Word. He must be led to know that the Bible is not a magical lodestar, a set of rules to be followed blindly, nor merely a list of propositions to be believed. He should accept it as God's means of revealing Himself through both the record of His actions in relation to man and the inspired words which interpret His actions. He must be helped to realize that his responses of faith, worship, and obedience to God will enable him to mature as a Christian. He can learn to grow in his knowledge of God through studying God's dealings with people in foreign cultures and other times, while at the same time realizing that the never-changing God is still active and real in his own times and experience. He can live in the realization of God's present activities and can actively obey His will in reliance on the Spirit's power which God provides.

Young people need to realize the important place meditation on the Word of God plays in the Christian life. In a cultural climate where quietness and thoughtfulness are not popular he must choose to be independently different and provide the mental field where the Holy Spirit can work effectively.

Youth years are ideal times in which to become acquainted with methods and tools of Bible study. Leaders must lead youth to develop and sharpen their study skills and to find satisfaction through personal discoveries in God's Word.

TO LEAD YOUTH THROUGH EXPERIENCES WHICH WILL ENABLE THEM TO TEST AND EVALUATE THEIR CHRISTIAN INSIGHTS AND DEVELOP A CHRIST-CENTERED PHILOSOPHY OF LIFE

One of the features of Christ's ministry was His reliance on more than hortatory words alone to accomplish His purposes. Many incidents in the gospels illustrate experiences through which He led the disciples in order to test their understandings. The Christian faith is built around interpersonal relationships. The teen years are years in which young people can grow in an understanding of themselves and of their relationship to God and others.

Varied worship experiences, for example, enable youth to evaluate their relationship with God. A variety of social experiences give opportunities for teens to test their relationships with others. Frank and honest appraisals of these experiences through individual counseling and group discussions enhance their value greatly.

Confronting youth with life as it is and affording them opportunities to serve in areas of special need will provide occasions to consider such questions as, Who am I? What do I want to become? What does God want me to do? What do I want out of life? In what way can God use my life? How can my life glorify the Lord?

TO HELP YOUTH FACE HONESTLY AND OPENLY ISSUES PERTAINING TO THE RELATION OF FAITH AND REASON

Children believe what they are told by people whom they trust. Young people have many doubts and desire reasonable explanations for what they believe. Doubting is a healthy youth experience. Without honest doubt and questioning, answers may be little more than clichés.

Youth need help in understanding the legitimate functions of reason and to develop discrimination in understanding the pronouncements of churches, theologians, ministers, and teachers. Lest youth be trapped by the glitter of contemporary rationalistic systems of thought, they need help to understand the limitations of reason and the possibility of its distortion by sin and self-interest.

Interest in discussions between scientists and theologians should not be avoided but used as a means of clarifying issues for youth and of helping them avoid spiritual shipwreck and intellectual dishonesty by knowing what truths they hold unreservedly and what interpretations they hold tentatively. Youth should be encouraged to dedicate their minds to their Lord as fully as they dedicate their other talents and energies.

When teens are given a learning climate where they may test, refine, and relate their beliefs to wider experiences of life, they tend to develop a firsthand rather than a "hand-me-down" faith in God and His Word.

TO DEVELOP IN YOUTH THE SKILLS NEEDED TO MINISTER TO OTHERS

Youth programs must do more than develop attitudes, beliefs, and Bible study skills. Education also involves teaching youth how to minister to others. Christian young people can be ministers, and they ought to be developed into such.

Youth are effective witnesses in many churches. Schools to equip youth in sharing Christ enroll thousands of eager learners. Training programs to develop other skills—teaching, caring for physical hurt, changing corrupt social institutions—are equally effective among today's young people.

A church makes a serious mistake in doing everything for its youth and not equipping them to do for themselves and for others. A muscle does not develop without exercise. Neither does a young Christian develop unless he is a doer as well as a hearer of the Word. A church program for youth must involve more than sitting and learning. Jesus told His disciples to teach, serve, and witness.

Youth Department Standards

A standard is a statement of a norm which exemplifies desirable characteristics of a program. Standards may be formulated in areas such as classification of persons, curriculum, methods of instruction, qualities of leadership, organization, programs, and ministries.

Since nurture is primarily the engagement of *persons* in processes which provide conditions in which God can work in lives, personal standards are of chief importance. Of secondary importance are standards which relate to organizational framework and program content.

PERSONAL STANDARDS

The attitude church workers take toward pupils is very important to successful youth work. Young people in the church should be motivated, not manipulated. They should be persuaded, not propagandized; viewed as persons, not things; and supported, not babied.

Meaningful involvement through many different types of free participation is essential if youth goals are to be achieved. Excessive pressure to conform to adult standards or to change in ways adults desire will not achieve Christian results in the nurture of youth. Freedom to choose either good or bad, and awareness of spiritual rather than human pressures are essential if youth are to mature.

This maturing will take place not in a rigid, condemning atmosphere, but in an atmosphere of love, acceptance, and freedom. This leads to standards for youth workers whose relationships with youth contribute significantly to this needed growth environment.

Youth workers should not be mere purveyors of precepts. They should be sympathetic, responsive human beings who respect youth for what they are and can be. They should be able and willing to face youth's problems with them. And rather than criticize the ways young people handle their problems, youth workers should be willing to counsel and to exhibit the kind of life youth can safely follow.

The youth worker should be well adjusted and responsible. The challenge of available, untouched spiritual resources to be used under the lordship of Christ should fire him with the kind of enthusiasm which youth can catch and fan into flame as they draw closer to Christ.[14]

ORGANIZATIONAL STANDARDS

Organizational and program standards and procedures should flow out of biblical objectives of ministry. For example, a basic principle underlying organization is that youth works should be so classified, arranged, and organized so that independence and responsibility are helped and promoted in a safe and supportive framework. Paul instructed and coached Timothy, and he observed Paul doing the ministry. Eventually, Timothy was prepared to assume a leadership role. Even then, the elders and deacons supported and assisted him as they engaged in the ministry together. An adult-dominated organization or a totally unguided organization must be avoided. The purpose of adult guidance is not so much to keep youth from making mistakes as it is to help youth learn from them.

If youth are guided and inspired they are capable of organizing and developing programs that are efficient, functional, and spiritual. Goals such as exhibiting the love of Christ, developing good personal relationships, and using time effectively should guide youth in organizing themselves in the church.[15]

PROGRAM STANDARDS

General standards foundational to the program include the following:

14. For more on personal qualifications of workers with youth, see chapter 11, "Adult Leaders of Youth."
15. For more on organization, see chapter 12, "Organizing for Youth."

maintain a good balance between preparing young people to serve Christ in the future and meeting needs and problems; develop a program which will lead youth to conform to Christian ideals and to reject unchristian standards; and help them remain open to the Holy Spirit and experience submission to and dependence on the body of believers. Emphasize throughout the program the indispensability of God's grace and power to do anything which will please Him, and encourage youth to submit their wills to God. Make the content of lessons and programs consist of that which is most essential and most appropriate for the spiritual nurture of youth.

Continually measuring each aspect of youth work in the local church by these standards can help workers gauge the effectiveness and quality of their ministry to young people.

SUMMARY

Clear youth department objectives and standards are essential for achieving ultimate purposes in a truly Christian way. Since it is God who is working in youth to enable them to will and do His pleasure, youth objectives should be stated as ways of helping young persons meet God in His Word and respond to Him. The youth worker as Christ's minister should desire to help youth face personally and responsibly the genuine message of God's Word. The major task of the church is to help its youth in the process of becoming spiritually independent and responsible Christian persons.

FOR FURTHER READING

Baruch, Dorothy W. *How to Live with Your Teen-ager*. New York: McGraw-Hill, 1953.

Bonner, Gary. *Marks of Maturity*. Nashville: Convention, 1972.

Brister, C. W. *It's Tough Growing Up*. Nashville: Broadman, 1971.

Brunk, Ada Z., and Metzler, Ethel Y. *The Christian Nurture of Youth*. Scottdale, Pa.: Herald, 1960.

Carroll, John L., and Ignatius, Keith L. *Youth Ministry: Sunday, Monday, and Every Day*. Valley Forge, Pa.: Judson, 1972.

Corbett, Janice M., and Johnson, Curtis E. *It's Happening with the Youth*. New York: Harper & Row, 1972.

Ezell, Mancil. *Youth in Bible Study/New Dynamics*. Nashville: Convention, 1972.

Garrison, Karl C. *Before You Teach Teen-Agers*. Philadelphia: Lutheran Church Press, 1962.

Little, Sara. *Youth, World and the Church*. Richmond, Va.: John Knox, 1968.

May, Helen. *Impactivity: Youth Program Resources.* Nashville: Broadman, 1974.

Morrison, Eleanor Shelton, and Foster, Virgil E. *Creative Teaching in the Church.* Englewood Cliffs, N.J.: Prentice-Hall, 1963.

"Religious Life of the Adolescent." *New Catholic World* 217 (September-October 1974): 194-239.

Richards, Lawrence O. *Creative Bible Study.* Grand Rapids: Zondervan, 1971.

———. *Youth Ministry: Its Renewal in the Local Church.* Grand Rapids: Zondervan, 1972.

Simon, Sidney B. *Value Clarification.* New York: Hurst, 1972.

Towns, Elmer. *Successful Biblical Youth Work.* Nashville: Impact, 1973.

"Youth and the Church." *Reformed Review* 24 (Winter 1971): 68-115.

4

A Historical Survey of Youth Work

Donald E. Pugh and Milford S. Sholund

SUNDAY SCHOOL FOR YOUTH

DURING THE NINETEENTH CENTURY the Sunday school was recognized in the United States by various Protestant denominations as the chief instrument for religious education. By 1950, the Bible was regarded as the primary curriculum material replacing the catechism though the latter was still considered important by some denominations.

The founding of the Sunday school is generally attributed to Robert Raikes in Gloucester, England, in 1780. He was motivated by a desire to teach the Bible to children who were neglected, underprivileged, and delinquent. Before long, Raikes's idea fired the minds of pioneers in America. The first Sunday school in the United States was started in 1785. There was much opposition from clergymen and the established churches. However, within fifteen years Sunday schools scattered along the Eastern seaboard were enrolling tens of thousands of children.

The extension of the Sunday school to include youth was begun in Nottingham, England, in 1798. Young working women gathered on Sunday mornings for religious instruction. Through correspondence the idea spread to America, and soon there were young people's classes throughout the eastern section of the country.

THE BEGINNINGS OF YOUTH GROUPS

Along with the growth of the Sunday school there were indications that a youth movement was developing within the churches. As early as the seventeenth century there were singing classes for youth. These classes were the forerunners of the Protestant church choir. Through these musical sessions, young people were drawn together for further religious activities.

DONALD E. PUGH, M.A., M. Div., is Managing Editor, Youth and Adult Divisions, Gospel Light Publications, Glendale, California.

MILFORD S. SHOLUND, Litt.D., is Director of Biblical and Educational Research, Gospel Light Publications, Glendale, California.

Social problems accelerated the formation of youth groups in churches. Alcohol ruined many pioneers on the plains and in the growing cities. The idealism of youth was a springboard for temperance societies. By 1829 there were more than a thousand temperance groups for youth in Philadelphia.

From 1787 to 1830 a missionary awakening arose among Protestants. Missionary societies swept over the continent. Among these groups were the following: New York Missionary Society (1796), Boston Female Society for Missionary Purposes (1802), and Witness of Baptist Youth Missionary Society of New York City (1806).[1] The famous Haystack Meeting of 1806 was instigated by a movement of young people who were destined to go to the ends of the earth with the gospel of Christ.

The modern youth movement in Protestant churches is an outgrowth of the first YMCA founded in 1844. Twelve young men met in London under the guidance of George Williams. The original purpose was religious in nature. By 1851, the work spread to the United States and Canada. Along with the appeal to young men there was one for young women—the YWCA—founded in London in 1855, and in New York City in 1858.

Theodore Cuyler quickened the pace of interest within the churches when he organized a young people's association in his church. Three ideas from Cuyler's original plan caught on in churches: (1) coeducational— the group should work with both young men and women; (2) weekly— the groups should meet every week; and (3) participative—committees composed of the young people should prepare weekly devotional meetings.

Churches throughout the eastern United States were eager to get young people involved in groups for memorizing Scripture and improving their Christian lives. During this period, the Sunday school movement was developing from an emphasis on Scripture memorization among children, to lectures on all sorts of biblical and related topics.

The evolution of educational theories implemented by Horace Mann in the public schools was soon impinging on the religious education movement. Considerable unrest developed with resultant searching for new ways of helping young people.

Christian Endeavor Society Organized in 1881

Francis E. Clark, pastor of the Williston Congregational Church, Portland, Maine, visited Theodore Cuyler's church in Brooklyn, New York,

1. *The Study of Education: Part 1, Christian Education Yesterday and Today* (Chicago: International Council of Religious Education, 1947).

and was inspired to organize the Young People's Society of Christian Endeavor (1881). The object of Christian Endeavor was "to promote an earnest Christian life among its members, to increase their mutual acquaintance, and to make them more useful in the service of God."[2]

The nondenominational character of Christian Endeavor groups was a bid for all Protestant churches to participate. The success of this society was unprecedented as a religious youth movement. However, in less than ten years (1889) denominations began forming their own groups. The Epworth League was formed from existing Methodist church societies (1889). The Baptist Young People's Union (1891) appealed to the loyalty of Baptist churches, and the Lutheran churches rallied their efforts around the Luther League (1895). Denominational programs were growing, and leaders used their skills in imagination, inspiration, and ink to guide and stimulate interest and fervor in local youth groups toward participation and constructive activities.

FACTORS AFFECTING GROWTH

Several characteristics of the young people's movement in the Protestant churches encouraged their growth: (1) fulfillment of the need for companionship inherent in young people moving to and living in the cities; (2) a sense of belonging, since most of the various groups required some kind of pledge or membership; (3) an involvement in responsibility by participating in the plans and programs (almost all the groups had a committee-centered approach); (4) the enthusiasm and hope which prevailed in the groups, for in that period (1880-1914) world conditions were conducive to a vigorous outlook for worldwide peace, prosperity, and progress; and (5) the democratic leadership which meant that young people themselves could participate in and direct their efforts.

1900-1930: EXPANSION AND DEVELOPMENT

The period from 1900 to 1930 was a time of expansion and development of the established patterns of young people's societies started by Cuyler in 1860. The typical local church youth society met weekly, usually on Sunday evening. The varied program covered topics on the Bible, Christian life, devotional readings, temperance, amusements, social problems, and world conditions. The increased activity and expression on the part of the young people in the evening program made it quite different from the Sunday school program.

In evaluating the various elements of religious education and their po-

2. H. Clay Trumbull, *The Sunday School—Its Origin, Mission, Methods and Auxiliaries* (Philadelphia: Wattles, 1888).

sitions in the program of the local church, Squires tells us that this typical contrast between the various phases of the youth program continued into the prosperous 1920s: (1) *informational emphasis*—Sunday school, 90 percent; Christian Endeavor, 10 percent; Boy Scouts and Girl Scouts, 25 percent; and weekday church school, 75 percent; (2) *worship emphasis*—Sunday school, 6 percent; Christian Endeavor, 15 percent; Boy Scouts and Girl Scouts, 2 percent; and weekday church school, 10 percent; and (3) *expressional emphasis*—Sunday school, 4 percent; Christian Endeavor, 75 percent; Boy Scouts and Girl Scouts, 73 percent; and weekday church school, 15 percent.[3]

GROWING PROBLEMS

The churches were reaching out for a complete program for youth but were limited by lack of volunteer leadership. Theological tensions were also growing in the churches. The heart of the theological controversy focused on two basic issues: the nature of Christ and the nature of man.

Leaders of youth were being educated in seminaries and colleges that were espousing liberal views of Christianity. Critical studies of the Old and New Testaments were in full bloom. Many of the conclusions of destructive higher criticism undercut faith in the sufficiency, authority, and finality of Jesus Christ and the Scriptures.

Inherent in the interpretation of the deity and humanity of Christ was the study of the nature of man. Charles Darwin in his book *The Origin of the Species* (1859) opened the gates of inquiry and research concerning the origin and nature of the human race. The enormous breakthrough in scientific studies in psychology confronted the churches with new ideas about the nature and potential of young people that soon affected programming and publications for young people's work throughout the churches.

In the field of religious education all these forces gathered strength in a great convention in Chicago in 1903 and organized the Religious Education Association. Internationally known leaders participated in the program. William Rainey Harper, first president of the University of Chicago, advocated more intelligent study in the use of the Bible. George Albert Coe had a genius for coining religious educational terms for the new liberalism. A prominent and provocative speaker at the convention was John Dewey, who had concepts about religion which differed radically from the conservative leaders who wanted a revival of Bible study in the churches.

3. Walter Albion Squires, *A Parish Program of Education* (Philadelphia: Westminster, 1923), p. 36.

The problem in the evangelical ranks was the lack of leadership. There was no "Moses" to lead them out of the "wilderness" of critical ideas about the Scriptures. In spite of many protests from evangelicals, there was no turning back the forces of cultural change in the American way of life as the revolutionary educational concepts captured the minds of youth leaders.

In liberal churches, evangelism was dissipated in trying to make young people Christian by giving them "refreshing experiences" rather than leading them to spiritual regeneration through the Holy Spirit. The basic teachings of the Bible on the sinfulness of human nature, the atoning work of Jesus Christ on the cross, and the call to worldwide evangelism were lacking in the purposes, plans, and programs of young people's organizations.

YOUTH WORK: LIBERAL AND CONSERVATIVE

Protestantism was divided not only into scores of denominations but into two theological camps: liberals and conservatives. The issues were debated and the lines drawn tighter. In 1922 the International Council of Religious Education formed as a merger of forty denominational boards and thirty-three state councils of churches. The work of ICRE was chiefly in local church programs, family life, and community religious education. The significance of the ICRE for youth work was twofold: theological overtones and organizational unification.

From 1922 to 1950 the ICRE through its youth department exerted an enormous influence on the development of denominational youth programs. In 1950 the ICRE merged with several other national and interdenominational agencies to form the Division of Christian Education of the National Council of Churches of Christ in the U.S.A. The United Christian Youth Movement, founded in 1934, provided guidelines for church youth groups to follow as they built their programs.

During this same period fundamental, conservative youth groups were carrying on in their respective denominations and in churches without a counterpart to the ICRE. There was no unifying agency through which they could express or expand their cause.

Between 1915 and 1935 youth work in both the Sunday school and Sunday evening youth groups dwindled. The spiritual depression throughout the land was equal to the economic depression that gripped America from 1930 to 1937. Even Christian Endeavor, so strong in 1910, was rapidly losing its grip in the thirties as an effective channel for the evangelical forces. The idealism of youth needed challenging leadership, but this was lacking.

DEVELOPMENTS SINCE 1935

Youth work during the next forty years was different from what anyone in 1935 could have safely predicted. Developments were in sharp contrast to the routine of many youth meetings. Parades, campaigns, rallies, small study groups, sensational appeals, coffeehouses, musical groups, recreation, camping, films, tours, missionary caravans—all these and countless other youthful expressions and enterprises constituted the motley assortment of youth work that was soon to appear in an era of economic depression, world war, affluent living, population explosion, race tensions, and moral and spiritual revolt. The clergy and laity were about to be "shocked" and "dismayed" with young people's work in their churches. The denominational machinery was not ready for the rapid changes in youth work. The typical church had "too little, too late" to satisfy the younger set swirling with the cultural changes that struck the United States during one generation. Throughout the nation young people were ready and willing to leave their religious moorings and try something new.

PARACHURCH YOUTH ORGANIZATIONS

The "something new" was the appeal of the parachurch activities and organizations. For more than seventy-five years the ministry among young people was closely associated with the local church or an interchurch agency. There were exceptions like the YMCA, YWCA, Boy Scouts, and Girl Scouts; but the rise of movements that were diverse, independent, religious, evangelical, and evangelistic was reserved for the revolutionary generation from 1937 to the present.

An example of this new effort was the Young Life Campaign launched in Texas in 1941. The founder, the Reverend James Rayburn, was burdened to reach high school young people on and off the campuses. He went directly to the leaders of the student body and school athletes with a personal, informal, casual approach. With a very positive response he soon found opportunity to expand to other schools, cities, states, and finally to the entire nation.

Young Life is only one parachurch movement. There are many other similar movements appealing to young people in and out of churches. Youth for Christ and Campus Life have effective ministries not only in the United States but around the world with high school youth. Campus Crusade for Christ, Inter-Varsity Christian Fellowship, and the Navigators minister primarily to college youth.[4]

4. For a detailed discussion of these and other movements see chapter 26, "Parachurch Youth Movements and Organizations."

NATIONAL ORGANIZATIONS

Within the framework of the Federal Council of Churches, a consolidation of youth emerged at the Cleveland Constituting Convention of the National Council of Churches of Christ in America on November 29, 1950. Youth work was placed under the newly formed Commission on General Christian Education. This arrangement lasted until around 1968 when many major denominations and the National Council of Churches changed the term *youth work* to *youth ministry*. At this point they also stopped carrying staff related to specific age levels and attempted to treat youth as members of the church. Their plan was to involve young people with adults in the program of the church. Many denominations discontinued a national program for youth but continued to develop resources for study and action within the local church.

The National Council of Churches continues to develop mission study resources for youth. In October 1975, almost forty denominational staff in youth ministry met in a four-day forum for sharing resources and leaders. It was the first meeting of its kind in six years. The Division of Education and Ministry of the NCC sees this pattern of planning to enable the denominations to come together as part of their service to the churches. They develop resources only when it can be done better by the NCC than by the denominations. They continue to be involved with denominations in the outdoor, leisure-time, and camping experiences for youth.

In 1942 the National Association of Evangelicals was founded in St. Louis. Harold Ockenga, pastor of the historic Park Street Church, Boston, headed the newly formed organization of evangelical denominations, churches, and individuals. The NAE emerged as a fellowship of evangelicals and a service agency in many areas related to church needs and problems arising in the World War II period. There was no concerted effort to build, organize, and serve the youth groups of the NAE's constituent denominations.

In 1945 the National Sunday School Association (NSSA) was organized in Chicago. James DeForest Murch, an incisive writer and interpreter of evangelical thought, advocated that means be created for evangelicals to express themsleves in Christian education. Under his skillful guidance, the NSSA found a hearty response from thousands of evangelicals. The NSSA, somewhat wary of centralized control, projected its main efforts through national and regional Sunday school conventions.

The Youth Commission of NSSA was formed in 1958. Ten years prior to that the Youth Commission had been a commission of the NAE and was known as the Association of Evangelical Youth International. The Commission was designed (1) to provide a national fellowship for youth executives and leaders; (2) to provide a year-round exchange center for the best in methods, materials, and procedures; (3) to conduct clinics and workshops at the annual spring convention of the NAE, at the annual NSSA convention, and elsewhere; and (4) to give attention to the collecting, evaluating, and communicating to the Christian public the facts about the needs of youth today. Promotional material for National Youth Week in January was produced annually and used by many denominations.

By 1974 very little activity was being carried on by the Youth Commission and NSSA. Meanwhile, various denominational leaders and programs have arisen to carry on Christian education and youth programming on denominational and local levels.

RENEWED EFFORTS IN CHURCHES

While change was taking place in national organizations attempting to serve denominations and churches, the work within the denominations and local churches continued to develop, expand, and change with the changing youth scene. The following are only a few examples of what has been happening:

The Southern Baptists reinforced their Training Unions for education in church membership. They set goals for enrollment and achievement which clearly indicated they were aware of the importance of training young people. Beyond training they emphasize the word *process*. They stress experiential learning which stimulates Christian growth, cultivates relationships with peers in small groups, and leads toward growth as church members and leaders.

The Methodist churches in their mergers shifted from Epworth Leagues to Methodist Youth Fellowships. The term "fellowship" became a common label for youth activities in churches. The denominational and regional offices implemented the MYF plans, programs, and publications. The spectrum of youth activities included everything from learning the Bible to discussing life-related teen problems and encountering the worldwide dilemma of war and peace.

The United Presbyterian Church in the U.S.A. identified a number of goals which help them in developing their understanding of youth ministry. These goals include the need to (1) involve youth with models of Christianity, (2) empower youth to speak for themselves in proclaiming the gospel, (3) identify Christian life-styles and how to cope with those who differ, and (4) have experiences that celebrate hope and love.

The Conservative Baptist Association of America does not have a national youth organization but encourages regional and statewide activities

for youth. Rallies held between Thanksgiving and Christmas include
sports, music, and missionary projects. Over the past twenty years the
young people of Oregon have given over $250,000 for missions. Many
summer service projects are available in mainland United States, Alaska,
Hawaii, Canada, Honduras, Argentina, and Mexico. Young people are
also involved in camp counseling and in aiding churches in their summer
ministries.

The North American Baptist General Conference moved in the 1970s
from dependency on youth materials to more free-lancing on the part of
youth groups. It was a move toward witnessing, outreach efforts of various
kinds, and more activistic social action endeavors. Lately there seems to
be a turning back, and youth workers are asking for help in organizing
and planning good youth programs. There is an obvious need to rethink
the purposes of the youth group, to identify goals, and then to determine
what would be the best way to accomplish those goals. Many are turning
to Bible study-discussion groups rather than to program-centered meetings.

Many other denominations (e.g., the Church of the Nazarene, which in
1974 celebrated the fiftieth anniversay of its Nazarene Youth Organization; and the Baptist General Conference) recognize that there is no way
to change the world without taking the young generation along. Just
about every conceivable type of ministry or program is being experi-
mented with in attempts to capture the imagination and energy of young
people in order to channel them into the evangelistic mission of the
church.

Never before has so much excellent material been available to help
churches train and equip young people to live the Christian life and discover ways to share the good news of Jesus Christ with others. Never before have so many colleges and seminaries offered majors in youth ministry to equip people to work with youth professionally. Never before
have so many seminars and workshops been conducted to help both young
people and volunteer teachers and workers who serve with young people.
Never before have there been so many varied opportunities for young
people to serve God and use their abilities and talents to reach others
for Jesus Christ.

This is not the whole story, however. Never before have young people
had greater temptation and opposition from the evil one undermining
the claims of Christ on the life of the individual. The forces of evil—
hedonism, atheism, materialism, secularism, humanism, drugs, the cults,
Eastern mystical religions, and the occult—all are making massive appeals
to young people. A highly stimulating environment, especially in the

cities, of amusement, music, athletics, corrupt literature and movies, and economic affluence, tend to make the typical church youth group seem tame, dull, and uninteresting. Alert churches using professionally trained youth leaders or ministers of education, along with dedicated volunteer youth workers, can provide young people with help and direction at such a critical time in their lives.

SUMMARY

The tendency toward specialization in teaching and training young people in Protestant churches in America began in the eighteenth century in singing and fellowship groups. The development of the Sunday school movement helped focus the attention of churches on the needs of their youth. Young people's societies of the late nineteenth century brought further evaluation as well as formalization of purposes and programs for youth. The shifting theological scene, the scientific revolution, two world wars and several "policing wars," and the inability of the churches to cope with the problems of family life—all these factors and many more created problems which challenged the best that American Christianity could give in leadership.

The potential of Christian youth calls for a deeper understanding of their needs and problems and a biblical, Christ-centered, and Spirit-em-powered ministry to them. Rather than despair because of obstacles and forces which work against Christianity, Christian leaders can rejoice in the movement of God's Holy Spirit in the lives of young people and con-tinue to provide the best we can to help them. That means the best models of Christianity in our own lives, the best helps and training possible, and constant supportive prayer. The future for youth ministry in the church seems unlimited.

FOR FURTHER READING

Christian Endeavor Essentials. Columbus, Ohio: Internat. Soc. of Christian Endeavor, 1956.

Cubberly, Ellwood P. *The History of Education.* New York: Houghton Mifflin, 1948.

Cully, Kendig Brubaker, ed. *The Westminster Dictionary of Christian Education.* Philadelphia: Westminster, 1963.

Eavey, C. B. *History of Christian Education.* Chicago: Moody, 1964.

LeBar, Lois E. *Education That Is Christian.* New York: Revell, 1958.

Leech, Kenneth. *Youthquake: The Growth of a Counter-Culture Through Two Decades.* London: Sheldon, 1973.

Little, Sara. *Youth, World and Church.* Richmond, Va.: John Knox, 1968.

Lynn, Robert W., and Wright, Elliott. *The Big Little School: Sunday Child of American Protestantism.* New York: Harper & Row, 1971.

A New American Reformation: A Study of Youth Culture and Religion. New York: New York Philosophical Library, 1973.

Price, J. M.; Chapman, J. H.; Carpenter, L. L.; and Yarborough, W. F. *A Survey of Religious Education.* 2d ed. New York: Ronald, 1959.

Richards, Lawrence O. *Youth Ministry: Its Renewal in the Local Church.* Grand Rapids: Zondervan, 1972.

Vieth, Paul H., ed. *The Church and Christian Education.* St. Louis: Bethany, 1947.

Zuck, Roy B., "Sunday Evening Youth Groups." *An Introduction to Evangelical Christian Education.* Edited by J. Edward Hakes. Chicago: Moody, 1964.

5

Research on Adolescent Religiosity

J. Roland Fleck

TODAY'S ADOLESCENT is the target of many efforts in religious education. However, very little organized, research-based information about the religious characteristics, values, interests, and concerns of adolescents is available to people concerned with reaching youth. One researcher addressing this problem noted that what the adolescent "thinks about his religion and the degree to which he observes its rules, and why, is possibly one of the least researched areas of contemporary American life."[1] One of the outstanding college textbooks in adolescent psychology, *Adolescence and Youth: Psychological Development in a Changing World,* by John Janeway Conger, devotes less than two pages out of 550 to adolescent religiosity.[2] In spite of this lack of systematic research, there is a substantial amount of research related to three areas of adolescent religiosity that will be examined in this chapter: (1) religious concepts, (2) religious orientation, and (3) religious values and concerns.

RELIGIOUS CONCEPTS

The research findings concerning the development of various religious concepts in childhood and adolescence clearly fit into a three-stage Piagetian developmental progression from the prelogical, global, egocentric, perception-bound thinking of Jean Piaget's preoperational child; to the concrete, literal, logical reversible thinking of the concrete operational child; to the abstract, theoretical, propositional thinking of the formal operational adolescent. Conceptions of God, prayer, religious denomination,

1. Bernard C. Rosen, *Adolescence and Religion: The Jewish Teenager in American Society* (Cambridge, Mass.: Schenkman, 1965), p. 2.
2. John J. Conger, *Adolescence and Youth: Psychological Development in a Changing World* (New York: Harper & Row, 1973).

J. ROLAND FLECK, Ed.D., is Associate Professor of Psychology, Rosemead Graduate School of Psychology, Rosemead, California, and editor of *Journal of Psychology and Theology.*

death, and religious thinking in general follow such a developmental sequence (see table 5.1) .

With the advent of formal operational thinking—usually around age
twelve but with marked individual variations—the adolescent develops a
number of mental capabilities not present in childhood. He now has the
ability for mature conceptual thinking. There is a shift of emphasis in
the adolescent's thought from the concrete to the abstract, from the real
to the possible. Thought is much richer, broader, and more flexible. In
like fashion, the adolescent's religious concepts reflect this accelerated
cognitive development.

GOD CONCEPT

Ernest Harms was the first researcher to present empirical evidence of
age differences in the conceptualization of God. Harms asked his subjects
(ages three to eighteen) to draw how God would look to them, if they
were to picture Him in their mind, or to imagine the appearance of the
highest being they thought to exist. Harms arrived at three broad classes
of drawings which were related to age (see table 5.1) . Adolescent religious
expression had much greater diversity and was more abstract, original,
unique, and personal than that of children. Young preschool children
pictured God in terms of their fantasy, and elementary school children
expressed God in terms of the concrete teachings and concepts of institutional religion.[3]

Jean-Pierre Deconchy employed a word-association procedure to study
the development of ideas about God in 4,733 French children ranging
from seven to sixteen years of age. The associations to the inductor word
God were grouped into twenty-nine categories and along three dimensions: attributivity, personalization, and interiorization. These three dimensions characterize the three stages of religious development identified
by Decanchy (see table 5.1) . The child thought of God chiefly in terms
of his attributes such as greatness, omniscience, omnipresence, creativity,
goodness, justice, and strength. In contrast, the emerging adolescent personalized God in terms of themes such as fatherhood, redeemer, and
master; the middle adolescent thought of God in terms of internal, sub-
jective, abstract themes such as love, trust, doubt, and fear. The God of
the child appears to be a transcendent God of his thoughts, whereas the
God of the adolescent appears to be a personal God of his life.[4]

3. Ernest Harms, "The Development of Religious Experience in Children," *American Journal of Sociology* 50 (1944): 112-22.
4. Jean-Pierre Deconchy, "The Idea of God: Its Emergence Between 7 and 16
Years," in *From Religious Experience to a Religious Attitude*, ed. Andre Godin
(Chicago: Loyola U., 1965).

PRAYER CONCEPT

Long, Elkind, and Spilka used an interview procedure in studying children's understanding of prayer.[5] One hundred sixty boys and girls between the ages of five and twelve were interviewed. In order to explore developmental changes in the form of the prayer concept, the following semistructured questions were employed: (1) Do you pray? (2) Does your family pray? (3) What is a prayer? (4) Can you pray for more than one thing? (5) What must you do if your prayer is answered? (6) If it is not? To explore developmental changes in the content of children's prayer activity and the fantasies and affect associated with such activities, the following set of six incomplete sentences and questions were employed: (1) I usually pray when ——; (2) Sometimes I pray for ——; (3) When I pray I feel ——; (4) When I see someone praying I ——; (5) Where do prayers come from? (6) Where do prayers go?

The results suggested three major developmental stages in the child's understanding of the prayer concept. These stages appear closely parallel to Piaget's preoperational, concrete operational, and formal operational stages (see table 5.1).

While neither the middle nor late adolescent was included in this study, prayer to the emerging adolescent was found to be abstract in the sense that it is regarded as an internal activity deriving from personal conviction and belief. Prayer is understood as a kind of private conversation with God involving things not talked about with other people. Prayer has become first and foremost a sharing of intimacies in which petitionary requests are of only secondary importance. In contrast, the preoperational child has only a vague and indistinct understanding of the meaning of prayer, and the concrete operational child conceives of prayer in terms of particular and appropriate activities (e.g., verbal requests). Prayer is very concrete and children in this stage never think beyond the mechanics of prayer to its cognitive and affective significances, which, to the adolescent, are the essence of prayer.

> With increasing age the content of prayer changed from egocentric wish fulfillment (e.g., candy and toys) to altruistic ethical desires (e.g., peace on earth). At the same time the affects associated with prayer activity become less impulsive and more modulated among the older children while prayer comes to be a deeper and a more satisfying experience. The fantasy activity associated with prayer changed from a belief that prayers were self-propelled missiles to the view that they were a form of direct communication with God.[6]

5. Diane Long, David Elkind, and Bernard Spilka, "The Child's Conception of Prayer," *Journal for the Scientific Study of Religion* 6 (1967): 101-9.
6. Ibid., p. 101.

RELIGIOUS DENOMINATION

David Elkind defined "religious identity" in terms of the spontaneous meanings children attach to their religious denomination. In three separate studies Elkind investigated the growth of the concept of religious denomination among Jewish, Catholic, and Congregational Protestant children.[7] Piaget's semiclinical interview technique was used as each of the more than seven hundred children was individually interviewed and asked six questions. The questions were, with the appropriate denominational terms inserted: (1) Is your family ——? Are you ——? Are all boys and girls in the world ——? (2) Can a dog or cat be ——? (3) How do you become a ——? (4) What is a ——? (5) How can you tell a person is ——? (6) Can you be —— and American at the same time?

It was possible to distinguish three fairly distinct stages in the attainment of religious identity which held true of Jewish, Catholic, and Protestant children. Again, these three stages appear closely parallel to Piaget's preoperational, concrete operational, and formal operational stages (see table 5.1) .

While again neither the middle nor late adolescent was included in this study, the emerging adolescent demonstrates an abstract, differentiated conception of his denomination. "It is abstract in the sense that these children no longer define their denomination by mentioning nonobservable mental attributes such as belief, faith, and understanding."[8]

> What is a Catholic? "A person who believes in the truths of the Roman Catholic Church." Can a dog or cat be a Catholic? "No, because they don't have a brain or intellect."[9]
>
> What is a Jew? "A person who believes in one God and doesn't believe in the New Testament."[10]
>
> What is a Protestant? "A person who believes in God and Christ and is loving to other men." Can a dog or cat be a Protestant? "No, because they can't join a church or understand what God is."[11]

In contrast, the concrete operational child has only a concrete conception of his denomination in the sense that he uses observable features or

7. David Elkind, "The Child's Conception of His Religious Denomination I: The Jewish Child," *Journal of Genetic Psychology* 99 (1961): 209-25; David Elkind, "The Child's Conception of His Religious Denomination II: The Catholic Child," *Journal of Genetic Psychology* 101 (1962): 185-93; David Elkind, "The Child's Conception of His Religious Denomination III: The Protestant Child," *Journal of Genetic Psychology* 103 (1963): 291-304.
8. David Elkind, "The Development of Religious Understanding in Children and Adolescents," in *Research on Religious Development,* ed. Merton P. Strommen (New York: Hawthorn, 1971), p. 678.
9. Elkind, "The Catholic Child," p. 188.
10. Elkind, "The Jewish Child," p. 212.
11. Elkind, "The Protestant Child," p. 295.

actions to define his denomination and to differentiate among persons belonging to different denominations.

> What is a Jew? "A person who goes to Temple or Hebrew school."[12]
>
> What is a Catholic? "He goes to Mass every Sunday and goes to Catholic school."[13]
>
> What is a Protestant? "They go to different churches," or "He gets bap-a-tized," or "He belongs to a Protestant family."[14]
>
> Can you be a Catholic and a Protestant at the same time? "No." Why not? "Cause you couldn't go to two churches."[15]

Elkind's investigations clearly indicate it is not until early adolescence that the child's conception of religious denomination corresponds to that of adults. Religious denomination to the young preoperational child is no more than a name that the child confuses with the names for race and nationality. During middle childhood, religious denomination comes to mean a form or behavior or a characteristic way of acting. With the emergence of adolescence, religious denomination or identity comes to be thought of as something emanating from within rather than from without the individual.

RELIGIOUS THINKING

Ronald Goldman studied religious thinking in two hundred white Protestant children in England (ten boys and ten girls at every age level from age six through sixteen).[16] Goldman constructed a "Picture and Story Religious Test" which consisted of three pictures (a family entering church, a boy or a girl at prayer, and a boy or girl looking at a mutilated Bible) and three Bible stories ("Moses and the Burning Bush," "The Crossing of the Red Sea," and "The Temptation of Jesus"). Each child was individually interviewed and following the presentation of each picture or story, the child was asked a standardized set of questions about the material. Goldman has identified three stages in the development of religious thinking that closely parallel the three Piagetian stages of interest in this chapter (see table 5.1).

Goldman's adolescent has the capacity to think hypothetically and deductively without the impediment of concrete elements. Thinking is now possible in symbolic or abstract terms. For example, Why was Moses afraid to look at God? "God is holy and the world is sinful." "The awe-

12. Elkind, "The Jewish Child," p. 212.
13. Elkind, "The Catholic Child," p. 187.
14. Elkind, "The Protestant Child," p. 294.
15. Elkind, "The Catholic Child," p. 188.
16. Ronald Goldman, *Religious Thinking from Childhood to Adolescence* (New York: Seabury, 1964).

TABLE 5.1

The Development of Religious Concepts

JEAN PIAGET	Ernest Harms (1944)	Jean-Pierre Deconchy (1965)	David Elkind (1961; 1962; 1963)	Long, Elkind & Spilka (1967)	Ronald Goldman (1964)	Gerald Koocher (1973)
	God	God	Religious Denomination	Prayer	Religious Thinking	Death
Preoperational Period (2-7 years)	Fairy-Tale Stage (3-6 years)		Global Undifferentiated Stage (5-7 years)	Global, Undifferentiated Stage (5-7 years)	Preoperational Intuitive Thought Stage (-7/8 Mental Age)	Egocentric Stage (6-9 years)
Concrete Operational Period (7-11 years)	Realistic Stage (7-12 years)	Attributivity (7-10 years) / Personalization (11-14 years)	Concrete, Differentiated Stage (7-9 years)	Concrete, Differentiated Stage (7-9 years)	Concrete Operational Thought Stage (7/8-13/14 Mental Age)	Concrete, Specific Stage (9-12 years)
Formal Operational Period (11-adulthood)	Individualistic Stage (13-18 years)	Interiorization (14-16 years)	Abstract, Differentiated Stage (10-12 years)	Abstract, Differentiated Stage (10-12 years)	Formal (Abstract) Operational Thought Stage (13/14- Mental Age)	Abstract, Generalized Stage (12-16 years)

someness and almightiness of God would make Moses feel like a worm in comparison."[17] In contrast, the elementary school child focuses on specific and concrete features of the pictures and stories. For example, Why was Moses afraid to look at God? "Because it was a ball of fire. He thought it might burn him." "It was the bright light and to look at it might blind him."[18]

DEATH CONCEPT

Gerald Koocher used an interview procedure in studying children and adolescents' understanding of death.[19] Seventy-five boys and girls ranging in ages from six to fifteen, and with at least average intellectual ability, were interviewed. In order to explore developmental changes in the form of the death concept, the following semistructured questions were employed: (1) What makes things die? (2) How can you make dead things come back to life? (3) When will you die? (4) What will happen then?

Changes in the direction of more realistic appraisals of death by the children were noted as levels of cognitive development advanced from preoperational, to concrete operational, to formal operational stages (see table 5.1). Adolescents made use of abstract and generalized reasoning in expressing their attitudes toward death, whereas, the child's responses tended to be either magical or concrete and specific.

CONCLUSION

From these research findings it can be concluded that until adolescence the child knows much more than he understands about God, prayer, religious denomination, and death. This conclusion is also no doubt true for other traditional religious concepts such as heaven, hell, soul, the devil, and the Trinity. Therefore, the child's verbalizations about religion should be interpreted with caution, since the verbalizations are not usually coupled with true understanding until the onset of adolescence.[20]

RELIGIOUS ORIENTATION

There have been two major attempts at defining the dimensions of personal religion: (a) Gordon Allport's intrinsic-extrinsic religious orienta-

---

17. Ibid., p. 60.
18. Ibid., p. 56.
19. Gerald P. Koocher, "Childhood, Death and Cognitive Development," *Developmental Psychology* 9 (1973): 369-75.
20. For a more complete review of the literature on the development of religious concepts in children, see J. Roland Fleck, Stanley N. Ballard, and J. Wesley Reilly, "The Development of Religious Concepts and Maturity: A Three Stage Model," *Journal of Psychology and Theology* 3 (1975): 156-63.

tion dichotomy,[21] and (b) Bernard Spilka's committed-consensual religious orientation dichotomy.[22] Both dichotomies seem to differentiate between those for whom religion is a thoughtful commitment and those for whom it is a formalized external response.

Allport conceptualized the intrinsic-extrinsic dichotomy as unidimensional and bipolar and referring to a difference in motivational characteristics. The extrinsically motivated person subordinates and tailors religious practices and beliefs to the satisfaction of personal motives. The intrinsically motivated person subordinates and tailors his motives and practices to the precepts of religion. In sum, "The extrinsically motivated person *uses* his religion, whereas the intrinsically motivated *lives* his religion."[23]

Spilka conceptualized committed and consensual religious orientation as separate dimensions representing broad differences in cognitive style or expression.

> The "committed" style involves a personal and authentic commitment to religious values wherein the full creed with the attendant consequences are internalized and expressed in daily activities and behavior.

> The "consensual" style involves a conformity or acquiescence to religious values wherein the full creed is not meaningfully internalized with respect to consequences for daily activities and behavior.[24]

Allen and Spilka differentiate between committed and consensual religious orientation in terms of five structural components: content, clarity, complexity, flexibility, and importance. In terms of these five structural components,

> The "committed" orientation, on the one hand reflects an emphasis on the abstract relational qualities of religious belief which tend to be nonambiguous, well differentiated or multiplex and diversity-tolerant. It would also involve a personal, devotional commitment to religious values which suffuse daily activities.

> The "consensual" orientation on the other hand reflects an emphasis on the concrete, literal qualities of religious belief which tend to be vague

21. Gordon W. Allport, *The Individual and His Religion* (New York: Macmillan, 1950); Gordon W. Allport and J. Michael Ross, "Personal Religious Orientation and Prejudice," *Journal of Personality and Social Psychology* 5 (1957): 243-443.
22. Bernard Spilka, " 'The Compleat Person': Some Theoretical Views and Research Findings for a Theological Psychology of Religion," *Journal of Psychology and Theology* 4 (1976): 15-24; Russell O. Allen and Bernard Spilka, "Committed and Consensual Religion: A Specification of Religion-Prejudice Relationships," *Journal for the Scientific Study of Religion* 6 (1967): 191-206.
23. Allport and Ross, "Personal Religious Orientation and Prejudice," p. 434.
24. Russell O. Allen, "Religion and Prejudice: An Attempt to Clarify the Patterns of Relationship," (Ph.D. diss., U. of Denver, 1965).

and global, nondifferentiated and bifurcated, relatively restrictive and diversity-intolerant. It would also involve a detached or neutralized, magical or possibly vestigial commitment to religious values.[25]

People may hold the same religious beliefs and perform the same religious practices but differ radically in how religion affects their lives. It is necessary to know not only what people say they believe but how these beliefs are held. The style of belief (i.e., committed-intrinsic and consensual-extrinsic) appears to be independent of the content of the belief.

Although the intrinsic-extrinsic and committed-consensual dichotomies have been tested with people of all ages except children, the majority of the studies have used middle and late adolescents (i.e., high school and college students). Therefore, the research findings concerning religious orientation apply directly to the adolescent years. Table 5.2 summarizes these major research findings and thus contrasts the characteristics and correlates of the committed-intrinsic and consensual-extrinsic religious orientations.

The contrasts between the two religious styles summarized in table 5.2 deal predominantly with three areas: (1) orientation toward the self, (2) orientation toward others, and (3) orientation toward God.[26] Adolescents whose religion is of the intrinsic-committed form tend to have positive orientations toward the self, others, and God. On the other hand, the extrinsic-consensual adolescent religionist tends to be characterized by negative self-views, distance from and negative feelings toward others, and similar negative images of God.

Committed-intrinsic youth have positive self-esteem, positive views of human nature, and feelings of personal power and control over their lives. Consensual-extrinsic youth have negative self-esteem, feelings of powerlessness, and feel a lack of control over their lives.

In interpersonal relationships, committed-intrinsic youth have positive regard for people, move toward people, perceive others as trustworthy, evaluate others individually without concern for social status, and are concerned about being helpful and serving others. On the other hand, consensual-extrinsic youth have feelings of greater interpersonal distance, move away from people, perceive others as less trustworthy, and evaluate others on the basis of social position and other materialistic concerns.

Committed-intrinsic youth view God as being loving, personal, and kind. Consensual-extrinsic youth perceive a negative God who is impersonal, distant, wrathful, and vindictive. Furthermore, committed-intrin-

25. Ibid., p. 14.
26. Spilka, " 'The Compleat Person.' "

TABLE 5.2

SUMMARY OF RESEARCH FINDINGS ON RELIGIOUS ORIENTATION

Research Study	Committed—Intrinsic Orientation	Consensual—Extrinsic Orientation
Allport and Ross (1967)[27]	Low prejudice	High prejudice
Allen and Spilka (1967)[28]	Low prejudice; High world-mindedness: a world view of the problems of humanity, with mankind, rather than the nationals of a particular country, as the primary reference group.	High prejudice; Low world-mindedness; Tendency to express ideas reflecting a lack of personal worth or meaningfulness, and a loss of self-determination or adequacy. Mistrust of other people
Strickland and Shaffer (1971)[29]	Internal locus of control	External locus of control
Maddock and Kenny (1972)[30]	Positive view of human nature; People perceived as trustworthy	Neutral view of human nature; People perceived as less trustworthy
Raschke (1973)[31]	Open-minded	Close-minded
Spilka and Mullin (1974)[32]	Positive self-esteem; Feelings of personal power; Feelings of control over one's life; Positive regard for people; Evaluates others individually on the basis of their own merits; Positive image of God—i.e., loving, personal, kind, and merciful	Negative self-esteem; Feelings of powerlessness; Feelings of lack of control over one's life; Greater interpersonal distance; Makes distinctions among people on the basis of social position, categories, and structure. Negative image of God—i.e., wrathful, vindictive, unloving, impersonal, distant, and controlling
Kahoe (1975)[33]	Low to moderate authoritarianism	High authoritarianism
Spilka and Minton (1975)[34]	Noninstrumental orientation to life; Concerned about being helpful and serving others and minimizes the importance of money. High regard for family life, social goals, and self-realization; Independent, creative, flexible modes of thinking	Instrumental orientation to life; Materialistic and self-aggrandizing success-achievement orientation; High concern for security and status; Cognitive simplicity, uncreative mode of thinking, and response to form rather than content
Kahoe and Dunn (1975)[35]	Absence of fear of death	Fear of death
Minton and Spilka (1976)[36]	Positive view of death as expectation of an afterlife of reward	Negative view of death as natural end, unknown, failure, pain, punishment, loneliness, and forsaking loved ones
Entner and Fleck (1976)[37]	Lower anxiety, higher empathy, greater emotional stability, and more trusting	Higher anxiety, lower empathy, greater neuroticism, and less trusting

sic youth have a positive, nonfearing attitude toward death; whereas consensual-extrinsic youth have a negative, fearful view of death.

The presence of the two contrasting religious orientations among youth is further substantiated by the research findings of Merton Strommen in *Five Cries of Youth*.[38] He concluded that the cry of self-hatred and the cry of the joyous are the dominant ones among high school youth. The joyous youth, whom Strommen equates with Spilka's religiously committed youth, have positive self-esteem, find meaning in life through relationships with others and God, and identify with a personal, loving God. On the other hand, self-hating youth have low self-esteem, inhibited interpersonal relationships, and anxiety over their relationship with God.*

Although they feel alienated from self, others, and God, Strommen's low self-esteem youth expressed a desire for opportunities to change these relationships. In fact high school youth who are not low in self-esteem also demonstrated a high interest in bettering their relationships with others, with God, and with themselves.[39] It appears that self-esteem and enhanced vertical and horizontal relationships are central concerns to a large majority of religious youth.

27. Allport and Ross, "Personal Religious Orientation and Prejudice."
28. Allen and Spilka, "Committed and Consensual Religion."
29. Bonnie Strickland and Scott Shaffer, "I-E, I-E, & F," *Journal for the Scientific Study of Religion* 10 (1971): 366-69.
30. Richard Maddock and Charles Kenny, "Philosophies of Human Nature and Personal Religious Orientation," *Journal for the Scientific Study of Religion* 11 (1972): 277-81.
31. Vernon Raschke, "Dogmatism and Committed and Consensual Religiosity," *Journal for the Scientific Study of Religion* 12 (1973). 339-44.
32. Bernard Spilka and Michael Mullin, "Personal Religion and Psychosocial Schemata: A Research Approach to a Theological Psychology of Religion" (Paper presented at the 1974 Convention of the Society for the Scientific Study of Religion, Washington, D.C., October 26, 1974).
33. Richard Kahoe, "Authoritarianism and Religion: Relationships of F Scale Items to Intrinsic and Extrinsic Religious Orientations," *JSAS Catalogue of Selected Documents in Psychology* 5 (1975): 284-85.
34. Bernard Spilka and Barbara Minton, "Defining Personal Religion: Psychometric, Cognitive and Instrumental Dimensions" (Paper presented at the 1975 Convention of the Society for the Scientific Study of Religion, Milwaukee, Wis., October 24, 1975).
35. Richard Kahoe and Rebecca Dunn, "The Fear of Death and Religious Atttitudes and Behavior," *Journal for the Scientific Study of Religion* 14 (1975): 379-82.
36. Barbara Minton and Bernard Spilka, "Perspectives on Death in Relation to Powerlessness and Form of Personal Religion," *Omega* 7 (1976): 261-68.
37. Paul Entner and J. Roland Fleck, "Religious Orientation and Mental Health" (Paper presented at the 1976 Convention of the Western Psychological Association, Los Angeles, California, April 8, 1976).
38. Merton P. Strommen, *Five Cries of Youth* (New York: Harper & Row, 1974).

*It should be pointed out that Strommen equates the prejudiced youth rather than the self-hating youth with Spilka's consensual religionist, but both the self-hating and the prejudiced seem to parallel certain characteristics of the consensual.

39. *Clergy-Youth Counseling Project*, National Institute of Mental Health, Final Report, cited in Strommen, *Five Cries of Youth*, pp. 28-29.

RELIGIOUS VALUES AND CONCERNS

Five significant attempts have been made in recent years to examine the relationship of religion to the values and concerns of American adolescents. Four of the studies deal only with high school students, but the fifth, *A Study of Generations*,[40] also includes college-age youth. These five studies are summarized in the following section.

BEALER AND WILLETS: THE RELIGIOUS INTERESTS OF AMERICAN HIGH SCHOOL YOUTH

Bealer and Willets[41] summarized the findings of three national studies dealing with adolescent religious behavior: (1) a Gallup poll of 1,300 high school students;[42] (2) the Purdue University Opinion Polls of 1957 and 1962,[43] and (3) Strommen's national sample of Lutheran high school youth.[44] Their conclusions can be summarized under five headings.

First, although American adolescents are most concerned about their own personal-social relationships, they are not unconcerned about religion and reveal a level of religious concern "clearly above that which one might garner from the more popular notions."[45]

Second, American adolescents are highly traditional and orthodox in their religious beliefs. Some express doubts but few completely reject conservative views. Also, a large majority accept the values and agree with the religious orientation of their parents.

Third, the typical adolescent is quite ignorant of basic tenets of his faith. "While the adolescent overtly supports both the established church and the basic tenets of Judaeo-Christian belief, he may very well know little of the 'factual' information concerning his religion."[46]

Fourth, the American adolescent "hedges" in his religious orientation. The overwhelming majority are quite willing to agree that the Almighty exists, watches, and perhaps controls the world. But there is marked reluctance to really trust this control and count solely upon it. They are not at all sure that "God will take care of them."[47]

40. Merton P. Strommen et al., *A Study of Generations* (Minneapolis: Augsburg, 1972).
41. Robert Bealer and Fern Willets, "The Religious Interests of American High School Youth," *Religious Education* 62 (1967). 435-44.
42. George Gallup and Evan Hill, "Youth: the Cool Generation," *Saturday Evening Post*, December 23, 1961, pp. 63-80.
43. Herman Remmers, "Teenagers' Attitudes toward Study Habits, Vocational Plans, Religious Beliefs, and Luck," Report of Poll No. 67, the Purdue Opinion Panel (Lafayette, Ind.: Division of Educational Reference, December, 1962).
44. Merton P. Strommen, *Profiles of Church Youth* (St. Louis: Concordia, 1963).
45. Bealer and Willets, "The Religious Interests of American High School Youth," p. 438.
46. Ibid., p. 440.
47. Ibid., p. 439.

Fifth, the previous four statements describe the "average" or "typical" adolescent. Yet there is clearly a wide diversity of religious commitment. "There are some youth who have deep religious commitment and act upon it and some few who show almost no religiosity."[48]

STROMMEN: PROFILES OF CHURCH YOUTH

Profiles of Church Youth[49] reports the results of the 520-item Lutheran Youth Research Youth Inventory given to a cross section of Lutheran high school youth in 1959 and 1962. The 1959 sample included four groups which have since merged and formed the American Lutheran Church: (1) American Lutheran, (2) Evangelical Lutheran, (3) Lutheran Free, and (4) United Evangelical Lutheran. The 1962 sample consisted entirely of youth from the Lutheran Church—Missouri Synod. A total of 2,952 participated in the study. Ninety percent of those contacted in the 1959 sample responded, and 82 percent of those contacted in the 1962 sample responded. In addition, 291 pastors and 2,475 laymen participated by providing estimates of the concerns and desire for help on the part of their denominational youth. Strommen reports specific findings in chapters 4-18 and thirty-six general conclusions in chapter 19 of his book.[50] The most significant of these conclusions are summarized as follows.

First, three-fourths of Lutheran youth believe: God loves them, forgives them, controls the future, and intervenes in the lives of men; Jesus Christ is God incarnate and the only way to salvation; and God's Holy Spirit continues His creative work in men's lives. There is some confusion about the concepts of justification by faith and forgiveness. A substantial minority lack understanding that salvation is by grace alone through faith in Jesus Christ, view sins as a series of controllable infractions, see the gospel as a mere guide to right living, and accede to the tenets of a generalized religion. Also nearly half of the youth believe forgiveness places them in an intermittent state of grace, withdrawn with each sin and restored upon confession. Half do not believe they live in God's forgiveness constantly. More than half doubt the certainty of their salvation. These youth seem to confuse feeling with forgiveness; that is, a person is forgiven only when he feels right in his heart.

Second, religious goals or values placed third behind social acceptance and health as values most desired by these youth. Among the highest rated religious goals were Christian parenthood, certainty of salvation, God's will, and bringing others to Christ. When the individual value items were

48. Ibid., p. 441.
49. Strommen, *Profiles of Church Youth.*
50. Ibid., pp. 232-45.

combined into clusters, three systems of values appeared: (1) achievement, (2) service, and (3) happiness. These three value systems correspond to the three life goals identified in the 1961 Gallup Poll of American youth (i.e., happiness, success, and service) .[51]

Third, the most troubling of all youths' concerns are feelings of (1) inadequacy and self-disparagement (three out of four Lutheran youth are troubled over emotional immaturities, social ineptness, and academic problems) ; (2) apartness from God (two of three Lutheran youth are troubled over their uncertain relationship with God) ; and (3) lack of acceptance by others (especially in relationship to teachers and school classmates) .

Fourth, cognitive beliefs and religious activities are unrelated to much or little involvement in questionable or immoral practices. A positive relationship exists between moral behavior and both the religious climate of the home and the personal dedication of youth, as revealed by earnestness in religious practices.

Fifth, the image that adults in the church, including pastors and youth workers, have of the concerns of youth bears little resemblance to the ranking of concerns that the youth report. Adults exaggerate youth concerns over family, dating problems, and involvement in questionable activities, whereas the Lutheran youth are more concerned about faith, unresolved guilt, Christian vocation, and marriage. Although lay adults and pastors show little perception of youth's needs, they demonstrate an eagerness both to know their youth and to give them needed help. Also where there is a greater sensitivity or atmosphere of concern for youth, greater health is found among the youth.

Sixth, medium-sized churches (500 to 999 members) have greater influence on their youth than smaller or larger congregations. Adults in these congregations seem to be more sensitive to the variety of problems troublesome to youth.

In summary, Strommen states:

> It has been assumed . . . that adults have a fair idea of the concerns of their congregational youth. The study has shown they have little understanding of where their youth need help. It has been assumed also that the problem and needs are much the same in all congregations—that a youth program effective in one congregation should be successful in all others. But the evidence has clearly established the need for a ministry that is unique to each congregation.[52]

51. Gallup and Hill, "Youth: The Cool Generation."
52. Strommen, *Profiles of Church Youth*, p. 244.

ZUCK AND GETZ: CHRISTIAN YOUTH: AN IN-DEPTH STUDY

Christian Youth: An In-Depth Study[53] reports the results of the 336-item National Sunday School Association Youth Survey administered during 1966 and 1967 for the purpose of assessing the characteristics, concerns, and opinions of a national sample of evangelical youth (grades 9-12). A total of 2,646 youth "who profess to know Christ as Saviour" were included in the sample. The sample was selected from 197 churches, 47.5 percent of the 415 churches originally selected. The churches sampled were drawn from the National Sunday School Association (NSSA) list of over five thousand churches. This is the only major research effort which reports the concerns and opinions of evangelical youth exclusively, and there are a number of important findings.

First, a large majority of evangelical youth are actively involved in religious practices: weekly Sunday school attendance (87 percent); weekly Sunday morning church (81 percent); weekly Sunday evening church (63 percent), weekly youth group meetings (63 percent), daily prayer (67 percent), and tithing (51 percent). The one exception is daily Bible reading with only 25 percent participating.[54] This level of religious participation is generally greater than what Strommen found with Lutheran youth.[55]

Second, evangelical adolescents ranked their parents as the most influential factor leading to their Christian conversion, but ranked parents lower as a factor contributing to their spiritual life and growth. In fact the youth were more regular in Sunday school and church attendance than their parents, and few of the teenagers reported their families as having regular family devotions.

Third, the five greatest areas of concern were in order: (1) Christian living (i.e., Bible study, prayer, witnessing, living up to Christian convictions), (2) self-acceptance, (3) family living, (4) church life, and (5) boy-girl relationships. Less than one in three evangelical youths was satisfied in the area of Christian living, but those involved in daily Bible reading and prayer reported greater satisfaction with many aspects of their lives: (1) churches' ministries to them, (2) boy-girl relationships, and (3) the credibility of evangelical doctrines.

Fourth, evangelical youths expressed more concern about their personal problems related to self-acceptance (e.g., academic ability, personal ade-

53. Roy B. Zuck and Gene A. Getz, *Christian Youth: An In-Depth Study* (Chicago: Moody, 1968).
54. Ibid., pp. 43-46.
55. Strommen, *Profiles of Church Youth*, pp. 41-45.

quacy, and social relationships) than they did about their families, their churches, or their relationships with the opposite sex.

Fifth, evangelical youth with non-Christian parents were more dissatisfied with their Christian living, their academic competence, their sense of personal adequacy, their social relationships, the lack of unity in their families, and the prospects of being happily married. They did not differ in moral practices, and were in fact more sensitive to religious experiences and goals.

Sixth, three out of five evangelical youths stated that they believe unquestioningly in certain doctrines common to most evangelical churches (e.g., virgin birth of Christ, Christ's bodily resurrection, the universality of sin, etc.). Also, those youth with the greatest exposure to religious activities and spiritual experiences expressed the fewest doctrinal doubts.

Seventh, these youth felt relatively satisfied with the various church activities, but expressed discontentment with adults who fail to live up to the truths they profess to believe. They felt the church was giving adequate counsel for their spiritual problems, but felt a need for more help from the church with dating and self-related problems.

Eighth, Zuck and Getz used verbatim the forty values and goals items from Strommen's study of Lutheran youth.[56] The values of the evangelical youth compare closely in rank with those of Lutheran youth, with social and religious goals ranked first and second by evangelical youth and first and third by Lutheran youth. "These two groups were hardly different in their value structure."[57] The findings were also similar to Gallup[58] and Strommen[59] in the ranking of the three systems of values: happiness goals ranking first, with service and success ambitions second and third.

Ninth, in an attempt to measure the ethical values and moral standards of evangelical youth, Zuck and Getz measured their approval of and participation in a wide variety of more or less questionable practices. The great majority of evangelical youth disapproved of most activities "definitely prohibited by biblical injunctions" (e.g., permarital intercourse, stealing, cheating, lying, etc.).[60] They were "divided in their acceptance and rejection of practices and issues not clearly delineated in the Bible" (e.g., social behavior, socio-political issues, dating, and marriage practices).[61] The approval of and participation in these latter practices increases with the year in school, but decreases with more active religious participation.

56. Ibid.
57. Zuck and Getz, *Christian Youth: An In-Depth Study*, p. 132.
58. Gallup and Hill, "Youth: The Cool Generation."
59. Strommen, *Profiles of Church Youth*.
60. Zuck and Getz, *Christian Youth: An In-Depth Study*, pp. 136-37.
61. Ibid., p. 143.

The extent of youth participation in disapproved practices varied wide-ly—i.e., from 84 percent for loss of temper to 4 percent for premarital sex. But the majority of "inconsistent youth" reported their involvement as little rather than some or much. "Generally the teens were quite consistent in that most of them did not participate in those activities which they disapproved."[62]

STROMMEN: A STUDY OF GENERATIONS

A Study of Generations[63] reports the results of a 740-item questionnaire assessing the beliefs, values, attitudes, opinions, and religious life-styles of a representative sample of 4,745 Lutheran adults between the ages of fifteen and sixty-five. These people were members in 1970 of congregations in the three major Lutheran groups in the United States: The American Lutheran Church, the Lutheran Church—Missouri Synod, and the Lutheran Church in America.

The researchers set out to study three generations: (1) those born before the end of World War I (ages fifty to sixty-five), (2) those born between World War I and World War II (ages thirty to forty-nine), and (3) those born after World War II (ages fifteen to twenty-nine). The major question under study was: "Did the wars change our national life drastically enough to demark demonstrably different generations within these age groupings?"[64]

Four distinct age-groups or generations emerged from the data: (1) fifteen to twenty-nine, (2) thirty to thirty-nine, (3) forty to forty-nine, and (4) fifty to sixty-five. Further statistical analysis of the fifteen to twenty-nine generation yielded three subgenerations of youth: (1) high school (ages fifteen to eighteen), (2) college (ages nineteen to twenty-three), and (3) post-graduation years (ages twenty-four to twenty-nine).[65] The remainder of this section focuses on the findings concerning the high school and college subgenerations.

High school youth as a subgeneration differed significantly from college-age youth, the older subgeneration of youth (ages twenty-four to twenty-nine), and all three adult generations on an interrelated set of dimensions. They are more peer-oriented, express more feelings of isolation and pressure, place high priority on self-development, see less purpose and meaning in life, and participate more extensively in questionable personal activities (exceeded only by college-age youth in this respect). They par-

62. Ibid., p. 161.
63. Strommen et al., *A Study of Generations.*
64. Ibid., p. 21.
65. Ibid., p. 23

.ticipate significantly more in congregational activity than college-age
youth and at the same level as the three adult generations.[66]

College-age youth as a subgeneration differ significantly on six characteristics. They are lowest in congregational activity, in the need for unchanging structure, the need for religious absolution, the desire to keep
socially distant from persons of different race and religion, and the tendency to exaggerate the truth claim of the church by identifying the truth
with only their denomination. They are highest in participation in questionable activities.[67]

The predominant pattern of generational tension contrasts the two
youngest subgenerations of youth (high school and college, ages fifteen
to twenty-three) versus the subgeneration of youth in transition (ages
twenty-four to twenty-nine) together with all three adult generations
(ages thirty to sixty-five). (See table 5.3).[68]

TABLE 5.3

PREDOMINANT PATTERN OF GENERATIONAL TENSION

Emphases of Ages 15-23	*Emphases of Ages 24-65*
More change in church and society	Less change in church and society
Variety	Norms
Acceptance of diversity	Exclusiveness
Anxiety and questioning	Certainty of belief
Little ability to affect decision-making	Power
Corporate responsibility	Individual responsibility

NOTE: Adapted from Merton P. Strommen, *A Study of Generations* (Minneapolis:
Augsburg, 1972), p. 259.

In conclusion, the areas of greatest difference and tension between youth
and adults include: (1) distrust of adults by youth; (2) priorities given
to different expressions of faith; (3) unwillingness of youth to delay gratification; (4) greater feelings on the part of youth for the needs of people;
(5) discrepancy between youth's rhetoric about their feelings for people
and youth's actions in helping people; (6) openness to change in congregational life and ministry with emphasis on the mission of the church,
the role of clergy, and appropriateness of worship practices; and (7) feel-

66. Ibid., pp. 230-31.
67. Ibid., pp. 232-33.
68. Ibid., p. 259.

ings of alienation from God, church, and life in terms of pessimism, isolation, and purposelessness.[69]

STROMMEN: FIVE CRIES OF YOUTH

Five Cries of Youth[70] reports the results of the 420-item Youth Research Center Survey given to a nationwide random sample of 7,050 high school age youth in 1970. The entire denominational spectrum was represented including American Baptist, Roman Catholic, United Methodist, Southern Baptist, Presbyterian, Lutheran, Church of Christ, Evangelical Covenant, and Episcopal, and also young people in Young Life. Answers to the 420 questions grouped themselves into five major categories, or cries, which define the areas of greatest concern in the lives of these high school youth: (1) self-esteem, (2) family unity and well-being, (3) welfare of people, (4) achieving favor, and (5) personal faith.

Cry of self-hatred. The cry of self-hatred is the most commonly voiced and the most intensely felt of the five cries. It rises out of feelings of worthlessness, self-criticism, and loneliness, and is a problem to one out of five (20%) church youth.

Strommen found eight feelings and concerns to be characteristic of the youth with low self-esteem. Three are feelings about oneself (self-relational): (1) distress over personal faults (self-criticism), (2) lack of self-confidence (personal anxiety), and (3) low self-regard. The other five are concerns about others (other-relational): (1) poor classroom relationships, (2) academic problems, (3) anxiety about God-relationship, (4) concern over family relationships, and (5) anxiety over relationships with the opposite sex.

Cry of psychological orphans. The major preoccupation of these youth is a troubled family and home situation. They are typical church youth except for their home life, and Strommen points to the parents as being primarily responsible for the disruption in the family. These youth want to be part of a stable family where acceptance, care, and love are expressed.

Strommen cites four major characteristics of these distressed homes: (1) family pressures such as separation or divorce of parents, illness, financial pressures, parent-youth strife, father absence, unemployment, and death; (2) distress over parental relationships including lack of communication and understanding between a youth and his parents, feelings of being treated like a child, and parental distrust or rejection of him and his friends; (3) family disunity including a frigid atmosphere and lack of understanding and consideration for one another; and (4) lack of social

69. Ibid., pp. 239-58.
70. Strommen, *Five Cries of Youth.*

concern among family members including being unresponsive to the needs of people outside their home and lack of involvement in any form of social action or helping activity.

Running away from home, delinquent behavior, and contemplation of suicide are among the most common self-destructive actions used by these youth to escape their distressed home situations. In fact, among the 458 youth from the most troubled homes, 57 percent stated they sometimes considered suicide.

Cry of social protest. The 335 socially concerned youth in the sample are distinguishable by means of five major characteristics. They are: (1) humanitarian, (2) oriented to change, (3) socially involved, (4) concerned over national issues, and (5) critical of the institutional church in which adults seem not to be "caring." They also tend to be intellectually brighter than the average church youth and are more likely to have parents who are in a profession. They do not differ from other church youth in doctrinal beliefs, religious practices, and involvement in the life of the congregation.

Cry of the prejudiced. These youth, about one in seven church youth, have adopted a sort of do-it-yourself religion that stresses achievement, right living, doing the best one can—that is, man's effort to achieve the favor of God. Strommen equates their religion to Spilka's consensual religious orientation and cites four major characteristics: (1) prejudice, (2) institutional loyalty (i.e., they are compliant members who are less likely to question what they are taught), (3) self-oriented values, and (4) concern over national issues.

Although their avowed religiousness (e.g., wanting a closer relationship with God, finding meaning and purpose in life, finding God's will, etc.) is well above average, their practices of personal piety (e.g., Bible reading, prayer, church attendance, giving, witnessing, etc.) do not differ from other church youth. They appear to talk a better religious game than they play. There is no visible evidence of the changed relationships they verbalize.

Cry of the joyous. The cry of joy is found in one-third of all church youth. It rises out of a sense of identity and mission that centers in the person of Jesus Christ. These youth have the feeling of being a whole person, identified with a God who loves them and people who care about them. Strommen equates their religion to Spilka's committed religious orientation and cites six major characteristics.

First, these youth are identified with a personal God, and for them Christianity is primarily a personal relationship. These committed youth who know a personal God: (1) participate actively in congregational and private religious activities, (2) pray especially for people needing God's special help, (3) seek God's help in deciding right or wrong behavior, and (4) reflect strong interest in help provided by the congregation. Their personal faith positively affects their ethical behavior, concern for others, outlook on life, attitudes toward parents, and sense of personal responsibility. They are also substantially higher in self-esteem than other church youth.

Second, these youth are active with God's people. Their involvement includes not only faithful church attendance, but faithfulness in personal religious practices such as Bible reading, prayer, financial giving, and corporate worship. They feel positive about what is offered by their religious community.

Third, these youth are motivated to grow and develop in their faith. They seek out experiences that will enhance their understanding of and relationship with God, their relationships with others, and their understanding of themselves.

Fourth, these youth feel morally responsible for the way they live and behave. They look to God for help in making ethical decisions and their beliefs are highly predictive of their actions.

Fifth, these youth want to serve others and find meaning in life through relationships with others and God.

Sixth, these youth have a hopeful and positive life perspective and feel hopeful concerning the future.

Summary. Strommen notes that the cries of self-hatred and joy are the dominant ones. "In them one meets a classic theme of alienation and reconciliation. The first cry is one of alienation from self, others, and God; the fifth is one of identification with God, his people, and their lifestyle."[71] The cries of self-hatred, family conflict, social protest, and prejudice are more characteristic of peer-oriented youth, who distrust adults and look to their own age-group for direction, than broadly oriented youth, who trust adults and relate well to all age levels.

Strommen further notes that adults underestimate the extent to which youth are concerned about their religious faith and relationship with God. They are also unaware of the close link between their own behavior and the needs of youth.[72]

CONCLUSION

It was hoped that a review of the research literature on adolescent religiosity would delineate difference between early, middle, and late adolescents in their religious concepts, religious orientation, and religious values

71. Ibid., p. 112.
72. Ibid., p. 125.

and concerns. Such changes and differences no doubt exist, but the empirical data available is not extensive enough to be sensitive to such developmental trends. Further cross-sectional studies are needed, but longitudinal data on changes in religious concepts, religious orientation, and religious values and concern is especially crucial.

FOR FURTHER READING

Allen, E., and Hites, R. "Factors in Religious Attitudes of Older Adolescents." *Journal of Social Psychology* 55 (1961): 265-73.

Argyle, M., and Beit-Hallahmi, B. *The Social Psychology of Religion.* London: Routledge & Kegan Paul, 1975.

Baker, W. W., and Koppe, W. A. *Children's Religious Concepts.* Schenectady, N.Y.: Union College Character Research Report, 1959.

Coleman, James S. *The Adolescent Society.* Glencoe, Ill.: Free Press, 1961.

Elkind, David. "The Development of Religious Understanding in Children and Adolescents." In *Research on Religious Development.* Edited by Merton Strommen. New York: Hawthorn, 1971.

Elkind, D., and Elkind, S. "Varieties of Religious Experience in Young Adolescents." *Journal for the Scientific Study of Religion* 2 (1962): 102-12.

Goldman, Ronald. *Readiness for Religion.* New York: Seabury, 1965.

Havighurst, R., and Keating B. "The Religion of Youth." *Research on Religious Development.* Edited by Merton Strommen. New York: Hawthorn, 1971.

Hollingshead, August. *Elmtown's Youth.* New York: Wiley, 1949.

Keary, Dermot. "Adolescent Spirituality." *Religious Education* 63 (1968): 376-83.

Keniston, Kenneth. *The Uncommitted.* New York: Harcourt, 1960.

Loukes, Harold. *Teenage Religion.* London: SCM, 1961.

Matteson, David. *Adolescence Today: Sex Roles and the Search for Identity.* Homewood, Ill.: Dorsey, 1975.

Parker, Clyde. "Changes in Religious Beliefs of College Students." In *Research on Religious Development.* Edited by Merton Strommen. New York: Hawthorn, 1971.

Piaget, Jean. *The Child's Conception of the World.* London: Routledge, 1929.

Rohrbaugh, J., and Jessor, R. "Religiosity in Youth: A Personal Control Against Deviant Behavior." *Journal of Personality* 43 (1975): 136-55.

Stewart, Charles. *Adolescent Religion: A Developmental Study of the Religion of Youth.* Nashville: Abingdon, 1967.

Van Dyke, P., and Pierce-Jones, J. "The Psychology of Religion of Middle and Late Adolescence: A Review of Empirical Research, 1950-1960." *Religious Education* 58 (1963): 529-37.

6

Adolescents in Socio-Psychological Perspective

Donald M. Joy

IT MAY BE THAT adolescence is a phenomenon produced by modern societies and technology. As one contemplates the social and psychological dimensions of the teenager's world, he should consider that man's favorite ways of living might, among other things, be severely complicating the task of growing up.

THE PHENOMENON OF ADOLESCENCE

For millennia, childhood was not marked off from adulthood in any clear way. Children were miniature adults and artists frequently represented them in this way. Much less was an in-between stage recognized or evidenced.

The relatively modern phenomenon of adolescence is defined as a psycho-social period beginning with the arrival of sexual potency and extending until economic and social independence is achieved. During those years the young person develops the body of an adult, but much of his childhood personality remains. And though he still needs love and acceptance, he no longer has the innocent belief that he is loved and accepted by everyone.

Today's adolescent is, in short, all dressed up with no place to go. His entire culture seems to shout to him: "Get lost! Go to college! Join the Army! Go anywhere but here; we have no job for you. We cannot tolerate your marrying until you are productive. Come back when you are twenty-five, and we will validate your citizenship in the form of acceptance and membership in our exclusive adult enterprises of marriage, family, jobs, and clubs." There is a sense in which college graduation or military ser-

DONALD M. JOY, Ph.D., is Professor of Human Development and Christian Education, Asbury Theological Seminary, Wilmore, Kentucky.

vice and discharge have become the rites of passage from childhood to adulthood. This ten-year extension of childhood which we call adolescence is a brightly packaged gift which our society gives to the child when he encounters pubescence (see figure 6.1).

Fig. 6.1. *Child becomes adult*

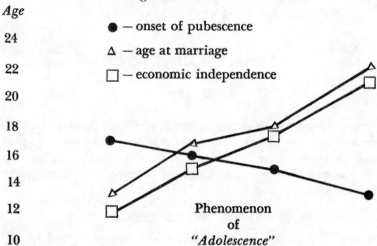

NOTE: This stylized drawing suggests how cultural variants of age at economic independence, age at marriage, and age at the onset of pubescence interplay to produce the phenomenon of adolescence in industrial and technological societies. It is ironic that pubescence strikes earliest in those cultures which hold off economic independence and marriage longest.

PUBERTY AND SEXUALITY

Puberty when defined by primary sexual exidences, begins in the male by first ejaculation and in the female by the first menstrual period. Secondary sex characteristics are more visible: breast formation and fattening hips in girls, the appearance of facial hair in boys along with the loss of body fat, elevated and enlarged cheek bones, and the cracking, changing voice. On the average, girls mature from twelve to eighteen months ahead of boys. The growth spurt which accompanies the onset of puberty thrusts many girls up to embarrassing height compared to boys of the same age; and late maturing boys may remain dwarfed in comparison, not only to the girls but to earlier maturing males. These radical variants in growth are among the most troublesome social factors the young teenager deals with. Girls will take comfort many times in knowing that few girls grow more than an inch in height after their first menstruation. And boys are often relieved to know that if they have not started shaving on a regular basis, they are still likely to grow several inches taller.

In defining puberty it becomes necessary to elaborate distinctly separate details regarding the two sexes.

The female sex system might be called a "process system." The maturing of the reproductive system puts in motion the release of the ovum on roughly a monthly cycle. This sexual functioning occurs without erotic or orgasmic events being intrinsic to the process. Theoretically a female could live to old age and die without experiencing erotic pleasure in relation to reproductive functioning. The female's sexual response system is learned and may be adapted to a wide variety of stimuli and to a wide range of frequencies of sexual experience. In our erotically saturated environment girls are generally ready to respond sexually from middle childhood.

The male sex system has sometimes been referred to as a "hydraulic system."[1] By hydraulic is meant that the reproductive functioning and orgasm are interlocked. The erection and ejaculation may occur spontaneously on first occasions, sometimes with great embarrassment. The "wet dream" is less traumatic. Self-manipulation is attractive to most boys after spontaneous erections begin. Sex play leading to orgasm may occur with friends of either sex, although most boys first play with other boys. The longer males go to school and the later they marry, the more likely they are to carry self-manipulation into later life.[2]

Arrival at puberty is increasingly early in North America and Western Europe. In 1840 the average girl's first menstruation occurred at age seventeen. In 1960 the age was thirteen, and by 1970 it was slightly earlier than age thirteen. (See figure 6.2). First orgasm in males is less observable and hence less reliable data is available, but the trend has been the same. Corresponding earlier differences in height and weight are also on record.

It has long been thought that early sexual maturity was a function of warmer climate, better nutrition, and genetic factors. While the latter two may be causative, it now appears that a major influence is light. The pineal gland, which is light-sensitive, produces melatonin—a blood chemical which is produced only during darkness and is believed to slow maturation, depress ovulation, and decrease secretion of ovarian and testicular hormones. It acts, in other words, as a braking system on the sexual development of the child. Early research suggests that even artificial light

1. Boyd R. McCandless, *Adolescents: Behavior and Development* (Hinsdale, Ill.: Dryden, 1970), pp. 14-15.
2. Generalizations drawn from main lines of Alfred C. Kinsey et al., *Sexual Behavior in the Human Male* (Philadelphia: Saunders, 1948).

Fig. 6.2. *Historical trends in age at menarche*

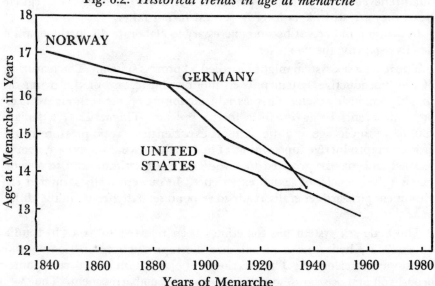

NOTE: Adapted from J. M. Tanner, "Sequence, Temper, and Individual Variation in Growth and Development of Boys and Girls Aged Twelve to Sixteen," in *Twelve to Sixteen: Early Adolescence,* edited by Jerome Kagan and Robert Coles (New York: Norton, 1972), p. 23.

inhibits the production of melatonin.[3] If extended research confirms this first report, it will be ironic that man's cleverness in rolling back darkness has accelerated the sexual development of our children and complicated all of our lives.

Though the male system may be regarded as "hydraulic," this is not to suggest that direct sexual stimulation is necessary for the health of the pubescent male. Seminal fluids, including live sperm, periodically over-flow into the urinary tract; indeed, the standard fertility test for young males is taken from an early morning urine specimen. This overflow, along with the spontaneous ejaculatory activities during both waking and sleeping, make direct stimulation unnecessary for physical well-being.

When the female and male sex systems are compared, it could be said, then, that the female sexual response system is basically psycho-social. That is, the female has only general hormonal inclination toward sexual awareness, but is highly responsive to learned and experienced sexual be-havior. The male, on the other hand, is more directly affected biologically, so that his system might be regarded as bio-psycho-social.

3. Gay Gaer Luce, "Trust Your Body Rhythms," *Psychology Today,* April 1975, pp. 52-53.

It becomes urgent, therefore, for both sexes, but especially for young males, that Christian parents and workers with youth not only clearly teach and explain biblical standards of sexual morality but also provide Christian, spiritual models in language, feelings, and expression.

While it is important that Christians avoid using secular research on sexual behavior as a baseline to suggest *what Christians ought to do,* it is nevertheless helpful to examine that research in order to understand *what people in general tend to do.* The intervention of God's grace can and should effectively transform the behavior of believers, but that transformation is all the more likely to be executed well if they can deal honestly with the standards and patterns of behavior which preceded the intervention of grace. It is also of maximum importance that Christian workers understand well the nature of man, both from the evidence of Scripture and from the evidence of creation. When both are reduced to their basic elements, they will confirm each other.

IDENTITY AND IMAGE

A popular news magazine reported that during the 1960s when young people were being jailed for their many forms of protest, one book more than any other was being carried into the cells. It was Erik Erikson's *Childhood and Society.*[4] The enormous popularity of Erikson with youth stemmed from his use of two words to describe an almost universal youth experience: "identity crisis."

Much writing and speaking has deplored the "generation gap." Doubtless some kinds of communication gaps exist between the generations, illustrated by Herbert Hoover's comment upon hearing that the United States now had close-up photographs of the moon and was going to place men on it. "I am part of a generation that doesn't understand that," he is reported to have said. But Alvin Toffler's *Future Shock* destroys simplistic ideas of a parent-teen generation gap.[5] The communications problem is much more complex. Changes are happening so fast that no one can live without gaps of all kinds being spawned between him and his world.

But the "identity crisis" language has a ring of truth. David Ausubel spoke of it in terms of "satellization."[6] The young child satellizes with his parents—regards them as indistinguishable from himself: "I'd rather be us than anybody I know!" is the cry of a well satellized young boy happy with his dad's selection of a new used car. The nonsatellizing child

4. Erik H. Erikson, *Childhood and Society,* 2d ed. (New York: Norton, 1963).
5. Alvin Toffler, *Future Shock* (New York: Random, 1970).
6. David Ausubel develops the satellization model from Freudian constructs. See his *Theory and Problems of Adolescent Development* (New York: Grune & Stratton, 1954), pp. 167-216.

who never develops close bonds of identity with his parents will be in for trouble not only during his adolescence, but probably for his entire lifetime.

With adolescence comes the "desatellization" of the child. He spins out from the orbit of parental identity and must define himself as distinct from them. This phase may be turbulent, often in direct proportion to (1) the failure of the parents to give him from childhood a sense of his worth as an individual and (2) the tenacity of the parents in restricting his free responsibility as a person. There is risk involved in allowing certain freedoms to children, but without that practice in child rearing, desatellization will come more abruptly and often with severe pain to all involved. One of the newer adages makes the point poetically: "If you love something, set it free. If it comes back to you, it's yours. If it doesn't, it never was."

In early adult years, Ausubel suggests, there normally will be a stabilization—a "resatellization." The young adult will strongly resemble his parents in values and life-style, though he will now be established in his own autonomous "orbit." All of this is reminiscent of Proverbs 22:6, which notes that the *child* who is trained up in the way he should go will not depart from that way *when he is old.*

Paul Tournier paints a similar picture but with distinctive elements.[7] He notes that the young child must be granted *privacy* if he is to become an *individual*—that the strength of his individuality is directly proportional to the respect he has received for his privacy: a locked box or drawer, respect for his privacy in his room, in the bathroom, and respect for his own "business" without prying every detail of his mind from him. But Tournier notices that the emerging adolescent needs to begin to share his secrets. Boys more often make their disclosures in a small group of close friends. Girls most often share intimately with only one or two very close friends—but the opening of the treasures of privacy marks the beginning of adult personhood. Sharing some personal secrets is an essential price of becoming a mature person. Such disclosures are most completely made within marriage, as two persons help bring each other to their highest experiences of personhood when they are most completely known. Tournier goes on to suggest that disclosure to God—totally and beyond our own capacity to verbalize about ourselves—brings the highest and finest expression of personhood achievement, in the acceptance of God's grace as we acknowledge the truth about ourselves.

Erikson sees the identity crisis as consisting of two magnetic poles.[8]

7. Paul Tournier, *Secrets* (Richmond: Knox, 1965).
8. Erik H. Erikson, "Eight Stages of Man," in *Childhood and Society*, pp. 219-33.

The adolescent tends to be pulled toward a stable picture of himself as a person of carefully defined characteristics—usually very much in the pattern of parents, or other parent-like adults in his life, who provide suitable models. But he is also pulled toward experimentation with pictures of himself that depart significantly from the values and charcteristics of those adults close to him. This tension Erikson represents by this formulation: identity vs. identity diffusion. Identity diffusion appears to be more dominant with youngsters who have lived with coercive control in their homes and where love and respect never won from them a sense of mutual respect and freely made commitment to the parental values.

James Coleman has chronicled the rise of peer influence in the child's life.[9] By the time the child is in the ninth grade, he tends to have reached the point at which his friends have their maximum power over him. According to Coleman's study, slightly more than half of young teens indicate that their friends influencc thcm more than their parents do on day-by-day decisions. This strength of influence will remain near this peak through high school and begin to wane during college.

The adolescent is easily caught in the magnetic pole of his peers and may experiment with their ways of valuing. He may run afoul of the law, spend a night in jail, and acquire a permanent police record all as a consequence of one minor flirtation with another picture of himself. This is an example of what Erik Erikson means by "identity diffusion"— the sampling of various kinds of behavior at variance with the dominant picture the young person has of who he is or who he eventually will become. It is important in ministry that the adolescent not be locked into a permanent identity by an isolated or hopefully temporary bit of behavior. Workers with youth do everyone a service in helping a youngster caught in this kind of situation to see that what he needs, and perhaps wants, to become may be very different from what his immediate reputation seems to be.

The rise of peer power over the adolescent provides him with both models and critics at a time when he is becoming painfully self-conscious about the image he is projecting. "I'd rather be dead than out of step with my generation!" one boy told his father. That kind of leverage is evident in the obedience of virtually all adolescents to peer-defined values regarding music and dress. And since high school students control a large part of the nation's money, manipulators of teen appetites in music and dress are always hard at work to tap this resource. In the late sixties, however, the adolescent world can be credited with reversing a syndicated decision about skirt length. The effect, which is still evident, was to break

9. James Coleman, *The Adolescent Society* (Glencoe, Ill.: Free Press, 1961).

the tyranny of the hemline dictators and to legitimize variety in fashion. Today's "acceptable" gear ranges from velour jeans through skirts of all lengths, to very formal wear—even all at the same occasion. Some teens delight in mixing formal with casual dress—a tuxedo with sneakers, for example—as if to assert independence from fad makers. Teens appear to have been less successful in the area of music. Their combos and rock bands tend to sound much alike. They have built, however, a music environment in which participation and performance is more the name of the game than is mere consumerism.

The adolescent's susceptibility to peer influence sets him up to be a pawn in the hands of hawkers who claim to sell what the teen needs: self-assurance, good looks, a good physique, and certification that he is the "cool" man or that she is the "cool" woman. Pushers of addictives such as tobacco and liquor have long made their appeals directly to the new market, no doubt knowing both their susceptibility and their long-term market value. Advertising across the decades changes in its content but remains constant in its appeal: whatever is regarded as the popular image is associated with the product.

Given the adolescent's identity and image needs, many churches place high priority on personnel and program to attract teens and bring them to Christ. If the teen tends to move with the crowd, to "swarm", then ministry might be formulated in such a way as to work with this characteristic instead of always doing battle with it. Walk in on a certain youth group in Plainview, Texas, for example, and observe a program that attracts virtually the whole youth population in the church and their friends. It is carried forward under the able ministry of the associate pastor and as a high priority for the total parish. Or walk through the upper floors of the education building of a leading evangelical church in Van Nuys, California, and see swarms of junior high and high school teens caught up in Sunday evening activities that make a lazy evening at home or mere "bombing around" seem pale and uninviting. Such forms of youth ministry have emerged as leaders have analyzed what the levers are which pressure kids and have moved to sanctify those levers and to use them for goal achievement in the kingdom of God.

CONSCIENCE AND CHOICE

The apron strings will be cut—either deliberately and cleanly or with rips and tears. With adolescence the emerging person moves into a phase of life which gives enough freedom of action for a teen to move beyond the gaze of parents and other significant adults. As a child, he was under both the responsibility and the control of his parents. Now he may continue to be the legal ward of his parents, but he is increasingly free from their control. He will now be consulting his personal and internal scales of values—most of which will be carbon copies of his parents' values if there have been positive and strong transactions and discussions during his childhood. In this process his conscience is strongly involved. Secular research for nearly fifty years has been studying the conscience—to learn how it acquires its value content and how it exercises control over behavior.[10] The conscience is a clearly biblical construct, an endowment unique to humans. The New Testament recognizes the Spirit-directed conscience as a true guide for action (Rom 13:5) but also recognizes that a conscience can be twisted and perverse (1 Cor 8:7). The emerging freedom of action granted to the adolescent makes it urgent that youth leaders understand the influences that pull at him when he is in the throes of moral choices.

The biblical model for child development places the infant in the custody of a pair of parents of opposite sex. Social science research now suggests that mother and father do have crucial roles in the formation of the child's conscience and value systems. Robert Sears was among the first to find a direct connection or correlation between a young boy's ability to resist temptation and the warmth of the relationship that existed between the boy and his father.[11] Boys whose fathers were cold and withdrawn and who resisted spending time with them tended to have a low resistance to temptation. After World War II, Eastern universities noted marked differences between the verbal and numerical scores of young men and women who were then enrolling and the scores of previous students. They traced the differences to the fact that these new students had been separated from their fathers because of overseas military duty. That initial discovery spawned extensive research into the effects of father absence on both boys and girls. Almost all the effects are directly connected to the moral behavior of the children.

Girls without fathers tend to fall into one of two categories of inappropriate heterosexual behavior. If the father has been lost by death, but was otherwise warm and affirming to his daughter, she tends to become shy and withdrawn—a wallflower lacking in social confidence. If the father was lost because of desertion or divorce, she tends to become inappropriately assertive with males—seductive, suggestive, desperate for male

10. See Robert R. Sears et al., *Identification and Child Learning* (Stanford: Stanford U., 1965).
11. See any of the works of Robert R. Sears, but especially his *Identification and Child Rearing*, noting the chapters dealing with resistance to temptation. See also the film *The Conscience of a Child*, in the series *Focus on Behavior*. It features Robert Sears as narrator and is available from most university audiovisual libraries.

affirmation of any kind. Both kinds of effects appear with high consistency regardless of the age at which the absence occurs, but the earlier the loss the more pronounced the effect tends to be.

Boys without fathers (or with fathers who for all practical purposes are inactive and noncommunicative) tend (1) to develop compensatory "masculinity": inappropriate and exaggerated aggression, consumption, and sexual exploitation; (2) to become effeminate, with a lack of interest in the usual male activities; (3) to become sexually inverted: homosexual in preference, with a more passive orientation than the typical male—the latter characteristic probably learned as part of the sex role acquired from his only parent, his mother; (4) to develop a defective conscience: unable to wait, high demand for instant gratification.[12]

Perhaps the most helpful research related to conscience is that which measures moral thinking. Jean Piaget first systematically studied moral thinking. He reported on Swiss children with whom he played marbles and discussed the rules of the game. He also used interview problem stories and asked children to solve them. He published his findings in 1932, under the title *The Moral Judgment of the Child*.[13] More than twenty years later, Lawrence Kohlberg extended Piaget's research by refining his observation procedures, advancing a series of six stages of moral thought, and extending his research to include adolescents and later adults.[14]

Such research suggests several important things for workers with children and young people:

1. Each person constructs a picture of reality in his mind, thus creating his own distinctive "cognitive structure" of reality.
2. There are three major levels of moral thought—major structural views of reality, each having two or more sublevels called stages and substages.
3. Progress through the levels is one-directional; all movement is upward;

12. These father-absent studies are summarized by E. Mavis Hetherington and Jan L. Deur, "The Effects of Father Absence on Child Development," in *The Young Child: Reviews of Research*, ed. W. W. Hartup and N. L. Smothergill, vol. 2 (Washington D.C.: Nat. Assn. for Ed. of Young Children, 1972), pp. 303-19. See also E. Mavis Hetherington, "Girls Without Fathers," *Psychology Today*, February 1973, p. 47.
13. Jean Piaget, *The Moral Judgment of the Child* (1932; reprint, Glencoe, Ill.: Free Press, 1965).
14. Lawrence Kohlberg, *The Development of Modes of Moral Thinking and Choice in the Years 10 to 16* (Chicago: U. of Chicago, 1958). The present author's research has probed the issues of conscience: Donald M. Joy, *The Effects of Value-Oriented Instruction in the Church and in the Home* (Ann Arbor, Mich.: University Microfilms, 1969); Donald M. Joy, "Some Clues about Advanced Early Moral Reasoning," unpublished paper, 1975; "Human Development and Christian Holiness," *The Asbury Seminarian* 28 (April 1976): 5-27.

no levels or stages are missed, though most persons eventually stop level growth and remain locked somewhere in the first two available levels.

4. Progress through the levels is contingent on biological ripening, but is not automatically produced by it. (Table 6.1 indicates the earliest and most likely ages at which transition into the various stages and levels may occur.)
5. Progress through the levels is contingent on formal operational cognitive ability, but is not significantly related to IQ.
6. Progress through the levels is most directly facilitated by the person's (a) experiencing a highly verbal environment in which moral issues are discussed; (b) taking or being thrust into responsibility; (c) having of necessity to make irrevocable moral choices, of living with them, and of interpreting them to others; and (d) taking responsibility for the care and welfare of persons other than himself.
7. Growth or movement from one level to another tends to generate inner turbulence. Sometimes this is sensed as doubt, a feeling that the secure world of the past is gone forever. Even agnosticism may be produced by growth in moral thinking, as the new "structure" emerges without clear categories for issues once thought to be "black and white."

Based on his experimental research with seventy-six boys between the ages of ten and fifteen years, Kohlberg identified three major levels of moral thinking. He called them preconventional, conventional, and post-conventional.[15]

The "preconventional" person may be well-behaved by cultural standards of right and wrong, but he interprets morality by the physical consequences which follow an act or an event: pain, pleasure, or a reciprocal exchange of favors. This is a typical level for children of ages five through ten, but becomes the permanent moral "home" of a large number of adults. Adults who become lodged here tend to be from downtrodden social or economic groups and from professions which reward arrogance, deception, ladder climbing, and payoffs.

The "conventional" person finds his definition of right and wrong in the expectation and rules of his family, tribe, group, or nation. He is concerned with conformity to their expectations, but later is concerned with maintaining, supporting, and justifying their values. This level is typical for adolescence, though many adolescents remain in level one orientation.

15. Lawrence Kohlberg, "The Cognitive-Developmental Approach to Moral Education," *Phi Delta Kappan,* June 1975, pp. 670-77.

TABLE 6.1
DEVELOPMENT OF MORAL THINKING

Level	Stage	Ages
LEVEL III Postconventional PRINCIPLE	**6 Universal Ethical Principle Orientation** A solitary conscience guided by self-affirmed universal principles on ultimate values.	25 to 35 (if at all)
	5 Social Contract/Consensus Orientation Voluntarily contracting persons arriving at corporate consensus, implement contract/code to protect the rights, dignity, and worth of individuals.	
LEVEL II Conventional AUTHORITY	**4½ Cynical Ethical Relativism Orientation** Optional stage: Confronted with pluralistic values, person concludes all are relative, becomes disoriented, not yet able to perceive ultimate principles, consorts for security.	16 to 25
	4 Maintenance of Order Through Law Orientation Laws are regarded as glue which holds society together. They are sacred because of this maintenance function. Leads to law for its own sake, legalism, and proliferation of laws.	12 to 25
	3 Interpersonal Concordance Orientation Concern for wishes and demands of other persons, outside locus of authority. "On my honor" characterizes this wish to live up to the expectations of significant others.	10 to 12
LEVEL I Preconventional PRUDENCE	**2 Instrumental Relativist Orientation** Right action consists of doing that which instrumentally satisfies my own needs. I have limited ability to perceive the needs of others—only insofar as meeting those needs meets my greater satisfaction.	7 to 10
	1 Punishment and Obedience Orientation Physical consequences of an action define its goodness or badness, no concern for intentions or for any underlying moral order.	5 to 8

Ages indicate earliest and more probable as range limits.

The "postconventional" level is characterized by a commitment to self-chosen, universal moral principles (as compared to "laws" of level two). These moral principles have validity, existence, and authority quite apart from any particular persons or groups who hold them or from any mere codified statement regarding moral behavior. Few persons seem consistently to function at level three moral orientation before the age of twenty-three years, and the more common age level for this typology is the thirties. Only a small percent of the adult American population would appear to function in level three consistently.

Transition from level to level requires substantial experience and growth into the new level. For the considerations of this chapter, then, it would appear that levels one and two must be regarded as the typical functional levels of adolescents.

A distillation of implications for workers with church adolescents from research on the development of moral thinking would include the following considerations.

1. Early teens and most high school persons are unable to consider the principled reasons behind many adult concerns for moral behavior. They see, instead, only the immediate physical consequences or the expectations of significant persons as sufficient motivation to behave in a certain way. This will mean that ministry requires the generous assignment of morally mature, attractive, and articulate adults to the teen ministries. These leaders must be able to establish and maintain a solid floor of moral expectations, to articulate them as positively as possible, to state the principled reasons why they themselves adhere to these standards of moral content, and they must be flexible enough to help young people recover from failure to live up to those expectations.

2. The adolescent should be helped to assume final responsibility for his own decisions and behaviors, with strong support and encouragement by parents, church counselors, and peers. Working through parents to secure teen participation in the church program or to place leverage on the adolescent to bring him to a certain decision or conformity is self-defeating to the adolescent's own growth and maturity. The adolescent tends to be well aware of his obligations and duties to parents and authorities; the youth adviser who can transcend these past leverages and inspire the adolescent to respond to more self-chosen and voluntarily participative decisions will do everyone a favor by helping release the teen to a new high point in his own maturity.

3. Watch for the adolescent who is arriving early at principled moral thinking. He will tend to be the more verbal, reflective, thoughtful type who has experienced a good deal of heavy responsibility and perhaps a

bit of pain. Such persons often succumb to doubt and drop out of youth activity in the church, or they find a highly personal experience of God's reality, often with mystical overtones. It is important to help treasure his personal relationship with God without attempting to force a carbon copy of that experience on all others in the youth group and without his thinking that his personal experience—rather than the specific teachings of God's Word—is the standard and basis of his spiritual life.

4. Try to calculate the adolescent's spiritual hunger and need to be oriented around level-two considerations. He will be needing to sense the new emerging authority of Christ and of Scripture, and the high expectation of the persons around him who make up the church—the youth director, his Christian peers, the great heroes of Christian faith present and past. If the teen is won to Christ, he will decide to place himself under new authority and will take responsibility for participating in a community under that same authority. He will elect to support, defend, and promote the kingdom of Christ as his new loyalty.

The adolescent's development brings him to the peak threshold for responding to the call to Christian commitment and discipleship. For the first time in his life he now truly begins to have (1) freedom of independent choice and action, (2) potential formal thinking powers, (3) a surging power of sexual maturity which tends to heighten moral sensitivity. Whatever responses he may have made to God up to this time, he is now confronted with the possibility of a truly personal and total commitment to his Lord.[16]

DISCIPLESHIP AND COMMUNITY

Foundational understandings of the adolescent's social and psychological characteristics will help youth workers comprehend his readiness for Christian discipleship and for participation in the church as the body of Christ.

The adolescent's emerging identity as a person distinct from parents and family places him, for the first time in his life, in a position to respond to the summons to Christian discipleship in autonomous, personal terms. During adolescence it is almost always more difficult for parents to be the direct bearers of that summons to their own children. This makes it urgent that ministries with youth not try to rest the program on the shoulders of parents of teens in the group. Such parents may serve well before or after their own teens have passed through the age bracket involved, but usually not during those years.

16. See Donald M. Joy, "Children, Salvation, and Dropout," *The Asbury Seminarian* 26 (October 1972): 20-35.

The adolescent's heavy reliance on peer values makes it urgent that ministries targeted on evangelism and Christian nurture of youth (a) establish an attractive teen program built around teens deeply committed to Christ, and (b) staff youth ministries with mature adult couples with young children and some whose children are grown, in order to anchor the adolescent in a multigenerational community of faith which will be both appealing and supporting.

Conclusion

Christian faith will not thrive unless it is passed along to the next generation. Jesus placed the child "in the midst," at the center of the community concern—the child of innocence who spontaneously and simply embraces the community and its beliefs. The adolescent is, in a sense, still a child as he launches into the adult years and takes responsibility for himself on wobbly social legs. Adults have their second chance in ministry with every child when he or she comes to adolescence; they may succeed this time in getting a hearing for the gospel. And this time if they are effective instruments of God, they may win him to Christ and to a long-term commitment to His work.

For Further Reading

Ausubel, David. *Theory and Problems of Adolescent Development.* New York: Grune & Stratton, 1954.

Blaine, Graham B., Jr. *Youth and the Hazards of Affluence.* New York: Harper & Row, 1966.

Coleman, James. *The Adolescent Society.* Glencoe, Ill.: Free Press, 1961.

Erikson, Erik H. *The Challenge of Youth.* Garden City, N.Y.: Anchor, 1965.

Gleason, John J. *Growing Up to God: Eight Steps in Religious Development.* Nashville: Abingdon, 1975.

Gold, Martin G., and Douvan, Elizabeth M. *Adolescent Development: Readings in Research and Theory.* Boston: Allyn & Bacon, 1969.

Goldman, Ronald. *Readiness for Religion: A Basis for Developmental Religious Education.* New York: Seabury, 1965.

Kagan, Jerome, and Coles, Robert, eds. *Twelve to Sixteen: Early Adolescence.* New York: Norton, 1972.

Kohlberg, Lawrence. "The Cognitive-Developmental Approach to Moral Education." *Phi Delta Kappan,* June 1975, pp. 670-77.

Kohlberg, Lawrence, and Gilligan, Carol. "The Adolescent as a Moral Philosopher: The Discovery of the Self in a Postconventional World." In *Twelve to Sixteen: Early Adolescence.* Edited by Jerome Kagan and Robert Coles. New York: Norton, 1972.

Masters, William H., and Johnson, Virginia E. *The Pleasure Bond: A New Look at Sexuality and Commitment.* Boston: Little, Brown, 1975.

McCandless, Boyd R. *Adolescents: Behavior and Development.* Hinsdale, Ill.: Dryden, 1970.

Muuss, Rolf E., ed. *Adolescent Behavior and Society: A Book of Readings.* New York: Random House, 1971. See especially Muuss's own chapter, "Adolescent Development and the Secular Trend."

Newman, Barbara. "The Study of Interpersonal Behavior in Adolescence." *Adolescence* 11 (Spring 1976): 127-42.

Offer, Daniel. *The Psychological World of the Teenager.* New York: Basic Books, 1970.

Strommen, Merton P. *Profiles of Church Youth.* St. Louis: Concordia, 1963.

Strommen, Merton P., ed. *Research on Religious Development.* New York: Hawthorn, 1971.

"Symposium: Ronald Goldman and Religious Education." *Religious Education.* (November-December, 1968):6.

Taylor, Marvin J., ed. *Foundations for Christian Education in an Era of Change.* Nashville: Abingdon, 1976.

Cassette Tapes

Ankney, Paul H., and Sund, Robert B. "Piaget for Educators." Chas. E. Merrill Co., Columbus, Ohio, 1976. Six tapes, handbook included.

Dobson, James. "Preparing for Adolescence." Vision House, 1507 E. McFadden, Santa Ana, Calif. 92705. Six tapes.

7

Cognitive Development of Adolescents

Lawrence O. Richards

THE PRINCE OF GRANADA, an heir to the Spanish crown, was sentenced for life to solitary confinement in Madrid's ancient prison, the Place of Skulls, for fear that he might aspire to the throne. He was given one book to read—the Bible.

The Prince of Granada apparently read the Bible hundreds of times. When he died after thirty-three years of imprisonment, he had covered the walls of his prison, using nails on the soft stone, with notations such as these:

> The eighth verse of the ninety-seventh psalm is the middle verse of the Bible.
>
> Ezra 7:21 contains all the letters of the alphabet except the letter J.
>
> The ninth verse of the eighth chapter of Esther is the longest.
>
> No word or name of more than six syllables can be found in the Bible.

This story was related by Scott O'Dell in *Psychology Today*.[1] How striking, as O'Dell pointed out, that during a lifetime of reading the Bible, in endless hours of loneliness, the Prince of Granada could cull only trivia from "the greatest book known to Western man."

The Prince of Granada was an educated man. He could read, write, and count. He asked a variety of questions, and he industriously probed for the anwers. He was, by almost any test, mentally mature.

It is important to keep the Prince of Granada in mind as we think together about adolescent cognitive development. The concern of this chapter is not simply to trace mental powers which emerge at various stages of life. Young people's developing capacities should be channeled

1. Scott O'Dell, "David: An Adventure with Memory and Words," *Psychology Today*, January 1968, p. 40.

LAWRENCE O. RICHARDS, Ph.D., is President, Renewal Research Associates, Phoenix, Arizona.

into meaningful interaction with God's Word as a revelation both of reality and of the person of God Himself.

Two researchers have provided important clues that help in designing Christian education of youth to fit youth's cognitive development. (See references at end of chapter for more information about their work.)

JEAN PIAGET

The work of Jean Piaget has received wide attention in education, particularly in the education of children. His main contributions have been in demonstrating that cognitive development proceeds in an invariant sequence across cultures. The ability to grasp and use concepts does not depend solely on what is taught to a child, but whether he has developed the mental capability to think in that way. One would not expect a six-year-old to play basketball on a par with teenagers; his muscles and physical control simply have not developed sufficiently for him to compete. Piaget has helped educators realize that the mind develops its own "muscles," at its own pace.

Piaget has also introduced several significant concepts about how learning takes place. One focuses attention on learning as a *transaction* between the person and his environment. That is, when confronted by elements in the physical or social environment, a person actively seeks to fit them into a world view. This involves restructuring both the understanding and the environment. In a sense, an individual imposes a "reality" on his environment, a reality of which he himself is a part.

The Prince of Granada took the Bible, that revelation of reality and truth given us by God, and saw it merely as a collection of verses, letters, and six-syllable words. In his transaction with Scripture, the Prince became a part of his "reality," and the part he took was that of scribe, mathematician, engineer in charge of manipulating symbols which were to him essentially meaningless.

Another significant concept that is basic in Piaget's thinking is that of *disequilibrium*. This is a state of tension or disturbance in which the elements of a person's world no longer seem to fit the "reality" which he has created. Disequilibrium can come from two sources, one of which Piaget tends to stress. The first source is change in the environment itself. Here is the introduction of new experiences, new information, new concepts. A person confronted by things which he can no longer fit into his old world view may be forced to reconstruct his perception of reality.

This first source of disequilibrium is one which the Christian educator has tended to rely on in evangelism and in teaching. Teachers have tended to feel that when they communicate biblical truth, this new data will lead to a change in understanding and commitment. All too often, however, truth communicated in only a *verbal* mode fails to introduce disequilibrium. Instead, individuals simply reject the information or mentally file it as irrelevant to life—even as the Prince of Granada daily came in contact with the great truths of God's Word, and daily ignored them.

The second source of disequilibrium is the one which Piaget tends to stress, and one which Christian education has tended to overlook. This source is the individual's own inner cognitive growth. When new capacities or "mental structures" develop, Piaget holds, then the individual will begin to "see" things in a different way. He will then seek a new way to integrate and rebuild his world; his personal picture of reality.

This process of disequilibrium introduced by changes *within* is probably one of the basic causes of adolescent doubt. The childhood faith suddenly seems inadequate. New issues are seen and grappled with. What was satisfactory to the nine-year-old is unsatisfactory to the fifteen-year-old, and the foundation of faith seems to shake. Viewed from a Piagean point of view, this kind of reaction is both normal and healthy. Out of doubt, faith will reconstruct a far more accurate and sound understanding of relationship with God, resting on more mature understanding. The real problems often come from adult failure to see this "doubting" time for what it is—a stage in growth—and from adult reactions which reinforce doubt rather than help the young person work through to a more adult understanding of Christian faith.

Piaget, then, introduces three vitally important concepts which help understand adolescent cognitive development, and which have implications for Christian education.

1. Cognitive growth progresses through invariant stages which are analogous to physical growth.
2. Learning involves a transaction between the person and environment, in which the person constructs a "reality picture" to explain the world and his place in it.
3. Disequilibrium, sourced in changes in the environment and/or developmental changes within the person, periodically leads to a restructuring of the person's view of reality.

What is striking is to realize how much of cognitive development takes place not in the childhood years but in the teens and twenties!

LAWRENCE T. KOHLBERG

Lawrence T. Kohlberg, professor of psychology at Harvard University,

TABLE 7.1

OVERVIEW OF KOHLBERG LEVELS AND STAGES

Level/Stage	Name	Approximate Earliest Age	Piaget Stage Required	Prerequisite Cognitive Tasks
Level 0 Stage O-A	Premoral Period Amoral Stage	Extends to 4	Sensorimotor and Pre-conceptual Sub.	
Stage O-B	Premoral Stage of Egocentric Judgment	To about 6	Preconceptual Sub. and Intuitive Sub.	
Level I Stage 1	Period of Preconventional Morality Punishment and Obedience Orientation	No earlier than 5 or 6, 7-8 likelier	Transitional from Intuitive Sub. to early Concrete Op.	Categorical classification
Stage 2	Instrumental Relativist Orientation	7-8 earliest 9-10 likelier	Concrete Operations	Reversibility (logical reciprocity)
Level II Stage 3	Period of Conventional Morality Interpersonal Concordance Orientation	10-11 earliest 11-12 likelier	Formal Operations Substage 1	Inverse of reciprocal; mutual simul. reciprocity
Stage 4	Law and Order (or Conscientious) Orientation	12-14 earliest 14-16 likelier	Formal Operations Substage 2	Able to order triads of propositions or relations
Stage 4½	(Stage of Cynical Ethical Relativism beyond conventional, but not principled)	H.S. earliest College likely	This is not true stage insofar as not part of invariant sequence. Only few go through it.	
Level III	Period of Postconventional, Autonomous, or Principled Morality			
Stage 5	Social Contract Legalistic Orientation	Early 20s Mid-late 20s likelier	Formal Operations Substage 3 Self-resp. exper.	Hypothetico-Deductive Reasoning. All poss. comb. of variables. Sys. relations.
Stage 6	Universal Ethical Principle Orientation	Unlikely before late 20s Early 30s likelier, if at all	Sustained resp. for welfare of others; irreversible real-life moral choices; high level cognitive stimulation and reflection.	

Prepared by John S. Stewart
Research and Development Program for Values Development Education
College of Education, Michigan State University
East Lansing, Michigan

NOTE: Reprinted from Lawrence O. Richards, *A Theology of Christian Education* (Grand Rapids: Zondervan, 1975), p. 184. Used by permission.

was intrigued as a graduate student by the implications of Piaget's thinking for moral development.

Kohlberg's impressive work in the past decade has demonstrated, to the satisfaction of many, that there are distinct parallels between moral and cognitive development, which probably indicate the dependence of moral development on cognitive development. Kohlberg has distinguished levels of moral thought that are parallel in nature to Piaget's cognitive structural levels, and has attempted to define an invariant sequence for moral development. In addition, Kohlberg has suggested that the equilibration process is basic to moral growth as it is to learning. The relationship between Piaget's and Kohlberg's schemas are shown on the accompanying table. While the specifics of the Kohlberg stages are suggestive for the theologian as well as the Christian educator, an exploration of these stages is not appropriate to this article. However, it is highly recommended that Kohlberg's writings be studied.

While Piaget has tended to stress inner development as the source of disequilibration, Kohlberg has addressed himself to the question of what kind of environment facilitates movement from one stage of moral thought to another. His research has been applied to the public school, and in a notable experiment, to a prison setting. His conclusions stress the need for opportunity (1) to explore moral dilemmas (thus *introducing* disequilibration as "pat" answers are challenged, and exposing persons to "higher level" thinking about the issue) and (2) to participate in a "just, moral community." This last suggestion stresses the need for higher-order moral principles to be expressed in the social environment of which the learner is a part, and thus exposure to them in practice as well as in theory.

THEOLOGICAL CONSIDERATIONS

The Christian educator needs to develop a healthy appreciation for behavioral science "research"; however, his theological considerations should still retain priority. The difficulty, of course, is to maintain balance. At times educators have become vigorously engaged in seeking proof-texts to support or to reject current secular thought; at other times educators have vigorously argued a theological position based on tragic misinterpretation of the biblical data. Often they have been guilty of unthinking acceptance of secular presuppositions.

What Christian educators need to do is to look at the broad picture sketched both by the behavioral sciences and Scripture, and seek the practical implications in whatever harmony may exist.

In looking at the picture sketched by Piaget and Kohlberg of cognitive and moral development, certain parallels with biblical basics become evident.

1. Growth is pictured in the Scriptures as a lifelong process. God is at work in the believer, working His own transformation, shaping him more and more toward likeness to Jesus Christ.

This reshaping process involves the total personality, including one's values, attitudes, emotions, and behavior as well as understanding. Yet understanding is definitely involved—and critical. "Put on the new self," Paul writes to the Colossians, "which is being renewed in knowledge in the image of its Creator" (3:10, NIV). In Romans, transformation is linked to the "renewing of your mind" (12:2, NIV). Strikingly, the Greek word *nous,* translated "mind," focuses attention in Romans 12:1-2 not on mental capacities (such as those exercised by the Prince of Granada), but on *"attitude, way of thinking* as the sum total of the whole mental and moral state of being."[2] In the same sense Ephesians 4:23 teaches that believers must adopt a new attitude of mind.

Christian growth seems to imply a *process in which one's world view is progressively reshaped.* This reshaping process, which constantly moves toward a more accurate perception of life and one's world from the divine viewpoint, is a distinctive and significant feature of biblical Christianity.

2. One of the themes stressed in Scripture is that the believer is to be *accepted* and *affirmed* by the Christian community, even when his present level of understanding or behavior is inadequate. "Welcome a man whose faith is weak," Paul writes in Romans, "but not with the idea of arguing over his scruples" (14:1, Phillips). The next verses ring with this spirit of acceptance. "Who are you to criticise the servant of somebody else?" (v. 4, Phillips). "Why, then . . . do you try to make him [your brother] look small?" (v. 10, Phillips). "Let us concentrate on the things which make for harmony, and on the growth of our fellowship together" (v. 19, Phillips). "We should consider the good of our neighbor and help to build up his character" (15:2, Phillips).

In this context (of doctrinal dispute over the eating of meat offered to idols) Paul focuses attention on an aspect of Christian experience the combatants had overlooked. Because growth is something that always involves time, a Christian need not insist that everyone in the fellowship conform at a given point in time to his own understanding. Instead, he can concentrate on *building a community in which growth will take place.* Christians can accept and handle differences, and even error, if our Christian community provides a context for growth through acceptance, affirmation, and love.

2. William F. Arndt and F. Wilbur Gingrich, *A Greek-English Lexicon of the New Testament and Other Early Christian Literature* (Chicago: U. of Chicago, 1957), p. 546.

3. Christian community is basic to development of a Christian *nous* ("mind"). Paul writes of teaching "unity in the faith and in the knowledge of the Son of God," of becoming "mature, attaining the full measure of perfection found in Christ." He goes on to insist that this growth takes place in the "whole body, joined together by every supporting ligament," which "grows and builds itself up in love, as each part does its work" (Eph 4:13-16, NIV).

The development of a Christian understanding of life is not something which takes place in isolation. The Christian community itself, giving living expression to the truths revealed in Scripture, *is* the "just, moral community" of the behavioral scientist, in which growth from one level of moral understanding to another is encouraged for all.

IMPLICATIONS

An approach to Christian education of youth can be based on the following insights rooted in contemporary research and in Scripture:

1. Growth is a progressive kind of thing. It moves from stage to stage, as mental development enables deeper and different understandings. A teacher of young people should not expect "instant maturity," or demand perfection. Providing "growing room" is important.

2. During adolescence significant times of disequilibration do come. Doubts and questions are natural and healthy elements in maturing. Youth workers should *encourage* rather than discourage open discussion of questions. And they should expose youth to more mature Christians, who can help raise their own level of understanding and commitment.

3. In times of disequilibration, a growing person needs help in working toward deeper understanding of faith and life. This help is *not* provided when an adult withdraws acceptance if a teen expresses doubt, or when an adult creates guilt by condemning those who seem to be deviates. In time of disequilibration, young persons have a special need for others. They need to sense in the lives of other Christians that stability, love, and confidence which provide maximum support and give testimony of the reality of those truths being questioned.

4. As a community, the church needs to express in its life-style the biblical realities revealed conceptually in Scripture. Experience of the truth is as important as exposure to concepts in that kind of cognitive development that focuses on *nous* rather than mere knowledge. In Christian education, youth workers need to become far more aware than they have been of the influence of other Christians on cognitive

development. And they need to place renewed stress on becoming a loving, supportive body of brothers and sisters in the Lord.

Contemporary and biblical studies into cognitive development can have a definite impact on the approach to ministry with youth. The focus of concern has shifted from an earlier emphasis on "what truths can be taught at a given age?" and "what methods are best in communicating concepts?" The emphasis now, and rightly so, should be more on the transformation of the teens' understanding (*nous*) and the development of his Christian world view and of his commitment. With this emphasis, youth workers need to be giving others time to grow, to be encouraging questioning during times of disequilibration, to be providing the community context in which truth can be experienced, and to be giving loving support in times of transition. These are vital aspects of teaching Christian truth to youth.

FOR FURTHER READING

Elkind, David. *Children and Adolescents: Interpretive Essays on Jean Piaget.* New York: Oxford U., 1970.

———. "The Development of Religious Understanding in Children and Adolescents." In *Research on Religious Development.* Edited by Merton P. Strommen. New York: Hawthorn, 1971.

Ginsburg, Herbert, and Opper, Sylvia. *Piaget's Theory of Intellectual Development: An Introduction.* Englewood Cliffs, N.J.: Prentice-Hall, 1969.

Goldman, Ronald. *Readiness for Religion.* New York: Seabury, 1965.

———. *Religious Thinking from Childhood to Adolescence.* New York: Seabury, 1964.

Hall, Brian P. *The Development of Consciousness: A Confluent Theory of Values.* New York: Paulist, 1976.

Kohlberg, Lawrence T. "Stage in Sequence: The Cognitive-Development of Approach to Socialization." In *Handbook of Socialization Theory and Research.* Edited by D. Goslin. New York: Rand McNally, 1969.

———. "Stages of Moral Development as a Basis for Moral Education." In *Moral Education: Interdisciplinary Approaches.* Edited by C. M. Beck, B. S. Crittenden, and E. V. Sullivan. New York: Newman, 1971.

———. "The Child as a Moral Philosopher." *Psychology Today,* July 1968, pp. 25-30.

———. "The Development of Modes of Moral Thinking and Choice in the Years Ten to Sixteen." Ph.D. diss., U. of Chicago, 1958.

———. "The Moral Atmosphere of School." In *The Unstudied Curriculum: Its Impact on Children.* Edited by N. V. Overly. Washington, D.C.: Association for Supervision and Curriculum Development, 1970.

———. "From Is to Ought." In *Cognitive Development and Epistemology.* Edited by Theodore Mischel. New York: Academic, 1971.

Kohlberg, Lawrence T., and Gilligan, C. "The Adolescent as a Philosopher: The Discovery of the Self in a Postconventional World." *Daedalus: Journal of American Academy of Arts and Sciences* 100 (Fall 1971): 1051-86.

Kohlberg, Lawrence T., and Witten, Phillip. "Understanding the Hidden Curriculum." *Learning*, December 1972, pp. 10-14.

Muuss, Rolf E. "Kohlberg's Cognitive-Developmental Approach to Adolescent Morality." *Adolescence* 11 (Spring 1976): 39-59.

Piaget, Jean. *Science of Education and the Psychology of the Child.* New York: Orion, 1970.

———. *The Moral Judgment of the Child.* New York: Free Press, 1965.

———. *To Understand Is to Invent.* New York: Crossman, 1973.

Pulaski, Mary Ann Spencer. *Understanding Piaget.* New York: Harper & Row, 1971.

Richards, Lawrence O. *A Theology of Christian Education.* Grand Rapids: Zondervan, 1975.

Wakefield, Norman. "Children and Their Theological Concepts." In *Childhood Education in the Church.* Edited by Roy B. Zuck and Robert E. Clark. Chicago: Moody, 1975.

8

Early Adolescence

Edward D. Seely

"I JUST DON'T UNDERSTAND THEM. They simply won't listen to a thing I say. They aren't logical; you can't reason with them. You try to make a reasonable point, and it goes in one ear and out the other!" A rather typical experience of parents of early adolescents between twelve and fourteen years of age, wouldn't you say?

Not so! And here is the crux of the problem. These are not the words of a parent about his or her children; they are the verbalized anguish of a young person concerning her relationship with her parents. Moreover, this experience is at the heart of much difficulty in the interpersonal interactions of junior high school people with their parents and teachers.

This is a rather significant communication problem—significant because both the young people and the subject matter of our transactions are important. The problem is compounded by the fact that many complex issues are interwoven. These must be understood and accepted if frustration is to be avoided and instructional and nurturant goals are to be attained. These complex issues revolve around three major developmental loci: physiological, sociological, and psychological growth factors. Understanding these factors will provide a framework for an approach to teaching this unsure, insecure, frequently worried yet fascinating, enthusiastic, and truly exciting age-group.

PHYSIOLOGICAL DEVELOPMENT

Man is not divisible into discrete parts which can be examined separately, much as an automobile mechanic, searching for trouble, might first take apart the distributor and look at it, then the carburetor and the solenoid and so on. Instead, all the parts of a human being are of a whole, serving not only a specific function limited to themselves but also other functions in relation to other parts. Hence, a human being is more than

EDWARD D. SEELY, Ph.D., Candidate, Minister of Education, Fifth Reformed Church, Grand Rapids, Michigan.

the sum of his parts. If we are to achieve an accurate understanding of his development, it must be kept in mind that each part is all this and more, the "more" being the interface which occurs between this part and each other part as well as all together.

As childhood wanes and puberty, the physiological trigger of adolescence, begins, many young people experience the occurrence of acne. The cause or causes of acne are not completely known, but it is felt that contributing factors include (1) hormonal changes which occur in adolescence and (2) hereditary tendency.[1] Nevertheless, the occurrence of acne is not only a *physiological* effect. For even the most superficial acquaintance with young people, if not one's own recollection of puberty, reveals an awareness of the powerful affective concern for this condition, in the anguish suffered by those afflicted, due to such *sociological* variables as concern for looking attractive to others and peer acceptance.

As might be expected, the physical growth and maturation of sexual organs and related aspects of the body constitute both the major biological dimensions of development in early adolescence and the cause of most of the worries of young people with regard to this area of life. While space does not permit an in-depth discussion, an overview of the most important aspects of biological concern must be kept in mind when structuring learning experiences for junior high young people.[2]

When, for instance, the teacher or leader observes a girl or boy being inattentive, writing, or drawing pictures on a piece of paper, he should not jump to the conclusion that the learner is disinterested in the subject matter (though this might be the case), dislikes the teacher (which also *may* be true*) or is a "bad" person (which is definitely *not* the case). Instead, he should approach the circumstance from the broader perspective and ask, "What is this girl or boy struggling with that is prompting such behavior?" Hence, instead of reprimanding the young person,† the leader

1. W. W. Bauer, *Today's Health Guide* (Chicago: AMA, 1965), p. 176.
2. For a more complete examination of these areas and their implications for Christian education, see the first three chapters of Edward D. Seely, *Teaching Early Adolescents Creatively* (Philadelphia: Westminster, 1971), pp. 17-68.

*While a young person may not like his teacher for a number of reasons, early adolescents want very much to be accepted by significant people (and a teacher is such a person in their eyes) and will therefore be trying, generally, to achieve acceptance rather than rejection even from a teacher they do not like a great deal. Pathological situations do arise which contradict this principle, but such situations do not constitute a norm.

†If the teacher or other youth worker feels certain that a young person is performing behaviors that are counterproductive to the goals of the class or group and prohibiting others from attaining important cognitive and affective outcomes, the leader should ask the offender to see him after class and refrain at all costs from the temptation to "put him down" in front of the group. In a one-to-one confrontation, the leader should lovingly and patiently try to help the teen understand the source of his concern and have a broader perspective of concern for others in the group.

should give him the benefit of the doubt. The leader should remember that even though the young person is sitting or standing there in relative quietude, inside himself, his body is surging into life-shaping formations, many of which, since he is a holistic being, create social and emotional conflicts.

What are some of these "life-shaping" formations which cause worries and subsequent aberrant behaviors in the classroom or youth group? Early adolescent girls are concerned with various aspects of menstruation and breast development. Boys are concerned about gonadal development and the change of their voices. Not only the changes themselves but the rate and degree of such change are causes of concern, complicated by the facts that individuals are very unique and that there is a wide range within which many occurrences can fall and still be considered normal. For instance, girls experience varying degrees of unevenness in breast development, and boys vary considerably in the size of their genitals. Such variance causes great concern especially to "late bloomers"; hence, locker rooms at school can be frightening, and worries that stem from these places and concerns can show up in the classroom at church. Therefore, the wise youth leader is aware of and sensitive to these teen concerns.

SOCIOLOGICAL DEVELOPMENT

As already pointed out, many of the attendant worries of the physiological aspects of development result from sociological factors. If young people were aware of the naturalness of uneven biological development, for example, they would not be as prone to place a stigma on this phenomenon. Another illustration of a problem overlapping the biological and sociological areas is the question of the use of drugs. Clearly, the effects from using drugs are personal and biological; however, one of the main reasons the drug issue is significant to early adolescents is because of their peers. If young people are unsure of themselves (with regard to what they believe and why) concerning moral matters, they are more susceptible to the pressure of peers to partake of forbidden fruit.

Another sociological factor which weighs heavily on the early adolescent is the transition from elementary to middle or junior high school. Some communities have middle schools (grades six through eight), and some are administered on a junior high basis (grades seven through nine). In either case the young person goes from upper elementary school, where he is more secure (being closer to home, often with just one teacher and being older than many other pupils) [3] to middle or junior high school,

3. John I. Goodlad and M. Frances Klein, *Looking Behind the Classroom Door* (Worthington, Ohio: Jones, 1974).

where he is less secure (being frequently farther away from home, often with different ethnic groups and several teachers and classes, and sometimes with difficut and important choices to make, as well as being among many young people who are older than he). For many youth this is a difficult experience, which causes understandable concerns that issue forth in behaviors which often try the patience of church teachers and leaders.

Youth leaders need to try to feel what their youth are experiencing in their everyday lives. Sometimes adults make the mistake of viewing life solely in terms of their own perspectives. When adults go to church after another week of high pressure business deals, or trouble with an overbearing boss or husband, or difficulty in determining where the money is coming from to make the next house payment, it is difficult for them to view the early adolescent's concern over a boyfriend who has begun to notice someone else as a very important issue, much less as a reason for causing trouble in class! However, when adults remember to view life from the perspective of the young people, it becomes obvious that both are made up of the same chemicals, sinews, and nerve endings. Teens have the same emotional feelings as adults, susceptible to the same kinds of (romantic, financial, and physical) stimuli. Therefore, they feel pain just as keenly as adults do. The same nervous system which will years later carry adult concerns now carries concerns that are just as weighty from their point of view.

It is wrong for an adult to dismiss with a wave of the hand a youth's intense feelings for the opposite sex as "puppy love" (which means it is of little consequence and to be forgotten about). That adult has just dismissed himself as a viable source of help in the sight of the young people who hear him say such mistaken and insensitive words. He probably has not destroyed his teaching ministry, due to the almost infinite desire of youth to be liked (and at some point he may reinstate himself as a person respected for his opinion) ; but until he demonstrates more perspectivism, sensitivity, love, and understanding of them as persons, his effectiveness is limited. He has taught far more in that statement than he may have realized, and because of the loudness of those words still ringing in their ears, the teens will hear little of whatever else he has to say. It is never too late to turn around, though, if he cares.

One final sociological factor is important to consider in working with middle school or junior high youth. Based largely on Piaget research[4] many communities have redepartmentalized their public schools and are grouping early adolescents according to a middle school format (grades six through eight). Other places retain the older junior high approach

4. See chapter 7, "Cognitive Development of Adolescents."

(grades seven through nine) . Still others have no intermediate school, but instead include grades six through eight as part of elementary school and include grades nine through twelve in high school. Even though churches frequently constitute collectively a larger institutional body than the schools, the latter are the sociological perspective through which early adolescents perceive formal education's norm. Hence, if young adolescents are in a middle school format and their church is on the junior high departmentalization, sixth graders may sense that the church and all it stands for is irrelevant, not even recognizing these young people as having attained the status accorded them by society. This could even have the worse effect of causing society to become more of a reference point than the church, a truly unfortunate situation and a potential concern which the church should begin to consider seriously.

PSYCHOLOGICAL DEVELOPMENT

In the transition from childhood into adolescence, the increased intellectual capacity of youth is second only to biological maturation in observability. Piaget has found that previously, from about ages seven to eleven or twelve, the child has been in the developmental stage he refers to as "concrete operations." This means that the thinking of the child in that age bracket has been limited to very concrete concepts involving tangible aspects of the present. Concrete-operational children cannot deal with complex verbal problems (e.g., if John is lighter than Harry, and John is heavier than Sam, who is the heaviest of the three?) , hypothetical problems (e.g., a logical argument requiring a perceptually untrue premise such as a question prefixed by the proposition, "Suppose that snow were black") , or problems dealing with the future.

By contrast, persons in the next development stage, known as "formal operations," are able to function mentally in all these ways. As the name of this period (beginning at about eleven or twelve years of age) implies, the early adolescent can consider the *form* of a concept apart from tangible or observable example. The development of this last stage marks the arrival at intellectual adulthood wherein the formal operational person can think abstractly, a factor which has many implications for catechetical and doctrinal education in the church. The insistence on teaching all the details of deductive, highly conceptual, and abstract doctrines before the beginning of "formal operations" produces conditions for frustration in the learner. As a result, the preadolescent, unable to sense the meaning of what is being taught, concludes that these concepts—and likely the whole church and what it stands for—are irrelevant to him and his life.

The early adolescent's capacity for greater perspective and increased understanding, combined with the surge of egocentrism characteristic of the attainment of a new stage, results in his becoming aware of the contrast between how things are and the way they should be. Thus here is one reason early adolescents usually have such a strong desire to discuss life issues and are very concerned about what is happening in the world today. The developing youth's awareness of their increased intellectual powers, untempered by the ability to take a more advanced perspective, often results in situations like the one mentioned at the beginning of this chapter. Their logical skills have progressed to the capacity of adult thinking, but they lack adult perspective. Alert teachers and youth workers will teach lessons and plan activities that challenge the youths' newly developing intellectual capacity to deal with life issues and to explore the biblical implications of such concepts, thereby enabling them to broaden their perspective and to employ that perspective in rational decision-making.

According to Lawrence Kohlberg, whose views are based on Piaget's basic theory,‡ what is "good" in the early adolescent's value system is what will maintain concord within his peer reference group. The things that are important and desirable to him are the things that please him or those with whom he has an affectional relationship. Churches will therefore do well to recruit teachers and youth leaders who are popular and looked up to by this age-group.

Kohlberg's research has implications not only for how adults communicate to the youth, but also for ways adults can help young teens develop higher levels of moral judgment. As youth discuss issues in their Sunday school classes and youth groups from the vantage point of what good Christians, their peer group, and loved ones think should be done, one can raise the question, Are these opinions of others correct opinions, and how do you know?

Also characteristic of early adolescents is the development of identity. A young adolescent today is much different from the way he was only a few years ago. He is more likely to realize that he has to fit all the pieces of himself—his physical, social, and psychological traits and relationships—into a unified uniqueness, an integrated whole.

One's identity is clarified through conversation with others. This is one

---

‡Kohlberg has built on Piaget's basic theory, not his 1932 study, *The Moral Judgment of the Child*. The scientific use of the term "theory" as employed herein, refers to a cogent explication of empirically documented evidence and not, as in the popular use of the term, a hunch or an opinion.

reason youth like opportunities for discussion.[5] Clarification of identity is also a reason for the heavy peer orientation which issues in the forming of cliques. In cliques, participants are protected from the discomfort of the major threat to identity formation, namely, role confusion. In the in-group, clear signs such as dress, skin color, and acceptable behaviors facilitate the stereotyping of desired characteristics, which in turn facilitates identity formation in a more concrete way. It should be remembered that these youth are not long out of the concrete operations stage, and since the stages are hierarchically integrated, such features reappear periodically even within the operations of more advanced thinking. The thoughtful teacher or youth worker will therefore employ natural groupings, since those groups serve an important developmental purpose. But the leader will also be sensitive to loners and to the desirability of helping those in in-groups to develop the sensitivity and perspective that will enable them to relate to others as well.

During this process of forging an identity out of the raw materials of life, the teacher of early adolescents has a crucial opportunity to help the youth consider the claims of Christ as an important part of those materials. Teachers and advisers of youth groups should emphasize that a person takes a big step toward wholeness when he includes Christ in his identity through accepting him as his Saviour and Lord. When he "puts on Christ" (Gal 3:27) and identifies with Him, he becomes as God originally intended him to be through Christ. Hence, young people can look at themselves and like what they see, an important teaching for this age-group, for they long to sense value and worth in their emerging self-concepts.

Similarly, young adolescents want very much to know how they and their church differ from other people in the world. They ask for input in their classes which deal with the uniqueness of their faith. Middle school and junior high teachers should provide for much discussion of these questions.

IMPLICATIONS

Theologians and biblical scholars have long discussed the difficulty in helping people understand the Scriptures' Hebrew frame of reference. This difficulty is a result of the powerful impact of the Hellenization of Western thought which greatly affects our concepts in this hemisphere even yet today. Similarly, educators frequently show concern over the

---

5. Some teachers who want to provide discussion opportunities for their youth are frustrated in not being able to create circumstances which facilitate such interaction in a class or group context. For suggestions on how to overcome this difficulty, see Seely, *Teaching Early Adolescents Creatively*, pp. 127-49.

potent effects of another Greek institution which has come down to us from that culture: the schooling model of teaching and learning, or what is somewhat more broadly referred to as formal education. As readers of the Bible know, neither the Old nor the New Testaments employed the schooling model, even though it was known and used during the period in which most of the Bible was written. According to the Word of God, the family had the primary responsibility for the education of its children (Deut 6:4-9; Eph 6:1-4).

And it still does. Yet the schooling model is here with us, and will be for quite some time, the prophets of its doom notwithstanding. Moreover, while the schooling approach (and its current use) is fraught with some very important and inherent flaws, it still provides opportunities for good learning. Clearly the provision of technological and other resources which facilitate learning but are not viable options for purchase for most families, as well as the opportunities for peer interaction, are positive contributions of school experiences.

What, then, are some of the inherent flaws? In the first place, learners, especially in the graded forms of the schooling approach, are usually assumed to be homogeneous in terms of their cognitive level of understanding, affective outlook on subject matter and activities, and rate of learning. Even the most cursory view, however, of any given class or group reveals to the contrary that with regard to any given subject some youth know a lot, some know a little, and some know almost nothing Other weaknesses include competitive tendencies (which are counterproductive to developing a "communion of the saints"), comparing one student with another (known as "norm referencing") rather than comparing each to a standard ("criterion referencing"), too small a part in decision-making accorded to most learners, and the assumption that attendance should be required.[6]

According to a well-known adage, you can lead a horse to water, but you can't make him drink. Similarly, teachers may compel students to attend Sunday school classes, but they cannot force their students to learn. Keeping students in classes and groups where they do not desire to be does them little good. What good does result is quite likely to be offset by negative effects, not the least of which includes dislike of and hostility toward parents (for making him go), teacher, church, and God (who, ironically, does not force man against His own will—see e.g., Rom 1:24). Moreover, such students are the cause of most discipline problems, the in-

6. See Ted. W. Ward and William A. Herzog, Jr., *Effective Learning in Non-Formal Education* (East Lansing, Mich.: Michigan State U., 1974), pp. 14-59, 72-77. See also Ted W. Ward, "Schooling as a Defective Approach to Education," unpublished paper circulated at Michigan State University.

effective handling of which by many teachers causes uneasiness, fear, and hostility in the other students, not to mention loss of learning.[7] In addition, the young people are now experiencing, as a result of their increased cognitive ability, a growing sense of independence which provides increased incentive to resist compulsion to attend and participate in situations that are not meaningful to them.

Kohlberg's research has indicated that early adolescents are at the level of development in which they are making values decisions on the basis of internal standards of motivation. They take a negative view of attempts to motivate by external sources. Hence, the teacher who wishes to reach young adolescents should try to begin where they are in their interests, experiences, and skills.

Yet ministers, superintendents, and parents usually hold the teacher responsible for creating learning in people who do not want to learn. Such wishful thinking is based on misunderstanding and idealism, as Robert Ebel has well said.

> There may be some teachers with a magic touch that can convert an uninterested, unwilling class into a group of eager learners. I myself have encountered such teachers only in movies or novels. Surely they are too rare to count on for solving the problems of motivation to learn, especially in some of the more difficult situations. For the most part, motivation to learn is an attitude a student has or lacks well before a particular course of instruction ever begins.[8]

How should youth workers deal with discipline problems presented by early adolescents? First, keep the above in mind and do not become defensive, feeling the situation is entirely the fault of the leader. For too long teachers have been held accountable for lack of classroom control, when such conditions are largely the result of inherent limitations of the schooling model and its contemporary use.

Second, be firm but loving, caring, and sensitive. Third, vary the approach, using many different methods and techniques[9] that involve the students actively in the learning process.§[10] Fourth, ask an offender to

7. Robert L. Ebel, "What Are Schools For?" *Phi Delta Kappan*, September 1972, pp. 3-7. See also Michael J. Dunkin and Bruce J. Biddle, *The Study of Teaching* (New York: Holt, Rinehart & Winston, 1974), pp. 134-35.
8. Ebel, "What Are Schools For?" p. 7.
9. See chapter 28, "Creative Methods."

§A high degree of involvement, including movement and physical activity, has been found by Piaget to be necessary for learning. Involvement also reduces the occurrence of discipline problems. Physical activity has been found by this writer and by others to reduce discipline problems as well as to aid learning. See Bill Truesdell and Jeff Newman, "Can Junior Highs Make It with the Wide Open Spaces?" *Learning*, November 1975, pp. 75-77.

10. Seely, *Teaching Early Adolescents Creatively*, pp. 100-103.

stay after class. Then when everyone else has gone, ask him why he is disrupting the class with his behavior, and try to help him work through those concerns. Ask also if he realizes that he is alienating himself from others in the class and inhibiting their learning. Above all, try to refrain from put-downs in front of the whole class for the obvious reason that that kind of action teaches how *not* to relate to one another as brothers and sisters in Christ. In concluding the conversation with the offender the leader should reaffirm his care for and liking of him, should ask him for his support in working together to have a good class, and should indicate that future reoccurrences will have to be discussed between the leader and him along with his parents.

If this last step is necessary, the following should be done: explain to the parents the above paragraphs in this section; indicate that they should not punish their son or daughter for his or her disinterest in the subject matter (is it really his or her *fault* for not being interested?) ; tell them that John or Sue will always be welcome when he or she *wants* to return (whether next week, next month, or as an adult in the adult educational program). His growth in Christ will still continue through family interaction, corporate worship and personal devotions or other contact with the Word, which contact is more likely since the negative affective obstacle has been removed. Moreover, if he discontinues in the class or group, inform the minister of education, the Sunday school superintendent, the Christian education board or whatever person or group is responsible for program planning in the church so that he or they can identify or develop some programs where those who are not interested in the formal opportunities available can find their needs met in other alternatives.||

This approach to discipline problems common among junior highs demands courage, but is effective.

Nonformal educational models such as camping are designed to challenge and meet the physical, social, and psychological needs of developing youth. Taken together, formal and nonformal modes of education promise exciting adventures in learning for early adolescents and their teachers.

Teachers and youth leaders who work with young adolescents can be en-

||If alternatives are not available, they should be created. If the minister of education is as busy as people in this profession usually are, several churches in a close geographical proximity could cooperate together with each one specializing in *an* aspect of church education to provide time for development of specific alternatives. Small churches that do not have a minister of education could form a cooperative in the above manner and with the help of ministers of education hired on a consultative basis, could develop a similar program format, or even hire their own professional educational leadership for such purposes.

couraged by the following prayer, composed by Emily Nicholson, which summarizes some of the major themes of this chapter. Adults who take this approach will find joy and success in teaching their early adolescents about Jesus Christ and His meaning for their lives.

> Lord, sometimes they *seem* so silly—
> My often argumentative, rarely angelic class.
> They make such big issues out of trivial things,
> When I am eager to lead them into the life-changing truths of
>   Your Word.
> At times I am tempted to snap them into silence with a few sar-
>   castic words.
> But I don't.
> Love prevents me from slamming shut the door of communica-
>   tion between us.
> I believe that what is frustrating to me can be a means of growth
>   for them.
>
> Please don't let me fail them, Lord.
> Though they like to express themselves,
> They expect me to have the answers to their awkwardly-phrased
>   questions about You and life.
> Give me the wisdom and patience to lead them to You
> So that each may enjoy the life-fulfillment You give Your children,
> And in an insecure world, let them realize that to know You is
>   to find security.[11]

FOR FURTHER READING

Duska, Ronald, and Whelan, Mariellen. *Moral Development: A Guide to Piaget and Kohlberg.* New York: Paulist, 1975.

Elkind, David. *Children and Adolescents: Interpretive Essays on Jean Piaget.* New York: Oxford U., 1970.

Erikson, Erik H. *Childhood and Society.* New York: Norton, 1963.

Ezell, Mancil. *Youth in Bible Study/New Dynamics.* Nashville: Convention, 1970.

Felske, Norma. *Teaching That Grabs Young Teens.* Wheaton, Ill.: Victor, 1976.

Flynn, Elizabeth N., and La Fasco, John F. *Designs in Affective Education: A Teacher Resource for Junior and Senior High.* New York: Paulist, 1974.

Holderness, Ginny Ward. *The Exuberant Years: A Guide for Junior High Leaders.* Atlanta: Knox, 1976.

Jenkins, Gladys Gardner; Shacter, Helen S.; and Bauer, William W. *These Are Your Children.* 3d ed. Glenview, Ill.: Scott, Foresman, 1973.

11. Copyright 1970, Scripture Press Publications, Inc. World rights reserved. Used by permission.

Joy, Donald M. *"Human Development and Christian Holiness."* A paper presented at the Wesleyan Theological Society sessions held at Atlanta, Georgia, in conjunction with the Christian Holiness Association Convention, April 2-4, 1975.

Kohlberg, Lawrence. "Understand the Hidden Curriculum." *Learning* December 1972, pp. 10-14.

———. "A Cognitive-Developmental Approach to Moral Education." *The Humanist*, November-December 1972, pp. 13-16.

Miller, Chuck. *Now That I'm a Christian.* 2 vols. Glendale, Calif.: Regal, 1974, 1976.

Piaget, Jean. "Piaget's Theory." In *Carmichael's Manual of Child Psychology*, vol. 1. Edited by P. H. Mussen. 3d ed. New York: Wiley, 1970.

Pulaski, Mary Ann Spencer. *Understanding Piaget: An Introduction to Children's Cognitive Development.* New York: Harper & Row, 1971.

Richards, Lawrence O. *A Theology of Christian Education.* Grand Rapids: Zondervan, 1975.

———. *You and Youth.* Chicago: Moody, 1973.

Seely, Edward D. *Teaching Early Adolescents Creatively: A Manual for Church School Teachers.* Philadelphia: Westminster, 1971.

Sime, Mary. *A Child's Eye View.* New York: Harper & Row, 1973.

Soderholm, Marjorie E. *Understanding the Pupil: Part III, The Adolescent.* Grand Rapids: Baker, 1957.

Stewart, John S. "Toward a Theory for Values Development Education." Ph.D. diss., Michigan State U., 1974.

Stoop, David A. *Ways to Help Them Learn—Youth.* Glendale, Calif.: Regal, 1971.

Wadsworth, Barry J. *Piaget's Theory of Cognitive Development.* New York: McKay, 1971.

9

Middle Adolescence

Rex E. Johnson

HIGH SCHOOL YOUTH are a threat to many people in the church. Parents worry about their sons' careers and daughters' marriages. Pastors worry about dress trends and worldliness. Sponsors and teachers worry about attitudes, trustees about destroyed property, older adults about change, and youth ministers about building the group.

"Youth" and "problems" mean about the same thing to some people. Perhaps it is time to begin thinking of the youth opportunity, the youth potential. Of course, teens' problems should not be ignored. But it is the privilege and responsibility of the church to discover the nature of today's high school teenagers, to work creatively to meet their needs, and to help them achieve their potential for Jesus Christ.

Ineffective ministries to people often can be traced to the attitude of the leader. Working with teenagers as the leader wishes they were, or as he thinks they ought to be, offers little hope for success. But discovering what life looks like to the teen, and accepting him as he is, promises much good.

The church must minister in distinctive ways to every age-group—from the infant through the senior citizen. But the middle adolescent years (roughly fifteen to eighteen) represent an especially critical period. To minister effectively to young people in their initial years of middle adolescence, youth leaders should be knowledgeable of the physical, emotional, mental, social, and spiritual characteristics of high school youth and the world in which they live.

Describing teenagers is like taking 35mm pictures at a motocross race. The whole scene keeps changing so much and so fast that description is dated before it is published. Also an accurate description of any one youth is difficult to generalize because the more a person observes about one youth the more he finds that those observations are not applicable to others. This points out the fundamental principle of individuality in youth work. The need, motives, attitudes, perceptions, and behaviors of each person differ.

REX E. JOHNSON, M.R.E., is Assistant Professor of Christian Education, Talbot Theological Seminary, La Mirada, California.

A true understanding of adolescence includes a recognition of the existence of individual differences. Surface similarities may often conceal crucial differences. An understanding of a given adolescent requires a wide and extensive knowledge of his past as well as his present physical and psychological environments. He must be viewed as an adolescent, but he must also be viewed as a human being, and his behavior as an adolescent must be interpreted with the aid of that view.

Brunk and Metzler point out some of the characteristics of this period in a young person's development:[1]

As youth enter middle adolescence, individual differences become more pronounced. The slow student reaches his intellectual level, so that school may be difficult for him. The brilliant young person may be ready for college by the time he is halfway through middle adolescence.

Hereditary characteristics of face and form introduce the appearance of the adult. Emotionally, some may be eleven- or twelve-year-olds, though their physiques are adult. Others, more precocious socially, may marry before the close of the period. Some gain economic independence and become job seekers, while others remain dependent even into the latter part of later adolescence. Many characteristics that are true of early adolescence may still be found in these ages, and many develop amazingly toward the maturity of later adolescence.

Between 1965 and 1975 a large population group, the post-World War II baby boom, experienced their teen years. The fact that there were so many teens created a major impact on society. Advertisers and merchandisers not only adjusted to the buying power of this large group, but in many cases, created market items for them. The term "generation gap" became popular, and social scientists began looking for the factors that brought about all this alienation.

While some of the concerns of youth in the past ten years were connected to current events many were concerns that have remained among youth after those events lost their currency.

The person or church who aspires to work with youth must be current in terms of response to cultural issues teens are facing, but must also be aware of concerns that have to do with development toward maturity regardless of the issues of the day.

Concerns that all teens face sooner or later, consciously or subconsciously, include coping with physical growth, intellectual maturation, growing in independence and responsibility, forming an identity, developing in sexuality, experiencing new emotional stimuli and mixed feelings, facing

1. Ada Brunk and Ethel Metzler, *The Christian Nurture of Youth* (Scottdale, Pa.: Herald, 1960), p. 44.

new values, reordering family relationships, responding to society, and responding to God. These ten concerns suggest an outline for the rest of the chapter.

COPING WITH PHYSICAL GROWTH

A young person approaches physical maturity in the midde adolescent years. Many of youth's so-called problems are due to what is happening in them by way of physical growth and changes in body chemistry. A minister to youth, though unable to do anything about physical growth and body chemistry, can have a marked influence on how an adolescent responds to these changes.

Girls normally mature physically earlier than boys, frequently gaining full height in early adolescence. Since they are also maturing in other ways ahead of boys their age, many girls are attractive to and attracted by boys two to five years older than themselves. While this often creates problems for the girls and their parents, it also creates pressures on young boys to accept roles they are not yet ready for.

Beside rapid growth in height, boys experience changes in primary sex characteristics such as obvious genital growth, ejaculation, wet dreams, and new sexual impulses. Along with these come secondary sex characteristics such as the growth of pubic and axillary hair, marked voice changes, the development of a beard, and those hated pimples.

Girls experience genital growth, enlargement of their breasts, pubic and axillary hair, new sexual impulses, menstruation, changes in body proportions, and of course complexion problems as well.

As a result of these changes there is an increase in energy that propels teens and leaves many parents weary. Teens often act without thinking and on impulse. Increased energy also brings increased appetite, impatience, awkwardness, and accidents. It also implies that youth ministers must be willing to be active people.

Individual differences in physical maturation are a challenge to understanding even in one family. They are also a source of problems themselves. De Jang observes that:

> Each individual differs as to when puberty begins and the pace it follows. Changes may begin "early" or at a "rapid" pace. Youngsters who are unhappy with their pace should not blame themselves because the timing and pace are out of their control. When the time does arrive, the sex hormones and the growth hormones act in concert to produce the vast changes of puberty![2]

2. Arthur J. De Jang, *Making It to Adulthood* (Philadelphia: Westminster, 1972), p. 15.

The girl who matures early is sometimes so much taller than her peers that she compensates with a slouched posture. She has menstruation (often an embarrassment) to deal with, and is sometimes a source of envy by her former friends. Her sexuality is often far more developed than her understanding of sexual roles and intimacy.

The girl who matures late faces rejection by her friends who only magnify her self-rejection. Sometimes she is simply left out.

The boy who matures late may see himself as inadequate and may be treated as incompetent even though he wants leadership. On the other hand, large boys tend to be given responsibility commensurate with their size rather than with their ability.

MATURING INTELLECTUALLY

Youth's horizons expand at this period. Earlier the teen was concerned primarily with himself, his personal wants. Now he begins to discover a world beyond himself, and to learn that satisfaction is found through relating himself to that world.

This growth in concern is accompanied by an increased capacity to learn. While the last word has yet to be spoken on the nature and accuracy of the IQ, it is obvious that not all teens grasp new concepts or stockpile knowledge for ready use with equal facility. But during mid-teen years the mind rolls up its sleeves for work.

At a time when teens' minds are maturing why is it that so many resemble bumps on a log in Sunday school and other Bible study situations? Are the truths taught from the Bible so difficult that young minds are overwhelmed? Obviously not! Many teens have learned not to think in church, but to accept. Then when ideas that have been accepted without thought and without values attached to them are challenged, youth often find them unacceptable.

Many teachers and youth ministers think of teaching as the process of filling their youths' minds with knowledge much as a cup is filled with water.

This approach is unsatisfactory, partly because of the rapid rate of forgetting but more because of the tenuous relationship between knowledge and behavior. A student could know all about the Constitution of the United States and be able to recite a list of the obligations of citizenship without being a good citizen himself. At least partly as a result of these shortcomings some educators devised a new concept of learning that viewed the student as an active participant in the process rather than a passive receptacle. The student was still expected to remember information, such as the characteristics of a good citizen; but, in addition, he was given an opportunity to live the role of a good citizen in the classroom.[3]

A problem arises when youth ministers or teachers equate learning by doing with crafts, art projects, or dramatic productions. All these are learning activities, but so are quiet research, writing, discussion, and responding activities. A learner does not need to be pasting up a collage to be learning. But if we can help young people use ideas instead of only remembering them, we will see them become learners, not just receptors.

Jean Piaget has shown that by middle adolescence, youth are able to handle abstract ideas and symbolism that were beyond their capacity before adolescence. This demands a rethinking of many of their foundational ideas, including what they have been taught in Sunday school. If Sunday school and their other church-related experiences challenge young people, they will be less likely to challenge and repudiate their basic beliefs. Helping youth rethink and then experience the validity of their faith is a major task of workers with youth.

GROWING IN INDEPENDENCE AND RESPONSIBILITY

An increase in independence is almost a characteristic of middle adolescence. Havighurst assigns two of the developmental tasks of the adolescent to areas of growing independence: achieving emotional independence of parents and other adults, and achieving assurance of economic independence. Several other developmental tasks also relate to independence and responsibility.[4]

The sixth-grader graduating from grammar school is seen as a child. The high school graduate is almost ready to be called an adult. The junior high youngster depends on his parents for food, his home, transportation, clothes, "spending money," and just about everything else. Even though junior highs may be adept at manipulating their parents to get what they want, parents have the final word.

The high school graduate may be ready to move away from home. He eats out often, drives the family car or even his own car, buys many of his own clothes with the money he earns. Many of his choices are not the choices his parents would make for him, but they go along with his choices anyway.

Obviously teens vary in the extent and pace of their independence. Also, families differ in the amount of tension created by adolescent growth in

---

3. Norris M. Sanders, *Classroom Questions: What Kinds?* (New York: Harper & Row, 1966), pp. 6-7.
4. Robert James Havighurst, *Human Development and Education* (New York: Longmans, Green, 1953), pp. 111-58.

independence. The critical factor is that of trust, especially a parent's ability to trust his or her own teens. With most parents, trust is built when their teen shows them growing self-discipline.

In figure 9.1 line AB indicates a teen's growth in independence, and line AC indicates his growth in self-discipline. Line AD shows a teen that is growing faster in independence than in self-discipline. Line AE shows a parent's expectations that his son grow in self-discipline before he is allowed increased independence. At any point in time, the relative distance between lines AD and AE is a measure of tension in a home.

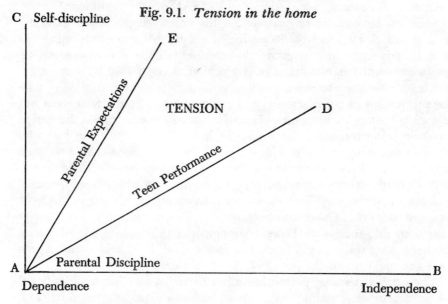

Fig. 9.1. *Tension in the home*

If a youth worker can help young people choose some ways to demonstrate self-discipline to their parents, both the teen and the parents will be grateful for reduced tension and the freedom to build trust. Whatever the parental expectations, the youth who are learning self-discipline faster than independence (whose performance line is higher than forty-five degrees from their independence line) are becoming responsible.

FORMING AN IDENTITY

Identity formation is not unique to adolescents. Toddlers shouting "Mine!" are working on their identity as are recently retired executives who cannot sit still. But adolescence is a particularly important period for identity formation.

An adolescent starts with the notion of who he is in relationship to his family. But as other people (especially peers) become more important to him, he looks to them for reassurance that what he thinks about himself is correct. Since the feedback he gets is often ambiguous and contradictory, he has the problem of deciding between his self-image and his impression of what others think of him. In the process of deciding, his self-image may begin to melt.

De Jang identifies some of the problems of identity diffusion: difficulty in making choices, depression and anxiety, concurrent urgency and futility resulting in problems with time, inability to concentrate, fear of competition, choosing a negative identity, and identity resistance.[5]

Some adolescents go to curious lengths and even desperate extremes in their search for identity. Rejection of old friends and establishing ties with friends whose life-styles are threateningly different is common. Rejection of family habits and ties is accepted as inevitable by our society but it is devastating to parents. Since self-image is so often linked in adolescents' minds to popularity with the opposite sex, youth who want but cannot get attention sometimes fantasize sexual experiences to the extent that they may confuse fantasy with reality. The result is the girl who claims to be pregnant, but whose story falls apart when cross-examined carefully, or the boy who brags about sexual exploits he never had.

A clue to identity diffusion may be heard in Christian adolescents' prayers for "strength." The young person who knows who he is in Christ assumes strength. Those who keep praying for strength forget the power that is already theirs—the power (strength) of the Holy Spirit who lives in them. One way to help Christian youth, then, is to help them experience and make use of the power of the Holy Spirit.

The Christian young person has a head start in forming his identity if he can accept what Scripture says about him as a person designed by God, responsible to God, and redeemed by the blood of Christ.

Developing in Sexuality

Puberty not only brings the development of primary and secondary sex characteristics. It also presents problems related to identity, motivation, feelings, values, and relationships.

With the rapid disintegration of our society's sexual values, some of the restraints on premarital sexual involvement have faded. This calls for at least two considerations for those who work with youth. One is how to help teens develop moral convictions strong enough to resist society's pressures combined with biological pressure. The other is how to help youth

5. De Jang, pp. 38-49.

who have sex-related problems such as premarital pregnancy, abortion, coping with guilt and guilt feelings, masturbation, sex-play, premarital sex, as well as concomitant identity and relationship problems.

How does one help a teen develop moral commitment, especially if the teen is not yet oriented to the authority of Scripture? First, the church must not shrink from its responsibility to parents and teens to teach clearly what the Bible says about sex. To maintain silence is to lose by default. Sporadic messages from the pulpit can never be as effective as a total program of sex education including biblical values, but even sporadic messages are better than total silence.

Probably the most effective help to developing moral commitment is the availability of many models of strong and intimate marriages. Youth who have not yet developed an orientation to scriptural strictures are often able to be influenced by married couples who have developed an intimate relationship and are not afraid to talk about their love for each other. These models of morality and purity stand in contrast to guilt feelings youth have who are beginning to experiment with sex-play. These models appeal to teens' developing idealism. This allows morality to be caught as well as taught.

Stone and Church, in a secular textbook, wrote the following:

> It may seem cold-blooded and anti-sexual to say that one should enter a sexual relationship open-eyed and clearheaded and after a certain amount of deliberation, but the alternative is likely to be psychologically damaging. Sex at its best is too marvelous a thing to be attained casually and indiscriminately. It requires full openness and intimate fusion between two persons, and one does not want to be intimate with just anybody. But without the intimacy and openness, sex becomes a matter of sensations which can be induced as well by self-stimulation as by contact between bodies. It is our contention that it is this intimacy which constitutes the "something else" that adolescents find missing from sex.[6]

If workers with youth are to help youth take a moral stand, they must be ready to share some of the "how to's" of sexuality such as how to dress attractively but modestly, how to say no firmly but politely, how to be considerate, how to decide when to stop.

It is most important that youth workers have training in counseling youth with sex-related problems. When a church starts helping youth develop moral commitment, it is likely to find that youth who are trying to cope with guilt will be ready for help. Hopefully the church can be redemptive when it's too late to say "thou shalt not."

6. L. Joseph Stone and Joseph Church, *Childhood and Adolescence*, 3d ed. (New York: Random, 1973), pp. 471-72.

EXPERIENCING NEW EMOTIONAL STIMULI AND MIXED FEELINGS

John seems a quiet, shy young man, all eyeglasses and floppy blond hair, sitting in the tenor section of the church choir. He excites neither trouble nor interest for the people around him. His infrequent talk is usually about sporting events. It is extremely important to him that his team should win; a loss by his school's team, or his state university, or his favorite professional team can make him morose and depressed for days. Not precisely unfriendly, he seldom opens a conversation; and when he responds to someone else's remarks, he talks a bit too loudly, a bit too fast, as though people might not hear him out unless he gets it all said in a rush of words.[7]

"I know a guy just like John," is a common response to hearing this description. "But why is he that way?" is the question that most often follows. Strommen pinpoints a common adolescent malady—feelings of worthlessness. He discusses how those feelings are built by distress over personal faults and lack of self-confidence, and how they are related to poor classroom relations, academic problems, family disunity, and anxiety about faith and the opposite sex.

At the same time an adolescent may sense the urge to rebel. But rebellion is bound to hurt someone, usually someone the adolescent loves. The result is usually turmoil, and everyone involved gets hurt, including the adolescent. Ginott describes the behavioral consequences.[8]

Another emotion that is not really new but is felt with new intensity in adolescence is disappointment and even outrage. The discrepancy between what many teens have been taught and the lives of their teachers suddenly becomes an issue. What society proclaims often appears ridiculously inconsistent with news events. Wagemaker writes about church leaders: "We talk about God's love, but we don't demonstrate it. We talk about helping people but we don't go to them or encourage others to go."[9]

Another emotion that many adolescents experience is anxiety. De Jang states that "developing a unique and workable identity is at the hurt of adolescent anxiety."[10] Anxiety may arise from unacceptable physical changes, as described earlier in this chapter. O. H. Mowrer believes that anxiety results when an adolescent fears the removal of love and approval by important persons in his life.[11] Of course, family trouble will raise

7. Merton P. Strommen, *Five Cries of Youth* (New York: Harper & Row, 1974), p. 12.
8. Haim G. Ginott, *Between Parent and Teenager* (New York: Avon, 1969), pp. 24-25.
9. Herbert Wagemaker, *Why Can't I Understand My Kids?* (Grand Rapids: Zondervan, 1973), pp. 21-22.
10. De Jang, *Making It to Adulthood*, p. 57.
11. Rollo May, *The Meaning of Anxiety* (New York: Ronald, 1950), pp. 107-8.

anxiety, and the responsibilities of impending adulthood may cause enough anxiety to elicit regression to the safer responses of childhood.

When young people set idealistic standards and then break those standards themselves, guilt and shame result. This guilt and shame is especially strong if the adolescent has expressed disappointment or outrage over the inconsistencies of adults. De Jang states:

> Young people walk a tightrope between guilt and shame. In breaking away from parents they are vulnerable to feelings of guilt. If they do not develop this autonomy, young people are able to avoid experiencing these feelings.[12]

So the emotions of adolescence—whether worthlessness, rebellion, turmoil, disappointment, outrage, anxiety, guilt, or shame—are strong. Even though these emotions are not foreign to children, their new intensity and the way they tend to gang up on a teen make adolescence a period of relative emotional instability.

FACING NEW VALUES

The 1970s have seen the beginning of a new interest in the process of developing values. In evangelical circles the chief interest until recently was in the content of learning. Then as interest turned toward the learner, the process of learning became an important area of consideration as well.

Many youth have rejected biblical content because they have not had the opportunity to be involved in the learning process. Study of the learning process has shown the importance of teens' developing personal values, especially in relation to morality.[13]

Particularly with the popularity of value clarification in the public school systems, the church needs to take a second look at its values and at its ways of helping youth develop their values. Kohlberg shows three orientations in moral thinking—orientation to prudence, orientation to authority, and orientation to principle.[14] He and others state that the earliest age a person usually finds orientation to principle is in his early twenties. Thus, youth workers are dealing with some youth whose orientation is to prudence, and many whose orientation is to authority.

Youth oriented to prudence are dominated by self-interest. Right and wrong are determined by physical consequences. If something satisfies a

12. De Jang, *Making It to Adulthood*, p. 64.
13. Donald Joy, *The Effects of Value-Oriented Instruction in the Church and in the Home* (Bloomington, Ind.: Indiana U., 1969). Available from University Microfilms, Ann Arbor, Michigan.
14. Lawrence Kohlberg, "Stages of Moral Development as a Basis for Moral Education" in *Moral Education*, ed. Clive Beck et al. (Toronto: U. of Toronto, 1970).

teen's needs, he considers it right. If he gets nothing out of it, he feels it is wrong to waste his energy. Intention is not considered because his perspective is egocentric. He assumes that if he does not get caught, his behavior was not bad; and if he gets by, he is proud and boastful.

Youth oriented to authority are concerned with what "significant others" think. Some are oriented to published codes including the Bible. Right and wrong are determined by the expectations of other people. Intention becomes all important, and perspective is reversible. Justice is reciprocal and equalitarian, demanding that things be put right.

Between the prudence level and the authority level of development, youth (as well as children) go through a period of stress and disequilibrium. As Joy says, "Level changes tend to be marked by a distinct crisis, a turbulence, and leap."[15]

Youth oriented to prudence may be attracted to a youth group by the "fun and games" that appeal to the satisfaction of their felt needs. Salvation is understood by them as being spared the physical pain of hell. Discipleship is next to impossible, and discipline must be immediate.

Youth oriented to the expectations of significant people may be attracted by youth or adults they esteem. Here the youth workers become important as models. Salvation is thought obtainable by doing what these significant people ask them to do—to say a prayer, to come forward, and so forth. Discipleship is important, and discipline might best be obtained by showing how misbehavior hurts the significant person or persons in a teen's life.

Youth oriented to codes may be attracted to a group by its quantity and quality of Bible study. Salvation is confessing sins in exchange for God's forgiveness. These youth may be ready to help disciple younger or more immature youth, and discipline might consist of showing discrepancies between behavior and biblical teaching.

Since youth tend to buy the values of their significant models, those models need to be sure their own values are genuinely biblical.

REORDERING FAMILY RELATIONSHIPS

A family in stress because of the presence of teens is seen by many parents as normal. If they can wait it out, parents expect to return to peace and quiet by the time their teens are in their twenties. Young parents are told, "Just wait till yours are teens."

As teens grow in independence and responsibility, as they form their own identity and develop physically, as they experience new emotions and

15. Donald Joy, "Developmental Levels as Potential for Religious Perspective" (Paper delivered to the Wesleyan Theological Society, Atlanta, Georgia, April 2-4, 1975).

mixed feelings, and as they face new values, they are bound to agitate the waters of peaceful family life. But where family life was not peaceful to begin with; where there was divorce and the loss of a parent or remarriage and the acquiring of a step-parent; where there was constant bickering; what does a teen who needs supportive relationships begin with? Fritze shows that only 20 percent of marriages can be defined as "happy" and "good."[16] Therefore, many teens in church as well as outside the church may feel the need for improved family relationships.

Many Christian teens who are otherwise successful in their walk with God are defeated in their family relationships. In time, their inability to live consistently, even at home, may draw them away from the church and from God.

A positive way of helping teens, then, is to work as closely as possible with their parents. Another way to help teens is to help teens explore ways they can respond positively to their parents. Even when their parents' demands go beyond reason, young people will respond positively if they have explored the implications of passages such as 1 Peter 2:9-25 and Ephesians 6:4.

Other ways of helping teens reorder their family relationships include helping them open channels of communication with their parents, helping them learn responsibility and apply their learning at home, helping teens who are in trouble with the law, teaching teens to love, helping them find ways of resolving conflicts, and helping them deal with their emotions.

RESPONDING TO SOCIETY

Possibly the greatest human influence in the life of a high school teen is another young person. At no other age will he rely so heavily on his peers. The clique becomes a way of life.

During midadolescence the peer group includes both sexes. Since there is no cure for this social instinct, youth workers will do well to utilize it. A youth program can hardly succeed where young people do not enjoy the company of each other.

This is not to imply that high school youth will not be friendly toward those outside their immediate circle of friends. But almost every youth has a few friends he prefers above others. They may quarrel, even to the extent of temporary severance of relationships, but before long all is forgotten and the group is intact once more.

It is an honor for any adult to become accepted into the collective confidence of such a group. Such acceptance is essential to effective youth

16. J. A. Fritze, *The Essence of Marriage* (Grand Rapids: Zondervan, 1969).

leadership. The leader's efforts will be analytically dissected by the group in private discussion, and judgment passed.

Since young people influence each other, it is important that the church help them form friendships within the fellowship of the church. Aggressive, happy young people provide the church with a most effective tool for influencing nonchurched teens.

RESPONDING TO GOD

The reality of a personal relationship with God is emotional as well as spiritual for young people whose lives are centered in Jesus Christ. Strommen describes them as follows:

> Joy . . . may take the form of quiet exuberance over the simple pleasures of living. Or it may be a shout of celebration and hope that contrasts with the despair and cynicism so often heard from twentieth-century man. It is the cry of youth whose joy is in a sense of identity and mission that centers in the person of Jesus Christ. As a minority group (about one-third of all church youth), they exemplify in what they value, believe, perceive, and do the impact of identifying with a personal God and a believing community.[17]

Such a faith-walk can be simultaneously profound and immature. It has profound effects on the life of the teen, yet is subject to ups and downs, to periods of fruit and periods of barrenness, to mistakes and doubts, to idealism and rationalization. A certain amount of inconsistency can be expected in a teen's response to God. But with time, meaningful relationships to other Christians, and a basic commitment to Jesus and His Word, maturity will come.

A marked form of inconsistency occurs in many churches as youth attend camps, retreats, or special meetings; respond to a challenge; and then are not discipled. This is the repeated story of many youth who drop out of church and away from their response to God. They come off a mountaintop experience to a routine world. They hope for change but have not learned how to walk with Jesus.

What do young people need to respond to God? They need to become acquainted with God. How? The Bible has a clear answer: "Christ in you" (Col 1:27). As teens see Jesus in the lives of their teachers (models), they will respond. Richards gives seven factors which enhance the teaching and learning of faith as life:

1. Frequent, long-term contact with the model(s)
2. A warm, loving relationship with the model(s)

17. Strommen, *Five Cries of Youth*, p. 92.

3. Exposure to the inner states of the model(s)
4. Observation of the model(s) in a variety of life settings and situations
5. Consistency and clarity exhibited by the model(s) in behaviors, values, and so forth
6. Correspondence between the behavior of the model(s) and the beliefs (ideal standards) of the community
7. Explanation of the life-style of the model(s) conceptually, with instruction accompanying shared experiences[18]

CONCLUSION

Workers with high school youth need to break out of old molds and modes of thinking about youth ministry and begin to think about it in new and bolder—and more biblical—ways. Youth workers are effective to the extent they know and work in accord with the characteristics of their teens and build ministries that are biblically solid in aims and objectives.

FOR FURTHER READING

Adams, James F., ed. *Understanding Adolescence.* 3d. ed. Boston: Allyn & Bacon, 1976.

Burton, Janet. *Guiding Youth.* Nashville: Convention, 1969.

Clark, Ted. *The Oppression of Youth.* New York: Harper & Row, 1975.

Committee on Adolescence, Group for the Advancement of Psychiatry. *Normal Adolescence.* New York: Scribner, 1968.

Drakeford, John. *The Awesome Power of the Listening Ear.* Waco, Tex.: Word, 1967.

Elbert, Edmund. *Youth, the Hope of the Harvest.* New York: Sheed & Ward, 1972.

Elkind, David. *Children and Adolescents: Interpretive Essays on Jean Piaget.* New York: Oxford U., 1970.

Erikson, Erik H. *Identity: Youth and Crisis.* New York: Norton, 1968.

Ezell, Mancil. *Youth in Bible Study/New Dynamics.* Nashville: Convention, 1970.

Garvice, T., and Murphree, Dorothy. *Understanding Youth.* Nashville: Convention, 1969.

Goldman, Ronald. *Religious Thinking from Childhood to Adolescence.* New York: Seabury, 1964.

Johnson, Rex E. *Ways to Plan and Organize Your Sunday School—Youth.* Glendale, Calif.: Regal, 1972.

Keniston, Kenneth. *Young Radicals.* New York: Harcourt & Brace, 1968.

Mager, Robert F. *Preparing Instructional Objectives.* Palo Alto, Calif.: Fearon, 1962.

Narramore, Bruce. *Help! I'm a Parent.* Grand Rapids: Zondervan, 1972.

18. Lawrence O. Richards, *A Theology of Christian Education* (Grand Rapids: Zondervan, 1975), pp. 84-85.

Offer, Daniel. *The Psychological World of the Teen-ager*. New York: Basic Books, 1969.

Popham, W. James, and Baker, Eva L. *Establishing Instructional Goals*. Englewood Cliffs, N.J.: Prentice-Hall, 1970.

——. *Planning an Instructional Sequence*. Englewood Cliffs, N.J.: Prentice-Hall, 1970.

Powell, John. *Why Am I Afraid to Tell You Who I Am?* Niles, Ill.: Argus, 1969.

Reed, Bobbie, and Johnson, Rex E. *Bible Learning Activities—Youth*. Glendale, Calif.: Regal, 1974.

Reed, Ed, and Johnson, Rex E. *Sunday School Teachers Planbook*. Glendale, Calif.: Regal, 1975.

Richards, Lawrence O. *You and Youth*. Chicago: Moody Press, 1973.

——. *Youth Ministry: Its Renewal in the Local Church*. Grand Rapids: Zondervan, 1972.

Sizemore, John T. *Blueprint for Teaching*. Nashville: Broadman, 1964.

Snyder, Ross. *Young People and Their Culture*. Nashville: Abingdon, 1969.

Stoop, David A. *Ways to Help Them Learn—Youth*. Glendale, Calif.: Regal, 1971.

Terkelson, Helen E. *Counseling the Unwed Mother*. Philadelphia: Fortress, 1964.

Westerhoff, John H., and Neville, Gwen Kennedy. *Generation to Generation*. Philadelphia: Pilgrim, 1974.

Yankelovich, Daniel. *The New Morality: A Profile of American Youth in the Seventies*. New York: McGraw-Hill, 1974.

10

Later Adolescence

Donald Williams

AN INTERESTING PARADOX exists today. College-age young people, though disillusioned with the church, are characterized by spiritual searching and commitment.

The revolutionary 1960s ended with the frustration of political hopes for a changed society. The promises of a new order, called the "Age of Aquarius," were shattered on the rocks of hard drugs, hard crime, hard institutions, and the hard realities of life itself, namely, making a living and growing up. With the termination of the Vietnam War, the focus for student rebellion was lost. It was said of Chaplain William Sloan Coffin of Yale University, "When this war ended, he died." Suddenly the campuses were quiet, the streets empty. A new generation arose with a post-Vietnam hunger for serenity and a post-Watergate cynicism toward life. By the mid-1970s a new selfishness determined the student world. Now there appeared the old passion of the 1950s for making it financially, but without that decade's idealism. It is likely that after this generation has acquired its share of the gross national product, another generation of idealists will emerge on top of the new affluence and security it provides.

The introversion of today's college generation, the failure of the pseudo-answers of the sixties, has led a significant minority into spiritual solutions to life. From the burned-out hulk of California hippies came the Jesus movement. Suddenly hard-core evangelism surfaced and tens of thousands of ex-revolutionaries, drug addicts, street people, college dropouts, and high school and college students were converted. Sociologically speaking, the Jesus movement was one expression of a spiritual hunger, also represented by the turn to Eastern religious mysticism and the occult. Theologically speaking, the Jesus movement was a genuine awakening among a student generation disenfranchised from both church and culture.

DONALD WILLIAMS, Ph.D., is Assistant Professor of Religion, Claremont Men's College, Pomona, California.

With the passing of the Vietnam War, the formal Jesus movement passed. Where it was welcomed or organized into some institutional form by the church, it endured. Where it depended on the revolutionary culture or a charismatic leader, it died. The result, however, of the general cultural upheaval of the sixties, and the evangelistic surge, has been a unique openness to the gospel among students. This openness comes from the following factors:

1. Disillusionment with the old materialistic values of Western culture
2. Skepticism over the old liberal idealism, and cynicism about the nature of man
3. The serious critique made of the technological society which has cracked the universal authority of the scientific world view
4. A new longing for spiritual life and openness to divine authority outside of man
5. An evangelistic climate where many want to know the unique claims of Jesus Christ and respect those who are "up-front" about Him
6. A new sense of Christian community and seriousness about a Christian life-style which has made Christianity a visible option for non-Christians
7. The interest in and return to more conservative and traditional views in society

All of this suggests that evangelical churches face unique opportunities for college-age ministry, and the growth of campus evangelical movements and evangelical church ministries bears this out.

This chapter is concerned with college-age youth (ages 18-22) though "later adolescence" extends, technically, from eighteen to twenty-four. Therefore, many of the following observations apply to this more inclusive age-group. People between the ages of eighteen and twenty-four are sometimes referred to as older youth or young adults. In addition to college students, this age division includes employed single young people and single military servicemen. Some youth in this age bracket live with their parents, some live on campuses, others have established their own homes, and still others live by themselves or with friends.

College-age youth are at decision-making crossroads. They are grappling with issues relating to self-support, life occupation, love, and marriage as well as a view of themselves, their friends, their country, the world, and life itself.[1] This is the "twilight zone in which persons can experiment with forms of adult life before settling down to new commitments

1. Much of the material in this section is adapted from Allen J. Moore, *The Young Adult Generation* (Nashville: Abingdon, 1969).

and patterns of life."[2] Henrietta Mears used to say that she preferred to work with college-age students because in their four or five years (18-22) many of them would make crucial decisions of life: What will I do? and Whom will I marry? While more elect a single life-style today, Mears's observations are still largely true.

Transition is the word to describe college and career youth. This transition is often made outside the family context. They are challenging the authority of parents, teachers, church, and civil leaders. They are bound by love to very few people, wheeling freely in loose patterns, and often anonymous in the big city or university. They have little sense of community responsibility. They are seeking to make up their minds about what they are like and what they want, so they are taking soundings of themselves and others. They want freedom to look around; yet they also want the security and delight of others. They are still experiencing the crisis of adolescence: breaking from the family while still wanting the security of the family. They seem to say, "Don't fence me in—but don't fence me out either."

Sexuality and sexual identity are consuming interests. With the use of contraceptives, the collapse of formal morality, and the marketing of sex, there is an overwhelming pressure on college-age youth today for sexual experience. Loneliness feeds this pressure as well, where physical intimacy can compensate for the lack of deeper intimacy and commitment. Sexual experience before marriage is now almost demanded by the secular culture as a "rite of passage" to manhood or womanhood. Popular music constantly glorifies sex for the sake of sex. Tremendous hurt is often the result. At the same time, interest in the opposite sex is natural and God-given. This is a peak period for concern about sex, love, and marriage.

Many college-age people experience a deep sense of guilt. The arrest rate for hard-core crimes is higher in the eighteen-to-thirty age bracket than in any other group.[3] Rootlessness is common because many youth in this age-group are not yet sure what they believe or should believe. In the last fifteen years, the eighteen-to-thirty group has increased 64 percent in America while the rest of the United States population increased only 17 percent. The church must either come to grips with this group or find its ministry drastically curtailed.

THE WORLD COLLEGE-AGE YOUTH LIVE IN

College-age persons are profoundly (though often unconsciously) af-

2. Ibid., p. 126.
3. Gertrude Selznick and John Larkins, *What Is Known about Young Adults?* Monograph 5 (Berkeley: Survey Research Center, U. of California), p. 1.

fected by the larger world in which all live. In the sixties they participated in a radical reshaping of part of that world, in the creation of the so-called "counterculture."[4] They now live in a certain tension between these two worlds.

The mass-culture is the culture of the scientific world view made functional through technology. In the early 1800s the steamboat was invented and the Industrial Revolution began. Science affected industry and also philosophy. Today most of the people in the United States live in the advanced stages of the Industrial Revolution. Cars, computers, color television sets are everywhere, and all these things share a common characteristic: they are impersonal.

On the tollways people drive up to a booth and drop thirty-five cents into the hopper, and a green light signals them through. On the light are painted the words, "Thank you." Is it the machine who gives the thanks? Or is it the guard in the change-making booth in the next lane, or the unseen superintendent of highways? Or are they oblivious to the existence of the drivers? To many people the "Thank you" is meaningless—contrived and impersonal.

People have become so accustomed to machines that can never meaningfully say "I'm sorry" or "Thank you" that people are conditioned to regard others around them as machines. People are valued for their *function* rather than their personhood. As Martin Buber has pointed out, people establish "I-it" relationships rather than "I-thou" relationships.[5] Worse yet, some people unconsciously regard God in this way too. They tend to feel that He is distant, and that the world He created is likewise mechanical and impersonal. Then they feel abandoned to a helpless life in a world of complicated, indifferent mechanisms where "research is the key to tomorrow."

The Industrial Revolution has done more than make life seem impersonal, however. It has also created rootlessness and mobility.[6] A person grows up in Detroit, goes to a university there and then gets a job in Los Angeles for five years, Dallas for two, Seattle for three, and Boston for four. By then he has no roots anywhere. The system offers him opportunity, but exacts its pound of flesh in payment.

The impersonal, rootless, multiple-choice feel to life around the college-age person profoundly affects his answers to all his basic questions. He cannot live indifferently to the formal and subtle influences of his culture.

4. See Theodore Roszak, *The Making of a Counter Culture* (Garden City, N.Y.: Doubleday, 1969).
5. Martin Buber, *I and Thou* (New York: Scribner, 1937).
6. Richard E. Gordon, Kathrine K. Gordon, and Max Gunther, *The Split-Level Trap* (New York: Geis, 1961).

In the sixties, numerous students became conscious of this and rebelled. Their reaction was not merely negative; they attempted to define a new life distinct from the mass-culture dominated by science and technology.

The heart of the "counterculture" was a new understanding of man. The scientific-world man was justified by his production and consumption; he was a functionary. For the counterculture, "post-modern man" was justified by his personhood; he was the end, not the means. Rather than stressing reason, order, and performance as values, the counter culture stressed freedom, spontaneity, and creativity. "Being" rather than "doing" was the goal of existence. This value shift created openness to Eastern spirituality, ecological sensitivity, and woman's liberation. Many dynamic changes were introduced into the mass-culture by the counterculture. Some college-age students live with full commitment to the old values of consumerism. Others reject the mass-culture, even with violence. Most stand stretched between the two worlds. While seeking the material rewards of the mass-culture, they seek the human and personal values represented in the counterculture.

In light of this, consider some of the psychological characteristics of college-age people.

THREE CRUCIAL QUESTIONS

The college-age person is neither adolescent nor adult, but a mixture whose proportions depend less on age than experience. He is therefore a surprising combination of maturity and immaturity. One minute he is pulling a prank on his girl friend. Fifteen minutes later he is asking a youth leader his opinion of the cosmological argument for the existence of God. Three crucial questions dominate this age of growing to maturity: (1) Who am I? (2) How do I relate to others? (3) What should I believe? In other words his questions concern *identity, interrelationships,* and *ideology.*

Identity: Who am I? A person's identity is who he or she is. To the motor vehicle bureau, identity is thought of in terms of name, address, age, sex, weight, color of eyes and hair, license number. But does this really tell who a person is? The question, Who am I? actually has to do with such things as personal worth and dignity. The mass-culture asks the question in terms of function, What am I good for? The counterculture asks the question in terms of being, Who am I? What is my worth as a person? Students fear that either way the answer is, "Nothing much."

Self-esteem is closely related to this. If a person decides that God has not created him for Himself and for a purpose in this world, he may be inclined to spend his life loafing or in frantic effort to create value out of what he owns and accomplishes. The depersonalized culture encourages this by hinting that people are replaceable and worth little as individuals. It says, "You're an IBM card," or "You're a dockhand." So a man wonders if he has a soul or if he is merely a five-fingered hand capable of picking things up and setting them down.

If the college-age person decides he is worth something, he will live on the growing edge of his life; otherwise, he will choose the receding edge and be like the person in one of Bergman's works who said that he dreamed he had returned to his mother's womb, and grown smaller and smaller until he disappeared.

Growth never happens without properly answering the question, Who am I? or perhaps, Who am I growing to be? Socrates, when asked formally to define man, said, "Man is not a vegetable," and would say no more. Pascal did say more: "Man is a reed, but a thinking reed."

Identity can be approached through the question, For what kind of life does my personality suit me? Emotionally, one might be fluttery, phlegmatic, volatile, or enthusiastic. Volitionally, he may be strong-willed or easily swayed. Intellectually, he may be an A student, or B, C, D, or F student. Socially, he may be a leader, second in command, follower, introvert, clown, party girl. Technically, he may be an engineer, professor, musician, linguist. He must find out these things about himself, guarding, however, against easy labels and narrow classifications. He must seek to be honest with his feelings, not fearing to be more and more in touch with his true self.

Essential to this question of identity is the influence of family background. A person basically views himself in the way his parents viewed themselves and him. He learned how to be a man, a husband, a father from watching his father. This he absorbed for better or for worse, and is some of both. In moving to maturity one must decide how much of his family he can accept as himself and how much he must reject.

The search for identity may set the student over against his parents and equals. Short liaisons with many groups are common. He may think, "I quit going because I don't know if I want to be like them." The college youth, now that he is away from home, is free to canvass the possibilities about whom to become. He may be lured into many traps. One of them is "I am what I buy." Another is "I am what I pretend." He may be one thing to himself, another to his parents, yet another to teachers, and another to friends and the opposite sex.

Existentialism attracts some later adolescents because it asks for authenticity, fiercely calling on a person to be himself. As the present conformity-minded age threatens to overwhelm individuality, youth are reminded that "to exist" means "to stand out from." This philosophy has been one of the sources of the countercultural revolt against the mass-society.

Contrary to the existentialistic view, the student who cheats (and many Christians do, at some time in the course of four years at college) is temporarily abandoning the quest for identity in favor of pretending to be something he is not. He flees reality for the dream world where he appears a more intelligent or diligent person than he is.

The student who is trying to be himself will often set himself against authority to some extent. It is part of growing up, part of the process of his trying to be himself instead of being merely an extension of his parents or others. Mears comments that this "rebellion" is a student's "natural need for independence that results as he matures."[7] Rebellion is part of the method by which students find themselves.

Solitude is another part of this method. Though self-understanding requires interaction with people, a student needs time alone to straighten out his thoughts about himself. Real commitments are almost always made in solitude.

Another part of the process of discovering one's identity comes from the presence of an adult guarantor. He is an adult friend of the student who encourages him to believe that he can make it through the confusions of the transitorial stage to adulthood.[8] He assures the student (1) that adulthood is worth the effort, and (2) that the student is worth enough to make the effort. No one buys a thousand-dollar setting for a ten-cent glass "diamond." The adult guarantor must help the student see that he is a million-dollar stone, and worth the expense of a thousand-dollar setting—adulthood. (The way the church can use this concept of the adult guarantor is developed in the last section of this chapter.)

Interrelationships: How do I relate to others? "Each human being who has only himself for aim suffers from a horrible void," André Gide has said. On the positive side, Christ told a scribe that the greatest commandment is to love God, and that the next greatest love is to others. Essentially the problems of interrelationships ("How do I relate to others?") concerns the college-age person's discovery of his relationship to God. By interrelationship is meant "the relationship in which people know one another, support one another, share . . . interest with another."[9]

7. Henrietta Mears, "Teaching College-Age Youth," in *An Introduction to Evangelical Christian Education*, ed. J. Edward Hakes (Chicago: Moody, 1964), p. 193; Edgar Z. Friedenberg, *The Vanishing Adolescent* (New York: Dell, 1959).
8. Moore, *The Young Adult Generation*, pp. 16-17.
9. Gibson Winter, *Love and Conflict: New Patterns in Family Life* (Garden City, N.Y.: Doubleday, 1958), p. 70.

The later adolescent is an "in-between" in the matter of interrelationships. He wants to be free of entanglements and responsibility, yet he wants the intimacy of close friendships. Some students, relating poorly to their own age-group, are afflicted by loneliness. Also, study is a lonely occupation, compounding the problem. The competition of the academic community separate students from each other. The student says, "I don't want to go with the crowd; I want to be myself. But I'm afraid that I can't. So I go with the crowd and pretend that it's just what I want." The place of an adult guarantor is strategic in encouraging the young person to be himself and love others.

The student is learning the answer to "How do I relate to others?" as he seeks to establish meaningful relationships with the opposite sex. He does this through casual friendships, dating, going steady. Not being sure who he is, or if he is a person of worth, the student hesitates to let others know him. Further, he hesitates to get to know others because of the responsibility which that knowledge would place on him. He also fears that if he establishes a personal relationship with someone, he will either give or receive hurt.

Maintaining proper interrelationships demands enough security so that one can give to others. But it is even more difficult to receive something *from* one's peers (such as thoughtfulness or forgiveness), for this challenges one to give something back, again a test of inner security. Interrelationship is the opposite of monologue. It means personally knowing the other person. Failure here leads to isolation. Most college students experience immense guilt over sins committed in the area of interrelationships. Paul Tournier's book *Guilt and Grace* is an excellent aid here (for publication information refer to list at the end of this chapter).

The secret to interrelationships is learning how to listen. This means listening not in order to advise, judge, or condemn, but listening in order to understand. Oddly enough, students sometimes provide an indirect commentary on their pastor's failure to solve his own problem of interrelationships. They say, "I can't speak to him because he's all business," or "I can't get a word in edgewise," or "He makes me feel so guilty," or "He doesn't understand me."

This may give a clue on how to serve college-age youth more effectively: Learn more about human relations. It is not by accident that Christ said that the mark of His disciples was love for each other (John 13:35). And in discussing evangelism, He prayed that the disciples "may be perfected in unity, that the world may know that Thou didst send Me" (John 17: 23, NASB).

Interrrelationship, then, is the reverse of the statement, "I belong to a party of one, because I live in a world of fear."

Ideology: What should I believe? A third question students ask is, "What should I believe?" They are trying to form a world and life view that makes sense out of their kaleidoscopic whirl of daily experiences. They wonder what it all means. This is closely related to the question of identity and interrelationship. How a person views himself and others depends on his reference points. In fact, the three questions are frequently asked together.

Until a person decides on his ideology, he lacks a "sorter" for his impressions of life. He is like a stranger to his own world and needs to find how to interpret life to have some kind of significance for the person. If he does not have an adequate world view, he has no vision, and fails to experience that alchemy that transforms the dreary round of life into an adventure of meaning and personal significance. The hundred freshmen in a church-related college were asked by their professor to put in writing their philosophy of life. Many of them admitted they had given the subject very little thought. Others expressed confusion or uncertainty in words like this: "Life to me is one great big mixed-up mess," or this: "At times I am not quite sure what I believe, if anything at all."[10] These responses were reported in 1960. Later, in 1974, 25 percent of the entering students at Stanford University answered the question, "Who has had the most important influence on your life?" with one response: Jesus Christ.[11]

J. Glenn Gray, a professor at Colorado College, feels that the real ideological problem facing students is "to discover some authority, both private and public, that will make possible authentic individuality."[12] Increasing numbers of students are finding the best world view in biblical Christianity.

THE COLLEGE-AGE PERSON AS A PROFESSIONAL

While the major thrust of this chapter is toward the college student, the church's ministry must also engage the nonstudent in his years of later adolescence. This is a specialized field not necessarily fulfilled by adding career people to a college ministry.

Professionals who have not gone to college are easily intimidated by college students, especially in their exaggerated intellectualism. Professionals also grow quickly beyond the socially delayed adolescence of college students. They feel removed from the "rah-rah" spirit. Furthermore,

10. Joseph M. Hopkins, "What Do College Freshmen Think about Life?" *Christian Herald*, May 1960, pp. 21-22, 61, 77-78.
11. As reported to this writer by Dr. Robert Munger of Fuller Theological Seminary and confirmed to him by the Registrar of Stanford University.
12. J. Glenn Gray, "Salvation on Campus," *Harper's Magazine*, May 1965, p. 54.

professional people are living in a world of intense social and perform-ance pressure. Their self-worth in the mass-culture is now often measured by salary, advancement, and job identity. As well, professionals have more time for social activity, more money to spend, and often their loneliness and social insecurity are intensified.

Having broken physically and financially from their families, profes-sionals feel more independent and mature than college students. The church must respond to their needs by seeing them as a crucial and grow-ing group. Many divorced people also find their way into single fellow-ships. They are in need of forgiveness and healing. Single professionals tend to be the great blind spot in adult ministry. Yet they are filled with potential for the cause of Christ. Programs must be designed to meet their social needs, teaching must be practical and relevant, and the church must become their "extended family."

THE COLLEGE-AGE PERSON AS A STUDENT

HIGHER EDUCATION IN THE UNITED STATES

In 1900 the average American left school to work when he was 12; in 1930 he left at 15; in 1960 at 18; by 1990 it will be 21.[13] The point is that the nation is investing more and more of its available energy in formal instruction, and changing the character of the work done to be more and more professional (and service-oriented). In fact, in 1900 only one in 1,100 was professionally trained. But in 1950 the ratio was one in 60.[14]

This has meant a flight from the humanities, which was only briefly ar-rested in the early 1970s, to professional specialties such as education, sci-ence, business, law, and medicine. The average student therefore spends less classroom time trying formally to understand himself and the world around him (the objective of humanities courses). This tends to retard the maturing process.

The demand for education, or at least for training, has produced aca-demic empires such as the University of California and New York Univer-sity. As a result it is now more difficult for students to know their profes-sors and administrators. At the same time, faculty labor under the de-mand to "publish or perish." Research not only enhances professional standing, it also lures federal and private dollars to the campus. Thus students often become quite secondary. Colleges are becoming gigantic knowledge factories. Some professors have grotesque ideas about what students are like simply because they have seldom had a down-to-earth conversation with any of them.

13. Christopher Jencks, "The Next Thirty Years in the Colleges," *Harper's Magazine,* October 1961, p. 128.
14. John W. Gardner, "The Great Hunt for Educated Talent," *Harper's Magazine,* January 1957, p. 49.

Another characteristic of enlarged universities is increased competition. Just as it is no longer distinctive to become a college student, so it is no longer easy to remain one. The "gentleman's C" is a thing of the past. Partly as a result of this, half of all who start college drop out.[15] The GPA (grade-point average) becomes a hard taskmaster. One recent response to this pressure was the attempt at suicide by sixty-seven students in one year at a university in the East.

Why are students working so hard? What is their goal? Most of them are not sure. This is reflected in an estimate of the typical freshman class, drawn by Christopher Jencks:

> 1% want serious scholarly or scientific training.
> 2% want a more general intellectual education.
> 5% want an introduction to an upper-middlebrow culture and upper-middle-class conviviality followed by technically distinguished graduate training.
> 20% want technical or semiprofessional training, painlessly.
> 20% merely want certification as ambitious and respectable professional employees.
> 50% don't know what they want, and will never get a degree, though they might "find themselves" during their stint in college.[16]

These percentages would change from junior college to unversity, from private college to public. Nevertheless, they are close enough to the target to cause church workers with college students to think seriously about their task.

THE MAIN DISTINCTIVE OF THE STUDENT

Youth leaders may be tempted to think that there are two kinds of college students: those who respect thinking and those who do not. But this would be a serious mistake. According to Nederhood:

> The distinguishing feature of an educated individual is not simply his having attended college; he is distinguished by the result of this attendance. . . . A college education should develop a thoughtful approach to life. Thoughtfulness, whether a present or a potential quality of each educated individual, is the quality which makes it necessary for the church to subject him to special scrutiny.[17]

Not every student is presently thoughtful. But almost all gain a potential for thoughtfulness that distinguishes them from most of those who

15. Jencks, "The Next Thirty Years," p. 121.
16. Ibid., p. 128.
17. J. H. Nederhood, *The Church's Mission to the Educated American* (Grand Rapids: Eerdmans, 1960), p. 55.

do not go to college. As a result, students respect thought, and want to be treated as thoughtful persons. In fact, they reserve their attention for that group of adults who will treat them as thoughtful people. In some cases students are no more thoughtful than nonstudents, but they think they are; and this prejudice must be recognized by those who want to communicate with them.

COLLEGE INFLUENCES

As discussed earlier, educated America is a distinct group, resting on a base of college education. To understand the student, therefore, is to understand a person who is more than a youth in transition. He is a student too.[18]

"The Church must seek to know the thought patterns, the prejudices, and the peculiar anxieties of the various types of American citizens. Moreover, the witnessing Church must seek to know what its message actually means to non-believers when they hear it."[19] The youth leader, by understanding the way his message strikes the collegiate non-Christian, will be better able to understand the problems of the Christian student, since both breathe the same campus air.

Four areas are worth considering: (1) the impact of science on students, (2) prejudices of the academic community, (3) misinterpretations of Christianity, and (4) the conflict between Christian students and secularism.

1. The scientific method dominates most of the assumptions and methods of higher education. It presupposes a closed universe of cause and effect (no supernatural) and the supremacy of man's reason to understand and control both his environment and himself. Science has led students to accept the following: (a) a wonder at the magnitude of the universe and also its impersonality; (b) the hypothesis of evolution (with religion being only one phase in man's development); (c) a psychological evaluation of people and their environment (Luther's theology would be examined in terms of his childhood rather than God's revelation to him); (d) a comparative approach to religion; (e) indiscriminate reading of popularized studies of religious data.

   The totalitarian hold of the scientific world view has been challenged by the counterculture, Eastern religions, and the occult as well as by Christian theology. Thus there are significant cracks in its

18. Also see chapter 25, "Reaching Youth in College."
19. Nederhood, *The Church's Mission*, p. 53.

monolithic hold on intellectual man which have opened many to the possibility of a supernatural world.[20]

2. The academic community holds three basic prejudices against Christianity: First, an instinctive negative reaction to anything which non-Christians feel demonstrates a *dogmatic* attitude. The tendency of Christians to speak in absolute terms often infuriates them, because they fear that the Christians have elevated opinion to fact. Secular intellectuals are often blind to their own presuppositions which they hold with as much eager faith as do Christians. The non-Christian's distrust of *theology* comes partly from this, too. Tentativeness is so much a characteristic of the scientific method that "Thus saith the Lord" sounds out of place. Again, secularists fail to see their own ideological commitments.[21] The church's emphasis on *faith* also rankles the academic community for which faith operates only in the area beyond recognized fact. "It is practically impossible for the educated to escape the impression that theology is but a massive systemization of personal opinion and fantasy."[22]

3. The academic community's meaning of the terms *God, Bible,* and *sin* differs from that of Christians,[23] so that the Christian student has to sort out the divergences. Many think of God as no greater than His universe; others look at Him as vague and distant. Thinking that He was only an effective moral teacher or an eschatological prophet, they feel that the church has made more out of Christ than He did Himself. The Bible is usually looked on as a literary masterpiece, though for some it is merely an illustration of a primitive view of the universe.

"Sin" is of great interest because everyone sees its effects, but "original sin" means only that sin is inevitable and does not stop every mouth before God (Rom 3:19). Sin is no longer measured by the divine law, and many hold that it is only a product of poor environmental conditioning. To present-day authors, sin does not convict men; it equalizes them.

4. Other elements in the present academic situation produce tensions for the Christian student. At college, people *ask,* thus asserting their freedom and detachment from the object of their inquiry. This is the essence of the dominant scientific method. The average Christian stu-

20. For a classic odyssey out of that determined world, see C. S. Lewis, *Surprised By Joy* (London: Fontana, 1959).
21. See, for example, the critique of the ideology behind biblical higher criticism in Walter Wink, *The Bible in Human Transformation* (Philadelphia: Fortress, 1973), pp. 1-15.
22. Nederhood, *The Church's Mission,* p. 97.
23. Ibid., pp. 102-11.

dent, however, has not *asked,* but has only *followed* an authority (parent, pastor, youth leader) .

Questions concerning ecology, sexual ethics, the role of women, racism, multinational corporations, and the institutional church fill the air of many four-year universities and colleges.

Since academic life invites skepticism, students are inclined to doubt. Doubting can be a valuable, hardheaded way of replacing secondhand convictions with firsthand ones, but some Christians tend to look at doubt as something to be ashamed of rather than as a trigger for firsthand study of a problem. Christians must see that God has given them minds so that they can evaluate alternatives, think them through, commit themselevs, and act.

In secular colleges, the Christian student's authority in the Bible may be ridiculed or ignored. He then feels that if an unsaved friend will not accept the infallibility of Scripture, he cannot use it with him. Non-Christian college youth may be helped toward accepting the infallibility of the Bible by first understanding the historical reliability of the Scriptures.[24]

These, then, are some of the influences brought to bear on the college student not because he is a young person in transition but because he is a student. It should be pointed out, however, that the secular college can be an immense stimulus to the Christian to become realistic about his faith, mature in his theological judgments, and sympathetic toward non-Christians. By the later seventies, evangelical student groups on major secular campuses often numbered in the several hundreds. Also, students in Christian liberal arts colleges and Bible colleges are confronting some of these same issues as they interact with these secularistic views in classroom discussions and as they witness for Christ in off-campus contacts.

THE CHURCH AND THE STUDENT

To minister effectively to older youth, church workers must know Christ personally, live in the power of the Holy Spirit, have a thought-through faith, be grounded in the Bible, understand students both in their persons and their world, and must seek to help them see the relevance of Christianity for every area of life including the intellectual, emotional, interpersonal, vocational, as well as the spiritual.

Pastors and youth workers must be intimately acquainted with both the Scriptures and the God of the Scriptures. To depart from the Bible is to

24. For an excellent presentation of the historical trustworthiness of the New Testament see F. F. Bruce, *The New Testament Documents: Are They Reliable?* 5th ed. (Grand Rapids: Eerdmans, 1967).

ignore reality. Even if a leader understands students well, he will have little to say if he is confused about God. Students respond to Christian leaders and activities if they sense and can see that Christianity, the church, and the Bible possess the qualities of *vitality and relevancy*.

Why do college students often say that the church is irrelevant? Surely not because God is irrelevant or because they are resistant to the faith. Perhaps it is because many "adult" Christians are playing religion rather than living a vital life with Christ under His lordship. If so, a student who is in search of the authentic sees adult Christians as plastic. As adults let Jesus Christ become the center of their lives, as they love and enjoy Him, as they trust His forgiveness, glory in His cross, and live in the power of His Holy Spirit, students will see the difference. Also, as adult commitment to Christ leads to commitment to others, the authenticity of their relationships in mutual love will be the telling sign of their discipleship.

Students may also consider the biblical message irrelevant because adults do not see students' problems from *their* viewpoint. Church leaders often fail to phrase their answers in the striking life-terms that show students that what they need is what God offers.

INSTRUCTION

The church must *teach*. This can be done through expository preaching, substantial Sunday school discussion classes, Sunday evening or weekly discussion groups, and, above all, by the open life and example of the teacher (see 1 Thess 2:7-8). Teachers should start with the truths of Scripture seen in their historical context, placing them in the larger theological framework of the faith, and then model their relevance from their own experience, applying all this to the specific needs of students. The needs itemized earlier in this chapter might be considered with regard to each passage studied. Teachers should help students work out a faith that interprets the facts of daily experience in the light of biblical revelation.

For example, many students have adopted the idea that the universe is impersonal and that God is vague and distant. The Bible then becomes only a record of His past action rather than the living Word for today. To counteract this, youth leaders should emphasize the doctrines of creation and providence, that is, that God created the world and each person, giving them abilities which they must use to His glory. He also upholds the world and guides it to His predetermined goal. Leaders should also stress that in Christ's first advent, God demonstrates His care for history, for humanity. In Christ's death, He took our sin, guilt, and punishment on Himself. Thus the incarnation and atonement prove that God cares, God comes, God acts. Moreover, Christ is risen and thus not locked into past history.

Youth leaders should also stress the person and work of the Holy Spirit, emphasizing His indwelling, empowering, and sanctifying ministries. Then God's providence, Christ's redemption, and the Spirit's power must be illustrated out of personal experience, demonstrating how these truths have become meaningful for them.

Pastors, Sunday school teachers, and other youth workers should also read information on current problems faced by students. They should read quality books describing older adolescents (including those from secular sources) and scan some of the novels and texts students are reading. There is also no substitute for spending time on campus, meeting students and their friends, reading the college newspaper, and knowing current campus issues.

LOVE

Through fellowship with other Christians in and out of the local church, students can discover their spiritual gifts and grow up together in Christ.[25] Here they find that they are an essential part of the church, gifted for ministry, and needing each other. Here they find also that they belong.

Christian students need not only each other; they also need, as suggester earlier, an "adult guarantor"—one who can guarantee the worth of adulthood as a goal, and convince the student that he is worthy to seek it. Spiritual adulthood, of course, is equal to maturity in Christ. "We proclaim Him [Christ], admonishing every man and teaching every man with all wisdom, that we may present every man complete [mature] in Christ" (Col 1:28, NASB).

A church should provide a climate where such a relationship between a college-age person and a Christian adult can develop. What kind of a person might this adult guarantor be? Ideally, it should first be a Christian father and mother, then a pastor, youth leader, or adviser, and perhaps later, a college or seminary professor or campus worker. Such an adult will model a vital Christian life, challenge students to be themselves and not just be carried by the crowd, and help bridge the transition from childhood to the adult world.

One such person leads a college-age group in a local church. He has these qualities:

1. *Sympathy* for young people. He understands them.
2. *A permissive spirit* both in class and in private conversation. Anything anyone says is received without the suggestion that it is unfitting or un-

25. See Ray Stedman, *Body Life* (Glendale, Calif.: Regal, 1972).

important. He honors every contribution. He is accessible, and he encourages students to come and talk with him.

3. *Humility.* He recognizes his own shortcomings. If a person is satisfied with himself, students will consider him unreal.
4. *Wisdom* about life. He has lived and learned from God through experience. This gives realism to what he says and does.
5. *Time.* Preparing discussion questions for his Bible class, conversing privately with his students, inviting them to meals at his home—these all take time.
6. *Enthusiasm.* While he is not young chronologically, he is young-hearted. He has a sense of humor, is adventurous, and not too rigid.
7. *Impartiality.* He seeks to be impartial with the members of his class. Some drop by his home three or four times a month. Some never come. All know they can come. (At the same time a youth leader may minister to a large fellowship where leadership training, focusing on certain students, is essential to reproduce the ministry).
8. *Love.* He and his wife let the students know that they are concerned for them. Love is felt. Love is verbalized. Love initiates. Love shares itself.
9. *Firmness.* He encourages students to resolve their own problems and to keep moving ahead in the maturing process. Yet he does it in a spirit of kind understanding.

Even if the student is given (1) information about God and life by way of preaching, Bible study, and conversation; and (2) love through association with a Christian community and an adult guarantor, another element is still needed—risk. Abraham believed God and left Ur. Moses believed and left Egypt. Noah believed and built an ark. Christian maturity develops as one responds to God's direction. "Playing it safe" is unchristian; one must learn to act in faith. Church leaders can encourage youth to become involved in the "risks" of the Christian walk.

One of the most common risks God asks Christians to take concerns witnessing. Here the student has to show love to someone he disagrees with, state his case clearly, pick himself up when he is defeated in argument, pray in secret for power and boldness, free himself from hypocrisy, seek an authentic private and public life, and trust the Lord for spiritual direction and power. Perhaps in no greater way does the Lord bring maturity to the Christian student on the secular campus than through the stimulus of witnessing. This also is true of the Christian student on a Christian college campus who witnesses to others off campus.

Identity, interrelationships, and faith are all bound together in the act of befriending non-Christians, winning the right to be heard, and speaking about Christ, judgment, and salvation.

The church can encourage students to witness by training them, praying for them, and helping them speak for Christ. Students should be encouraged to join a campus group of witnessing Christians. They need to be with a group such as some who are charged by God with the responsibility of evangelizing the campus. This forces them to face God in remarkable ways.

Risk is also experienced as Christian students become involved in the complex social issues of the day. A Christian view on ecology, affluence, population growth, and world hunger must be hammered out and programs of action proposed. Racism and poverty cannot be ignored. This means hard work, conflict, and misunderstanding. Christ's lordship must be confessed and lived out in all of life. Risk (or to say it another way, faith) must be demonstrated in the hard situations if the college student is to grow spiritually.

SUMMARY

This chapter has sought to show that college-career students are in transition from adolescence to adulthood, a process generally going on between the ages of eighteen and twenty-four. They are asking three questions: Who am I? How should I relate to others? and What should I believe?—the three I's of identity, interrelationships, and ideology.

Churches should help older youth become mature in Christ. Churches can (1) help college-age persons answer their three great questions from a biblical standpoint, (2) surround older youth with a loving fellowship of Christians, and (3) stimulate them to "risk" themselves in faith, in personal evangelism and in care for the world.

FOR FURTHER READING

Apologetics and Doctrine

Anderson, J. W. D. *Christianity: The Witness of History*. London: Tyndale, 1969.

Denney, James. *The Christian Doctrine of Reconciliation*. London: James Clarke, 1959.

Guinness, Os. *The Dust of Death*. Downers Grove, Ill.: InterVarsity, 1973.

Henry, Carl F. H., et al. *Quest for Reality: Christianity and the Counter Culture*. Downers Grove, Ill.: InterVarsity, 1971.

Lewis, C. S. *Mere Christianity*. New York: Macmillan, 1943.

Lewis, Gordon R. *Decide for Yourself: A Theological Workbook*. Downers Grove, Ill.: InterVarsity, 1970.

Little, Paul. *Know Why You Believe*. Wheaton, Ill.: Scripture Press, 1967.

Machen, J. G. *Christianity and Liberalism*. Grand Rapids: Eerdmans, 1923.

McDowell, Josh. *Evidence That Demands a Verdict*. San Bernardino, Calif.: Campus Crusade For Christ, 1972.

———. *More Evidence That Demands a Verdict*. San Bernardino, Calif.: Campus Crusade For Christ, 1975.

Packer, J. I. *Knowing God*. Downers Grove, Ill.: InterVarsity, 1973.

Pinnock, Clark. *Set Forth Your Case*. Chicago: Moody, 1971.

Ramm, Bernard. *Special Revelation and the Word of God*. Grand Rapids: Eerdmans, 1961.

Schaeffer, Francis. *Escape from Reason*. Downers Grove, Ill.: InterVarsity, 1969.

———. *The God Who Is There*. Downers Grove, Ill.: InterVarsity, 1968.

Sire, James. *The Universe Next Door: A Basic World View Catalog*. Downers Grove, Ill.: InterVarsity, 1976.

Stott, J. R. W. *Basic Christianity*. Grand Rapids: Eerdmans, 1959.

Bible Study

Ezell, Mancil. *Youth in Bible Study/New Dynamics*. Nashville: Convention, 1970.

Manley, G. T., and Oldham, H. W., eds. *Search the Scriptures*. Chicago: InterVarsity, 1955.

Miller, Chuck. *Now That I'm a Christian*. 2 vols. Glendale, Calif.: Regal, 1974, 1976.

Palmer, Earl. *Salvation by Surprise: Studies in the Book of Romans*. Waco, Tex.: Word, 1975.

Richards, Lawrence O. *A Theology of Christian Education*. Grand Rapids: Zondervan, 1975.

Williams, Donald. *Celebrate Your Freedom: An Introduction to Inductive Study and Commentary on Galatians*. Waco, Tex.: Word, 1975.

Wollen, Albert J. *Miracles Happen in Group Bible Study*. Glendale, Calif.: Regal, 1976.

Understanding and Teaching Older Youth

Board, Stephen. "Campus Trends: 1976." *Eternity*, June 1976, pp. 18-21.

Clark, Ted. *The Oppression of Youth*. New York. New York: Harper & Row, 1975.

Eddy, Edward D., Jr.; assisted by Parkhurst, Mary Louise, and Yalcovakis, James S. *The College Influence on Student Character*. Washington, D.C.: American Council on Education, 1959.

Erikson, Erik H. *Identity: Youth and Crisis*. New York: Norton, 1968.

Fordham, Forrest B., and Alessi, Vince. *Teaching Older Youth*. Philadelphia: Judson, 1959.

Hoge, Dean R. *Commitment on Campus: Changes in Religion and Values over Five Decades.* Philadelphia: Westminster, 1974.

Mead, Margaret. "Problems of the Late Adolescent and Young Adult." In *Survey Papers,* 1960 White House Conference on Children and Youth.

Mears, Henrietta. "Teaching College-Age Youth." In *An Introduction to Evangelical Christian Education.* Edited by J. Edward Hakes. Chicago: Moody, 1964.

Moore, Allen J. *The Young Adult Generation.* Nashville: Abingdon, 1969.

Nederhood, J. H. *The Church's Mission to the Educated American.* Grand Rapids: Eerdmans, 1960.

Richards, Lawrence O. *Youth Ministry: Its Renewal in the Local Church.* Grand Rapids: Zondervan, 1972.

Roszak, Theodore. *The Making of a Counter Culture.* Garden City, N.Y.: Doubleday, 1969.

Satir, Virginia. *People Making.* Palo Alto, Calif.: Science and Behavior, 1972.

Selznick, Gertrude, and Larkins, John. *What Is Known about Young Adults?* Monograph 5. Berkeley: Survey Research Center, U. of California.

Skoglund, Elizabeth. *Where Do I Go to Buy Happiness?* Downers Grove, Ill.: InterVarsity, 1972.

Snyder, Ross A. *Young People and Their Culture.* Nashville: Abingdon, 1969.

Strommen, Merton P. *Five Cries of Youth.* New York: Harper & Row, 1974.

Strommen, Merton P., ed. *Research on Religious Development.* New York: Hawthorn, 1971.

"The New Youth." Special report. *Life,* fall 1977.

Tournier, Paul. *Guilt and Grace.* New York: Harper & Row, 1962.

Voelkel, Jack. *Student Evangelism in a World of Revolution.* Grand Rapids: Zondervan, 1974.

Yankelovich, Daniel. *The New Morality: A Profile of American Youth in the Seventies.* New York: McGraw-Hill, 1974.

11

Adult Leaders of Youth

William R. Goetz

"HE'S REALLY GREAT! I feel I can express an opinion, or ask him for spiritual help and really get it. He cares about us."

"I like him all right; but when it comes to being a youth sponsor, he's just not with it!"

"I don't know why he even bothers being a youth leader. I don't think he even likes us."

Teens discussing "solid" Sam, "fumbling" Fred, and "phony" Phil—three successful (and not so successful) adult workers with youth. Their comments indicate that not every adult who works with young people in the church clicks with teens.

Many factors contribute to genuine success in this difficult role. These factors include personal qualifications, training, spiritual maturity, and awareness of the duties of one's task.

IMPORTANCE OF GOOD ADULT LEADERSHIP

A lack of adequate leadership in youth work showed up very pointedly in the nationwide survey of teen dropouts from church conducted by the Research Commission and the Youth Commission of the National Sunday School Association in the 1960s.

More than half the dropouts' complaints against Sunday school pertained to the teachers.[1] One problem with youth meetings, said 15.5 percent of the dropouts, was poor adult leadership. Dropouts also expressed dissatisfaction with leaders who do not seem to be interested in young people or who seem to be unable to understand them.

On the other hand, scores of Christians (among them many of the leaders of evangelical churches in America) have pointed to the help

1. Roy B. Zuck, "Why Do Teens Quit Church?" *Link*, March 1963, p. 11.

WILLIAM R. GOETZ is Senior Pastor, Sevenoaks Alliance Church, Abbotsford, British Columbia, Canada.

given them as youth, by capable adult leaders. They have described this help as being life-changing in its influence.

Strong, spiritually healthy youth groups, classes, and organizations can be attributed, in large measure, to strong, understanding, spiritual adult leaders. Experience has shown that the adult leader is the key to the success of the youth organization which he guides.

"Four indispensables are to be found in every successful youth group," Gunnar Hoglund writes. They are "program, organization, morale, and leadership—but the greatest of these is leadership."[2] And of the two types of leadership in youth groups—adult leadership and youth leadership—the adult is of greater importance, since proper adult guidance can develop and strengthen youth leadership.

Young people need adult friends in whom they can confide and whose example they can follow. Church youth workers who "measure up" can meet this need in a unique sense.

This is borne out in the response of dropouts to the final question in the previously mentioned NSSA survey. To the query, "What do you think churches need to do to improve their ministry to young people?" many dropouts replied in effect, "Enlist better adult leaders!"[3]

The fundamental importance of reliable, spiritual leadership is also illustrated profusely in the Bible. Moses, Joshua, Gideon, David, and other godly men and women are examples of good leadership in Israel. The apostles gave the early church sound spiritual leadership.

In similar ways God calls today for consecrated adults who will recognize the importance of ministering to youth—adults who will accept it as a commission from God and who will accomplish the task in the strength God imparts.

Function of Adult Workers

The basic function of the adult worker with youth is to guide toward spiritual maturity those youth entrusted to his care. Spiritual maturity begins with the new birth, and subsequent spiritual growth in Christ continues until "we all attain to the unity of the faith, and of the knowledge of the Son of God, to a mature man, to the measure of the stature which belongs to the fulness of Christ. . . . We are to grow up in all aspects into Him, who is the head, even Christ" (Eph 4:13, 15, NASB).

Spiritual maturity involves not only knowing Christ conceptually but also growing daily in Him through His Word and prayer, and being equipped to render effective service in the will of God.

2. Gunnar Hoglund, *Youth Groups* (Chicago: Harvest, 1967), p. 23.
3. Roy B. Zuck, "Why Do Teens Quit Church?" *Link*, April, 1963, p. 5.

The number of young people who progress toward this goal will vary from church to church. Almost every group will have three kinds of youth: those who are moving toward spiritual maturity, those who are in varying degrees of rebellion against God, and those who are basically "neutral."

The adult leader of youth is one of the channels—a very important one— through which the Holy Spirit desires to work in the lives of young people to accomplish His will. Thus the adult worker with teens is a guide, a counselor, a leader fulfilling his role as an instrument of the Holy Spirit, to help lead youth toward greater spiritual maturity.

QUALIFICATIONS OF ADULT LEADERSHIP

What sort of person is qualified to be a leader of youth? Who will serve acceptably as a Sunday school teacher of teens, a club leader or guide, a youth fellowship sponsor, or a camp counselor?

Qualifications will differ slightly, depending on the educational agency served. And yet a number of basic, essential qualifications are desirable for all adult workers with young people.

Salvation and an exemplary Christian life. It is obvious that a youth worker must know and love Christ if he is to lead others to know Him. Only the new birth can create within an individual the God-given love essential for effective youth leadership: love for God, for His Word, and for those who have been committed to the leader's care.

The leader must model the attitudes, the feelings, the values, the enthusiasm, and the dedication which he seeks to develop in youth. What the leader is overrides any other factor in youth ministry.[4] His verbal skills or ability to fulfill organizational roles are of only secondary consideration. Youth are quick to detect—and to despise—hypocrisy. The inconsistency of adults was the second-ranking complaint made by the dropouts surveyed by the National Sunday School Association.[5]

As Lawrence Richards has well said:

> Too often in the contemporary church youth and adults come together only within the church walls, or on occasions where they *talk about* the Christian life—not live it. And so very often we develop young people who can talk a good faith, but who have no capacity to express faith through their life in the world. We have such young people in large measure because they have had opportunity to hear adults talk about their faith—not to live it in the real world.[6]

4. Lawrence O. Richards. *Youth Ministry: Its Renewal in the Local Church* (Grand Rapids: Zondervan, 1972), p. 123.
5. Zuck, "Why Do Teens Quit Church?" April 1963, p. 7 .
6. Richards, *Youth Ministry*, pp. 123-24.

Real love for and sympathetic understanding of youth. Genuine love will often accomplish with youth what nothing else will. Love will overlook the thoughtlessness, moodiness, and ingratitude of which youth are capable. The worker who shows love will be honored with the privilege of confidence entrusted by youth: counsel sought and advice accepted.

Understanding that teens are in a period of change—physically, mentally, socially, and often spiritually—is an important key in dealing with youth. A youth worker improves his leadership if he makes a sincere effort to understand the problems, viewpoints, conflicts, dreams, needs, and fears of young people.

This suggests the quality of contemporaneity—the ability to get along with today's teens, to sense something of the peculiar problems of young people in this generation, to be on the "wave length" of present-day youth. This is not to suggest that a leader must necessarily be young in years. In fact, some older adults work better with youth than do some younger adults.

When the dropouts responding to NSSA's survey discussed what they would prefer in adult leaders, they requested adults who understand youth.[7] Such understanding involves the ability to discern personal needs and tactfully offer help without being inquisitive and nosy.

A firm foundation in the Word of God. The leader should build his philosophy of ministry on biblical principles, realizing that the answers to young people's needs and problems are given in God's Word. Consequently, an important qualification of a leader of youth is a good grounding in the Bible. This does not necessarily mean a Bible college education, but it does mean familiarity with the truths, doctrines, and precepts of the Bible.

Time and capacity for hard work. Youth work, if it is to be done properly, takes time and hard work. The youth leader should possess an abundant capacity for work and be willing to make personal sacrifices in the interests of his youth. Adequate lesson preparation takes time and effort; club work, properly done, is most demanding on one's energies and time; an effective youth group requires hours of tactful coaching; and a youth camp can occupy one's entire vacation period. The youth leader must be available.

These facts need to be realized by would-be adult workers with youth. The cost should be counted, and the requirement of a large expenditure of time and effort realistically faced.

Faithfulness and dependability. It is "required in stewards, that a man be found faithful" (1 Cor 4:2). How important that a youth worker be

7. Zuck, "Why Do Teens Quit Church?" April 1963, p. 5.

found faithful when the spiritual welfare of young people is in his hands! Without dependability, the most impressive qualifications lose their luster. For if the adult worker is not faithful to his responsibilities and dependable in discharging them, he cannot hope to lead youth aright. Faithfulness in other areas of church life should be a prerequisite to the privilege of youth leadership.

Spiritual and emotional maturity. A sensible and emotionally balanced person possesses qualities to which youth respond with respect. These include drive, ambition, enthusiasm, good judgment, and a sense of humor. A pleasing personality and organizational ability are also contributory. The ability to see the potential in young people, to appreciate and patiently develop it, is a part of these important qualifications.

Willingness to learn. Adults who work with youth can learn with them by being open for help and instruction which will enable them to know and serve their young people better. This should include reading helpful books, attending conferences and training sessions, and talking with other youth workers.

Ability to counsel youth. A youth worker needs more than a burden for and an interest in young people; he also needs to be able to help them with their problems.

Acquaintance with and adherence to cardinal rules of counseling promote confidence and trust in adult leaders. These include the following: never betray a confidence; do not express shock at what a teen tells you; do not ask too many questions; never preach; do not expect a pleasant time with every counselee; and do not be disappointed if obvious results are not always produced.

Counseling includes listening well, questioning tactfully and wisely (so that the young person can see his problem for himself), and guiding the counselee in finding answers to his needs in God's Word.[8]

Awareness of the total church program and his share in it. The alert leader should realize that his service with his teens is a part of a larger, total ministry of the church. The well-rounded, total church ministry provides for instruction, worship, training, and fellowship for each individual. Each agency ministering to young people should fulfill its part of the whole; no agency should feel it is *the* whole or even the most important segment of that whole.

Specific ministries like camping, club work, teaching, or directing church youth musical groups naturally demand special qualifications suited to these requirements. The specific service will suggest these special necessary qualities.

8. Also see chapter 30, "Counseling Adolescents."

Each youth worker may feel that he does not match perfectly the foregoing characteristics and qualifications. Nevertheless these are ideals toward which he may aspire. Growth in them will contribute toward his own spiritual maturity and improvement in his service to youth.

RECRUITMENT OF YOUTH WORKERS

Recruiting people to work with youth is not easy. Not all adults readily respond to the challenge of working with young people. And not all adults should!

Recruitment should be the task of the board of Christian education so that the total needs of the church may be kept in view, and so that the best possible personnel for each job can be secured. As Carroll and Ignatius have observed:

> How serious are you about recruiting your best adult? Let's find out. What if the most qualified person in your church is a popular teacher of an adult class, chairman of a women's group, a board member, etc.? *Are you willing* to release him/her from the present involvement so he/she can be totally free for ministry with youth? . . . *Are you willing* to design his/her work load so he/she can give a significant amount of time to working with youth?[9]

If individual church agencies are left to "compete" for the available potential leaders, the probability of an orderly fitting of persons to proper responsibilities is decreased, as are the chances for successful recruitment.

The board which is faced with personnel needs in its youth departments should follow a carefully planned sequence of activity in all recruitment efforts. First, the board members should prayerfully seek God's direction and blessing in the important task of recruiting youth workers.

Next, a list should be made of the persons who might qualify, taking into consideration the necessary qualifications. Then, the list of possible candidates should be rated and aligned on the basis of that rating.

The representative of the board appointed to the task should then make an appointment with the person (or persons, in the case of couples) first on the list. Recruitment for a job of the magnitude of youth worker should be done through a planned personal contact.

From a list of desirable qualities and the services performed by a youth leader, a church may define the role of a youth leader in a printed job description. Such a statement could explain the opportunities one has for personal growth and Christian service in working with youth, as well as acquaint him with some of the problems youth leaders often face. It

9. John L. Carroll and Keith L. Ignatius, *Youth Ministry: Sunday, Monday, and Every Day* (Valley Forge, Pa.: Judson, 1972), p. 35.

should also indicate to whom the leader is responsible and the extent of the authority to act which he possesses.

The candidate should be urged to consider the proposition prayerfully and to reply within a reasonable length of time. If he says no, the recruiter may go on to the next person on the list. The recruiter must be careful about pressuring people into a task as demanding as that of youth worker.

Several things can be done to create a favorable climate for the recruitment of youth leaders in a church. One is to impress on the congregation the importance of this ministry and the necessity for able leadership. An occasional sermon on the heritage of and responsibility to youth in the church will be helpful.

Using the church bulletin, bulletin boards, and pulpit announcements to keep the youth ministries before a congregation is one effective way of increasing awareness of and concern for youth. A special dedication service of leaders once a year can be a meaningful and helpful event.

The use of young people's groups in church services on special occasions—such as Youth Week, Pioneer Girls Sunday, or Boys' Brigade Sunday—will also help build an awareness of the work. Making the youth ministries and their adult leaders the subject of prayer in the midweek services will lead to a climate in which recruitment will be much easier.

TRAINING OF YOUTH WORKERS

The recruitment of adults for work with youth is only the beginning of a church's responsibility to those leaders. Local church Christian educators who believe that youth leaders have a significant task to perform will see that they are given as many training opportunities as possible. The following are some of the possibilities:

Ensuring that the job to be done is clearly understood by the leader. The supply of a written job description, and the necessary materials, records, and reviews will show leaders good leadership in action.

Encouraging leaders to attend conferences, workshops, seminars, clinics, and leadership institues. The alert Christian education leader will see to it that as many of his youth leaders as possible attend such gatherings. Churches near large centers where national or regional Sunday school and Christian education conventions are held can take advantage of these opportunities.

Conducting local church leadership training classes. Many churches conduct one or more such training classes annually. Some offer these as a training hour or Sunday school class for as many as three quarters in a year. Prospective leaders are enrolled and present leaders are brought in on a rotation basis.

Providing reading materials and audiovisuals. A number of excellent books, filmstrips, and cassettes are available to use as aids in leadership training classes. For suggested books, see "For Further Reading" at the end of this chapter. For films, filmstrips, and cassettes, contact evangelical publishing houses and film companies that produce helps for youth workers.[10]

Some denominational Christian education headquarters produce leadership training programs. Recognition by the denomination is usually granted to youth leaders who meet the requirements of those courses.

If a church is not large enough to conduct a class for the few youth leaders within it, other arrangements can be made. One of these is to consider the possibility of combining forces with several other area churches for a class or series of classes. Another is to schedule weekend retreats of youth workers from several churches for the purpose of training in departmental or agency workshops. Another alternative is the suggestion that follows.

Enrolling leaders in correspondence courses or personal study courses. The leadership training provided and required by the Christian Service Brigade (Box 150, Wheaton, Ill. 60187) and Pioneer Girls (Box 788, Wheaton, Ill. 60187) is an example of the value of this type of training. This sort of help can be a definite boon to youth workers. Many of the excellent correspondence courses available through the Moody Bible Institute will be beneficial to adult workers with youth.

Christian Service Brigade, Pioneer Girls, and Success With Youth also offer assistance by mail in training leaders. Some denominational headquarters do the same.

Directing youth leaders to read helpful youth periodicals. Even a small church can subscribe or encourage youth leaders to subscribe to and read some of the many excellent youth magazines available. Often much youth know-how can be absorbed by keen adults through such reading.

Training can be accomplished if the leaders of the church attach sufficient importance to it and truly seek ways to provide it for their adult youth workers.

RELATIONSHIPS OF ADULT WORKERS AND YOUNG PEOPLE

The relationship between adult leaders and their youth should be a warm, friendly one, marked by proper respect for each other. The adult should not stand on his dignity as an adult, nor should he adopt a hail-fellow-well-met, backslapping pseudoteen attitude. He should be himself. Teens appreciate adults who are good sports, ones who can act their age and yet permit teens to act theirs.

10. For addresses of these organizations, see chapter 29, "Materials for Working with Youth."

Winning and earning the respect of teens is basic to a lasting, friendly relationship. Love, understanding, concern, and encouragement can be given by visiting with the youth, following up on absentees, being open to listen to and counsel them, keeping them busy and involved, and making room for them in one's home and in the church.

Another aid to a good relationship is tactful discipline as it may be needed. Youth respect the leader who will kindly but firmly insist on what is right and who at the same time helps them work out their own standards for conducting their activities.

The leader leads with his life. Leadership by example, according to Chuck Miller, has four steps to it: "First, the leader does it *for* the youth. Next, the leader does it *with* the youth. Then, the youth do it *with* [under the supervision of] the leader. Finally, the youth do it *without* the leader."[11]

Youth need to experience through an adult's ministry to them the reality he is attempting to communicate. Building such a relationship will take time and effort, but the influencing of one life by another cannot be done by "remote control." It will require the personalized attention of the leader to each youth. If a youth leader says, "Who is sufficient for these things?" let him be reminded that this kind of relationship and equipping of the youth is to be his desired *goal*.

DUTIES OF YOUTH WORKERS IN SPECIFIC CHURCH AGENCIES

While the function of all adult workers is basically the same—to guide youth to spiritual maturity—the duties of the workers vary within the different agencies of the church.

DUTIES OF SUNDAY SCHOOL TEACHERS

1. Attend Sunday school each week—on time.
2. Prepare lessons thoroughly and prayerfully, avoiding use of the teacher's manual in class. Teach interestingly, with a variety of methods.
3. Get to know each class member well, both as a member of the age-group with general characteristics and as an individual.
4. Share in planning class activities and attend social events.
5. Spend time with students by arranging for personal, outside-of-class contacts. Be ready to counsel youth.
6. Set a good example by attendance at church services.
7. Develop greater facility in teaching and youth work by attending conferences and other training sessions.
8. Pray earnestly for themselves, their teaching, and their young people.

11. Cited in Richards, *Youth Ministry*, p. 132.

DUTIES OF YOUTH-GROUP SPONSORS

Duties of sponsors vary depending on the age level served.[12] With juniors and younger children, adults have to assume more responsibility, but must be willing to allow the children to assist as far as is feasible. Strong adult leadership is necessary in young teen groups, but here the teens can be involved more fully in leadership responsibilities.

High school youth need leaders who are able to coach them and encourage them to lead and learn.

Older youth can fully assume responsibility, with adult help available as needed. Adult duties in light of these facts include the following.

1. Attend youth meetings. Be regular and twenty minutes early.
2. Attend planning-group sessions. Be prepared to offer advice as necessary. Be positive.
3. Attend social activities of the group. Use these as opportunities to get to know each person and build relationships.
4. Be a good example by church attendance and involvement.
5. Take every opportunity to improve ability to sponsor effectively the group. Attend training sessions and conferences.
6. Pray earnestly for themselves, for their group, and for each young person.

DUTIES OF WEEKDAY CLUB LEADERS

The duties of adult leaders of weekday clubs can vary a great deal because of the wide age spread in club groups and their variety of approach.[13] However, certain basic duties are similar:

1. Be present early for all club meetings. Join in informal pre-meeting activities.
2. Be sure that *all* is in readiness for the activities, crafts, achievement tests, and message. Be available to lead and direct outdoor club activities.
4. Counsel and guide youth in their achievement program.
5. Learn to know youth well in total-life situations such as in camping and sports.
6. Pray.

12. Also see chapter 19, "Youth Programs."
13. The leaders' manuals published by denominational and nondenominational weekday club organizations usually include specific duties for adult leaders of weekday clubs. For more on this subject, see chapter 20, "Weekday Clubs."

DUTIES OF FULL-TIME MINISTERS OF YOUTH

Because specific duties will vary from one church to another, it would be unwise to formulate a fixed pattern, but these suggestions may prove helpful.[14]

1. Organize, supervise, and coordinate the total youth ministry.
2. Recruit, disciple, train, and direct the ministries of lay workers.
3. In cooperation with the minister of education and the board of Christian education, formulate the philosophy and policies for youth ministry. The philosophy of youth work should identify with and undergird the life and ministry of the local church.
4. Develop job descriptions for all lay workers and periodically evaluate the descriptions so they remain current and useful.
5. Evaluate the success of the ministry by biblical criteria. For example— Are youth trusting Christ as Saviour? Is there an excitement and interest in the study of the Scriptures? Are young people being discipled so that they are reproducing Christians? Are they concerned about the needs of others?
6. Keep abreast of trends and methods in Christian education.
7. Work with and instruct parents in their ministry in the home which must be recognized as the primary agency of Christian education.
8. Meet weekly with the minister of education (if there is one), biweekly with the pastor (weekly if there is no minister of education on the staff) and monthy with the board of Christian education.
9. Be responsible to the minister of education, the pastor, and the board of Christian education.

DUTIES OF OTHER LAY LEADERS

Church camp directors, counselors and workers; directors of youth choirs or musical groups, recreational directors; and others naturally have specific duties related to their tasks.

A CHURCH'S APPRECIATION OF ITS YOUTH WORKERS

Those who work with youth will find their satisfaction and reward in a youth's confidence, in the privilege of seeing a teen's problems solved, or in the joy of watching youth grow spiritually.

A Christian education board would be wise in planning some form of public recognition and thanks to youth workers. An ideal time for this is

14. Adapted from a job description for Minister to Students, developed at Lake Avenue Congregational Church, Pasadena, California, March 1, 1968.

National Youth Week or some other week when the church's ministry to youth is spotlighted. Some churches prepare citations of appreciation and present them to all who have served faithfully. Or appreciation can be voiced during services of dedication, when adult workers are publicly committed to their responsibilities and when the prayers of the congregation are solicited for them.

Personal words or notes of appreciation from pastors, ministers of education, or other church leaders are also in order. Regardless of how it is expressed, thanks should not be overlooked, for youth work is difficult. Adult workers are as human as anyone else, and just as subject to discouragement. Often a sincere commendation will lift a discouraged worker.

SUMMARY

Youth workers should remember the importance of being faithful—faithful to the Lord and to those whom He has called them to serve. For all who are faithful, in the strength which God provides, there awaits the prospect of His commendation in that day when the results of faithful labor will be revealed: "Well done, thou good and faithful servant" (Matt 25:21).

FOR FURTHER READING

Brigade Leader (magazine). Wheaton, Ill.: Christian Service Brigade.

Carroll, John L., and Ignatius, Keith L. *Youth Ministry: Sunday, Monday, and Every Day*. Valley Forge, Pa.: Judson, 1972.

Coleman, Robert A. *The Master Plan of Evangelism*. Old Tappan, N.J.: Revell, 1963.

Corbett, Jan. *Creative Youth Leadership*. Valley Forge, Pa.: Judson, 1977.

Crowe, Jimmy P. *Church Leader Training Handbook*. Nashville: Convention, 1974.

DeHaan, Richard. *Those Wonderful Difficult Years*. Wheaton, Ill.: Victor, 1973.

Eims, LeRoy. *Be the Leader You Were Meant to Be*. Wheaton, Ill.: Victor, 1975.

Gangel, Kenneth O. *Competent to Lead*. Chicago: Moody, 1974.

———. *Leadership for Church Education*. Chicago: Moody, 1970.

———. *So You Want to Be a Leader*. Harrisburg, Pa.: Christian Pubns., 1973.

High School Leader's Resource. Vols. I and II. Wheaton, Ill.: Scripture, 1969, 1971.

Hoglund, Gunnar. *Youth Groups*. Evanston, Ill.: Harvest, 1967.

Holley, Robert. *Diagnosing Leader Training Needs*. Nashville: Convention, 1974.

Hyde, Douglas. *Dedication and Leadership.* South Bend, Ind.: Notre Dame, 1966.

Jenkins, Jerry B. *You Can Get Thru to Teens.* Wheaton, Ill.: Victor, 1972.

Kilinski, Kenneth K., and Wofford, Jerry C. *Organization and Leadership in the Local Church.* Grand Rapids: Zondervan, 1973.

Kuhne, Gary W. *The Dynamics of Personal Follow-Up.* Grand Rapids: Zondervan, 1976.

LeBar, Lois E. *Focus on People in Church Education.* Westwood, N.J.: Revell, 1968.

Maslow, Abraham. *Motivation and Personality.* New York: Harper & Row, 1970.

Mattson, Lloyd D. *Camping Guideposts.* Chicago: Moody, 1962.

McDonough, Reginald M. *Working with Volunteer Leaders in the Church.* Nashville: Broadman, 1976.

Ortlund, Raymond C. *Lord, Make My Life a Miracle.* Glendale, Calif.: Regal, 1974.

Palmer, Bernard. *Pattern for a Total Church.* Wheaton, Ill.: Victor, 1975. Chaps. 4, 5.

Pell, Arthur R. *Recruiting, Training, and Motivating Volunteer Workers.* New York: Pilot, 1972.

Peterson, Eugene H. *The Youth Pastor.* Tempe, Ariz.: Success With Youth, n.d.

Pioneer Girls Guide. Wheaton, Ill.: Pioneer Girls, 1963.

Powell, Terry. *Making Youth Programs Go.* Wheaton, Ill.: Victor, 1974.

Richards, Lawrence O. *You and Youth.* Chicago: Moody, 1973.

————. *Youth Ministry: Its Renewal in the Local Church.* Grand Rapids: Zondervan, 1972.

Sanders, J. Oswald. *Spiritual Leadership.* Chicago: Moody, 1968.

Schaller, Lyle E. *The Change Agent.* Nashville: Abingdon, 1972.

Soderholm, Marjorie E. *Understanding the Pupil: Part III, The Adolescent.* Grand Rapids: Baker, 1961.

Todd, Floyd, and Todd, Pauline. *Camping for Christian Youth.* New York: Harper & Row, 1963.

Towns, Elmer. *Successful Biblical Youth Work.* Nashville: Impact, 1973.

Webster, Dan, and McAllister, Dawson. *Discussion Manual for Student Relationships.* Glendale, Calif.: Shepherd Productions, 1975.

Zuck, Roy B., and Robertson, Fern. *How to Be a Youth Sponsor.* Wheaton, Ill.: Scripture Press Foundation, 1960.

Cassette Tapes

"Discipleship." Youth Specialties, 861 Sixth Avenue, San Diego, Calif. 92101.

"Five Successful Youth Workers Tell You How." David C. Cook, 850 N. Grove Avenue, Elgin, Ill. 60120.

12

Organizing for Youth

Donald S. Aultman

TRADITION BUILDS high walls! The enthusiasts for the status quo are found in the organizational aspects of youth work as in every area of ecclesiastical endeavor. However, philosophy—the why and what of ministry—must precede practice. When the goals of worship, instruction, fellowship, and expression—both within and without the body of Christ—have been carefully articulated, then and only then should organization be contemplated.

Whether organizing "from scratch," or reorganizing a presently unsatisfactory situation, the focus must be on what is happening to people, not on programs and meetings. Ministry is people; therefore, policies, procedures, and programs are means to the spiritual development of youth. Churches are not in the business of training youth for organization roles. They should be taught to love and minister to *people*. God is concerned about what kind of *persons* they are becoming. The following discussion is to be interpreted from that perspective.[1]

Youth leaders should be sure that the local church youth activities—including Sunday school classes and departments, youth groups, socials, service projects, retreats, camp—are so organized that they achieve biblical aims in the best possible way. This will call for constant evaluation. Organization once adequate, and programs once appealing, may become outmoded unless they are constantly evaluated and, if necessary, reshaped and updated. While certain guiding principles of Christian education do not change, the implementing of those principles should not become static. To maintain vitality, youth activities must be Christ-centered and

1. See Lawrence O. Richards, *Youth Ministry: Its Renewal in the Local Church* (Grand Rapids: Zondervan, 1972), chapter 18; and John L. Carroll and Keith L. Ignatius, *Youth Ministry: Sunday, Monday, and Every Day* (Valley Forge, Pa.: Judson, 1972), chapter 4.

DONALD S. AULTMAN, Ed.D., is Associate Professor of Psychology, Lee College, Cleveland, Tennessee.

life-related. But they should *also* be based on the best principles of organization.

ORGANIZATIONAL PRINCIPLES

To be meaningful to young people an organization must be structured for *quality* and *growth*. It should therefore follow principles which assure a program that is well ordered and full-orbed, and which draws youth into activities that provide for participation, fellowship, biblical instruction, worship, discipleship, and evangelism.

The organization should be purposeful. Any youth organization in the local church should have a distinct purpose, a definite raison d'etre. Organization should exist for the sake of people, not people for the sake of organization.

Two primary tests of organization are: Is it essential, efficient, flexible?[2] and, Will it contribute to the development of spiritual leadership?[3] The rapid proliferation of programs and multiple youth agencies demands that youth leaders ask, Are these activities really necessary to meet the needs and interests of young people? If an organization or activity cannot be justified as to purpose, then continuation of it may well be questioned. "Any organization which exists for its own sake and does not contribute to better program is superfluous."[4] To be functional, a youth organization must be flexible. For efficiency, organizational framework should be held to a minimum. Each youth agency must be able to function freely without infringing on related agencies. Structure should be viewed not as repeating itself on a predetermined cycle but evolving to that which is the next logical step in response to identified objectives.

Historically, youth work has been related to people ranging in age from twelve to twenty-four. It has been suggested, however, that the increasing tempo of maturation in young people, new forms of youth education and entertainment, and the prosperity of teens earning billions of dollars annually have made youth more sophisticated and are consequently gradually lowering the age of participating youth in the church. But this chapter will consider the traditional years of twelve to twenty-four as the age bracket for the church's youth division.

Since the size of a church determines the number of specific age groupings, it is necessary to build on a flexible base that can be adapted to large and small groups. The following age divisions can be adjusted as the size of the congregation increases. Age or grade groups here are treated as departments in any agency of the church.

2. Carroll and Ignatius, *Youth Ministry*, pp. 46-47.
3. Richards, *Youth Ministry*, p. 343.
4. Paul H. Vieth, "The Local Church Organized for Christian Education," in *Religious Education*, ed. Marvin J. Taylor (Nashville: Abingdon, 1960), p. 249.

A new department may be formed when there are fifteen or twenty young people of a particular age or grade group.

Fig. 12.1. *Departmental divisions*

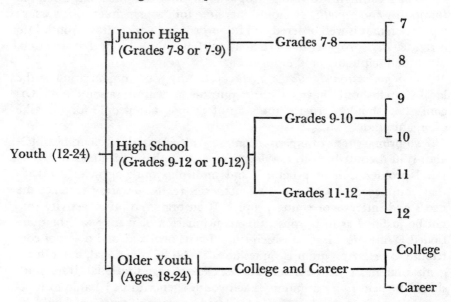

Smaller churches may be limited to a single youth department, whereas larger churches might have as many as three to five departments. Of course in large churches some agencies (e.g., Sunday school) may need more divisions than other agencies. The point here is to be sure that the youth organizations are flexible so that they can divide as they grow in number.

While the small church has unique organizational problems, it also has some definite advantages. The term "small church" is used as a reference to churches with less than one hundred members and less than five meeting rooms. The most obvious problems are lack of facilities, groups too small for advanced organization, lack of creative leadership that is adequately trained for youth work, a "small-church complex" with consequent failure in attempts to duplicate large church programs and compete with community programs.[5]

It can readily be observed that most of these problems can be turned to advantages. A small church need not try to compete with community programs or duplicate large church efforts. In a small group, members can easily get acquainted, thus forming lasting friendships ideally suited

5. Rachel Swann Adams, *The Small Church and Christian Education* (Philadelphia: Westminster, 1961), pp. 16-19.

for Christian fellowship. Adams suggests that a small church has these advantages:

1. The home becomes a natural setting for many church groups.
2. The small church can use the out-of-doors for teaching.
3. The small church can use its total environment for teaching.
4. There is concern across age lines (also wider acquaintances and friend-ships).
5. The family unit is more easily identified and nurtured in the small church.
6. The values of small group participation are more easily achieved.
7. Creativity can be stimulated in the use of facilities, personnel, and resources.[6]

The small church should specialize in doing an adequate job with fewer agencies, providing programs that will involve its youth in worship, study, training, and fellowship. It is erroneous for a small church to assume that effective youth work can be done only in large groups.

When initiating new youth groups in a church where no set patterns have developed, the following suggestions may be helpful: (1) have a stated purpose that is acceptable to youth and adults—this should consti-tute a challenge to their spiritual life that will fire their imagination and make them resourceful; (2) relate the group to the church through official channels; (3) provide resources that will yield productive ideas and pro-gramming aids; (4) let the youth be involved in the decision-making pro-cess; (5) as soon as possible organize separate groups for junior highs, high school youth, and college-age youth (when they are all in one group, the older ones tend to drop out or the younger teens feel dominated) ; (6) carefully develop with the youth what is expected of them—give them the guidelines, keeping the rules simple, expecting cooperation and allowing freedom within this framework.

The scope should be comprehensive. The organization should provide activities for youth of all ages, taking into account their varied interests as well as their spiritual, social, and intellectual needs.

> With respect to each person, organization is properly comprehensive when at the program planning level he may be seen as a whole person, and provision made for his total Christian education. Individual persons will usually be related to more than one agency. For example, a junior-high-school boy may be in the Sunday church school, the vacation church school, Boy Scouts, junior-high fellowship, church membership class, and

6. Ibid., pp. 14-16. Also see Virgil E. Foster, *How a Small Church Can Have Good Christian Education* (New York: Harper, 1956), chaps. 6-7.

Fig. 12.2. *Organizational diagram*

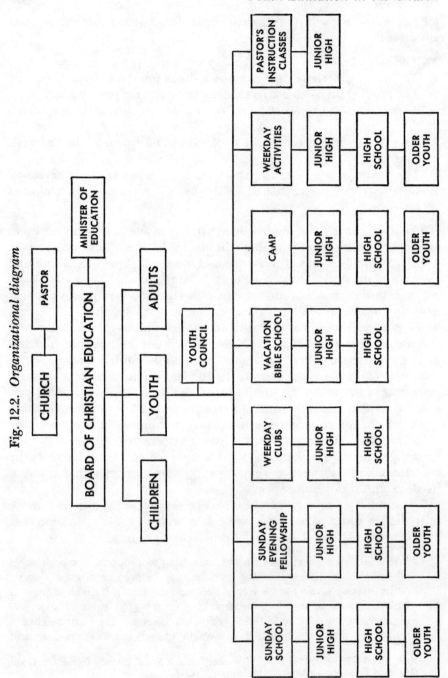

attend the church service of worship. Good organization should make possible planning for the total interests and needs of this boy and should help each agency contribute its share without conflict or overlapping with others.[7]

Providing a comprehensive youth program calls for coordinating the various functions. But a church must be careful not to diagram an organizational and programming scheme which looks good on paper, but is not workable. Coordination should be viewed against the demands of the teens' home and school life and not against the background of theoretical programming. If a plan cannot easily be implemented in practice, it would be best to reconsider its value to the total youth endeavor.

Of course, the primary concern is for quality, for spiritual results in the youth activities. This is that which puts fiber on the skeletal framework of an organizational plan. Many churches provide for the following educational functions through these (and other) agencies: (1) study of the Bible and Christian doctrine—Sunday school and pastor's instruction classes; (2) training in Christian living and leadership—weekly youth groups and weekday clubs; (3) spiritual, social, and physical development—weekly activities; (4) evangelism and Bible study—vacation Bible school.

The program should be church-related. Youth work in the church exists to help the church in its mission of evangelism and edification. Each group should be seen as a part of an overall educational program, administered by the board of Christian education, which in turn is answerable to the congregation or official church board. The organizational diagram illustrates this fact and summarizes the organizing principles discussed.

Some churches have a youth council. This consists of an adult representative from each youth agency. This would include the junior high, high school, and college-age departmental superintendents in the Sunday school, the head sponsor of each of the three youth groups, the head leader of each of the youth weekday clubs, and the minister of education (and/or youth minister), and the pastor. All the council members may be on the board of Christian education, or only the council chairman may be on the board.

The function of the youth council is to provide resources, recruit leadership, coordinate, and evaluate the activities of all the youth agencies. It may also plan functions that would include all three age-groups (junior high, high school, and college-age) where all three may be involved. Examples of such functions would be a youth retreat, a career clinic, or a work project.

7. Vieth, "The Local Church," p. 249.

In churches not large enough to require a youth council, these coordinating functions may be done by one person. He may be known as the youth chairman or youth coordinator.

Some large churches have a junior high coordinator, a high school coordinator, and a college-age youth (or older youth) coordinator. Each of these three leaders is responsible for overseeing and correlating the total educational program for his particular age-group.

ADMINISTRATIVE FUNCTIONS

Seven administrative functions are necessary if a group is to succeed. Ineffectiveness in church group programming can usually be traced to poor work on one or more of these functions. They are planning, organizing, executing, supervising, coordinating, publicizing, and evaluating.

Planning should be done by capable persons who are aware of the objectives of the group. *Organizing* should be in keeping with the basic principles already discussed. *Executing* is putting into practice the objectives of the group. *Supervising,* the oversight and directing of a project, should be done by someone who knows the aims of the planners and who has the authority and insight to suggest changes where needed. *Coordinating* the program insures harmony and helps avoid unnecessary overlapping and competition. *Publicizing* makes the church community aware of the what, when, and where of every activity. *Evaluating* the program can be a means of measuring quality, progress, and attainment of goals.

The following questions may be asked when seeking to evaluate a youth agency or activity: Is it Christ-honoring? Is it leading young people to Christ for salvation? Is it helping them grow spiritually? Does it have a purpose distinct from the other youth activities and is this known and understood by the youth and their adult leaders? Does it provide opportunities for personal social adjustment? Does it employ the best in educational techniques? Does it provide opportunities for seeking Christian answers to basic life problems? Are the needs and interests of young people being met?

LEADERSHIP GUIDELINES

It has become increasingly apparent that young people do not leave church because they have no interest in religion but because the approach of the church has failed to interest them. The greatest single need in youth work is for youth leaders who will give themselves to the exhausting task of seeking to understand, love, and guide the impressionable lives of young people.

Youth leaders let youth belong. Young people learn best when they "belong" to a group which seems significant to them. When youth are asked about the kind of group they prefer, they usually indicate that they like a group with a feeling of oneness, a sense of belonging, and an atmosphere of warm friendliness.

Youth leaders let youth share. Teens gain a sense of belonging to an organization as they have opportunity to share in it and contribute to it. This means that adult leaders must avoid the two extremes of a dictatorial, do-it-all kind of control and a laissez-faire, onlooking, do-nothing attitude.

The adult must be a sponsor, a guide. But this role is often misunderstood.

> He is not a dictator who decides exactly what the group ought to do. He is not a clown, who woos and wins with his great personality. The sponsor is an advisor. He is a manager or, better still, a coach. . . . The sponsor is very busy behind the scenes. . . . He is always there.[8]

This principle applies primarily to Sunday evening groups,[9] but it also relates to Sunday school teaching. A Sunday school teacher of teens should not "do all the talking" nor should he let the class ramble aimlessly in endless discussions. Instead he should be a guide and a stimulator, helping the young people discover the truths of God's Word for themselves. As the teacher guides, the teens *share* in the discovery of God's truths.[10]

Though the leadership is to be shared with the youth, some planning must be done by the adults alone.

> Would that not rob youth of "participation"? No! Clear thinking will suggest that this over-all survey by adult workers in no wise overlaps youth's own areas for planning. There are some things youth cannot do! Likewise, there are some things—those within the experience range and abilities of the age level of youth involved—adults should not rob them of their chance to do. But short-sighted "letting youth do it all" may mean failure on the part of adult workers to attain a level of youth work worthy of a Christian church.[11]

Youth leaders let youth participate. Youth agencies and activities should be organized to allow for maximum participation by the young people.

Many young people have qualities of leadership far beyond their op-

8. Donald S. Aultman, *Guiding Youth* (Cleveland, Tenn.: Pathway, 1965), p. 75.
9. For more on the sponsor's role, see chapter 19, "Youth Programs." Also see Roy B. Zuck and Fern Robertson, *How to Be a Youth Sponsor* (Wheaton, Ill.: Scripture Press, 1960), chaps. 2-3.
10. Also see chapter 15, "Guiding Youth in Bible Study."
11. Clarice M. Bowman, *Ways Youth Learn* (New York: Harper, 1952), p. 38.

portunity to exercise them. To capitalize on the dynamics of the peer group relationship and teens' yearning for adult acceptance, the adult sponsor should let young people take part. But he must know them individually, so he can know in what ways they can best participate. Outstanding youth leaders are keenly sensitive to the autonomy of youth and are committed to techniques which would not violate it.[12]

The wise youth leader or teacher will (1) let each member of the group or class know that he is accepted, (2) create an atmosphere of responsible freedom in which there is opportunity to discuss freely, (3) identify with the youth, (4) reach young people at their point of need, and (5) come to know the young people and their families.

In Sunday school and youth groups, young people appreciate opportunities to be officers—presidents, secretaries, treasurers. They enjoy taking part in Sunday school opening assemblies, and in ministering musically in youth groups and church services.

In youth groups, leadership can be shared as teens serve on committees and planning groups. There are better reasons for committees than "we have always had them and couldn't get along without them." These reasons include the following: (1) to get the work done, (2) to develop young people's leadership potential, and (3) to train young people in teamwork, in working with others. Some of the possible committees in youth groups include missionary, social, publicity, membership. The planning of programs should be in the hands of planning groups, with each young person in a group.[13] Of course at camp, banquets, socials, rallies, teens may be given responsibilities on various short-term committees.

VITAL RELATIONSHIPS

The *pastor* is related to the youth work as an ex-officio member of the youth council and the board of Christian education. He should be a personal friend to youth and available for counseling. As the spiritual leader and chief administrator of the church he should be apprised of all program plans in regular reports from the adult leaders. He should respond by demonstrating a positive interest in all the youth activities.

The *minister of education* is the chief resource person to the youth work. As the administrator of the total educational program he should be aware of all youth projects and activities. Relating the plans of the board of Christian education to the various youth leaders, his advice and evaluation should help steer the entire youth program. He attends youth

12. Merton P. Strommen, *Five Cries of Youth* (New York: Harper & Row, 1974), p. 118.
13. See chapter 19, "Youth Programs."

meetings and social functions as time permits. In some larger churches these functions are carried on by a full-time or part-time youth director in addition to or in place of the minister of education.[14]

Informed *parents* can lend significant assistance to the youth program. The adult leaders should keep teens' parents informed about youth activities and policies, enlist the prayer support of Christian parents, get to know the parents, urge them to cooperate with the youth program, and occasionally ask them to assist in various youth activities.

Since the Sunday school is the agency most likely to reach the largest number of youth, the youth *departmental superintendents* have an important relationship to the total youth program. They should become personally acquainted with the young people and should encourage their participation in all aspects of the church's youth program.

The *Sunday school teachers* should be close friends and advisors to youth. As key people in the educational program, they have a major responsibility in the ministry to youth. To many teenagers, Sunday school is one of the most boring hours of their entire week. If teaching methods are noncreative, if young people are treated like children, and if Bible study is irrelevant, dull, and less challenging than public school studies, teens find it difficult to get excited about Sunday school. Therefore, it is the responsibility of Sunday school teachers to teach creatively, to treat young people as adults, to make the study of God's Word challenging and teen-slanted.

Finally, the total youth program should be related to the church through the *board of Christian education.* All adult workers with youth should be approved and/or appointed by the board of Christian education.

SUMMARY

All youth activities should be worthy of the gospel and should be representative of the purposes and standards of the church. Youth should be led to recognize that they are under the umbrella of the church and, as such, should participate in the work of the Lord on a churchwide basis. That such a relationship to the church can be deeply appreciated by young people is borne out by a sixteen-year-old who said, "I feel I am becoming more and more a part of my church." This is the purpose of organizing for youth—to help them grow in the Lord as they take part in (and thus sense that they are a part of) God's program of evangelism, worship, instruction, and service.

14. See chapter 11, "Adult Leaders of Youth," for duties of the full-time youth minister.

FOR FURTHER READING

Adams, Rachel Swann. *The Small Church and Christian Education.* Philadelphia: Westminster, 1961.

Aultman, Donald S. *Guiding Youth.* Cleveland, Tenn.: Pathway, 1965.

———. *Learning Christian Leadership.* Cleveland, Tenn.: Pathway, 1960.

Bormann, Ernest G., and Bormann, Nancy C. *Effective Committees and Groups in the Church.* Minneapolis: Augsburg, 1973.

Brilhart, John K. *Effective Group Discussion.* 2d ed. Dubuque, Iowa: Brown, 1974.

Byrne, H. W. *Christian Education for the Local Church.* Grand Rapids: Zondervan, 1963.

Carroll, John L. "One of These Days We've Got to Get Organized," *Baptist Leader,* January 1967, pp. 4-6 .

Carroll, John L., and Ignatius, Keith L. *Youth Ministry: Sunday, Monday, and Every Day.* Valley Forge, Pa.: Judson, 1972.

Gangel, Kenneth O. *Leadership for Church Education.* Chicago: Moody, 1970.

Getz, Gene A. *Sharpening the Focus of the Church.* Chicago: Moody, 1974.

Havelock, Ronald G. *The Change Agent's Guide to Innovation in Education.* Englewood Cliffs, N.J.: Educational Technology Pubns., 1973.

Johnson, Rex E. *Ways to Plan and Organize Your Sunday School—Youth.* Glendale, Calif.: Regal, 1971.

Kilinski, Kenneth K., and Wofford, Jerry C. *Organization and Leadership in the Local Church.* Grand Rapids: Zondervan, 1973.

LeBar, Lois E. *Focus on People in Church Education.* Old Tappan, N.J.: Revell, 1968.

Newby, Donald O. "The Church's Ministry to Youth." In *Religious Education,* ed. Marvin J. Taylor. Nashville: Abingdon, 1960.

Richards, Lawrence O. *Youth Ministry: Its Renewal in the Local Church.* Grand Rapids: Zondervan, 1972.

Smith, Bob C. *When All Else Fails . . . Read the Directions.* Waco, Tex.: Word, 1974.

Strommen, Merton P. *Five Cries of Youth.* New York: Harper & Row, 1974.

Sullivan, James L. "What Organization Can Do for a Church." *Church Administration,* October 1971, p. 42.

Taylor, Marvin J., ed. *Foundations for Christian Education in an Era of Change.* Nashville: Abingdon, 1976.

Towns, Elmer. *The Successful Sunday School and Teachers Guidebook.* Carol Stream, Ill.: Creation House, 1976.

Worley, Robert C. *Change in the Church: A Source of Hope.* Philadelphia: Westminster, 1971.

Cassette Tapes

"Y. E. S." (Youth Education Service), Success with Youth, P. O. Box 27028, Tempe, Arizona 85281.

13

Evangelism of Youth

Russ Cadle

AT THE BEGINNING of a school year, an eleventh-grade boy met a new teen rider on the school bus. On the twice-a-day bus rides, the two got better acquainted. The high school junior was a Christian and the new student, a sophomore, was not. The Christian deftly turned their conversation to spiritual matters. After a few weeks, he led his friend to Christ.

A junior high girl attended a series of training sessions at her church on how to share the gospel effectively. Later over the phone she introduced a friend to Jesus Christ.

A college student, out to have a good time with sex, alcohol, and drugs, gradually came to the realization that these experiments are not worth their cost, that they were not filling his inner void. A fellow student invited him to a Bible study in their dorm, and after several studies, the non-Christian received Christ as his Saviour.

These examples demonstrate two truths:

1. Non-Christian young people *are* interested in the gospel.
2. Christian young people can lead their peers to Christ.

Billy Graham has said that in recent years a higher portion of those attending his evangelistic campaigns are young people, compared with ten years ago. The ministry of Campus Crusade for Christ has demonstrated that many young people readily respond to God's plan of salvation when it is presented lovingly, clearly, and cogently in the power of the Holy Spirit.

Sunday school teachers, camp counselors, weekday club leaders, youth program sponsors, and pastoral staff members can all verify the fact that many adolescents genuinely want to "make sense" out of life and death. Of course, many teens hide their concern behind a facade of indifference

RUSS CADLE, M.A., Doctor of Ministry candidate, is Minister of Education, First Presbyterian Church, North Palm Beach, Florida.

or in some cases even antagonism. But numerous surveys of young people in the United States have unveiled facts about teens' religious values and spiritual interests.[1] Young people—of junior high, high school, and college age—are looking for meaning, are seeking answers to deep questions about God and life, and are therefore responsive to the gospel.[2]

How can that adolescent's spiritual interest be tapped by the local church? What can be done to win more young people to Christ? How can churches equip their Christian teens to win their peers to Christ?

BE SURE THEY KNOW THE MESSAGE

Evangelism is the persuasive presentation of the gospel for the purpose of bringing people to Jesus Christ, for salvation from sin. Evangelism is not, as liberal theologians say, simply the process of informing people that they *are* Christians. Nor is evangelism a social action kind of process, designed to better man's environment socially, physically, and culturally.

The Bible makes it clear that people without Jesus Christ are eternally lost (Rom 3:23; 6:23). They are condemned already (John 3:36) and are spiritually dead, unable to help themselves (Eph 2:1-2). They cannot satisfy the demands of God's righteousness by their own efforts (Isa 64:6; Eph 2:8-9).

The gospel is the good news of God's saving grace through Jesus Christ. Thus the person presenting the gospel to the lost is called an evangelist, a bearer of good news. Jesus Christ died on the cross for man's sin (1 Pet 2:24; 3:18), as a ransom or payment for the penalty of sin (1 Pet 1:18; Matt 20:28) and in man's place. This was the supreme demonstration of God's love (Rom 5:8).

Through faith in Christ man becomes free from the penalty of sin (Rom 8:1) and a child of God (John 1:12). Through a simple act of trust in Jesus Christ (Acts 16:31) as one's personal Substitute on the cross, he is redeemed by God's grace and enjoys forgiveness of sin (Eph 1:7) and possesses eternal life (John 3:16).

LIVE THE MESSAGE

Paul Kokulis is a lawyer who has been teaching a high school Sunday school class at Fourth Presbyterian Church, Washington, D.C. for fifteen years. He has personally led many young people to Christ and has had a profound impact on literally hundreds of others. His home is open each Friday evening to any teenager who wants to drop by to chat, watch TV, or just sit around and be part of his family. He and his wife, Carolyn,

1. For details on this subject, see chapter 5, "Research on Adolescent Religiosity."
2. Also see chapter 1, "Adolescents in an Age of Crisis."

and their four children are a living demonstration of how a home can be a missionary outpost to the unsaved. Many teens have told this writer that their love for Christ has grown as they have *observed* "Mr. K" love his family and share his personal, busy time with them.

One of the greatest means of winning non-Christian young people to Christ is to live—to model—the Christlike life. The spiritual appetites of many teens have been whetted by seeing a Christian adult or teen follow Christ's commands in his daily life. They have said, "I wanted what I saw in his life—that peace, joy, and purpose that I knew was missing in my own life." Conversely, many unsaved people have been "turned off" to Christianity by watching Christians whose lives were inconsistent with what they professed to believe.

The apostle Paul advised Timothy, "Let no man despise thy youth; but be thou an example" (1 Tim 4:12). The local church can contribute to the training of teen evangelists by teaching them the importance and how-to of a Christlike, Spirit-filled walk.

Work with Parents

God has given parents the responsibility for the spiritual welfare of their children (Deut 6:7; Eph 6:4) and the privilege of influencing the home for Christ (2 Tim 1:5). The family rather than the church is the primary agency for spreading Christianity. There is nothing a person can do for Christ which will count for more than the maintenance of a truly Christian home.[3]

In order for parents to teach the Bible effectively to their children and teens, those parents must first love the Lord and have His message in their own hearts (Deut 6:5-6). As Howard Hendricks has put it, "We cannot impart what we do not possess!"[4] One of the greatest comments this writer ever heard from a teenager was, "My dad has always strived to live out what he expects his kids to do. He backs up what he says."

Deuteronomy makes it clear that parents should teach God's Word to their offspring formally (i.e., systematically and regularly), and informally (i.e., by discussing scriptural principles informally and casually). "You shall teach them diligently . . . and shall talk of them" (Deut 6:7, NASB). After a teen has been won to the Lord, godly parents can help their youngster grow in Christ by discipling him. One college-age girl on the staff of Fourth Presbyterian Church, Washington, D.C., said one summer, "My mom led me to Christ when I was twelve years old, and my parents have been discipling me ever since." This kind of parental disciplining can be

3. Howard G. Hendricks, "Miers Memorial Lectureship," Fourth Presbyterian Church, Washington, D.C., May, 1975.
4. Ibid.

done by parents as they discuss their teens' problems with them, comment informally (at dinnertime and other times) on issues from a biblical perspective, and encourage youth to attend and participate in church activities, to study the Word, pray, witness, and live a Spirit-filled life. The church can help equip parents of teens for this evangelizing and discipling ministry in the home through such means as meetings, seminars, retreats, camps, and cassette tapes.[5]

Provide Worship, Instruction, and Fellowship as a Basis for Evangelistic Fervor

Perhaps the reason many congregations are weak in evangelism is that they have failed to provide adequately for worship, instruction, and fellowship. After the three thousand came to Christ on the day of Pentecost, they "were continually devoting themselves to the apostles' teaching [instruction] and to fellowship, to the breaking of bread and to prayer [worship]" (Acts 2:42, NASB). Concern for others' needs and for evangelism (Acts 2:43-47) seemed to flow from this community of believers who were striving to be rightly related to God and to others.

Some of the most significant evangelism this writer has observed in the youth ministry at Fourth Presbyterian Church has occurred when the pastors—Dick Halverson, Bob Strain, Eddy Sweison, and the writer—have been rightly related to God and to each other. The ministry to dads all over the metropolitan area through a breakfast called "Dads' Breakfast Club" grew out of a growing concern of the pastors. Today a core of dads is spearheading this significant ministry where dads can hear the godly role and responsibility of being a husband and father. This ministry grew out of fellowship. The same is true for "moms' teas," father-child outings or banquets, family seminars and retreats.

Love for Christ is basic to an effective witness. Youth leaders who want their Christian teens to witness for Christ should first get those young people to grow in their love for Christ. Then the witnessing will flow out of a heart of love. Richards emphasizes this point in this way:

> The love motivation in witness is, however, as much vertical as horizontal. Love for others takes on evangelistic meaning only when it is balanced by love for Christ as well. Thus an effective witnessing emphasis in youth ministry presupposes that, through involvement in Scripture and Body relationships, young people are growing in their own relationship with the Lord. As one of my friends emphasizes, "Witness must be the overflow of a life that Jesus has filled up." Jesus said, "The man who believes

5. For more on the role of parents in the church's youth ministry, see chapter 33, "Working with Parents of Youth."

in me, as the scripture said, will have rivers of living water flowing from his inmost heart" (John 7:38, Phillips).[6]

Jesus Christ, nearing the end of His public ministry, pulled the disciples aside and told them that He was giving them a new commandment: "Love one another, even as I have loved you. . . . By this all men will know that you are My disciples" (John 13:34-35, NASB). The mission is one of love—the love of Christ being demonstrated and lived out in everyday relationships and activities through the power of the Holy Spirit. This is the heart of evangelism to youth.

UTILIZE THE TOTAL CHURCH MINISTRY

SUNDAY SCHOOL

This teaching arm of the church has the responsibility of providing instruction for the saved so that they may grow to spiritual maturity. To accomplish this, curriculum materials must be selected which provide opportunities for such teaching, and teachers must be trained to capitalize on such opportunities. Evangelistic opportunities occur when teachers befriend teens outside the classroom, in class get-togethers, and personal contacts.

SUNDAY YOUTH PROGRAMS

Sunday youth programs provide additional opportunities for youth to invite friends to "their own" meetings. But perhaps the greatest assistance in evangelism is the instruction and practical experience afforded in training Christians for personal evangelism. Gospel teams may be formed, instructed, trained, and then sent out to reach other youth for Christ.

WORSHIP AND EVANGELISTIC SERVICES

The regular church services offer opportunities for decision and/or public witness, formally or informally, and give teenagers a chance to bring unsaved friends in contact with a skilled presentation of the gospel. Some churches schedule rallies, retreats, or conferences designed particularly to reach young people. Special decision days afford a time for teens and others to make a decision or give public witness to a previous decision for Christ. Youth sitting together in the sanctuary is of strategic importance in developing espirit de corps in ministry with and to them.

WEEKDAY ACTIVITIES

Numerous activities are conducted by churches on weekdays, such as

6. Lawrence O. Richards, *Youth Ministry: Its Renewal in the Local Church* (Grand Rapids: Zondervan, 1972), p. 282.

clubs, study groups, recreational activities, and special interest groups. These can be geared to provide opportunity for personal contact and counsel which Sunday activities may lack. Effort should be made to reach "fringe followers" and unsaved youth and to lead them into a meaningful relationship to Jesus Christ.

CAMPING

The advantages of weekday activities over Sunday contacts are magnified even more in camping situations because of round-the-clock contact, close living, natural setting, on-your-own feeling, and comparative isolation—all of which provide multiplied opportunities for counseling and winning the unsaved.[7]

OTHER AGENCIES

The church library can have an evangelistic influence by providing books on Christian biography, doctrine, apologetics, Bible study, and Christian fiction. Choirs and ensembles have been a means of evangelism both among those participating and those who listen. Then there are many other evangelistic organizations at work in the neighborhood and on campus.

Adult workers with youth should be alert to opportunities the Lord provides for them to witness and win non-Christian youth to Himself. For example, one youth leader saw three or four boys playing basketball in the afternoon on a schoolground. He asked them if he could play with them. They agreed. After getting acquainted with them while playing ball, he bought them cokes at a nearby drugstore. Then he invited them to attend the Sunday school class he teaches. Result: the boys were in his class the next Sunday! All that the church does should be geared for evangelism and edification—to win others to Christ and then build them up in Christ.

Train a Nucleus of Teens

A local church can have a two-pronged evangelistic thrust toward youth: (1) through efforts such as those mentioned above that present the gospel directly to the unsaved, and (2) through training Christian young people in the church to witness to and win their peers.

The latter is often overlooked by churches, and yet this is very effective in youth evangelism. Teens, more so than many adults, can reach other teens because they speak the same language, have common interests, spend time together, and are not looked on as professionals.

7. Also see chapter 27, "Camping."

However, not all the Christian young people in a church will be interested in learning how to witness and in being involved in evangelism. Therefore, youth leaders may need to be content to work with a nucleus of interested young people. One youth minister asked six young people individually if they would like to take part in a discipleship training program on Sunday afternoons. He set the standards high. Faithful attendance, memorization of Scripture, and commitment of time were requirements. This hand-picked group studied the basics of the Christian life, developed a close-knit fellowship as they prayed for each other's needs, and studied the Bible and shared together. After a few months they studied how to witness effectively. Then the leaders encouraged them to share the gospel with others during the week. As people received Christ through the teens' witness, the enthusiasm of the young people grew. Then the group was eager to learn how to disciple their new converts.

This is an example of how a nucleus of teens can be trained and channeled in spiritual growth and outreach.

The Lord did a similar thing in His ministry. In addition to His ministry to the masses (e.g., Mark 6:44) and to individuals (e.g., John 3 and 4), He selected a nucleus of men—the disciples—whom he trained and involved in service (Mark 3:13-14).

Briscoe has commented on the importance of discipling a nucleus:

> There is a principle of Christian activity that the church in her mad quest for visible results has tended to overlook. She has been so busy totaling up statistics that she has lost sight of the value of the individual. She has been so intent on building large congregations that she has forgotten how small the Lord's congregation was when He left for heaven. She has majored so completely on the mass that she has overlooked the potential of the nucleus.
>
> Jesus showed us this in His ministry. He put on various spectaculars for the crowds and they came by the thousands. He even put on free bread and fish suppers and on one occasion provided free wine all around. They flocked to Him, but according to Him (and He should know) they came for the excitement and the entertainment value—not for the spiritual blessing.[8]

Briscoe applies this to youth work as follows:

> The value of the individual must never be overlooked, and the potential of the dedicated nucleus must be rediscovered. That's why I insist that it does not matter if all your kids don't get excited about an aggressive movement to the unreached. They are helping you select your nucleus! Some

8. Stuart Briscoe, *Where Was the Church When the Youth Exploded?* (Grand Rapids: Zondervan, 1972), p. 95.

youth pastors have told me that if they don't run the right kind of a program to keep the kids amused, the parents get after them, and in some
instances that I know of, have had them fired. "What do I do then?" they
have asked. "Praise God!" I replied. "Praise God that you got out of the
entertainment business which you should never have been in, and that
now you are free to get into the business you are supposed to be in—the
business of producing disciples who will reach the unreached."

"But suppose I do go for a nucleus of kids, and concentrate on them.
What happens to the others?" That is a common question that I have
been asked. My reply is that you should have someone look after the
slower moving ships, while the faster moving ones go into training. It
may mean a duplication of work, but that in itself is no argument for not
doing it.[9]

Know Problems Teens Face in Witnessing

To encourage young people to share the plan of salvation, it is important to know why they do not witness. Richards discusses four reasons
cited by young people for not witnessing.

> The reason most often mentioned was fear. There was a deep concern
> for what other kids would think. Potential ridicule, fear of making a fool
> of oneself, uncertainty about acceptance if they should speak of Jesus
> Christ in personal relationship terms, all loomed large in youth's decisions
> to remain silent. Knowing the power of the peer group . . . and youth's
> need to belong, we can be sympathetic with such doubt and fears.
>
> A second reason youth advanced was lack of "know-how." "I wouldn't
> know how to begin," or "I wouldn't know what to do if someone asked
> a question," or "I don't know enough Bible verses," appeared on the ma-
> jority of papers. While teens could point to training classes in the church,
> to role-play experiences in youth groups, and even to Sunday school units
> on "how to witness," they felt totally inadequate for the task. The concept
> of witness as a simple sharing of what Christ means to them as persons,
> of an introduction of one friend to another, seemed foreign.
>
> A third problem that loomed large was a lack of relationship with non-
> Christians. Few teens who responded spoke of non-Christian *friends*.
> Many explicitly said they "didn't know any unsaved kids well enough to
> speak to them" about Christ. Like their elders, the associations of Chris-
> tian young people were often circumscribed by the church crowd. Know-
> ing others than these as friends—the kind of friends who come over to
> your home or who you hang around with when you have free time—was
> unusual.
>
> A final problem was a sense of aloneness. Nearly all the teens expressed
> a belief that other Christian young people ought to witness, too—but
> nearly all said also, "If I were to witness I'd be the only one around doing

9. Ibid., p. 97.

it." The obligation of involvement in personal evangelism is something all give lip service to. And something most do *not* carry over in action.[10]

Fear of ridicule, ignorance of know-how, no non-Christian friends, aloneness—can these problems be overcome? Perhaps one way is by taking young people witnessing. A Campus Crusade for Christ high school conference held in Texas between Christmas and New Year sought to help young people overcome all four problems. The conference leaders trained the teens in how to share the gospel, and then all the teens—several hundred of them—went in groups of twos in house-to-house witnessing. This method overcame lack of know-how (through the training session and the actual practice), fear of ridicule, and aloneness (through each teen having the support of another young person with him). And even the problem of no non-Christian friends was overcome (through going door to door).

Many people have found helpful the "Four Spiritual Laws" booklet, published by Campus Crusade for Christ, Arrowhead Springs, San Bernardino, California 92403. A similar booklet being widely used is "How to Have a Happy and Meaningful Life," published by Dallas Theological Seminary, 3909 Swiss Avenue, Dallas, Texas 75204.

USE A VARIETY OF EVANGELISM OUTREACHES

The following is a list of some of the means churches have utilized and can utilize to reach out to unsaved young people with the gospel:

Canvassing	Year of voluntary service
Visitation	Fishermen clubs
Open-air meetings	Billboard posters
Mission services	After-game socials
Vacation Bible school	Game nights
Christian peace corps	Hobby or craft clubs
Traveling choirs	Campus forums
Breakfast clubs	Prayer cells
Singspirations	Camp counseling
Gospel films	Literature distribution
Youth centers	Summer mission safaris
Weekend conferences	Campus teas or coffees
Retreats	Study groups
Evangelistic seminars	Radio, TV programs
Gospel teams	Sorority and fraternity meetings
Vacation evangelism	Weekday club activities[11]
Dial-a-teen telephone ministry	

10. Richards, *Youth Ministry*, p. 280.
11. For information on witnessing on college campuses, see chapter 25, "Reaching Youth in College."

These are most effectively used when Christian young people are involved in these activities—in both the planning and the carrying out of them. Thus non-Christian young people see Christian teens "in action." These endeavors can help youth overcome the problem of not having unsaved teens among their acquaintances. By participating in a planned activity to which non-Christians are invited or which is taken "to" the unsaved, Christian youth have a ready-made audience.

Many dedicated Christian youth are more at ease and more successful in evangelism of children than in reaching other teens. Young people may take part in the following and other activities that give opportunity for presenting the gospel to children:

Child evangelism clubs	Park open-air meetings
Vacation Bible school	Beach evangelism
Camp counseling	Gospel fairs
Children's church	Children's rallies
Home Bible clubs	Weekday clubs[12]

CONCLUSION

The interest of young people in spiritual things, the religious sensitivity of adolescence, the response of teens to God's plan of salvation—all these factors challenge youth workers to be "fervent in spirit" (Rom 12:11) in sharing the world's greatest news—how to have eternal life through Jesus Christ—with one of the most receptive age-groups, young people!

FOR FURTHER READING

Allen, Roland. *Spontaneous Expansion of the Church*. Grand Rapids: Eerdmans, 1962.

Banks, Melvin E. *Winning and Keeping Teens in the Church*. Chicago: Urban Ministries, 1970.

Benson, Dennis. *Electric Evangelism*. Nashville: Abingdon, 1973.

Briscoe, Stuart. *Where Was the Church When the Youth Exploded?* Grand Rapids: Zondervan, 1972.

Coleman, Robert A. *The Master Plan of Evangelism*. Old Tappan, N. J.: Revell, 1963.

Gesell, Arnold, et al. *Youth: The Years from Ten to Sixteen*. New York: Harper & Row, 1956.

Halverson, Richard C. *Be Yourself and God's*. Grand Rapids: Zondervan, 1971.

Hendricks, Howard. *Say It with Love*. Wheaton, Ill.: Victor, 1973.

Henrichsen, Walter A. *Disciples Are Made—Not Born*. Wheaton, Ill.: Victor, 1974.

12. For details on ministry to children, see Roy B. Zuck and Robert E. Clark, eds., *Childhood Education in the Church* (Chicago: Moody, 1974).

Little, Paul. *How to Give Away Your Faith.* Downers Grove, Ill.: InterVarsity, 1962.

Miller, Chuck. *Now That I'm a Christian.* 2 vols. Glendale, Calif.: Regal, 1974, 1976.

Ortlund, Raymond O. *Lord, Make My Life Count.* Glendale, Calif.: Regal, 1975.

Packer, James I. *Evangelism and the Sovereignty of God.* Downers Grove, Ill.: InterVarsity, 1961.

Richards, Lawrence O. *Youth Ministry: Its Renewal in the Local Church.* Grand Rapids: Zondervan, 1972.

The Dynamics of High School Evangelism. San Bernardino, Calif.: Campus Crusade for Christ.

Stott, John R. W. *Christian Mission in the Modern World.* Downers Grove, Ill.: InterVarsity, 1975.

Towns, Elmer. *Successful Biblical Youth Work.* Nashville: Impact, 1973.

Voelkel, Jack. *Student Evangelism in a World of Revolution.* Grand Rapids: Zondervan, 1975.

Webster, Dan, and McAllister, Dawson. *Discussion Manual for Student Discipleship.* Glendale, Calif.: Shepherd Productions, 1975.

———. *Discussion Manual for Student Relationships.* Glendale, Calif.: Shepherd Productions, 1975.

Wilson, Carl W. *With Christ in the School of Disciple Building.* Grand Rapids: Zondervan, 1976.

14

Discipling of Youth

Warren S. Benson

THE CHOOSING of the disciples marked one of the climactic turning points in the ministry of Jesus Christ. His plan was simple, yet its results were extraordinary. In commenting on this strategy Elton Trueblood states,

> It is no exaggeration to say that Christ's decision to select the Twelve was one of the crucial decisions of the world. There is no reason to suppose that we should ever have heard of the Gospel apart from this carefully conceived step. Since Christ wrote no book, He depended entirely upon the faithfulness of the prepared group. Not all of them understood Him or proved faithful, yet, in the end, the method succeeded.[1]

The making of disciples was not only practiced by our Lord but it is to be perpetuated by His church. The Great Commission makes this eminently clear. Of the four action verbs recorded in Matthew 28:19-20—going, making disciples, baptizing, and teaching—only *mathēteusate,* "make disciples," a finite verb (main verb) is in the imperative mood. The other three verbs are actually participles, modifying and explaining the main verb. The grammatical construction leads one to the conclusion that the central goal of the Great Commission is to make disciples. Going, baptizing, and teaching are contributory means to that end. But one must not stop with Matthew's gospel.[2]

The parallel passages in the other gospels do not contradict the Matthew account, but rather give further clarification regarding the means. Mark 16:15-16 emphasizes that preaching the gospel is necessitated in the making of disciples.* The Lukan passages (Luke 24:47-48; Acts 1:8)

1. D. Elton Trueblood, *The Lord's Prayers* (New York: Harper & Row, 1965), p. 36.
2. George W. Peters, *A Biblical Theology of Missions* (Chicago: Moody, 1972), pp. 172-73.

*While the ending of Mark (16:9-20) continues to be debated due to the fact that several good ancient manuscripts do not record these verses and are therefore suspect,

WARREN S. BENSON, Ph.D., is Associate Dean of Academic Affairs and Professor of Christian Education, Trinity Evangelical Divinity School, Deerfield, Illinois, and formerly Minister of Education and Minister of Youth for twelve years in local churches.

add the "witnessing" dimension, and John contributes the "sending" aspect (John 20:21). As Peter Wagner has well said:

> Sending, going, preaching and witnessing are all pre-soteric (before salvation) activities; baptizing is con-soteric (along with salvation but not *producing* salvation in a sacramentalist sense); and teaching is post-soteric (after salvation). None are ends in themselves, but all relate to the goal of mathēteusate.[3]

The verb form *manthanō*, "to learn," occurs only twenty-five times in the New Testament, and only six times in the gospels where one would have expected it most as a mark of discipleship. The noun *mathētēs*, "learner, pupil, disciple," occurs 264 times in the New Testament, exclusively in the gospels and Acts. It is used to indicate total attachment to someone in discipleship.[4]

Making disciples includes both evangelism and edification. A most common error is to equate this thrust *only* with teaching and its resultant spiritual growth in another. Conversely, making disciples is more than winning people to Christ.[5] The biblical balance is difficult to achieve.

The apostle Paul gives us a good working definition of discipling in 2 Tim 2:2 (NIV), "And the things you have heard me say in the presence of many witnesses entrust to reliable men who will also be qualified to teach others." The discipling process is one of reproducing in others what the Holy Spirit is developing in the discipler, so that they will reproduce it in a third generation.

The preeminent example is Jesus and the twelve. The Saviour intended for the disciples to produce His likeness in and through the church. Through them and others like them His ministry in the Spirit would be duplicated in an ever-enlarging circumference. By this strategy, a life on a life, reaching the world was only a matter of time and their faithfulness to Christ's plan.[6]

Discipling, then, must be seen as germane and mandatory, not incidental and optional, to a ministry with youth. The days of majoring in programming and personalities should be past, for an era of the "peopleizing" process has begun. A clarification of additional terms is in order

---

the present ending is well documented from second and third century writings. See William L. Lane, *The Gospel according to Mark* (Grand Rapids: Eerdmans, 1974) and William Henricksen, *Exposition of the Gospel according to Mark* (Grand Rapids: Baker, 1975).

3. C. Peter Wagner, "What is 'Making Disciples'?" *Evangelical Missions Quarterly,* Fall 1973, pp. 283-93.
4. Dietrich Muller, "Disciple," in *The New International Dictionary of New Testament Theology*, ed. Colin Brown (Grand Rapids: Zondervan, 1975), 1: 486.
5. Wagner, "What Is 'Making Disciples'?" pp. 292-93.
6. Robert E. Coleman, *The Master Plan of Evangelism* (Old Tappan, N.J.: Revell, 1963), p. 102.

at this point in the discussion. The following definitions proposed by
Gary W. Kuhne are noteworthy.

> A disciple is a Christian who is growing in conformity to Christ, is achiev-
> ing fruit in evangelism, and is working in follow-up to conserve his fruit.[7]

> Discipleship training is the spiritual work of developing spiritual maturity
> and spiritual reproductiveness in the life of a Christian.[8]

> A multiplier is a disciple who is training his spiritual children to reproduce
> themselves.[9]

A multiplier or discipler is one who is involved in the process of discipleship training. Dawson Trotman, founder of The Navigators, was a
multiplier. During the first half of this century he was one of those who
pioneered in recovering the ministry of producing reproducers. Trotman
discipled and influenced a number of people who have made strategic
contributions to the cause of evangelical Christianity. To his dying breath,
most of his ministry was with youth and young adults.

QUALIFICATIONS FOR MAKING DISCIPLES

Disciple-makers are people whose lives evidence certain basic characteristics. Many could be presented, but these seem to be of particular significance.

AN EXEMPLARY LIFE

The apostle Peter states that leaders of the church are to be good examples (1 Pet 5:3). This includes a consistency of life. The most powerful
influence a parent has with a child is in the area of modeling the truth.
The multiplier's life-style will be inculcated into that of the one being
discipled. A lack of discipline in his life will be perpetuated in another's.

Strommen, in his *Five Cries of Youth,* finds it highly significant that
sociological variables which are often cited as reasons for the "breakdown
of the home" are of little importance. Matters such as socioeconomic level,
mobility, or size of family are minimal in their impact. Parental modeling
is crucial.[10]

COMMITMENT TO CHRIST'S LORDSHIP

The lordship of Christ must be a practical reality in the lives of would-

---

7. Gary W. Kuhne, *The Dynamics of Personal Follow-up* (Grand Rapids: Zondervan, 1976), p. 21.
8. Ibid., p. 22.
9. Ibid.
10. Merton P. Strommen, *Five Cries of Youth* (New York: Harper & Row, 1974),
    p. 44.

be disciplers (Luke 9:23-27). If actualized, they will reproduce that commitment in others. A rebel will produce rebels. Proverbs 23:9 (NASB) states, "Do not speak in the hearing of a fool, for he will despise the wisdom of your words." One can only transmit the authority to which he himself submits. A study of Philippians 2:5-11 reveals that Jesus Christ lived in absolute submission to the authority of His Father. Being Christ's disciple meant far more than joyfully accepting the Messianic promise; it required the surrender of one's whole life to the Master in absolute submission to His sovereignty (Matt 20:26-28). The development of a servant's heart will be the result. Christ embodied this principle as He washed the disciples' feet (John 13). Because of the age differential and psychological advantage in working with youth, leadership and servanthood must be carefully interpreted biblically and then modeled.

DEPENDENCE ON THE HOLY SPIRIT

In John 17 Jesus spoke thirteen times of the disciples and the authority which the Father had given Him. He was making it clear that authority is given, not taken. The Holy Spirit will cause others to recognize one's authority in church leadership and/or in the discipling process. As leaders live under the sovereignty of Christ and in dependence on the Holy Spirit, those with whom they work will respond to their discipling of them. Peters observes, "Jesus made the Twelve first into disciples before he made them into apostles. Followship preceded apostleship. Learning preceded teaching.[11]

The disciples learned to be dependent on the Holy Spirit: first, by the model of the Master; second, through the teachings of Christ to them, particularly in the upper room before the resurrection and ascension (John 14; 16); and third, by experiencing the Spirit's power as they engaged in ministry. They permitted the Holy Spirit to have complete command of their lives as they realized how dependent they were on Him. Only the Spirit can teach spiritual truth in any teaching/discipling opportunity (John 16:13; 1 Cor 2:12, 13).[12]

PRIORITIES AND VALUE SYSTEM BIBLICALLY BASED

The first step in building a discipleship ministry concerns priorities. Priorities determine the way leaders invest their time. Priorities establish criteria that assist in analyzing which things are important and which activities are urgent but of less significance.

11. George W. Peters, *Saturation Evangelism* (Grand Rapids: Zondervan, 1970), p. 32.
12. See Roy B. Zuck, *Spiritual Power in Your Teaching* (Chicago: Moody, 1972), chaps. 2-3.

The primary priority is one's walk with God (Ezra 7:10; 1 Tim 4:16).
Ronald A. Jensen interviewed over two hundred Christian leaders asking
them how much time they spent in personal Bible study and prayer daily.
Eighty-five percent were not spending as much as fifteen minutes a day
in both. The reason they gave for such a low-level priority was, "We're
just too busy. We have too much to do."[13] This is a frightening prospect
for the evangelical church. A relationship with God is foundational to all
other relationships and activities. A love for the Word of God and a desire
to teach it to others should be natural consequences of this relationship.

The second priority for a man or woman of God is a successful family
life (Deut 6:4-7; Psalm 78:1-8; 1 Tim 3:4-5). A "full" ministry for a
married person demands a godly home life. Hendricks comments:

> Your home life cannot be separated from your ministry. This is the
> thrust of Paul's argument in his first epistle to Timothy. Don't put a man
> in spiritual leadership until his home life passes examination, for if a
> man does not know how to rule his own house, how can he rule in the
> house of God. The home is a personal proving ground for ministers.
> Show me a man who keeps a cutting edge in public and I will show you
> a man who keeps a cutting edge in private. Many a man tries to use his
> public ministry as a cover for failing in the basic responsibilities God has
> given him at home. Sooner or later he is almost certain to face incredible
> dissonance.[14]

A discipler of youth must first succeed in loving and caring for his wife
or husband, and children. The church, a youth group, and individual
young people with acute problems are to be accorded time only after one's
own family has been given initial consideration. The family first provides
a fantastic opportunity for modeling the biblical value system. Eli who
discipled Samuel fell short of being an ideal model, for his own sons did
not respond to him or respect Eli's authority (1 Sam 2:23). Quite possibly, Eli had trained Samuel in the basic religious duties but had never
helped Samuel to know God personally. Youth workers encounter the
same dilemma.

Society groans with changes facing the family that eventuate in youths
feeling disinterested, disconnected, and perhaps even hostile to the people
and activities in their environment. This feeling of disconnectedness results in alienation.[15] A multiplier should keep this in the forefront of his

13. Ronald A. Jensen, "Gearing the Local Church for Discipleship" (D.Min. thesis,
    Western Conservative Baptist Seminary, Portland, Oregon, 1974), p. 67.
14. Howard G. Hendricks, *Say It with Love* (Wheaton, Ill.: Victor 1972), p. 72.
15. Urie Bronfenbrenner, "The Origins of Alienation," *Scientific American* 231 (Au-
    gust 1974): 53.

thinking as he constructs a ministry of discipling and programming both to his family and church youth.

The third priority concerns one's ministry to the youth group, the local church, and society in general.[16] It is the predilection of this writer that a multiplier's investment of time and effort within this third priority should center on the youth ministry though the others are important as well. Whether in a full-time or lay, part-time capacity one cannot do all of them well. After he has made this decision he has one more crucial decision to make: Should he follow the Saviour's modus operandi, or capitulate to the parental "mass" concept of ministry, or attempt a blending of these philosophies? Many youth workers fail at this point. Unless they have a biblical philosophy of ministry, the inevitable activity and aimless treadmill will drive them out of youth work.

It can be readily demonstrated that Jesus in His ministry followed the principle of concentration.[17] First, the Master spent more time with Peter, James, and John than with the other disciples. Secondly, He invested Himself in the Twelve. Third, His ministry was to the Seventy, and finally, Christ worked with the masses. But, some will say, "I am not allowed the luxury of the Saviour's philosophy. I answer to the board of deacons, board of elders, board of Christian education, or the youth council. And they want results, spelled S-T-A-T-I-S-T-I-C-S."

Others will point out, "Yes, but Christ was God. He understood people as we do not. The Saviour had time that we do not have and the disciples observed Him in all the dimensions of life." True, in no way can leaders today equate what He could do with what they can accomplish. But as Christ promised the disciples, the Holy Spirit is with Christians to give them perspective, leadership, and guidance regarding priorities.

The Holy Spirit will guide a discipler to know the persons in whom to pour his life. Guidance will come through several factors. The first avenue to take in determining who is ready for discipling is prayer. Christ spent at least one night in prayer over choosing His disciples (Luke 6: 12-13). No doubt He spent considerable additional time in prayer regarding these crucial decisions. Second, follow-up (discipling) will of itself filter out the unfaithful and the halfhearted. Some who start will

16. David Roper, comp., "Principles of Ministry," Appendix C in Bob C. Smith, *When All Else Fails . . . Read the Directions* (Waco, Tex.: Word, 1974), pp. 128-30.
17. See Robert Coleman, *The Master Plan of Evangelism;* A. B. Bruce, *The Training of the Twelve* (Grand Rapids: Kregel, 1971); Gary Kuhne, *The Dynamics of Personal Follow-up;* Carl W. Wilson, *With Christ in the School of Disciple Building* (Grand Rapids: Zondervan, 1976). Walter A. Henrichsen, *Disciples Are Made—Not Born* (Wheaton, Ill.: Victor, 1974); and Alfred Edersheim, *The Life and Times of Jesus the Messiah* (Grand Rapids: Eerdmans, 1972).

disqualify themselves by missing appointments, Scripture memory assignments, etc. Third, look for youth who have a hunger for spiritual growth. Such a person will be consistent in his devotional life and Bible study assignments through the initial follow-up period. Fourth, if he is a new Christian, he will gain an understanding of what has taken place in his life. This searching, believing heart will desire God's best, God's will. Fifth, one who is alert and questioning has good potential for becoming a faithful trainee. Discern the attitude behind the Socratic thrust. Good verbal feedback is important.

Many disciplers face several problems that the Master also encountered. One was a relatively short tenure of two and one-half to three years of ministry with the same group of people.† This did not discourage Him because He had a plan. In addition, Christ also received parental pleas from at least one mother regarding her sons' place in the kingdom. Christ handled the dilemma firmly but kindly.[18]

Ultimately most of the questions and difficulties can and must be answered in light of the leader's biblical ladder of priorities. That is not to circumvent the reality of the problems mentioned above. Realistically, an individual or a team of people must establish a ministry to the many while concurrently discipling the few. The total group is the pool from which those who will be discipled emerge. In actuality, then, a ministry to both "groups" must be sustained, not because of a fear or intimidation from church boards or parental pressures, but because of a biblical philosophy of the ministry.

As indicated previously, the youth group is to be viewed priority- and philosophy-wise in conjunction with the total local church body and society. Youth are not a separate entity in themselves. They are to be treated as an integral part of the local church. Departmentalization—while it has contributed much of value—has sometimes gone to seed. One of the marks of maturity of a youth fellowship is their involvement in the total life of the church. Youth leaders often err in this area and they are urged to critique their ministry from this perspective.[19]

A second mark of maturity of youth, and of adult leaders as well, is its concern for and involvement with people who do not know the Saviour. Youth groups should have a strategy for evangelism in which a genuine

†The earthly ministry of the Lord was approximately three and one-half years in length. The biblical data is insufficient to establish firmly how long the disciples or even the first four (Peter, Andrew, James and John) were with Him.

18. See D. Bruce Lockerie, "The Mama Zebedee Complex," *Evangelical Beacon,* November 12, 1974, pp. 10-11.
19. See Addison H. Leitch, "Accent on Youth," *Christianity Today,* December 3, 1971; and "Apologia for Accent on Youth," *Christianity Today,* March 3, 1972.

love for people is evidenced, rather than just a concern for their spiritual "scalps" (1 Tim 3:7). Attitudes of youth workers toward non-Christians are readily conveyed nonverbally.

Fig. 14.1. *A discipling church*

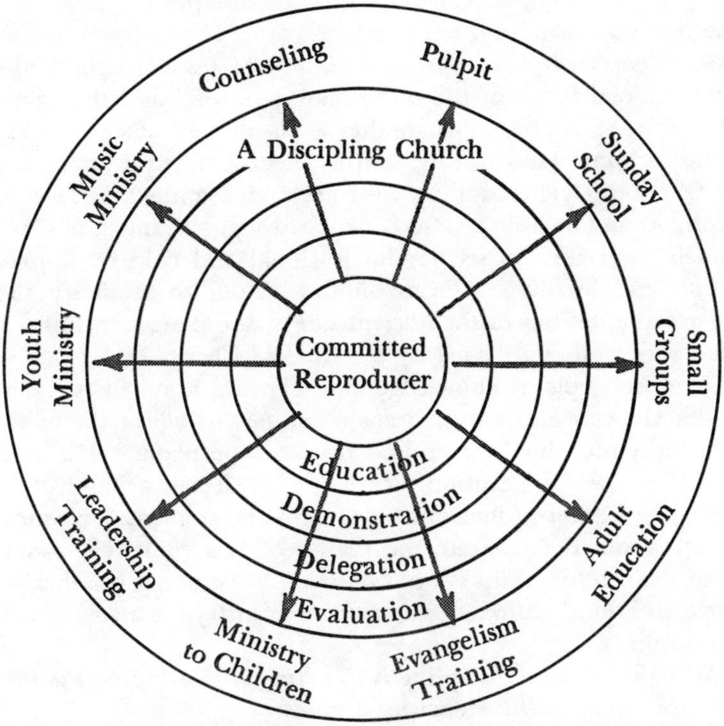

Ronald A. Jensen, "Gearing the Church for Discipleship" (D. Min. thesis, Western Conservative Baptist Seminary, 1974), p. 54.

THE PROCESS AND PRACTICE OF MAKING DISCIPLES

GUIDELINES FOR THE PROCESS

Henrichsen suggests four guidelines essential in the process of discipling young people.[20]

The first guideline in discipling is to *major in principles more than methods.* This is a matter of emphasis. With the disciples (Luke 8) Christ often gave principles of ministry, but He did not always specify methods. Therefore, He encouraged them not to be slaves of traditional methodology but to be open to new and better ways. Change can become

20. Henrichsen, *Disciples Are Made—Not Born,* pp. 118-30.

a threat, but if biblical principles form the basis of what is done, then disciples will be eager for fresh and creative avenues of carrying out the ministry. The trainee gains perspective and develops convictions by probing into the whys of what is done. Take time for discussing deeply so that the principles become part of the fabric of the disciple.

The second guideline in discipling is to *major in meeting the needs of others more than in the teaching of techniques.* Jesus met both the felt needs and the real needs of the blind man (John 9) and the woman at the well (John 4). He began where they were—in need of sight and water. Each came to know Him in salvation as they were ready to trust Him.

Many Christians view training in a classroom context as learning to master content and techniques. As Ted Ward suggests, much of Christian education is patterned on secular institutional and cultural approaches to teaching and learning. "From Sunday school to seminary the approaches are adaptations of the ancient Greek academic traditions—traditions that were well established by the time of Christ."[21]

The Greek concepts of knowledge and learning stood in striking contrast to the Hebrew Scriptures. Jesus chose not to adopt them; He deliberately built no school nor raised funds to perpetuate His teaching through an endowed institution. Rather, He selected a handful of disciples and lived among them, using "teachable moments" to inculcate biblical truth and demonstrate the reality of His content through the meeting of their needs. This is what one should be doing whether within the context of a local church, a parachurch ministry, or a structured academic situation.

The third guideline in discipling is to *major in developing the thought processes more than skills.* Henrichsen states:

> Jesus Christ is far more interested in what we are than what we do. "It is for you to be; it is for God to do," provides a simple but wise piece of advice. The Saviour wants to reprogram our computer, to change our whole thought process.[22]

The Pharisees epitomized the antithetical stance which Christ wanted the disciples to resist. In order for the Master to have sovereign control in their lives, they were in need of observing His servant posture and submission to His Father. Change in the experience of the disciples came slowly and subtly. As their thinking processes were corrected, the imparting of character was operationalized and their value systems were profoundly altered. Center on bringing their philosophy of life into conformity with the Scriptures, and their convictions and perspective will

21. Ted W. Ward, "To Reform Christian Education: Six Criteria" (Unpublished paper, 1976), p. 1. ·
22. Henrichsen, *Disciples Are Made—Not Born,* p. 123 .

follow. Remember, the inconsistencies of adolescents render them incapable of total stability. Flexibility and an understanding spirit in youth workers will be constantly tested.

The fourth guideline in discipling is to *major in how to trust God more than teaching theories about God.* This is not a "negation" of theology. Theology is eminently practical. Such a dichotomy is unbiblical. Rather it is a matter of emphasis. Theology should be taught life-relatedly. Emphasis on knowing is to be acompanied by an emphasis on doing. Human development is a holistic matter—youth leaders cannot split off one aspect of the person with whom they deal. Enhancement of mental processes, such as recall of information, is an insufficient goal of discipleship training.[23] If leaders of youth know and trust God deeply, their young people will capture the concept. Growth is a painful process and all possess tendencies toward mediocrity. In working with youth, coasting is catching. Knowing and trusting God are "partners" of perspective and conviction. They will assist in checking natural inclinations toward passivity.

Examine the lives of the great leaders of the past—Moses, Daniel, Elijah, Peter, and Paul. Conviction and perspective were the touchstones in establishing their places in the biblical hall of fame.

PRINCIPLES FOR THE PRACTICE

There are nine basic principles to apply in the discipling process.[24]

First, establish clear objectives. To construct lucid aims and goals the worker with youth should first understand himself. Socrates said, "Know thyself"; the Romans said, "Control thyself"; and Christ said, "Deny thyself." The follower of Christ may jump to the emphasis of His injunction to "deny thyself" and disregard the other two. However, on examination the thinking disciple discovers a biblical orientation for all three emphases. In actuality, these three statements progress like an exploding chain reaction. Self-control is impossible for the person who does not know himself, because control demands a knowledge of objectives, motives, and capabilities. The one who understands himself can better control and deny himself for the purpose of personal improvement by (1) eliminating weaknesses that dissipate his effectiveness, and (2) by capitalizing on strengths.[25]

23. Ward, "To Reform Christian Education," p. 3.
24. The nine principles cited have been employed by Howard G. Hendricks in the discipling process at Dallas Theological Seminary over a twenty-five year teaching and discipling ministry. These principles are used by permission, and discussion of each is the author's material.
25. Sidney S. Buzzell and Mark J. Krug, "Couple to Couple: Discipleship in Duplicate" (Unpublished project, Dallas Theological Seminary, 1974), p. 1. A number of their ideas in discipling are utilized in this chapter. Used by permission.

As a person knows himself and establishes his priorities and value system, assisting others to reach biblical goals is somewhat simplified. It is helpful to write out a plan for taking someone else through the process of structuring objectives. The amount of time involved, the type of relationship, the biblical background, and the stage of Christian growth will vary with each trainee.

Gary W. Kuhne suggests four types of relationships:[26] (1) relationship one-to-one ; (2) counseling one-to-one; (3) structured one-to-one; and (4) partnership one-to-one.

The purpose of the *one-to-one relationship* is simply to build rapport and develop a warm climate. The content is unstructured and not necessarily spiritual in nature. The primary object is to spend quality time playing sports, having meals together, attending meetings or sports events, and so forth. Modeling the Christian life before the one being discipled is the key (Mark 3:14; 1 Thess 2:1-16) .

The objective of *counseling one-to-one* is character development. Being with a person enables one to discern areas which need to be surfaced and dealt with in order to promote consistent spiritual growth. This is a difficult but crucial part of a ministry with youth. Good habit patterns in devotions, prayer, Scripture memory, and sharing one's faith are to be encouraged. To make this contribution to another demands winning the right to be heard through spending time with him weekly and demonstrating the quality of a disciplined life.

The goal of a *structured one-to-one relationship* is to lay a foundation of biblical truth in one's life. This is usually equated with the term *follow-up*. Kuhne suggests that basic doctrine, the how-tos of growing in Christ, and techniques of outreach should form the corpus of the material taught. A time period should be determined with a view to establishing a partnership one-to-one relationship with the individual, which often is the next step in the discipling process.

The aim of the *partnership one-to-one relationship* is to insure consistency of life and spiritual reproduction. This usually occurs later in a new Christian's development. The one you are discipling has become a self-starter and has developed an independence through spiritual growth. Therefore, the element of mutual edification is now involved to a greater degree. Partnership one-to-one is less time-consuming than the other types, and can often be combined with some other activity. This relationship is characterized by mutual prayer and study, mutual sharing, and mutual counsel. While being largely unstructured in format, it is necessary for continual multiplication. Only the rare high school person has

26. Kuhne, *Dynamics of Personal Follow-up*, pp. 139-41. The discussion of the types of relationships reflects Kuhne's impact on the writer's thinking.

reached this level of maturity, but a number of collegians and single young adults are ready for this type of relationship.

However, a major question remains. When in the discipling process should each type of training relationship be utilized? A valid answer comes by studying the stages of growth in the life of a maturing Christian. Then the types of relationships can be related to the stages of growth.

John indicates three stages or categories of growth with great clarity: children, young men, and fathers. "I write to you, dear children, because your sins have been forgiven on account of his name. I write to you, fathers, because you have known him who is from the beginning. I write to you, young men, because you have overcome the evil one" (1 John 2: 12-13, NIV).

The children are the new converts. The first goal of a ministry with youth who are infant Christians is the establishment of fellowship with God. A new Christian must develop in this most basic and profoundly important spiritual relationship. The second is the launching of a vital involvement with other Christians. The encouragement and protection one receives from the church, the body of Christ, is extremely valuable. Therefore, this calls for ministering to him initially with a structured one-to-one approach as well as a relationship one-to-one approach.

The young men are the growing young Christians whose needs differ from those of new, infant Christians. Two additional goals are included for them. They need to develop a consistency of life and an effective outreach. They need more information regarding doctrine, apologetics, and witnessing. The counseling one-to-one relationship will be contributory, as dialogue with a more mature believer will help him shape up the weak areas of his life. As the young Christian grows and matures, both structured one-to-one and relationship one-to-one will be dispensed with, and counseling one-to-one will predominate in terms of the relational style. Many of the young people who have been reared in the church will be found at this stage of development, but considerable variance will be discovered from one to another.

The fathers, i.e., the mature Christians, will need little structured one-to-one or relationship one-to-one. The needs of this stage are best met by counseling one-to-one which usually evolves into the partnership one-to-one dimension.[27]

A caution for all youth workers would be that one should ask God for the leading of His Spirit in attempting to evaluate the type of relation-

---

27. For a biblical perspective on understanding where potential disciples of Christ might be in their spiritual pilgrimage, see Robert Coleman, *The Master Plan of Evangelism;* and Carl Wilson, *With Christ in the School of Disciple Building;* and engage in a careful study of 1 John and 1 Corinthians 2—3.

ships and the biblical ministry that each individual needs. Be prepared
to be flexible and make changes where necessary. This writer has found
that a study of the gospel of Mark in conjunction with Coleman's *The
Master Plan of Evangelism* (see reading list at end of chapter) is an excellent combination in the discipling process. Establishing clearcut objectives is mandatory in maximizing a ministry.

Second, recruit as individuals; train as a team. "Jesus went up into the
hills and called to him those he wanted, and they came to him. He appointed twelve—designating them apostles—that they might be with him
and that he might send them out to preach" (Mark 3:13-14, NIV). The
Bible not only provides God's message to men but also instructs regarding
the methods of the Master and those of His disciples and apostles. In the
recruiting process Jesus selected a few, the twelve, from the company of
followers pressing around Him. And he called them individually or in
groups of two. He had to keep the group small enough to work with
them effectively. This did not mean that others were excluded from following Him. The seventy (Luke 10:1); Mark and Luke, biblical writers;
James, Jesus' own half-brother (1 Cor 15:7; Gal 2:9, 12) are notable examples of this. However, there was a rapidly diminishing priority given
to those outside the twelve.[28] Yet, in a local church ministry, a discipleship philosophy of ministry is seldom encouraged unless a solid and vital
ministry is sustained to the total group. As stated previously, this is stark
realism and it must be acknowledged, particularly in the youth area.

As Coleman observes, "it would be wrong to assume that Jesus neglected
the masses. Such was not the case. Jesus did all that any man could be
asked to do and more to reach the multitudes."[29] But victory is never won
by the multitudes. Youth workers, professional and lay, must train leadership for "works of service" (Eph 4:12, NIV).

Of the twelve men chosen by the Lord, only three made any knowledgeable impact on the church. One, in fact, was a traitor and even he
was chosen by "Him who knew what was in men." They were twelve men
with wide-ranging differences in their backgrounds and personalities.
Christ did not surround Himself with a group of "yes men." Each man
was selected individually because of his unique contribution to the team.
In fact, the biblical record indicates some were chosen more for what they
did to others than for what was done for them (e.g., the despised publican,
Matthew). It was only as they were molded into the others that their
lives were significant. The methods of the Master have only recently
been "discovered" by the social learning theoreticians.

28. Coleman, *Master Plan*, pp. 24-25.
29. Ibid., p. 27.

Most often, discipleship training begins on a one-to-one basis. As youth grow in Christ, put them together in groups with a mature person leading. A team or group relationship will do at least four things for them: (1) a support system of love and encouragement is provided; (2) instruction of each other results; (3) they discipline one another; and (4) some informally disciple one or two of the others.

In developing a functioning team of disciples, the attitudes of love, humility, and likemindedness become increasingly important (1 Pet 1: 22; 1 John 3:14-18, 4:20-21; Phil 2:2-3). Christ built a group of men who were committed not only to Him but also to each other. The team relationship and attitudinal development tend to eliminate the offensive aspects of cliques. However, never waste time or breath "preaching" against cliques. They are a valuable source of security for adolescents in particular, and for adults as well. Sociometrically speaking, cliques among youth often reflect the cliques of their parents.

Proper attitudes need expression through action. As they minister first to one another they then will become conscious of the needs of "significant" others and seemingly insignificant others (Acts 2:44-47; Rom 15:7; Gal 6:2; Eph 4:31-32; Heb 10:24-25; James 5:16).

Third, develop dependence on the Lord; develop independence of the leader. Men like power over other men. The tendency toward paternalism is ubiquitous. The individual who has unintentionally built a power base among youth must never forget that they are the disciples of Christ, not his disciples. The natural tendency of adolescents to cling to the adult who listens, undertsands, is concerned, and gives of himself, does not provide the panacea. Rather, the dependency tends to flourish and concretize, and the leader may enjoy the personal cult of spiritual cripples that develops, or else he may not know how to correct the situation graciously and eliminate the parasitic attachment.

Jesus Christ confronted the same dilemma. The disciples came to depend heavily on Him. In his classic study of discipleship training, A. B. Bruce observes that the gospels cumulatively report only thirty-four days of activity in the total ministry of Christ. To the question of what the Lord did with the rest of His time Bruce suggests that Jesus spent the bulk of His unaccounted-for hours with His disciples, teaching and training them.[30] Therefore, their dependence on the God-man is understandable.

In John 16:7 (NIV) the Saviour delivered a distasteful paradox to the disciples: "But I tell you the truth: It is for your good that I am going away. Unless I go away, the Counselor will not come to you; but if I go,

30. A. B. Bruce, *The Training of the Twelve.*

I will send him to you." How could the disciples possibly be better off
without Him? Obviously, this was part of His perfect plan. The more
relevant and crucial question is: If Jesus Christ saw the need to turn His
men over to the guiding ministry of the Holy Spirit, where does this leave
present-day disciples? They are monumentally dependent on the Lord
and the ministry of the Holy Spirit!

Long before He left the disciples, Christ started developing a sense of
"independent dependence." Matthew chapters 10, 14, and 17 record three
incidents where the twelve were on their own. However, an interesting
model for youth ministry is given in Mark 6:7-13, 30-34 as Jesus sent out
the disciples two-by-two, instructing them to "take nothing for the journey
except a staff" (verse 8, NIV) and assuring them that all their needs would
be supplied. He had carefully trained them in terms of what to do, but
they had to exercise their faith regarding God's power. They pursued
their mission and then reported enthusiastically to Him. Undoubtedly
He helped them analyze what had been done and how it was accomplished
(their work and His power), so that following the ascension, the Holy
Spirit could prompt them regarding the message and the methods (John
16:13). At the conclusion of discipling someone, help the person think
through what he has been taught and what has been with him so that he
can understand the ministry of being a multiplier. Write the process
down—and thus "stars" will more likely become servants.[31]

The multiplying ministry of some youth leaders is marked by their
practice of transferring disciples with whom they have been working into
the care of another person. The management principle of the span of
control, the one-to-six ratio—i.e., no one can have more than six people
reporting to him and still perform a work of excellence—is applicable
here. If the Saviour had twelve "reporting" to Him, then six might be a
good maximum for today. The youth minister who works directly with
three couples, one each with junior high, high school, and college, is
already up to capacity in terms of management standards. While the
excitement is in ministering directly with young people, one must remember that the number which one person can disciple is limited. If
the youth minister attempts to work closely with too many, his own family become the losers, and that is antithetical to biblical teaching.

The minister to students must strategize in order to maximize his ministry. This is done best by developing a cadre made up of collegians and
other single adults and couple-sponsors who have been discipled by the
professional. Each one of them, if the 2 Timothy 2:2 process is part of
their philosophy of life, should be assigned three to five junior highers,

31. Buzzell and Krug, "Couple to Couple."

high schoolers, or collegians. For instance, a female sponsor could be assigned three high school girls, preferably ones who are in the same year in school and attend the same high school. As these three girls are discipled, they will develop a caring concern for others. They should each choose two girls from their high school, one who is from their church and one who does not know Christ. This builds in the responsibility factor and gives each one a ministry to a Christian who needs to be cared for and eventually discipled, and to a non-Christian who needs to be cared for, brought to the Saviour and in time, discipled. The sponsor meets with or is in communication with her original three at least weekly.

A college man may be assigned three junior high or high school boys, if possible, from the same school and in the same grade. He then meets with them weekly on an individual or group basis, utilizing the various types of discipling relationships described previously in the chapter.

The minister of youth will sustain a ministry to the youth who take leadership roles and then personally disciple only one or two of the same sex as the minister. These would be youth who are particularly difficult to work with. If one understands and follows a multiplying philosophy of ministry, he will tend to remain at a church for a longer tenure. One then is free to provide the resource assistance that he alone can give in both the programming and discipling area of youth work.

Fourth, allow enough freedom for them to grow. Some disciplers fail to possess a sufficient data base to impart the correct biblical knowledge and information to those being discipled, and therefore, they depend on their relational skills.[32] Others have constructed a rigid, inflexible curriculum through whose hoops every disciple must jump. Both are incorrect. The ministry is to people, not machines. Workers with youth should be supersensitive to their growth patterns. Then determine the curriculum for maximal but unhurried maturation. Young people come to the discipler from diverse backgrounds and with radically different information banks and interest levels. On devising an individualized curriculum for one person, be ready to accelerate or slow down in light of where he is and how he progresses.

Mandatory in the teaching-learning process is the opportunity for the disciple to use what is being received cognitively. This suggests that Bible study, discussion, outside reading, Scripture memory, and listening to tapes are not the end-all. For the internalization of truth to take place, involvement in the real world of being with non-Christians and sharing one's faith is highly contributory. In Christ's ministry with the twelve He

---

32. See Kuhne, *Dynamics of Personal Follow-up*, pp. 141-206, for excellent curriculum suggestions for "children" and "young men" in the faith.

modeled the message and the methods, had them participate in the work under His observing eye, and then sent them out first by twos and eventually on their own. After the young people are involved with the disciples in teaching and evangelistic situations, in time this will become part of the very nature of their being.[33] The experiential dimension affords the disciple the opportunity to fail. Some failure is inevitable. Talk about the reality of failure before it happens. Explain that there are two reactions to failure: defeat or determination. The person who is defeated by failure has most often failed because of not learning from past downfalls. The other type of individual evaluates why, builds good habit patterns, and determines, with God's help, not to repeat the mistake.

A classic example of allowing a disciple the privilege of freedom is the Paul-Timothy relationship. Paul sent this young man to Ephesus to pastor the church. In his freedom Timothy did some things well but also made many mistakes. Paul wrote two letters, First and Second Timothy, due to the fact that failure was a distinct possibility. The discipler allowed the young pastor the freedom to experiment without neglecting him. Paul gave instructions and encouragement while never letting Timothy forget his love for him. He stayed with him until success and growth were assured.[34] Youth are prone to misuse their potential. Stay with them through the prickly parts of development.

Fifth, expect resistance as a part of growth. Psychologists are quick to concur that adolescence almost always produces some turmoil, whether overt or covert, in the experience of youth.[35] However, as a general law of social and personal development, social learning theorists such as Albert Bandura assume there is continuity in human growth patterns and in the learning process and that no basic changes or clear-cut new stages in the mode of thinking appear at any age-level. With this, stage theorists of development such as Gesell, Freud, Erikson, and Piaget, disagree.[36] Nevertheless the psychological area of an adolescent's existence inevitably brings some anxiety.

In contrast to Bandura's claim that turmoil and anxiety are exceptional rather than normal, Cattel and Scheir found that during adolescence a noticeable increase in anxiety distinguishes that period from childhood

33. D. James Kennedy, *Evangelism Explosion* (Wheaton, Ill.: Tyndale, 1970).
34. See Douglas Hyde, *Dedication and Leadership* (South Bend, Ind.: U. of Notre Dame, 1964), pp. 42-45, 111-20, for techniques used by the communists for challenge and growth experiences of new recruits. The communists have used some biblical methods better than Christians have.
35. See chaps. 1 and 5—10 for discussions of this phenomenon.
36. Rolf E. Muuss, "The Implications of Social Learning Theory for an Understanding of Adolescent Development," *Adolescence* 11 (Spring 1976), p. 67.

and adulthood. "In the normal person, free anxiety is very high in adolescence and drops sharply as adulthood is reached.[37]

While the pronouncements of psychologists concerning the exigencies of adolescent development and the impact of anxiety should be read with care, the Scriptures give additional perspective on this universal symptom.

> Be self-controlled and vigilant always, for your enemy the devil is always about, prowling like a lion roaring for its prey. Resist him, standing firm in your faith, remembering that the strain is the same for all your fellow-Christians in other parts of the world. And after you have borne these sufferings a very little while, the God of all grace, God Himself who has called you to share his eternal splendour through Christ, will himself make you whole and secure and strong. All power is His forever and ever, amen! (1 Pet 5:8-11, Phillips).

Resistance is predictable when spiritual growth is flourishing. Just when that seemingly deeply committed young person is moving into high gear, the carburetor stalls and he becomes blasé about Bible study, prayer, and sharing. The youth leader should not forget either the psychological or the biblical explanations for these inconsistencies. For both reasons, but particularly because of the work of Satan, opposition is to be expected. J. Dwight Pentecost has said,

> Many of God's children live a defeated life because they do not recognize the nature of the adversary and the kind of conflict in which they are engaged. Our adversary is so cleverly and subtly camouflaged many do not even recognize his existence. There can be no victory until we recognize the nature of the war.[38]

Teen disciples need to know the biblical evidence of the nature and subtlety of this foe. Talk about this resistance to growth before it appears. For a battle of supernatural proportions, supernatural assistance is needed. Study Galatians 5:16-26; Ephesians 6:1-17; James 1:2-18 and 1 Peter 5:8-11. Discuss the sources of resistance, the weapons available, the value of failure, and the assurance of God's power. Expect disciples to disappoint, and the discipler need not be ashamed to admit when he has disappointed them.

David Roper reminds youth workers to "maintain a strong support base for them. Provide help as they need it. Pray for them, write them, and be available for counsel."[39] However, do not let this opposition lower

---

37. R. B. Cattell and I. H. Scheir, *The Meaning and Measurement of Neuroticism and Anxiety* (New York: Ronald, 1961) as cited in Muuss, "Implications," p. 68.
38. J. Dwight Pentecost, *Your Adversary the Devil* (Grand Rapids: Zondervan, 1969), p. 138.
39. David Roper, "Making Disciples," Appendix A in Bob C. Smith, *When All Else Fails . . . Read the Directions* (Waco, Tex.: Word, 1974), p. 119.

severely the level of expectation of them. Laziness or juvenile rationalization may be present. Roper's succinct admonitions should be heard
again. "Don't be afraid to be hard on these men; God's men will bounce"
(Mark 8:18, 33; 9:1-8, 19).[40] In the discipling practices of Jesus Christ
and Paul, they dealt in love and firmness, in tenderness and toughness
(2 Thess 2:7-12). Strive for that biblical balance. These times are strategic for advancement.

Sixth, expose them to other gifted men. Professional fields often have
an intricate system of referrals that enable the general practitioner to
complement and enhance his care of a patient or client by employing
the skills of the specialist. In discipling young people, youth leaders
should not hesitate to use referrals and thereby expose them to other
gifted Christians. The pastor, some members of the board of elders, and
other godly men and women in your church and in other churches may
assist in this role.

Paul sent Timothy and Epaphroditus (Phil 2:19-30) to the church at
Philippi. Paul indicates that he had no one else like Timothy "who takes
a genuine interest in your welfare" (verse 20, NIV). Timothy cared
about people and he had a contribution to make. Epaphroditus had been
sent by and had represented the Philippians as he assisted Paul in the
ministry. However, he became homesick for the Philippians.

Pride and a case of myopia cause multipliers to stumble on this point.
Christ's body, the church, is an interdependent organization. Each member of the body has a definite function which is designed to aid in the
growth of the other members. One must not become trapped in the folly
of failing to teach disciples to benefit from other men and women God has
placed around them for their benefit and enrichment. It takes all the
saints to know all the dimensions of the knowledge of God. In actuality,
they are not your disciples; they are God's. The leadership "technique"
taught in Philippians gives the proper viewpoint: "Do nothing out of
selfish ambition or vain conceit, but in humility consider others better
than yourselves" (Phil 2:3, NIV). The entire learning environment is to
reflect the unity of a true community.[41]

Seventh, stress interpersonal relationships. Moses engaged in a ministry
of discipleship training. He knew he would not enter the promised land,
and he was aware that someone else would be given the inexpressible joy
of leading the people into it. Moses began to spend time with Joshua.
He counseled and encouraged and instructed him regarding the ways of
God (Exod 24:13; 33:11; Deut 3:28; 31:7-8, 23; 34:9). Joshua was trained
to give leadership to God's people.

40. Ibid.
41. Ward, "To Reform Christian Education," p. 4.

When a discipler opens his life to others and they begin to study the Word of God together, they will begin to share where they hurt and have needs. Some leaders, however, reject this approach and it is to be admitted that an overemphasis on the experiential and the confessional aspects presents dangers. But the loving and discerning multiplier of men will provide guidance regarding the depth and type of sharing. Two areas in which youth tend to share unwisely are those of private family information and sexual exploits and hang-ups. However, there are so many benefits that come from bearing one another's burdens (Gal 6:2; James 5:16) that sharing is strongly encouraged with the exception of these and other areas that may be deemed off limits. Richards, in commenting on the efficacy of sharing, observes:

> Bearing one another's burdens implies at least two corollaries: first, that we care deeply about the troubles and needs of other believers, and seek to shoulder them in prayer, in encouragement, in expressed concern. And second, that the burdens of believers are shared with others. The only way I can know of the needs of a person is if he tells them to me. If he shares. So this "one another" phrase tells us much about love in action. Trusting love honestly and openly expresses its needs and weaknesses and burdens to others: responsive love rejects criticalness and condemnation to express concern and care. Love takes the neighbor's burden as its own.[42]

Christians are also "to admonish one another" (Rom 15:14). The word *admonish* means to warn and instruct with the general connotation of "helping through warning and rebuke." Love is expressed by welcoming (Rom 15:7), showing respect (Rom 12:10) and rebuking. Human beings have a natural proclivity to avoid confrontation, but genuine love speaks the truth in a warm and gracious manner (Eph 4:15). As interpersonal relationships mature, opportunities to assist young people in evaluating themselves proliferate. Youth often carry considerable guilt, insecurity, and anxiety. They need ministers and lay people who can interact with them without anxiety, who possess the ability to accept and love persons who have not yet grown to love or to accept themselves.

The supportive, loving concern of believers gathered in body relationship is, together with the Word of God, the primary means God uses to remold believers from within—a dynamic, divine power that growth in Christ demands they experience in life together as a new community; a community created and marked by love.[43]

42. Lawrence O. Richards, *Youth Ministry: Its Renewal in the Local Church* (Grand Rapids: Zondervan, 1972), p. 226.
43. Ibid., p. 231.

Eighth, magnify roles over gifts. God is more interested in the person one is becoming than in the spiritual gifts he possesses. His desire for each believer is that he become Christlike. The more like the Saviour the youth leader becomes, the less pressure he will put on himself to locate or be preoccupied with his exact gift or gifts. The qualities of a godly man are far clearer in Scripture than his ability to be positive regarding his spiritual gifts. Paul did not instruct Timothy and Titus to look for men with certain spiritual gifts. Rather they were to find men who possessed spiritual qualifications.[44] This is not to depreciate the validity of gifts nor to impugn their importance in the local church. However, some have become so confused in the area of gifts that they have capitulated in frustration. This is particularly true in the youth area.

One's role—the capacities one functions in the local assembly—is determined by the direction and will of God. It is the Holy Spirit's way of placing us in relationship with other people in the body of Christ. For instance, one of the functions all Christians have is that of being a servant (Mark 10:45; John 13:1-11). Jesus Christ came in the stance of a servant. If a Christian has the heart of a servant, then the effectiveness of the exercise of his gift, whatever it may be, will enrich the church. Concomitantly, the young people with whom he works will acknowledge that one's relationship with God is more crucial than the knowledge of one's spiritual gift. Teach them how they might know what their gifts are and provide experiences in service so that the identification process may be accurate.[45]

Trust the Holy Spirit to work in their lives. Provide them with counsel and encouragement. As they progress, move them into positions with increasing responsibility. To produce reproducers they must experience the ministry they can have with their peers. Never rob them of the thrill of introducing a friend of theirs to Christ. Give them that privilege and they will respond in diligently shepherding that person to spiritual growth. The ministry of multiplication then becomes more than a slogan of discipleship.

Ninth, recognize God's ability to change people. Like Moses under the guidance of God, Elijah also chose a young man to train as his successor. An important matter for a youth worker to consider is what will happen to the young people when he leaves. Is his ministry that of performing and leading and theirs that of spectating and following? Will some youth have been discipled, equipped to do the work of the ministry? Has spir-

---

44. Gene A. Getz, *Sharpening the Focus of the Local Church.* (Chicago: Moody, 1974), p. 114.
45. See Rick Yohn, *Discover Your Spiritual Gift and Use It* (Wheaton, Ill.: Tyndale, 1974); Leslie Flynn, *19 Gifts of the Spirit* (Wheaton, Ill.: Victor, 1974); and Ray Stedman, *Body Life* (Glendale, Calif.: Regal, 1972).

itual power been transmitted? Ultimately it is God who changes people. We are dependent on Him. The Holy Spirit has come to change people into Christ's likeness. But He also works through believers as models of God's truth.

A most valuable asset in youth ministry is an incurable confidence in God's ability to change people. Teenagers, even collegians and young adults, will fail and will frustrate leaders and sometimes drive them close to despair. However, God is at work. He will accomplish what He alone can do. God does not call workers to be a success; he calls them to be faithful. Project what a man can become. Richard Halverson gives some needed words of assurance.

God Calls a Man

Gives him a vision . . .
Anoints him for its fulfillment.
Obedient to the call in the light of the vision and the power of the anointing—his labors are blessed with unusual results.
Others take notice . . .
Want to get in on the act.
They ask the man how he did it (the assumption being that if they did as he did, they would achieve as he achieved).
He begins to analyze what he did—comes up with the methods which were born out of the call, the vision and the anointing.
If enough people ask him how he did it—he'll publish a manual setting for the methods he used.
Then anybody can buy the manual—apply the methods—and get the same results . . . or so the idea goes.
Somehow the call—the vision—and the anointing are forgotten or ignored or subordinated to the mechanics.
As though God could not do another thing with another man.
As though God had run out of calls or vision or power.
As though God had no new ways to do what had never been done before.
How distinct the servants of God in the Bible—how different their ways of doing things—how incredible their effectiveness . . .
When each was himself as God called and envisioned and anointed him to be.
God has not changed. He wants to do the same today with those who will yield to Him—to be led by Him—allow Him to teach them His ways.[46]

Youth workers must be open to God to develop their own strategy of discipleship based on the needs of young people and their personal vision and motivation. The strategy presented in this chapter is a suggested model with variations that may be adapted to a variety of situations. For

46. Richard Halverson, *Perspective*, November 10, 1971. Used by permission.

too long discipleship training has been a distant second to programming. Long-term results come through the discipleship process. As Wiersbe suggests, youth ministry, to be biblical, must be "personal not institutional, real not artificial, practical not theoretical, creative not manufactured, courageous not timid, involved not isolated, and patient not immediate."[47]

FOR FURTHER READING

Bruce, A. B. *The Training of the Twelve.* Grand Rapids: Kregel, 1971.

Coleman, Robert E. *The Master Plan of Evangelism.* Old Tappan, N.J.: Revell, 1973.

Edersheim, Alfred. *The Life and Times of Jesus the Messiah.* Grand Rapids: Eerdmans, 1972.

Getz, Gene A. *Sharpening the Focus of the Local Church.* Chicago: Moody, 1974.

Henrichsen, Walter A. *Disciples Are Made—Not Born.* Wheaton, Ill.: Victor, 1974.

Hyde, Douglas. *Dedication and Leadership.* South Bend, Ind.: U. of Notre Dame, 1964.

Kuhne, Gary W. *The Dynamics of Personal Follow-up.* Grand Rapids: Zondervan, 1976.

Miller, Chuck. *Now That I'm a Christian.* Vols. 1, 2. Glendale, Calif.: Regal, 1974, 1976.

Ortlund, Raymond C. *Lord, Make My Life a Miracle.* Glendale, Calif.: Regal, 1974.

Richards, Lawrence O. *Youth Ministry: Its Renewal in the Local Church.* Grand Rapids: Zondervan, 1972.

Skinner, Betty Lee. *Daws.* Grand Rapids: Zondervan, 1974.

Smith, Bob. *When All Else Fails . . . Read the Directions.* Waco, Tex.: Word, 1974.

Strommen, Merton P. *Five Cries of Youth.* New York: Harper & Row, 1974.

Webster, Dan, and McAllister, Dawson. *Discussion Manual for Student Discipleship.* Glendale, Calif.: Shepherd Productions, 1975.

Wilson, Carl W. *With Christ in the School of Disciple Building.* Grand Rapids: Zondervan, 1976.

Cassette Tapes on Discipleship

The Navigators, P.O. Box 1659, Colorado Springs, Colo. 80901.
Youth Specialties, 861 Sixth Avenue, San Diego, Calif. 92101.

---

47. Warren W. Wiersbe, "Biblical Basis of Youth Ministry" (Message preached at the Success with Youth Seminar, Detroit, Michigan, March, 1973).

15

Guiding Youth in Bible Study

Ardith Hooten and Emily Nicholson

A GENERAL REVIVAL of religious interest is sweeping the youth culture to-day. Youth are asking basic questions about the meaning of life. But due to the influence of fanatical cults which are rooted in mysticism or pseudo-Christian teaching, young people often accept false anwers as truth.

Alison's case is not atypical.[1] Reared in a religious home, she lost interest in religion during high school. But, as a college freshman, she was plagued by guilt feelings. Wrestling with unresolved spiritual problems, Alison was an easy prey for the religious cult that swept her into their discussions about behavior, dress, religious beliefs, and life goals. They dealt with "things I needed to think about," Alison explained. They also quoted Scripture, out of context and distorted, to support all they said. "This got me so turned around I didn't know if anything I was doing was right," she admitted. It took Alison and her parents a year of agony and soul-searching before she was finally freed from the demonic grip the cult had on her mind and emotions.

Alison is one of the more fortunate ones—she escaped from the soul-destroying, personality-wrecking cult that had literally enslaved her. But according to anthropologist Irving Zaretsky of the University of Chicago, an estimated 250,000 young Americans have "given over their lives" to cults. Another million maintain "some sort of continuous contact with them," often cutting off all ties with family and friends as proof of their devotion. The problem is growing, affecting not only college students but high school young people as well.

1. Charles Remsberg and Bonnie Remsberg, "The Rescue of Alison Cardais," *Good Housekeeping*, April 1976, pp. 108, 134-41.

ARDITH HOOTEN, M.A., is High School Curriculum Editor, Scripture Press Publications, Wheaton, Illinois.

EMILY NICHOLSON, B.A., formerly Young Teen curriculum editor for Scripture Press Publications, Wheaton, Illinois, is now a free-lance writer.

William Rambur, president of the Citizens Freedom Foundation, an organization of parents whose children have been or are presently involved in a cult, estimates that 1,800 fanatical cults like the international organizations of the Children of God, Hare Krishna, the Guru Maharaj Ji's Divine Light Mission, and the Sun Myung Moon's Unification Church, are now operating in this country. They recruit thousands of gullible followers through massive publicity campaigns, or crisscross the country on so called "evangelistic" missions.[2]

According to a national study by the Who's Who Among American High School Students Association, 88 percent of the top high school students in the United States believe in a personal God, and 82 percent believe religion is still relevant in today's society.[3] But believing in God and being religious does not ensure young people that they have found God's premise for possessing eternal life or for enjoying the abundant life Christ promises His committed followers (John 10:10).

Many cults spout Scripture to trap naive seekers into believing they have the right answers to "the meaning of life." But to Christ's church, the body of Christ, indwelt by His Holy Spirit and entrusted with teaching the revealed Word of God, falls the responsibility of leading seeking young people to Christ ("the way, the truth, and the life," John 14:6) and then of guiding them to handle "accurately the word of truth" (2 Tim 2:15, NASB).

The goals Christ gave His followers for carrying on His work till He comes are: (1) to make disciples, and (2) to teach them to observe all His commands (Matt 28:19-20). How does the body of Christ best reach these goals? Through the ministry of teaching.

In every local gathering of the body of Christ there are always those to whom the Holy Spirit has given the gift of teaching (1 Cor 12:27-28). But having a call to teach is just the beginning of the teaching-learning process described and illustrated in various places in Scripture.

The following scriptural studies (1 Thess 2:4-12; Col 1:9-10) are based on Paul's ministry to early Christians. They provide valuable insights into the person of the teacher and the way an effective teacher structures his class to foster student responses and spiritual growth.

THE PERSON OF THE TEACHER

In writing to the Thessalonian Christians, Paul outlined five important areas in which a person should qualify for a teaching ministry.

2. Ibid., p. 134.
3. *Youth Today*, April 1975. (Currently named *Youth Letter*, published by The Evangelical Foundation, 1716 Spruce Street, Philadelphia, Pa.).

Pattern for Teaching Ministry *1 Thessalonians 2:4-12* (NASB)
1. CALLING "Approved by God to be entrusted with the gospel" (2:4)
2. Motive "We speak, not as pleasing men but God, who examines our hearts" (2:4). No "flattering speech" nor seeking "glory from men, either from you or from others" (2:4-6).
3. RELATIONSHIP "Gentle among you, as a nursing mother tenderly cares for her own children" (2:7). "Having thus a fond affection for you, we were well-pleased to impart to you not only the gospel of God but also our own lives, because you had become very dear to us" (2:8). "You are witnesses, and so is God, how devoutly and uprightly and blamelessly we behaved toward you" (2:10).
4. METHODS "Exhorting and encouraging and imploring each one of you as a father would his own children" (2:11).
5. GOAL "So that you may walk in a manner worthy of the God who calls you into His own kingdom and glory" (2:12).

How do the areas Paul outlined apply to a person who wants to teach youth effectively?

1. CALLING

A teacher must receive his calling from God—not man—and take his responsibility seriously.

A teacher's *calling* grows out of his relationship with the Lord. His love for Christ compels him to accept his position as Christ's personal representative, knowing he has been commissioned with God's message of reconciliation (2 Cor 5:14-21). His commitment to the Lord and His will motivates him to seek God's presence in prayer, to rely on His power realistically, and to read God's Word with an increasing longing to know his Lord better.[4] Since he has found in Christ the one relationship that

4. Ada Zimmerman Brunk and Ethel Yake Metzler, *The Christian Nurture of Youth* (Scottdale, Pa.: Herald, 1960), p. 2.

surpasses all others in joy, comfort, self-revelation, life-fulfillment, and practical guidance, he longs for teens to experience a relationship with Christ for themselves. For these reasons, a teacher of spiritual truths needs to feel his specialness. Special—not in his own abilities and Christ-likeness, necessary as these qualities are—but to be special in his understanding of the Holy Spirit's work in his own life and in his unshakable faith that the Holy Spirit can also do a great work in the lives of the teens he is teaching.

2. MOTIVES

He must be motivated by love for and a desire to please God.

Naturally a teacher's relationship with God affects his *motives* for teaching.

A Sunday school publishing house editor who conducted a survey among local Sunday school teachers of high school teens reveals the following motives for teaching: "I like kids"; "I enjoy kids' company and want to know them better"; "It's an outlet for Christian service"; "I was asked to teach"; "The class produces growth in me"; "I am a schoolteacher so I took the class because they needed a teacher."[5]

Paul was not affected by motives such as these; instead he made pleasing God his aim (1 Thess 2:4-6). And pleasing God doesn't mean merely being active in religious activities. It means responding to God in love and allowing Christlike love to be the motivating factor for all Christian service—including teaching.

3. RELATIONSHIP

A teacher must develop and express a Christlike love in his relationship with his students.

Right motivation for teaching stems from love for Christ and obedience to His commands. This opens up an entirely different *relationship* with others. "Love one another; as I have loved you" (John 13:34) Christ told His first followers and all succeeding ones.

How did Jesus love? Selfishly? In a performance-centered way with His eye on what He got out of it? No, Jesus' love was costly. It involved loving even at personal loss—and giving that others might gain. Jesus loved, and consequently died for people while they "were yet sinners" (Rom 5:8). This is the kind of relationship Paul illustrated when he said, "We were well-pleased to impart to you not only the gospel of God but also our own lives, because you had become very dear to us" (1 Thess 2:8, NASB).

5. Ardith Hooten, *Survey of Sunday School Teachers for High School Youth*, 1975.

How does a teacher develop this kind of love? Good resolutions often fly out the window when confronted with an absolutely impossible-to-love-in-my-own-strength young person. And that is just the secret. Christ has equipped His body to carry on His work by giving to each believer His gift of the Holy Spirit. As a believer gives himself over to the Holy Spirit's control, he finds that the Holy Spirit produces His fruit in his life—the first part of the cluster is *love* (Gal 5:22-23) . This love is graphically depicted in 1 Corinthians 13. A teacher who studies this chapter will find that these love characteristics develop into practical guidelines in his relationship with young people.

A loving teacher does not see himself as the "great authority" to his students. He knows he is also a learner in a state of constant growth and change in his relationship with his Lord. He knows he cannot change the attitudes or actions of his young people. Neither can he make the Bible come alive to them nor produce spiritual growth. This knowledge keeps him humble as he assumes the role of an instrument of the Holy Spirit.[6]

As a Sunday school teacher, he takes his role as a model seriously. He realizes that young people's ideas of what God can do in a person's life may depend on what they see God doing in their teacher's life. Students' ideas of the reality and relevance of the Bible to their lives may depend on how they see the Bible fitting into their teacher's life. Since the Holy Spirit really does the teaching (John 16:13) a human teacher simply helps by arranging the circumstances to facilitate the Spirit's effectiveness. Arranging of circumstances includes getting youth actively involved in inductive Bible study, in-depth discussions, and meaningful activities that can cause them to consider how biblical truth applies to their lives. By getting youth "into" the Word, a human teacher sets the stage for the Holy Spirit to do His work in motivating students to respond to God and His Word.[7]

A loving teacher goes out of his way to become familiar with the everyday world of his students. He tries to keep aware of the present youth culture—life-style, motivations, and goals—for he knows this is the world his young people face when they leave his class. He does not minimize the influence this "culture" has on his students nor make light of the conflicts it often produces even in his most "spiritual" students.[8]

A loving teacher sees his teens as individuals—not stereotypes. Although

6. Ardith Hooten and Paul Heidebrecht, *Teaching Today's Teens* (Wheaton, Ill.: Victor, 1976), pp. 31-32.
7. Ibid.
8. Lawrence O. Richards, *You and Youth* (Chicago: Moody, 1973), pp. 80-81.

he is familiar with the general characteristics of the age-group he is teaching, he doesn't try to squeeze his young people into a mold they are supposed to fit. For instance, a young teen may be surprisingly mature in accepting responsibility, while a high school teen or college person may buckle under at the slightest touch of "being on his own" or "thinking for himself."

A loving teacher knows his young people's needs—generally and specifically. He prayerfully tailors his lessons to help throw light on God's provisions for those needs.

Youth's general needs include: (*a*) receiving salvation; (*b*) knowing God, His will and ways, and how He directs each individual personally as he desires God's plan to unfold for him; (*c*) growing and maturing spiritually—learning to relate to other Christians and unbelievers in Christlike ways; (*d*) knowing how to appropriate God's wisdom, guidance, and strength in overcoming pressures, problems, and temptations; (*e*) learning to accept themselves as individuals of worth who can make meaningful contributions in others' lives; (*f*) being accepted as a person and as part of a group; (*g*) establishing a biblical value system; and (*h*) finding a purpose for their lives.[9]

A loving teacher has a good understanding of the specific needs of the age-group he teaches. For instance, young teens especially need a caring teacher who can identify with and lovingly accept their often up-and-down moods, their hunger to belong to the group, their groping for a self-identity, and their desire to be independent though this desire is coupled with a fear of the unknown, mature world "out there." Young teens constantly ask, though not in specific words, "Who am I? Why am I here? Where am I going with my life?"

Though many of these young teen characteristics carry over into the high school years, older teens are more independent and more concerned about the future than young teens. They appreciate a teacher who relates to them as a friend, but whose Christian maturity they can draw on and respect. High schoolers relate best to a teacher who can take in stride their clowning around, their constant drive for activity, their preoccupation with the opposite sex, and their questions and doubts about the validity and relevance of the Bible, God, and Christian faith. A high school teacher should be a good listener, be flexible, have a keen sense of humor, and be able to guide teens through doubts and rebellion to establish a faith in God that stems from a genuine inner love response and not a superimposed set of rules.

9. Norma Felske, *Teaching That Grabs Young Teens* (Wheaton, Ill.: Victor, 1976), pp. 11-12.

If teens have not established a faith of their own by the time they reach college age, they will be even more vulnerable to worldly, cult, and occult influences. A teacher of college and career age young people must be keenly aware of the many false philosophies their students constantly face and be prepared to guide them in developing a solid Christian apologetic. He may also need to provide "a home away from home" to give warmth and security to young people who are away from home for the first time. An understanding, listening ear will be helpful as he seeks God's wisdom in guiding students through problems with self-worth, singleness, relationships, sex, parents, grades, loneliness.

Because they need to exercise increasing independence and develop their potentials, both high school and college young people need ever broadening opportunities for Christian service and leadership.

In addition to knowing the general needs of the particular age-group he teaches, a loving teacher knows even more about the individuals in his class. He knows what each individual is facing *now*. For instance, he knows and cares that Gary's father lost his job, Tom had a tiff with his best friend, and Carl is "bombing out" of math and his father barely speaks to him as a result.

On the other hand, a loving teacher is never nosey. He relies on the Holy Spirit's promptings for mutual sharing. He knows his relationship with his teens is a two-way street, and he shares his life as transparently as he accepts his teens' sharing their lives with him.

A loving teacher spends time with his students. It is not the amount of time spent that matters, but the quality of time spent and the teacher's attitude of really caring about and wanting to be with his students.

One busy teacher of inner-city girls, who were scattered across a large city, learned to make every contact meaningful. "Some of our deepest confidences were exchanged at the water cooler between Sunday school and church," she admitted. But the love-bonds forged then remain strong even now that the girls are young women.

A loving teacher treats each young person with respect and, as a result, refrains from putting him down or betraying a confidence.

A loving teacher is flexible and able to keep himself and his students in the proper perspective by maintaining a sense of humor.

One teen was going through a critical stage, when she evaluated everything and everyone—and usually reacted negatively. Though her adult confidante often felt like "setting her straight," she prayed for patience and for the Holy Spirit to produce His fruit of love and tolerance in the girl's heart— for the girl was a sincere Christian. A year passed. Then one day after a frank discussion on some of life's issues, the girl said, "I don't know what's wrong with me. I seem to have changed my mind about so many things and people."

Her adult friend smiled and said, "Well, for one thing, you're not six-teen anymore." A loving teacher remembers that no one is thirteen or sixteen or twenty-one forever. Young people mature, grow in tolerance, and usually change their opinions many times in their progress along the bumpy road from adolescence to adult status.

4. METHODS

A teacher must develop specific teaching techniques based on his under-standing of and love for his students' needs and on his desire to com-municate God's message to them.

See chapter 28 for creative methods that foster maximum student par-ticipation, thus involving them in personal encounters with God and His Word.

5. GOAL

A teacher must keep in focus the goal of leading teens to Christ and en-couraging spiritual growth.

The means a teacher chooses are the means by which he, as the Holy Spirit's partner, helps young people reach the goal of living "lives worthy of the God who is calling you to share the splendour of his own kingdom" (1 Thess 2:12, Phillips).

STRUCTURING THE CLASS TIME FOR SPIRITUAL GROWTH

A teacher uses all the means at his disposal to communicate God's Word to his class because he knows that God's Word works effectively in all be-lievers (1 Thess 2:13). In his prayer for the Colossian Christians, Paul graphically describes how the Word of God works effectively in believers (Col 1:9-10). This spiritual growth should be taken into consideration when structuring the class hour.

How will a teacher who teaches for spiritual growth structure the class-time?

1. PREPARATION

He realizes teaching is spiritual work and must be done through a spir-itually prepared person.

The apostle Paul constantly prayed for his "students" (Col 1:9). Prayer is an important part of a teacher's *preparation.* He must not think of prayer as a few brief words muttered, however sincerely, when he has finished planning his lesson for a class period. He takes seriously Jesus' words: "It is the man who shares my life and whose life I share who proves

Pattern for Spiritual Growth *Colossians 1:9-12* (NIV)		
1. P R E P A R A T I O N	**PRAYER** "We have not stopped praying for you" (1:9)	
	3. P L A N	**FOCUS** (students' interests, felt and real needs)
		DISCOVER (Bible truth) "We have not stopped . . . asking God to fill you with the knowledge of His will" (1:9) (life implications) "through all spiritual wisdom and understanding" (1:9)
		RESPOND (personal applications) "that you might live a life worthy of the Lord and may please Him in every way"
2. P U R P O S E	**TEACHING AIM:** changed lives (1:10-12) Bear fruit (action) "bearing fruit in every good work" Know God better (knowledge) "Growing in the knowledge of God" Mature spiritually (spirit) "So that you may have great endurance and patience" Enjoy life with God (attitude) "and joyfully giving thanks to the Father" Receive full inheritance as God's child (soul) "Who has qualified you to share in the inheritance of the saints"	

fruitful. For the plain fact is that apart from me you can do nothing at all. . . . But if you live your life in me, and my words live in your hearts, you can ask for whatever you like and it will come true for you. This is how my Father will be glorified—in your becoming fruitful and being my disciples" (John 15:5-8, Phillips) .

A teacher should begin his preparation by first prayerfully applying the lesson to himself, and then bringing each student and his needs to the Lord so He can definitely direct the teacher's preparation. As he does this, he is opening the door in a practical way for the Lord to work in each student's life.

E. M. Bounds's exhortation, though spoken to pastors, aptly fits the person who is carrying out the ministry of teaching today: "What the Church needs today is not more machinery or better, not new organizations or more and novel methods, but men [teachers] whom the Holy Ghost can use—men [teachers] of prayer, men [teachers] mighty in prayer. The Holy Ghost does not flow through methods, but through men. He does not come on machinery, but on men. He does not anoint plans, but men— men of prayer."[10]

Lois LeBar has written, "In order to teach others, we must be in vital union with Christ and be filled with the Word and the Spirit. We must live in the part of the Word we teach until it becomes a living part of ourselves, until it is being worked out practically in our own everyday lives. Only then are we free to listen to and respond to others. Only then can we use the Word flexibly in relation to the spontaneous demands of our class."[11]

2. PURPOSE

He builds the lesson around a clearly defined aim.

Paul had a definite aim in mind as he ministered. Every lesson is built around an *aim*.[12] Stated in terms of a lesson aim, the life response should be something the teacher wants to see happen in the lives of his students as a result of their personal encounters with God and His Word. The life-response aim is usually stated in terms of behavior or action—an outward expression of an inward response to God. For instance, the life-response aim for a lesson on giving might be: to motivate teens to give of themselves and their material possessions in a specific outreach ministry of their church.[13]

10. E. M. Bounds, *Power Through Prayer* (Chicago: Moody, n.d.), p. 8.
11. Lois E. LeBar, *Education That Is Christian* (Westwood, N.J.: Revell, 1958), p. 196.
12. Hooten and Heidebrecht, *Teaching Today's Teens.*
13. For more on this subject, see chapter 3, "Objectives and Standards for Youth Work."

3. PLAN

He plans for a teaching-learning process that helps get youth into God's Word and God's Word into youth.

With this life-response aim clearly in mind, a teacher can begin planning for in-class guided discovery learning—a Bible-based, life-related, teaching-learning process that helps get youth into God's Word and God's Word into youth.

In the guided discovery learning process, the methods chosen should help students: (*a*) *focus* attention on the lesson topic; (*b*) *discover* Bible truths and their practical applications for youth today; and (*c*) actively *respond* to God as He reveals Himself and His will to them through the Bible truth discovered. Of course, methods are not ends in themselves; they are means to an end. Used correctly, methods are carefully planned activities led by the teacher to guide students toward a specific life response.

This way of teaching God's Word is designed to meet learner needs, not to display a teacher's talents. It becomes a process of discovery for each learner who is actively involved in discovering and applying truth to himself. He is not passively sitting by while only the teacher goes through the process and receives the blessing.

(*a*) *Focus. The aim of this part of the lesson plan is to motivate students for the day's Bible study by focusing on youth interests and needs to be dealt with by the Bible passage.*

Methods which might accomplish this aim include role play, case study, question and answer, skit, personal testimony, thought questions, agree/disagree, and debate.

(*b*) *Discover. The aim of this part of the lesson is to guide teens in discovering specific Bible truth and how it relates to teen life today.*

Having just focused on some interest, need, or questions that relate to the Bible passage, teens should be motivated to discover what the Bible has to say. This step appeals mainly to youths' intellects and focuses on what the students should *know* as a result of this Bible study. A teacher who uses this opportunity to lecture is usually doomed to disappointment. Just as the Holy Spirit indwells every believer, so does He instruct every believer. A teacher who assumes his role as the Holy Spirit's partner will also trust the Holy Spirit to teach teens through the personal study of the Word. A teacher should help students dig out biblical facts and principles for themselves, using such questions as, What does it say? What does it mean?

Many methods can be effectively used here: question and answer; Bible search either by individuals or by groups; research reports; outlining;

paraphrasing; lecture can also be effective but should be used only occasionally and for some truths which the teacher will need to state or clarify.

Who, what, when, and *where* questions help students discover facts as they study the Bible passage in its full context, trying to understand what the author was saying to his original readers before determining what the passage means for Christians today. *Why* and *how* questions help students link what they have discovered in the Word with their own experiences. The methods chosen here should guide teens in thinking about and verbalizing and even creatively expressing specific ways the Bible truth studied can make a difference in their attitudes and actions toward God, themselves, and others.

Now teens are ready for the ultimate aim of the lesson—personal response to God.

(c) Respond. This part of the lesson plan helps teens respond in obedience to God concerning the Bible truth just studied.

This step in the lesson appeals to teens' *emotions* and *wills*—what teens should *feel* and *do* in response to the truth studied.

From personal experience, a teacher should know that transfer of Bible truth to life does not come automatically. Exhortations to obey, or true illustrations of people who have obeyed some Bible truth are no guarantee that teens will do what they know they should do. The teacher must help each teen make a personal application of God's Word and give an opportunity to put that application, or response, into practice. Some methods that can be used effectively to do this are decision cards which personally express what the teen decides, creative writing assignments, personal evaluations, personal sharing, and personal and/or group projects.

Focus, discover, respond add up to a total learning experience that is a discovery from beginning to end. The lesson begins by surfacing teens' felt and real needs. Teens then turn to the Bible to discover how God's plan for the ages can meet their needs. Finally, each teen is given an opportunity to respond personally to God as He has revealed His will in His Word. This heartfelt response to God gives God the opportunity to change the teens' lives.

A teacher who allows the Holy Spirit to use his life as an investment in youths' lives will find that he wants to, and does, give his teens many things (refer to 1 Corinthians 13 again) :

He gives part of his time;

  a share in his money and material things;
  his love;
  his respect;
  his patience;

his prayers;
himself.

But his greatest gift to his young people will be leading them into the joy of the most satisfying relationship they will ever experience—a personal, growing relationship with Jesus Christ.

FOR FURTHER READING

Bowman, Locke E. *How to Teach Senior Highs.* Philadelphia: Westminster, 1963.

Brunk, Ada Zimmerman, and Metzler, Ethel Yake. *The Christian Nurture of Youth.* Scottdale, Pa.: Herald, 1960.

Drakeford, John B. *The Awesome Power of the Listening Ear.* Waco, Tex.: Word, 1967.

Edge, Findley B. *Helping the Teacher.* Nashville: Broadman, 1959.

———. *Teaching for Results.* Nashville: Broadman, 1956.

Felske, Norma. *Teaching that Grabs Young Teens.* Wheaton, Ill.: Victor, 1976.

Getz, Gene. *Audiovisual Media in Christian Education.* Chicago: Moody, 1972.

Gorman, Alfred H. *Teachers and Learners: The Interactive Process of Education.* 2nd ed. Boston: Allyn & Bacon, 1974.

Hooten, Ardith, and Heidebrecht, Paul. *Teaching Today's Teens.* Wheaton, Ill.: Victor, 1976.

Horne, Herman Harrell. *Teaching Techniques of Jesus.* Grand Rapids: Kregel, 1971.

Jenkins, Jerry B. *You Can Get Thru to Teens.* Wheaton, Ill.: Victor, 1973.

Johnson, Rex E. *Ways to Plan and Organize Your Sunday School—Youth.* Glendale, Calif.: Regal, 1971.

LeBar, Lois E. *Education That Is Christian.* Westwood, N.J.: Revell, 1958.

LeFever, Marlene D. *Turnabout Teaching.* Elgin, Ill.: David C. Cook, 1973.

Reed, Bobbie, and Johnson, Rex E. *Bible Learning Activities—Youth.* Glendale, Calif.: Regal, 1974.

Richards, Lawrence O. *Creative Bible Teaching.* Chicago: Moody, 1970.

———. *69 Ways to Start a Study Group and Keep It Growing.* Grand Rapids: Zondervan, 1973.

———. *You and Youth.* Chicago: Moody, 1973.

———. *You the Teacher.* Chicago: Moody, 1972.

———. *Youth Ministry: Its Renewal in the Local Church.* Grand Rapids: Zondervan, 1972.

Stoop, David A. *Ways to Help Them Learn—Youth.* Glendale, Calif.: Regal, 1971.

Zuck, Roy B. *Spiritual Power in Your Teaching.* Chicago: Moody, 1963.

16

Youth in Personal Bible Study

David H. Roper

AN INVITATION TO A NOBLE TASK

BIBLE STUDY is an ennobling adventure. According to the book of Proverbs, "It is the glory of God to conceal a matter, but the glory of kings is to search out a matter" (Prov 25:2, NASB). God delights in hiding treasure in His Word. It is our kingly task to search it out for ourselves and teach others how to bring forth out of that treasure "things new and old" (Matt 13:52, NASB). Luke wrote that the believers in Berea were more noble than those in Thessalonica "for they received the word with great eagerness, examining the Scriptures daily, to see whether these things [the things that were being taught] were so" (Acts 17:11, NASB). The Bereans appreciated the effort of their teacher (in this case the apostle Paul) and received his words eagerly, but their final authority was the Old Testament, and they evaluated every teaching in light of their firsthand investigation of the Word. Luke says that because of this attitude they were *noble*.

UPSIDE-DOWN BIBLE STUDY

During the Middle Ages the acme of wisdom was to reproduce what the church Fathers taught about the Bible, or to find the teachings of the Fathers in the Bible. For example, St. Benedictine wrote, "Scripture should be read and with it the exposition of the Fathers as a final explanation." And later in the nineteenth century, Victor Hugo wrote, "Learn what you should believe and then go to the Scriptures to find it there."

They turned the process upside down! And by this strange inversion they developed a system of Bible study that completely stifled individual investigation of the biblical text. Eventually, all interpretation of the

DAVID H. ROPER, Th.M., is a Ph.D. candidate in Near Eastern studies at the University of California, Berkeley.

Bible was based on the authority of *tradition* (the teachers of the Fathers and findings of the various councils), *translation* (in this case the Latin Vulgate), and *teacher* (the pope). They literally put the Bible under lock and key. Can it be that the vestiges of this system of interpretation are with us today?

LEARNING TO LIVE

The task of teachers of and workers with youth, basically, is to motivate young people to enjoy Bible study, and to teach them to understand or interpret the Scriptures so that they can live by them. And the task is crucial because one's relationship to Christ is linked to his understanding of the Word, as these verses indicate: "So faith comes from hearing, and hearing by the word of Christ" (Rom 10:17, NASB); "Many other signs therefore Jesus also performed in the presence of the disciples, which are not written in this book; but these have been written that you may believe that Jesus is the Christ, the Son of God; and that believing you may have life in His name" (John 20:30-31, NASB); and "Jehoshaphat stood and said, 'Listen to me, O Judah and inhabitants of Jerusalem, put your trust in the Lord your God, and you will be established. Put your trust in His prophets and succeed" (2 Chron 20:20, NASB).

Christ's words in John 5:39-40 (NASB) can keep us from confusing the process of Bible study with the product: "You search the Scriptures, because you think that in them you have eternal life; and it is these that bear witness of Me; and you are unwilling to come to Me, that you may have life."

The purpose of all Bible study, therefore, is to direct us to Christ and His power for living a new life. Paul wrote that "the goal of our instruction is love" (1 Tim 1:5, NASB), a new style of life derived from the indwelling life of Christ, not from mere facts or knowledge of the Bible. Paul wrote to Timothy about those who "wrangle about words," that is, make the investigative process the end (2 Tim 2:14-26). A preoccupation with Bible study itself is useless and ruinous (v. 14); leads to ungodliness rather than godliness (v. 16); upsets the faith of some (v. 18); and produces quarrels (v. 23). To approach Bible study this way is to be a workman who ought to be ashamed. On the other hand, God's approved workman handles the Word accurately (Gr., "cuts straight to the goal"). He uses the Word to teach, reprove, correct, and train (himself and others) in order that God's man may be an adequate instrument, ready for any demand (2 Tim 3:16). And therefore he has no reason to be ashamed.

READY TO LISTEN

The Scriptures are designed to reveal Christ and His will. It seems obvious, therefore, that an open heart is a primary consideration in Bible study. If a young person is unwilling to respond to the truth, then the entire process breaks down. Sometimes young people ask for help in studying the Bible because they are finding their own study unproductive. They believe that they merely lack a method that will open the Word to them. The first question to ask such persons is, "Are you willing to submit to what you discover?" Bible study is not merely an intellectual process. It is a spiritual issue.

God only reveals truth to those who are prepared to respond in obedience to it. Jesus' instruction to His disciples along these lines was, "Do not throw your pearls before swine" (Matt 7:6, NASB). That is a strong metaphor and its meaning is crystal clear. Truth is a precious thing and God will not allow it to be trodden underfoot or profaned in any way. The consistent witness of Scripture is that God withdraws light from those who spurn it (see, e.g., Isa 6:9-10; 8:16-17; Matt 13:10-17). But God lavishes truth on those who are hungry for it and willing to abide in it.

HEALTHY APPETITES

"Like newborn babes, long for the pure milk of the word that by it you may grow in respect to salvation" (2 Pet 2:2, NASB). Believers are to long for the Word as a newborn longs for milk. That desire can be stymied, however, by sin, much like sickness causes babies to lose their appetite. "Therefore, putting aside all malice and all guile and hypocrisy and envy and all slander, like newborn babes, long for the pure milk of the word" (1 Pet 2:1-2, NASB). Sins such as malice, guile, hypocrisy, envy, and slander are spiritual microbes that take away one's appetite for the Word. A Christian can regain his spiritual appetite for Bible study by recognizing and confessing sin in his life.

A NUMBER ONE REQUIREMENT—THINK

Bible study is not easy. The procedures are not difficult to explain, but the actual process of study involves patient labor. If there is a method of Bible study suggested in the Scriptures, it is found in 2 Timothy 2:7 (NASB), "Consider (Gk., 'keep putting your mind to') what I say, for the Lord will give you understanding in everything." Bible study, then, is a two-part process: our part is to think; God's part is to grant understanding. God always rewards diligent, mental spade work.

BASIC STEPS TO BIBLE STUDY

The following are some basic steps that will help youth workers guide teens in digging into the Word on their own. These steps are applicable for all occasions of teen Bible study whether in groups (Sunday school classes, youth groups, weekday clubs, camps, etc.) or individually. And they are relevant to junior highs, high schoolers, and college-age youth.

STEP 1: SELECT WITH THEM A UNIT OF STUDY

The unit may be a verse, paragraph, or chapter. Normally, a paragraph is a good place to begin. Sometimes, however, the verse, paragraph, or chapter divisions are in the wrong place. These divisions, as is generally known, are not part of the original texts. The Bible was not divided into chapters until A.D. 1205 and into verses until A.D. 1571. Though these divisions cannot be relied on completely for their accuracy, they do make a good place to begin. Of course, the passage to study may already be determined by curricular materials if a pubilsher's curriculum is being followed.

STEP 2: TEACH THEM HOW TO READ

Many young people lack zeal in Bible study simply because they do not read patiently or very accurately. They miss details because they do not read the passage enough times to see what it is actually saying.

Encourage young people to get accustomed to reading a passage between ten and twenty times. Obviously, it may not be possible for them to read a large section of Scripture that many times at one sitting, but it is feasible with smaller segments. G. Campbell Morgan, one of the greatest Bible expositors who ever lived, stated that this one principle was revolutionary to his early Bible study and is the basis of all accurate biblical interpretation.

A question Jesus frequently asked the Jews was, "Have you never read the Scriptures?" Of course they had. But in their reading they failed to see what was really there. Jesus in his controversy with the Sadducees based his entire argument for the resurrection (a fact which the Sadducees denied) on a present-tense verb (Matt 22:32). Jesus had an eye for detail. He knew how to "read" the Scriptures; the Sadducees didn't.

Basic to effective reading of the Bible is the ability to observe the details of the text. The following excerpt is a good example of the process of careful observation, illustrated by Alexander Agassiz, a great naturalist and teacher.

It was more than fifteen years ago that I entered the laboratory of Professor Agassiz, and told him I had enrolled my name in the scientific school as a student of natural history. He asked me a few questions about my object in coming, my antecedents generally, the mode in which I afterwards proposed to use the knowledge I might acquire, and finally, whether I wished to study any special branch. To the latter I replied that while I wished to be well grounded in all departments of zoology, I purposed to devote myself specially to insects.

"When do you wish to begin?" He asked.

"Now," I replied.

This seemed to please him, and with an energetic "Very well," he reached from a shelf a huge jar of specimens in yellow alcohol.

"Take this fish" said he, "and look at it; we call it a Haemulon, by and by I will ask you what you have seen."

With that he left me, but in a moment returned with explicit instructions as to the care of the object entrusted to me.

"No man is fit to be a naturalist," said he, "who does not know how to take care of specimens."

I was to keep the fish before me in a tin tray, and occasionally moisten the surface with alcohol from the jar, always taking care to replace the stopper tightly. Those were not the days of ground glass stoppers, and elegantly shaped exhibition jars; all the old students will recall the huge, neckless glass bottles with their leaky, wax besmeared corks, half-eaten by insects and begrimed with cellar dust. Entomology was a cleaner science than ichthyology, but the example of the professor who had unhesitatingly plunged to the bottom of the jar to produce the fish was infectious and though this alcohol had "a very ancient and fish-like smell" I really dared not show any aversion within these sacred precincts, and treated the alcohol as though it were pure water. Still I was conscious of a feeling of disappointment, for gazing at a fish did not commend itself to an ardent entomologist. My friends at home, too, were annoyed, when they discovered that no amount of eau-de-cologne would drown the perfume which haunted me like a shadow.

In ten minutes I had seen all that could be seen in that fish, and started in search of the professor, who had, however, left the museum; and when I returned, after lingering over some of the odd animals stored in the upper apartment, my specimen was dry all over. I dashed the fluid over the fish as if to resuscitate it from a fainting fit, and looked with anxiety for a return of a normal, sloppy appearance. This little excitement over, nothing was to be done but return to a steadfast gaze at my mute companion. Half an hour passed, an hour, another hour; the fish began to look loathsome. I turned it over and around; looked it in the face—ghastly; from behind, beneath, above, sideways, at a threequarters view—just as ghastly. I was in despair; at an early hour I concluded that lunch was necessary; so with infinite relief, the fish was carefully replaced in the jar, and for an hour I was free.

On my return, I learned that Professor Agassiz had been at the museum, but had gone and would not return for several hours. My fellow students were too busy to be disturbed by continued conversation. Slowly, I drew forth that hideous fish, and with a feeling of desperation again looked at it. I might not use a magnifying glass; instruments of all kinds were interdicted. My two hands, my two eyes and the fish; it seemed a most limited field. I pushed my fingers down its throat to see how sharp its teeth were. I began to count the scales in the different rows until I was convinced that that was nonsense. At last a happy thought struck me—I would draw the fish; and now with surprise I began to discover new features in the creature. Just then the professor returned.

"That is right," said he; "a pencil is one of the best eyes. I am glad to notice, too, that you keep your specimen wet and your bottle corked."

With these encouraging words he added,

"Well, what is it like?"

He listened attentively to my brief rehearsal of the structure of parts whose names were still unknown to me; the fringed gill-arches and movable operculum; the pores of the head, fleshly lips, the lidless eyes; the lateral line, the spinous fin, and forked tail; the compressed and arched body. When I had finished he waited as if expecting more, and then, with an air of disappointment:

"You have not looked very carefully; Why," he continued more earnestly, "you haven't seen one of the most conspicuous features of the animal, which is as plainly before your eyes as the flesh itself. Look again, look again!" And he left me to my misery.

I was piqued; I was mortified. Still more of that wretched fish. But now I set myself to the task with a will and discovered one new thing after another, until I saw how just the professor's criticism had been. The afternoon passed quickly, and when towards its close, the professor inquired:

"Do you see it yet?"

"No," I replied. "I am certain I do not, but I see how little I saw before."

"That is next best," said he earnestly, "but I won't hear you now; put away your fish and go home; perhaps you will be ready with a better answer in the morning. I will examine you before you look at the fish."

This was disconcerting; not only must I think of my fish all night, studying, without the object before me, what this unknown but most visible feature might be, but also, without reviewing my new discoveries, I must give an exact account of them the next day. I had a bad memory, so I walked home by Charles River in a distracted state, with my two perplexities.

The cordial greeting from the professor the next morning was reassuring; here was a man who seemed to be quite as anxious as I that I should see for myself what he saw.

"Do you perhaps mean," I asked, "that the fish has symmetrical sides with paired organs?"

His thoroughly pleased, "Of course, of course!" repaid the wakeful hours of the previous night. After he had discoursed most happily and enthusiastically—as he always did upon the importance of this point, I ventured to ask what I should do next.

"Oh, look at your fish!" he said, and left me again to my own devices. In a little more than an hour he returned and heard my new catalogue.

"That is good, that is good!" he repeated, "but that is not all; go on." And so for three long days he placed that fish before my eyes, forbidding me to look at anything else, or to use any artificial aid. "Look, look, look," was his repeated injunction.

This was the best entomological lesson I ever had—a lesson whose influence has extended to the details of every subsequent study; a legacy the professor has left to me, as he left it to many others, of inestimable value which we could not buy, with which we cannot part.[1]

Suppose someone revealed the location of a fabulous treasure chest, outfitted ten young people with shovels, and sent them out to dig. However, he failed to tell them the depth at which the chest would be found. Those who located it would do so not because they had a special shovel, but because they persisted. In a similar manner, effective Bible study requires observation and persistence. It is an arduous and time-consuming process, but the results are certain for those who persist. Encourage teens to read and reread a Bible passage until they see "wonderful things from [the] law" (Psalm 119:18, NASB). Encourage them to have paper and pen handy to jot down their observations or note their observations in their Bibles as they read.

STEP 3: SHOW THEM HOW TO OBSERVE THE STRUCTURE OF LANGUAGE

Observe words. Are certain words (or synonymous or similar words) repeated? Repetition of a term or idea may give teens a clue to the meaning of a passage. For instance, note the number of times the same word occurs in the following passage: "For men will be lovers of self, lovers of money, boastful, arrogant, revilers, disobedient to parents, ungrateful, unholy, unloving, irreconcilable, malicious gossips, without self-control, brutal, haters of good, treacherous, reckless, conceited, lovers of pleasure rather than lovers of God" (2 Tim 3:2-4, NASB). From the repetition of this word, it becomes obvious that the problem with the men Paul was referring to was one of misdirected love.

1. Appendix, *American Poems* (Houghton Odgood, 1880).

Note the order and sequence of words. The order of words in a sentence, particularly words that are arranged in series can be significant. For example, note 2 Timothy 3:10-11 (NASB): "But you followed my teaching, conduct, purpose, faith, patience, love, perseverance, persecutions, sufferings, such as happened to me at Antioch, at Iconium and at Lystra; what persecutions I endured, and out of them all the Lord delivered me!"

The arrangement of these terms seems to be deliberate and suggests that Paul is leading Timothy to a particular conclusion.

Define words that are unknown or difficult to understand. Have teens look up difficult words in an English dictionary or Bible dictionary. Or they may want to define the words by their use in Scripture, using a Bible concordance. In studying a word, it is helpful to note first how the human author uses it elsewhere in the book being studied, and then to note how he uses it in other writings. After that, the word can be observed in other portions of Scripture. The surest guide to the meaning of a word is how the author uses that term in the particular book being studied. For example, if a student is trying to determine the meaning of the term "entrusted" in 2 Timothy 1:12, a concordance would reveal that the word occurs three times in that epistle: in 1:12, 14; and in 2:2. Then it can be discovered that the same word occurs a number of times in 1 Timothy. Since both books were written to the same individual, it can be assumed Paul used the term consistently; thus something about the word can be learned by its use in his first letter.

Another way to define words is to compare translations. For example, the New American Standard Bible translation of 2 Timothy 2:15 reads: "Be diligent to present yourself approved to God as a workman who does not need to be ashamed, handling accurately the word of truth." How does one handle the word accurately? The Jerusalem Bible reads, "has kept a straight course with the message of the truth." The Beck version reads, "as he teaches the Word of truth in the right way." Comparing translations will often help a person understand the shades of meaning of the original word behind the translation.

At times the very passage being studied may define an unknown or difficult word. In 2 Timothy 3:17 (NASB) the term "adequate" is defined by the following phrase "equipped for every good work."

Observe grammar and syntax. In order to be effective in their Bible study, teens need an elementary understanding of the parts of speech in a sentence (grammar) and their relationship to one another within the sentence (syntax). It is essential to know something of English grammar and syntax in order to understand the argument of a passage. The following brief review, using various Scripture portions from 2 Timothy (NASB), will refresh their thinking.

The parts of speech are as follows, with the italicized words in parentheses illustrating the various parts:

Nouns denote a person, place, or thing (*"Paul* an *apostle* of *Christ Jesus,"* v:1).

Verbs tell or assert something about a person, place, or thing ("I *thank* God ... as I ... *remember,"* 1:3).

Adverbs modify (describe, limit, or qualify) verbs, adjectives, or other adverbs ("He *eagerly* searched," 1:17).

Pronouns substitute for nouns in order to avoid the monotony of repeating the same noun ("The Lord grant mercy to the house of Onesiphorus for *he* often refreshed me," 1:16).

Prepositions are placed before nouns or pronouns to relate them to other words. They are words such as *in, on, by, with, to, for, from, through, into.* There are approximately sixty English prepositions. ("Guard, *through* the Holy Spirit, who dwells *in* us," 1:14.)

Conjunctions join together words, phrases, or clauses ("Kindle afresh the gift of God ... *for* God has not given us a spirit of timidity," 1:7).

It is important to note several facts about nouns. In *number,* nouns may be singular or plural (e.g., "our *works,"* 1:9, plural, "His ... *purpose,"* 1:9, singular). Also *gender* denotes whether a noun or pronoun is masculine (*"he* was in Rome," 1:17), feminine ("she"), or neuter ("it"). In *person* the subject varies in its relationship to the speaker. The speaker may indicate himself (first person, *"I* have fought the good fight," 4:7), or the one addressed (second person, *"you,* be sober," 4:5), or a person or object referred to (third person, *"they* will not endure," 4:3).

Adjectives modify nouns ("The standard of *sound* words," 1:13). The *indefinite article* denotes any one of a class of objects (*"a* holy calling," 1:9), whereas a *definite article* designates the noun as known or particular (*"the* will of God," 1:1).

Several facts may be noted about *verbs.* As to *voice,* the verb may view a state or action as either performed (active, "I *remind* you," 1:6) or received (passive, "I *was appointed,"* 1:11). The *mood* of a verb reflects the attitude of the speaker or actor. The *indicative* mood is used to state a fact or ask a question ("I *suffer* hardship," 2:9). The *imperative* mood is used to express a command or entreaty (*"Be strong* in the grace that is in Christ Jesus," 2:1). The *subjunctive* mood expresses doubt, contingency, or possibility ("They *may come* to their senses," 2:26). The *tense* of a verb indicates the time of action. English has six tenses, but the three most important are past ("I *have kept* the faith," 4:7); present, ("I am *being poured out,"* 4:6) ; and future ("They *will* not *endure,"* 4:3) . *Adverbs* may modify the verb ("The Lord . . . will bring me *safely* to His heavenly kingdom," 4:18) .

It is also important to observe the relationships that exist between various parts of speech. Conjunctions frequently indicate what sort of connection exists between words, phrases (incomplete sentences used as members of a compound or complex sentence) , and clauses. Relationships can be classified as follows:

Series or progression, designated by: *and, moreover, furthermore, likewise, then* ("It will lead to further ungodliness, *and* their talk will spread like gangrene," 2:17) .

Contrast or alternative, designated by: *but, on the other hand, nevertheless* ("and thus they upset the faith of some. *Nevertheless,* the firm foundation of God stands," 2:18-19) . In this example the contrast is this: the faith of some is being upset; however, by contrast, God's foundation is unshakable) .

Conclusion or inference, designated by: *therefore* ("You *therefore,* my son, be strong," 2:1; on the basis of certain facts presented before, be strong) .

Reason or cause, designated by *because, since, for* ("In the last days difficult times will come. *For* men will be lovers of self," 3:1-2; the last times will be difficult because men will love themselves, etc.) .

Result or purpose, designated by: *that, so that, in order that* ("No soldier in active service entangles himself . . . *so that* he may please the one who enlisted him as a soldier," 2:4; his purpose for remaining unencumbered is to please the one who enlisted him) .

Condition, designated by: *if* ("*If* a man cleanses himself from these things, he will be a vessel for honor," 2:21; one will be an honorable vessel on the condition that he cleanses himself from these things) .

Comparison, designated by *even as, as, as so, than, like, just as* ("Their talk will spread *like* gangrene," 2:17; the comparison introduces an analagous thought or illustration to explain the action or thought of the main clause.)

STEP 4: OBSERVE THE CONTEXT

The next major step is to see the passage in its proper context. In order to do this, have the teens read the paragraphs immediately before and after the unit. Then enlarge the setting by reading the chapters that precede and follow the unit. In some cases it may be necessary to read the entire book. And ultimately, of course, the entire Bible forms the setting for any unit of study. However, for practical reasons it is usually sufficient to read the immediate context (paragraph or chapter surrounding the section being investigated). It is helpful to note particularly any conjunctions or connective devices that introduce the unit. For example, 2 Timothy 2:1 (NASB) opens with the statement, "You therefore . . . be strong in the grace that is in Christ Jesus." The chapter division would suggest a new subject. However the presence of the conjunction "therefore" would indicate that the new material in this chapter is a conclusion based on certain facts given in chapter one. Thus, in order to interpret chapter two correctly, the student would need to know the facts in chapter one. Context is very important because much of Scripture is a reasoned argument rather than a homily of isolated facts. Understanding the context of any passage will help young people grasp the flow of the passage.

STEP 5: OBSERVE THE HISTORICAL/CULTURAL SETTING

The next step is to understand the historical-cultural background of the passage. In one sense this step is another aspect of context, although at this point the concern is historical rather than literary. The Bible, of course, is rooted in history. These things "happened" to people in Bible times (1 Cor 10:6). Their writings, therefore, are colored by place, time, circumstances, and the prevailing view of their time.

Knowing the author and those he is addressing is helpful. Teens can transfer mentally to biblical times and reconstruct their environment, by asking these questions: Where were they located geographically? Why were they there? What were they doing? What was the political, social, and religious climate of that day? What is the purpose of the author? What did he have in mind? What problems existed in the church at that time? A good Bible dictionary is an indispensable tool for uncovering this sort of information.

STEP 6: INTERPRET THE PASSAGE

Now that the young people have read and observed the passage in its grammatical-historical-cultural setting, they should have some understanding of its meaning. Following are some principles for guiding teens in interpreting the passage.

Assume the normal, socially accepted meaning of words. God has spoken to man in conventional language. Therefore, normal rules of grammar and syntax can be applied to the language of the Bible. The Bible should be interpreted as any other piece of good literature would be approached. Without question, the Bible is a unique document, and therefore cannot be regarded as a normal piece of human literature. However, God chose to convey truth through the medium of human language, and all languages are subject to laws and are not arbitrarily understood. The uniqueness of Scripture does not mean that the sense of a passage is gained by reading it backwards or vertically or by skipping every other word. Nor can the reader make words mean anything he wants them to mean. We are subject to the laws that govern that language. Therefore interpret Scripture according to the way language is conventionally understood. Interpret history as history, poetry as poetry, figures of speech, allegories, metaphors, and other symbolic languages as those literary forms would normally be used. The safest course is to assume a literal meaning for Scripture unless it is obvious that a symbolic meaning is intended.

Scripture is the best interpreter of Scripture. Bring all of Scripture to bear on the passage studied. Other passages in the same book may be helpful, along with material by the same author. Since the Bible is a harmonious whole, any single passage must fit into the overall teaching of Scripture. The Reformers called this principle the "analogy of faith." By that they meant that truth in one portion of the Bible must correspond or be analogous to truth in other portions. In other words, the Bible agrees with itself. There are no internal contradictions. A unit of study may be compared with analogous teaching elsewhere in the Word, by checking cross references for parallel passages (cross references are found in the margins of most Bibles). Any interpretation that clearly contradicts the uniform teaching of Scripture should be discarded.

STEP 7: APPLY THE TRUTH

This step, of course, is the necessary conclusion of all Bible study. Application is true worship. Jesus said the Father seeks worship that is inward, "in spirit," and based in "truth" (John 4:23). Worship is essentially response to revelation. God's Word is not intended to be good advice or one possible option for life. It is a revelation to which man must respond. Therefore Bible study is not the end of the process but merely the means by which we discover and respond to God's will.

When young people have completed a study of any passage of Scripture, have them ask themselves these applicational questions:

Is there some command here which I must obey?
Is there some promise which I may claim?
Is there some sin I must avoid?
Is there some danger to which I must be alert?
Is there some fact to share with a friend?
Is there some truth which I should ponder?
Is there some encouragement for the days ahead?

READY TO STUDY

For personal Bible study, teens should be encouraged to find a quiet place and time during the day when they can study uninterruptedly. Tools essential for Bible study include a Bible (preferably a New American Standard Bible or other modern translation) ; pen and paper; and a Bible dictionary, a concordance, and an English dictionary. These tools, though somewhat expensive, are an invaluable investment for future Bible study.

The diligent student of God's Word works as carefully as a person panning gold. He diligently searches for and sifts that which is of value to him. Such diligence in study will show teens that the Bible is a priceless possession, more valuable than money or food (Psalm 19:7-10; 119:72).

FOR FURTHER READING

Ezell, Mancil. *Youth in Bible Study/New Dynamics.* Nashville: Convention, 1970.

Gettys, Joseph M. *How to Enjoy Studying the Bible.* Richmond, Va.: Knox, 1956.

Jensen, Irving L. *Independent Bible Study.* Chicago: Moody, 1963.

Job, John B., ed. *How to Study the Bible.* Downers Grove, Ill.: InterVarsity, 1972.

Miller, Chuck. *Now That I'm a Christian.* Vols. 1, 2. Glendale, Calif.: Regal, 1974, 1976.

Perry, Lloyd M., and Walden, Howard. *How to Study Your Bible.* Westwood, N.J.: Revell, 1958.

Richards, Lawrence O. *Creative Bible Study.* Grand Rapids: Zondervan, 1971.

Traina, Robert A. *Methodical Bible Study.* New York: Ganis & Harris, 1952.

Vos, Howard F. *Effective Bible Study.* Grand Rapids: Zondervan, 1956.

Wald, Oletta. *The Joy of Discovery in Bible Study.* Rev. ed. Minneapolis: Augsburg, 1976.

17

Youth in Worship

Julie A. Gorman

ANY TREATISE on worship must begin and end with God. The sum total of all efforts of worship must be for relating to Him. Worship centers on God! Worship is to God! Worship is for God! Worship satisfies God! To worship this One who is above all others is the most rewarding experience in which youth can participate.

Worship implies involvement in relationships with God and others. The Scriptures delineate three basic relationships for man. The primary relationship is that of man to God, a relationship restored in Christ. Like a clarion call from the beginning of time, Scripture emphasizes the priority of this relationship. Jesus' life and ministry were to the end that men know God. "This is eternal life, that they may know Thee" (John 17:3, NASB). All other relationships pale in the significance of this highest of commitments.

But knowing God means that God adopts us and relates us to others in the family of God. As second priority in our relationhips, He calls us to love others who know God. We worship shoulder to shoulder with all who know Him. Consistent with His desire that all may know and worship Him, God designed a third priority relationship—that of sharing God's love with an unbelieving world. Youth is a period of expanding relationships. Therefore, to guide youth in worshiping—to expand their horizons in understanding and appreciating God in His first priority—is a most exciting commitment.

If worship is to be the dynamic of an exciting relationship with God Himself, why then the lackluster image of worship in much of Christendom today? It has been described by various authors as "a lost art," "a missing jewel," and something "replaced by program."

Isaac Watts thought of heaven as a land where "congregations ne'er break

JULIE A. GORMAN, M.A., is Minister of Children and Family at the Whittier Area Baptist Fellowship, Whittier, California.

up and Sabbaths never end." Many have seen a grim humor in this description, and have sympathized with the little girl who told her mother she wanted to go to the other place, where there was "more going on."[1] Leaders of youth need to convince the next generation that worship is the action where there is "more going on" than in any other sphere of experience. True worship, as God intended it, is the most exhilarating and satisfying expression that a man can have. The word *worship* ought to quicken the believer's pulse, call forth joyous memories of wholeness, of being fulfilled with the Presence of the One for whom he was made. The psalmist expresses his delight this way: "Then I will go to the altar of God, to God my exceeding joy" (Psalm 43:4, NASB). This is the goal of worship—to get to God and to find Him to be "exceeding joy."

WHAT IS WORSHIP?

The English word *worship* is derived from the Anglo-Saxon *worthship*. It is defined by Webster as "courtesy or reverence paid to worth; hence, honor, respect." The original languages of the Scriptures carry the root meaning of "bowing down in homage." In surveying its biblical usage Richards observes that "the primary focus seen in worship . . . involves the response of God's people attributing worth to God for who He by nature is."[2] Worship acknowledges God's value, placing high esteem on His attributes and functions. It is responding to Him by saying, "You are great!"

TWO FILTERS

Jesus highlighted two factors in worship: "God is spirit; and those who worship Him must worship in spirit and truth" (John 4:24, NASB). Declaring God's worth must involve a man's heart, not just a cold, dispassionate rehearsal of His magnitude. True worship is for lovers of God whose hearts are passionate toward Him because of His Spirit within them fanning the flames of that relationship. The Spirit is the enabler when it comes to expressing the worthiness of God. "No one can say, 'Jesus is Lord,' except by the Holy Spirit" (1 Cor 12:3, NASB). The Spirit's encouragement and influence energize our spirits to declare Him worthy (Phil 3:3). He promotes our right attitude toward God and cultivates our enthusiasm and appetite for God so that "in spirit" we rise up to call Him blessed.[3]

1. Raymond H. Huse, *The Soul of a Child* (New York: Eaton & Mains, 1914), p. 121.
2. Lawrence O. Richards, *A Theology of Christian Education* (Grand Rapids: Zondervan, 1975), p. 286.
3. Raymond C. Ortlund, *Lord, Make My Life Count* (Glendale, Calif.: Regal, 1975), p. 41.

Worship is also built on a rationale—we are to worship *in truth*. The worshiper, using his mind to draw actively on all he knows about who God is, verifies what God has revealed about Himself. According to truth revealed and in true accord with what he believes about that truth, the Christian worships God "in truth." The Word of God serves as the guide and source of truth. Worship is not a function performed by all. It is the expression of the presence of life existent in the relationship between God and man. It may be labeled "for believers only."

TWO RESOURCES

Worhip is by lips and by life. It is a whole person experience. Matthew 15:8-9 (NASB) quotes the uselessness of one without the other: "This people honors Me with their lips, but their heart is far away from Me. But in vain do they worship Me, teaching as their doctrines the precepts of men." Tozer capsules this concept of a life of worship:

> Keep reminding God in our times of private prayer that we mean every act for His glory. . . . Let us practice the fine art of making every work a priestly ministration. . . . Paul's sewing of tents was not equal to his writing of an Epistle to the Romans, but both were accepted of God and both were true acts of worship. . . . It is not what a man does that determines whether his work is sacred or secular, it is why he does it.[4]

Worship is *to* God; worship is *for* God.

WHY WORSHIP?

John gives a resoundingly clear answer for making worship imperative, not optional—the Father is seeking worshipers (John 4:23). That is the first answer to the question, "Why worship?" Can there be any more compelling reason for youth to worship? In worship both parties are satisfied (Psalm 36:8-9).

> Worship is the highest and noblest act that any person can do. When men worship, God is satisfied! "The Father seeketh such to worship Him." Amazing isn't it? And when you worship, you are fulfilled! Think about this. Why did Jesus come? He came to make worshipers out of rebels. We who were once self-centered have to be completely changed so that we can shift our attention outside of ourselves and become able to worship Him.[5]

A second answer to the question, "Why worship?" is that the Scriptures give numerous injunctions to worship. "Come, let us worship and bow down; let us kneel before the Lord our Maker" (Psalm 95:6

4. A. W. Tozer, *The Pursuit of God* (Harrisburg, Pa.: Christian Pubns., 1948), pp. 123, 127.
5. Ortlund, *Lord, Make My Life Count*, p. 37.

NASB) ; "Worship the Lord in the splendor of holiness" (Psalm 96:9, NASB margin) ; "Exalt the Lord our God, and worship at His holy hill; for holy is the Lord our God" (Psalm 99:9, NASB). The Bible also gives frequent examples of worship, such as: Israel, Exodus 33:10; Moses, Exodus 34:8; Christ's disciples, Luke 24:52-53.

The benefits of worship to the worshiper are verified both biblically and historically. These benefits include "fulness of joy [and] pleasures forever" (Psalm 16:11, NASB) and "honor for those who honor God" (1 Sam 2:30, NASB). Frank Laubach declares: "But why do I constantly harp upon this inner experience? Because I feel convinced that for me and for you who read there lie ahead undiscovered continents of spiritual living compared with which we are infants in arms."[6] For youth with their venturesome spirit, the church must unveil those "undiscovered continents of spiritual living" that can be seen only by worship-filled vision. God seeks youthful worshipers.

THE FORMS OF WORSHIP

BOTH PRIVATE AND CORPORATE

The Scriptures illustrate that centering on God in worship may be either a private or a corporate experience. Both are necessary in a youth's walk with God. To encourage and instruct youth in getting to God regularly on their own is to build mature men and women in Jesus Christ. The habit of personal devotion to God Himself can make the difference as to whether young people win or lose in the daily struggle of living for God. Both Daniel 6 and Psalm 1 exemplify the strength of the believer who daily focuses on God privately. George Fox wrote, "It is a wonderful discovery to find that you are a temple, that you have a church inside of you, where God is. In hushed silence, attend to Him. 'The Lord is in His holy temple!' "[7] He is in believers! Youthful worshipers need to be taught how to "practice the presence of God." Jesus Himself maintained a deliberate flow of time with men encompassed by focus on God. The frequent retreats to mountains or lonely places serve as "presence oases" in the midst of deserts of unbelief and need.

Equally stressed by God's Word are the times of group worship where believers become one in their responses of worthiness to the King. In corporate worship, youth can experience the reality of Jesus' desire for oneness among believers.

One hundred pianos all tuned to the same fork are automatically tuned,

6. Frank C. Laubach, *Letters by a Modern Mystic* (Westwood, N.J.: Revell, 1958), p. 16.
7. Cited in Ortlund, *Lord, Make My Life Count*, p. 14.

not to each other but to another standard to which each one must individually bow. So one hundred worshipers met together, each one looking away to Christ, are in heart nearer to each other than they could possibly be were they to become "unity" conscious and turn their eyes away from God to strive for closer fellowship.[8]

Corporate worship is not going through an order of service, nor is it evaluating the participants in front, nor checking to see who is there. Worship is for God. Everything that is done there must be for God. "Whether the people in the congregation ever discover it or not, they are the actors. The up-front people are the prompters, whispering cues as needed—and God is the Audience, looking on to see how they do."[9]

> Worship means attributing worth to deity. This is best accomplished when we talk to God rather than about God. By definition sermons, announcements or any part of a service addressed to the congregation belong in another category. The church is at worship when the assembly speaks directly to God in praise or thanksgiving regarding His matchless qualities.[10]

Formal corporate worship services should be planned to enable the participants to get to God. The structure, however it may be organized, needs to include elements that are addressed to God. "Opening exercises, "special entertainment," and "song fests" are usually not worship. Worship is meeting God and centers all attention on Him.

Several occasions in the educational program of the local church provide opportunities for young people to participate in meaningful worship experiences. These include the youth programs, midweek prayer meetings, camping experiences, and of course the Sunday morning and evening church services. These experiences in group worship can help a teens own private worship of the Lord.

THE TEACHING OF WORSHIP

Why teach worship rather than just letting it happen? In the Garden of Eden God communicated to man the way he could please him. In Israel's exodus from Egypt, God undertook an extensive education of His people as to how He wanted to be worshiped. Succeeding events and teachings added information and expressions of worship. But even today, many who have gone to church for years have not yet learned to worship. Instruction on the meaning of worship from God's viewpoint is foundational to teaching youth ways to worship.

8. Tozer, *Pursuit of God,* p. 97.
9. Anne Ortlund, *Up with Worship* (Glendale, Calif.: Regal, 1975), p. 13.
10. Richards, *A Theology of Christian Education,* p. 289.

HOW CAN WORSHIP BE TAUGHT?

Since God is the author and cultivator of worship, the best curriculum and course outline may be found in the Scriptures. God communicated what was important, and then allowed man to experience the wonder and joy of getting to Him. Expose youth to biblical experiences of worship, looking for what the worshipers said about God, what they did to express their responsiveness, and the results accompanying each worship encounter. Study such passages as Exodus 15; 1 Chronicles 15–16; 29; 2 Chronicles 5–7; Isaiah 6; Revelation 7; 19. Investigate the private worship experiences of David (Psalm 34), Moses (Exod 33), and Daniel (Dan 6). A sample study follows.

PSALM 66: A STUDY IN WORSHIP

Read through the psalm looking for the theme of the psalmist's worship (praise to God for His deeds).

1. According to this psalm, what has God done?
   a. His feats of history demonstrate miraculous protection (v. 6).
   b. He executes sovereign ruling (v. 7).
   c. He demonstrates omniscience and awareness of world affairs (v. 7).
   d. He provides preservation in living (v. 9).
   e. He provides security for the believer (v. 9).
   f. He tests His people (v. 10).
   g. He puts difficulties into our existence (vv. 11-12).
   h. He provides restoration in abundance (v. 16).
   i. He hears prayer (v. 19).
   j. He responds in lovingkindness (v. 20).

   What are some of God's deeds in our lives?

2. How does the psalmist suggest that one worship this Mighty Doer?
   a. Shout joyfully (v. 1).
   b. Sing (vv. 2, 4).
   c. Marvel at His deeds (v. 3).
   d. Tell each other what God has done for us (vv. 5-9, 16).
   e. Bless Him (v. 8).
   f. Declare His praise (v. 8).
   g. Come to Him with offerings (vv. 13, 15).
   h. Follow through on promised commitments (v. 13).

   What are ways we can worship God for His deeds in our lives?

   How can we call others to "come and see the works of God" (v. 5, NASB) and to "come and hear . . . what He has done" (v. 16, NASB)?

3. What principles of worship are found here?

Who is the focus of the worship service in this psalm?

What is worship, according to this Scripture passage?

What attitudes does this passage suggest are necessary for worship?

What does this psalm teach about the expression of worship?

How can we experience what the psalmist experienced?

In light of the criteria and principles found in biblical accounts of worship, lead youth into a study of the elements of worship.

ELEMENTS OF WORSHIP

Scripture. What part did Scripture (or knowledge about God that came from Scripture) play in the above worship experiences? Study biblical passages on the attributes of God, such as His love, justice, creativity, holiness, eternality, wisdom, sufficiency, sovereignty, immutability, omniscience, omnipotence, omnipresence, truthfulness, faithfulness, infinity, goodness, mercy, unity, grace, patience, and trustworthiness. Or study God's activities, including His works as protector, shepherd, builder, creator, friend, counselor, father, promise-maker, physician, lover, provider, head, forgiver, and listener.

Experience a worship service using only Scripture. Use it to call people to God, to call on God, to extol Him with His own words, to sing His glories, to speak a litany of praise to Him. Instill the concept of excellence and meaning whenever Scripture is to be read. This means practice before using it in worship so that participants can concentrate on God rather than be self-conscious in reading. Teach the meaning of the Scriptures before they are used to praise.

Prayer. "Pray with the spirit and . . . pray with the mind [understanding] also" (1 Cor 14:15 NASB). Study biblical prayers for content and expression. Teach youth to write prayers that will lift others to God. Instill the concept of praying with as well as for others, of praying enthusiastically and with volume enough to lift the last row to God. Study prayer hymns as expressions of worship and silent prayer as a means of knowing God. Use the letters of the alphabet to praise the attributes and abilities of God (e.g., God, You are Almighty, Alpha, Blesser, etc.). Teach that prayer is: adoration (Psalm 111:1); confession (Psalm 51); thanksgiving (1 Thess 5:17-18); and supplication (1 Tim 2:1-2; 1 John 5:15).

Music. The book of Psalms offers a rich study on the place and use of music in worship. First Corinthians 14:15 reminds worshipers that songs are to be sung with the mind and with the spirit. In light of this, survey hymns and choruses for worship. Categorize these in terms of two questions: To whom is this hymn addressed? What function does it fulfill? (Praise?, Confession?, Inspiration?, Challenge?). Experiment with the power of music to call forth different attitudes and responses as it is played for worship. Music performed, like music participated in, must always call the believers to God, not to the person singing or playing. The books of First and Second Chronicles present God's plans for the ministry of music in the house of God. The choir is seen there as offering their service to God—not as entertaining the onlookers; their qualifications and responsibilites are also noted.

Offering. Look for the role of the offering in the previously mentioned Scriptures on worship experiences. Study the kinds of offerings that people made to God and discuss why these acts of giving are seen as worship by God.

Sermon, Story, Devotional. While frequently found in a worship service, this instructional element is not addressed to God and hence is not a part of the worshiper's adoration of Him. Rather, such information should be viewed as God speaking to the worshiper. The Word of God can speak truth to the believer who then responds in further worship. It is possible to plan a worship service, omitting this element, and to lead the participants in addressing God alone. What is important is that when any of the instructional items are included, opportunity for response must also be included. As believers, we need to listen to God and then respond to Him.

GENERAL PRINCIPLES IN WORSHIP

1. *Coordination.* Worship sequences that are selected on a theme build intensity of experience and reinforce meaning. Select a function or attribute of God as a basis for choosing which elements will be used in worship.

2. *Vertical dimension.* Is God central? Construct worship by using those ingredients which focus on God.

3. *Preparation.* Teach preparation of heart for worshiping God. Also teach preparation for leading others in worship. To lead others in worship requires preparation and practice. Think through transitions between elements.

4. *Participation.* Worship is not a spectator event. Too often the leaders perform and the audience evaluates. Involve worshipers in as many ways as possible in preparing, responding, joining the up-front prompters, following the words as music is played or sung. Build worship so that others can participate. After three minutes of leader-led prayer, a worshiper's mind begins to wander. Plan that he remain involved.

5. *Variety.* The poet-lover declares, "How do I love thee? Let me count

the ways." As lovers of the eternal God, Christians must continually find more modes of expressing their adoration to Him. The familiar ways are helpful because worshipers find expression comfortable through them. But the new expressions are also valuable because they bring fresh meaning to our responses. Worship need not always be quiet and meditative. "Shout for joy," declares the psalmist. "Clap your hands." Let youth worship Him with the energy and enthusiasm of the young. A loud worship service with guitars praises God as magnificently as a quiet one with organ music as long as it is genuinely directed to God.

6. *Leadership in the background.* Worship is to God. Leadership needs to become the unobtrusive enabler that helps people get to God. Announcing hymn numbers for those who have an order of service, vigorously leading songs, and introducing participants cause the worshipers to focus on mechanics and men. The more a worship experience is visibly "led," the less is the freedom to concentrate on God alone. Included below is a sample of a formal worship service.[11]

SERVICE OF MEDITATION
    We have come to meet with the Lord. Let us declare our holy intention with silence and reverence in the Sanctuary. Read the Scripture lesson of the morning. Meditate on the hymns. Draw near to God in prayer as we prepare for our ministry to the Lord.
Organ Prelude: Jesus, Lover of My Soul
Pastoral Welcome
Silent Prayer
Choral Call to Worship
SERVICE OF PRAISE
    Hymn: Praise the Lord! Ye Heavens
    Praises to God
    Gloria Patri
    Organ Praise
SERVICE OF PRAYER
    Choral Meditation: If My People
        If My people, which are called by my name
            shall humble themselves and pray, and
            seek My face, and turn from their wicked ways;
        Then will I hear from heaven, and will
            forgive their sin, and will heal their land.
    Pastoral Prayer and Choral Response   Praise & Confession to God
    Hymn: Dear Lord and Father of Mankind
SERVICE OF GIVING
    Organ Offertory

11. Adapted from Lake Avenue Congregational Church, Pasadena, California.

SERVICE OF PROCLAMATION
Reading of God's Word: Jonah 1 and 2
Message: "Confessions of Jonah"
SERVICE OF RESPONSE
Hymn: Who Is on the Lord's Side?
Benediction and Choral Response
Organ Postlude: Come Thou Almighty King

SUMMARY

While the elements of worship can be taught, the impetus for worship grows out of a youth's relationship with his God. The strengthening and enjoyment of this personal relationship will enhance each occasion of worship. Worship which is an encounter with God becomes the most satisfying spiritual experience believers can have.

> I cannot get God by holding Him off at arm's length like a photograph, but by leaning forward intently as one would respond to one's lover. Love so insatiable as the love of God can never be satisfied until we respond to the limit.[12]

FOR FURTHER READING

Armes, Woodson, and Ames, Sybil. *What Is Worship?* Nashville: Convention, 1965.

Blackwood, Andrew. *The Fine Art of Public Worship.* Nashville: Cokesbury, 1939.

Dobbins, Gaines. *The Church at Worship.* Nashville: Broadman, 1962.

Gudnason, Kay. *Complete Worship Programs for College Age.* Grand Rapids: Zondervan, 1956.

Laubach, Frank C. *Letters by a Modern Mystic.* Westwood, N.J.: Revell, 1958.

Miller, Randolph Crump. *Education for Christian Living.* Englewood Cliffs, N.J.: Prentice-Hall, 1956.

Ortlund, Anne. *Up with Worship.* Glendale, Calif.: Regal, 1975.

Ortlund, Raymond C. *Lord, Make My Life Count.* Glendale, Calif.: Regal, 1975.

Packer, J. I. *Knowing God.* Downers Grove, Ill.: InterVarsity, 1973.

Richards, Lawrence O. *A Theology of Christian Education.* Grand Rapids: Zondervan, 1975.

Rinker, Rosalind. *Prayer, Conversing with God.* Grand Rapids: Zondervan, 1959.

Tozer, A. W. *The Knowledge of the Holy.* New York: Harper, 1961.

——. *The Pursuit of God.* Harrisburg, Pa.: Christian Pubns., 1948.

Verkuyl, Gerrit, and Garner, Harold E. *Enriching Teen-Age Worship.* Chicago: Moody, 1950.

Wilson, John F. *An Introduction to Church Music.* Chicago: Moody, 1965.

12. Laubach, *Letters,* p. 58.

18

Youth and Music

E. Dee Freeborn

"THINGS ARE DIFFERENT NOW." So went the words of an old familiar chorus and so goes the world of youth and music. Changes in the last two decades have been staggering. The world of music has witnessed and experienced a revolution in styles, content, and performance that are unparalleled. Many agree that the genesis for such change came with the music of the Beatles in the early 1960s. Beginning in England, their music quickly found its way to the United States, to the delight of youth and the dismay of many church leaders. This nation has not been the same since.

With the explosion of youth music came a burgeon in the commercial music industry. Suddenly folk and pop gospel music were popular and profitable. In the religious as well as the secular world, fortunes were being made by the artists as well as the companies. Meanwhile, heroes of the youth music world came and went.

Certainly, heroes have their place. However, when it comes to Christian-entertainment heroes and their message of affluence, super-ability, and stunning beauty, many Christian leaders are questioning the false values which are often transmitted. In addition, many young people have been turned off or disillusioned by such superstars, knowing that they themselves will never look as good as their hero, sing as well, or play the guitar as well. On the youth music scene, we have to deal with the continuing encroachment of show business values.

An issue youth workers must face is the role of music as worship and sacrifice versus the role of music as performance for spectatorship and entertainment. In answering the question, What is the job of a Christian musician? Harold Best asserts, "To make his music first to God. It's his offering and sacrifice."[1] It is the difference between "doing" music for

1. Harold Best, "Music: Offerings of Creativity," *Christianity Today* (May 6, 1977), p. 12.

E. DEE FREEBORN, B.D., is Assistant Professor of Christian Education, Nazarene Theological Seminary, Kansas City, Missouri.

God, "making it big" so that one can "witness" for Him, or offering one's music to God in worship. Certainly some Christian musicians, by their personal commitment and their excellence in the field, witness with authenticity. Willing to pursue their music with dedication and discipline, they give it back to God in adoration, letting Him use it or not as an avenue of witness.

Out of the emphasis on performance comes also an expected stress on technical professionalism. In conventions and seminars on Christian music, workshops are offered on "Choosing Sound Systems," "Singing in the Studio," "Promotion," and "Stage Presence."

The whole question of commercialism and show business performance throws into penetrating light the question of values. Because of the power of music and musicians to educate and/or manipulate youth, the question of values is a continuing challenge. Wayne Rice has stated this problem well:

> Show business (i.e., the entertainment industry) provides the public with an escape from reality, yet the Gospel does just the opposite. Show business is a world of make believe—false fronts, make-up men and "beautiful people," while the Gospel is truth that hopefully does away with the false fronts and honors the ordinary, the lowly, the un-beautiful. A show business approach to presenting the Gospel non-verbally contradicts the very Gospel being presented.[2]

Harold Best sounds a similar alarm:

> Today we are inundated by an unprecedented quantity of music, literature, films, and art. In music the market overflows with anthems, folk music, cantatas, and that unscrupulous aggregate of pseudo-rock-folk-pop called "contemporary." Among these the ratio of quantity to quality is appalling. And it is all supposed to support a so-called radicalizing Gospel. Its advertising abounds with superlatives and "with it" slogans, as if to repeat back to the world in its own jargon such fallacies as that the value of a thing is determined by what it is called, not what it intrinsically is. So we mix entertainment with the crucial task of exposing a person to the whole force and weight of the Gospel.[3]

Though one may not agree totally with such an evaluation, it *is* cause for serious reflection.

In the same train of thought is the consideration of the person of the musician, and especially the one who will lead others through the avenue

2. Wayne Rice, "Rockin' Out in the Rockies," *Wittenburg Door* (October/November 1976), p. 5.
3. Harold Best, "There Is More to Redemption than Meets the Ear," *Christianity Today* (July 26, 1974), p. 16.

of song. The leader's values and life-style are important in any consideration of music and youth. In ministry, the integrity of the music leader
and the depth of his commitment to the living God through Jesus Christ
are crucial. The prime responsibility of the Christian is to glorify God,
to seek Him, and to enjoy Him (Rom 11:36, 1 Pet 4:11). Those who
would lead youth through music must continually evaluate themselves to
determine if this is their chief concern. Spradlin gives this sound counsel:

> If you expect to involve yourself in a personal relationship with God and
> yet do not recognize that your heart, as *was* Christ's, must be set safely
> on responding to God (as opposed to performing for Him on your own
> initiative), you cannot expect your life or your ministry to manifest the
> evidence of God's fullness in it.[4]

In a discussion of youth music one is driven back to view the underlying
issues at stake, though certainly all of them cannot be covered in this
brief treatment. Before he becomes involved in the mechanics of a music
program—directing choirs, choosing music, planning tours, creating ensembles, finding and developing soloists, formulating budgets, and the
like—a Christian musician must take a hard look at scriptural standards
and present-day culture and values and at how these impinge on his concepts of youth music and its place in ministry.

THE YOUTH MUSIC LEADER

Before examining philosophy and criteria for choosing music, some attention should be given to the role of the leader. The leader of music for
youth may be the youth pastor or minister to youth, youth director, minister of music, or an interested layman who loves youth.

Don Hustad provides suggestions for a job description for the youth
music leader.[5] Using the gifts mentioned in Ephesians 4:11-12, Hustad
aims his remarks at the minister of music, but they have validity for the
youth music leader as well. As a "prophet," the music leader will be concerned with choosing music whose texts do the most to bring God's Word
to the participants. He will be careful to work at helping youth grow in
their knowledge of the Word through music. As an "evangelist," the
music leader will be concerned that the message, which brings people to
God, will not be lost in the music, which may bring young people to the
performance. In a real sense, the leader of youth music has a great opportunity to be involved as a "pastor." Music provides an effective avenue

4. Bryon Spradlin in *What Do You Say to a Naked Spotlight?*, ed. Stephen Hilson
   (Melville, N.Y.: Belwin-Mills, 1972), p. 207.
5. Don Hustad, "Music Speaks . . . But What Language?" *Christianity Today* (May
   6, 1977), p. 16.

for shepherding and ministering as a believer-priest. Close to this concept is that of "teacher," probably the most important role to be played by the music leader.

In a more structured format, Easterling suggests the following outline of desired goals and objectives for the leader of youth music in a local church.[6]

1. He must encourage a growing musical knowledge as a basis for skill development, including the ability to read the music score; improvise and create music; use standard conducting patterns in leading hymn singing; interpret terms and symbols indicating dynamics and tempo; recognize the structure and form of music as represented in hymns, anthems, cantatas, and oratorios; reproduce rhythmic notation; and follow music directions.

2. His teaching should assist youth in developing the ability to use the singing voice correctly and expressively; to read the music score accurately; reproduce rhythmic notation; sing with a pleasing tone quality; sing with musical sensitivity; improvise and create music; sing with satisfaction during and following voice change; recognize faulty intonation; interpret terms and symbols indicating dynamics and tempo; recognize structure and form in music; develop a concept of appropriateness for music used in congregational services and meetings of church organizations; and sing in a music group with choral finesse.

3. He should encourage youth to develop the ability to play an instrument skillfully, artistically, and expressively. This includes the ability to read the music score; reproduce rhythmic notation; play a melody or accompaniment on some kind of instrument; improvise and create music; recognize faulty intonation; interpret terms and symbols indicating dynamics and tempo; recognize the purpose of instrumental music in the church; attain a superior tone quality; recognize music structure and form as represented in hymns, anthems, cantatas, and oratorios; and recognize the appropriateness of music used in congregational services and meetings of church organizations.

4. He should assist youth in developing the ability to lead others in musical experiences through the proper understanding and appreciation of music. This includes their ability to read the music score; sing confidently a voice part with other vocal and instrumental parts; improvise and create music; use standard conducting patterns in leading hymn singing; recognize faulty intonation; interpret terms and symbols indicating dynamics and tempo; recognize the purpose of music in the

6. R. B. Easterling, Jr., *Church Music for Youth* (Nashville: Convention Press, 1969), pp. 23-24.

church; recognize superior tone quality as produced by different voices and instruments; recognize music structure and form as represented in hymns, anthems, cantatas, and oratorios; and recognize the appropriateness of music used in congregational services and meetings of church organizations.

Choosing Music for Youth

One of the most serious tasks of a youth music leader is that of choosing music. Both lyrics and music become items of serious consideration. How does one judge such items as the words and message? By what criteria are the musical forms of the day to be evaluated? Orjala has suggested a list of criteria for such an important assignment.[7]

In evaluating lyrics, the first criterion is "theological adequacy." Some leaders may not be paying enough attention to this critical area. Certainly there is the constant danger that without adequate care and attention to words and their theological impact, leaders may very well confuse and misdirect youth. No doubt there is some connection here with the rise in "folk theology" and related shallow thinking which has been witnessed in recent years.

Closely aligned with this problem is that of overdoing certain theological themes to the neglect of others. For instance, some musical forms seem to major on personal salvation and the second coming, to the exclusion of other subjects which make up the whole of the Christian gospel.

On the other hand, as Orjala points out, there is a limit to the extent to which the theological criterion should be applied. The music can hold only so much theological content, and writers ought to be given some right of poetic license and use of modern metaphors as long as they are consistent with Scripture.

A second criterion to be applied to lyrics is their literary quality.

A third criterion is what Orjala terms "contemporary identification," by which he refers to spontaneity of style and contemporaneity of language. Though Orjala is concerned about the "over-seriousness" of some lyrics in traditional church music, his main concern is that much church music is not written in English that is readily understood. This may point toward a coming hymn crisis in which many of the old hymns, written in an English little used today, may find minimal acceptance, and only those written in modern English and those most loved by the people will survive.

Moving from lyrics to music, Orjala suggests four criteria for evaluation.

---

7. Paul Orjala, "Secularism and Church Music" (unpublished paper presented at the Church Music Symposium held at Nazarene Theological Seminary, January 27-28, 1977), pp. 10-11.

The first is again the question of "theology." Can the music help convey the Christian message to the intended hearers, or is it too closely identified with that which is incompatible with the Christian faith? More will be said about this in the comments on rock music.

Second is the technical criterion. Does the music come up to minimal levels of style and quality? Certainly folk-pop contemporary music ought to be expected to measure up to the same standards as any other musical art form.

A third criterion is that of communication. As Orjala puts it, "Does it meet the test of identification, acceptance, appropriateness, and cultural fit?"

The fourth criterion is the pragmatic. Does the music help people in meeting their needs? Do they understand it and identify with it? Is the church growing in right directions because of its help?

These seven criteria for judging lyrics and music give the youth music leader basic guidance in making responsible music evaluation. Contrary to such statements as Cook's that "it's not what or how you are performing that counts most; it's what you are getting done for eternity,"[8] most youth leaders will realize the serious implications of their work and ministry with teens and will be interested in more than just a pragmatic, and usually superficial, assessment.

In selecting music, the leader needs to be aware of the power of music not only to communicate but to manipulate. When a person is convicted of sin by the Holy Spirit and moves toward repentance and forgiveness, it is an emotional as well as a cognitive experience. One may be tempted to use music that simulates the same feelings, thus substituting the power of music for the power of God.

THE QUESTION OF ROCK MUSIC

At present, no other topic is capable of stirring so intense a difference of opinion among church members as the use of the rock idiom in church music. Some, no doubt, thought it would pass, but it has not. For the leader of teen music, rock and its related phenomenon, broadly called "contemporary music," will need to be reckoned with on more than just emotional grounds.

Cook quotes John W. Peterson as saying, "We should not be afraid of new music. The important thing is that the music, whatever its style or form, is linked to the absolute of the Word of God."[9] In the same article

8. Robert A. Cook, "That New Religious Music," *Moody Monthly* (April 1977), p. 43.
9. Cook, "That New Religious Music," p. 41.

Cook quotes Paul B. Smith of People's Church, Toronto, who says, "In music of any kind the name of the game is communication; and if we are not reaching people with our message through our music, then it has missed its point completely."[10]

An important question to be asked is this: Does the music do more than just carry the message? In other words, can the music itself, at least by association, convey a message antithetical to the Christian gospel?

In response to the assertion that the church has borrowed secular forms through the years, as did Martin Luther in particular, Best makes this observation:

> Borrowing to him (Luther) was only a small part of a rich means of expression. When he borrowed, he borrowed excellence only and left mediocrity to the devil. A skilled musician and a composer, he looked with the greatest admiration to the best music of his time, that of the composer Josquin des Prez. If Luther's total position were injected into the contemporary discussion of church music, it would make him very unpopular.[11]

Concerning the discussion of culture and the associations which become attached to certain forms of music, Best writes:

> Music has no moral meaning, no theological or philosophical meaning. But when a certain kind of music is done repetitively in a certain place, it comes to mean that place, that context. Music is abstract until you begin by repetition to link it to a certain circumstance, environment, or event. Then it begins to mean the event itself. Thus the term "sacred music." We have certain expectations about how sacred music should sound, not because there's an intrinsic thing called sacred music, but because by association we've come to expect certain things.[12]

It would seem, then, that borrowing may or may not be a good argument in the case of Luther and others. The historical context must be taken into account. It simply is not enough to say that earlier church hymn writers borrowed from their secular world; one must consider what they borrowed, its place in that culture at that time, and why they borrowed a particular form.

In the case of the associations attached to musical forms, it would seem that there is more to the argument than just the statement, "The style doesn't matter so long as the words are good."

Along this same line of reasoning, Rosfeld argues from a more technical approach, using the term "connotations," by which he means the associa-

10. Ibid.
11. Best, "There Is More to Redemption than Meets the Ear," p. 16.
12. Ibid., p. 15.

tions made between the music and some point of experience. The associations will often be essentially the same in meaning for all members of a society. Based on this approach to analysis, taken from Leonard Meyer's work *Emotion and Meaning in Music,* Rosfeld says,

> I would suggest that some secular musics have such strong connotative and kinetic non-Christian signification that these meanings persist when this music is brought into the sanctuary. I am not including all secular music in this judgment but I believe the large body of music referred to as "rock" does fall into this category.[13]

A kinetic aspect of rock music is the rhythm, which Rosfeld also believes poses problems for the music leader. Believing it to be a prime factor in such music and that it appeals to the senses, often beyond the control of rational evaluation, he finds it to be a powerful "musical language." Then he warns,

> Since it is so powerful, you may ask, is it not the ideal medium for a Christian message? No, because of its direct sensual thrust and its capacity to cause its devotees to relinquish self-control, the driving rock beat has some similarities to the music used by cults in African-influenced cultures which stress the giving of the self to spirit possession. But the Christian religion demands intellectual involvement and textual primacy in its message. We do not use hypnotic repetition to achieve the Holy Spirit's possession; we commit ourselves by a *conscious act of the will.* There is a big difference.[14]

Music ought to communicate in the culture's terms, but it must be careful to avoid associations that would be in opposition to, or in any way dilute or misdirect, the Christian message.

CONCLUSION

Few ministries provide more opportunities for influence than that of working with youth through music. The revolution in the music world has opened up greater possibilities of freedom in creativity and involvement—creativity in musical forms, in styles of presentation, in the writing of music not only for but by young people. Involvement has opened up to the extent that almost everyone, not just the super-talented, can be comfortable in some form of musical expression.

Youth workers have a great opportunity for teaching through music. Concepts of Christian life-style and doctrines of the faith can be shared as never before. What a tremendous opportunity to help young people learn what it means to worship God genuinely!

13. Rosfeld, "Secularism and Church Music," p. 4.
14. Ibid., p. 5.

Avenues for witness are unprecedented. With the continuing rise in the popularity of gospel music, the time is right for thoughtful, loving, telling witness through song.

"Speak to one another with psalms, hymns and spiritual songs. Sing and make music in your heart to the Lord, always giving thanks to God the Father for everything, in the name of our Lord Jesus Christ" (Eph 5:19-20, NIV).

FOR FURTHER READING

Best, Harold. "Music: Offerings of Creativity." *Christianity Today*, May 6, 1977, pp. 12-15.

Church Musician. Sunday School Board of the Southern Baptist Convention.

Hilson, Stephen, ed. *What Do You Say to a Naked Spotlight?* Melville, N.Y.: Belwin-Mills, 1972.

Hustad, Donald P. "Music Speaks . . . But What Language?" *Christianity Today*, May 6, 1977, pp. 16-18.

Ingram, Madeline D., and Rice, William C. *Vocal Technique for Children and Youth.* Nashville: Abingdon, 1962.

———. *A Guide for Youth Choirs.* Nashville: Abingdon, 1967.

Larson, Bob. *Rock and the Church.* Wheaton, Ill.: Creation House, 1971.

Lovelace, Austin. *The Youth Choir.* Nashville: Abingdon, 1977.

Meyer, Leonard. *Emotion and Meaning in Music.* Chicago: U. of Chicago, 1956.

Osbeck, Kenneth W. *The Ministry of Music.* Grand Rapids: Zondervan, 1961.

Routley, Erik. *Words, Music and the Church.* Nashville: Abingdon, 1968.

———. *Twentieth Century Church Music.* New York: Oxford, 1964.

Wilson, John F. *An Introduction to Church Music.* Chicago: Moody, 1965.

Wittenburg Door. October/November, 1976.

YOUTH MUSIC RESOURCES

Alexandria House
P. O. Box 300
Alexandria, Indiana 46001

Augsburg Publishing Company
57 E. Main Street
Columbus, Ohio 43215

The Benson Company
365 Great Circle Road
Nashville, Tennessee 37228

Broadman Music
127 Ninth Avenue North
Nashville, Tennessee 37234

Lillenas Publishing Company
P. O. Box 527
Kansas City, Missouri 64141

Sonshine Productions
501 East Third Street
Dayton, Ohio 45401

Word Records
P. O. Box 1790
Waco, Texas 76703

Youth Specialties
861 Sixth Avenue
San Diego, California 92101

Flammer/Shawnee   Zondervan/Singspiration
Delaware Water Gap   153 Louis Street, Northwest
Pennsylvania 18327   Grand Rapids, Michigan 49502

19

Youth Programs

Mark H. Senter III

THE YOUTH GROUP is alive and well in the last half of the twentieth century. The following examples illustrate this fact.

- Washington, D.C.: Each Wednesday morning, over two hundred high school people are drawn to a 6:30 Teen Breakfast Club to eat, fellowship, and hear biblical truth presented.
- Park Ridge, Illinois: Six hundred young people pack the church on Wednesday evenings, and another six hundred come on Thursday nights to identical three-hour youth-group meetings involving competition, musical and dramatic presentations, and straight talk from the Word of God.
- Trumbull, Connecticut: For eight years a musical group called the "Eastsiders," have taken summer trips to such places as Florida, Texas, California, the Midwest, and Alaska ministering the gospel through music arranged by their youth director.
- Arlington Heights, Illinois: Forty-three high school people and sponsors pedaled around Lake Michigan on bicycles rented from a Christian camp and gave evangelistic concerts each evening.
- Van Nuys, California: A local church employs four youth directors for their high school department alone.
- Snow Mountain Ranch, Colorado: Over fifteen hundred young people and sponsors attended a national youth conference sponsored by one of the nation's smaller evangelical denominations.

Why is all of this happening? A brief look at the recent history of the ministry to youth by local churches might be in order.[1]

Following World War II there was a rapid rise in ministry to young people outside the local church. Youth For Christ, Young Life, and, in

1. For more on this subject, see chapter 4, "A Historical Survey of Youth Work," and chapter 26, "Parachurch Youth Movements and Organizations."

MARK H. SENTER III, M.A., is Pastor of Christian Education, Wheaton Bible Church, Wheaton, Illinois.

time, Campus Crusade for Christ arose to reach high school and college students for Christ. Captivated by new methodologies and the commitment they produced, many of the key young leaders channeled their spiritual energies away from the local church and toward these parachurch organizations. Creativity abounded. Organizations were built. Ministries grew and churches began to accept what was happening.

In time local churches decided that their ministries could be strengthened if they would add to their staffs young men who were specialists in working with that group which had come to be known as "teenagers." Seminaries and Bible colleges became the recruiting places for potential youth workers. These men, not having had a strong youth ministry in their own churches, began modeling their ministries after the meaningful experiences which they had enjoyed in their parachurch organizations.

Youth ministry began to change. More churches began hiring full-time and part-time help. Christian Endeavor, which dominated youth work for so many years, began to give way to new concepts of youth work. Bible quizzing was introduced as an important part of denominational programs. Traditional youth choirs were transformed into sharp-looking, pleasant-sounding musical ensembles. Inductive Bible study became a way of life for certain groups. Drama was introduced. Personal evangelism was emphasized as young people went out with their leaders to tell others about Christ. The youth group had bloomed. It was never to be the same.

An interesting sidelight of this movement was the trend of parachurch organizations toward more direct evangelism and social involvement. No longer did they have to entertain the discontented children of the saints; their job was now more clearly defined—to present the whole gospel to the "now generation."

ESSENTIAL ELEMENTS OF MINISTRY

Meanwhile, back at the local church, youth pastors began seeking a biblical mandate for their ministries. In order to evaluate their ministry to youth adequately, they needed a standard by which to judge their priorities. The story of the church in the book of Acts provided just such a standard. Toward the end of the second chapter is a brief but powerful description of the basic elements which should appear in the local church wherever it is doing God's work. These elements should be part and parcel of the local youth ministry.

Luke told his readers that the believers "were continually devoting themselves to the apostle's teaching" (Acts 2:42, NASB). The ministry of the local church to young people must include the *learning* of biblical truth. This may be done through explanation or investigation, but it must be included.

The believers were also devoting themselves to *fellowship* (Acts 2:42). They shared their joys and sorrows and even their physical possessions with one another. This is a model which the youth group needs to follow. Some call it "community," others call it "love," sometimes it's referred to as *"koinonia,"* but no matter what it is called, it must be there.

A third element found in this early band of believers was *praise* (Acts 2:47). The days following Pentecost had become a celebration. Perhaps they were praising God for their salvation; perhaps it was for their fellowship or the teaching of the apostles; but more than anything else it must have been for God Himself. In a day when God has been relegated by many to the place of a "buddy," young people need the perspective of worshipful praise.

The final element found in the passage is that of *ministry* resulting in evangelism. Luke states that the "Lord was adding to their number day by day those who were being saved" (Acts 2:47, NASB). Ministry began when one believer ministered to another believer as need arose, and it ended with the place being crowded with new believers. Similarly, a healthy ministry to young people will include the salvation of their peers.

The Role of the Youth Group

As one looks at the educational agencies of the church, it is important to delineate the specific functions of each in order to insure that these four basic elements of healthy church life—teaching, fellowship, worship, and ministry/evangelism—are adequately covered on all age-levels. Worship needs should be met primarily through the corporate services of the church, though these needs may also be met on retreats, in camps, in small-group experiences or even through service opportunities. Learning experiences should be emphasized in the Sunday school, though they will happen elsewhere as well.

The youth group is left then with two primary responsibilities: fellowship and ministry. It is on these two functions that the youth group should focus.

Perhaps the best way to describe the youth group is as a laboratory for the Christian life. The youth group is an ideal place for helping teens discover and experiment with spiritual gifts. Spiritual gifts are channels for ministry, and young people need to discover which channels are theirs through being provided with many opportunities to minister to the body of Christ as well as to the world. In a laboratory one may fail, especially at first, in attempts to perfect a skill. So it must be with a youth group. Young people must have the freedom to fail—and to try again.

In the past the word *ministry* when applied to young people has been synonymous with stuffing bulletins, leading singing in youth group meetings, and trimming the hedges around the church. Today, however, ministry is being thought of in a much wider scope. Evangelism, comforting of the sick, ministries through music and drama, preaching and teaching, helping on specific projects, and many other forms of ministry are common today. The youth group has become a laboratory for developing spiritual gifts.

Another way in which the youth group serves as a laboratory is in relationship to experiencing truth. Through their formative years children perceive truth as words to be learned. As young people enter into their teenage years, their capacity to deal with abstract concepts tends to allow their minds to call these truths into question. It is extremely important that at this point in their development, young people have the freedom to express their doubts in a noncondemning atmosphere. Further, it is desirable that experiences be provided that allow young people to "live out" biblical truths as an outgrowth of learning situations. This implies, of course, a close tie between Sunday school and the youth group.

A third way in which the church youth group is like a laboratory is that it is a testing ground for Christian love. The non-Christian world in which young people live mocks love and substitutes shallow and often meaningless relationships. Young people have heard about love, but now is the time to experience love. There is a need to experience real *koinonia*. The youth group, more than any other agency in the church, is responsible to see that it happens. It is within the youth group that a positive counterculture needs to be formed that will affect the entire youth society.

MODELS OF YOUTH GROUPS

There are perhaps six distinct models of youth groups. Of course, the very nature of a model is such that it very seldom exists in its pure form. The model is helpful, however, in identifying basic elements which may then be applied in various ways within a program structure. It is in this light that the following models are offered:

The Christian Endeavor Model. Perhaps the oldest and most widely used model, especially in smaller churches, is the Christian Endeavor model, which is built around the idea that young people from the church are trained for leadership in the church through taking the responsibility of preparing and presenting programs to the youth group.[2] Traditionally this has happened on Sunday evenings when a team from within the youth

2. Fern Robertson, "Sunday Evening Youth Programs," in *Youth and the Church*, ed. Roy G. Irving and Roy B. Zuck (Chicago: Moody, 1968), pp. 214-17.

group leads a meeting relating to a given theme. Major publishing houses provide printed materials which serve as guides to young people and sponsors alike in their preparation for the various meetings. Activities for the group are centered around the Sunday evening meetings but also include socials, service projects, and retreats.

Fig. 19.1. *Christian endeavor model*

PHILOSOPHY

Train youth to serve the Lord through serving the group, specifically through the preparation and presentation of programs.

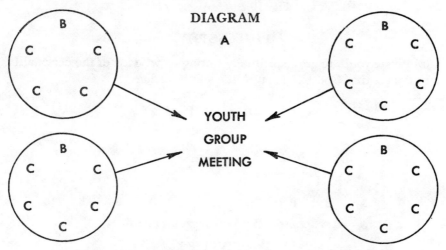

A = Sponsor; B = Team captains; C = Team members

ACTIVITIES

Small group preparation
Large group meetings
Social activities

The Hero Model. As local churches began employing youth directors, their youth groups tended to move away from the use of materials prepared by the publishing houses. The new breed of youth leaders tended to shape the youth group around their particular gifts and abilities. The philosophy of this model is as widely varied as the personalities involved. However, a common denominator seemed to be the basic desire on the part of youth leaders to use their God-given gifts to encourage spiritual growth on the part of young people. The youth-group meeting tended to remain the focal point of the group but strong emphasis was placed on personal relationships established between the youth director and the young person. The youth director was likely to visit the high school campus or other places where the youth group and their friends tended to congregate. The result was that young people gravitated to this person who really cared about them, and the ministry of the church to local youth was expanded. Of course, youth-group activities still included socials, service activities, and retreats, but these became occasions for strengthening relationships so that personal (one-to-one) ministry could happen at a later date.

Fig. 19.2. Hero model

PHILOSOPHY

Motivate youth to grow spiritually through a wise use of the personality and talents that God has given to the youth leader.

DIAGRAM

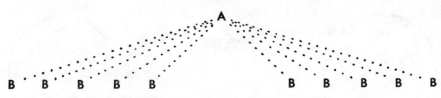

A = Sponsor; B = Youth group members

ACTIVITIES

Large group meetings
Large group socials
Evangelism done in meetings
Personal relationships established through follow-up
    conversations

The Evangelism Model. In some churches youth workers are chosen on the basis of their commitment to evangelism.[3] The youth group reflects this priority. In some cases the gospel is preached each week and public invitations are given whenever the youth group meets. In other cases, the group meetings become a training ground for personal evangelists, climaxed by evangelistic outreaches through coffee houses, socials, missionary

3. Elmer L. Towns, *Successful Biblical Youth Work* (Nashville: Impact, 1973), pp. 141-46.

trips, sharing the gospel in local shopping centers, and in personal contacts with friends at school. The common bond among all of the variations within the evangelism model seems to be an intense desire to reach the world in this generation.

Fig. 19.3. *Evangelism model*

PHILOSOPHY

Train youth to reach an ungodly world for Christ in their lifetime.

DIAGRAM

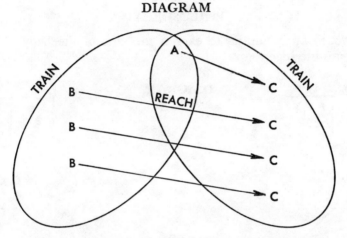

A = Sponsor; B = Youth group members being trained; C = Target
(young people being won and trained)

ACTIVITIES

Sharing the gospel
Training sessions
Growth groups
Evangelistic spectaculars
Social activities

The Involvement Model. The late 1960s was a period of activism among American youth. The question was not so much a matter of whether or not to become involved, but where. About the same time there came an emphasis on gifts of the Holy Spirit, most notably taught by Stedman in in his book *Body Life*.[4] Some youth workers put these two factors together

4. Ray C. Stedman, *Body Life* (Regal, 1972).

by emphasizing that young people discover their spiritual gifts by becoming involved in ministry situations.[5] Opportunities were provided to build up the body of Christ through music, drama, tutoring, multivisual presentations, puppet shows, missionary trips, evangelistic efforts, and aiding members of the church who had physical needs. The Sunday evening group meeting became an opportunity to prepare for definite, attractive, attainable ministry goals. Social activities and teaching/learning experiences tended to support and reinforce the ministry situations.

Fig. 19.4. *Involvement model*

PHILOSOPHY

Give youth opportunities to express the gifts of the body of Christ through ministering groups.

DIAGRAM

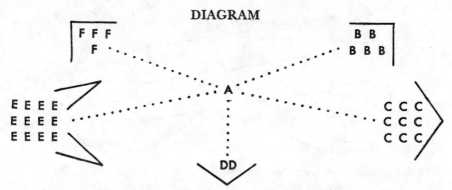

A=Sponsor; B-F=Groups of young people with similar interests who minister to the group or to others outside the group.

ACTIVITIES

Module planning
Module ministry
Feedback
Social activities

The Discipleship Model. Coleman's book, *The Master Plan of Evangelism,*[6] was another significant factor in youth work during the late

5. Mark H. Senter III, *Guiding Youth in Project Ministries*, Christian Education Monographs: Youth Workers Series, no. 6 (Glen Ellyn, Ill.: Scripture Press Ministries, 1971).
6. Robert E. Coleman, *The Master Plan of Evangelism* (Westwood, N.J.: Revell, 1963).

1960s. The emphasis of the book was not so much on world evangelism as on the training of disciples to become God's men in the world. The emphasis of this type of youth ministry switched from one person ministering to many, to that of one person ministering in depth to a few people who in turn would minister in depth to a few other people who would minister to others, until many people had been discipled. Many of the principles were drawn from the training strategy used by the Navigators under the leadership of Dawson Trotman.[7] The weekly meetings reflected this

Fig. 19.5. *Discipleship model*

PHILOSOPHY

Train youth to be God's people who will reproduce their lives in the lives of others (2 Tim 2:2) .

DIAGRAM

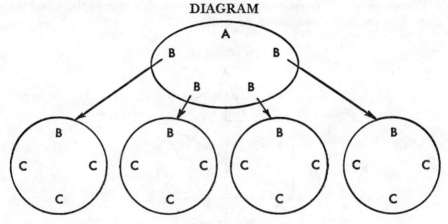

A = Sponsor; B = First-generation disciples; C = Second-generation disciples.

ACTIVITIES

Group Bible studies
Ministry within the group
Ministry from the group
Informal fellowship
Evangelism
Structured socials

7. Dawson Trotman, *Born to Reproduce* (Lincoln, Neb.: Back to the Bible, 1970), pp. 41-42.

emphasis. Bible teaching and sharing were stressed. Ministry and social functions tended to be an outgrowth of the small groups, though there still remained appropriate places for all-group social functions.

The Relevancy Model. In some churches, especially those in which social action was emphasized, the Sunday evening meetings became opportunities for arousing the social consciences of the high school people. Structure tended to be minimal and the effectiveness of the idea tended to be tied directly to the ability of the discussion leader to bring productive results from the meetings. In an age of activism, such as in the late 1960s, this model produced, on occasion, highly motivated learning and meaningful service.

Fig. 19.6. *Relevancy model*

PHILOSOPHY

Encourage youth to wrestle with the issues which confront them and the church in the midst of a watching world.

DIAGRAM

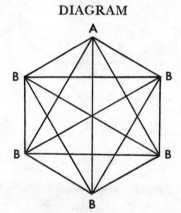

A = Sponsor; B = Young people

ACTIVITIES

Group discussions
Social activities
Ministry projects

THE ROLE OF ADULT LEADERSHIP

One of the most important factors in causing youth ministry in a local church to progress is the proper type of adult leadership. A church may have the finest group of young people imaginable but without solid, spiritual, and aggressive adult leadership, the group will seldom rise above mediocrity. Zuck and Robertson speak of the ideal youth sponsor as a coach.[8] Towns compares the sponsor to the director of a play in his emphasis on The Hero and Evangelism Models.[9] Both of these concepts convey the idea of a person who has a rather extensive knowledge of how a job should be done and how to guide young people who have natural potential but need to have it properly channeled.

There are, perhaps, three types of adult leaders or sponsors for a given youth group. In smaller churches, these functions may all be combined into one or two people. In larger churches a number of people will perform increasingly more specialized roles.

The *permanent sponsor* is the person designated by the Christian education board of the church to work with the youth of the church. He is permanent in the sense that he has been designated to work with the youth group for at least one year. It is preferable, however, that the permanent sponsor of high schoolers work with the youth group for at least one high school generation. This would be a four-year commitment in churches where the local high schools include grades nine through twelve. In many churches the permanent sponsor would be the youth director. In other cases a young adult who would be willing, after his formal education is ended, to spend three or four years working with the youth group before taking on heavy family responsibilities, may be ideally suited for the position. In other cases, it could be a mature college or seminary student or middle-aged couple who could best meet the needs of the young people. In all cases, however, the permanent sponsor must be a person who has a special love for young people and a willingness to invest the time necessary to allow young people to mature in their relationship to God, the local fellowship of believers, and the world for whom Christ died.

The primary responsibility of the permanent sponsor is in building relationships, establishing goals, planning, and motivating. Many permanent sponsors tend to omit the first two steps and to begin with the planning function.[10] Then when the young people are not motivated to become involved in the activities of the group, the sponsor tends to feel that he is not cut out for youth work. The truth lies more in the fact that he started at the wrong place in his attempt to minister to young people. He needs to take the time necessary to find out where the young people are

8. Roy B. Zuck and Fern Robertson, *How to Be a Youth Sponsor* (Wheaton, Ill.: Scripture Press, 1960), pp. 13-14.
9. Elmer L. Towns, *Successful Youth Work* (Glendale, Calif.: Regal, 1966), p. 137.
10. Lawrence O. Richards, *Youth Ministry: Its Renewal in the Local Church* (Grand Rapids: Zondervan, 1972), pp. 137-38.

in their personal and group development. Most frequently this is best done through personal conversations in which the sponsor concentrates on hearing what the young people are saying. Frequently the sponsor will find that he must spend four to six hours a week with young people apart from formal meeting time. In doing so he gains the ability and sensitivity necessary to establish goals which are compatible both with the needs of the youth group and with his own gifts and abilities.

A second type of sponsor is the *discipling sponsor*. This is a person or persons selected by the permanent sponsor to extend his ministry to more people on a more personal basis. The need for this second type of sponsor arises usually as a result of the numerical growth of the youth group. Sometimes this need will arise immediately. At other times it will not occur for more than a year. As a general rule, one discipling sponsor is needed for every eight to twelve young people in the group. Like the permanent sponsor, the discipling sponsor needs to commit himself to a minimum of one calendar year of working with the youth group and four informal hours with young people each week.

The responsibilities of the discipling sponsor are to extend the ministry of the permanent sponsor in developing personal relationships and in motivating young people toward the four basic functions of the local church: teaching/learning, fellowship, worship, and ministry. He will serve as a constant source of feedback from the young people to the permanent sponsor and will provide creative input as the permanent sponsor develops goals and outlines a model of youth ministry for the group.

The *temporary sponsor* is a third type of sponsor. He is a person who has been asked by the permanent sponsor to do a specific job for a limited amount of time. He might be asked to coach a play or direct a musical. He might be asked to sponsor a retreat or train the group for a specific task. However, when the specific task is done, then the temporary sponsor no longer has responsibilities within the group. Temporary does not mean interim, nor does it imply lack of ability or capacity. On the contrary, the temporary sponsor should be much more qualified than the permanent sponsor in the area in which he has been asked to serve.

THE ROLE OF PEER LEADERSHIP

Within any youth group at least three types of leaders emerge among the teens: formal or elected leaders, informal or opinion leaders, and cultivated or servant-leaders. There is a tendency for youth sponsors to rely on the first type, react to the second type, and long for the last type of leaders. The wise sponsor, however, will be well advised to use the dynamics of all three types of leaders to accomplish the goals established for the youth group.

The role of elected youth group officers is being seriously questioned in some circles today. The criticism has been made that the election of officers is a popularity contest, pure and simple; that election is based much more on the people one knows than on whether one is spiritually mature. Others have suggested that those elected are too frequently environmentally conditioned to provide the proper answers and exhibit the expected life-style, so they provide leadership for only a limited circle of similarly conditioned people.

Granting the validity of these observations, others have found elected youth group officers to be of great benefit to the total growth of the youth group. Elected officers tend to reflect the essential nature of a youth group. If the officers are social climbers, it is most likely that the rest of the group wishes they could be too. If the officers have a difficult time relating to the average non-Christian at school, it is quite likely that the rest of the group would be afraid if they were put into a social situation with an average non-Christian group at school. If this is true, then the sponsor would be well advised to start with the elected officers in an attempt to determine the group's needs and to motivate the group to deal adequately with these needs.

In every group there seems to be one or two people who hold no elected office but who are able to sway the mood of the group with only a word or two, spoken at the appropriate time. They tend to be on the fringe of the group both spiritually and socially. They tend to ask the questions which others are thinking but are afraid to ask. They are the ones who are going through a form of critical reevaluation of their faith and who have the potential for emerging as exciting and dynamic leaders in the days ahead.

The natural reaction to the informal leader is to rebuke such a leader for his attitude or actions, and sometimes this is necessary. The wiser course of action is to begin building personal relationships with the informal leaders based on mutual respect and understanding so that the opinion leader will begin to influence the group in positive directions or at least not hinder the positive directions of the group.

Perhaps the ideal type of peer group leadership is that of the servant-leader.[11] This is the young person who does not come to be ministered to, but to minister. The breed is rare. For the most part these leaders must be carefully cultivated by godly leadership over a period of time. This is done by example. It is done through a process of discipleship. For the most part, people will not recognize this type of leader until he is gone.

The role of peer group leadership in a local youth group cannot be overemphasized. Young people need to be a part of the decision-making

11. Ibid., p. 125.

process in order for them to feel a desire to become involved. If the only things young people are allowed to do in terms of leadership are to plan socials and prepare weekly programs, then apathy tends to set in midway through the high schooler's junior year, if not before. But if young people perceive themselves as part of the decision-making process, then their commitment and involvement tends to intensify.

What then is the relationship between the adult sponsor and the youth group leader? Zuck and Robertson's illustration of the coach-player relationship perhaps best explains it.[12] But perhaps the illustration should be taken a step further. The peer group leader is like the captain of the team. He is the quarterback who takes everything his coach has taught him, calls the play in the huddle, and inspires the team to produce at the line of scrimmage. The coach will never again be a quarterback. He must content himself with training eleven younger men to do their jobs and do them well, and then trust that their quarterback will guide them to victory. Christ had his eleven, too. They were called disciples.

DETERMINING WHICH MODEL TO USE

As plans are being made for the future of a youth group, there is the tendency either to extend the system of youth ministry currently being employed by a church or to grab a new model of youth work and impose it on the group. Both approaches tend to insure, at best, continued mediocrity in the youth program, and at worse, catastrophe.

The permanent youth sponsor would be well advised to sit down with perceptive adults, Sunday school teachers, youth sponsors, and mature young people and ask some probing questions about the needs of the young people, the youth group, and the adults who are working with the young people of the church.[13] These questions should include the following:

1. What are the greatest spiritual needs which our young people have? Social needs? Mental needs? Physical needs?
2. How many members of the group have a meaningful relationship with the Lord Jesus Christ?
3. What types of family relationships are represented in the group and what needs do these relationships indicate?
4. How well have the group members accepted themselves as individuals and as a group?

12. Zuck and Robertson, *How to Be a Youth Sponsor*, pp. 13-14.
13. Kenneth O. Gangel, *Leadership for Christian Education* (Chicago: Moody, 1970), p. 48.

5. How well do the young people relate to each other and to adults, especially within the body of Christ?
6. What type of grasp do the young people have on principles of spiritual growth?
7. What kind of attitudes do the young people have toward the youth group? Toward the church? Toward authority in general?
8. What have been the greatest successes and failures in the lives of the young people as individuals? As a group?

These questions may be answered in individual conversations, in small group discussions, or by means of questionnaires. The important factor is that the needs of the young people be adequately determined before any attempt is made to establish or revise any particular model of youth ministry.

Once the group's needs have been established satisfactorily, the next step is to suggest changes in behavior which would be desirable for the young people, the group, and the adult leadership. These changes should be a direct outgrowth of the needs which have been identified. They should be specific and measurable. It would be wise if they were worded in such a way that everyone would know if the behavioral objective has been attained when the goals are reviewed at a later date. Some questions which might be helpful here may include these:

1. If I were Jesus Christ, what change would you expect me to make in your life? In the group? In the adult leadership?
2. Six months from now, where do you think the Lord Jesus would want us to be in relationship to each of the needs identified? In a year? In two years?
3. How will we know if, by the grace of God, these goals are attained?

Some people may object that this approach leaves no room for the working of the Holy Spirit. However, the contrary is true. These are mere goals and if the Holy Spirit chooses to work in a manner different from the way in which He originally directed the sponsors to move, the glory goes all the more to Him. The problem tends to come when nothing happens at all, and then this planning process appears to highlight the fact that the Holy Spirit has not been working in the lives of the group members.

The third step in planning for the future of a youth group is to identify the obstacles which are presently hindering the youth group from accomplishing the goals suggested. This is not an easy task. The temptation will be to raise the standard types of problems such as these: "The adults do not care about the youth of the church," or "the teens aren't spiritual enough," or "they've had poor youth sponsors." These criticisms may or may not be valid but the obstacles usually run much deeper. These are some questions which might be asked:

1. To what degree is the church as a whole committed to the four basic elements of biblical church development?
2. To what extent does the youth group reflect the commitments of the church?
3. With what degree of permanency and with what depth of personal relationship have previous sponsors committed themselves to the youth group? The present sponsors?
4. Do the young people expect God to work? Why?
5. Do parents expect God to work? Why?
6. Are there adequate sponsors to effect the goals suggested?
7. Are there other Christians ministries in the community which are meeting the same or similar needs?
8. What type of leadership presently exists within the group?

As obstacles are identified, they can be dealt with in a direct manner. Sometimes this will demand that objectives be modified because they are unrealistic. At other times goals will be scrapped all together. But usually this process will allow a youth group to begin to move in a realistic manner toward the goals identified.

The final step is to establish a program which will meet the needs that have been identified and move toward the goals which have been established for the group. It is doubtful that any single model of the youth group identified above would specifically meet the needs of any local youth group. Even if a certain model would meet those needs, it is possible that the model would have to be modified from year to year or at least every three or four years.

Programs should never be sacred. The day they cease meeting the needs that have been identified is the day the programs should be modified. Periodically an evaluation should be made to be sure the program is actually doing what it was intended to do. The following are some questions which may be helpful in determining which models or combination of models to use:

1. What models of youth ministry have worked in the recent past?
2. What type of natural talent is possessed by the group members and the sponsors?
3. How much time can the sponsors devote to the youth program?
4. How much money can be spent by the youth group?

5. How frequently can the group get together without hurting the quality of family life and the teens' schoolwork?
6. What is the most significant contribution the group can make to the body of Christ this year in terms of learning, worship, fellowship, and ministry?

CONCLUSION

The youth group is the product of people. The best youth-group models, program materials, and youth-group treasuries will never produce by themselves a significant ministry to young people. The key now as in the first century will be people ministering to people: sponsors involved with young people in both informal and formal situations; parents taking their time to enjoy their young people and to support the youth sponsors. Then it will be that the Holy Spirit will take the written Word and produce men and women of God. The youth group merely provides a situation in which this can happen naturally.

FOR FURTHER READING

Books

Browning, Robert L. "The Church's Youth Ministry." In *An Introduction to Christian Education.* Edited by Marvin J. Taylor. Nashville: Abingdon, 1966.

Carroll, John L., and Ignatius, Keith L. *Youth Ministry: Sunday, Monday, and Every Day.* Valley Forge, Pa.: Judson, 1972.

Christian Education Monographs: Youth Workers Series, no. 1-8. Glen Ellyn, Ill.: Scripture Press Ministries, 1970-71.

Coleman, Robert L. *The Master Plan of Evangelism.* Westwood, N. J.: Revell, 1963.

Colburn, Ralph J. *Secrets of Success in Youth Work.* Redondo Beach, Calif.: Christian Workers' Service Bur., 1956.

Corbett, Jan. *Creative Youth Leadership.* Valley Forge, Pa.: Judson, 1977.

Ezell, Mancil, and Ezell, Suzanne. *Being Creative.* Nashville: Broadman, 1974.

Hoglund, Gunnar. *Youth Groups.* Chicago: Harvest, 1967.

Johnson, Rex E. *Ways to Plan and Organize Your Sunday School—Youth.* Glendale, Calif.: Regal, 1971.

Kennedy, D. James. *Evangelism Explosion.* Wheaton, Ill.: Tyndale, 1970.

Kuhne, Gary W. *The Dynamics of Personal Follow-Up.* Grand Rapids: Zondervan, 1976.

May, Helen. *Impactivity: Youth Program Resources.* Nashville: Broadman, 1974.

Middleton, Barbara, ed. *Respond.* Vol. 4. Valley Forge, Pa.: Judson, 1975.

Ortlund, Raymond C. *Lord, Make My Life a Miracle!* Glendale, Calif.: Regal, 1974.

Powell, Terry. *Making Youth Programs Go.* Wheaton, Ill.: Victor, 1974.

Reed, Bobbie, and Johnson, Rex E. *Bible Learning Activities—Youth.* Glendale, Calif.: Regal, 1974.

Reed, Ed, and Reed, Bobbie. *Creative Bible Learning for Youth.* Glendale, Calif.: Regal, 1977.

Richards, Lawrence O. *Youth Ministry: Its Renewal in the Local Church.* Grand Rapids: Zondervan, 1972.

Robertson, Fern. "Sunday Evening Youth Programs." In *Youth and the Church.* Edited by Roy G. Irving and Roy B. Zuck. Chicago: Moody, 1968.

Stoop, David A. *Ways to Help Them Learn—Youth.* Glendale, Calif.: Regal, 1973.

Strommen, Merton P. *Five Cries of Youth.* New York: Harper & Row, 1974.

Towns, Elmer L. *Successful Biblical Youth Work.* Nashville: Impact, 1973.

Wilson, Carl W. *With Christ in the School of Disciple Building.* Grand Rapids: Zondervan, 1976.

Yaconelli, Mike, and Rice, Wayne. *Ideas.* Nos. 1-17. San Diego, Calif.: Youth Specialties, 1968-76.

——. *Right-On Ideas for Youth Groups.* Grand Rapids: Zondervan, 1973.

——. *Way-Out Ideas for Youth Groups.* Grand Rapids: Zondervan, 1971.

Youth Leaders Resource Guide. Teen Dynamics Seminar Notebook. Wheaton, Ill.: Youth For Christ, n.d.

Youth Letter. (a monthly publication). 1716 Spruce Street, Philadelphia, Pa. 19108.

Zuck, Roy B., and Getz, Gene A. *Christian Youth: An In-Depth Study.* Chicago: Moody, 1968.

Zuck, Roy B., and Robertson, Fern. *How to Be a Youth Sponsor.* Wheaton, Ill.: Scripture Press, 1960.

Cassette Tapes

"Discipleship." Youth Specialties, 861 Sixth Avenue, San Diego, Calif. 92101

"Five Successful Youth Workers Tell You How." David C. Cook, Elgin, Ill. 60120.

"Y.E.S." (Youth Education Service), Success with Youth, P. O. Box 27028, Tempe, Arizona 85281.

20

Weekday Clubs

Virginia Patterson

DO CLUBS HAVE A PLACE IN OUR SOCIETY?

HANSON AND CARLSON suggest that the "boys' and girls' clubs have probably existed for hundreds of years."[1] They go on to say that although youth groups are probably as old as the human race, the rise of nationwide organizations with stated purposes and objectives is a modern structure. If groupings of youth in clubs have always existed, is it not reasonable to assume that they always will in one form or another?

The 1970 White House Conference on Children included a report to the President with recommendations on various issues relating to children. One of those recommendations was stated in this way:

> We must change our national way of life so that children are no longer isolated from the rest of society. We call upon all our institutions—public and private—to initiate and expand programs that will bring adults back into the lives of children and children back into the lives of adults. This means the reinvolvement of children of all ages with parents and other adults in common activities and responsibilities.[2]

A club program can be part of the answer to this recommendation and concern of the government. A club environment would bring adults and children together in a learning together and being together situation.

Government is not the only group concerned with providing programs and activities for youth. Educators too are realizing that "many agencies outside the formal structure of the school are making contributions to the education of our children."[3] Cremin suggests, "No serious discussion of

1. Robert F. Hanson and Reynold E. Carlson, *Organizations for Children and Youth* (Englewood Cliffs, N.J.: Prentice-Hall, 1972), p. x.
2. Stephen Hess, *Report to the President, White House Conference on Children* (Washington, D.C.: U.S. Government Printing Office, 1970), pp. 243-44.
3. Sara Anne Robertson, *Pioneer Girls: A National Religious Club Program, A Case Study* (Diss. proposal presented to the faculty of the graduate school, Northern Illinois U., July 1975), p. 1.

VIRGINIA PATTERSON, M.A., M.S., Doctoral candidate, is President of Pioneer Girls, Wheaton, Illinois; and President of Leader Enrichment, Wheaton, Illinois.

contemporary educational policy can afford to ignore them."[4] Passow indicates agreement with Cremin when he states, "Authentic learning can take place in a wide variety of settings, many of them remote from the school house."[5] Some of these other institutions that contribute to the learning process are the church and all of its avenues, the family, peers, and all experiences in which a child or teen is involved, including clubs.

Knox, Rice, and Dessler, in *A Rationale for a Christian Girls' Club,* point out some sociological factors that would be natural for introducing a club program graded for children and young people from grades two through high school:

> Second graders are practicing the art of making and keeping friends by beginning to pair off into short-lived sets of "best friends" and loosely grouped associations of children of the same sex.
>
> Third and fourth graders are becoming more group-conscious, and are forming deeper relationships with one another in and out of school. Informal clubs, with rapid turnover are common. "Best friends" split overnight; . . . there is a growing ability to work together and a building toward more stable relationships.
>
> Why not take advantage of this natural experimentation in working and being together by providing them with a club-type setting for them to learn about themselves and their world together. Give them a chance to channel their enthusiasm or exploration and learning, by developing their abilities while they want to learn, and are amenable even desirous of adult guidance. No one has to motivate them to come to a program—they are only waiting for an invitation.
>
> Fifth and sixth graders seem to think that life is great fun when doing things with the gang. Seventh and eighth graders can be found frequently with a few friends, just being together. Gangs, secret clubs, and crowd cliques, or just comfortable two's and three's appear in the pre and early adolescent way of life.
>
> . . . it seems that a club or get-together which capitalizes on girls' natural inclination to congregate would definitely be justified, and worthwhile.
>
> A junior high age youth seeks self-identity while participating in a clique-like group and in doing whatever everyone else does.
>
> As one matures the group performs a more task-oriented function. For senior high youth, groups or clubs are formed because those involved like to do the same kinds of things. Instead of being together and then doing something, one wants to do something and hence seeks out others to be with.[6]

4. Lawrence A. Cremin, *The Genius of American Education* (New York: Vintage, 1965), p. 14.
5. A. Harry Passow, "Reforming America's High Schools," *Phi Delta Kappan* 56 (May 1975): 589.
6. Dorothy Knox, Barbara Rice, and Mary Dessler, *A Rationale for a Christian Girls' Club* (Wheaton, Ill.: Pioneer Girls, 1972), pp. 3-4.

These observations indicate that there are some inherent social developmental needs that can quite readily be met in a club context.

Do clubs have a place in our society? From a historical standpoint, from the government's analysis of the needs of today's children, from the viewpoint of certain educators, and from a sociological perspective, the answer is yes. Clubs do have a place in our society.

What Are Some Values of Church-Related Clubs?

Two factors in our society have created a lack of Christian adult models for children and youth to imitate: the working mother and weekend father, and the high rate of mobility that has left most of our offspring without extended families. They no longer have grandparents, aunts, and uncles to interact with on a daily or even weekly basis. Statistics show that the working mother is becoming the norm rather than the unusual thing:

> The proportion of married women in the labor force continues to rise, increasing from 26 percent of all wives in 1953 to 42 percent in 1973.
>
> Figures of the U.S. Bureau of Labor Statistics for women in the labor force who have working husbands, reveal that 50 percent of all wives with children aged 6 to 17 are now working. In 1953, the figure was 39 percent.[7]

It is not unusual for a child to begin being left in day care centers when he is only a few weeks or months old in order for the mother to work. With the increasing divorce rate one-parent families will continue, and that one parent may not always be the mother. Because of the stress on planned parenthood, an increasing number of families have only one child. In view of these changes in American society, children will continue to have fewer and fewer adult examples in their formative years.

The White House Conference on Children addressed itself to this problem of children being isolated from adults:

> The isolation of children from adults simultaneously threatens the growth of the individual and the survival of the society. . . . It is primarily through observing, playing, and working with others older and younger than himself that a child discovers both what he can do and who he can become, that he develops both his ability and identity. . . .
>
> By isolating our children from the rest of society, we abandon them to a world devoid of adults and ruled by the destructive impulses and compelling pressures both of the age-segregated peer groups and the aggressive and exploitative television screen.[8]

What more ideal opportunity is there to provide Christian adult models

7. EP News Service, June 15, 1974.
8. Hess, *Report to the President*, p. 242.

than by using every avenue possible through the church. Weekday club programs provide an excellent opportunity that will bring Christian adults into the lives of children and youth.

Young people of the present generation have far more leisure time than did their parents and grandparents, and they are not content to waste it or have it filled with meaningless activities. "The use to which leisure time is put is becoming seen more as an investment than a time passer. The activity engaged in must be rewarding and satisfying."[9] This says that the church cannot merely expand and initiate programs and activities that are not satisfying. Church leaders need to determine the needs, abilities, and interests of the young people for whom they want to provide programs and then initiate activities that meet their needs, that are capable of developing their abilities, and that are challenging to their interests.

A weekday club program gives churches opportunity to confront youth with the claims of Jesus Christ for salvation and for spiritual living. In a club, Bible study becomes meaningful when teens begin to see how biblical principles apply to every aspect of life, both in the club and outside the club setting. The various activities learned in the club experience are meaningful and worthwhile not only for learning new skills and perfecting existing ones at the time, but also for the significance that those skills and experiences will have to the individual in the future. A club program can be a meaningful, satisfying use of leisure time for many young people, and more significantly, can have a profound spiritual impact on many teens.

Is it possible for the church to provide programs and activities that are appealing to their own young people and that at the same time attract teens from the community? Does the church and its programs have an effect on today's youth? Dean Kelly states that "religion is everywhere; man cannot manage long without it."[10] J. Milton Yinger comes to the same conclusion: "It is widely held by students of society that there are certain functional prerequisites without which society would not continue to exist. . . . Most writers list religion among the functional prerequisites."[11]

Church-related programs were ranked high by young people recently, as reported by John and Phil Weedin: "When asked to rank effectiveness of various youth organizations in their own development, 490 Saline

9. Jules Pagano, "Conclusion," *Adult Leadership,* October 1974, pp. 108-9.
10. Dean Kelly, *Why Conservative Churches Are Growing* (New York: Harper & Row, 1972), p. 37.
11. J. Milton Yinger, *The Scientific Study of Religion* (New York: Macmillan, 1970), p. 21.

County (Missouri) 9th and 10th graders said: 'Most effective was church youth groups. Next in order were little league, 4-H, Boy Scouts, Girl Scouts.' "[12] Church-sponsored weekday clubs for teenagers can capitalize on this interest of youth·in spiritual things through group Bible studies and discussions of spiritual truths and biblical principles. Many children and young people have been attracted to the Saviour and have grown spiritually through an appealing club program.

In summary, a weekday club program for young people has these values: it brings youth and adults together, it gives teens adult models to emulate, it provides meaningful leisure activities, it can reach non-Christian youth in the community, and it can help Christian teens develop spiritually.

WHAT CLUBS ARE AVAILABLE TO THE CHURCH?

In the chart beginning on page 291, only Protestant youth groups or clubs have been included. Those which have been omitted are national groups such as Scouts, Campfire Girls, YWCA and YMCA, Boys' and Girls' Clubs of America; vocational clubs such as 4-H; Masonic youth organizations such as Rainbow Girls, DeMolay, Job's Daughters, and Key Clubs; and various other national youth organizations which have as their purpose and aim something other than religious orientation.* *Organizations for Children and Youth,* by Hanson and Carlson (see "For Further Reading" at the end of this chapter) contains complete information on these youth organizations.

The youth club organizations included in the chart are those which have the greatest appeal to Protestant evangelical churches. These clubs are classified as: (1) denominational clubs and (2) nondenominational clubs which operate within the local church structure. Clubs that operate outside the context of the local church (e.g., Young Life and Youth For Christ, International) are discussed in chapter 26, "Parachurch Youth Movements and Organizations."

As to the potential number of children and youth who may become involved in these church-related clubs, one needs to consider the total population of those children and youth in the United States and the population of those enrolled in school. This kind of view gives an idea

12. John G. Weedin and Phil M. Weedin, "The Concerns of Youth," *Journal of Extension* 12 (Winter 1974): 14-20.

*A few nonevangelical religious-oriented groups are the following: Jewish youth groups include the B'nai B'rith Youth Organization, National Federation of Temple Youth, United Synagogue Youth, and National Council of Young Israel; the Church of Jesus Christ of Latter-day Saints (Mormon church) sponsors a weekly activity program called MIA (Mutual Improvement Association); the Roman Catholic church sponsors a variety of youth organizations including the Catholic Youth Organization (CYO), Junior Program of the Catholic Daughters of America, and the Columbian Squires. (Some Catholic parishes sponsor Scouts and Campfire Girls.)

of the potential number of children and youth who could be reached by a church club program. The following tables give this information:

TABLE 19.1

POPULATION BY SEX AND AGE[13]

Age	Boys	Girls	Total
5-13	18,700,000	18,000,000	36,700,000
14-17	8,100,000	7,800,000	15,900,000
18-20	5,300,000	5,500,000	10,800,000
Total	32,100,000	31,300,000	63,400,000

TABLE 19.2

EDUCATION BY SEX AND AGE[14]

Age	Boys	Girls	Total
7-9	5,759,000	5,522,000	11,281,000
10-13	7,315,000	7,025,000	14,340,000
14 + 15	2,878,000	2,762,000	5,640,000
16 + 17	2,369,000	2,331,000	4,700,000
Total	18,321,000	17,640,000	35,961,000

The following chart of selected church-related clubs was compiled through brochures and introductory materials available from each group; questionnaires were also used with follow-up by telephone. Details of some groups, which did not respond to the questionnaire or the request to receive materials, were drawn together from a previous study done a few years ago by Pioneer Girls, Inc., and updated with bits of information that could be gleaned from various sources such as encyclopedias, books, and firsthand information. The list, though not necessarily including the club organizations of all evangelical denominations and all nondenominational organizations, does give an overview of the variety of aims, activities, and materials available for club work with adolescents.

WHAT GOALS SHOULD A CLUB PROGRAM INCLUDE?

An examination of the chart on the following pages reveals that the aims of these organizations, while similar, are stated in various ways. Ideally a club program for adolescents should include the following goals.

13. *Statistical Abstract of the United States, 1974* (Washington, D.C.: U.S. Dept. of Commerce, Bureau of the Census, 1974), p. 10.
14. Ibid., p. 108.

CHURCH-RELATED CLUBS

Date Organized	Brief Description of Organization	Stated Aims	Major Activities	Materials Produced
1956	**Assemblies of God** 1. *Missionettes* (girls' program). Currently 11,350 local units, with membership of 135,000 Age levels: Daisies, ages 5-6 Primaries, ages 7-8 Juniors, ages 9-11 Seniors, ages 12-15 Sponsors selected by pastor and Missionettes coordinator Suggest size of clubs be limited to 12 for best success. (If more than 12 are in a club, it should be divided.) "Its Christ-centered weekday activities build upon and supplement other phases of church youth work."	To interest the girl in the things of God, to help her acquire a knowledge of missionary endeavor, to help her find a place of service and develop Christian character, to provide training and experience that will help her become a creditable member of the Women's Ministries of the Assemblies of God	Bible study and memorization of Bible portions Study of character-building materials Handwork projects Social activities Opportunity to complete an achievement program and work on extra-activity badges—cooking, nature, campcraft, sewing, music, citizenship, homemaking, personal development	Leadership manual Manuals for sponsors of age levels Handbooks for Primaries, Juniors, Seniors. Handwork packets for Daisies Publications "Missionettes Memos" (quarterly) Filmstrip: "Kim's Kaleidoscope" Catalog brochure listing supplies (books, badges and awards, etc.)
	2. *Royal Rangers* (boys' program) Age levels: Buck-a-Roos, ages 7-8 Pioneers, ages 9-11 Trailblazers, ages 12-14 Air, Sea, & Trail Rangers, ages 15-17	To instruct in Bible doctrine, to challenge to Christian service, to inspire to faith in the beliefs of the church, to satisfy boys' basic need for activity	Recreation Camping Hiking Skills Crafts	Buck-a-Roo Handbook Pioneer Handbook Trailblazer Handbook Air-Sea-Trail Rangers Handbook Royal Rangers Leader's Manual Adventures in Camping

Date Organized	Brief Description of Organization	Stated Aims	Major Activities	Materials Produced

1945	*AWANA Youth Association*
	
	Nondenominational week-day club program
	
	5,200 clubs in 1,400 churches
	
	Boys:
	  Pals, grades 3-5
	  Pioneers, grades 6-8
	
	Girls:
	  Chums, grades 3-5
	  Guards, grades 6-8
	
	Girls and boys:
	  Shipmates (high school)
		To get as many boys and girls as possible from the local community into the AWANA club and under the sound of the gospel of the grace of God, whereby they may have the opportunity to accept Christ as their personal Saviour
		
		To prepare clubbers to accept the responsibility of spreading the gospel through leadership, service, and witness
			Bible memory work
			Game time
			Olympics
			Bible drills
			Crafts
			Songs
				Buck-a-Roo Leader's Handbook
				Junior Leader's Handbook
				High Adventure, a magazine for boys, published quarterly
				Uniforms
				Awards
				
				Pals handbooks:
				  Hunter (3rd grade)
				  Brave (4th grade)
				  Warrior (5th grade)
				Pioneers handbooks:
				  Explorer (6th grade)
				  Trailblazer (7th grade)
				  Ranger (8th grade)
				Chums handbooks:
				  Papoose (3rd grade)
				  Maiden (4th grade)
				  Princess (5th grade)
				Guards handbooks:
				  Compass (6th grade)
				  Lifeline (7th grade)
				  Anchor (8th grade)
				Leaders' handbooks
				Basic Training Course
				Signal (magazine for leaders)

Date Organized	Brief Description of Organization	Stated Aims	Major Activities	Materials Produced
1941	*Baptist General Conference* 1. *Girls Meeting God* 340 churches using program 16 state groups 10,500 total membership Program for girls: Primary, grades 2, 3 Junior, grades 4-6 Junior Hi-Senior High, grades 7-12 2. *Boys' Program* (follows Christian Service Brigade program and materials)	To help each girl know God's love and find Jesus as her Saviour, teach each girl to know God's Word, enable each girl to develop a Christian life-style, involve each girl in meaningful church relationships, encourage girls to express God's love to others	"Meeting God": Bible study "Creative ministries": crafts, recreation, music, prayer partners, parties, etc. "Missions ministries": study, involvement, projects "Award ministries": personal growth, achievement, choice of projects and experiences	Leadership Growth study units (2) for training Curriculum for weekly club meetings Introductory guidelines Manuals for leaders Handbooks for Primary-Junior and Junior Hi-Senior High Items for sale: sweatshirts, pins, stationery, New Testaments, awards for achievement
1960	*Christian Reformed Church* *Calvinettes* Offers four 2-year programs: Busy Bees, ages 7, 8 or 8, 9 Jr. Calvinettes, ages 9, 10 or 10, 11 Sr. Calvinettes, ages 11, 12 or 12, 13 Adv. Calvinettes, ages 13, 14 or 14, 15	To create a sense of belonging, participation, and creativeness and to develop greater interest in church life; to find oneself; to find God	Bible study, skills and crafts, recreation, retreats, cookouts, camp life	*Touch* for girls *Cable* for women Leader training materials

Date Organized	Brief Description of Organization	Stated Aims	Major Activities	Materials Produced
1937	*Christian Service Brigade* Provides programs by which the local church can reach out to boys through Christian men Stockade, ages 8-11 Battalion and Task Force, ages 12-18 "Discipleship in Action" (Operates on discipleship principles with emphasis on low leader-boy ratio) Nationwide scope with representatives located throughout the US (Also large Canadian organization)	Slogan: "Building Men to Serve Christ" Purpose: assist local churches to motivate and prepare Christian men to influence boys to accept Jesus Christ as Saviour and follow Him as they mature into Christian manhood Programs designed to help boys find Christ as personal Saviour, grow as Christians and achieve Christian manhood, develop a biblical perspective, make friends and learn from the give-and-take of group activity, benefit from the influence and example of Christian men, develop and experience leadership, and multiply themselves through effective witness for Christ	Weekday meetings usually held in the local church Physical and mental challenges geared to boys' interests and needs; thoroughly integrated with Bible study and memorization; linked together by a structure of individual and group achievement Preadolescents working on activity projects under adult guidance A wide range of developmental activities aimed toward personal growth and Christian maturity for adolescents	Handbooks for boys: *Builder Trails* (ages 8, 9) *Sentinel Trails* (ages 10, 11) *Observer*, age 12 *Adventure Trails* (ages 12-15) *Frontier Trails* (ages 15-18) Training guides for teen-agers and adults: *Leading Now* (teens) *Understanding and Reaching Boys* *Leading Boys in Battalion and Stockade*; program resources and planning guide Periodicals: *Brigade Leader* (magazine for adults) *Dash and Venture* (magazines for boys) Full range of awards, sportswear, and supplemental items

Date Organized	Brief Description of Organization	Stated Aims	Major Activities	Materials Produced
	Free Methodist Youth			
1939	*Christian Youth Crusaders* Adopted by the Wesleyan Church in 1960 and by the Pilgrim Holiness Church in 1964 Plans for 3 age divisions	Winning youth early to God and church; evangelism, Christian nurture; fun program with purpose; developing total Christian personality as in Luke 2:52	Camp program, Bible study, hobbies, crafts, skills, service, recreation	Guidebooks
	International Church of the Foursquare Gospel Club ministry handled through department of Christian education Candlelighters, ages 4, 5 Cupbearers, ages 6-8 Cadets, ages 9-12 Recommends to its churches both the Pioneer Girls and the Christian Service Brigade programs	Seek to develop leadership and talents		Printed materials available but not described

Date Organized	Brief Description of Organization	Stated Aims	Major Activities	Materials Produced
1951	*Wisconsin Evangelical Lutheran Synod* *Lutheran Pioneers, Inc.* Headed by the congregation's pastor as spiritual leader and adviser Service group which supplies the local clubs ("Trains") and districts with literature, devotional aids, filmstrips, suggested programs, uniforms, insignia, and many other supplies Between conventions the ten-man National Council, elected by the Trains, conducts the business of Lutheran Pioneers, Inc. Currently 377 churches are using LP For boys: Buckaroos, ages 6-8 Lutheran Pioneers, ages 9-12 Troopers, boys who have been confirmed Currently 6,000 boys involved	Provides youth with a program in keeping with the purpose of the church, that includes Scripture-based teaching and application Aims: good citizenship; knowledge of outdoors and the beauties of God's creation; first aid and its application; skills and crafts to help prepare our youth for adulthood; hiking, swimming, lifesaving, nature study, signaling, measuring, map reading, stalking, safety in handling knife, axe, and firearms; any other useful skills of interest to the adolescent youth	Local "Trains" meeting together with other local "Trains" in a district and coordination of many joint activities and projects	*Handbook for Boys* *Leader's Handbook* *Preaching and Prayers for Pioneers* Lutheran Pioneer Informational Packet available to those who wish information on starting an organization in their church Other materials available

Date Organized	Brief Description of Organization	Stated Aims	Major Activities	Materials Produced
1947	*Mennonite Conference* (Goshen, Ind.) 1. *Girls Missionary and Service Auxiliary* Ages 9-14 Groups meet once a month or more Some groups are self-supporting while others are subsidized by the Women's Missionary and Service Commission	The Girls Missionary and Service Auxiliary is under the Women's Missionary and Service Commission The purposes of WMSC are to unite the women and girls of the Mennonite Church and to coordinate their activities, help women and girls find and share faith, encourage regular and disciplined Bible study, encourage strengthening the quality of family life, develop an awareness and appreciation of our Anabaptist heritage, help women and girls discover, develop, and utilize their individual gifts; help develop leadership potential among women and girls; encourage cultivation of person-to-person relationships, motivate creativity in planning programs and activities, respond as Christ's representatives to community and worldwide needs	A variety of service, material aid, and money projects	*Devotional Guide* (published annually)
	2. The second program sponsored by the Mennonite Church is for boys and girls Wayfarers, girls, ages 9-14 Torchbearers, boys, ages 9-14 The General Conference Mennonite Church, Newton, Kansas, uses the Wayfarer and Torchbearer programs.	An achievement club program that provides wholesome group activities and develops individual skills and responsibility	Crafts; games; camping-hiking skills; personal skills; service to home, community, and church	*Wayfarer Guidebook* *Wayfarer Leader's Manual* *Torchbearer Guidebook* *Torchleader's Manual* Membership cards Record sheets Awards

Date Organized	Brief Description of Organization	Stated Aims	Major Activities	Materials Produced
1939	**Pioneer Girls, Inc.** An interdenominational weekday club program for girls, with clubs in 2,500 churches in 60 denominations in the US and Canada, and clubs in 20 foreign countries Has 24 camps in the US and Canada	Slogan: "Christ in every phase of a girl's life" To provide a Bible-based, Christ-centered girls' program that results in personal growth for the girl in her total life and prepares her for Christian service	Bible explorations Scripture memorization Songs/music Crafts/arts Games/sports Nature Outdoor education Sewing Communications/media Personal development Family involvement Service projects for church, community, and family	*Trails* (magazine for elementary grades) *Reflection* (magazine for junior and senior high) *Perspective* (leaders' magazine) Awards
	Voyagers, grade 2	To help girls begin their voyage into a widening world of new experience and exposure to the Bible		Handbook: *Launch Out* Program packets (elective curriculum)
	Lavaliers, grades 3-4	To help girls discover they are uniquely created by God to glorify Him in what they do, say, and think; to apply the Bible to life in meaningful ways; to help girls develop new skills		Handbook: *Stepping Stones* Program packets (elective curriculum)
	Trailblazers, grades 5-7	To help the girl cross over from childhood to teens smoothly through skill-building activities; to help her mature in her relationship to God, self, and others		Handbook: *The Bridge* Program packets (elective curriculum)
	Shikari, grades 7-9	To help young teens face and think through vital decisions in light of biblical principles; to provide activities which will allow girls to put these biblical truths into action		Handbook: *Crossroads* Program packets (elective curriculum)

Date Organized	Brief Description of Organization	Stated Aims	Major Activities	Materials Produced
	Explorers, grades 9-12	To help girls become skilled in individual and group Bible study; to have them explore a variety of interest areas; to assist them in assuming club leadership; to involve them in service to others		*Potpourri* *Explorer Exchange* Program packets (elective curriculum)
		The programs are written to present Christ as Saviour and Lord, train girls to study and to apply Scripture to daily life, enable girls to form relationships helpful toward personal growth, develop the whole person by providing group and individual experiences, involve girls in the fellowship of a local church, and equip girls to reach and serve their church, community, and world for Christ		*Pioneer Girls* *Leaders' Handbook*
1930s	*Reformed Church in America* *Girls' League* 190 churches Wants to provide a coed program for teens Reformed Church Women are introducing Pioneer Girls materials to their churches and Girls' Leagues. They are interested in promoting Pioneer Girls to their churches which have no youth clubs.	To create interest in Christian missions (overseas and home), and in social concern and action	Bible study, service projects	Guides' manual Missions and Bible study magazine

Date Organized	Brief Description of Organization	Stated Aims	Major Activities	Materials Produced
1916 1962 1975	*Salvation Army* 1,323 centers 271 churches using program: Sunbeams, ages 6-10 Guards, ages 11-14 Senior Guards, ages 15-18	To develop happy, resourceful persons and useful citizens; to instill knowledge of and love for the Word; to provide a true meaning and purpose for life in Jesus Christ; to guard one's soul, mind, and body	Crafts, hobbies, service, skills, Bible study, recreation, community knowledge, education, and worship services	Leadership training manuals Pamphlets, uniforms, handbooks, program helps, tests Staff materials: *The Leader* *The Signal* Correspondence courses (4) Test helps
1960	*Word of Life Clubs* Sponsored by Gospel-preaching churches Church-centered, church-governed, laymen-led Junior and senior highers, grades 7-12 Club meetings may be in church on Sunday evenings or in the church or in homes during the week	To establish patterns of godly living in the life of the Christian teenager; and to establish godly patterns of a meaningful Bible study, a daily quiet time, Scripture memorization, Christian reading, personal and mass evangelism, and Christian service	Bible study Scripture memorization Christian service projects Roundups	Six-year curriculum: This I Believe series Leaders' Guide and Supplement Quiet Time diary Scripture memory system You Can Help a New Christian

1. *To present Jesus Christ as Saviour and Lord to the unchurched youth of the community.* A club gives the church a natural outreach into its own neighborhood. However, in inviting unchurched youth to be involved in a club program, they should understand that it is a Christian club where the Bible will be studied. Youth workers should not be guilty of attracting people through gimmicks or a false front of entertainment.

In presenting Jesus Christ, workers must keep in mind that they cannot force another person to accept Christ. They should not manipulate or pressure anyone into such a decision. Instead, they must do their part and then allow God to do His work in His time.

2. *To train teens to study the Bible for themselves and to apply scriptural principles to every area of their lives.* A commitment to serious Bible study is an identifying mark of the strong Christian. Therefore, club leaders need to be serious about the business of training teens to study the Scriptures. Bible study is more than listening respectfully while a leader reads or explains it. The leader's task is not to describe the various landscapes of truth he has seen on his journeys into Scripture, but to assist each youth in launching his own personal excursions into the truth. Each person needs to wrestle with Scripture firsthand, to probe it, experiment with it, question it, generalize from it, translate it into terms he understands, analyze it, synthesize it, research its implications, and evaluate his life in terms of its demands.

Because the Bible is the only ultimate authority for all matters of doctrine and Christian living, it is imperative that every believer be saturated with the teachings of this Book. He must go to it often and dip into it deeply—so deeply that more happens than the generation of a warm feeling toward God. Lasting transformation of lives and steadfast growth toward a mature faith come from the renewing of the mind rather than from the stirring of the emotions (Rom 12:2; 2 Tim 3:14-17).

The Christian needs to be intellectually convinced of the truth of Christ's deity, His efficacious work on the cross, His resurrection, His present power, His position as Judge of all, His legitimate claims to sovereignty in their personal lives. Intellectual conviction of these truths will stand firm when emotions have wavered.[15]

3. *To develop discipling relationships between adults and teens.* The determining factor in personal development is personal relationship. Character and personality tell on others. The people with whom an individual develops personal relationships will exert certain influences, even apart from any conscious effort toward that end.

This is not referring to one person telling another what to do, or be-

15. *Pioneer Girls Leaders' Handbook* (Wheaton, Ill.: Pioneer Girls, 1975), p. 145.

lieve, or be. Instead, this is the unavoidable mingling of character as two people become friends. Friends influence each other.

Now, this is what happens when adults and teens become friends. The character of one tells on the other. The examples of Paul and Timothy, of Christ and His disciples, illustrate how this is so. As the relationship deepens, the influence intensifies, the training quickens.

Leaders aware of this are faced with two challenges. One challenge is to stretch, reach, and grow in character. Youth will follow the model of what their leaders are, not what they say.

Does a club leader say his teens should witness to their friends? Does he witness? Does a club leader say his teens should have a strong prayer life? Do they hear him freely and joyously speak to the Father? As they listen to him pray, what will they learn as proper topics for prayer?

And so it is with every aspect of life. What the leader is, the youth will become.

The second challenge for the leader who knows the force with which one character touches another is to cast aside fear of relationships. Is the leader willing to be a friend—a deep friend—with the teens he leads? Is he willing to share himself with them in the lowliest, humblest ways? Is he willing to be both salt (antiseptic, preventing corruption, purifying) and light (guiding, warming, attracting)? To do either, he must allow his young people to get close to him.[16]

4. *To provide activities and experiences that develop the whole person.* In order to minister to the whole person, leaders must provide club programs chock-full of a variety of activities. God is pleased when adults minister to youth, helping them to grow toward perfection in *all* the ways in which it is possible for human beings to grow.

Mankind's greatest achievement is to know God, to love Him supremely, and to serve Him fully. Human capacity for love and service is enhanced when minds are keen and trained, when knowledge and interests are broad, when bodies are sturdy and disciplined, when emotions are wholesome yet strong, when social functioning is easy and winsome. Helping a teen grow in all these ways is part of a full-orbed spiritual ministry.

As a youngster, Jesus grew. He grew in wisdom and in stature. And He grew in favor with God and man. He must have been a marvelous boy to have around. He must have been a pleasure to see and to be near. He was as grand a boy in every way as one could be. It was not a weak body He offered to God. It was not a lazy, thoughtless mind. It was not a shy, introverted manner, nor a bullying, hateful one. He grew physically, mentally, and socially. He grew in all these ways simultaneously while

16. Ibid., p. 187.

stretching Himself to do His Father's will. In His wholeness He was well-pleasing to God, and people were attracted to Him.

In the same vein, a "whole" club program, deliberately planned to help adolescents grow physically, mentally, emotionally, socially, and spiritually, will attract other teens. Satisfying club experiences that touch every aspect of life for good will keep them coming week after week. As they come, a rich, varied club program says to a youth, "All of life is from God. All of life can be grand and abundant. God has given us all things richly to enjoy. Exult in it; praise Him in it; be all you can be in every way—for His glory."

As a man, Jesus' earthly ministry clearly showed His concern for the total person. He healed. He taught. He comforted. He loved and served. He interacted easily with people from every level of society. He provided food. He relieved mental and emotional anguish. He carefully guided individuals to care for one another in families or other intimate social groups. He did all this while *at the same time* He nurtured spiritual insight and carefully trained His followers to carry on His work. His ministry was not compartmentalized; He ministered to the whole person.[17]

5. *To involve youth in the total church ministry.* The commission of the local church is to evangelize and to nurture through discipleship. Ephesians 2:19-22; 4:11-16 and 1 Peter 2:1-10 speak to this truth. They speak of those who are His as a body, a building, a people, a nation. These passages contain such phrases as "builded together for an habitation of God," "all the building fitly framed together," "whole body fitly joined together." Club leaders have gifts which God is using to minister to their youth. But Christ has also distributed different gifts to other members of the church, including Christian teens. All are needed to help teenagers reach full Christian maturity.[18]

6. *To equip the youth with leadership skills to serve his church, community, and world for Christ.* Service and outreach go hand in hand. What kinds of experiences should teenagers be given in a club in order to fulfill this goal?

"To equip" means to develop the knowledge, attitudes, and skills necessary to know what the task is and to be able to do it.

"Outreach" means going into all the world with the gospel. It means witnessing in one's own Jerusalem, Judea, and Samaria—and the remote places in the world; actively searching out the ways to represent Jesus Christ among people who do not know and honor Him; actively seeking

17. Ibid., p. 228.
18. Ibid., p. 254.

through the power of the Holy Spirit to bring them into fellowship with the Father, and with the Son, and with a body of Christians.

"Service" means developing eyes which see and hands which do whatever is necessary to help, comfort, minister, or mature others. It is learning to be a servant-leader.

"For Christ" gives the motivational key to serving others and spreading the gospel. It is the motivation exemplified in Jesus Christ. It is aimed at meeting all of man's needs through Christ.

Leaders of youth are in a unique position to help the upcoming generation become fearless witnesses, on fire for their Saviour. This can be done by consciously teaching witnessing skills. This can build confidence so that witnessing is no longer frightening or mysterious. Most Christians know that they *should* witness, but are unable to take effective action because no one has shown them how to do it. Giving attention to how to witness does not imply that one is neglecting the role of the Holy Spirit in salvation—the one who empowers the witness, speaks through him, and gives the results.

Witnessing should be the natural outcome of a proper relationship to God. It should be an enjoyable experience for teens lovingly to persuade others to come to love the Saviour who loves them![19]

What Distinctive Features Should a Club Program Include?

An effective club program should be designed to meet both needs and interests of young people, and should provide the following features.

1. *A climate that allows teens the freedom to question, analyze, discuss things that bother them, and express their own fears, anxieties, doubts, and concerns.* The Bible has the answers to a young person's desires, questions, and concerns, but he must be able to study by questioning and analyzing the scriptural principles in light of their practicality to him today.

The climate must also be such that the young person is able to establish meaningful relationships with his adult leaders. The most effective way to teach Christian principles and behavior is through modeling. A young person must have significant adults after whom he can model, imitate, and pattern his life.

2. *A varied program that will meet the needs and interests of event-or experience-oriented youth as well as achievement-oriented ones.* Both kinds will be among any group of teenagers. The achievement-oriented teen will be motivated by competition and symbolic awards. But the event- or experience-oriented one will be motivated by the activities he is engaged

19. Ibid., pp. 265, 275.

in. For him, merely being with the group is satisfying. The event-oriented youth wants to learn and grow and develop new skills and have new experiences, but it is not important to him to receive an award for the experience. The learning or doing or just the event itself is sufficient reward. Neither kind of person should be made to feel guilty for the kind of motivation that inspires him. Neither should either one be forced to fit into the mold of what motivates the other.

3. *Individual and group experiences.* An adolescent "needs the support, approval, and proximity of age-mates in order to satisfy the need for companionship."[20] He also needs "someone to go around with, someone to confide in, someone to give him support in his ventures."[21] And the group can give him this. But each one also needs to learn how to be alone, how to do things alone, and how to develop his own individual interests and potential that may not be met through group activity. Some teens love group activity and thrive on competition, while others prefer to develop their own abilities apart from group pressure.

4. *Activities and experiences that are considered by the youth as meaningful and worthwhile.*

The activities should be such that each young person is able to see how Christ is to be an integral part of everything he does in life. Christ does not dichotomize life into secular and spiritual; He integrates all of life through the spiritual.

The activities must allow youth to learn new skills and have new experiences without fear of failure or harmful criticism. Each person must be encouraged and allowed to become more proficient in his areas of specific interest or ability.

Ideally, what he experiences and learns in the club setting will be seen as transferable to other areas of his life, such as school, home, and job.

How Should a Club Program Be Chosen and Started?

The following steps should be taken in determining which club program to select and in starting one.

First, determine the needs of the young people in the church. What programs of the church are being well-received and are holding the interest of the youth? What programs flounder and never seem to get off the ground? Are the values and goals of a youth club program, discussed earlier in this chapter, being adequately provided for teens? If not, would a club program be an answer?

20. Harold W. Bernard, *Adolescent Development in American Culture* (New York: World Book, 1957), p. 452.
21. Marguerite Malm and Odis G. Jamison, *Adolescence* (New York: McGraw-Hill, 1952), p. 121.

Second, consider the goals of the church for the next year and for the next five or ten years. Would a club program help accomplish those goals or hinder the progress? And what kind of club program will enable the church to achieve the results it desires? Are the goals of the club program consistent with the goals of the church?

Third, consider the philosophy of the local church in regard to evangelism and Christian growth. Is it the responsibility of the church to reach out into the community to those who are unchurched and unsaved, or is it the church's responsibility to teach and nurture those who are already there, or both? And what method of evangelism should be used—the more personal approach, or the kind that draws large numbers? Should counseling and instruction allow for personal interaction between adult leaders and teens individually or can adequate instruction be given in large groups? What kind of content is necessary for evangelism and nurture?

Fourth, determine whether enough adults are available for working in a club program. Does the club program provide adequate materials for training the leaders to run the clubs?

Fifth, study the materials published by club organizations. Note the unique features of each program and its philosophy of evangelism and Christian nurture. Then choose the program that will most nearly meet the needs of the church and its young people and the young people in the community.

Sixth, recruit and train leadership. They are the key to having an effective club program that will meet the needs of today's young people.

For Further Reading

Freedman, Anne. "Changing Ethics, Changing Schools, Changing Jobs." *Adult Leadership* 23 (October 1974): 104-8.

Ginott, Haim. *Between Parents and Teenagers*. New York: Macmillan, 1969.

Gross, John G., and Weedin, Phil M. "The Concerns of Youth," *Journal of Extension* 12 (Winter 1974): 14-20.

Hanson, Robert T., and Carlson, Reynold E. *Organizations for Children and Youth*. Englewood Cliffs, N.J.: Prentice-Hall, 1972.

Lampner, Carl. "An Approach to Religious Youth Work." *Dissertation Abstracts*, 26/02, p. 4579.

Levenson, Dorothy, and Spillane, R. R. "The Rights of Children." *Teacher*, December 1974, pp. 26-27, 74.

Lockerbie, D. Bruce. "Christian Schools: Whole Truth for Whole Persons." *Christianity Today*, September 15, 1972, pp. 11, 12, 14.

Murphree, Garvice, and Murphree, Dorothy. *Understanding Youth*. Nashville: Convention, 1969.

The National Commission on Resources for Youth, *Resources for Youth Newsletter,* March 15, 1975, pp. 1-7.

Schimel, John L. *The Parents' Handbook on Adolescence.* New York: World, 1969.

Snyder, Ross. *Young People and Their Culture.* Nashville: Abingdon, 1969.

White House Conference on Children, 1970. *Report to the President, White House Conference on Children.* Washington, D.C.: U.S. Government Printing Office, 1970.

Youth Letter. (a monthly publication). 1716 Spruce Street, Philadelphia, Pa. 19108.

Youth Report. April 1974, and May 1974.

Zuck, Roy B., and Clark, Robert E., eds. *Childhood Education in the Church.* Chicago: Moody, 1975. Chapter 21.

21

Recreational Activities

Edward L. Hayes

PROBLEM OF INCREASED LEISURE

INCREASE IN LEISURE TIME has been heralded as a blessing to mankind. "Leisure for everybody," writes Neumeyer, "may prove to be the most revolutionary thing that has ever happened."[1] Never before in the history of civilization has leisure been so widespread as it is now. This is especially true in the United States. Youth have been traditionally viewed as vulnerable to the excesses created by increased leisure time.

It should be remembered that leisure has always been used in one of three ways: (1) idleness; (2) activity lacking constructive qualities, often leading to the deterioration of character; or (3) opportunity for the enrichment and enhancement of life.[2] Thus it may be assumed that the extent to which leisure is used constructively depends on how well individuals are prepared for it.

The claims of recreationists may be summarized as follows: (1) recreation is vital in changing attitudes; (2) recreation is useful in improving social efficiency—individuals learn to relate to one another through play; (3) recreation develops a sense of well-being and of proper mental health; (4) recreation promotes relaxation; and (5) recreation is a primary means of helping individuals acquire skills.

Current preoccupation with the culturally damaging effects of urbanization, mobility, excessive use of TV as a substitute for reading and relating, commercialization of play, and the destructive forces of socially unaccepted forms of leisure all point to the necessity of forming a Christian view of leisure.

1. Martin H. and Esther S. Neumeyer, *Leisure and Recreation,* 3d ed. (New York: Ronald, 1958), p. 3.
2. Charles K. Brightbill and Harold D. Meyer, *Recreation* (New York: Prentice-Hall, 1953), p. 37.

EDWARD L. HAYES, Ph.D., is Academic Dean and Chairman of the Department of Christian Education, Conservative Baptist Theological Seminary, Denver, Colorado.

Within the past several decades there has also been a resurgent interest in the arts and crafts. This cultural explosion has occurred as a counter force to technological dominance. Making things for oneself, questing for quality of life experiences add up to a new mood in American youth.

The relationship of leisure and recreation is readily seen. While leisure implies free time, recreation includes any way people spend their leisure. In a broad sense, forms of recreation are free activities, and many leisure pursuits have some recreational value.

The place of recreation in modern society cannot be fully understood unless the significance and development of leisure are also considered. The dawn of leisure is hidden in antiquity. The desire to play seems almost universal. However, two important factors led to the rise of leisure and recreation: the division of labor and the emergence of a leisure class. Stratification of class society led to the emergence of an aristocratic, elite group whose main objective was play. Indulged in by the feudal lords of Europe, leisure time in the Middle Ages took on wider significance. Knights gave tourneys, and gentlemen practiced fencing and hunting, while people in general indulged in a plethora of activity.

The reaction of the churches of the Reformation was a natural consequence. Alarmed by the brutality, debauchery, and unconstructive recreational activities, churches took a firm stand against certain forms of sports, dances, theatricals, and betting. This reaction culminated in a general taboo of pleasure-seeking.

The modern-era, with technological change and urbanization, has produced more free time than ever before. Leisure of children and youth has increased considerably. The reduction of child labor, the extension of the school period, the deferment of marriage, and the introduction of modern living conditions reducing numerous time-consuming chores have played their part in giving youth new leisure. Young people find themselves with time on their hands. Relaxed parental control; conflict with traditional standards, prohibitions, and taboos; spontaneity and freedom, all combine to aggravate the problem of a young person's use of free time.

The Relationship Between Recreation and the Church

Leisure and recreation have always been tied closely to religion. The Olympian Games of ancient Greece had their origin in the religious tributes to Zeus. The dilemma between religion and play, as epitomized by the Greek use of play activity *toward* God and the Roman activity *away from* God in brutal and corrupt entertainment, is of long standing. While the Reformation freed churches from unswerving dogmas and intolerances, work was honored and play was frowned on. Idle hands were considered the devil's workshop. And repeatedly churches have spoken out against varied forms of recreation.

But today most churches encourage wholesome recreation. Churches have always been concerned with the way their young people use their leisure hours. The church supper and Sunday school picnic have given way to a variety of acceptable recreational activities. Many churches also provide special recreational facilities, and a growing number of churches have come to consider recreation a major concern of church programming and administration.

The ecological dimensions of play and the use of God's created resources have brought new opportunities and responsibilities to churches and communities. Recreation is no longer seen as merely having fun. It involves stewardship of time, of land and mineral resources, of energy, and the protection of a fragile environment.

A CHRISTIAN VIEW OF RECREATION AND LEISURE

Recreation and Christianity have sometimes been thought to be incompatible. Asceticism has died a slow death. In the face of radically upset patterns of life and the proliferation of recreational opportunities for new-found leisure, the church needs a Christian interpretation of recreation and leisure.

The early efforts of E. O. Harbin to set forth a philosophy of recreation were commendable.[3] Any present or future discussion of the subject must of necessity build on his well-laid foundations.

A Christian interpretation of recreation and leisure can be built on three premises: (1) the wholeness and sanctity of life, (2) the sanctification of time, and (3) the necessity of character-building. These premises have little meaning apart from a working definition of recreation.

Recreation involves any activity voluntarily engaged in during leisure and motivated by the personal satisfactions which result from it. For the Christian, recreation is brought into the spectrum of the new life in Christ, in which physical, mental, and spiritual development are valued. The goals of recreation and education are similar. Maturity in Christ becomes a holistic idea, rather than a fragmented, programmed notion.

The wholeness and sanctity of life. Man is not a splinter. A Christian view of man sees him as created in God's own image, a sinner by nature and choice, potentially godlike in character through redemption, and useful to both God and others. The wholeness of man suggests that what he does to his body, soul, and spirit is either harmful or helpful. To the

3. E. O. Harbin, *The Recreational Leader* (New York: Abingdon-Cokesbury, 1952), chapter 2, "A Philosophy of Recreation," pp. 19-24.

Christian the treatment of the body is always subject to the scriptural truth that the body is the temple of the Holy Spirit. Whatever a Christian engages in mentally is to be brought always into captivity to Christ (2 Cor 10:5). Salvation by Christ refers to the total man—not just his soul. Therefore, the Christian attaches a sacredness to all of life.

The sanctification of time. Unlike the spaceman to whom all hours are alike, the Christian values times and eternity. Every hour is unique and endlessly precious. The ancient Hebrews attached holiness to time, and Christ taught His disciples to care for eternity. Clear dichotomies do not always exist between good and bad uses of time. Often the distinction should be made between the better and the best use of time. The proper use of time can be spiritually beneficial, therapeutic and thus rehabilitative. Churches can and ought to help people use time properly. Pope John XXIII, in September 1959, issued a letter in which he stated what can be considered a Christian interpretation of time: "According to the Christian vision of life, all time—working and leisure time—is a value entrusted by God to the freedom of man, who must utilize it to the glory of God."

Quite understandably the Catholic position regarding life and practice centers in church and divine authority. The Christian, accepting the Scriptures as the only rule of faith and practice, finds no contradiction between a wholesome use of recreation and his faith in Christ. While the Bible denounces idleness and indolence, it is full of expressions of joy, fullness of life, and temperate use of the body and time. The incompatibility of recreation and Christianity is to be found only in the abuse and disuse of leisure time and the human body.

The necessity of character-building. A biblical view of education and recreation places the building of character in an important place in church programming. The older school of thought that character education was the starting point of the regenerative Christian experience is rejected by most evangelicals. A Christian view of character growth begins with nurture leading to conversion. Growth in character, character researchers discovered, is not automatic, and the mere knowledge of "rightness" does not produce right behavior. Only the inner dynamic life of the Holy Spirit operating in the believer will produce the fruit of the Spirit, the character traits of a Christian.

The importance of recreation to character-building may be seen in relieving social and personal tensions, demonstrating desirable moral habits, developing a sense of loyalty, and contributing to a sense of values useful to society.[4]

4. Ibid., pp. 25-35.

The place of recreation in deterring delinquency should not be minimized. At the same time, it should not be overremphasized. Brightbill has stated the following:

> To be sure, a youngster cannot be using his leisure constructively (as in wholesome recreation) and get into trouble at the same time. This is not to say, however, that delinquency can be erased, or even substantially reduced, by merely multiplying the number of recreation centers or clubs for youth. It is not as simple as ping-pong versus sin![5]

The Christian use of recreation is not eliminating delinquency so much as it is helping to hold the line against character disintegration by providing for character development, achievement, and recognition. The delinquent must first be changed inwardly. This does not preclude the role of recreation in bringing the delinquent to a place where the gospel can be communicated and received.

In summary it may be stated that recreation can provide youth with a wonderful opportunity for an enriched, abundant, and satisfying life. Through properly guided recreation, character may be both fostered and displayed. Genuine character change, however, must come from within. Environment, while it may be beneficial and may serve to create a climate for spiritual change, cannot regenerate. "Christian recreation," writes Harbin, "should develop individuals who behave like Christians because of inner controls that "constrain" them to be good rather than because of outer pressures that compel them."[6]

RECREATION AND THE CHURCH PROGRAM

How can recreation be utilized by a local church? Should a church provide facilities on its property for recreation? These two questions are important ones and are rather pivotal to any discussion of recreation and youth.

The query, "How can recreation be utilized in the church?" is misleading. Recreation, properly understood, is not a tool, device, gimmick, or bait for the unsuspecting. It is not mere amusement, entertainment, participation in games or sports. To hold such views is to be victimized by outdated interpretations. The church which seeks to use recreation in such ways is guilty of relegating recreation to lower levels. A high view of recreation sees recreation as a natural outflow of recreative activity motivated by enjoyment, personal satisfaction, enrichment of life, character and personality growth, and growth in Christlikeness.

5. Charles K. Brightbill, *Man and Leisure: A Philosophy of Recreation* (Englewood Cliffs, N.J.: Prentice-Hall, 1961), p. 272.
6. Harbin, *Recreational Leader*, p. 26.

A church would do well to give serious thought and planning to the following considerations: (1) the church has a responsibility to help its young people to see that recreation is a necessary element in Christian experience; (2) the church has a responsibility to help its young people discern between right and wrong choices of recreational activity; (3) the church has a responsibility to help its young people properly use their leisure time wherever they may find themselves; and (4) the church has a responsibility to set an example to the community and the world. Its use of recreation may be evangelistic, but only in the sense that individuals are attracted to activities which reflect a Christian use of leisure.

Often young people's activities, club programs, and attractive facilities are included in the church's program only as bait to lure people to the church. This use of recreation is not Christian. Used as a "hidden persuader," recreation is cheapened, and the gospel is viewed as related to and dependent on gimmicks. Evangelism ought to make use of what is supernatural—the winsomeness of the gospel lived out dynamically in a changed life. Let it be perfectly clear, the Christian's whole life should be given to bringing glory to God. This life purpose finds its expression in worship, work, and play. The non-Christian will be converted by the power of God. He will be convinced when he sees God's principles embodied in real Christian lives. Wholesome recreational activities, while they may afford a context in which youth may observe the reality of the Christian experience, ought to be an expression of that Christian reality and not a device to be used. The question then is one of motivation—and any use of free time that is forced is not recreation, at least not by this definition.

Should a church provide recreational facilities? This question is discussed more fully later in this chapter but a few guiding principles may be useful here. Those who answer yes to this question argue that since society is corrupt, the church must make every provision for the recreational time of its youth. Consistent with this view is the conviction that the church has every right to provide for the total life of the individual including his recreation. But this viewpoint tends to make the church a "Christian ghetto," with undue demands on a person's time. An extreme position in this regard would hold that the church has the right to bring the member into physical proximity for protection from the evils of society. Such a view, of course, is monastic.

On the other hand, others maintain that it is not the church's business to engage in recreational programming of its members, or to invest in expensive gymnasiums and other recreational facilities. The church must first be itself, it is argued. If it expends effort on tangents, it ceases to be a church. But, on the other hand, the provision of such facilities enables the church to become all things to all youth.

Obviously there are weaknesses in both viewpoints. Would it not appear practicable to build a working philosophy of youth recreation on elements from both viewpoints? Certainly a church is to be a church. In so doing it is to help young people be Christians twenty-four hours a day. It is to equip them to do their work as believers in the world. It is to provide for the expressions of fellowship, and in so doing may provide certain facilities to foster this within the life of the church. Wherever possible the church may serve the community needs of youth by providing the finest of facilities within the framework of church policy, purposes, and financial ability.

Recreation can become a dynamic part of the church when church members become aware of the need and place of recreation in Christian living. Its role may be fulfilled in enriching human life, developing and deepening fellowship, maintaining good morale, attracting new members, and complementing the whole program.

PROGRAMMING FOR CHRISTIAN RECREATION

It has already been stated that recreation does not consist merely of games, sports, and social activities. The church recreational leader will make his first mistake by assuming such to be true. Such an activity-centered concept may serve to fill the calendar with fun nights, swimming, bowling, and the like, but the recreational needs of youth may not best be served.

Programming for youth recreation must first take into account the basic age groups and sex differences of youth. The young teen (ages 12-14) may lack physical coordination and skill to enter into highly competitive sports. Individual interests and supportive group activities which do not tend to emphasize sex differences in recreation are to be fostered. High school and college-age youth enjoy feats of skill, group activity with both sexes, and vicarious experiences of watching others perform. There is almost no limit to the recreational possibilities of Christian youth regardless of age.

Programming for youth must account for the basic characteristics of recreation: (1) activity, (2) variety of form, (3) use of unobligated time, (4) voluntary participation, (5) flexibility, (6) purposeful behavior, (7) promotion of socially accepted and thoroughly Christian behavior.[7]

7. Harold Meyer, Charles Brightbill, and H. Douglas Sessoms, *Community Recreation: A Guide to Its Organization,* 4th ed. (Englewood Cliffs, N.J.: Prentice-Hall, 1968).

Programming for youth recreation, furthermore, must take into consideration the various categories of recreation. The following classification is often used by recreational leaders:

> Arts and crafts
> Drama
> Games, sports, and athletics
> Hobbies
> Music
> Outdoor recreation
> Reading, writing, and speaking
> Social recreation
> Special events
> Volunteer service[8]

Another and perhaps more useful classification may be as follows:

> Camping and outing activities
> Competitive sports
> Creative-cultural activities
> Physical activities
> Social activities

No single classification is complete. Any arbitrarily devised list of program possibilities in recreation will leave much to be desired, but the reader may benefit from the following partial listing of recreational possibilities:

CREATIVE-CULTURAL ACTIVITIES

Arts and Crafts	Metalcraft	Bells
Basketmaking	Model airplanes	Books
Bead craft	Painting	Buttons
Block Printing	Photography	Coins
Cabinetmaking	Pottery	Furniture
Carving	Rugmaking	Glassware
Ceramics	Sand painting	Guns
Costume design	Sculpture	Indian craft
Drawing	Sketching	Keys
Dyeing and Coloring	Tincraft	Paintings
Embroidery	Toymaking	Ships
Etching	Weaving	Stamps
Knitting	Wood carving	Drama
Leatherwork	Collecting	Charades
Macrame	Antiques	Festivals

8. *The Recreation Program* (Chicago: Athletic Inst., 1954).

Impersonations
Informal dramatics
Making scenery
Marionettes
Mask making
Masquerades
One-act plays
Pageants
Pantomimes
Parades
Play reading
Puppetry

Stage craft
Story plays
Storytelling
Three-act plays
Mental activities
  Book clubs
  Debates
  Discussion groups
  Forums
  Guessing games
  Lectures
  Mental games
  Public speaking

Puzzles
Reading
Study groups
Television watching
Tricks
Musical activities
  Bands
  Barbershop quartets
  Ensembles
  Glee clubs
  Orchestras
  Solo instruments

SOCIAL ACTIVITIES

Banquets
Basket suppers
Beach parties
Carnivals
Conversation
Dinners
Family reunions
Parties
  Birthday

Block
Costume
Seasonal
Pencil and paper games
Picnicking
Potluck suppers
Scavenger hunts
Table games
  Anagrams

Caroms
Checkers
Chess
Crokinole
Dominoes
Monopoly
Parcheesi
Pickup sticks
Treasure hunts

CAMPING AND OUTING ACTIVITIES

Bait and fly casting
Barbecues
Boating
Camping
Canoeing
Clambakes
Corn roasts
Crafts from native ma-
  terials
Fish fries
Hiking
Horseback riding
Hosteling
Mountain climbing

Nature study
  Astronomy
  Bee culture
  Birdhouse building
  Caring for pets
  Collecting
    Animals
    Birds
    Bugs
    Flowers
    Minerals
    Mosses
    Rocks
    Snakes

Gardening
Making nature trails
Rifle shooting
Skeet shooting
Skiing
Snowshoeing
Snow tracking
Tobogganing
Trapping
Visiting zoos
Walking
Wiener roasts

PHYSICAL ACTIVITIES

Archery
Badminton

Baseball
Bicycling

Bowling
Box hockey

Boxing
Croquet
Darts
Deck tennis
Driving
Fencing
Field hockey
Football
Golf
Handball
Horseshoes
Ice skating

Jacks
Kite flying
Lacrosse
Mass games
Ping-Pong
Racquet ball
Roller-skating
Rope skipping
Rope spinning
Shinning
Shuffleboard
Soccer

Softball
Speedball
Squash
Stunts
Tennis
Track and field
Tumbling
Volleyball
Wading
Water polo
Weight lifting
Wrestling

COMPETITIVE SPORTS

Archery
Archery golf
Badminton
Baseball
Basketball
  Foul shooting
  Spot shooting
  Twenty-one
Bowling
Curling
Distance running
Fencing
Fly and bait casting
Football
Golf
Gymnastics
Handball

Hockey
  Field
  Ice
Horseshoes
Hurdles
Jump events
  Pole vault
  Running high jump
  Running hop, step
    jump
  Running long jump
Lacrosse
Paddle tennis
Ping-Pong
Relay races
Riflery
Rowing
Shuffleboard

Skiing
Soccer
Speedball
Sprints
Squash
Swimming and diving
Tennis
Touch football
Trap and skeet shoot-
  ing
Volleyball
Water polo
Weight events
  Discus throw
  Javelin throw
  Shotput
Wrestling

ORGANIZING FOR CHURCH RECREATION

Most churches have the basis for a recreation program if they have a Sunday school, youth groups, or weekday club programs. Providing for Christian recreation is part of the program of these groups. Some committee or group is desirable, however, to correlate, coordinate, and, if need be, increase recreational activities.

The recreation committee. Appointed or elected by the church, this committee would work closely with the board of Christian education and leaders of the various groups working with young people to provide an adequate youth recreation program. The scope of this committee's responsibility would extend beyond youth recreation to churchwide concerns as well.

A chairman should be chosen who has demonstrated his interest in church recreation and who has proven himself faithful in church activities. Membership may be small, consisting of three to six people representing various age-groups in the church. Young people of high school or college age may well serve on this committee since much of the church recreational program benefits them directly.

The committee is responsible to the board of Christian education for planning and carrying out the church's recreational program. Some of the duties of the committee may include the following:

1. Making a survey of recreational interests
2. Creating interest in Christian recreation
3. Surveying church facilities to see what areas or rooms can be adapted to recreational activities
4. Planning a church calendar for the year, which provides for balanced fellowship and recreational activities for the year in consultation with group leaders
5. Promoting an occasional all-church recreational activity
6. Helping secure proper equipment and providing for the administering of the program, utilizing facilities and equipment

Most churches may not have developed their recreational program to the point that a committee will be needed, so the burden of providing for a balanced recreational diet may rest on the board of Christian education. In small churches group leaders, adult sponsors, and other interested persons may demonstrate their concern for Christian youth recreation by pooling their talents and efforts to see that adequate recreational opportunities are provided under the auspices of the church.

The organization may be minimal or expansive, depending on the size of the congregation, the needs of the youth, community factors, and the will of the congregation.

This discussion has been included because it is felt that any organized youth recreation program ought to be a part of the total church endeavor.

Providing adequate leadership for youth recreation. The need for specialized training of recreational leaders in churches has been recognized only recently. Communities usually make provision for certified recreational leadership to supervise playgrounds and other recreational centers. Any church which views recreation as more than simple social gatherings may do well to consult with community leaders on all facets of recreation.

Leadership training materials for recreational leadership are abundant at the community level. Only recently, however, have churches attempted to provide specialized help to church recreational leaders. Efforts of the

Church Recreation Service of the Southern Baptist Convention have been outstanding, and materials prepared by this excellent agency may be helpful to any church which desires to improve its recreational program.

A few larger churches which have well-developed recreational programs hire trained personnel for supervising recreation. But most churches rely on volunteer leadership to work with youth. Every youth worker, teacher, or sponsor ought to appreciate the place of recreation in the lives of youth. Lay workers can receive help in being better recreational leaders. Concerning desirable personality traits, a recreational leader (1) is fair and impartial, (2) plays no favorites, (3) has a good sense of humor, (4) plays and mingles with the group, (5) is interested in each person, (6) possesses a cheerful disposition, (7) is patient, (8) does not "fly off the handle," (9) praises good work, (10) encourages the slower ones, (11) dresses appropriately, (12) is always willing to help, (13) is punctual, (14) is courteous, and (15) has varied interests.[9]

But the Christian recreational leader must possess more than these traits. He must know how to help the group grow *spiritually* through the experiences of play and fellowship.

The effect of supervision can do much toward improving the program. Rapport between leader and group calls for a two-way road of respect. The pastor, youth director, Christian education director, or other leader in charge of church recreation will help leaders become better leaders with young people if the leader's work is evaluated and adequate assistance is given. Teachers planning class parties, sponsors and youth officers planning banquets, young people planning meaningful use of free time—all these personnel need resources. Church leaders will seek to be as well informed as possible on the various facets of church recreation.

BUILDING FOR CHURCH RECREATION

Recreational facilities are no panacea for a weak educational ministry with young people. Planning for building space should come only after careful study of the existing educational and recreational programs. "Recreational facilities will not assure an adequate church recreational ministry. Rather, the strength of a program will determine the need for additional facilities."[10]

Principles for providing recreational facilities. The following principles reflect wise use of recreation in the church and may be helpful to church leaders who are planning for new educational and recreational facilities.

9. H. Dan Corbin, *Recreation Leadership*, 2d ed. (Englewood Cliffs, N.J.: Prentice-Hall, 1959), p. 23.
10. Bob Boyd, *Building for Church Recreation* (Nashville: Church Recreation Service & Church Architecture Dept., S. S. Board of the Southern Baptist Convention), p. 3.

1. Every church can and should provide for recreation.
2. Provisions for church recreation should be an integral part of the total educational program.
3. Recreational facilities should be provided only after the needs of the basic educational organizations have been met.
4. Recreational facilities should complement those activities of a wholesome nature provided by the community.
5. Need for facilities should be considered before cost.
6. Cost of leadership must be considered in initial planning. Good leadership is far more important than buildings.
7. The cost of maintenance should be considered in the early planning stages of any recreational building.
8. Whenever possible, plans should allow for later expansion and modification of the facilities.
9. Planners and architects alike should make extensive use of recreational specialists.
10. Planning of any recreational area should take into consideration its use by all the age-groups of the church family.[11]

Churches with limited facilities. Some churches with vision have determined to keep expenses at a minimum and utilize community facilities wherever possible. Bowling, skating, swimming, and golf facilities are often available to church groups. There are the wide open spaces of public camps and forest preserves, parks and recreation areas which every church can put to greater use.

Churches can utilize parking lots, grassy areas, vacant buildings, basements, and church members' homes. A church may not need a gymnasium. Facilities may be available that will be more satisfactory. The following are some possibilities:

1. Larger rooms which may be cleared for parties and table games
2. Wide halls suitable for shuffleboard, portable bowling, or Ping-Pong
3. Small rooms where craft activities may be conducted
4. Below-grade area which might be cleaned up, painted, and equipped as a recreational area
5. The sanctuary or an assembly room where religious drama may be presented
6. Residential property by the church
7. A hut built by the church for scout or other youth groups
8. Former recreational space which has been misused or abandoned
9. Unused buildings in the area (vacant schools, churches, offices)

11. Ibid., p. 6.

10. Outdoor areas:
    (a) Grassy areas for volleyball, croquet, horseshoes, archery, and badminton
    (b) Parking area suitable for skating, badminton, basketball, tennis, shuffleboard, tetherball
    (c) Undeveloped church property
    (d) Vacant lots for softball, baseball, and touch football
    (e) Nearby city parks which can be reserved
    (f) Nearby schoolgrounds and facilities
    (g) Large flat roof areas with sufficient structural support to allow conversion to recreational space
11. Community and commercial facilities which may be used by the church[12]

Building new facilities. Planning must precede expansion. No extensive recreational building ought to be built until the following questions are carefully considered: (1) Does the church really need a special building, or can other buildings, rooms, or outdoor space be utilized? (2) Is the church merely duplicating what is already available in the community? (3) How will the church supervise the building and its use? The last question is often overlooked. In some ways it is best not to engage in a full-scale recreational program in a gymnasium if it is poorly planned and inadequately supervised. Professional assistance should be sought before any large-scale building of recreation facilities is undertaken.

SUMMARY

The new importance of recreation is dawning. The fact that youth are becoming more and more aware of their tomorrow with its "free time" ought to cause churches to look seriously on recreation not as a cure-all for church ills, nor as a necessary evil to "keep young people in the church," but as a dynamic force to be utilized for the growth of persons and the glory of Christ.

FOR FURTHER READING

Books

Baumann, Clayton. *125 Crowd Breakers.* Glendale, Calif.: Regal, 1974.
Boyd, Bob M. *Recreation for Churches.* Nashville: Convention, 1967.
Brightbill, Charles K. *Man and Leisure: A Philosophy of Recreation.* Englewood Cliffs, N.J.: Prentice-Hall, 1961.
Brightbill, Charles K., and Meyer, Harold D. *Recreation.* New York: Prentice-Hall, 1953.

12. Ibid., pp. 4-5.

Bucher, Charles A. *Recreation for Today's Society*. Englewood Cliffs, N.J.: Prentice-Hall, 1974.

Carlson, Bernice. *Recreation for Retarded Teenagers and Young Adults*. Nashville: Abingdon, 1968.

Carlson, Reynold Edgar. *Recreation in American Life*. Belmont, Calif.: Wadsworth, 1972.

Corbin, H. Dan. *Recreation Leadership*. 2d ed. Englewood Cliffs, N.J.: Prentice-Hall, 1959.

Edgren, Harry D. *1000 Games and Stunts*. New York: Abingdon, 1960.

Eisenberg, Larry and Helen. *Omnibus of Fun*. New York: Association, 1956.

Harbin, E. O. *The Recreation Leader*. New York: Abingdon-Cokesbury, 1956.

———. *The Fun Encyclopedia*. New York: Abingdon, 1940.

Jacobsen, Marion. *Good Times for God's People*. Wheaton, Ill.: Scripture Press Foundation, 1952.

Kaplan, Max. *Leisure in America: A Social Inquiry*. New York: John Wiley, 1960.

Kraus, Richard G. *Recreation and Leisure in Modern Society*. New York: Appleton-Century-Crofts, 1971.

———. *Recreation Today*. New York: Appleton-Century-Crofts, 1966.

May, Helen. *Impactivity: Youth Program Resources*. Nashville: Broadman, 1974.

Meyer, Harold; Brightbill, Charles; and Sessoms, Douglas. *Community Recreation: A Guide to Its Organization*. 4th ed. Englewood Cliffs, N.J.: Prentice-Hall, 1968.

Neumeyer, Martin H., and Neumeyer, Esther S. *Leisure and Recreation*. 3d ed. New York: Ronald, 1958.

Plyant, Agnes D. *Church Recreation Program*. Chicago: Athletic Institute, 1954.

Recreation and the Church. New York: National Recreation Association, 1946.

Rice, Wayne, and Yaconelli, Mike. *Right-in Ideas for Youth Groups*. Grand Rapids: Zondervan, 1973.

Wilson, Bill, and Tedesco, Paul, eds. *Kid Keepers*. Grand Rapids: Baker, 1975.

Yaconelli, Mike, and Rice, Wayne. *Ideas*. Nos. 1-17. San Diego: Youth Specialties, 1968-76.

———. *Way-out Ideas for Youth Groups*. Grand Rapids: Zondervan, 1971.

Significant Journals

Church Recreation Magazine. Church Recreation Department, Southern Baptist Convention, 127 Ninth Avenue, North, Nashville, Tennessee 37234.

Journal of Health, Physical Education and Recreation. American Association for Health, Physical Education, and Recreation, National Education Association, 120 16th Street, N.W., Washington, D.C. 20036.

Sources of Information

Association Press, 297 Broadway, New York, New York 10007.

Athletic Institute, 705 Merchandise Mart, Chicago, Illinois 60654.

Burgess Publishing Company, 7108 Ohms Lane, Minneapolis, Minnesota 55435.

Church Recreation Department, Baptist Sunday School Board, 127 Ninth Avenue, North, Nashville, Tennessee 37234.

National Recreation and Park Association, 1601 North Kent Street, Arlington, Virginia 22209.

22

Missionary Education of Youth

Bill Bynum

LITTLE INSIGHT is needed to recognize how desperately the world is plagued by unmet needs. Youth are as aware of this as are adults—perhaps even more so. Youth are eager to act, but they need a sense of direction. Missionary education of youth should provide more than the awareness of human need to know Christ as Saviour. It should also give teens opportunity to develop skills in sharing and to grow in such expressions of God's love.

THE PLACE OF MISSIONARY EDUCATION WITH YOUNG PEOPLE

The missionary task of the church is evangelistic—bringing others into a personal relationship with the Lord Jesus Christ. As the Word of God reveals, all believers (adults and youth) are to be witnesses for Christ. The local church exists for the twofold purpose of (1) winning people to Christ, and (2) helping believers become grounded in the Word, built up in the faith, and skilled in witnessing and service.

The program of the church must therefore include missionary education in order to encourage and challenge young people to witness by life and by verbal testimony.

Christian youth can be encouraged to share their experience in Christ in a number of ways: by a life filled with the compassion of Christ; by a practical, workable knowledge of the Word of God which fortifies this experience and gives depth to that witness; and by a desire to see this experience duplicated in other lives as they give forth the good news.

This missionary spirit is noted in three major aspects of a Christian young person's life: (1) conversion, resulting from someone else's witnessing to him; (2) awareness of the will of God—a plan and purpose for his life; and (3) obedience to the will of God, expressed in service. Being in the will of God means being, in a sense, a missionary regardless of one's vocation or geographical location.

BILL BYNUM, D.R.E., Ed.D., is Chairman of the Department of Christian Education, Talbot Theological Seminary, La Mirada, California.

THE CHALLENGE OF MISSIONARY EDUCATION FOR YOUNG PEOPLE

But why should the church be concerned with providing missionary education for young people? Several factors may be mentioned in answer to that question.

1. *The nature of adolescence.* Many of the physical, mental, emotional, social, and spiritual characteristics of young people can be channeled into missionary interests. Moreover, many of the needs of teens can be met by an active missionary educational program. The concerns of youth today, as summarized by Merton P. Strommen, aptly fit the purpose of missionary education:

> They can be distinguished by means of five major characteristics. They are: (1) humanitarian, (2) oriented to change, (3) socially involved, (4) concerned over national issues, and (5) critical of the institutional church, in which adults seem not to be "caring."[1]

Furthermore it is a fact that a large proportion of missionaries respond to the call to missionary service while in their teen years.

2. *World conditions.* Newby states that the world situation in which youth find themselves is characterized by change, confusion, and consternation.[2] Churches should help young people see that answers to these world problems and to their own problems are found in Christ. As teens' lives are changed by Christ, the missionary program of the church should instill within youth the desire to make Christ known to others around the world.

3. *The indigenous principle.* The missionary endeavor abroad has been operating successfully under the "indigenous church" concept for a number of years. If this philosophy has strengthened national churches by developing believers and spreading the gospel, surely the same philosophy will work here "at home." If young people are encouraged in their various church-related activities to be self-supporting, self-propagating, and self-governing, the missionary concept will not be so foreign to them.

Applying the indigenous principle to youth work involves making missions an integral part of the church's program, and not an appendage to it. When we encourage young people to plan and execute means whereby the missionary spirit can be manifest, the indigenous principle of self-propagation is being followed. As we do this, missions may become the permeating spirit of the church and not just an afterthought.

1. Merton P. Strommen, *Five Cries of Youth* (New York: Harper & Row, 1974), p. 53.
2. Donald O. Newby, "The Churches' Ministry to Youth," in *Religious Education: A Comprehensive Survey*, ed. Marvin J. Taylor (Nashville: Abingdon, 1960), pp. 124-25.

4. *The nature of learning.* Youth learn best through involvement. David A. Stoop shows that exploration and involvement are two of the higher and more active stages of learning:[3]

Fig. 22.1. *The learning process*

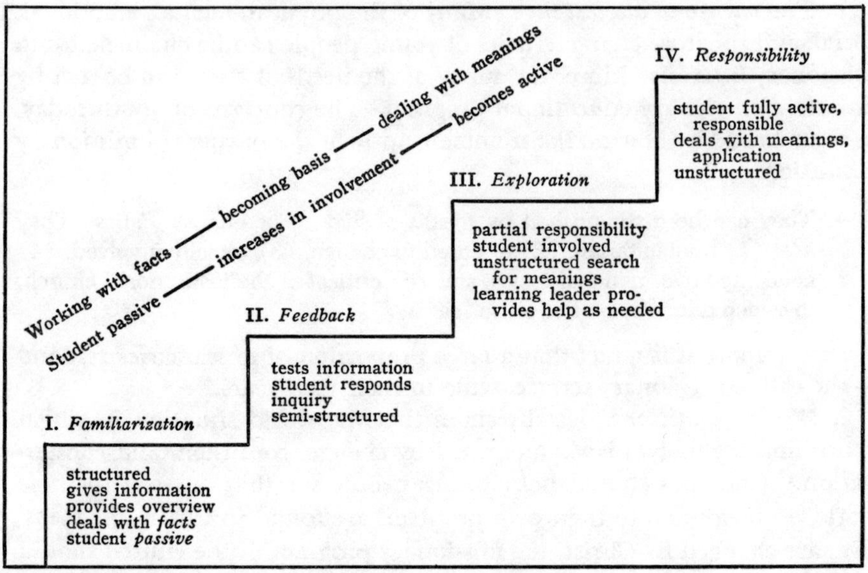
Working with facts —— becoming basis —— dealing with meanings
Student passive —— increases in involvement —— becomes active
I. *Familiarization*
structured
gives information
provides overview
deals with *facts*
student *passive*
II. *Feedback*
tests information
student responds
inquiry
semi-structured
III. *Exploration*
partial responsibility
student involved
unstructured search for meanings
learning leader provides help as needed
IV. *Responsibility*
student fully active, responsible
deals with meanings, application
unstructured

Reprinted from *Ways to Help Them Learn—Youth* by David A. Stoop. © Copyright 1971 by Gospel Light Publications, Glendale, Calif. 91209. Used by permission.

The knowledge or cognitive aspect of education—*familiarization*—coupled with the affective, appreciation, or valuing level—*feedback*—produce an important base in missions education. Building on those levels, however, teens genuinely "learn" missions when they are *exploring* the subject and assuming *responsibility* in missionary activity.

Objectives and Principles of Missionary Education with Youth

The following goals are basic to a successful missionary program with youth:

1. Developing in youth an awareness of the purpose and plan of God for their lives. A knowledge of this plan can help lead teens to follow God's will in obedient service.
2. Helping teens know and practice the great objective of the church by witnessing for Christ by lip and life.

3. David A. Stoop, *Ways to Help Them Learn–Youth* (Glendale, Calif.: Regal, 1971), p. 40.

3. Leading young people into a concern for the spiritual needs of others around the world and into sacrificial support of missions, by expending abilities, efforts, money, and time.
4. Providing frequent opportunity for young people to give their lives to the Lord for specific missionary service.

These four goals may be grouped into one overall objective: to bring young people to the place of spiritual maturity wherein there is total commitment of life to the purpose and program of God—personal discipleship and the extension of the church.

These aims are met through (1) *apprehension* or knowledge of the Scriptures, of the concept of discipleship, the conditions of mankind throughout the world, the history and program of missions, and the program of the local church and denomination; (2) *appreciation* and understanding of others and their spiritual needs, of the duty and privilege of discipleship and service, the relevance of the gospel, what constitutes a missionary call, and the needs, requirements, and programs of various mission boards; (3) *activities* which allow for self-expression in a positively scriptural and purposeful way, which provide Christian fellowship so vital to young people, which enhance character development and leadership training, and which promote the missionary spirit.

The planning and carrying out of a missionary educational program among youth will be successful to the extent that these principles are followed:

1. Encourage adult workers with youth to be missionary-minded and vitally interested in the missions program of the church.
2. Provide missionary education through the existing organizations for youth such as Sunday school,[4] camp, weekday clubs, vacation Bible school, youth groups. Leaders in these groups should be encouraged to coordinate their efforts.
3. Make missions an integral part of the church's total program. Stress that missionary service involves commitment to the will of God and discipleship in service at home and abroad.
4. Teach missions throughout the year, not just seasonally or occasionally.
5. Involve youth in missionary activities "at home" in your church, neighborhood, and town. This makes missionary service more tangible. In some churches, a missionary committee (consisting of several youth and an adult) in the youth group plans such activities.
6. Encourage youth not to look down on others in an attitude of con-

4. See the leaflet "How to Emphasize Missions in the Sunday School," published by World Vision, 919 West Huntington Drive, Monrovia, California 91018.

descending pity, but to have instead a God-given compassion and intelligent concern for their spiritual needs.

7. Relate missionary education to the age-groups being taught, and provide for knowledge, inspiration, and conduct-responses.

8. Help young people see that dedication to the will of God is the ultimate purpose of true missionary education—not merely the giving of money, time, or talents. Conversion is in answer to Christ's call, "Come unto Me"; discipleship answers His command, "Follow Me"; and both should be climaxed with obedience to the exhortation, "Serve the Lord with gladness."

PROGRAM ELEMENTS IN MISSIONARY EDUCATION FOR YOUTH

As mentioned earlier, missionary education provides opportunities for many kinds of learning experiences. A well-rounded missionary educational program incites young people to think, feel, will, and do—to see and hear, to desire, to decide, and to act. This includes (1) familiarization and feedback, (2) exploration, and (3) responsibility in missionary activity.

Familiarization and feedback are those opportunities to learn through the experiences of others and through interaction with others.

Stories are always of great benefit, and there are multitudes of books with missionary stories, biographies, adventures, which challenge the minds and hearts of even the least inquisitive. Include books on these subjects in the church library. In Sunday school opening assemblies, occasionally have reports by teens on missionary books they have read. The magazine *Wherever*, published by TEAM, Box 969, Wheaton, Illinois 60187, is directed to college-age youth and young adults on missions. Copies are available free.

Visual helps such as pictures, posters, and objects are valuable tools for the missionary educator. Using these with a lecture or demonstration increases the extent of learning. Visuals help missionary speakers explain their work, the geographical location, the customs of foreign peoples. Many mission boards have a number of visual aids along this line.

Tape recordings are very useful in vicarious learning. Playing a recording from a missionary creates interest and intrigue. Teens also enjoy "writing" to nationals or enjoy missionaries by tape. Some junior highs enjoy having a pen pal in a foreign land.

Drama, when used to promote missions, has great appeal and strengthens learning. A skit, dialogue, tableau, or play might be given on the life of a contemporary or historical missionary, or on how a missionary ascertained the purpose of God for his life. Drama also allows for additional learning experiences as the young people participate in its production. This is more of a direct experience with its own specific values to the learner.

Related to dramatics is the use of *readings*. The oral interpretation of missionary material or a dramatic interpretation in monologue can be very impressive.

Recreation offers a different kind of educational experience for youth, which at first may not be immediately recognized as a means of missionary education. But at teen socials the playing of games representative of various countries can unconsciously give young people a greater worldwide perspective.[5] Or an entire social or a banquet may be planned around a missionary theme, including food, games and costumes typical of foreign lands; a missionary speaker; or film.[6]

The possibilities of *exploration* and the observation of missions are unlimited. These teaching-learning experiences take a little more time and effort and are therefore often slighted. *Flats* (missionary pictures mounted for use) and *graphics* (charts and graphs) can be sources of information and challenge to action, if well prepared and wisely used. A "World Religions Kit," including several interesting charts on world religions, is available from the Church Literature Department, Baptist Sunday School Board, 127 Ninth Avenue, North, Nashville, Tennessee 37203. The *National Geographic Magazine* is an excellent source of pictures on missions. (Attractively display these on posters and bulletin boards.)

Films and filmstrips with a missionary emphasis are "legion." *The Audio-Visual Resource Guide* (New York: Friendship Press) lists several hundred films and filmstrips directly related to missions. Many evangelical mission boards—both denominational and independent—as well as several evangelical film producers have produced numerous films and filmstrips on various aspects of missionary endeavor and on various mission fields.[7]

Exhibits include displaying such items as maps, flags, curios, stamps, coins, Christian literature in other languages, dioramas, and missions scrapbooks.

Field trips are an invaluable teaching tool. Occasional excursions to the headquarters of missionary agencies give young people information

5. See E. O. Harbin, *Games of Many Nations* (New York: Abingdon, 1954) and the Fun and Festival Series of booklets (New York: Friendship).
6. For a catalog of numerous, inexpensive accessories for use at parties and banquets to create a missions atmosphere, write to The Wright Studio, 5264 Brookville Road, Indianapolis, Indiana 46219.
7. See chapter 29, "Materials for Working with Youth," for a listing of evangelical film producers.

and understanding of the missionary task beyond mere listening techniques.

RESPONSIBILITY

During summers and vacation periods more and more youth leaders are taking carefully selected Christian young people from their churches both to observe and to accept responsibility in missionary activity. These direct experiences are taking place in such places as Mexico, Guatemala, Alaska, Arizona among the American Indians, and overseas. Thus young people have firsthand opportunity to see how missionaries work, to learn of conditions in these locales, and to contribute to the work of missions by helping in work projects, conducting services, visiting homes. Certainly an excellent way to create enthusiasm for missions is an actual visit to a mission field.

The opportunity of hearing missionary speakers and talking with them is an excellent means of fostering teens' interest in missions. In fact, it is significant that in a survey of 709 missionaries, 58 percent of them said they received their call through a missionary.[8]

Three programs being used to involve youth in responsible and direct experience in missionary activity during the summers are worthy of mention. One is the Rural Outreach Program under the auspices of the American Missionary Fellowship (formerly the American Sunday School Union). This program gives young people training and experience in conducting vacation Bible schools and in camp counseling. This organization also engaged in inner city ministries with youth. The Practical Missionary Training program (a ministry of the Central American Mission) offers the same type of expression but takes place in an actual missionary situation outside the country. This is also true of the MAC (Missionary Assistance Corps) of the Conservative Baptist Association. Information may be obtained by writing to the American Missionary Fellowship, 1816 Chestnut Street, Philadelphia, Pennsylvania 19103; Practical Missionary Training, 8625 La Prada Drive, Dallas, Texas 75228; and the Conservative Baptist Foreign Mission Society, Box 5, Wheaton, Illinois 60187.

The enthusiasm and strength of learning through such firsthand experiences should not be underestimated. Every youth counselor should give some thought to what he might do along this line with his young people.

Worship, a vital aspect of the church's activity, offers a number of ed-

8. J. O. Percy, "Where Are the Recruits?" in *Missions Annual, 1959* (Ridgefield Park, N. J.: Interdenominational Foreign Mission Assn., 1959), p. 34.

ucational opportunities directly related to missions. This includes numerous hymns and gospel songs related to dedication and to the missionary purpose and vision. The fact that the reading of the Scriptures should have a place in this instructional task hardly needs emphasis. Prayer can also be missionary in spirit as intercession for missionaries and for worldwide needs is brought to the Lord. Each youth group or Sunday school class should have a young person record the group's missionary prayer requests and answers. This will help make young people aware that God does work through prayer and that their lives and the lives of those in specific areas of service are affected by it.

Stewardship is ultimately a missionary concept. Some teen Sunday school classes have taken on partial support of a missionary, a national orphan, or a missionary child. Others have given toward a specific project such as the purchasing of a typewriter for Japan or a set of books for India. Rural teens have raised calves, sold them, and given the money to missions. But the sacrificial giving of money to support missionary programs is only one aspect of stewardship. According to the Bible, stewardship includes the giving of one's self for the purposes of God. Consequently the use of one's time and talents—life itself—is a part of Christian stewardship and of missions.

Youth can be involved in missionary *activities* right at home—in the church or community. The most readily available activity is the church visitation program. Leaders can encourage teens to express their concern for the lost by participating in door-to-door evangelism. Training the youth in how to witness will result in their increased empathy and interest.

Opportunities for missionary outreach in the community are unlimited. An excellent source of ideas to stimulate the thinking of those interested in touching their communities is the book *The 70's Opportunities for Your Church.*[9]

In the summer young people can be encouraged to volunteer their services for improving the appearance of a room in the church. Teens make good painters and hangers of drapes! Or the offices of missionary organizations may need assistance in stuffing and addressing envelopes. Other activities may be suggested by the church missionary committee.

It is important to involve youth in *special missionary programming*. For example, during a missionary conference, a teen banquet may be planned in which missionaries would be seated with the young people to converse with them about missions. Some churches have young people enter a poster-making contest prior to a missionary conference. Other

9. James Daniel and Elaine Dickson, *The 70's Opportunities for Your Church* (Nashville: Convention, 1969).

churches involve teens in booth-making contests. And still others have used teens in manning the booths.

A few churches have sponsored an annual School of Missions—a week of courses on missions, with a program for the various departments and a combined meeting several nights in the week for the entire congregation.

Special days can be used for missionary instruction, including Christmas, Thanksgiving, and a missions day in Sunday school once a quarter. Teens can be encouraged to give a special "missionary Christmas offering" for some missions project. Some groups suggest that Christmas cards to church members be eliminated and that the money saved in this way on cards and postage be given to the project. Other activities such as sharing foodstuffs with needy families are also practiced by many churches. Other seasonal events can be used to great advantage by creative, missionary-minded leaders.

Also *youth programs* may deal with various questions related to missions, such as these: What is a missionary call? Are the heathen lost? Who are some of the great missionaries of the past and present? What are the various avenues of missionary service? (aviation, education, evangelism, literature, medicine, radio). Why do so few young people volunteer for missionary service? What opportunities for missionary service exist in our own nation? How can young people best prepare for missionary service? Are foreign countries closing to missions? For those who may be seriously anticipating entering missionary ministries as a vocation, valuable information on various types of vocational opportunities in missions may be obtained from Inter-Cristo, Box 9323, Seattle, Washington 98109. Short Terms Abroad, Box 575, Downers Grove, Illinois 60515 publishes a free directory on numerous vocational opportunities overseas for one- or two-year terms.

SUMMARY

Missionary education is central in the Scriptures and essential in Christian education. It is vital to the spiritual growth of young people. The foregoing suggestions are presented to stimulate youth leaders to investigate the many areas in which missions can be taught and ways by which each young person can be challenged to present himself "a living sacrifice . . . unto God" (Rom 12:1).

FOR FURTHER READING

Adeney, David H. *The Unchanging Commission*. Chicago: InterVarsity, 1956.
Allen, Roland H. *Missionary Methods: St. Paul's or Ours?* Grand Rapids: Eerdmans, 1962.

Building Blocks . . . for the Missionary Program of the Church. Wheaton, Ill.: Conservative Baptist Mission Societies.

Cook, Harold R. *Introduction to the Study of Christian Missions.* Chicago: Moody, 1954.

———. "The Missing Link in Missionary Recruitment," *Moody Monthly,* December 1964, pp. 20-21, 45.

Culley, Paul G. *The Missionary Enterprise.* Wheaton, Ill.: ETTA, 1954.

Daniel, James, and Dickson, Elaine. *The 70's Opportunities for Your Church.* Nashville: Convention, 1969.

Engel, James F., and Norton, H. Wilbert. *What's Gone Wrong with the Harvest?* Grand Rapids: Zondervan, 1975.

Glover, Robert Hall. *The Bible Basis of Missions.* Chicago: Moody, 1964.

Griffiths, Louise B. *Wide as the World: Junior Highs and Missions.* New York: Friendship, 1958.

Harner, Nevin C., and Baker, David D. *Missionary Education in Your Church.* New York: Friendship, 1950.

Henderson, Jack. *Missions and the Church.* Santa Ana, Calif.: Wycliffe Bible Translators, 1972.

Little, Sara. *Youth, World and the Church* . Richmond, Va.: Knox, 1972.

Lovering, Kerry, comp. *Missions Idea Notebook.* Cedar Grove, N.J.: SIM, n.d.

Missionary Idea Kit. Wheaton, Ill.: Conserv. Bapt. Mis. Soc., 1969.

Pearson, Dick. *Missionary Education Help for the Local Church.* Palo Alto, Calif.: Overseas Crusades, 1966.

Pierce, Robert. *Emphasizing Missions in the Local Church.* Grand Rapids: Zondervan, 1964.

Ranck, J. Allan. *Education for Missions.* New York: Friendship, 1961.

Stott, John R. W. *Christian Mission in the Modern World.* Downers Grove, Ill.: InterVarsity, 1975.

"Try These Foreign Games," *Tips* (Baptist General Conference), November 1964.

Voelkel, Jack. *Student Evangelism in a World of Revolution.* Grand Rapids: Zondervan, 1974.

23

Youth Serving the Church

Robert A. Crandall

THE CHURCH can be a great school of Christian living and service for her youth.[1] She can provide answers to their questions, a faith for their quest, and an avenue for their abilities. Often, however, the opportunity for service is lacking. "It is lacking, not for want of vision on the part of the young people nor because the older persons have failed to dream dreams."[2] Every youth leader has the responsibility of helping the church see the worth of her youth, and in turn helping youth dedicate themselves to the work of the church.[3]

Byrne has pointed out that service activities are beneficial both to the church and to the young people in it:

> Participation in service activities has many advantages, among which are contributions to the social happiness of others, character-forming elements, and practical training for the membership in actual practice of gospel truths and obligations.[4]

THE NEED OF YOUTH FOR SERVICE

Significant service in the church can provide for many of the basic needs of youth.

Youth need a sense of purpose. They not only need a creed to believe but a cause which demands their fullest effort. "One great need in youth work is to help youth gain a sense of mission and purpose."[5] "Where

1. H. W. Byrne, *Christian Education for the Local Church* (Grand Rapids: Zondervan, 1963), p. 27.
2. Kathryn L. Higley, "Go Forward and Serve," *Workers with Youth* 18 (October 1964): 38.
3. Ada Zimmerman Brunk and Ethel Yake Metzler, *The Christian Nurture of Youth* (Scottsdale, Pa.: Herald, 1969), p. 114.
4. Byrne, *Christian Education*, p. 30.
5. Merton P. Strommen, *Profiles of Church Youth* (St. Louis: Concordia, 1963), p. 234.

ROBERT A. CRANDALL, Ph.D., is General Director of the Department of Christian Education, Free Methodist Headquarters, Winona Lake, Indiana.

youth have seen themselves as the church in action, they have moved out in power, often to the surprise of their elders."[6] Through challenging Christian service teens see what can be accomplished by God through dedicated lives and talents.

Youth need a sense of participation. One reason young people drop out of church is that they find it boring, uninteresting, and lacking sufficient activities.[7] In many churches youth are only spectators, forced to observe without opportunity to contribute. Wise youth leaders recognize that involvement is one of the keys to working effectively with adolescents. As Bradford points out, "A simple sense of participation often adds the essential meaning and purpose to life that breaks lackadaisical indifference."[8] Every young person in the church can have a place of service, regardless of talent or ability. But be advised—if adults convey to youth that the teens' talents are more important than their spiritual temperature, the youth ministry is perverted. Obedience is always better than sacrifice. Service is to flow from the intrinsic motivation of a warm relationship with Jesus Christ.

Youth need practice. Learning is often accompanied by trial and error. But proficiency is gained as one performs the service or task. Service training, therefore, provides teens with necessary practice.

Youth need to produce. They need the opportunity to achieve and accomplish. Much of the church's ministry is intangible and thus largely immeasurable. But through service projects a young person can see what his contribution means in the life and outreach of the church.

Youth need praise. Recognition of achievement is important. Through well-performed service a young person can win some honor, public acknowledgment, or a word of personal commendation from the teacher or leader.

Unless the church meets these needs of her young people, she runs the risk of losing them. For this reason, service projects of various kinds should be explored and encouraged. Finding a place of service for spiritually motivated adolescents may well require some imagination and initiative. The maxim "Use me or lose me" is as appropriate today as ever. But again, what impels them to serve is crucial.

Years ago, in his book *Church Work with Young People,* Harry Thomas Stock listed six opportunities the church has for helping youth meet their needs. The last one he mentions is "to promote opportunities in sharing

6. Robert L. Browning, "The Church's Youth Ministry," *An Introduction to Christian Education,* edited by Marvin Taylor (Nashville: Abingdon, 1966), p. 187.
7. Roy B. Zuck, "Why Do Teens Quit Church?" *Link,* March 1963, p. 6.
8. Jack Bradford, "The Care and Keeping of Young People in the Church," *Christian Life,* May 1962, p. 59.

significant service."[9]   In providing such opportunities, the church can meet the needs of her youth and hold them. Talents will be utilized and abundant energies channeled. In this way the need of youth for the church and the need of the church for her youth will both be met.

Promoting service opportunities may not be easy, but it is important. As Frederick W. Stewart has written:

> It is a large challenge! How best to serve youth and to let youth serve in turn, while at the same time keeping the church, as it must ever be, a chronological cross-section of society, with every age represented. . . . The fact is that emotional life, aesthetic life, mysticism, idealism, and opportunity for service—these are normal adolescent needs, which will die out, if not satisfied, and the church can best meet these needs.[10]

Furthermore, many Christian young people *welcome* rather than reject opportunities to serve the Lord in tangible ways. As Browning points out, "Ministering to others, the life and work of service, is much more highly valued by youth than we have supposed."[11]

SERVICE AS A LEARNING EXPERIENCE

A well-balanced program for youth consists of instruction, worship, fellowship, and service.[12] Together these help accomplish the comprehensive aims of Christian education which include "making one's contribution to the church, reaching lost men, and assuming responsibility as a Christian citizen in the community and the world."[13] These aims can hardly be fulfilled without service, for learning in Christian nurture occurs through life's experiences as one shares ideas and deeds.[14] Service therefore becomes a method of learning, an expression through activities which give to the didactic presentation symbolic or practical meaning.[15] Youth-group meetings can thus "carry out the implications of the Sunday school class in the form of learning to solve practical problems and service projects."[16]

Youth want to be doing something. After a period of training they

9. Harry Thomas Stock, *Church Work with Young People* (Boston: Pilgrim, 1929), p. 10.
10. Frederick W. Stewart, *A Study of Adolescent Development* (Philadelphia: Judson, 1954), pp. 164-65.
11. Browning, "The Church's Youth Ministry," p. 187.
12. Lois E. LeBar, "Curriculum," in *An Introduction to Evangelical Christian Education*, edited by J. Edward Hakes (Chicago: Moody, 1964), p. 93.
13. Ibid.
14. Robert R. Boehlke, *Theories of Learning in Christian Education* (Philadelphia: Westminster, 1962), p. 22.
15. Victor Hoag, *The Ladder of Learning* (Greenwich, Conn.: Seabury, 1960), p. 140.
16. LeBar, "Curriculum," p. 94.

should be given opportunities for putting that training to work. Peter Person reminds us that "the most important permanent learning does not come by way of textbook and lectures, but through actual doing."[17]

In Christian education a balanced curriculum should include instruction in Christian service and leadership.[18] Leaders of youth are aware that today's adolescents desire a religion which is relevant and practical. For this reason, unselfish service, as a Christian learning experience, can be a stabilizing factor when teens face periods of questioning and doubt.

PHILOSOPHIES OF SERVICE FOR YOUTH

The effectiveness of service opportunities depends on the philosophy of service held by the adult leaders, and how well that philosophy is transmitted to the young people with whom they are working. Christian service should certainly not be mere activity for activity's sake. Nor is it merely performing some task to earn status in a youth organization.

An adequate philosophy of service by which to guide youth should have three characteristics. It must be *Christ-centered, others-directed,* and *church-channeled.*

Christian service begins with the awareness that Christ was a servant. In all His earthly ministry Jesus gave Himself for others. Christian young people should be impressed with the idea that as followers of Christ they must be known in the world for their life of service.[19] One youth manual has challenged young people in these words: "The church's ministry is that of its Lord. As the people of the church we are called to a life of service."[20]

Iris Cully suggests that youth leaders convey the idea that deeds of loving service are not to be performed because God loves us and expects us to return His love in this manner. Rather, love for God is shown because the persons cannot do otherwise. Love for God is a gift to be shared.[21] The sharing of this gift, love in action, is Christian service. The danger of reducing the intangible love of God to a set of suggestions in a program activity guide is a real one. It is easy to get sidetracked into the performance of service for some lesser motive. "Religious training must be oriented to the experience of joy in service to God."[22]

17. Peter P. Person, *The Church and Modern Youth* (Grand Rapids: Zondervan, 1963), p. 66.
18. See chapter 19, "Youth Programs."
19. W. L. Jenkins, *A Message Concerning the Church's Ministry with Senior Highs* (Philadelphia: Board of Christian Ed., United Presbyterian Church), p. 34.
20. Ibid., p. 24.
21. Iris Cully, *The Dynamics of Christian Education* (Philadelphia: Westminster, 1958), p. 154.
22. Jan Waternik, *Basic Concepts in Christian Pedagogy* (Grand Rapids: Eerdmans, 1954), p. 134.

Love to Christ will find expression in service to others. Young people should see little of self-aggrandizement in a particular service activity. For this reason those who offer rewards for service should be very careful to outline the greater reward of serving others. We must transmit to our youth the idea that we are persons who have received particular gifts from God to be employed in service to others.

It is important that the church serve as a channel for youth's Christian service. A youth group too often functions as an auxiliary rather than as an integral part of the church. There is the danger that service projects will become peripheral rather than pertinent to the life of the church. While young people will often be organized and grouped for practical purposes, their service activities should always be seen as an important part of the church's ministry.[23]

MOTIVATING YOUTH FOR SERVICE

A biblical philosophy of service must be the basis for motivation. Christ is the model for biblically motivated servanthood. He gave Himself to others, and the disciples watched Him do the ministry. Their observation of the quality of His life and His selfless manner profoundly influenced them. As adult and youth disciplers model the truth, the normal response of committed young people will be to imitate them. However, all youth are not at that stage of spiritual development. While most young people are "eager to do something," they may not manifest an interest in serving. Or they may wish to adopt an unsuitable project.

The general approach to the three adolescent age-groups will vary. These approaches might be stated in this way: for junior highs, "Service is what you *should* do"; for high schoolers,, "Service is something you *could* do"; for college-age youth, *"Would* you do service?" Perhaps these different approaches, together with specific suggestions for motivation, can best be considered by viewing each group separately.

JUNIOR HIGHS

The young adolescent has a strong sense of group loyalty, is a hero-worshiper, and has intense joy in personal accomplishment.[24] "He has a vision for service. He wants to do something for the Lord. He is ready to act, but he does not know what to do."[25]

Action in this group, therefore, can be secured through the personal appeal of the teacher or leader whom the adolescent idolizes, through en-

23. Jenkins, *Message,* p. 45.
24. Marjorie E. Soderholm, *Understanding the Pupil: Part III, The Adolescent* (Grand Rapids: Baker, 1962), pp. 22-23.
25. Ibid., p. 32.

couragement to support the project adopted by the group. Since youth in this age-group need considerable guidance, and are generally responsive to it, an appeal on the basis of "oughtness" is effective. But there is danger in overdoing it. Pressure is resented, while practical suggestions are rewarded.

HIGH SCHOOLERS

Middle adolescents have an increasing desire to help others, especially those less fortunate than they.[26] Since they often view service as something to be done for people far away, they need to see the possibilities for serving the Lord in their own church, youth group, and community. Teenagers are also creative, idealistic, open to suggestions by their peers, and eager to belong to a well-organized social group.[27]

For these reasons teens in this group should be encouraged and allowed to use their initiative in selecting a project. But an adult, by dropping suggestions to key young people, can give real though indirect guidance. Whatever the project selected, reponsibility for organization, publicity and follow-through should be carefully assigned. The key to gaining response from this group is to channel energies by showing what can be done, thus getting them personally involved.

COLLEGE-AGE YOUTH

College-age people, properly challenged, relish opportunities to serve and manifest a crusading zeal.[28] Yet if a later adolescent thinks he does not have a particular talent, he may feel there is no place for him in the Lord's work.[29] He may also question the significance of certain service.

To activate college youth, request their assistance, provide service opportunities, and make them feel the importance of the tasks.

The following are some practical suggestions for selecting a youth project.[30]

Some Dos:

1. Be alert for a need to be met. If one cannot be found, check with the pastor.
2. Investigate thoroughly whatever problem has presented itself. Seek the help of adults who know. Appoint committees to collect all the information needed.

26. Ibid., p. 51.
27. Ibid., pp. 45-46, 49.
28. F. L. Reynolds, "You and the Class of '62," *Christian Herald*, May 1962, p. 60.
29. Soderholm, p. 86.
30. Adapted from *Senior High Fellowship Handbook* (Richmond, Va.: Knox, 1962), pp. 250-52.

3. Decide exactly what is to be done. Outline a course of action. Assign responsibilities definitely.
4. Arrange for as many people as possible to participate.
5. Watch for opportune moments that suggest action, such as when the completion of one project may suggest another to follow.
6. Carry through on plans, revising them as necessary, and doing further study as needed.
7. Evaluate the work done, as to its effect on others and on the group.
8. Do each project in a spirit of prayer.

Some Don'ts:

1. Don't begin a project from a selfish motive. If it is done in that way, it may be of little help to the group or others.
2. Don't plunge into something without knowing what it is all about and without careful and prayerful planning.
3. Don't attempt to "sell" the group on something "cooked up" for them; instead, carefully motivate interest by planning with the teens. Concentrate on the need to be met, the privilege of serving, and the potential for participation by everyone.
4. Don't give up. Plans may need to be changed, but it is important to see that the project is successfully completed. Select projects within the ability of the group so they can be carried through.
5. Don't carry out the project *for* the young people. Instead, do it *with* them.
6. Don't select all projects of one type. Giving Thanksgiving baskets and Christmas toys year after year, and doing nothing else, may kill the interest of your group in becoming involved in other kinds of equally meaningful projects.

PRINCIPLES FOR SELECTING SERVICE PROJECTS

In selecting projects, and in challenging young people to become involved, keep the following principles in mind.

1. Service to others is an expression to them of our love for Christ. Jesus commands us to love, but that love has to be expressed. Service, then, is the vehicle through which we may express love to Christ and to others. Christians are the body of Christ—not just a body of believers, but the arms and legs, face and hands, of Christ in the world today.
2. Service to others, if it is truly to reflect love, must never be forced. There will be, in every youth group, some who will not want to participate in service projects. Their level of commitment is not as deep

as that of those who willingly take part, and eagerly look forward to services they may render.

3. Some service projects lend themselves to the involvement of a group of young people. Other projects require only one or perhaps two or three. Be careful not to expect the entire group to become involved in a project which should be handled by individuals.

4. Service projects should not take the place of social events. A youth group should not be taken to a nursing home to sing to elderly persons, instead of being taken to the beach. These activities should be scheduled without conflict so that the teens can do both.

5. Careful adult guidance is needed in selecting service projects that will relate to the youths' abilities, and which may be carried out in the amount of time allowed. However once the project is underway and the young people have been given careful instruction and guidance, they should be allowed to follow through on their own.

6. Service projects should be a training ground for young people. As they become involved in service projects which their leaders suggest, the young people should become more and more aware of opportunities for service on their own.

7. Projects should vary according to age-groups involved. Junior highs do not have the same level of commitment as older youth, and therefore are usually not capable of handling projects that require a lot of time and continual follow-through. On the other hand, college-age youth require projects that are challenging and through which they can feel a vital contribution is being made to a person, to a family, or to the church. Senior high young people are somewhere in the middle.

SELECTING SPECIFIC PROJECTS

Possibilities for service projects are everywhere. Some needs may be obvious. But the most urgently needed service is not always apparent. Research, by asking the pastor or community leaders, or by making a survey, may be required.

The handbooks and service brochures of many denominational youth organizations and of parachurch organizations such as Christian Service Brigade list a variety of ideas. Bowman lists eighty-three service project ideas.[31] Other resources for general and specific service projects are listed under "For Further Reading" at the end of this chapter.

Below are some possible projects youth may perform for the church,

31. Clarice M. Bowman, *Ways Youth Learn* (New York: Harper & Row, 1952), pp. 154-60.

in the community, or as special summer services. Some of these may be carried out for the pastor or other church leaders. Some are related to worship, and others to an outreach ministry of the church.

These suggestions are by no means exhaustive. Any youth leader or group, by using imagination, may be able to select something which fits their group better than any of these. Originality in selection is halfway to success, since the group is thus already involved.

The age-group to which each project seems most likely suited is designated by the following code: J = Junior high; H = High school; C = College-age youth. Some projects may be carried out by more than one group while some others seem limited to one. And some projects are suited more to an individual, while others may involve the entire group.

MINISTERING TO THE CHURCH

1. Assist with church janitorial work (J H C).
2. Assist the pastor and/or the pastor's wife with personal and/or household chores to give them more time for church work (J H).
3. Help direct traffic at the church parking area (J H).
4. Operate projection equipment at special services, and be responsible for its care and maintenance (H C).
5. Provide transportation to church for invalids or children (H C).
6. Purchase visual education equipment, hymnals or chorus books, carpeting, other necessary items for the church and Sunday school (H C).
7. Assist children's workers or teachers in storytelling, preparing teaching equipment, gathering materials (H C).
8. Provide flowers for the church, and distribute them to shut-ins following the service (J H C).
9. Care for hymnals, Bibles, and other worship equipment (J H).
10. Assist with the secretarial work of the church for the pastor, church secretary, Sunday school superintendent, minister of music (H C).
11. Publish a church newspaper (J H C).
12. Establish and sponsor a scholarship fund for a deserving student at college or seminary (C).
13. Sponsor an overseas orphan (H C).
14. Keep in touch with men and women of the church who are members of the armed forces (H C).
15. Establish, sponsor, or assist in a church nursery (J H C).
16. Visit newcomers in the church (H C).
17. Provide ushers for church services (H C).
18. Operate a baby-sitting service for parents so they can attend adult functions of the church (J H).

19. Form a youth choir or help sponsor a children's choir (H C) .
20. Begin or help maintain a church library, including a visual aids section (H C) .
21. Sponsor a youth-conducted evangelistic series (H C) .
22. Sponsor a missionary project, such as raising funds for a specific need or collecting and mailing needed items (J H C) .
23. Paint and distribute signs and posters for the church (J H C) .
24. Supply music for Sunday school and/or church services (including vocal and instrumental solo or ensemble) (J H C) .
25. Compile a church directory showing names, addresses, and telephone numbers of officers of various organizations and departments; and a listing of regularly scheduled services (J H C) .

MINISTERING TO THE COMMUNITY

1. Visit all newcomers in the community (H C) .
2. Organize group activities for older members of the church (C) .
3. Make recordings of special church services and take them to shut-ins (J H C) .
4. Make tray favors for hospitals and rest homes for special days, or for any ordinary day, as a special surprise (J H) .
5. Conduct services in jails, hospitals, rest homes, sanitariums, or other institutions (H C) .
6. Launch a branch Sunday school, with guidance from the pastor or Sunday school superintendent (H C) .
7. Conduct a community census to secure prospects for Sunday school or church (H C) .
8. Distribute invitations to special meetings (J H) .
9. Provide for services in abandoned churches or unchurched areas, with cooperation and approval of the pastor (H C) .
10. In rural areas have a "Lord's Acre" project (growing a crop on a portion of land, turning proceeds over to church) (J H C) .
11. Prepare a float for a community parade (J H C) .
12. Assist in preparing and manning a church-related booth at a county fair or community exposition (J H C) .
13. Launch and participate in a high school Bible club (H) .
14. Conduct a "news service" to report church activities to local papers (H C) .
15. Collect food, used clothing, and used repairable toys for benevolent institutions; then sort, mend, repair, paint, ship (J H C) .
16. Distribute gospel portions or devotional materials in hospitals, rest homes, county homes (J H) .

17. Minister to migrant workers (H C).
18. Collect items to send to Goodwill Industries, Salvation Army (J H C).
19. Give assistance to community welfare and service agencies (H C).
20. Join in a community clean-up campaign (J H C).
21. Offer a gift of love—a workday (H). Send letters to families residing in the neighborhoods of the teens in the group, and/or to church members or others. The letters should read: "Dear friend: The members of our church youth group want to show appreciation for our special friends on a workday. Do you need help in any way? Do you need your windows washed? Do you need help getting groceries? Would you like a baby-sitter half a day? On the enclosed card, check whether you would prefer morning or afternoon on Saturday— (designate a date)."
22. Have a "rake and run" (J H). Get a bus full of teens with rakes. Stop the bus at the yard of an older person. Have all the kids get out and rake. If the person is at home, have a teen go to the door to explain what they are doing. If no one is home, leave a note.
23. Have a "snow and blow" (J H C). This is the same as "rake and run" except that it is done in the winter where there is snow. The young people take snow shovels, and shovel snow from walks and driveways of persons not able to do it themselves.
24. Give a cup of cool water in His name (H C). Along the beaches, have the fellows carry coolers on their backs and the girls carry paper cups. They walk along the beach, offering a cup of cool water in His name, to persons lying on the beaches.[32]

MINISTERING IN THE SUMMERS

1. Serve as counselors or workers in church-sponsored summer camps (H C).
2. Provide scholarships for a week at camp for some youngster(s) who would otherwise not be privileged to attend (C).
3. Assist in vacation Bible school (J H C).
4. Help with construction or maintenance on camp or conference grounds (J H C).
5. Form a crusade team to tour a district or a state, conducting Bible schools in unchurched areas or helping to revitalize other work (H C).
6. Assist with cleaning, painting, repairing, varnishing of a local church, including yard work and the maintenance of the parking lot (J H C).
7. Help pay the way of a person participating in voluntary missionary service (short-term) or in a summer work camp (H C).

32. Suggestions 21-24 are ideas adapted from Youth Specialties, 861 Sixth Avenue, San Diego, California 92101. Used by permission.

8. Form a work group to go to a nearby mission or smaller church that needs help in painting, redecorating, cleaning (H C).
9. Have a gardening project and give proceeds to church—boys could raise a vegetable garden; girls could grow flowers (J H C).
10. Help with leadership of summer playground activities in the community (H C).
11. Visit a foreign mission field to assist missionaries in needed projects (H C).
12. Sell Christian books in downtown high-rise apartments (H C).

MINISTERING TO SPECIAL NEEDS

1. Help the elderly. Many older people in retirement or convalescent homes are lonely and in need. Youth groups can let these people know someone cares. Each young person may "adopt a grandparent." The young person would visit the "grandparent" once a week, read to him, take him for a walk, take him a small gift or fresh flowers and, if possible, take him to church on Sunday. All the young people involved in the "adoption" program could fix some special snacks or plan a party for the entire group once or twice or more a year, with the approval of the management of the home. Quiet games may be played, and a talent show, skits, or other program may be offered for entertainment. Special music and a devotional may be included (H C).
2. Help the poor, the hungry, the unemployed. Youth groups can conduct food drives or clothing drives. One youth group had a "way-out weight-in." The group divided into scavenger teams. The team that collected the most weight in food for needy families won the competition. Another youth group used their offerings to purchase a reserve supply of food. This was stocked in utility cupboards in the basement of the church. When a family was hit by sudden tragedy or unemployment, the food was given to them free (J H C).
3. Help victims of tragedy (J H C). If a fire, tornado, or earthquake should strike a home in the community, encourage the youth to conduct food and clothing drives or to secure bedding or other necessities for the needy family (J H C).[33]

A new area of service open to young people through most denominations and several interdenominational agencies today is the service at home to community or denominational needs, and service abroad on a short-term basis.[34] The "at home" programs are usually open to any

33. These three ideas are adapted from materials produced by Youth Specialties. Used by permission.
34. For more on involving young people in missionary service, see chapter 22, "Missionary Education of Youth."

young person who is in high school. The overseas programs are generally restricted to those who are recent high school graduates or of college age. While overseas assignments are perhaps more glamorous, at-home projects offer opportunities for young people to assist small struggling churches, to work in home missions projects, and to help in areas of their community where there is real need. These young people go out in task forces, under adult supervision, to do such things as to give a small church a coat of paint, to fix up the parsonage lawn, to putty windows, to add weather stripping to a Christian school building.

MINISTERING THROUGH FUND-RAISING PROJECTS

One way young people can assume responsibility for church and community needs is by financing worthy endeavors. Recently young people have been involved in all types of projects to help raise money for church or community causes. They have sponsored walk-a-thons, bike-a-thons, run-a-thons, telethons, rock-a-thons (in rocking chairs), and other imaginative energy-expending programs for which people contribute. Then there are car washes, bake sales, and slave days, house-to-house sales or canvassing, programs, and so forth.

REWARDS FOR YOUTH SERVICE

There are rewards in service both to the participating individual and to the church. To the young person there is the reward of personal satisfaction and the opportunity of preparing for service in the future. The enjoyment of Christian fellowship, the learning of social graces, and the acquiring of leadership experience are possible by-products of service activities. While there may be some honor or public recognition, the greater commendation is our Lord's "Well done, thou good and faithful servant" for young people who have performed a task to the glory of God.

Perhaps in some respects the local church is more a beneficiary of service activities than the youth themselves. With each song rendered, each witnessing venture experienced, each visit made to a shut-in, each box of clothing packed, youth are maturing in preparation for adult leadership. As Stoughton has said, "God's best lieutenants of tomorrow will be those youth who serve Him in the ranks of today."

Hopefully through such activity many young people will be called into vocational Christian service. Many people who later became ministers or missionaries participated meaningfully in the life of the church when they were teens.

The assimilation of youth into the work of the congregation tends to infuse it and them with enthusiasm. Youthful zeal often stimulates lethargic adults.

SUMMARY

The church's greatest resource of reproduction is through the winning and discipling of her own youth. These youth may at times lack motivation. However, the potential is there. Happy is the church—and happy are the youth in it—that provides its young people with the opportunity to serve Jesus Christ.

FOR FURTHER READING

Bowman, Clarice M. *Ways Youth Learn.* New York: Harper & Row, 1952.

Bradford, Jack. "The Care and Keeping of Young People in the Church," *Christian Life,* May 1962, pp. 58-59.

Corbett, Jan. *Creative Youth Leadership.* Valley Forge, Pa.: Judson, 1977.

Design for Diligent Witness. Official Guidebook for Free Methodist Youth. Winona Lake, Ind.: Free Methodist.

High School Resource Guide. Vols. 1, 2. Wheaton, Ill.: Scripture Press, 1969, 1971.

Hoglund, Gunnar. *Youth Groups.* Chicago: Harvest Publications, 1967. Chapter 8.

Junior High Crusader's Guide. Winona Lake, Ind.: Free Methodist, 1961.

May, Helen. *Impactivity: Youth Program Resources.* Nashville: Broadman, 1974.

Middleton, Barbara, ed. *Respond: Resources for Senior Highs in the Church.* Valley Forge, Pa.: Judson, 1975.

Murray, Herbert J., Jr. "Youth Are the Church Now!" *Baptist Leader,* January 1967, pp. 24-25.

Richards, Lawrence O. *Youth Ministry: Its Renewal in the Local Church.* Grand Rapids: Zondervan, 1972.

Senter, Mark H. III. *Guiding Youth in Project Ministries,* Christian Education Monographs: Youth Workers Series, no. 6. Glen Ellyn, Ill.: Scripture Press Ministries, 1971.

Smith, Jeanne K. "Should Senior Highs Teach?" *The Christian Educator* (April-June 1963): 3-4, 20.

Strommen, Merton P. *Bridging the Gap.* Minneapolis: Augsburg, 1973.

——. *Five Cries of Youth.* New York: Harper & Row, 1974.

——. *Profiles of Church Youth.* St. Louis: Concordia, 1963.

——. *A Study of Generations.* Minneapolis: Augsburg, 1972.

Towns, Elmer. *Successful Biblical Youth Work.* Nashville: Impact, 1973.

"Vocational Guidance Series." Nashville: S. S. Board, Southern Baptist Convention.

"Vocational Series." Fort Worth, Tex.: Radio and Television Commission, Southern Baptist Convention.

Yaconelli, Mike, and Rice, Wayne. *Ideas*. Nos. 1-17. San Diego: Youth Specialties, 1968-1976.

Youth Letter. (a monthly publication). 1716 Spruce Street, Philadelphia, Pa. 19108.

24

Denominational and Interchurch Activities

David A. Hockenberry

THIS IS A NEW AGE—so called because of the rapid changes taking place in every part of the current American life-style. Technologically, man has reached the moon. Physiologically, "miracle drugs" are used every day for curing and eliminating dreaded diseases. Educationally, learning is pupil-centered rather than teacher-centered. Psychologically, a person's very psyche seems to have been tampered with, and things once considered bad are now upright and good. Philosophically, young minds are accepting different standards of morality.

In spite of these supposed "advances" young people still face many problems. Alarming statistics about young persons experiencing depression, using "escape drugs," being committed to psychiatric institutions, and committing suicide show that needs go deeper than technology and environment.

How should local churches respond to this new generation of youth? How can church denominations meet the demands of leadership for this new generation?

Young people need opportunities to develop to their full potential. Therefore, denominations and local churches should keep in mind the "whole" person when preparing programs, ministries, and activities.

Activities usually connote busyness—"If the youth are busy, then something good is happening." This, however, is a false presumption because activity does not guarantee maturity. The fact that a denomination or church offers a variety of programs and activities does not necessarily mean that young people are interested or involved and learning.

The denomination can no longer develop programs and ministries only with the hope that they will be implemented at the local church. It must take into consideration that programs become part of the total

DAVID A. HOCKENBERRY, M.Div., M.C.E., is Pastor of Glacier Baptist Church, Kalispell, Montana.

youth ministry of that denomination or church and should be designed to meet the needs of the whole person.

To understand the ingredients of a total youth ministry, it is necessary to understand the makeup of a whole person. Being made in the image of God (Gen 1:26), youth need to be exposed to experiences that will help them become whole. In addition to physical development, they need to mature in their spiritual lives, expand their intellectual potentials, increase in emotional stability, and enlarge their social awareness. The denominational thrust must include resources and training that will assist youth and leaders in these areas of developing into whole, mature persons.

How can this happen? How can a denomination develop programs and activities that include these elements?

First, the board of Christian education of a denomination should appoint a task force of persons to research the youth of that denomination to determine what youth want and need. This will help eliminate meaningless and expensive programs and allow more time and funds for ministries that are compatible with youth needs.

Second, a solid foundation needs to be built that encompasses a practical philosophy for youth ministry. In architecture before any structure goes up, a study is made of the depth to dig, the amount of materials needed, the number of employees needed, and when to begin building. Similarly, in youth ministry several foundational factors need to be considered:

What is the denomination's philosophy for youth ministry?
What are the needs of the local churches' youth?
What activities and ministries can the local church itself implement?
What programs and ministries can the denomination provide that cannot be provided by the local church?
Who is available to plan these ministries?

These and other foundation building questions need early answers for a fruitful youth ministry.

Third, well-defined goals need to be established for youth ministry. These will give insight and direction into the kind of programs and activities for which to plan. Local churches, district leaders, and the denomination should understand and work closely together toward accomplishing mutual goals.

Fourth, an adequate training ministry must be developed simultaneously with all programs and activities if maximum results are to be realized. If leaders are trained to use the resources relevant to each program and activity, the total youth ministry will become more effective.

Thus, the total youth ministry is more than activities and programs. It is everything that is done with and by youth—in the denomination and in the local church. It is a composite of many groups of individuals of different ages and ministries, people who are concerned about helping youth become complete individuals, persons growing up in every way unto Christ (Eph 4:15). These include Sunday school teachers, parents, grandparents, pastors, coaches, brothers, sisters—everybody is part of the total youth ministry. A total program for youth, then, needs to include several emphases designed to guide youth toward maturity.

First, youth need to discover who they are as persons so that they can grow personally while becoming disciples of Christ. Young people need to learn how to establish a personal value system and to develop open and honest relationships based on the Word of God.

Second, teenagers should be learning that service to others in the name of Christ is the normal way of life. Leading persons to Christ, meeting people's needs, and ministering to the body of Christ is not a tacked-on experience done sporadically, but is to be a natural part of daily living. Call it evangelism or outreach, youth need opportunities for sharing their faith with other persons.

Third, this new generation of young people needs to be challenged with what interests them. For too long, programs and activities have been limited in scope. Leaders have planned activities around what they think youth need instead of asking young people what they want. Larry Richards says: "It is vital in planning for ministry with youth that we understand the styles in which youth tend to think and feel and shape our ministries to what they are, not what we might think they ought to be."[1]

Leaders must take time to learn about individuals and their interests in order to provide experiences that will minister to them where they are living. Interests can range from Bible study to auto mechanics to bird watching. They are as varied as the number of people and resources in a church or denomination. Interest ministry may be a new concept. Perhaps it sounds somewhat secular, not belonging in the church. However, interest ministry is simply helping youth develop their interests into ministry in Christ's name. Its purposes are threefold: (1) to present Jesus Christ as Saviour and Lord in an appropriate and appealing way to every young person in the denomination and church; (2) to help youth rediscover the thrill of learning through involvement in voluntary study areas of interest—art, carpentry, mechanics, music, athletics, poetry, and others; and

1. Lawrence O. Richards, *Youth Ministry: Its Renewal in the Local Church* (Grand Rapids: Zondervan, 1972), p. 14.

(3) to strengthen youth in all areas of the Christian life by providing opportunities for them to associate with mature Christians.

Fourth, there are times when youth need to "celebrate," that is, to magnify and glorify Christ in such activities as worship, drama, recreation, fun, music, picnics, camping, and retreats.

In summary, denominations and interchurch activities should provide opportunities, experiences, and places where Christian youth can grow personally, have opportunity to minister to other persons, be challenged to develop their interests into a ministry, and be free to celebrate the Christian life using their God-given personalities, gifts, and talents.

THE DENOMINATIONAL YOUTH PROGRAM

From this understanding of youth needs and a total youth ministry, existing denominational and interchurch activities can be evaluated, and suggestions can be made for other youth ministries.

A few years ago the denominational youth organization was linked more closely than now with the weekly youth group program in local churches. The typical organization centered around youth-group presidents and vice-presidents. Likewise, regions or districts elected youth to various offices. Thus the denominational organization consisted of regional or district representatives and a few interested adults who met periodically to plan and give direction to the overall youth ministry.

To meet the needs of a new style of ministry for youth today, the character of this leadership is changing. Many denominational youth organizations now have a task force for developing youth ministry. This group of regional or district leaders and youth manage youth ministry on a denominational level. Appointed by the board of Christian education, such a task force is composed of adults currently working with youth (Sunday school teachers, coaches, counselors, club leaders); adults interested in youth (parents, laymen, etc.); and young people themselves. Their responsibility is to make sure that a balanced youth ministry is taking place in the local church and community. They will need to understand that the old philosophy of youth ministry—preparing youth to be the church of tomorrow—will not work in this new generation. Today's young people want to be part of the action now.

Along this line William A. Yon stated the following:

> So long as the church believed that its primary task was to maintain its own institutional life in order to provide nurture for those within it, youth were necessarily assigned subordinate roles, since they obviously lack the experience and judgment to manage the business affairs of this mammoth institution. But when the church's primary concern shifts from institu-

tional maintenance to mission in the world, then the young person takes his place alongside the adult as another soldier on the firing line.[2]

Youth ministry is more than preparing youth to become a part of the church of tomorrow. They are part of the church now and need to be considered with all other members of the body of Christ. Young people can contribute. They want to become involved in ministry in their church, school, family, neighborhood, and the world.

Some denominations hold super youth conferences every year. These large gatherings supplement local church and state get-togethers. These not only provide a natural setting for fellowship and fun, but individuals or small groups can personally develop in interest areas such as music, art, sculpturing, crafts, and sports. This type of setting also provides opportunities for witnessing and sharing personal faith with people of the hosting community.

A great number of youth organizations conduct contests on a denominational level. Having contests just for the sake of competing, however, is wrong. But contests that offer a viable service to youth, where they can minister through God-given abilities and talents, do have a place.

Many denominations publish various materials for their youth programs. However, written programs can be a hazard. Programs soon become a bore to youth and leaders if they are not designed with youth needs in mind. Too often they are used by leaders as crutches for personal creativity, or they are used indiscriminately because of a "lack of something to do."

While written materials offer helpful suggestions, they should be used only in relationship with the purpose of the total youth ministry. Leaders should always ask how the program will meet the needs of the young people. Does this program best meet those needs? What are the alternatives? Youth activities on a denomination level, whether a weekend rally, a retreat, a camp, or a conference must have goals and objectives that meet needs and enhance the total youth ministry.

THE DENOMINATIONAL SUNDAY SCHOOL MINISTRY

In spite of such efforts as interchurch attendance campaigns, Sunday school attendance in many denominations is rapidly declining. Why? Could it be that denominations and churches have placed an almost impossible burden on the Sunday school? In many groups the Sunday school is relied on to do the entire educational job. It is expected to evangelize, teach, recruit, train, and send out youth into missions all over the world.

2. William A. Yon, *Student World* (Geneva: World Student Christian Federation) 56 (1963), p. 307.

With declining attendance, it is evident that it cannot do the job alone. It needs help. Not that Sunday school is no longer important. It, like all ministries, needs to be continually evaluated and updated.

As an essential educational agency of the church, the Sunday school's purpose is to teach, but differently from a few years ago. With the changing emphasis in education from a teacher-centered to a learner-centered approach, the classroom needs to become more than a content and information center. It needs to provide young people with experiences where they are discovering for themselves truths from God's Word and making application to their own spiritual, intellectual, emotional, and social needs.

David Stoop says that "youth are looking for involvement and for meaning in life. This means that the teacher of youth must resist the temptation to limit his teaching to the lecture. He must lead youth to the level of exploration and responsibility where they can work with meanings and be involved in the life-changing process of learning."[3]

True, the Sunday school should be one avenue for challenging youth with Christ and His claims on their lives, but the total responsibility for training youth leaders cannot be left in the lap of the Sunday school. Other agencies, persons, and ministries must become part of the total ministry in reaching youth with the whole gospel.

THE BOYS' AND GIRLS' CLUB MINISTRIES

Many denominations have discovered the value of boys' and girls' club ministries. A club program is unique in that it meets children and youth where they are living. A complete club ministry also includes junior high and high school youth. It offers opportunities for evangelism, self-discovery, and learning at interest levels. It ministers to needs in churches, families, and communities. It offers opportunity for one-to-one relationships. In addition, denominational club ministries often have rallies, retreats, training conferences, and conventions.[4] All parts are for the benefit of helping Christian leaders and youth to grow personally, to touch other persons in need, to develop in interest areas, and to celebrate life as God has intended.

THE LEADERSHIP TRAINING MINISTRY

A large part of every denomination's activities is training leaders to implement the ministries developed for the denomination's churches. The plan for training leaders is different in every group. Some denominations

3. David A. Stoop, *Ways to Help Them Learn—Youth* (Glendale, Calif.: Regal, 1971), p. 45.
4. Also see chapter 20, "Weekday Clubs."

set aside special weekends each year for leadership training. Youth with leadership responsibilities receive training and inspiration to better effect their ministry in the local church. Other denominations sponsor times when leadership specialists are invited to share their ideas and concepts for youth ministry.

These concepts are often sound. But they have primarily focused on developing youth, with little emphasis on developing youth leaders. With the changing philosophy that youth ministry includes more than youth, the goals for leadership training are changing. If youth are to realize their potential, then it is necessary to help people who work with youth reach *their* potential. Therefore training youth leaders is as important as training youth. Denominations are establishing district or regional training centers where leaders can receive information and training. Here they can learn about such things as the importance of the self-image, what makes an effective youth worker, how to communicate the gospel, and how to implement youth activities and ministries in the local church. Denominational officials seek to present a wide-ranging schedule of topics and methods that will help leaders improve themselves and their ministry while working with youth.

Interchurch Youth Activities

Local churches unaffiliated with a denomination can obtain fellowship by seeking out like-minded churches in the neighborhood or community or state and arranging for joint activities.

Whether or not a church belongs to a denomination, its youth can participate in the following forms of interchurch youth activities.

THE CAMPING MINISTRY

Denominations sponsor extensive camp and assembly programs where young people can spend a week, a month, or even an entire summer in learning about God, the Bible, and themselves; and just having fun. In fact, camp has become a foremost area of evangelism for youth as well as an effective means of leading Christian young people to commit their lives to Christ.

As in other ministries, camping is going through change in order to meet today's needs. A typical daily camping program includes Bible study, classes on Bible doctrine, sports, swimming, and a special speaker. This has met some needs. Many have accepted Christ; others have grown in their Christian life. However camping programs are also moving into other specialized ministries, ministries where evangelism, fellowship, and training are still very much a part. Some camping programs center around special interests such as music, sports, crafts, homemaking, art, poetry, sculpturing, books, or evangelism. These special interest camps allow for greater participation at all levels. A trained staff is necessary in order to carry on such an extensive ministry, but results are good. In this style of camping, the individual becomes more important and ministry is more on a one-on-one basis. Denominational youth leaders should give guidance and direction to the camping program and see that a wide variety of ministries are integrated into the camping ministry.[5]

WEEKEND CONFERENCES

In most denominations the weekend conference is growing. Many teenagers feel personally inadequate. They have fears about failure, being left out by their families and peers, not having enough ability to participate fully in life, no place to go, and no idea about what to be. Weekend conferences can help adolescents begin to discover themselves, God, and other persons. Regions or districts are continually planning for spring, fall, or other conferences. These get-togethers can be for churches in an entire state or for a number of churches in one area. Several hundred churches may take part, or as few as two or three churches can participate.

In planning such a conference or convention the nature of the event must first be determined. The purpose and goals of the conference will determine the selection of such things as location, recreation, and accommodations. Traditionally, weekend conferences have been speaker-centered, with the implied thought, "If we get a good speaker the conference will be an automatic success." Special speakers, however, should not be only a tacked-on part of the schedule, but should be integrated into the whole purpose of the conference. This means that the planning committee must provide the speaker with careful and adequate instructions (in writing) as to what it has in mind, several months in advance of the conference. In some weekend conferences a speaker may not be needed. What is included in the program will depend on the needs to be met and the goals and objectives of that ministry.

Planners for weekend conferences will also need persons to help in advertising, registration, housing, food, and recreation. It is no small job to put on a weekend conference, but the final results of changed lives and other lives being channeled in the right direction makes it all worthwhile.

WEEKEND RETREATS

At retreats people can meet at deeper and more meaningful levels when they have time to become acquainted with one another, relate to one another, and minister to one another.

5. See chapter 27 for more information on camping ministries.

Youth retreats differ from weekend conferences and conventions in two ways. First, they are usually held in an outdoor setting rather than in a church or similar building. In fact, many denominational camping facilities are busy year-round with weekend retreats. Second, weekend retreats can range from large youth gatherings to small groups for specialized ministries. In fact, the uniqueness of weekend retreats is the opportunity of getting away for a purpose. That purpose may be worship or prayer or relaxation or a combination of these. It may also be the time for a group of persons to come together to plan for other ministries in the church or denomination.

Retreats can be held at any time. Three-day weekend holidays are popular because they allow longer periods of time to minister. Retreats can also be held for a single day or part of a day apart from the ordinary routines.

If a retreat is to be successful, its planners must consider the following factors:

Purpose. Too often retreats are poorly planned with the only reason being that "we always have a retreat over Memorial Day weekend." Thinking through the purpose will help determine what activities to include.

Place. Knowing the purpose will help in choosing the place for the retreat. If a large group is planned for, it might be best to look for a camping situation or hotel or retreat center. If a small planning retreat is to be held, a cabin or even some person's home might be sufficient. Whatever the place, it should have adequate room for recreation, food, accommodations, and planning sessions.

Personnel. Retreat leaders need to understand the nature and potential of small interpersonal groups. Do not get caught with too many youth and not enough trained leaders to supervise and carry out a successful time of large and small group ministries. Be sure to provide cooks, nurses, lifeguards, and interest-ministry specialists. Some of these jobs, of course, can be handled by young people themselves.

SPECIAL EVENTS

Special events such as afternoon picnics, beach parties, Easter sunrise services, boat excursions, hayrides, hikes, and many other similar ministries are some worthwhile ventures an interchurch youth program can assume. All should be considered in relation to a total youth ministry.

SUMMARY

Denominational and interchurch activities are important in helping youth learn about themselves, how to relate to God, and how to accept other persons. A purposeful, well-planned youth ministry will include relevant and meaningful denominational and interchurch ministries designed to meet the needs of the "whole" person.

FOR FURTHER READING

Little, Sara. *Youth, World, and Church.* Richmond, Va.: Knox, 1968.

Nelson, Virgil, and Nelson, Lynn. *Retreat Handbook.* Valley Forge, Pa.: Judson, 1976.

Richards, Lawrence O. *Youth Ministry: Its Renewal in the Local Church.* Grand Rapids: Zondervan, 1972.

Schaller, Lyle E. *Creative Church Administration.* Nashville: Abingdon, 1975.

Snyder, Ross. *Young People and Their Culture.* Nashville: Abingdon, 1969.

Stoop, David A. *Ways to Help Them Learn—Youth.* Glendale, Calif.: Regal, 1971.

Tournier, Paul. *The Meaning of Persons.* New York: Harper & Row, 1957.

———. *The Whole Person in a Broken World.* New York: Harper & Row, 1964.

25

Reaching Youth in College

David M. Howard and Paul E. Little

THE UNIVERSITY WORLD is an enormous mission field today in North America. The significance of students to our society cannot be overestimated. The impact of students on society during the activism of the late 1960s was profound. While the atmosphere on campuses has changed radically since those days, the fact remains that students are an increasingly important segment of society that must be reached for Christ.

THE SIZE OF THE FIELD

Educational experts predict that by 1983 the United States will have 8,940,000 students enrolled in all institutions of higher learning working on degree credit, and another 1,637,000 in institutions of nondegree credit. This is a total of 10,577,000 students in tertiary education.[1] Actually this is little different from the student population projected for 1977. For a variety of reasons, such as lower birth rate and increasing interest in vocational training instead of liberal arts college, the student population is expected to remain fairly constant in the coming decade.

But even without dramatic growth the univeristy world is still a field of immense importance. It will take creative insights to keep up with it and daring strategies to reach it for Christ.

Today's students are tomorrow's leaders. A college student won to Christ today may be a Christian lawyer, doctor, engineer, politician, professor, minister, or missionary tomorrow. The greatest manpower pool in the world for foreign missions is found on the campuses of North Amer-

---

1. "20-Year Trends in Higher Education," *The Chronicle of Higher Education,* September 2, 1975. See also Kenneth A. Simon and Martin M. Frankel, *Projections of Educational Statistics to 1983-84* (Washington, D.C.: Center for Education Statistics, US Dept. of HEW, 1974).

DAVID M. HOWARD, LL.D., is Assistant to the President, Inter-Varsity Christian Fellowship, Madison, Wisconsin.
The late PAUL E. LITTLE, M.A., was Assistant Professor of Evangelism, Trinity Evangelical Divinity School, Deerfield, Illinois.

ica. While the Third World is becoming increasingly aware of its foreign mission responsibilities, there will continue to be a need for North Americans in missions. Each year thousands of Christian students enter secular campuses. When we add those who will come to Christ through their witness, the potential of the missionary force coming out of universities is exciting to contemplate.

UNDERSTANDING THE FIELD

In reaching mission fields, whether geographical or in a particular enclave of society, there must be an understanding of the field and an identification with it before an effective approach can be made.[2]

What is the typical secular university student like today? Variations and exceptions can be found, but many of the following descriptions characterize students today.

First, students today are in a *quest for authority*. The overwhelming activism of the late 1960s was a revolt against all authority. This revolt was directed against government, school, church, family, and "the establishment" in general. However, students today have begun to realize that when all authority is eliminated one is left in an impossible vacuum. This vacuum is being filled today in one form or another in a quest for authority. This may take the form of looking for a "guru" or some other outlet through Eastern mysticism. Sometimes it takes the form of a commitment to the occult where submission is given to those with specific occult powers.

This characteristic lays the groundwork for a direct presentation of Christianity based on the authority of the Word of God. Whether or not they accept the Bible as the Word of God, the fact is that today's students are looking for authority in some form or another.

Second, there is an *intense personalness* among students. Students want to know each other for who they are and want to be known on the basis of their own merits. There is a quest for deep friendships. The cell group or sharing-group concept is widespread.

The desire for personal relations is noted in such things as students giving only their first name when introduced to a stranger. It is far more common for a student to do this rather than to give his or her full name. This is because a student wants to be known for who he or she is rather than for family or other relationships. Another indication is the greatly increased freedom in sexual relationships. While there is a wide variety of reasons for this, one reason is unquestionably the desire for a deep personal relationship even if this is only on the physical level.

Third, *interest in vocation* is on the increase again. Students today are

2. Also see chapter 10, "Later Adolescence."

going to college to prepare to become part of society—not to try to destroy society. Therefore, they are planning to work within the system even though they may wish to change that system from within. Consequently, there is an increasing desire to find meaningful studies in relationship to the future.

Fourth, *there is great uncertainty about the future.* The speed with which change is taking place in society leaves a student breathless. Sociologists now assert that most people will change vocation three or more times in their lifetime. This makes a student uncertain as to what he is doing in college in spite of his interest in vocation. It also leaves one increasingly uncertain as to the immediate future after college. Far more students today have no idea about what they are going to do after graduation than was true of previous generations.

Though we live in a so-called Christian country, the average university student is biblically illiterate. Evangelistic discussions in a fraternity or dormitory are sometimes begun by asking students how they would define Christianity to someone from another country who had no objections to Christianity but simply was ignorant of it. Replies are shocking in that the person and work of Christ are seldom intelligently related to being or becoming a Christian.

A non-Christian student from a Pennsylvania college was riding with a Christian student. They passed a sign along the road which said, "Jesus saves." The non-Christian in all sincerity said, "That's something I've never thought of before. If Jesus was thrifty, I should be too!"

The fact of biblical illiteracy has important implications for the ways Christians communicate the gospel to non-Christian students. It must be in nontraditional vernacular language for the benefit of those who haven't learned "Protestant Latin," as Eugene Nida has called Christianity's traditional jargon.

Students often think they have rejected Christianity, but in conversation it soon becomes apparent that they have rejected simply a caricature of the real thing. Many students think of Christianity as essentially a negation of life. This false idea must be countered by the communication of the abundant life Jesus offers (John 10:10) without in any way hiding the cost of discipleship. No man can hang on to his sin and follow Jesus Christ; his desires change when he becomes a new creation.

A generation ago reactions were very strong against faith of any type. It was considered unscientific and intellectually naive to have faith. However, this is now changing. The increasing interest in the metaphysical and the nonmaterial world is evidence of this. The fact that Transcendental Meditation is sweeping the country and being accepted in intellectual, educational, and political circles is further evidence of this fact. Therefore, Christians need not be so much on the defensive today when they talk about faith.

Few have ever heard the factual basis and evidence on which the Christian faith is based and have not realized that in Christianity faith goes beyond reason but not against it. They are amazed, for instance, to hear the evidence for the resurrection and the evidence for the reliability of biblical documents. Unfortunately, many Christian students are equally amazed to encounter the same evidence and are quite relieved to realize that they don't have their "heads in a bucket" after all!

This latter fact points up the painful truth that many churches have done less than a first-class job in preparing students for the intellectual climate of the thinking non-Christian world. Many churches have tended to give young people answers to the wrong questions—questions they are not asking. This conclusion has been confirmed by an experiment Paul Little used to conduct on Christian college campuses. "Let's imagine," he would say to the students, "you're a fraternity or dormitory group on a secular campus. I'll give a talk which I give on the secular campus and we'll have a question period just as we do there. You can ask anything you want and remember that we'll assume you're a non-Christian group." The questions these students ask, which they *think* the non-Christian would ask, are quite different from those encountered regularly in talking to unsaved youth. They tend to be much more biblically oriented and not really as basic as those in Sigma Chi or Sproul Hall.

But university students, like people everywhere, have a hunger for God. It is often undefined and unrecognized, but it can be brought into focus by relating the problems of life to the source of those problems—separation from God (the result of rebellion against the Creator). Secular researchers confirm this also: "When we talked to the students about religion we found that many of them began the discussion by declaring that they felt strongly a need for some kind of a religious faith or philosophy to give meaning to their lives and to bridge the gap between the manifest occurrences of daily life and the ultimate meaning of these occurrences."[3]

The fields of the university campus are white for harvest now as perhaps at no other time in history. The disillusionment following Vietnam, Watergate, and so many other problems have left students groping for something beyond themselves. The depravity of man is scarcely debated any longer. Rather, it is accepted on the incontrovertible evidence of

3. R. K. Goldsen et al., *What College Students Think* (New York: Van Nostrand, 1960), p. 156.

society today. This, in itself, paves the way for the presentation of the gospel. Christians believe that Christ is the answer. But if He is to be heard, Christians must communicate the gospel in relevant terms. It is encouraging today that society and Christianity are on the same wavelength, at least on this first point of the sinfulness of man.

WINNING A HEARING

Getting an audience for the gospel on the university campus is the key problem. The most brilliant speaker may be communicating the gospel dynamically, but if no one is listening but the Christians, little has been accomplished in terms of evangelizing campus youth.

Effective mass evangelism in any field is based on effective personal evangelism, both before and after the effort. However, evangelism cannot be limited to the circle of friends of the Christian student, even though it begins there. Paul says in 2 Corinthians 9:6 (NASB) : "He who sows sparingly shall also reap sparingly; and he who sows bountifully shall also reap bountifully." The Christian student's objective should be to communicate the gospel effectively over the course of a year to as many students and faculty as possible.

How it is done is as important as *that* it is done. *How* it is done will also determine *whether* it can be done in the increasingly confused climate of church-state relationships as they apply to public, tax-supported institutions. For instance, students on a state university campus were denied permission to sponsor a lecture on the subject "Is the Bible true?" on the grounds that this would violate the principle of separation of church and state. Several months later, however, they were permitted to have a lecture on the subject "Are the New Testament documents reliable?"

Since students are reacting against traditional forms, a Christian will gain a much wider hearing for the gospel by going where they are rather than asking them to come where he is. In other words, since few non-Christians come to evangelical churches, the latter must gain entrance to the places where students live and carry on their activities.

Evangelistic bull sessions in fraternities, sororities, and dormitories are a very effective way to get a large non-Christian audience. Although fraternities and sororities reached a low ebb for awhile, they have revived in the recent years. Membership is up, houses are being reopened, and competition for acquiring memberhip is increasing. Consequently, this platform for discussion groups is once again opening up. These discussions can be arranged by contacting the fraternity, sorority, or dormitory council presidents, suggesting the availability of a half-hour program consisting of a fifteen-minute talk followed by a fifteen-minute open question period.*

The topic should be provocative, such as "Are Christianity and Transcendental Meditation Compatible?" or "Can Jesus Christ Be a Guru Today?" The more a topic expresses a question or some idea that is actually in the non-Christian's mind, the more it will attract people to the discussion.

The question period has special appeal for students. They are accustomed to discussion, and if the word gets around that the house agnostic will be there and controversy is likely to occur, this additional spice draws the otherwise disinterested student to the meeting. It is important to note that *why* people come to such a discussion is not important. The fact that they come is all-important. After hearing the gospel intelligently presented and discussed, many of them are touched by the Holy Spirit. Interest deepens, and some come to the Lord. Obviously, if they never come in the first place, this does not happen.

Answering questions is not nearly the problem it appears to be at first. The questions asked are remarkably limited in range and surprisingly predictable.[4]

The discussion should be concluded promptly at the close of the half hour with the leader suggesting that he will be glad to remain to talk further with any who still have questions. Most will stay on but it will be on their time, voluntarily (rather than because they were forced to stay) ; and out of courtesy to a speaker who kept faith with his time commitment.

Just before adjournment the speaker should offer further information to those who want it. This can be done by showing booklets like *Becoming a Christian,* by John Stott; *Is Christianity Credible?* by Kenneth N. Taylor; *One Way to God,* by Brian Maiden; *What Is Christianity?* by John W. Alexander; and *Transcendental Meditation,* by David Haddon.[5] He can leave blank index cards on a table or have each person coming to the discussion receive one as he comes in. The speaker might suggest that anyone wanting a free copy of "booklet 1," or "booklet 2" will receive one by jotting down his name and address and the number of the booklet (s) he wants. Giving numbers for the booklets avoids the problem of the student having to remember a long title.

---

*Groups such as Campus Crusade for Christ (Arrowhead Springs, San Bernardino, Calif. 92403), Inter-Varsity Christian Fellowship (233 Langdon Street, Madison, Wis. 53703) and The Navigators (Glen Eyrie, Colorado Springs, Colo. 80901) are carrying on effective ministries on college campuses.

4. Paul E. Little's book, *How to Give Away Your Faith* (Downers Grove, Ill.: Inter-Varsity, 1966) includes an excellent summary of the type of questions students ask.

5. All of these booklets are available from InterVarsity Press, Box F, Downers Grove, Ill. 60515.

This way of "drawing the net" does several things. First, it leaves the total initiative up to the individual in response to the work of the Holy Spirit. The student never feels coerced into something. This is very important in university work. If there is even the slightest touch or suggestion of emotionalism or pressure, there can be and usually is a severe reaction. If students smell even the tiniest trace of "sawdust," they revolt.

Second, this approach allows students to get the information later if, as often happens, the speaker gets tied up in an animated conversation with a vocal agnostic. If the speaker is going to be on campus the next day, he can indicate he will be available for interviews. He can name a prominent lounge or room on the campus everyone would know how to locate, and then say, "I'll be there to meet you any time you indicate on your card." Christian students or the speaker can take the booklets requested to the individuals the next day. By turning in a card, spiritual interest may be indicated, and further conversation may result at the time the booklet is delivered. If the student does not want to talk, he is not forced to, and the booklet is merely left with him.

Another method that has had increasing success in recent years is the use of a book table. On campuses all across the country books are sold in the student union, in the quadrangle, in the main mall, or at other central locations on campus. Every conceivable political stripe is represented by book stalls, including Young Socialists, radical Marxists, Gay Liberation, Women's Lib, and John Birchers. Christian students have seen this as an opportunity to sell the Scriptures and Christian books. Sometimes sales are not large, but the openings given for direct witness for Jesus Christ are great.

EFFECTIVE FOLLOW-UP

Evangelistic Bible studies are an effective follow-up to these discussions. They can also be started with a prior discussion. In this case, one or two students invite their friends to study the New Testament with them informally. This can be done by personal door-knocking or by displaying posters. It is essential to have the majority in the group non-Christians so that a free and permissive climate will be established. If the non-Christians feel outnumbered and view themselves as targets rather than participants, they will clam up and probably not return. The leader should first lay down a few ground rules, such as this: "The thing we want to do tonight is discover what this passage of the Bible actually says. Whether one agrees with it or not is another question and can be discussed after the study." By laying down this ground rule at the outset, a number of tangents can be avoided. By carefully prepared questions the leader enables the participants to discover for themselves what he or she would point out if lecturing to them. Several useful guides with pretested questions are available.[6]

Evangelistic Bible studies are not an end in themselves but a means to an end. In any given Bible study, seldom does the passage being studied involve a systematic or complete presentation of the gospel. Students have come to the Lord through Bible studies where there has been personal follow-up. Systematically and prayerfully each non-Christian should be visited on a friendly and informal basis. They can be drawn out as to their own understanding of the gospel, and any gaps in information can be filled in. As the Holy Spirit leads the student, he or she should be invited to respond personally to the claims of Jesus Christ. This step should be carefully explained.

After several students have been won to the Lord, it is wise to establish a Bible study group to train these new converts in the basic teachings of the Scriptures and in basic principles of Christian living.[†]

In considering these group approaches, it is imperative to go through proper channels. University authorities are rightly jealous of their prerogatives. Whenever there is an existing campus Christian group which is officially recognized by the university, it will be wise to work through it. The university does not generally look with favor on uncoordinated efforts or activities which seem to duplicate those already established.

Where there is no group it is well to contact the dean of students, become acquainted with him, and explain the broad purpose and plan for the group. If any repercussion gets back to the dean before such a contact is made, the problem can be infinitely complicated, more so than is the case if one takes the initiative first.

University administrators are not necessarily prejudiced against evangelicals. A common attitude is one of indifference. Their major concerns are *how* something will be conducted and that student interests be protected from any form of pressure. If a youth worker realizes that the dean must answer to the president, parents, and unhappy students for any reverberations, he can fully appreciate the dean's position.

6. See for example, J. I. Packer, *Knowing God* (Downers Grove, Ill.: InterVarsity, 1973) and *Knowing God: Study Guide* (Downers Grove, Ill.: InterVarsity, 1975); Gordon Lewis, *Decide for Yourself: A Theological Workbook* (Downers Grove, Ill.: InterVarsity, 1970); *Discussions on the Life of Jesus Christ* (Downers Grove, Ill.: InterVarsity, 1962). The discussion technique is spelled out by James Nyquist in *Leading Bible Discussions* (Downers Grove, Ill.: InterVarsity, 1967).

†For this purpose The Navigators have ten study books called *Studies in Christian Living;* Inter-Varsity has *Grow Your Christian Life* plus numerous other study guides; and Campus Crusade for Christ has a ten-book study called *Ten Basic Steps toward Christian Maturity.* See "For Further Reading" at the end of this chapter.

THE CHURCH AND THE CAMPUS

Local churches can have a vital ministry to college youth. Churches should keep in contact with Christian students studying on the campus. Rather than pressure these Christian students to be at the church every time it opens its doors, the church should encourage them to spend time as missionaries with non-Christian students who may be reached in no other way. Christian students need training in evangelism to help them overcome the all-too-common tendency to stay in the "holy huddle."

Granted a genuine, vital relationship with Jesus Christ, apart from which no practical instruction will be of much help, Christian college students must know certain definite things. For instance, they need to realize that *separation* from the world is not the same as *isolation* from the world. They need to have practical instruction in how to live without compromise in a non-Christian world, where the behavior pattern is different from that in Christian circles. On the one hand, they need to avoid compromise, and on the other hand, "oddballism," which results from making minor issues major ones in one's Christian witness. They must know how to respond to invitations to participate in activities in which they will not feel free as Christians. For example, how do they react to the increasing sexual freedom in dormitory life on their campus? How do they react to the use of drugs among their friends.[7]

Most Christians are insecure with non-Christians because of insufficiency in one of three areas:

1. They do not know how to approach non-Christians, win their friendship, and swing the conversation from mundane things to spiritual issues.
2. They are not exactly sure what the gospel is. It is like a mathematical problem they have understood in class but are unable to explain clearly an hour later to the friend who cut class. They have believed the gospel and have been changed by it, but are unable to verbalize it clearly enough to someone else so that he too can have the same experience of personal relationship with Christ. Careful instruction in the facts of the gospel and where they can be documented in the New Testament is needed.
3. Many are afraid of being unable to answer questions asked by non-Christians. Instruction in questions and answers, as well as how not to push the panic button when they cannot answer a particular question, is necessary vital equipment.

7. For specific practical suggestions see Paul Little, *Lost Audience* (Downers Grove, Ill.: InterVarsity, 1959).

The Campus Crusade for Christ (Arrowhead Springs, San Bernardino, Calif.) has been especially successful in its evangelistic ministry to college students through the use of the *Four Spiritual Laws* booklet. This gives collegians a tangible tool to help them in presenting the gospel and has been greatly appreciated.

In addition to those whom the students and members of the church bring to services, other students can be attracted by a relevant program. Attractive, creative posters on campus are one good way a church can let students know what they are doing. The campus newspaper is also a key link in effective church and campus communication.

A separate *class for college students in the Sunday school* can be very effective. This gives them their own peer group with which to study. However, it should be noted that in some churches today there is a trend toward the mixing of ages in Sunday school classes. It may turn out to be more valuable for a college student to be involved with both younger people and middle-aged or elderly adults in biblical discussions in Sunday school. Some teachers are having increasing success with this method. It is vitally important, however, that whoever teaches the class should be someone capable of communicating to college students and also drawing them out in honest discussion.

A *series of Sunday evening messages on Christian evidences* would be both instructive to Christians and thought-provoking for non-Christians.

A *collegiate club on Sunday evenings* can be useful also. A dynamic, relevant program on topics which are on people's minds can have a spiritual impact. Recognized scholars in their fields can relate Christianity to their academic disciplines and comment on the relevance of the gospel to the affairs of the day. Full opportunity for questions and discussion should be a major feature of this type of program.

Christian literature provided by a local church for its college youth can be of real spiritual help. A church library could make books available on Christian evidences, doctrine, witnessing, the Bible and contemporary issues (such as mysticism, the occult, a Christian's involvement in politics). Some churches may find it a worthy investment to subscribe to one or more Christian collegiate magazines for their older youth.[8]

The tone or atmosphere of the church itself is another factor in reaching students. Are students welcomed or are they tolerated? Are they resented because they do not contribute financially and are unable to shoulder major responsibilities in the church? Are they judged because of their hair length or style of clothing? Such intangible attitudes are quickly sensed by students. A positive tone can be set by providing transportation

8. See the list of periodicals at the end of this chapter.

from the campus to the church or by making an effort to arrange for students to have dinner in the homes of church members. Only those who have experienced the monotony of institutional life and food will know what a welcome relief a meal and a few hours in a home can be! But by far the most important point will be for the church to create an atmosphere of acceptance where students will feel welcome regardless of their particular life-style.

A local church should keep in touch with its students who are attending schools in other towns. This can be done through the pastor writing to students, through the church office mailing the weekly church bulletin and other literature to students, through adult "prayer partners" corresponding with one or more students assigned to them for prayer and correspondence. These students should also be incorporated back into the life of the local church when they return home on vacations. This means not simply acknowledging their presence but, rather, seeking to involve them in the activities and ministries of the church. There should also be regular prayer for them in the church during the school year as well as during vacation.

REACHING INTERNATIONAL STUDENTS

The more than 300,000 foreign students and doctors from 170 countries who are now living in the United States are looking for friendship. A recent survey shows that 98 percent of them said that the one thing they wanted more than anything else during their time in America was one solid friendship with an American student or family. But only 15 percent of them said they had actually achieved such a friendship. No one should make an overture of friendship to a foreign student unless he is prepared to see him or her regularly until the person returns home. "One-shot" friendships are extremely frustrating to someone from overseas and often lead to disillusionment. No pressure should be put on a foreign student to attend church or to become a Christian. Where there is genuine friendship, however, it will be perfectly natural to discuss and share the Christian faith. The student will usually want to go to church with his host if he is sure that the host is truly his friend, and the friendship will not hinge on his response to the gospel. Strategic leaders from overseas often become believers in Christ in living rooms as Christians love them, live the Christian life, and talk to them of Christ as there is opportunity.[9]

International Students, Inc. (Star Ranch, Star Ranch Road, Colorado

9. For further specific suggestions on dos and don'ts in contacting and developing friendships with and witnessing to foreign students, see *A Guide to International Friendship,* from Inter-Varsity Christian Fellowship, 233 Langdon Street, Madison, Wis. 53703. (Single copy free.)

Springs, Colorado 80901) is doing evangelistic work among students in the United States who are from foreign lands. They are anxious to help families who decide to share their houses and lives with overseas students.

SUMMARY

The university campus in every part of the world is one of the most exciting and strategic frontiers in missions today. There is a need for more full-time student workers as well as for those who in the course of other ministries will include the campus in their scope. Opportunities abound for thouands of other people to open their hearts, homes, and local churches to those who are pursuing truth. By so doing they will be the means of many coming to know the One who is the Truth.

FOR FURTHER READING

Books and Articles

Boa, Kenneth D. *God, I Don't Understand*. Wheaton, Ill.: Victor, 1975.

Board, Stephen. "Campus Trends: 1976." *Eternity*, June 1976, pp. 18-21.

Discussions on the Life of Jesus Christ. Downers Grove, Ill.: InterVarsity, 1962.

Engel, James F., and Norton, H. Wilbert. *What's Gone Wrong with the Harvest?* Grand Rapids: Zondervan, 1975.

Grow Your Christian Life. Downers Grove, Ill.: InterVarsity, 1973.

Lewis, Gordon. *Decide for Yourself: A Theological Workbook*. Downers Grove, Ill.: InterVarsity, 1970.

———. *What Everyone Should Know about Transcendental Meditation*. Glendale, Calif.: Regal, 1975.

Little, Paul. *How to Give Away Your Faith*. Downers Grove, Ill.: InterVarsity, 1966.

———. *Know What You Believe*. Glen Ellyn, Ill.: Scripture Press, 1970.

———. *Know Why You Believe*. Downers Grove, Ill.: InterVarsity, 1967.

Nyquist, James. *Leading Bible Discussions*. Downers Grove, Ill.: InterVarsity, 1967.

Packer, J. I. *Knowing God*. Downers Grove, Ill.: InterVarsity, 1973.

———. *Knowing God: Study Guide*. Downers Grove, Ill.: InterVarsity, 1975.

Sire, James W. *The Universe Next Door*. Downers Grove, Ill.: InterVarsity, 1976.

Stott, John R. W. *Basic Christianity*. Grand Rapids: Eerdmans, 1958.

Studies in Christian Living. Colorado Springs, Colo.: Navigators, 1964.

Ten Basic Steps toward Christian Maturity. San Bernardino, Calif.: Campus Crusade For Christ, 1968.

Voelkel, Jack. *Student Evangelism in a World of Revolution*. Grand Rapids: Zondervan, 1974.

Pamphlets

Alexander, John W. *What Is Christianity?* Downers Grove, Ill.: InterVarsity, 1967.

Haddon, David. *Transcendental Meditation.* Downers Grove, Ill.: InterVarsity, 1976.

Little, Paul. *Guide to International Friendship.* Madison, Wis.: IVCF, 1971.

Maiden, Brian. *One Way to God.* Downers Grove, Ill.: InterVarsity, 1974.

Stott, John. *Becoming a Christian.* Downers Grove, Ill.: InterVarsity, 1950.

Taylor, Kenneth. *Is Christianity Credible?* Downers Grove, Ill.: InterVarsity, 1951.

Monthly periodicals

Baptist Student. Southern Baptist Convention, 127 Ninth Avenue North, Nashville, Tennessee 37234.

Worldwide Challenge. Campus Crusade for Christ. Arrowhead Springs, San Bernardino, Calif. 92403.

HIS. InterVarsity, Box F, Downers Grove, Ill. 60515.

The Chronicle of Higher Education. 1717 Massachusetts Avenue, N. W. Washington, D.C. 20036.

Youth Letter. 1716 Spruce Street, Philadelphia, Pa. 19108.

26

Parachurch Youth Movements and Organizations

Vic Glavach and Milford S. Sholund

IN ORDER TO UNDERSTAND the significance of this chapter, one must first recognize that the church is both a spiritual body and a social institution. Romans chapter 12 begins with two verses which relate the familiar challenge to Christians to be separate from the world in terms of priorities, life-styles, and allegiances. But the often overlooked bulk of Romans 12 relates to the *relationships* Christians are to have with one another and with society.

The church is the body of Christ, with life and power bestowed by God. It knows no racial, economic, political, or organizational boundaries, except to exclude those which would deny the existence of God and the deity of Jesus Christ. All who admit their sinfulness in Adam and receive redemption through Christ are members of this spiritual body.

But the church has also become a social institution with both the strengths and the weaknesses of such a structure. Part of the reason for this is that Christians live in relation to one another. Very few can or should or want to avoid social contacts. And as Christians have associated with one another, they have formed local groups for the purposes of worship, fellowship, service, and evangelism. In our society the church, as a social group, is recognized and somewhat accepted. It enjoys privileges, it owns property, it has an organized structure and program. In this sense it has become an institution.*

*Philosopher Eric Hoffer makes some noteworthy observations about movements and institutions. He suggests that movements are relatively unstructured and that people are drawn to them because of ideals, emotion, and/or social conditions. However, as movements grow they inevitably become organized and lose some of their vitality. Organization is a necessary step in the maintenance of the effectiveness of a movement, but it also kills some of the spontaneity of the movement. In a sense the movement

VIC GLAVACH, M.A., is Assistant to the President, Youth For Christ International, Wheaton, Illinois.

MILFORD S. SHOLUND, Litt.D., is Director of Biblical and Educational Research, Gospel Light Publications, Glendale, California.

Parachurch, or extrachurch, movements, then, do not imply appendages to the body of Christ. Although they are often outside the social institution known as the church, they are not outside the body of Christ.

The development of parachurch youth movements and their relationship to the church is a story of innovation in response to need. The organized church, whether a denomination, a fellowship, or a local congregation, has sought to meet the needs of those in the body of Christ and to bring light to a world in need of reconciliation. However the very fact that the church is institutionalized has frequently mitigated against its establishing new programs which are specifically designed to reach beyond the confines of the traditional church organization to the world in which Christians live. This is not an indictment of the church, but merely a recognition of the limited effectiveness that any institution can have on the general population, particularly with relation to religious matters and to adolescents.

Innovation has come as Christians, acting singly and in groups, have assumed the responsibility given them by Christ to carry the gospel to those who have not experienced the love of Christ. In this way the church *has* acted and has been instrumental in the formation of movements outside the institutional church.

Fortunately the Holy Spirit works through many channels to accomplish God's work. However, it is unfortunate that the church as an institution often has not recognized God's work beyond its organizational boundaries. With each succeeding generation the qualities of trust and love and recognition of the diversity in the body of Christ must be learned anew by both the institutional church and those who have ventured forth in new parachurch movements.

Christian youth work in America cannot be appreciated, explained, or evaluated outside the context of the churches. From the beginning Jesus Christ has ordained that the church, a local body of believers in Christ, should be the essential instrument through which He would work and witness in every generation. The norm for the ministry of these churches is described in the New Testament.

loses life through systematization. The final stage of life for a movement is institutionalization. This occurs when the movement has obtained acceptability and has established for itself a place in society. At this point the impact of the idea which gave birth to the movement may lose its effect on society.

Some segments of the church have experienced this metamorphosis. The life is not gone from them, but their acceptability has become, in many cases, a hindrance to the accomplishment of their mission. Therefore, movements have sprung up within the church which inject new life. The parachurch youth movements have been effective in this way. But even as these movements have become organized and accepted, they have progressed along the path to organization and, in some cases, institutionalization.

Christian youth work grew up through the eighteenth and nineteenth centuries in the United States within the framework of the institutional church. This skein of church policy and practice became for many ecclesiastical leaders sacred threads that should not be broken. Many leaders, locally and nationally, committed themselves to honoring programs of the institutionalized church. The result was often a ministry which lacked responsiveness to the needs not only of society but also of the church itself.

It is no surprise, then, that in the growth of Protestant churches in the United States there should be aberrations and some occasions when efforts to do the work of Christ effectively should occur outside of the channels of the institutional church. The parachurch movement is interwoven in the denominational and independent spirit of American Protestantism.

OBJECTIVES OF PARACHURCH MOVEMENTS

Parachurch movements and organizations as used in this chapter refer to those efforts that are made by individuals and members of religious organizations to minister through an association that is not controlled by officially delegated representatives from local and/or denominational bodies. "Para" in this sense means outside the official institution of the church but not outside the life of the universal church.

Parachurch youth movements are an evidence that God is no respecter of churches per se. These organizations are an effort of individuals and groups of individuals to express the will of God, to desire to witness and work in response to God's call and the needs of others. Some have often sensed a vacuum in the vitality and vision of churches. Others have recognized the limitations of the institution and have sought to overcome those limitations. The parachurch youth movement is, in a sense, a peculiar phenomenon among churches in a nation that has provided a congenial setting for religious freedom. It is not meant to rival the institution but to be an extension into fields where the institution cannot go or has not gone, much as the missionary is an extension of the domestic institutional church.

A relationship of mutual respect and appreciation among organizations is, admittedly, a delicate balance to be maintained. Along with our religious freedom and the rugged individualism which seems to be characteristic of the United States, we have fostered the spirit of competition in our "free enterprise" approach to religious activities, and organizations have developed too often into divisions akin to those identified by the apostle Paul in Corinth, where some were of Apollos, some of Paul, some of Peter, and still others of Christ. Even allowing for legitimate doctrinal differences we still experience rivalries between denominational groups, individual churches, and parachurch organizations. The institutionalized church has not been totally in error in criticizing parachurch groups for establishing rival pseudochurches.

One movement which has survived a difficult beginning and has become a part of the institutionalized church is the Sunday school. The Sunday school was once the foremost parachurch movement. Sunday schools, as we know them today, have not always been supported by and integrated into the denominational life of the churches.

Edwin Rice, noted authority on the Sunday school movement, states:

> The churches not being ready for such a movement, it was practically necessary to establish it on a voluntary and union basis. Rooms were hired for holding its schools in rented halls. Denominational organizations were jealous of their prerogatives. At first, therefore, this new scheme was rejected by the churches, though accepted by individuals. . . . It thus became a movement sustained by laymen.[1]

The Sunday schools in America in the early nineteenth century were born spontaneously in the hearts and minds of the laymen, quite distinct from the clergy. These laymen were not agitating for new organizations and groups for instruction. They sought more effective outreach and instruction than they often found in the churches. Early Sunday schools were attempts to infect culture with righteousness in relation to God and to man.

The Sunday schools grew by leaps and bounds for forty years (1785-1825) as a parachurch movement before the Protestant Episcopal Sunday school societies were projected as a union in 1826 in Philadelphia under the leadership of Bishop White. Shortly thereafter the Methodist Episcopal Sunday School Union began (1826).

The American Sunday School Union, founded in 1816, from the beginning had certain marks of the parachurch groups that were to follow and to become such mighty forces for Jesus Christ.

The American Sunday School Union was not antidenominational, for the members of the union were individual members in good standing with their respective denominations. The ASSU was not undenominational, since its members belonged to and participated actively in local churches. The ASSU was not interdenominational in the sense of being supported and directed by representatives officially elected and recognized by denominational groups. It was nondenominational.

Another point of significance was the internal organization of the ASSU. Rice wrote, "It is significant that the managers of the Union

1. Edwin Wilbur Rice, *The Sunday School Movement and the American Sunday School Union* (Philadelphia: Amer. S. S. Union, 1917), p. 45.

[ASSU], in their first report, recognized their responsibility to submit a report of their proceedings not to the public, but to the members of the society."[2]

Known since 1974 as the American Missionary Fellowship, the society is active as a mission to areas in our country where there are no well-established local churches. It now includes evangelism, medical work, and education. Its present outreach extends to 2,700 churches each year.[3]

The American Missionary Fellowship is one evidence that a parachurch organization can become an asset to the churches, and that such an organization can be useful for more than one generation. But, even though the Sunday school has become successfully integrated into the life and program of the institutionalized church, such integration is not necessarily the goal of all parachurch movements. As noted earlier some of the most effective work of the church, the body of Christ, must take place outside the institutional church.

The nineteenth century witnessed the birth of a number of parachurch organizations which continue today. The American Bible Society (1816), the YMCA (1844), and the YWCA (1855) were among those of national stature. Many notable leaders in churches were active in these organizations. The birth of these groups grew out of the desire to multiply effectiveness in meeting the needs of others, and the American penchant for forming new groups for all kinds of endeavors and interests.

Alexis de Tocqueville (1805-59), noted French writer, in his work *De la democratic en Amerique* wrote:

> Americans of all ages, all conditions, and all dispositions, constantly form associations. They have not only commercial and manufacturing companies, in which all take part, but associations of a thousand other kinds—religious, moral, serious, futile, extensive or restricted, enormous or diminutive. The Americans make associations to give entertainments, to found establishments for education, . . . to send missionaries to the antipodes. . . . Wherever, at the head of some new undertaking, you see the Government in France, or a man of rank in England, in the United States you will be sure to find an association.[4]

If de Tocqueville thought the United States was exploding with organizations in 1856, what would he exclaim today? More than 12,600 *national* associations are listed in the *Encyclopedia of Associations.*[5] Another 1,900 are listed as either "inactive," "defunct," or "missing"!

2. Ibid., p. 85.
3. Margaret Fisk, ed., *Encyclopedia of Associations* (Detroit: Gale Research, 1975), p. 7.
4. Toqueville, Alexis de, *Democracy in America*, trans. Henry Reeve (New York: Oxford U., 1947), p. 319.
5. Fisk, *Encyclopedia of Associations*, p. 1116.

At the end of the nineteenth century, the main efforts in religious work among young people were channeled through established churches and denominations. The denominations were large enough to organize, sustain, and direct youth ministries which drew out the loyalty and participation of their own local church groups. The larger denominations pooled their resources for youth and related areas on an interdenominational basis in the formation of the International Council of Religious Education (1922) and the subsequent development in the organization of the United Christian Youth Movement (1934).[6]

The period of 1910-1940 was sterile for lack of energetic involvement of young people in the practical meaning of the redemptive purpose of Jesus Christ for their lives and their peers. The liberal wing of Protestantism emphasized social action in a manner which reduced emphasis on the need for personal redemption. The fundamentalist wing of Protestantism was torn by wretched arguments that resulted in bitter divisions and disappointments. The inability of responsible adults in church life to solve their problems and to discharge their responsibilities in religious education and training for leadership left the young generation without a solid theological foundation and without a corresponding conviction concerning the meaning of the Christian cause.

God has not left His church and His world without a witness. What the Lord could not get done through the formal, organized channels of the Protestant church organization He was pleased to do in a measure through parachurch movements.

In the face of a lack of clear Christian distinctives in much early twentieth-century youth work, many fundamental leaders and groups emerged beginning as early as the mid-1930s. By the post-World War II years they were growing in effectiveness and influence, aided by the interest in matters of life and eternity generated by the war. Groups such as Christian Service Brigade, Young Life, Youth For Christ, Word of Life, Hi-BA, and others sprung up spontaneously during this time. The cultural changes in the United States influenced their development positively and negatively. The popularity of organized religion in the fifties resulted in their acceptance by those who did not restrict God's work to the organized church.

But during the sixties the fruits of the postwar materialism were manifested in an apathy among the general population toward spiritual and religious matters. In the midst of this climate a new movement developed and ultimately influenced the entire nation—the Jesus movement. Emerging almost spontaneously in various regions of the country, it seemed to gain its main impetus from west coast influences. The California life-style

6. See chapter 4, "A Historical Survey of Youth Work."

had affected religion. This was no institutional activity but a gospel of liberation in Christ—liberation from drugs, materialism, and world views which denied the spiritual. Simultaneously the church and American culture began experiencing a new interest in Jesus Christ. Rock musicals, Jesus rallies, house churches, Jesus newspapers, charismatic gifts, Christian communes, and mass baptisms in lakes, rivers, and oceans became part of the national news.

As with previous movements, this also spawned new organizations, mostly local in nature, and often relating to one another through the travels of the "Jesus people," those young people who met Christ as a result of the movement. A new emphasis on the unity of believers emerged from this movement, perhaps partially explaining the relative lack of development of new, large national organizations. Indeed, many existing organizations and churches are experiencing an influx of believers who became Christians not as a direct result of their efforts but because of the effect of the "Jesus movement."[7]

The scope of the activities of parachurch youth organizations is as varied as young people themselves. There are groups designed for physical improvement, mental stimulation, social interaction, emotional growth, and/or spiritual impact. There are groups designed for boys or for girls; some are coeducational; some are local, others regional, national, or international. Some groups require membership; others seek only for attendance at meetings. Many groups appeal to small group activities; others specialize in gigantic efforts. There is no way they can be strictly classified according to age, purpose, or plan. The *fact* of the existence of influential parachurch groups in American church life among youth cannot be denied. Estimates of their *value* and *significance* have varied depending on the viewpoint of the appraiser.

DEVELOPMENT OF SPECIFIC PARACHURCH GROUPS

Some parachurch groups were started as social welfare-educational groups, but have been assimilated into the programs of many local churches. The Boy Scouts of America (1910) and the Girl Scouts of America (1912) were not initiated by leaders who were trying to be competitive with existing religious groups. Through the years, however, churches have made arrangements to accommodate and use these groups in their programs.

Some groups originated abroad. The Inter-Varsity Fellowship (IVF) was first begun in Great Britain by Christian leaders and students on col-

---

7. For more on this subject, see sources under "For Further Reading" at the end of this chapter.

lege campuses and later introduced in the United States by British and
Canadian students. The Inter-Varsity Christian Fellowship of America,
organized in 1941, sponsors activities related to evangelism, Bible study,
prayer, spiritual growth, and world missions.

Another parachurch movement begun among collegians in America is
Campus Crusade for Christ. Founded in 1951, this movement has an aggressive evangelistic approach to college and university students. As the
response to their ministry grew, leaders of Campus Crusade broadened
their program to include outreach to laymen, military personnel, athletes,
and high school students. Today this organization is a veritable evangelistic conglomerate, with worldwide activity and impact.

Some groups limit their ministry to high school youth. Two of the
better-known groups are Young Life Campaign (1941) and Youth For
Christ International (1944), both active in the United States and overseas.

Young Life Campaign conducts group meetings in homes for high
school youth, operates camps for teenagers, and annually directs an institute for training leaders for the movement. Youth For Christ International has expanded its ministry to include crusades, conferences, camps,
high school Campus Life clubs, literature (*Campus Life* magazine), ministry to troubled youth (described later), and projects in fifty-two countries run almost entirely by nationals. Full-time YFC personnel are trained
professionals, having been educated in college or Bible school and having
received training at a summer institute and in year-long internship experiences.

There are also extrachurch groups with specialized activities and objectives. The Fellowship of Christian Athletes (1954) directs its ministry
to athletes. The FCA sponsors specialized conferences on evangelism and
the Christian life. It also provides outstanding sports personalities and
coaches to speak and to give Christian testimonials at churches, rallies,
banquets, and other youth programs. The FCA encourages young people
to serve the cause of Christ through the church of their choice. FCA calls
attention to the priority of Jesus Christ in a person's life, stresses the importance of Christian attitudes on and off the playing field, and points out
the importance of physical and spiritual fitness.

Another group with a specialized ministry is The Navigators, founded
in 1933 by Dawson Trotman. This organization conducted an extensive
ministry to men and women in military service during World War II.
This was done through a program of guidance in personal Bible study,
Scripture memorization, Christian witnessing, small-group Bible study,
and Christian fellowship. Continuing their work in this area, The Navigators have enlarged their program to include a wide variety of worldwide

ministries—such as the preparation and supervision of many of the printed materials that are used in the counselor training and follow-up ministries of the Billy Graham Evangelistic Association. The Navigators also conduct a year-round program of laity leadership training at their national headquarters in Colorado. They sponsor specialized summer camps and conferences, and have representatives engaged in a broad range of Christian activities in many countries of the world.

Quite a different approach to meeting the needs of youth is shown in the Christian Service Brigade for boys, and in the Pioneer Girls. These two national organizations originated in the Chicago area, the former in 1937, and the latter in 1939. Their programs include Christ-centered activities, using a club approach similar to Boy Scouts and Girl Scouts. From the beginning, each of these groups has been directed by an incorporate board of laymen. The intention and practice have been to conduct each club on the local church premises. In this respect these two extrachurch groups have been geared to the local church. The clubs are subject both to a local church committee and to the policies of the national extrachurch organization. Another similar church-related club organization for boys and girls is the Awana Youth Association, begun in 1945.[8]

In the 1960s evangelical Americans became aware of the ministry of Francis Schaeffer and his wife Edith who had moved in 1948 from a pastorate in St. Louis, Missouri, to Switzerland. Their ministry among children grew to that of a center of intellectual and spiritual inquiry of particular interest to young adults. Dr. Schaeffer's studies, lectures, and books on the development of modern thought and culture were the result of a journey prompted by the realization that children were most vulnerable in a world where basic presuppositions no longer reflected the biblical view of man and creation. The ministry developed into a type of hostel where pilgrims from all around the world visited, studied, worked, and found an intellectually sound faith in the God of history who, in the words of Schaeffer, "is there."

Schaeffer's influence on twentieth-century evangelicalism is yet to be measured, but his apologetic brought many from the experience of grappling with eighteenth- and nineteenth-century issues to an awareness of the fact that a thoroughly biblical faith is defensible and is, indeed, necessary. The balanced gospel, integrating the intellectual, spiritual, social, and physical, which is practiced at L'Abri (French for 'shelter') is duplicated at other centers springing up in other locations around the world.

Several independent groups are working among disadvantaged and de-

8. Also see chapter 20, "Weekday Clubs."

linquent youth. Youth for Christ has developed a youth guidance program emphasizing neighborhood ministries, institutional services, court referrals, and group homes. Youth Development, Inc., directed by Jim Vaus, a former wiretapper, works in the heart of Harlem, New York. Youth Adventures, Inc. (Portland, Ore.), founded by Howard Busse, ministers to teens primarily through residential treatment and counseling. Youth Guidance, Inc. (Pittsburgh, Pa.) has a rehabilitation ministry to delinquent boys through counseling, camping, recreation. Young Life successfully operates somewhat similar ministries among both affluent and poorer youth because they emphasize personal ministry to the total person, as do Youth For Christ and other groups.

In addition to groups with activities in specific local areas of the United States are those which have built up effective ministries in wider regions of our country and have even, in some cases, expanded overseas as a result of their missionary zeal. Word of Life is one such group. Begun informally in 1934 through Bible studies, street meetings, and meetings in interested churches in the Northeast, Word of Life under the leadership of its founder Jack Wyrtzen was legally incorporated in 1946. It now includes camps on five continents, Bible clubs in North American churches, Word of Life Bible Institute, and other ministries utilizing various media to reach youth with the gospel.

Hi-BA (High School Evangelism Fellowship) is another such ministry, which began as a regional emphasis in eastern United States but now includes ministries in Japan also. The strength of their work includes the conviction that they equip teens for personal evangelism.

The extrachurch youth movement has not been limited to Protestant churches. The *Encyclopedia of Associations* indicates that there are at least 728 religious groups in addition to church and denominational bodies.

FUNCTION OF PARACHURCH GROUPS

The question naturally arises among churchmen: Why do these parachurch groups for youth arise, and how should they be evaluated?

The answer to the first query is quite clear. Parachurch groups arise to meet a need. If they do not meet a need, they soon dwindle or die because of the resistance and opposition of established church youth groups.

The answer to the second question depends on many factors. Some clergy and churches oppose parachurch groups for various reasons. Some ministers and congregations merely tolerate them. Others decide to encourage them and support them. The criteria for deciding what to do will obviously have to be established by local churches and by denominational leaders.

Charges have been made by pastors, community leaders and denominational executives that the parachurch groups were antichurch, narrow, emotional, temporary, and personality-centered. After years of experience and reputation, most of the leaders of parachurch youth groups have been found to be responsible members and also leaders in local churches. They function on the basic conviction that Christian youth work should be related somehow to the churches. The problem as they see it, however, is that the field of non-Christian young people is greater than the institutional church can reach. Special efforts must be made to bring the gospel to them in ways that they can understand and appreciate.

Perceptive youth leaders with more than forty years of experience and observation have indicated that extrachurch organizations can and often do provide Christian leaders like no other groups have done.

The following analysis by V. Raymond Edman, former chancellor of Wheaton College (Wheaton, Ill.), specifically discusses the development of one extrachurch organization (Youth For Christ), but his observations throw light on the strengths and weaknesses of many extrachurch youth movements.

> When Youth For Christ appeared dramatically on the religious scene in 1944, some evangelical leaders began to criticize it. Others postponed their criticism with the belief that the new "baby" was basically healthy and in time would grow up to make a large contribution to the cause of Christ. Youth For Christ is now [1959] in its 15th year, and I believe it is ready for a frank appraisal. Having worked with the organization and its leaders from the early days, but never as an official part of it, I think I have sufficient detachment to be objective, and enough knowledge to be factual. . . .
>
> The prophets of doom who announced that Youth For Christ would soon fade from the scene have, in some cases, changed their line to "The results are not lasting!" Undoubtedly in those early years many may have made a decision for Christ who were not properly nourished for Christian growth. But the fact that there are pastors, missionaries, and Christian workers today who *were* won to Christ in YFC meetings years ago is proof of fruit. . . .
>
> Whatever a local pastor or lay Christian might say about Youth For Christ, there is much that must be said for it: Youth For Christ is composed of leaders who believe unreservedly in the power of the gospel and the importance of prayer. Any secular organization with so little machinery would have collapsed in a year! Without the imposing structure of denominational prestige or financial support, Youth For Christ has made a phenomenal impact on cities and on entire nations.

It is to be commended for maturing without institutionalizing, maintaining its emphasis on youth, putting evangelism and world missions in the foreground, and depending on the power of God. . . .

One gets the impression that Youth For Christ, like Topsy, "just grew." First came the Saturday night rallies, then high school clubs, Bible quizzes, teen talent contests, a ministry to juvenile delinquents, teen films and literature, and other programs. . . .

Youth For Christ is an organization that has the program, passion, and potential for world evangelism despite all its weaknesses and past faults. . . . I am prone to agree with Youth For Christ leaders that "unless we win teen-agers today, there may be no Church tomorrow."[9]

SUMMARY

The effect and benefit of the parachurch youth movement in the life of the church can be observed through both a proliferation of evangelistic and mission groups and an infusion into church youth programs of ideas tested and proven by parachurch groups. Arising from the loosely knit early Youth For Christ organization alone have been other organizations of varying ministry emphasis. For example, former YFC leaders went on to develop Gospel Films, Ken Anderson Films, The Billy Graham Evangelistic Association, congresses on evangelism (inspired by the YFC-sponsored Congress of World Evangelism in Brussels in 1950), Overseas Crusades, International Students, Inc., Trans World Radio, Greater Europe Mission, World Vision International, and Youth Evangelism Association.[10]

Parachurch youth organizations have innovated in programming, often to their detriment, but ultimately for the benefit of the church and its youth programs. Because they are not bound by any tradition other than their own, they have been able to develop camping ideas, youth clubs, contemporary music with a Christian message, Bible quizzing, gospel teams, and other sometimes zany ideas, such as using live animals in rallies. The unusual nature of some activities (e.g., the Campus Life "Scream in the Dark," a Halloween fun house of Youth For Christ) often has drawn the ire of the religious establishment, but the increasing enthusiasm with which some church bodies use other ideas like Bible quizzing and gospel teams attests to the usefulness of parachurch groups in religious life.

If these trends continue, the institutional church should be experiencing an increasingly effective ministry among young people. A deeper ministry among youth, emphasizing reconciliation with both God and man and a ministry to the total person, is characteristic of the programs of many of

9. V. Raymond Edman, "Has Youth For Christ Grown Up?" *Christianity Today*, August 31, 1959, pp. 13-14. Copyright © 1959. Used by permission.
10. James C. Hefley, *God Goes to High School* (Waco, Tex.: Word, 1970), pp. 58-70.

INFORMATION ON SELECTED PARACHURCH ORGANIZATIONS

Name	Address	Year Founded	Geographical Area	Age Groups
Awana Youth Association	3215 Algonquin, Rolling Meadows, Illinois 60008	1950	US, Canada, ten foreign countries	Third grade through high school
Campus Crusade for Christ International	Arrowhead Springs, San Bernardino, California 92403	1951	International	Children-adult
Christian Service Brigade	P. O. Box 150, Wheaton, Illinois 60187	1937	US and Canada	8-18
High School Evangelism Fellowship (Hi-BA)	46 West Clinton, Tenafly, New Jersey 07670	1944	Northeast and Japan	High school
Inter-Varsity Christian Fellowship	233 Langdon Street, Madison, Wisconsin 53703	1941	US	College
The Navigators	Glen Eyrie, Colorado Springs, Colorado 80901	1933	US and 34 foreign countries	Children-adult
Pioneer Girls, Inc.	P. O. Box 788, Wheaton, Illinois 60187	1943	US and Canada	Second grade through high school
Word of Life International	Schroon Lake, New York 12870	1946*	International	Children-adult
Young Life Campaign	P. O. Box 1519, Colorado Springs, Colorado 80901	1941	International	High school
Youth Adventurers, Inc.	P. O. Box 4791, Portland, Oregon 79242	1962	Pacific Northwest	14-18
Youth Development, Inc.	P. O. Box 9429, San Diego, California 92109	1959	US	11-18
Youth Guidance, Inc.	2831 Laketon Rd., Pittsburgh, Pennsylvania 15221	1964	Pittsburgh area	8-15
Youth Evangelism Association	4715 Rainbow Blvd., Shawnee Mission, Kansas 66205	1943†	Kansas and Missouri	Junior high and high school
Youth For Christ International	P. O. Box 419, Wheaton, Illinois 60187	1944	US and 54 foreign countries	High school

*Begun in 1934 and incorporated in 1946.
†Begun informally in 1943 and founded in 1973.

the larger movements. This emphasis in methods is widely successful in ministries to young people in a world which is desperately in need of God's very personal and affirming love.

For Further Reading

Altbach, Philip G., and Peterson, Patti M. "Before Berkeley: Historical Perspectives on American Student Activism." In *Annals of the American Academy of Political and Social Science*, 395, 1-14, 1971.

Bollback, Harry. *The House that Jack God Built*. Schroon Lake, N.Y.: Word of Life, 1972.

Cailliet, Emile. *Young Life*. New York: Harper & Row, 1964.

Cannon, William. *Jesus Revolution: New Inspiration for Evangelicals*. Nashville: Broadman, 1971.

Christian Endeavor Essentials. Columbus, Ohio: International Society of Christian Endeavor, 1965.

Ellwood, Robert S., Jr. *One Way: The Jesus Movement and Its Meaning*. Englewood Cliffs, N.J.: Prentice-Hall, 1975.

Enroth, Ronald M., et al. *Jesus People: Old Time Religion in the Age of Aquarius*. Grand Rapids: Eerdmans, 1972.

Hakes, J. Edward, ed. *An Introduction to Evangelical Christian Education*. Chicago: Moody, 1964.

Hefley, James C. *God Goes to High School*. Waco, Tex.: Word, 1970.

Johnson, Merle A. *The Kingdom Seekers*. Nashville: Abingdon, 1973.

Keniston, Kenneth. *Young Radicals*. New York: Harcourt Brace, 1968.

King, Pat. *Jesus People Are Coming: The History and the People of the Jesus Movement*. Plainfield, N.J.: Logos, 1971.

McFadden, Michael. *The Jesus Revolution*. New York: Harper & Row, 1973.

Mead, Margaret. *Culture and Commitment*. New York: Doubleday, 1970.

Moore, Allen J. *The Young Adult Generation*. Nashville: Abingdon, 1971.

Newby, Donald O. "The Churches' Ministry to Youth." In *Religious Education: A Comprehensive Survey*, edited by Marvin Taylor. New York: Abingdon, 1960.

Pederson, Duane. *Jesus People*. Glendale, Calif.: Regal, 1971.

Rice, Edwin Wilbur. *The Sunday School Movement and the American Sunday School Union*. Philadelphia: Union, 1917.

Roszak, Theodore. *The Making of a Counter-Culture*. New York: Doubleday, 1971.

Russell, Eunice. *The Development of Pioneer Girls' Philosophy*. M. A. thesis, Wheaton College, 1959.

Schaeffer, Edith. *L'Abri*. Wheaton, Ill.: Tyndale, 1969.

Westerhoff, John H., and Neville, Gwen Kennedy. *Generation to Generation*. Philadelphia: Pilgrim, 1974.

27

Camping

William D. Gwinn and Lloyd O. Cory

CALLING TIME-OUT

NOW AS IN BIBLICAL TIMES man has needed to call time-out, so that he can evaluate his walk with God, gain a renewed perspective for his life, and be refreshed physically and spiritually. A change of pace and a change of place are periodic necessities for every person. Christian camping has become one of the most effective ways to provide for this need. In unsurpassed natural settings of all kinds, people of all ages are choosing to come aside from the normal routine and distractions of life, even as our Lord often did. Seasonal and year-round camp ministries have sprung up at an incredible rate. The unthreatening atmosphere of love, acceptance, discovery, and simulated family life, characteristic of most camps, has made them special places for personal evaluation, affirmation, and decision.

BRIEF HISTORY OF CHRISTIAN CAMPS AND CONFERENCES

No one knows for sure when the first Christian camp convened. But there are a few published facts about early Christian camps and conferences in America.

The founding Pilgrim fathers wrote about their first meeting in the new land: "It was decided on the morrow that a small party would go ashore and select a campsite. . . . A campsite was selected on high ground."[1] This too was rugged survival camping.

Some trace the ancestry of Christian conferences back to the old-time camp meetings. These gatherings, which consisted largely of meetings and meals, may have begun just prior to 1800. Through them many people became Christians and grew spiritually.

1. L. B. SHARP, "The Role of Camping in Our American Heritage," *Camping*, February 1942, p. 33.

WILLIAM D. GWINN, M.Div., is Executive Director, Mount Hermon Christian Conference Center, Mount Hermon, California.
LLOYD O. CORY, A.B., is Vice-President, Editorial Department, Scripture Press Publications, Wheaton, Illinois.

The first youth camps in America may have started during the Civil War. Frederick Gunn, dubbed "father of the American camping movement," was headmaster of the Gunnery School for Boys in Washington, Connecticut. Often he let his lads sleep outside so they would feel more like soldiers. In 1861 Mr. Gunn led his troops to nearby Milford-on-the-Sound, where they camped out for two weeks. His program consisted of a combination of military training, hiking, boating, and fishing. He operated this first school camp each summer until 1879.

In 1880 Rev. George Hinkley took seven boys from his church out camping. According to existing records this encampment on Gardener Island, Wakefield, Rhode Island, was the first church-sponsored camp. Pastor Hinkley figured correctly that the informal living in God's great outdoors would help break down barriers so that he could get closer to his boys and win them to the Lord. His campers had Bible teaching, educational and sports activities, and evening services.

The YMCA, which started out strong evangelistically, originated organizational camping in 1885. The Y's Camp Dudley, on New York's Lake Champlain, is the oldest boys' camp still operating.

About this time D. L. Moody started a Bible conference in Northfield, Massachusetts. The Winona Lake (Indiana) Bible Conference and the Mountain Retreat Association (later Montreat, near Asheville, N.C.) began in the 1890s. Bible conferences tried to provide a relaxing atmosphere, but their primary task was Bible study. Their founders started them because they were convinced that many churches were not doing an adequate job of teaching the deeper truths of the Word.

In the 1920s and 1930s, Bible conferences generally switched from tents to permanent buildings. Many conferences began to sponsor boys' and girls' camps on the outskirts of their properties.

Church-sponsored camping programs started taking hold after World War I. This movement has been growing ever since, except during World War II, when male leaders were scarce.

The American Camping Association soon began to provide as one facet of its program a loosely knit fellowship of church-related camps. Three or four sectional affiliations of evangelical camps and conferences sprung up across the United States, and some of their members were linked also on an annual basis through a camping section of the National Sunday School Association. Because of the rapid growth of camps and conferences, the need was felt for an international affiliation of evangelical camps and conferences. In 1963 leaders from across the United States and Canada met together to form the Christian Camp and Conference Association International, later to be identified by the simpler label of Christian

Camping International. CCI is an interdenominational organization with a strong evangelical statement of faith. It sponsors a magazine, sectional/regional/divisional (national) /and international conventions, and field consultations. Its headquarters in Illinois services over four thousand members in more than fifty nations.[2] Standards of excellence are set which encourage camps to establish quality facilities and programs and provide for their camps' health and safety needs. Many Christian Camping International members also retain their membership in the American Camping Association, which has pioneered the call for high standards.

DEFINITION OF CAMPS AND CONFERENCES

Drawing lines of demarcation among the many different kinds of camps and conferences is difficult. However, certain patterns emerge. The term *conference* generally is applied to a meeting-centered, speaker-centered approach, though many ingredients of a camp may be present. The term *camp* generally is applied to an activity-centered, counselor-centered approach, though speakers often are still employed. "Camps" fall into two classifications—*facility* and *outdoors*.

BIBLE CONFERENCES

A Bible conference is a rather formal organization designed to accommodate whole families. Families may live together in cottages or larger lodging units, and often children's and youth activities are provided. Most Bible conferences have at least one large auditorium, big enough to hold a normal quota of temporary residents plus a "drive-in crowd." Outstanding Bible teachers, evangelists, missionary speakers, and musicians provide the spiritual input in formal meetings. Bible conferences also provide facilities for dining, recreation, and fellowship. Increasingly, electives, seminars, and small groups are being employed as a supplement to the major platform hours. While the *revelational* aspects of truth remain primary, the *relational* implications of truth are being stressed more and more. The unity and togetherness of the family is being stressed and encouraged in conference programming.

FACILITY CAMPS

Most church camps fall into this category. Permanent buildings are provided, even though the outdoors may be utilized considerably. Programming philosophy ranges widely from large groups of up to five hun-

2. Christian Camping International, Box 400, Somonauk, Illinois, 60552. Executive Director, Ed Oulund.

dred to small camps of thirty-five to fifty; from more heavily programmed formal instruction times, much like a "conference," to a minimum of formal instruction with much elective opportunity and time for relational involvement and individual counseling. In almost all cases, however, the small cabin group with a counselor remains the key, and Christ-centered biblical teaching is the indispensable basis of each entire day.

OUTDOOR CAMPS

Outdoor camps range from primitive camping on one site to wilderness experiences which employ equipment but use no permanent facilities, other than possibly a base camp for equipment storage, orientation, and debriefing. The key words here are *stress, adventure,* and *wilderness,* where the outdoor setting is employed to the fullest as an unsurpassed laboratory setting. The counselor is responsible for activity, instruction, supervision, Bible teaching, and spiritual counseling; and often he serves also as a nurse, cook, and more. His qualifications and training are unusually critical, due to the more hazardous and decentralized nature of this type of camping. Specialty programs involving bicycles, canoes, or whatever, are another expression of nonfacility camping. The greatest growth in camping today is in the area of wilderness camping. In it life-changing results have been unusually impressive, especially with troubled and spiritually "fed-up" youth.

CENTRALIZED AND DECENTRALIZED CAMP PROGRAMS

The two kinds of program approaches are centralized and decentralized. In a centralized program the director and his aides map out mass activities for the whole camp.

A decentralized program, which is more complex, allows small groups (as cabin units) a degree of choice in activities. The decentralized program puts more emphasis on the informal, personal contacts between counselor and campers than does the centralized program's carefully planned large-group activities. Good decentralized camping calls for a crew of godly, well-trained counselors and a director who always keeps track of what each small group is doing.

As one would expect, the programs of outdoor adventuring camps are usually more decentralized than those of conference-type camps. Most evangelical church-camp programs have been basically centralized, with a few decentralized hours sprinkled into a week's activities. The trend of recent years, however, has been toward stronger counselor teams and more decentralization.

CLASSIFICATION OF CAMPS BY DURATION AND LOCATION

DAY CAMPING

Day camping is conducted on a daytime basis, with campers going home to sleep. Especially popular with preteens, day camping has several advantages over resident camping. For one thing the cost of operating a day camp is nominal. The basic requirements are a creative director, a bus, and some recreational equipment. Another advantage of day camping is the absence of the emotional tension caused when younger campers are separated from their parents for a week or so. Parents see that day campers get to the church or other starting point daily, at perhaps 9:00 A.M. Campers usually bring bag lunches; the director furnishes the beverage. They bus to a park, forest preserve, lakefront, or other spot. The program may consist of hiking, handcraft, Bible stories, nature study, or attending a pro ball game or a museum. Campers are returned to the starting point between 3:00 and 5:00 P.M. Once a week there may be a campfire, to which parents are invited. Day camping is proving to be an excellent way to reach children and subsequently their non-Christian parents for the Lord.

OVERNIGHT CAMPING

Overnight camping calls for the campers sleeping out, but spending their days at home, work, or school. While day camping appeals to the eight to eleven age-group, overnight camping has more attraction for older campers. Though generally conducted for only one night, overnight camping is sometimes repeated several nights in a row, or several times in a week or month. (Another kind of overnight camping takes place within the framework of a resident camp. This occurs when a group of resident campers and their counselor leave the main campsite for a camp-out.)

TRIP CAMPING

As its name implies, trip campers do not settle in one location. They keep on the move, pitching camp in different spots. Trail campers travel on foot, burro, or horseback, often in remote wilderness areas offering isolation, ruggedness, and beauty. Other trip campers slice through the water in canoes or boats. And bicycle camps are becoming increasingly popular. Still others cover greater distances in mechanized caravans, using cars, trailers, and "campers" that perch atop pickup trucks.

RESIDENT CAMPING

The most widespread form of Christian camping is resident camping, conducted on a twenty-four-hour day-and-night basis. There are three primary kinds of resident camping: long-term (two to four weeks), short-term (four to seven days), and weekend.

VARIOUS TYPES OF CAMPS

Though the following varieties of camps may be conducted on day camp, overnight camp, or trip camp basis, the large majority operate as resident camps. Some are centralized in their programs, whereas others are decentralized.

BOYS', GIRLS', AND COED CAMPS

Most Christian camping is resident camping. And most Christian resident campers are between the ages of eight and seventeen. As already pointed out, camps range from platform to wilderness, from centralized to decentralized. Some children's camps are more refined with paved trails, intercom systems, big classrooms, and floodlighted ball fields. Others are rugged, back-to-nature, weatherbeaten, pup-tented camps, with primitive outside facilities. Judging from apparent spiritual results over the years, there are various valid ways to run camps. When it comes to lasting results, what matters most are the camp's men and women leaders, not the facilities or the methods used. Clearly the Lord is not limited by or tied to man-made methods. When God works in campers' lives, He works through dedicated, radiant staff members who believe, live by, and teach God's Word. This does not mean that camping know-how is unimportant. It does mean that staff commitment—a Spirit-driven desire to win, challenge, and train campers for Christ—is more basic than the camp's facilities and its leaders' knowledge of camp operations or nature lore.

FAMILY CAMPS

In today's hectic world, families have become so fragmented, even in departmentalized church programs, that family togetherness has become one of the most needed and effective goals in all of Christian camping. It has become apparent that the camp setting is uniquely suited to refresh and nurture families.

Family members spend much time together in family groups—sleeping, eating, playing, praying, studying, and interacting together. Opportunities are also provided for peers to be together periodically at the various age levels, but the unity of the family is protected in most programming. Sleep-outs under the stars, cookouts, projects, creative competitiveness in recreational events, campfires, and numerous other activities are utilized to help estranged families become comfortable with one another and open to biblical teaching. Family camping also strengthens families already accustomed to being together. Family campers have time to be taught, to dig into God's Word for themselves, to meditate and apply biblical truth, and to evaluate the goals, values, and priorities of their homes and individual lives.

Some family camping is done in smaller groupings in state and national parks, and of course many families go camping by themselves. All forms of family camping provide opportunity for "vacation with a double value"—a good time of relaxation coupled with solid spiritual nurture.

OTHER RESIDENT CAMPS

In addition to boys' camps, girls' camps, coed camps, and family camps, many specialized forms of camping are being carried on by evangelicals. And every year new ways to utilize camping to further the gospel are being developed. Here are some of these specialties:

1. Leadership training (camps geared for in-depth discipleship)
2. Work camps (usually service-oriented, for high schoolers)
3. Athletic and music or writers' camps (special appeal, need strong resource teams)
4. Collegiate camps (to reach and train college students)
5. Conferences for single career adults
6. Men's and women's retreats (to meet marriage, family, and vocational needs)
7. Married couples conferences and marriage workshops
8. Camps for elderly
9. Camps for handicapped (provide fresh incentives for many)
10. Camps for retarded (happiness fosters progress)
11. Camps for underprivileged
12. Camps for delinquents

CHRISTIAN CAMPING GOALS

Some camp directors operate with vague goals and indefinite objectives. They can be compared to an archer who hopes to score a bull's-eye but does not bother to take careful aim. His chances of hitting the mark are remote.

Fortunately, the majority of Christian camp directors keep the most important goals, evangelism and Christian nurture, uppermost. Many, however, seem to forget that their campers' main goal is something different—to have fun. In a successful camp all three of these goals are met.

Nearly all sin starts out as fun. Camp is an excellent place to teach that a lot of fun can be had without indulging in iniquity. Camp counteracts the prevalent idea among many young people that Christianity is dull, old-fashioned, blah.

The main aim of evangelical camping is that the Holy Spirit will lead campers without Christ into a personal relationship with Him as Saviour and Lord. Counselors pray and teach and exemplify the truths of God's Word, seeking to establish friendly beachheads in campers' heads and hearts, to help win them to Christ. Many non-Christian Sunday school students, plus many unchurched campers, receive the Saviour at camp. Camp is the strong right arm of evangelism for many churches. It is often the place of *harvest* for seed sown long before by a faithful parent, pastor, youth worker, or friend.

Because of the *concentrated* period of time involved, and the *laboratory* nature of the experience, Christian campers often grow more rapidly in a camp week than in any setting other than a Christ-centered home.

DEVELOPMENT OF CAMPERS

Spiritually. Camp should not be a relatively unimportant, tacked-on activity—merely a good opportunity for parents to get rid of their off-spring for a week or so. For a good camp is a veritable proving ground for Christianity. Leaders show Christian campers how to develop a solid faith that keeps working, remove the "knocks" from their speech, iron wrinkles out of their behavior, and align their lives with God's Word. In general terms, camp leaders seek to lead every camper's total life toward maturity in Christ, taking him further up the inclined plane of Christian growth than he was when he arrived at camp.

Mentally. In a properly programmed camp, campers have much more time to be alone, to think, than they have in other parts of their church's program. Counselors should encourage them to spend part of this alone-time with God's Word and its author, tucking away Bible knowledge, memorizing Scriptures that can help them all their lives.

Campers also stretch their mental muscles as they learn firsthand about flora and fauna, crafts, first aid, and perhaps work on the camp's news sheet.

Physically. Camp is one place in Christian education where adventure abounds. With no TV sets around, "spectatoritis" is at a minimum. Campers get lots of exercise, both on land and in the water. They have plenty of time and opportunity to expend pent-up energies. This greatly enhances the receptivity of campers to the gospel and Christ's claims on their lives.

Socially. Camp is a great leveling place. For instance, neither wealth nor family prestige stand an uncooperative camper in good stead. His peers work hard at chipping off his personality's rough edges. "Iron sharpens iron, so one man [camper] sharpens the face of another" (Prov 27:17, Berkeley) .

Thanks to the living-together setup at camp, cabin groups as a rule are soon welded together. Campers learn to appreciate others whose abilities, temperaments, race, and views are different from their own. Many camp-formed friendships endure through the years. In coed camps a significant percentage of campers manage to meet their future life partners.

Emotionally. Campers gain a new perspective on life by being away from home. Most of them make progress in emotional independence from their parents.

Camp should be a glad and happy time for campers, a time when they have fun and also really get to know Christ, the true source of inner peace and joy. Their camping experiences should help them develop a strong confidence in God and what He can do through them. Many parents and Sunday school teachers find camp to be a turning point; their young people come home knowing "the strength of the Spirit's inner re-inforcement" (Eph 3:16, Phillips), and are better prepared to face life's problems. An amazingly high percentage of Christians and Christian leaders verify that the most significant decisions of their lives were made at camp.

TRAINING OF LEADERS

Training counselors. One reason counselor training is important is quantitative: It is a significant ministry in and of itself to literally thousands of students. The other reason counselor training is vital is qualitative: The counselor of a small group wields great influence over his campers. He or she is the key! Humanly speaking, the camp's effectiveness will rise or fall with the counselor. He not only tells but models what Christ means to him. Unlike a leader at Sunday school, children's church, Sunday evening youth group, weekday club, or vacation Bible school, a camp counselor cannot leave his charges after an hour or three. There is no place for a counselor to hide till the next day or week. He is vulnerably on display both day and night. Since campers tend to pattern their actions after their counselors, an untrained or spiritually weak counselor can wreck a camp program. As the specialists in waterfront and cooking need training for their tasks, the counselor needs training as a specialist in spiritual matters. He also must be able to manage small-group activities, unaided.

Prospective counselors should know their camp's standards for counselors, which should be based on that camp's philosophy. Here is one list of counselor qualifications:[3]

3. Adapted from Joy MacKay, "The Counselor Training Program for the Established Summer Camp" (M.A. thesis, Wheaton College, 1962), pp. 35-37.

1. Know Jesus Christ as Saviour and maintain a vital, growing relationship to Him as Lord.
2. Have a love for the age-group involved.
3. Be able to lead a camper to Christ.
4. Radiate Christ, being a mature staff member who is worthy of emulation.
5. Understand the philosophy and aims of the camp and seek to carry them out.
6. Be loyal to the camp, its director, and its policies.
7. Be able to work well with other leaders.
8. Assume responsibility cheerfully and be conscientious in performing duties.
9. See extra work to be done and do it without being told; be willing to do tasks not required in your job analysis.
10. Be familiar with the out-of-doors; feel at home there and be able to help campers feel at home too; know your way with map and compass; recognize night sounds of the woods; understand what to do when it rains on an overnight.
11. Be able to teach some camp skill.
12. Like campers and enjoy being with them, since campers quickly distinguish a counselor who really enjoys their company from one who patronizes them.
13. Understand campers, as a group and as individuals; take time to listen to each one.
14. Possess good health and vitality.
15. Know your own capabilities and limitations.
16. Be flexible and resourceful, adjusting easily to new situations.
17. Be neat in appearance and keep your belongings in good order.
18. Be at least nineteen years of age, having had two years of college or its equivalent.[4] (This last qualification is reduced to one year of college in many camps, usually because of leadership shortage. Most states now require by law that counselors be at least eighteen.)

A counselor training schedule will vary according to the proportion of new counselors, whether counselors are volunteers or summer-long, the length of the camp, the availability of the site, the distance the staff must travel to camp, and the extent to which the director believes in such training. Some phases of training can be covered by mail and, in the case of camps with local staffs, by meetings in town. But a large part of the instruction, to be fully effective, must take place at the campsite.

4. "Standards Report of Camping Practices—Resident Camps" (Martinsville, Ind.: Amer. Camping Assn.), p. 2.

Here is an outline of a fairly complete plan for training counselors:[5]

COUNSELOR TRAINING PLAN

Method	Time	Content
1. By correspondence	Begin sending letters three to four months before camp starts.	Upon receipt of application send: welcome letter, counselor contract, counselor memo or challenge. Upon receipt of signed contract send: job analysis, second memo or challenge, list of books to read, Bible study helps. Then send: third memo or challenge, counselor training helps, cabin devotion helps, campfire message suggestions, health form.
2. Pre-camp training (at location near the counselors' homes)	Weekend	Discuss aims and philosophy of camp, psychology of handling campers. Pass out recommended bibliography. Discuss how to prepare Bible studies. Make activity assignments. Make cabin assignments. Go over program in general.
3. Pre-in-camp training (at camp)	One week or ten days before campers arrive	Take time to get to know each other better. Go through a daily schedule. Develop evening programs. Discuss morale, health, safety. Become familiar with site and environs. Gain experience in nature, craft, and trip programs. Make camper duty charts; note kitchen procedures. Practice a cookout.

5. Adapted from Joy MacKay, *Creative Camping* (Wheaton, Ill.: Victor, 1977), pp. 162-33.

Method	Time	Content
4. In-service training (while camp is in session)	Thirty-minute counselors' meeting each day; also interviews and evaluations	Discuss music in camp. Hold divisional meetings. Enlarge on the aims and philosophy of the camp's program. Allow time for counselors to prepare; get cabins ready. Impart spiritual challenge. Pray together. Plan how to deal with specific problems and weak points. Give help when difficulties arise. Schedule regular interviews and evaluations with counselors. (Note: Give a spiritual challenge with every contact.)

Training campers to be leaders. Camp is becoming known as a prime place to develop latent leadership abilities. Most young people in good Christian camps develop spiritually, mentally, physically, socially, and emotionally. Changes frequently come in campers' lives with ease and rapidity, partly because of the continuity of experience in a controlled environment.

Camp is perhaps the most logical place in the church program to develop the four Cs of leadership:

Confidence, in self and in God, is fostered by the campers' countless opportunities for learning by doing. Wise counselors let their charges help plan hikes, choose teams, lead song services, build a simple outdoor chapel, which help to discover their gifts and develop a sense of self-worth.

Curiosity runs high, as young people come to camp expectantly, with their learning readiness at a high peak. Many seek adventure in the woods, in lakes and rivers, and some in exploring God's Word.

Conscience is exercised and developed as the Holy Spirit speaks to individuals. He keeps a camper wrestling with his own conscience and helps him develop a sense of right and wrong based on the Scriptures.

Communication of God's message is stimulated in Bible hours, casual contacts, and cabin discussions. Campers have lots of time to practice expressing the gospel clearly.

Probably most future camp leaders are now campers. There is no better place than camp for training tomorrow's staff members. Counselor training programs in various forms are spreading from camp to camp. It is hoped that a camp can "grow its own" future counselors as well as prepare young people for other leadership roles for Christ.

Trainees are older campers who work as assistants to counselors. They generally live with a cabin group, take special classes in Bible and/or camping skills, practice leadership skills, often work a few hours a day at a camp maintenance job, and sometimes take the counselor's place so that he/she may have free or study time. Like all staff members, trainees should be sent a job description before camp, receive supervision during camp, and be evaluated at the close of the training period.

Many campers become counselor trainees, then counselors, later interns in a camp, and finally full-time staff members.

WIDENING OF EVERYONE'S HORIZON

Camp spells adventure, new skills, and exploration to young people who are a bit restless in their often-plastic cities and suburbs. Counselors should make sure that camp does not disappoint them. Eunice Russell advises:

> Your example . . . is pivotal here. You can make simple hikes and stunts adventuresome just by contagious enthusiasm. Your own curiosity at a tadpole squirming in the shallow edge of the lake, or a milkweed pod ready to burst—your interest in learning to paddle a canoe or hit the archery target—may stimulate an interest in a new field or skill. If you succeed in carrying over the same spirit of adventure into exploration of the Bible, you will help to break down the "compartmentalization" that may exist in some minds: "This is fun," and "this is spiritual" (with the implication that the latter is dull).[6]

Compass-orienteering, ax-wielding, fire-building, horsemanship, riflery, sailing, archery, swim instruction, skin- and scuba-diving, conservation, and outdoor cooking are a few of the many skills campers may develop. There are unlimited possibilities common to various sites, and each camp must creatively discover these. Wise directors reserve certain privileges (as overnights) for junior highs, others (as canoe trips) for high schoolers. Such a progression program (which includes degrees of attainment in waterfront, archery, riflery, and other skills) helps get campers back year after year.

For many years Christian camps disregarded skill activities in camp as a valid use of time and money. At best they were treated as *means* only to another *end*. Though everything that happens in camp is aimed at cultivating a twenty-four-hour-a-day, seven-day-a-week awareness of Christ's

6. Eunice Russell, *How to Be a Camp Counselor* (Wheaton, Ill.: Scripture Press Found., 1959), p. 5.

lordship, camp activities can also be *ends* in themselves, developing a sense of accomplishment. In such an atmosphere, young hearts open wide to the God who declares each person important to Him. A further by-product of a strong activity program in camp is the natural life-on-life opportunity which the instructor has with each camper. This can be a great reinforcement to the ministry of the camper's cabin counselor, and might even be the most important relationship of the week to a given camper, who may respond less enthusiastically to his particular counselor.

Most campers come from cities or suburbs and are accustomed to the urban setting. They are more familiar with street lights than the lights of the heavens. At camp, in the blackness of night, as they peer up toward God's sky, the world's pull is weaker, God's pull stronger (Psalm 19:1).

With the strong emphasis today on protection of the environment, it is heartening to know that camps have long been pioneers in the field. It is important to develop a regard for enjoying, maintaining, and enhancing the beautiful natural features common to a particular site. What an added privilege to do so in the context of becoming more closely related on a personal basis with the Creator of it all!

Eventful camp days never die. Long after a camper is harnessed with adulthood's weighty problems, he occasionally relives golden days spent at camp. He recalls the loving care of his counselor, paddling across the still lake at sunrise, sneaking a cold frog into his buddy's bunk, and the last night in camp—the presence of God that felt warmer than the campfire—and his determination to live more obediently under Christ's lordship.

CAMP ORGANIZATION AND ADMINISTRATION

In simple terms, organization is planning one's work; administration is working one's plan. Sad to say, camp organization and administration are sometimes viewed as necessary evils attached to Christian camping.

Increasingly, camp overseers are realizing that a businesslike operation is essential to effective witness. A camp's Christian testimony is bolstered by businesslike contacts with forest rangers, deliverymen, salesmen, health and welfare inspectors, camp staff, and the camper's parents.

The field of camp organization and administration is broad. There are at least as many ways to organize and administrate camps as there are different types and kinds of camps. A given camp's organizational setup and administrative activities will depend on whether it is a day camp, a resident camp, a wilderness camp, or some other type of camp; whether its program is basically centralized or decentralized; and the training and backgrounds of the people in charge.

Doubtless all competent camp directors would concur that good camps result from good planning. Here is a checklist of a director's planning and performance duties which applies to many camps:[7]

BEFORE CAMP

1. *Determine responsibility.* A committee or board should stand behind every camp, meet regularly, keep records, report to its superior organization, appoint the camp director.

2. *Decide camp location.* Choose rented or self-owned site. Let "master planning" be the key word in all steps of progress.

3. *Determine objectives.* See "Christian Camping Goals" earlier in this chapter.

4. *Set up organizational framework.* Depict the personnel structure on a chart; select people carefully, based on qualifications; delegate jobs in an orderly manner. Develop job descriptions.

5. *Decide camp fees.* Factors include amounts of subsidization and donated food, labor, upkeep, improvements. Fees should be set to cover all operating costs and all Campership Funds developed to subsidize those with financial needs.

6. *Be sure you're insured.* No camp should operate without medical and hospital coverage, vehicle, fire, and liability insurance.

7. *Mark age and sexual divisions.* Decide on age groupings, whether camp will be coed or sexually segregated, whether two or more age-groups will operate on the grounds simultaneously with separate programs.

8. *Get the word out.* Camp promotion includes posters, letters, brochures or folders, rallies, camp banks or stamp books, contests with camperships as prizes, church bulletin news releases, photos on bulletin boards, slide or movie presentations.

9. *Line up staff.* Sign up counselors, cooks, athletic director, waterfront personnel, dishwashers, nurse, and others.

10. *Plan daily schedule.* Base this on the goals for your campers' lives. Beware of overscheduling.

11. *Take care of last-minute details.* Check the staff, campgrounds, preregistration progress, mess hall, and canteen supplies. Bible study materials and visual aids, physical exams, health cards, transportation.

12. *Train the counselors.* See suggestions under "Training counselors" earlier in this chapter.

7. Condensed from *Camp Director's Handbook* (Wheaton, Ill.: Scripture Press Found., 1959), pp. 4-22.

DURING CAMP

1. *Make opening day smooth.* Be efficient and friendly in housing and orienting campers, making them feel at home. Provide a camp bank.
2. *Keep praying; be enthusiastic.* These two go hand in hand.
3. *Insist on good records.* Over the long pull, records do much to make or break a camp. File registration information, food, and equipment transactions.
4. *Play fair with campers.* Outline rules (as few as possible), orally and in writing, to campers. But don't expect fifteen-year-olds to act like thirty-five-year-olds. Give each discipline case a full hearing, with love and forbearance. Lower the boom only when necessary. Be consistent. Take the long-range view.
5. *Hold daily staff meetings.* See in-service training suggestions earlier in this chapter.
6. *Take problems in stride.* Delegate tasks; anticipate troubles.
7. *Keep a spiritual accent.* Athletics, fun times, and the like should not become "king of the hill," but should contribute toward the development of Christlike character.
8. *Give farewell counsel to campers.* Allow ample opportunity for those who have put off spiritual decisions to talk with their counselors. Warn campers about the emotional letdown they may face when they get home. Encourage them to become involved in a Bible-believing church. Brief them on how to witness wisely to school classmates, parents, and others. Encourage counselors to brief parents at pickup time.

AFTER CAMP

1. *Let churches know what happened.* Using camper evaluation forms, let the camper's Sunday school teacher (or a church visitation worker if the camper does not attend) know about his apparent spiritual, athletic, and social progress.
2. *Write some letters.* Right after camp write a form letter to parents, telling how the camp worked to build Christian character in their son or daughter; suggest that they write, if they have suggestions for improving camp. Also send personal thank-you notes to all staff members. Urge counselors to maintain contact with campers, especially those with special needs.
3. *Evaluate.* How effective were the Bible classes, age divisions, outdoor activities, the approach to non-Christians? Ask the campers on closing day to fill out an unsigned questionnaire, giving their opinions of camp's different activities.

4. *Lay groundwork for next year.* Report to the board or committee what transpired. Determine the dates of next year's camp. See that next year's director is selected before Christmas and that essential information is placed in his hands.

THE RELATIONSHIP OF CAMPING TO THE LOCAL CHURCH

Christian camping has become an integral part of almost all growing churches and denominations, as well as a major tool in most missionary work across the world.

Because of the extended amount of time provided for instruction, and the laboratory nature of the entire experience, churches have found camping to be an indispensable supplement to the ministry in the local church, second only to the Christian home as a place to impart and demonstrate Christian education in a total fashion. Many think of their camps as an extension of their own church plant. Rather than being in competition with the local church program, camping has become another expression of that program, either for purposes of evangelism or nurture or both. Many pastors attend retreats or week-long conferences with students or families from their churches, often taking their own family along. The deepened relationships, the opportunity for a pastor to be a person with his people, and the relaxed opportunity to delve more deeply into biblical truth are among the many values received.

Increasing care is being taken by all camps to work cooperatively with pastors, youth ministers, and camp coordinators. Since follow-up must and should be left largely to the churches, every effort is made to inform the churches of what transpired at camp, so that the progress experienced at camp can be considered in future ministry to that camper.

RESPONSIBILITIES OF A CAMP COORDINATOR

A logical first step, in integrating camping into a church's overall program, is to appoint a camp coordinator to the board of Christian education. The camp coordinator may have these responsibilities:

1. He learns the present "camp score" in his church by taking a survey to find out how many, and who, are going to private secular camps, Y camps, agency Bible camps, sports camps, and the camp (if any) that his church sponsors or recommends.
2. He keeps abreast of camping trends; he finds out if a nearby Christian camp may serve his church.
3. He keeps the Christian education board and various other church agencies informed about this camp, its schedule, and its program.

4. If nearby Christian resident camps are crowded (or nonexistent), he investigates the possibilities of getting together with other churches and starting a day camp or resident camp. Or he may initiate camping in his own church on a small scale by organizing a weekend church family camp, snow camp, or youth retreat.

5. He encourages competent collegians and young adults in the church to serve as counselors at the camp their young people will attend, if the camp does not provide the staff.

6. He helps line up workers for readying and improving camp.

7. He tries to correlate (not duplicate) the camp program with his church's year-round program. He makes sure that his church is not in one corner, the camp in another, without either knowing what the other is doing. He sees the need for continuity through the year in Bible teaching, so his campers do not study Samuel, for example, in Sunday school, vacation Bible school, weekday clubs, and camp.

8. He promotes camp attendance by brochures, posters, audiovisuals, a savings plan, announcements, precamp rallies. He sees that camp is not pigeonholed till summer, but is talked about most of the year.

9. He gives the Christian education board an itemized estimate of camp-related expenses as part of the church's total Christian education budget. (This may include camperships for needy young people.)

10. He counsels with those who will soon attend camp, to help them make the most of their coming experiences.

11. After camp, he provides public opportunities for campers to share the benefits of their experiences and their enthusiasm, perhaps in a "camp echo" testimony service.

12. He helps campers fit camp learning experiences into their more mundane lives at home and school.

13. He gets ex-campers active in church agencies and perhaps Youth For Christ, Young Life, Campus Crusade, Inter-Varsity Christian Fellowship, The Navigators, and similar organizations that can help them continue to grow spiritually.

14. He checks to see that the pastor and the campers' Sunday school teachers read the camper evaluation forms filled out by counselors and sent to the church. (If he receives some unchurched campers' evaluation forms, he contacts the young people for his church.)

15. He finds outlet opportunities for those whose camp experiences have helped qualify them for service.

Summary

Christian camping presents exciting, only partially explored opportunities for winning, challenging, and training people for Christ. May hundreds of additional God-directed leaders start new Christian camps and may the existing camps have the faith to expand as God guides. May they know what God wants them to do, and check often to see how well they are measuring up to their goals of decisions for Christ, development of campers, training of leaders, and the widening of everyone's horizon. As they do this, results will show up in local churches, families, neighborhoods, campuses, places of work—and around the world.

For Further Reading

Bibliography for Camp Leaders. Chicago: National S. S. Association Camp Commission, 1962.

Camp Director's Handbook. Wheaton, Ill.: Scripture Press Foundation, 1959.

Cory, Lloyd O. *The Pastor and Camping,* Christian Education Monographs: Pastors Series, no. 3. Glen Ellyn, Ill.: Scripture Press Foundation, 1966.

Ensign, John, and Ensign, Ruth. *Camping Together as Christians.* Richmond, Va.: Knox Press, 1958.

Evangelical Camp Resources. Chicago: National S. S. Assn. Camp Commission, 1962.

Genné, Elizabeth, and Genné, William. *Church Family Camps and Conferences.* Philadelphia: Christian Educ. Press, 1962.

Goodrich, Lois. *Decentralized Camping.* New York: Assn. Press, 1959.

Hammett, Catherine, and Musselman, Virginia. *The Camp Program Book.* New York: Natl. Recreational Assn., 1951.

How to Be a Camp Counselor. Wheaton, Ill.: Scripture Press Foundation, 1959.

Journal of Christian Camping. Somonauk, Ill.: Christian Camping International. Published quarterly.

Lynn, Gordon. *Camping and Camp Crafts.* New York: Golden, 1959.

MacKay, Joy. *Creative Camping.* Wheaton, Ill.: Victor, 1977.

————. *Raindrops Keep Falling on My Tent.* Wheaton, Ill.: Victor, 1972.

Mattson, Lloyd. *Camping Guideposts.* (Christian Camp Counselor's Handbook). Chicago: Moody, 1962.

————. *Way to Grow.* Wheaton, Ill.: Victor, 1973.

Nelson, Virgil, and Nelson, Lynn. *Retreat Handbook.* Valley Forge, Pa.: Judson, 1976.

Reimann, Lewis. *The Successful Camp.* Ann Arbor, Mich.: U. of Michigan Press, 1958.

Saunders, John. *Nature Crafts.* New York: Golden, 1958.

Tinning, Graham, ed. *Yearbook of Christian Camping.* Van Nuys, Calif.: Christian Camp and Conferences Assn., 1965.

Todd, Floyd, and Todd, Pauline. *Camping for Christian Youth.* New York: Harper & Row, 1963.

Wright, H. Norman. *Help! I'm a Camp Counselor.* Glendale, Calif.: Regal, 1968.

Filmstrips

"Christian Camping." Burbank, Calif.: Cathedral Films. Color, four filmstrips, and two 33⅓ rpm records.

Additional resources

Helpful information is available from the "Tinning Resource Library," Christian Camping International Headquarters, Somonauk, Illinois; includes cassettes, magazines, books.

Counselor manuals from camps with existing counselor training programs are excellent resource material, as are colleges with camping course libraries. Also, most camps maintain a library of some of the best literature in the field of camping and related support subjects.

28

Creative Methods

Marlene D. LeFever

IN A RECENT "Terrific Teacher" contest, teens across the United States and Canada nominated church workers they felt were worthy of this honor. Over and over students emphasized two characteristics. First, they were certain their leaders loved them. Second, the leaders made the study of the Bible and how to live the Christian life interesting, relevant, varied.

The first characteristic indicated the teachers were living Christ before their students. They were picking up His reflection. In the second, the teachers were showing an understanding of the age level, the educational process, the teaching methods available to them. Christian leaders model the most creative Teacher. Their classes and youth groups should sparkle with age-graded ideas, in-depth, creative Bible study, realistic methods that help teens apply what they have studied.

Contrary to the thinking of some, the word *methods* is not synonymous with tricks that cover up poorly prepared lessons. Some educators have gone as far as to say that without participative methods, carry-over learning does not take place. Methods, when correctly used, can guide a student to study God's Word for himself.

Using creative methods, however, requires more from the teacher. Note these "requirements":

1. No longer is the teacher the central focus of the classroom. He gives up some of his authority to become a guide and resource person.
2. The teacher must know his material thoroughly. As students study the Bible for themselves and become involved in the learning process, they will have questions, opinions, problems. This approach is not as "safe" as lecturing or using other teacher-centered activities.
3. Using creative methods requires spending more preparation time beyond actual studying. Materials must be gathered and the classroom

MARLENE D. LeFEVER, M.A., is Administrative Youth Editor, David C. Cook Publishing Co., Elgin, Illinois.

must be arranged so that the students will have maximum success in using the method.

4. An effective use of creative techniques is aided by an awareness of Christian and secular sources on creative teaching.*

5. The teacher must be selective. Only methods which honestly forward the aim of the lesson should be used. Just as a modern version of the Bible might help a teen see a new truth, so a new method often helps a student discover a truth he missed or did not think was applicable to his life.

It is impossible in a single chapter to explain completely every participative method available to the teacher of teens. It is also improbable that the list will ever be completed. It is always growing. Jesus used visual aids (e.g., the transfiguration); lecture (e.g., the Sermon on the Mount); individualized study (e.g., Peter walking on the water); group activities (e.g., the disciples going out two by two); inductive study (e.g., the disciples' slow realization that Jesus was the Christ); object lessons (e.g., the withered fig tree); and others. Many of these may be used along with other methods which Jesus' students would not have understood, such as simulation and script development for audiovisual tape recorders. In fifty years, teachers should have a longer list of teaching methods than they have today. The message remains the same. Jesus Christ desires that teens make Him both Saviour and Lord of their lives. But the ways to communicate do change as teachers learn more about the educational process.

This chapter focuses on student-centered methods—methods in which the student takes an active part in the learning process. It is with these types of methods that many Christian leaders need to develop expertise.[1]

Each of the following methods can be mastered by the nonprofessional Christian leader. All are inexpensive and can be used successfully within the time limitations of most Sunday school classes and youth meetings. Each method has carry-over value; that is, each will help students put what he has learned into practice in the hours each week he is not in church.

As one reads of various methods, he should ask himself, "How would my students respond to this method? What would they learn from it? With what teaching objective in the near future could I use this method?"

*For example, *Instructor* and *Educational Leadership* are two magazines of a secular nature that can be helpful. *Instructor* (Instructor Park, Dansville, NY 14437) is primarily geared to elementary age levels. Teachers of junior highs will find this easy-to-read magazine helpful. *Educational Leadership* (Association for Supervision and Curriculum Development, 1701 K Street, N.W., Washington, D.C. 20006) is an excellent, scholarly magazine to help adults dealing with young people stay on top of what is happening in secular education.

1. Material on the use of audiovisuals is included in chapter 29, "Materials for Working with Youth."

Dramatic Methods

Roleplay and mime yield close to 100 percent class participation. Two or three are actively involved while their peers watch and learn and prepare to take part in the discussion which will follow.

Both roleplay and mime force students to use biblical truths which previously may have been only head knowledge.

Steps in using classroom dramatics successfully include these:

1. Establish a classroom climate in which students feel secure.
2. Be enthusiastic.
3. Be prepared for an imperfect first experience. In order to expose students to what can happen in a roleplay, the teacher should take part in the first few. Play one of the roles and feed the fellow roleplayer questions to which he can respond. Plan to use roleplays several meetings in a row until students have mastered the technique.
4. Maintain control over students. Dramatic methods can be fun, but teens must see that these roleplays and mimes are serious training for the Christian life.

ROLEPLAY

The following is an example of two roleplay situations complete with objectives.

Measurable classroom objective: that teens demonstrate how biblical principles can be used to help them deal with problems in their Christian lives.

Carry-over objective (in which the Holy Spirit guides and teaches): that teens will begin to search the Bible for themselves and apply what they find to their own lives.

Characters: two Christians.

Assignment: The Christian teen with whom this problem is shared should help the other Christian find biblical principles that will help him deal with the problem and suggest practical ways in which these principles can be implemented.

Roleplay introduction number one: "I've been a Christian for years, and it's a little hard to take God as seriously as the people who have recently met God. Their lives were pretty messed up, and Christ brought about a big change for them. God works in new Christians' lives, and my life just plods along in the same humdrum way it always has. How can I get more enthusiastic about my Christian life?" (Psalm 51:8, 12).

Roleplay introduction number two: "I have no desire whatsoever to go into full-time Christian work, and sometimes I get the feeling that this makes me less of a Christian than the people who do feel this calling. Is full-time Christian work always God's best for a person? If so, I want it, but how can I get the desire to do it? If it isn't, how can I get rid of my guilt feelings?" (Gal 6:4) .[2]

Many Christian curriculums use roleplays in their teachers' guides and teaching aid packets, but some teachers will want to use this method more extensively by writing their own. Follow these steps:

1. Decide on the subject. This, of course, will correlate with the aim of the day's lesson. Subject areas which lend themselves easily to roleplay are morality, Christian life-style, witnessing, parent-teen relationships.
2. Decide on a one- or two-sentence incident dealing with the subject. Be careful not to pick one so similar to one actually experienced by a class member that he will recognize it.
3. Write the roleplay. The following formats are not difficult.
   (a) Write in the first person. The final sentence should be a question which will enable the other person in the roleplay to respond immediately.

   Example: "I don't like the way I act, and I don't think others do either. How can I help people find Christ when they can't stand to be around me?"

   Example: "My friend is sleeping around. What can I say to her that will help her see the stupidity of what she's doing without my losing her friendship?"

   (b) In several sentences, set up a situation. Then give each player additional information which they are to use in the roleplay. The other players should not be aware of this information.

   Example: A brilliant black girl has agreed to tutor a white girl. Although they attend the same church, neither has previously had much to do with the other. Things are tense at the first session, and even worse at the second. Finally one says, "Look, we aren't going to be able to work together until we talk about our feelings and figure out what to do about them. What do you really think about me?"

   Additional information to the black girl: You feel superior to the white girl and have always felt she snubbed you. However, you enjoy tutoring and want to do a good job. Deep down you have wished this girl would notice you. She comes from a well-to-do family, and her friendship could lead to party invitations and an introduction to the "in" group.

2. Roleplays taken from the roleplay simulation game, "Guidance" by Marlene D. LeFever, included in *Senior High Creative Teaching Aids* (Elgin, Ill.: David C. Cook, 1976).

Additional information to the white girl: You feel superior to
the black girl, and have always felt she snubbed you. However,
you do need to pass, and deep down, you admire her brains. You
feel like you could benefit from a friendship with her, especially
since it's now the "in" thing to know people from different races.

4. Write discussion questions to use following each roleplay. For example, in the above roleplay, you might include these questions: What
unchristian motives were shown by each girl? Why is it often difficult
to act in a Christlike manner?

MIME

Mime, derived from the Greek word meaning "to imitate," is dramatic
action in which players use motions rather than words to share experiences
with the audience.

Mime forces students to express their emotions and use their faces and
bodies to communicate Christian truth. Mime, since there are no words,
deals with general rather than specific situations and concepts. A good
mime, for instance, will be as understandable to a Japanese-speaking audience as to an English-speaking one. Students, as they watch, are forced
to interpret the action, decide the implications of the action, and verbalize
and support their opinions in the discussion which should follow classroom mime.

Expose students to this method by having them perform the following
situation, called "Two Alone."

Two Alone

A sad-faced girl walks around the stage with her arms outstretched as if
she is trying to touch something. Finally, unable to find anything or anyone, she goes to the center of the stage, squats down, and places her head
on her knees.

A happy girl, smiling and obviously excited about life, skips on stage.
She goes to the sad girl and tries to get her attention.

Finally the sad girl looks at her. The happy girl indicates that she would
like to play, to be her friend. The sad girl reaches out to touch the happy
girl, but draws back at the last minute. Without getting up, she inches
away from the happy girl.

The happy girl's smile fades. Suddenly she has an idea. She runs off-
stage and returns with a flower. She holds it out to the sad girl.

After a brief pause, the sad girl takes it, and the happy girl is delighted.
She sits beside the sad girl and acts out the motions of talking. It is obvious the sad girl isn't listening. Sad girl's eyes wander, and she slowly begins picking the petals off the flower.

The happy girl looks disturbed and tries to get her attention, to get her to stop. Finally when there are no petals left, the sad girl lowers her head again.

The happy girl's smile fades. She stops talking and gesturing. Slowly she goes to an unoccupied corner and sits down. She shrugs her shoulders and puts her head on her knees.

The discussion after the mime may include these questions: What did the flower symbolize? Share a time when you were like one of the two girls in the mime—either rejected or rejecting; how did you feel? Why? In what ways could the attitudes of one or two in the youth group affect the feelings and effectiveness of the entire group?

After your students have been exposed to mime, give them general topics around which to develop original mimes. These need not be written. Topics would include the salvation experience, the power of prayer, the concept of Christian service.

CHORAL READING

Choral reading is an easy, effective dramatic form to use with youth. Readings can be developed around a specific topic or taken directly from Scripture. Have your group try the following choral reading.

_____ For God did not send His son into the world to condemn the world, but in order that the world might be saved through Him.

_____ Not to condemn the world

_____ But that the world might be saved

_____ God so loved the world

_____ Condemn

_____ Save

_____ Condemn

_____ Save

_____ Save, save, save

_____ For God so loved the world that He gave His only Son

_____ In order that the world might be saved through Him.

Duets, solos, total group, all male, all female: any number of different vocal combinations can be used. Students will want to mark volume and key words to be emphasized.

Choreography can make a choral reading even more effective. Voices can come from different sections of the room. Students can act out (mime) their roles. For example, a group of students representing those who are saved in the above reading might begin with their backs to the audience and slowly as they realize that God has provided salvation, they could turn and raise their hands in joy toward heaven.

Students could make slides or a film to illustrate their choral reading. For example, a world condemned by sin could be illustrated with slides made from newspaper photographs. A world saved could be shown with the happy faces of class members.

METHODS OF TESTING

TESTING FOR CONTENT

Content testing is important, for if students are to apply biblical principles, they must be aware of the facts from which these principles are derived. The biblical stories yield examples of men who faced very contemporary problems. From the study of their lives and the response God made to their actions, teens can discover more about what He expects from them.

Often team games can challenge young people to learn the facts. Have students develop original team games built around Bible content. They may want to use athletic sports as models. For example, what rules would be necessary for two teams to play Bible tennis?

Content games are excellent for building class and team spirit.

SELF-TESTING FOR PERSONAL VALUES

Content testing should not be the only testing method used by teen leaders. It matters little if students can name all the disciples if their lives show a lack of discipleship qualities.

Teens need to become aware of what their personal values really are— not just what other Christians say they should be. They need to know what they believe and what they would publicly affirm. They need to know what values and beliefs they would be willing to act on.

Unlike many secular educators, Christian teachers present a values system which is constant. Truth and right do not fluctuate with an individual's philosophy or the accepted attitudes of society. Christian teachers present the gospel as the only eternal workable life system. By giving tests which help teens focus on their values, teachers help teens clarify what they believe. The Bible is the standard by which they can evaluate what they discover.

There are many different kinds of tests which can help a student evaluate what he personally believes.[3] Often they can be used to help a student

3. Sidney B. Simon, Leland W. Howe, and Howard Kirschenbaum, *Values Clarification: A Handbook of Practical Strategies for Teachers and Students* (New York: Hart, 1972).

see his need to discover what God says about an issue. They can lead into Bible study. They can also be used following Bible study to help a teen identify areas in which he needs to make a life response to God. The following are some examples of tests for self-evaluation.

Mark the line. The far left side represents total honesty. The far right represents total dishonesty. Place a dot on the line to indicate how honest you are.

Values voting. How many of you think Christians should watch TV more than an hour a day? (Discussion may follow voting. A student may abstain from voting if he wishes.)

Rank order. List in the order of preference where you would most like to be on a Sunday morning.

_____ in bed
_____ at a picnic with parents
_____ in Sunday school
_____ on a breakfast date

Rank these Christian problems, placing the one you consider most serious first.

_____ unchristlike thoughts
_____ gossip
_____ gluttony
_____ sexual misconduct

Either-or forced choice. Describe yourself as accurately as you can.

Are you more of a yes or a no?

Are you more a giver or a taker?

Unfinished sentences. (This test helps students review and explore some of their goals, ideas, doubts, beliefs—the things which indicate their values.)

I feel best about myself when _____

If I could change one thing about myself, I would change _____

The results of these tests may be private, or if the students wish, they may be shared with the group. General group discussion about the reasons behind some choices (such as the rank order and the values voting) can help students further clarify what they believe.[4]

4. For information on how a person develops a working set of values and for examples of dilemma stories which are being used on a secular level to help students develop a set of ethics, see Ronald E. Galbraith and Thomas M. Jones, *Moral Reasoning: A Teaching Handbook for Adapting Kohlberg to the Classroom* (Anoka, Minn.: Greenhaven, 1976).

TESTING FOR CHRISTIAN ACTION AND RESPONSES—SIMULATION GAMES

Simulation games try to make reality more simple than it is, to seemingly reduce its size so that players can better understand the aspect of reality covered in the game. Through these games a student experiments with life.

For example, in a poverty game which divides students into rich, middle-class, and poor groups, those assigned to poverty may begin to feel frustration and anger when all their efforts to succeed are blocked, when they see that in spite of all their efforts they will never better their position in the game. They may become bored, uninterested in continuing. For the first time students may empathize with those for whom poverty is not a game.

Simulation is one step removed from reality. Students are usually willing to participate since it is a game; the risk factor is minimized. In the security of a game atmosphere, learning takes place.

These games give young people opportunities to put Christian principles into practice. Of course they often fail. Yet even failure can lead to learning as they discuss why their actions were wrong. And they often determine to do better when faced with a real-life situation. For example, in a cooperation simulation, five students are given pieces of five squares to assemble. No student may talk or indicate in any way that he needs a piece another person has to complete his square. The other person must notice his need and donate the piece. Students' actions demonstrate how difficult it is to be concerned with the other fellow's needs and to keep from being frustrated when one person fails to see what piece will complete another's square. Following this simulation game, students are ready to discuss situations or ways in which Christians should demonstrate a spirit of cooperation.[5]

DISCUSSION METHODS

A Christian view of abortion, the difficulties of living out Christ's command to love others, the significance of current events to a Christian lifestyle, and a thousand other subjects need to be discussed openly by teens and their leaders. For some, the ability to stimulate and guide discussions comes naturally. For many it is a skill to be polished. These principles will help:

5. For descriptions of secular simulation games now available (many of which are easily adapted for use in Christian youth programs), see David W. Zuckerman and Robert E. Horn, *The Guide to Simulation/Games for Education and Training* (Information Resources, P.O. Box 417, Lexington, Maine 02173). Also see Miller, Snyder, Neff, *Biblical Simulations* (Valley Forge, Pa.: Judson, 1973).

1. Be sure students have the necessary knowledge (content background) to participate intelligently in a discussion.[6]
2. Choose a discussable topic dealing with the aim of the lesson. Discussion is more than students answering content questions. (For example, What are the parts in the Christian's armor and what does each piece symbolize?) In a good discussion, teens use the knowledge they have learned from the Bible and add to this—by applying it, sharing a personal experience, and giving an interpretation. (For example, Which part of the Christian's armor do you find most useful in school? Why? What practical suggestions could you give another teen who is having trouble keeping his armor in good repair and is ready to change?)
3. Listen to the teens as they talk. They will learn from each other, and the teacher will learn from them. And often a teen will learn from himself, for as he verbalizes what he believes it will become more a part of his life.
4. Encourage each student to participate. Often asking, "What do you think?" of a quiet student will be enough to get him involved. Conversely, do not allow one person to monopolize the discussion.
5. Share yourself. The teacher should participate and guide but not dominate the discussion. A youth leader's skills as a discussion guide can be increased, by participating in adult level discussions. In that way, he can discover what he likes in other leaders and what is ineffective. And he can experience some of the same fears his students feel when they dare to share themselves with their peers.

TYPES OF DISCUSSION

1. *Buzz groups* (*three to ten students*). A chairman and secretary-reporter are selected to lead and record group ideas about an assigned topic. The secretary-reporter will later report the group's key ideas to the total class.

2. *Brainstorming*. Small groups are given a task, such as to solve a problem or come up with a teen project. Members suggest as many ideas as they can think of while a secretary records them. Then the group chooses or combines the best ideas, polishes them, and presents them to the total class.

The above two methods can be used week after week with success. Those which follow are most effective when used less frequently.

3. *Predecessor discussion*. With the group seated in a circle, the leader makes a statement about the topic to be discussed. The next person adds

6. See chapter 15, "Guiding Youth in Bible Study."

to the idea, clarifies it, or even asks a question. The third person does the same, and the pattern continues until the group has exhausted what they have to say. Anyone who has nothing to add may say, "I pass." For example, before a study on the Holy Spirit, the leader may use this method to show how little they know about this Person of the Trinity. Then, following Bible study, the group may hold another predecessor discussion on what they have learned and the significance of these facts. This is one form of a technique often called "circle response."

4. *Panel discussion.* Three to six people speak on an assigned subject. Later the discussion is opened for anyone to share opinions and interact with the panelists. Occasionally it will be impossible for a good resource person to attend the meeting. Tape his contribution. This, of course, is second best since much of the benefit of this discussion comes from interaction with the panelists.

5. *Interview.* There are several types of interview that may be used.

   (a) *Homework interview.* Ask each teen to interview one person on an assigned topic and report on the results of that interview. Assignment suggestions: (1) Talk with one person in the church neighborhood who does not attend this church and ask him "What is your opinion of the church?" and "On what do you base your opinion?" (2) Talk with a Christian old enough to be your grandparent and ask him what he considers to be the most important thing for a Christian teen to learn *early* about life.

   (b) *Class interview.* Set up interviews between teens and visiting missionaries, Christian businessmen, politicians, etc. It often sparks discussion if teens come prepared with one question they would like to ask.

   (c) *Triad interview.* Students interview each other. Divide the class into groups of three. Assign a topic question, such as, "Which Bible story is most relevant to you right now, and why?" A interviews B while C listens. B interviews C while A listens. C interviews A while B listens. Teens report to the other groups on what they heard, not what they said.

IDEAS FOR USING PICTURES IN DISCUSSIONS

Begin a picture file. Pictures can be an equalizer in a discussion, enabling those who are new or who have little background to participate. Pictures also are a great method for helping students who are frightened or unaccustomed to discussion to get involved.

1. *What happens next?* Hand out a different picture to each small

group, and ask students to brainstorm what might happen next in their picture if _____ (Gear the discussion to the topic of the meeting.) For example, if you are studying the Christian's responsibility to others, you might give each group a picture from the newspaper of people in trouble (burned home, injured, abandoned, elderly) and ask teens what might happen next if one person in the picture or just out of camera range is a Christian.

2. *Enter the picture.* Ask students to pretend they have been placed in a picture for a certain amount of time. As always, gear the assignment to the lesson aim. For example, if you are studying the Christian's responsibility to the poor and oppressed, you might give each group a poverty picture. Ask teens to brainstorm "If you were placed in this picture situation by God for one month, what would you try to do and why? What obstacles might you face? How would you try to overcome them?"

3. *Face-to-face pictures.* Keep a picture file of faces in which people show a variety of emotions. When you use these in class, have small groups deal with the person in the picture as if he or she were present. This is an excellent picture technique to help teens practice witnessing in a nonthreatening situation. They would decide as a group how best to share the gospel with the person in the picture. What points would they want to make clear? What questions might the person have? If, for example, the face shows anger, how would they try to eliminate that emotion in order to make the person more responsive to the message?

4. *Giggle pictures.* Collect cartoons and cut off captions. (Christian magazines are excellent sources.) Have students write original captions dealing with the thrust of the day's lesson.

CREATIVE WRITING

When teens share their feelings and ideas in writing, they are more likely to appropriate these Christian concepts personally. Creative writing also gives them a form through which they can communicate Christ to others. Creative writing can alert the teacher to problems students may be having, and to special abilities teens have which should be encouraged.

WRITING PRAYERS

Writing prayers is a valuable life-response activity which allows students to react in love, joy, decision to God. Follow these suggestions in initiating this activity.

1. Let teens know they will not be asked to share their prayers aloud unless they wish to do so.

2. Suggest they write their prayers using the same language they use when they talk.
3. Challenge participants to be honest. Sometimes teachers encourage dishonesty by assuming everyone in the class is ready to write a prayer to God. Most students caught in this dilemma will write something they don't believe in to avoid being conspicuous. Always supply an alternate activity. A teacher might ask students to write thank-You notes to God following a lesson on Thanksgiving. At the same time, he might suggest that those who don't honestly feel thankful and those who don't yet have a prayer relationship with God write an ending to the sentence, "The most important thing I learned from today's lesson is _____."
4. Encourage students to pray as specifically as possible.
5. Develop ways students' written prayers can continue to be part of their learning experience after they have shared them with God.[7]

For example, each student might take his prayer promise home and read it each time in the coming week he is tempted to break it. Or prayer poems could be included on the back page of the church bulletin.

ADDITIONAL CREATIVE WRITING IDEAS

Original parables; original songs (words to an existing tune or original words and music) ; poetry using biblical forms; class and church newspaper articles (also class editorials for city newspapers) —there are so many exciting ways to use creative writing with young people. Quiz them on what they are doing in school and what they enjoy doing. Note the types of reading they do and their ability to express themselves vocally; gear projects and assignments to their skill level.

PROJECTS

One of the most effective methods of uniting a group and teaching teens to live out God's Word is to help them structure projects that are spin-offs of concepts they have been studying.

To be an effective group learning experience, a project must:

1. involve anyone in the group who wants to become involved. There must be opportunities for leaders and followers. There must be opportunity for creative growth and for development along more prescribed lines.
2. be Christ-centered.

7. Marlene D. LeFever, *Turnabout Teaching* (Elgin, Ill.: David C. Cook, 1973), p. 119.

3. be others-directed.
4. be carried out concurrently or immediately following the Bible study which prompted the activity.
5. have somewhat measurable results. Results can be measured in terms of what the class was able to accomplish for others and in terms of how the project forced participants to grow.

The following are some project ideas:[8]

1. Reading/visiting programs to the elderly.
2. Babysitting for church and neighborhood mothers who cannot afford to pay a sitter.
3. Missions service project (raising money for a specific project).
4. Youth missionary project. Teens raise money to send a teen in the group to a mission field for a summer. Arrangements should include accountability on both sides. The teens should let their representative know what they expect of him in his summer ministry. They should expect a full report when he returns. In turn the teen going should let class members know he expects letters and prayer support.
5. Church service participation. Students could help with certain portions of the Sunday morning worship service. For example, they could develop a choral reading on the day's Scripture or read acrostic prayers on the sermon's topic.
6. Clean-up projects (neighborhood, church, elderly people's chores which are often difficult for them).

SUMMARY

This chapter has to expose the teacher of teens to a few of the many methods available to you as you teach God's message. Practice and perfect these. Add others. Most important, keep in constant touch with the Master Teacher and work to make your life more and more a reflection of His.

FOR FURTHER READING

Books

Benson, Dennis C. *Recycle Catalogue.* Nashville: Abingdon, 1975.
———. *Gaming.* Nashville: Abingdon, 1971.
Bowman, Locke E. *How to Teach Senior Highs.* Philadelphia: Westminster, 1963.
Bratt, John. *Springboards for Discussion.* Grand Rapids: Baker, 1972.
Clark, D. Cecil. *Using Instructional Objectives in Teaching.* Glenview, Ill.: Scott, Foresman, 1972.

8. For more on projects, see chapter 23, "Youth Serving the Church."

Dalglish, William A. *Media Two for Christian Formation.* Dayton, Ohio: Pflaum, 1970.

Edge, Findley B. *Teaching for Results.* Nashville: Broadman, 1956.

Ezell, Mancil. *Youth in Bible Study/New Dynamics.* Nashville: Convention, 1970.

Ezell, Mancil, and Ezell, Suzanne. *Being Creative.* Nashville: Convention, 1974.

Flynn, Elizabeth W., and La Fasco, John F. *Designs in Affective Education: A Teacher Resource Program for Junior and Senior High.* New York: Paulist, 1974.

Gangel, Kenneth O. *24 Ways to Improve Your Teaching.* Wheaton, Ill.: Victor, 1975.

Getz, Gene A. *Audiovisual Media in Christian Education.* Chicago: Moody, 1972.

Gorman, Alfred H. *Teachers and Learners: The Interactive Process of Education.* 2d ed. Boston: Allyn & Bacon, 1974.

Joy, Donald M. *Meaningful Learning in the Church.* Winona Lake, Ind.: Life & Light, 1969.

Krutza, William J., and DiCicco, Philip P. *Facing the Issues.* 3 vols. Grand Rapids: Baker, 1969-70.

————. *Youth Face Today's Issues.* Grand Rapids: Baker, 1970.

LeFever, Marlene D. *Turnabout Teaching.* Elgin, Ill.: David C. Cook, 1973.

Leypoldt, Martha M. *40 Ways to Teach in Groups.* Valley Forge, Pa.: Judson, 1967.

————. *Learning Is Change.* Valley Forge, Pa.: Judson, 1971.

Mager, Robert F. *Developing Attitudes Toward Learning.* Belmont, Calif.: Fearon, 1968.

McPhee, Norma. *Discussion Programs for Junior Highs.* Grand Rapids: Zondervan, 1974.

Middleton, Barbara, ed. *Respond: Resources for Senior Highs in the Church.* Vol. 4. Valley Forge, Pa.: Judson, 1975.

Miller, Donald E.; Snyder, Graydon F.; and Neff, Robert W. *Using Biblical Simulations.* Vols. 1, 2. Valley Forge, Pa.: Judson, 1973, 1975.

Reed, Bobbie, and Johnson, Rex E. *Bible Learning Activities—Youth.* Glendale, Calif.: Regal, 1974.

Reed, Ed, and Reed, Bobbie. *Creative Bible Learning for Youth.* Glendale, Calif.: Regal, 1977.

Richards, Lawrence O. *Creative Bible Teaching.* Chicago: Moody, 1970.

————. *69 Ways to Start a Study Group and Keep It Going.* Grand Rapids: Zondervan, 1973.

————. *You and Youth.* Chicago: Moody, 1973.

Seagren Daniel R. *Tune In . . . Discussion Starter for Youth Groups.* Grand Rapids: Baker, 1972.

Seely, Edward D. *Teaching Early Adolescents Creatively*. Philadelphia: Westminster, 1971.

Stoop, David A. *Ways to Help Them Learn—Youth*. Glendale, Calif.: Regal, 1971.

Torrance, E. Paul, and Myers, R. E. *Creative Learning and Teaching*. New York: Dodd, Mead, 1973.

Towns, Elmer. *The Successful Sunday School and Teachers Guidebook*. Carol Stream, Ill.: Creation House, 1976.

Wilson, Ron. *Multimedia Handbook for the Church*. Elgin, Ill.: David C. Cook, 1975.

Yaconelli, Mike, and Rice, Wayne. *Ideas*. Nos. 1-16. San Diego: Youth Specialties, 1968-1976.

———. *Right-On Ideas for Youth Groups*. Grand Rapids: Zondervan, 1973.

———. *Way-Out Ideas for Youth Groups*. Grand Rapids: Zondervan, 1971.

Zuck, Roy B., and Robertson, Fern. *How to Be a Youth Sponsor*. Wheaton, Ill.: Scripture Press Foundation, 1960.

Cassettes

"Eight Successful Teachers Tell You How." David C. Cook Publishing Co., Elgin,, Ill. 60120.

"Five Successful Youth Workers Tell You How." David C. Cook Publishing Co., Elgin, Ill. 60120.

Papers

Encounter: The Challenging World of Youth. Published by The National Research Bureau, 424 N. Third Street, Burlington, Iowa 52601.

Youth Report. Published by Grafton Publications, 667 Madison Avenue, New York, N.Y. 10021.

29

Materials for Working with Youth

Werner C. Graendorf

PRINCIPLES FOR SELECTING AND USING YOUTH MATERIALS,
AUDIOVISUAL MEDIA, AND ROOMS AND EQUIPMENT

PUBLISHED TEACHING AND PROGRAM MATERIALS

SOME YOUTH WORKERS, because of their own creativity, require little if any published material to carry on an effective ministry with young people.

On the other hand, a large percentage of workers find good materials a major asset in their work. For them, such materials offer a variety of helps:

1. A basis for developing meaningful teaching by providing direction on what to teach and how to organize and conduct the teaching.
2. Guidance for balanced, systematic ministry through materials organized by time and growth patterns (thus avoiding both neglect of essentials and unnecessary duplication).
3. Idea stimulation for encouraging personal creativity in program and material. (The best materials and programs are those adapted to each group's needs and interests.)
4. Visual and content stimulation for young people through attractive contemporary materials that encourage both group participation and personal study.
5. Opportunity to keep current through contact with new ideas and directions.

Essentially, published youth materials represent resources. For the worker with youth who has them available and knows how to put them to good use, they provide a constant source of teaching and program content, communication ideas, and creative stimulation.

Guidelines in Choosing Youth Materials. What are some of the things

WERNER C. GRAENDORF, Ph.D., is Chairman of the Department of Christian Education, Moody Bible Institute, Chicago, Illinois.

to look for in determining the materials to use? There are two preliminary considerations:

1. What does the leader want the materials to accomplish? This means he has some purposes or goals in mind for using the materials, for example, to develop youth leadership, to understand basic Bible doctrines, to apply biblical principles to teenage concerns, or similar areas. Answering this question helps focus the type of material desired.
2. What are the theological/Christian living standards of the local church? The youth teacher or sponsor is in a crucial position for guiding youth's thinking and decisions in vital Christian areas. The choice of materials needs to be guided by established standards.

Beyond these preliminary considerations there are additional helpful criteria:

1. The materials should be Christ-honoring. They should clearly reflect the centrality of Christ, point to Him as personal Saviour, and should have a cumulative effect of motivating teens toward living wholeheartedly for Him.
2. The materials should be Bible-based. They should clearly reflect an evangelically sound view of the Bible as the Word of God, and build concepts of teaching on its authority.
3. The materials should take into account the interests, needs, and abilities of the students. Materials should capture the interests of teens, answer their needs, and be geared to their ability levels. Bowman cautions, "Unwittingly, adults tend to think of what *they* like: what appeals to them."[1]
4. The materials should help teens understand Christian concepts and develop Christian convictions. From the use of materials young people should come to understand more about God (His being and nature, His plans and purposes, His ways) , man, the world, the church, Christian living. Good lesson materials help young people develop these teachings as their own beliefs and convictions.
5. The materials should deal with life problems. Since life is a continual series of decisions, major and minor, the student needs to know how to make creative use of God's truth in meeting his life needs. Lesson and program materials ought to guide teens in discovering God's truths for themselves and relating them to their current problems.
6. The materials should provide adequate scope and sequence of both content and experience. Curriculum materials are concerned with de-

1. Clarice M. Bowman, *Ways Youth Learn* (New York: Harper, 1952), p. 76.

termining the amount (or scope) and sequence of content and experience. The total youth curriculum must cover a certain amount of fact and understanding, and a certain range of experience. This body of content and experience must be arranged in logical, understandable order for best results.

7. The materials should be structured to allow adjustment and flexibility in use.
8. The materials should be attractive in appearance and contemporary in design.

When choosing Sunday school lesson materials, the teacher of teens should also consider the structure of individual lessons. The following are some positive features:

1. The lessons should have clearly stated purposes (lesson aims).
2. The lessons should capture attention and motivate the student to learn.
3. The lessons should provide for natural transitions from known truths to new truths.
4. The lessons should encourage student participation.
5. The lessons should develop student insight.
6. The lessons should encourage the student to respond to insights gained.
7. The lessons should promote carry-over into the week.
8. The lessons should help the teacher prepare for the following:
   a. Student readiness: preparing the student for involvement in the lesson by capturing attention, arousing curiosity, developing a feeling of need for the content and experience, relating the new to the old (known).
   b. Bible presentation: looking into the Word of God to understand clearly the passage being studied.
   c. Bible exploration: exploring and analyzing Bible teaching to discover its meaning and relevance. This may include discussing the meanings of various Scripture passages and experiences to bring new insight; seeing relationships and exploring new ideas through a visual presentation; researching; and engaging in activities.
   d. Bible application: seeing how biblical truths or principles relate to present-day living for the young person. Breadth precedes depth. He may "see" the truth worked out in *one* specific way through a life situation, story, or problem. He may relate its application to many other situations. Then through these he gains insight into his own situations and is better equipped to respond to the truth and appropriate it to his life.

e. Pupil response: helping the pupil respond to the Christian truth or principle he has appropriated by expressing commitment to it, and assuming responsibility for carrying it out. True belief convinces and convicts to the point of change. True learning experiences bring new insights and understandings, new attitudes, new convictions, new actions.

AUDIOVISUAL MEDIA IN YOUTH WORK

Our society is media-oriented, and our youth have grown up in this context. For them, television and tape cassettes are a way of life. Communication by moving color and sound is a normal part of learning experience. It is essential, therefore, for the youth worker to recognize these facts as he guides in communicating the Christian life and message to this generation of young people. His challenge is to take advantage of contemporary audiovisual media in working with young people, without compromising Christian standards of quality or allowing them to become substitutes for warm personal relationships.

It is also important to remember that while the more sophisticated media such as the tape cassette are given prominence, there is a whole field of audiovisual communication means that are relatively inexpensive and simple to use. It is not necessarily the equipment that makes communication effective, but the ability of the communicator to use effectively whatever means are available. In this sense, it is well to remember the example of Christ as He took advantage of the resources in His environment to communicate through audiovisual means.

What Audiovisuals Do for Youth Work:

1. Audiovisuals arouse interest and hold attention because they appeal to teenage desire for action and adventure.
2. Audiovisuals help overcome the communication barriers of verbalism—words too far removed from experience for understanding—by building a concrete basis for abstract thinking.
3. Audiovisuals bridge the islands of individual differences by providing clarification toward common understanding.
4. Audiovisuals make an impact on the emotions by bringing pupils into vivid contact with the real thing.
5. Audiovisuals provide stimulus for pupil participation in group activities, discussion, follow-up projects.
6. Audiovisuals promote meaningful learning by making what is taught important, clear, and practical.

7. Audiovisuals encourage learning retention by helping provide new-
   ness, sensory stimulation, emotional tone, personal satisfaction.
8. Audiovisuals add useful variety.

Types of Audiovisuals for Youth Work. One of the remarkable things
about audiovisuals is that it is difficult to limit them to any specific age-
group. While object lessons, for example, are usually associated with
children's work, they can occasionally provide effective communication
for youth. The same is true of such materials as pictures, models, and
puppets. Actually, the creative youth worker can adapt almost any audiovisual for use with young people. However, there are some broad categories that will help suggest materials to use:

1. *Projected visuals.* These include films, filmstrips, slides, transparencies
   for overhead projectors, and possibly videotapes. Besides the normal
   use of presenting material, projection equipment also offers possibilities for *youth-led* projects.
2. *Nonprojected visuals.* In this category is the whole range of pictures,
   photographs, charts, maps, and what are sometimes categorized as
   graphics. Again, this listing offers opportunity for both visual presentation of material and creative involvement on the part of young people. Here is a wide field for youth photographers and artists; and
   visual expression in many forms and from a variety of perspectives.
3. *Audio materials.* The focus here is on the cassette tape recorder. Besides its use with professionally prepared materials, the tape recorder
   allows for great creativity in youth work. It can be used for interviews,
   taping special events, providing music and special sound effects, and a
   variety of other teaching and training opportunities.

While these categories touch the major part of the audiovisual field,
various other materials such as objects and puppets should also be included.

PRINCIPLES FOR PROPER USE OF AUDIOVISUALS

1. Make the audiovisual work for the group. This means that the leader
   must know what he wants the audiovisual to accomplish in the lesson
   or program.
2. Preview materials to be used. Taking time to preview such materials
   as films and tape recordings enables the leader to use the material accurately and to best advantage. It also guards against being embarrassed by unexpected material.

3. Check out equipment involved. This can mean, for example, having chalk for chalkboard use or making certain there is a screen for a slide presentation.
4. In materials such as films, plan the introduction and follow-up to fit best into the overall program. This may mean asking discussion questions or appointing observation teams.
5. Get young people involved in the audiovisual use. Take advantage of the opportunities for them to plan, develop, draw, program, and participate in the full range of audiovisual experience.
6. Continue to develop the ability to use audiovisuals effectively. Audiovisuals can do much to enhance one's ministry with youth. It is well worth the time and effort to become adept in their use. For example, here are some simple suggestions for material presentation and display:
   a. When drawing or printing before the class, do it quickly, in time with verbal commentary. Prepare complicated layouts and large amounts of material in advance. Be sure that what is done can be seen and is legible.
   b. When displaying materials simultaneously with verbal commentary, plan for simplicity, clarity, good lighting. Avoid clutter and confusion. Display the material at proper eye level. Keep printed material for explanation short, simple, uniform.

In working with audiovisuals the youth worker will find these books helpful: *Audiovisual Media in Christian Education,* by Gene A. Getz (Moody, 1972) and *Multimedia Handbook for the Church,* by Ron Wilson (David C. Cook, 1975).

Rooms and Equipment for Youth Work

The teaching environment is an important factor in Christian education. The rooms we meet in and the atmosphere they provide can either help or hinder the effectiveness of our youth ministry. Winston Churchill said, "We shape our buildings and then our buildings shape us."

Attractive facilities for teaching, worship, fellowship, and recreation on the youth level do much to emphasize the church's interest and concern for its young people. For some churches this may mean separate chapels, lounges, and possibly gymnasiums. How much of this is done depends on the philosophy and budget of the individual church. However, every church needs an awareness of the importance of adequate facilities (not necessarily luxurious!) to attract and minister to young people. Some practical suggestions follow.

Plans for rooms and equipment must take into account the need for pleasant surroundings and comfort. We cannot minimize the impact of the physical on the senses and through the senses on our mental and emotional states. Untidiness, disrepair, and violations of good decor can produce a distaste—perhaps indiscernible, but nonetheless real—which results in apathy or disorderly conduct. It may also reflect on spiritual witness as young people evaluate church standards.

Physical comfort can also contribute to learning by eliminating distractions which interfere with concentration: heat, cold, stale air, cramped positions, crowded conditions, inability to see or hear adequately, and competing noise. Efforts to provide correct temperature and humidity, adequate ventilation, proper lighting, comfortable seating, and a degree of soundproofing are well worth the work in the rewards of increased learning.

Plans for rooms and equipment must take into account the need for utility and flexibility. To plan well, some very practical questions must be considered. Who will use the rooms and for what purposes? What will be the largest group and the smallest group to use the room? How much space should be allotted to each person? What various functions will the room need to serve? Will chairs with desk arms be needed or will folding chairs be better? How many electrical outlets will be needed— and where? How much area should be window space—for ventilation, for spaciousness, for utilization of outdoor beauty? What storage cabinets, shelves, closets will be necessary? What space will be needed for displays and activity—bulletin boards, chalkboards, tables? Which rooms will be used for audiovisuals? Where should coats be hung? Where should lavatories, youth library, and service facilities for refreshments be located? The aim in all this planning should be to gain maximum service from available space.

A well-proportioned room can have a three-to-two ratio of length to width. Rooms should be ample, but not vast, producing neither a sense of overcrowding nor lostness. Young people need between fifteen and eighteen square feet of floor space per person. A recommended class size for junior high groups is ten to fifteen pupils and for high school groups, fifteen to twenty. Equipment should include the following items:

1. Adult-size chairs. Desk-arm chairs are preferred, though some folding chairs should be available. Chairs should be movable; they should be in rows for some occasions, in circles or semicircles for discussion and study, and in smaller circles for buzz groups.

2. Tables, ten to twelve inches higher than chairs. Folding, rectangular tables which are easily moved and stored are especially practical.

3. Chalkboards, preferably moveable and of eye-easy green with yellow chalk.
4. Display boards and materials, such as flannelgraph boards, magnetic boards, large flip-charts, prepared charts, tack boards—either portable or permanent wall type.
5. Easels to hold display boards and materials.
6. Other audiovisual equipment and materials such as projection equipment, maps, pictures.
7. Recreational equipment.
8. Divider screens to section off small groups.

Planning for economy and utility also means planning for adaptability. Rooms and equipment should be planned to serve a full week program, with space adaptable for multipurpose use. Thus teen clubs on a week-night may meet in the same rooms used for instruction on Sunday. The adaptability principle takes into account also the need for modifying and enlarging for growth.

Planning for rooms and equipment offers opportunity for ingenuity. Sometimes minor adjustments make for major improvements. Paint and draperies can create a cheerful, relaxed atmosphere. Convenient coat-racks can eliminate disorder and disturbance. Portable furnishings such as movable or foldaway worship units, a library on wheels, rolling storage units for folding chairs and tables, and cabinets on casters have the advantage of being movable to whatever room or part of the room they are needed or of being removed entirely for storage. In fact, with ingenuity in planning floor and wall space, one room might provide a movable lounge, sliding-door library, cabinet kitchenette, behind-doors worship-center unit, and recreational space. With adequate storage space, such a room could provide for a wide range of exciting youth activities!

A Basic Guide to Youth Materials

This section is designed to be a practical introduction to resources for working with youth. It suggests categories, sources, and address listings to guide youth workers in selecting materials.

There are essentially two types of youth material sources. There are youth material publishers, such as Scripture Press, who offer a wide variety of printed helps. Then there are youth organizations, such as Youth For Christ International, who maintain youth ministries, of which printed materials are a part.

Normally, resources from publishers can also be obtained through local Christian bookstores, while materials from youth organizations are often handled directly. Included at the end of this chapter is a basic listing of twenty sources along with a listing of film suppliers. Beyond these sources there are, of course, the distinctly denominational suppliers for groups with denominational affiliation or contact.

Youth materials can be placed in several major categories on the basis of their use. These include materials: (1) for Sunday school, (2) for Sunday evening youth meetings, (3) for weekday club work, (4) for leadership/discipleship emphasis, and (5) for special interests, including periodicals. Listed below are selected sources and examples of materials available, grouped in the five categories just mentioned.

MATERIALS FOR SUNDAY SCHOOL

The following are major independent suppliers of Sunday school materials for junior high (young teen) and high school youth:

> David C. Cook Publishing Company (Elgin, Ill.) .
> Gospel Light Publications (Glendale, Calif.) .
> Scripture Press Publications (Wheaton, Ill.) .
> Standard Publishing Company (Cincinnati, Ohio) .
> Urban Ministries (Chicago, Ill.) with materials specifically
>   for blacks.

Each of these publishers lists a variety of student study materials, audio-visual helps, and teacher materials. The advantage of using the materials of a Sunday school publisher is the provision for planned, organized study and materials that can usually be related to a total Sunday school curriculum.

A continuing development in youth curricula is the use of paperback book/magazine style format for lesson material. Usually the material is presented in contemporary youth style and artwork. For example, twelve lessons for youth on the book of James are published by Gospel Light as a paperback, *Will the Real Phony Please Stand Up,* by Ethel Barrett.

While the Sunday school publishers' materials are basically geared to a Sunday school context, much of the material is also adaptable for use in weekday Bible studies.

MATERIALS FOR SUNDAY EVENING YOUTH MEETINGS

Baptist Publications (Denver, Colo.) . IN/Time and HI/Time quarterly program packets are published, along with advisors' guides. Also included are four-program Theme Paks with micro-books.

David C. Cook Publishing Company (Elgin, Ill.) . Program books for junior highs and senior highs include introductory material and program ideas and plans for each Sunday of the year. Also included are teen-time topic packets, with ideas for four or five meetings in each packet.

Scripture Press Publications (Wheaton, Ill.). Offers a broad range of youth program materials, known as high school and young teen "selectives." These are unit studies of usually four programs each on a wide variety of topics such as victorious Christian living, Bible study methods, developing leadership skills, devotional life, teen-parent relations, dating and marriage, witnessing, and worship. Sponsors' guides are also available for each topic. Also helpful for leaders in working with young people are the leaders' resource books.

Standard Publishing Company (Cincinnati, Ohio). A variety of program books for youth are published.

Success with Youth (Tempe, Ariz.). Provides basic youth program materials for junior high (Alpha Teens) and high school (Omega) youth. These include materials from publicity posters to achievement awards. New programming resources are published three times yearly for the participating groups. Sponsors' helps are included.

Youth For Christ International (Wheaton, Ill.). Campus Life Club materials (in the club and directors' manuals) provide a variety of program suggestions and ideas. The YFC *Symposium on Youth* manual is an excellent source for both youth worker resource and youth program materials. It was developed as part of the YFC teaching symposium for parents and youth leaders, and offers a wide range of youth work helps.

MATERIAL FOR WEEKDAY CLUBS

Material for weekday clubs is represented by three national club organizations. These materials are normally related to the club programs.[2]

Awana Youth Association (Rolling Meadows, Ill.). The Awana coed Shipmate Program provides extensive Bible study and activity program resources in loose-leaf manual form, such as the Shipmates Activity Planning Guide.

Christian Service Brigade (Wheaton, Ill.). This organization provides program manuals for members and program resources for leaders.

Pioneer Girls (Wheaton, Ill.). This organization provides numerous materials for working with girls in a club program.

Each of these three organizations has leadership training resource materials available.

2. For more on these organizations and their materials see chapter 20, "Weekday Clubs."

MATERIALS FOR LEADERSHIP/DISCIPLESHIP TRAINING

The materials in this section have potential use in the program represented by each of the three previous categories, as well as in programs that are supplementary to or distinctive from them. Thus some churches might have teen discipleship classes apart from their regular youth-group programs while others include discipleship emphasis in the regular youth meetings.

InterVarsity Press (Downers Grove, Ill.). Inductive Bible study guides especially designed for college level are useable also by high school youth who are ready for more solid study.

The Navigators (Colorado Springs, Colo.). They publish a nine-booklet series on Christian living (44 lessons) designed to develop personal Bible study. They also produce a three-unit topical memory system with helpful guidebooks.

SPECIAL MATERIALS

Back to the Bible Broadcast (Lincoln, Neb.). Booklets and individual study courses can be used by a group wanting to place inexpensive and attractive booklets in members' hands. Also available are several correspondence courses for youth.

Bible Club Movement (Upper Darby, Pa.). *Steps to Maturity* is a solid three-year Bible study course for young people, providing an extensive youth-oriented apologetic for Christian faith and life. Illustrated manuals are available for students and teachers.

Word of Life Clubs (Schroon Lake, N.Y.). Word of Life provides a doctrinal series of Bible studies for youth. The *This I Believe* series has forty-five lessons and includes a leader's manual.

Youth For Christ International (Wheaton, Ill.). *The Way* is an illustrated, widely used edition of *The Living Bible* developed specifically for young people by Youth For Christ International.

The following periodicals are recommended for teens: *Campus Life* (Youth For Christ International), with contemporary approach in content and style; *Venture* (Christian Service Brigade), with articles and information for the older boy; *Young Ambassador* (Back to the Bible Broadcast), with materials especially suitable for junior highs.

SELECTED SOURCES OF YOUTH MATERIALS

Youth Organizations

Awana Youth Association, 3215 Algonquin Road, Rolling Meadows, Ill. 60008.

Bible Club Movement, 237 Fairfield Avenue, Upper Darby, Penn. 19082.

Campus Crusade for Christ International, Arrowhead Springs, San Bernardino, Calif. 92414.

Christian Service Brigade, Box 150, Wheaton, Ill. 60187.

The Navigators, P.O. Box 1659, Colorado Springs, Colo. 80901.

Pioneer Girls, Box 788, Wheaton, Ill. 60187.

Word of Life Clubs, Schroon Lake, New York 12870.

Young Life, 720 West Monument Street, Colorado Springs, Colo. 80901.

Youth For Christ International, Box 419, Wheaton, Ill. 60187.

Publishers

Back to the Bible Broadcast, Box 82808 Lincoln, Nebr. 68501.

Baptist Publications, 12100 West Sixth Avenue, P.O. Box 15337, Denver, Colo. 80215.

David C. Cook Publishing Company, 850 North Grove Avenue, Elgin, Ill. 60120.

Gospel Light Publications, Inc., 110 West Broadway, Glendale, Calif. 91204.

Harvest Publications, 1233 Central Street, Evanston, Ill. 60201.

InterVarsity Press, Box F, Downers Grove, Ill. 60515.

Judson Press, Valley Forge, Pa. 19481.

Moody Press, 820 North LaSalle Street, Chicago, Ill. 60610.

Scripture Press Publications, Inc., 1825 College Avenue, Wheaton, Ill. 60187.

Standard Publishing Company, 8121 Hamilton Avenue, Cincinnati, Ohio 45231.

Success with Youth, P.O. Box 27028, Tempe, Arizona 85282.

Urban Ministries, Inc., 9917 South Green Street, Chicago, Ill. 60643.

Youth Specialties, 861 Sixth Avenue, San Diego, Calif. 92101.

SELECTED SOURCES OF FILMS FOR YOUTH

Broadman Films, 127 Ninth Avenue North, Nashville, Tenn. 37234.

Cathedral Films, 2921 West Alameda Avenue, Burbank, Calif. 91501.

Concordia Films, 3558 South Jefferson, St. Louis, Mo. 63118.

Family Films, 14622 Lanark Street, Van Nuys, Calif. 91402.

Gospel Films, Box 455, Muskegon, Mich. 49443.

Guidance Associates, Box 5, Pleasantville, N.Y. 10570.

Johnson-Nyquist Productions, 18410 Eddy Street, Northridge, Calif. 91324

Ken Anderson Films, Box 618, Winona Lake, Ind. 46590.

Moody Institute of Science Films, 12000 E. Washington Blvd., Whittier, Calif. 90606.

Paulist Productions, P.O. Box 1057, Pacific Palisades, Calif. 90272.

Teleketics, 1229 South Santee Street, Los Angeles, Calif. 90015.

Youth For Christ International, "Media Guide for Ministry and Training" in the *Symposium on Youth* manual.

FOR FURTHER READING

Brown, James W.; Lewis, Richard B.; Harcleroad, Fred F. *AV Instruction: Media and Methods.* New York: McGraw-Hill, 1973.

Dale, Edgar. *Audio-Visual Methods in Teaching.* New York: Dryden, 1969.

Getz, Gene A. *Audio-visual Media in Christian Education.* Chicago: Moody, 1972.

McMichael, Betty. *The Library and Resource Center in Christian Education.* Chicago: Moody, 1977.

Wilson, Ron. *Multimedia Handbook for the Church.* Elgin, Ill.: David C. Cook, 1975.

30

Counseling Adolescents

Gary R. Collins

To SOME PEOPLE, counseling conjures up images of men with long beards and foreign accents analyzing disturbed patients who sprawl out on a couch. To others, counseling implies the power to ask personal questions, to dispense free adivce, to change people's lives, to quote condemning Bible verses and sometimes to bask in the glory of being a problem-solver. Overdrawn as these pictures may be, they point to a confusion in many minds concerning what counseling really is.

Stated simply, counseling involves a helping relationship between at least two people. One of these people, known as the counselor, or helper, seeks to encourage, guide, or in other ways assist another person to deal more effectively with the problems of life. In essence, counseling involves the giving of friendship, but there is something more. Unlike casual friend-to-friend relationships, counseling occurs when one person is in need of help but the other is not. In counseling there is a minimum of casual chit-chat and a more intensive discussion of the counselee's problem or needs.

For Christians, the ultimate goal in counseling is to see counselees become maturing disciples of Jesus Christ who are able to cope effectively with the problems of daily living. A number of sub-goals in counseling relate to enabling counselors to move counselees to this end. These include changing the counselee's attitudes, behavior or values; teaching new skills; helping the counselee to express emotions or confess sins; giving support and encouragement; guiding as decisions are made; helping the counselee to understand himself or herself; and equipping the counselee to mobilize his or her resources in times of crisis or special need.

It should not be assumed that counseling adolescents differs in any significant way from other kinds of counseling. The problems of adolescents

---

GARY R. COLLINS, Ph.D., is Professor of Pastoral Counseling and Psychology, Trinity Evangelical Divinity School, Deerfield, Illinois.

are unique, of course, but the counseling of young people is largely the same as any other type of helping. According to research reports, the basic element in all counseling is to build a close relationship. That's not all there is, of course, but once a counselor builds a relationship with an individual or group, he is well on the road to becoming an effective people-helper.

Who Makes a Successful Counselor of Adolescents?

Several years ago an important study was published in which professional counselors were compared to nonprofessionals.[1] The results of this research were startling since they demonstrated that the nonprofessionals could do as well at counseling or better than the so-called experts. The difference between a competent and incompetent counselor, it was discovered, had nothing to do with such things as years of training, age and sex of the helper, or preference for some one counseling theory. The effective counselors were those whose lives were characterized by a few very basic personal traits. These conclusions, which have been confirmed by subsequent research, have important implications for youth workers who counsel adolescents. The first and most important step in counseling adolescents is for counselors to develop the following characteristics in their lives. These, in turn, will enable them to build effective counseling relationships.

UNDERSTANDING

One cannot hope to help people until he begins to understand their problems, from their point of view. Recently this writer watched one of his students in a practice counseling session. After two or three minutes of listening, the student launched into a long advice-giving speech which didn't help at all because he had not taken the time or effort to see the problem as the counselee saw it. Learning to understand is difficult, especially when older people counsel adolescents. It is hard to appreciate the adolescent's perspective and sometimes adults dismiss teenagers' problems as being of minor importance. It is well to remember, however, that if the counselee sees his life as having a problem, then there *is* a problem whether or not this appears to be so from the perspective of the counselor.

WARMTH

This involves caring for the counselee in spite of his or her actions and personality. It is an attitude which says, "I might not agree with how you act, but I am genuinely concerned about you as a person and want to

1. R. R. Carkhuff, "Differential Functioning of Lay and Professional Helpers," *Journal of Counseling Psychology* 15 (1968): 117-28.

help—without ridiculing, criticizing, or condemning you." Such an attitude is difficult to fake. If one really cares for a person, as Jesus did when He showed compassion, this will shine through. If he doesn't care, this will be communicated as well, and it will hinder his counseling effectiveness.

All of this does not imply that counselors are to overlook sin in the counselee's life. Sin is wrong and must be dealt with, but as Jesus did with the woman taken in adultery, it is possible to love and accept the sinner, without condoning the sin in any way.

GENUINENESS

This involves honesty, "shooting straight" with the counselee, and being oneself. Theres is no place in counseling for phoniness or for taking a "holier-than-thou" stance. The counselor's task is to speak the truth as he sees it, but to speak in love and gentleness.

Several years ago, a well-known psychologist named Gordon Allport wrote that the greatest therapeutic agent of all is love.[2] Love, he wrote, is something that professional counselors do not know much about but it is something which exists as the very basis of Christianity. In many respects, the understanding, warmth, and genuineness that are so important in counseling, are actually different aspects of the love Christ gives to His followers. If one really wants to counsel adolescents, it is important that he love them—even when they are unlovely or unappreciative of his love.

WHAT DOES A SUCCESSFUL COUNSELOR DO?

Most counselors, at some time, have longed for a good "cookbook"—a tested collection of recipes for dealing with each problem that comes along. Some people have even tried to write counselor cookbooks but such efforts invariably fail because every counselee is unique. It is very helpful to have an understanding of specific adolescent problems—that is partially the purpose of this book—but when counseling, it is good to remember that each adolescent must be dealt with in a different way.

There are some general guidelines, however, about what to do in counseling. Research and the conclusions of experienced counselors have uncovered a number of helping skills which are worth using with all counselees, regardless of the nature of their problems.

LISTENING

This, as every counselor soon learns, is basic to the counseling process,

2. Gordon W. Allport, *The Individual and His Religion* (New York: Macmillan, 1950), pp. 90-93.

but keeping his mouth shut is very difficult! It is much easier to tell people what they should do, and at times all counselors slip into the dangerous habit of preaching at their counselees or giving answers to questions they are not asking. To give genuine help, counselors must give undivided attention to the counselee, listen patiently to what is said both verbally and through his or her actions and mannerisms, ask questions sparingly, and make every effort to understand. Often during the course of talking, the counselee will find his or her own answers and will discover that a concerned listener was the only thing needed to solve a problem.

RESPONDING

It should not be assumed, of course, that the counselor never says anything. He can make a variety of helpful responses which clarify issues, help the counselee see something in a new light, and move the counseling to a successful conclusion.

Near the beginning of counseling, it is generally agreed that one's responses should communicate understanding. "I see," "I'm with you," "Uh huh," are examples. At times he might wish to ask for clarification ("Can you tell me more about that?" or "What do you mean by the word 'smashed'?") and sometimes he might summarize the counselee's feelings ("That must have made you angry") or summarize the content of what has been said ("It sounds like you have trouble getting along with almost everyone at school"). Later, as the counselor gains more understanding, he might offer some interpretations ("Down deep you seem like an angry person" or "I wonder if you really have some serious doubts about your salvation").

In all of this it is important that the adult be alert to the adolescent's feelings, thinking, and behavior. Each of these three can be significant and a part of the person's problem might be overlooked if one focuses attention only on how the counselee feels, what he or she thinks, or how he or she acted in some sinful or other self-defeating way.

STRUCTURING

This refers to the act of telling counselees how the counseling will proceed. In professional counseling it is important to explain such things as what to expect during the sessions, how much counseling will cost, or how to make appointments. In counseling adolescents, this structuring is much less important, but even so, it helps to give some guidelines, especially if the counselee does not know what to expect. "Why don't we discuss your concerns for an hour or so over a coke," one might say, "then we can decide if we want to talk more later." This lets the counselee know how the adult plans to operate and can quickly clear up any misconceptions that he or she might have.

CONFRONTING

This word sometimes gives the idea of a counselor "reading the riot act" to the counselee and telling him to "shape up." Such a technique only angers the counselee and is rarely very helpful.

It is more realistic to think of confrontation as the counselor's pointing out discrepancies in the counselee's life. The counselor might point out sin ("You are a Christian but look what you are doing"), inconsistencies ("You say you want to get good grades but you don't study," "Have you noticed that you tell people how much you care, but in practice you never have time for others?") or value discrepancies ("I've noticed that you seem to want to be a good Christian, but you run around with a rather rebellious bunch of kids").

Confronting is best done after a good relationship has been built. At times it is helpful to use the Scriptures to point the counselee to his or her sinfulness and to show how one can change. Confrontation, with or without the Scriptures, should be done in a spirit of love, followed by a discussion of how the counselee sees the situation and how he or she might change. It is not very helpful to hit people with Bible verses, tell them to change, and then beat a hasty retreat before they have opportunity to respond. That's a cowardly way to confront.

SELF-DISCLOSURE

At times the counselor must be honest enough to reveal that he or she has problems too. Open self-disclosure is a risky thing, especially for youth leaders, but to share some of their own struggles (including the failures and victories) can be very beneficial to the counselee. He or she can see that the leader is human too, but that he is growing in maturity and in his relationship with Jesus Christ. Even a quick reading of Paul's epistles shows that Paul did this repeatedly. His own openness must have been an encouragement to his readers and it gave him an opportunity to model what the maturing believer should be like.

TEACHING

In many respects, counseling is a special form of teaching—a highly individualized form of Christian education.

Teaching, of course, occurs in a variey of ways. People are instructed by lectures and by being told what to do, but this is not always an efficient way for learning unless it is followed by practical experience in which the counselee can put the new learning into practice.

More recently, emphasis has been placed on the giving and withholding of rewards or reinforcements in counseling. In that approach, a counselor tends to respond with praise or expressions of interest when a counselee says something of which the counselor approves. Similarly, he ignores, criticizes, or otherwise avoids rewarding things that he does not want to hear. He directs the course of counseling in subtle ways, therefore; but it is difficult always to reinforce desirable behavior and not reinforce behavior or words which are considered undesirable. In counseling adolescents, reinforcement is not as powerful as some writers claim.

More effective as a teaching technique, this writer believes, is modeling. Here the counselor demonstrates what is acceptable behavior and shows how one can successfully cope with the stresses of life. This was one of Paul's major means of teaching ("Be imitators of me," he said in 1 Cor 11:1, NASB) ; Jesus used it, and parents are instructed to do the same (Deut 6:6-7). Clearly this is an important part of counseling adolescents. Words in counseling are very important but here, as in other situations, actions often speak more loudly than words (1 Cor 4:16; 11:1; Phil 4:9; 1 Thess 1:6-7; 2 Thess 3:7, 9).

FOCUSING ON THE IMMEDIATE

"Immediacy" is a term which refers to the counselor's ability to discuss with the counselee exactly what is going on between them as they talk. "I think you're bucking me. I feel frustrated," "I'm not sure you're being really honest," are immediacy responses. These enable the counselee to understand himself or herself better and they make communication easier. It is risky to talk on such an intimate level but it has been found to be very helpful to counselees, and it leads to good counseling progress.

KEEPING CONCRETE

Counseling is most productive if the discussion focuses on specific feelings, ideas, and actions. Assume, for example, that a counselee wants to "get along with people," "grow spiritually," or "be happier." These are legitimate goals, but they are vague and difficult to tackle. It is best, therefore, to deal with more concrete goals. Instead of an ambiguous discussion of "getting along with people," one might ask the counselee to think of one or two specific people with whom he or she has a conflict, and then to think of some practical, tangible things that could be done to relate to these people. Presumably, when the counselee learns to relate well to one or two people, there can be a slow expansion of this learning to others. Whenever possible, it is better to work on specific problems than vague goals.

In the past, several writers have suggested that counseling
low some kind of predetermined phases in order to be succe
danger exists in listing a series of counseling steps, lest the counselor try
to fit his helping into some artificial mold. Nevertheless, there do seem
to be specific, overlapping stages in counseling, each of which is clearly
illustrated in the Bible.[3]

> *Building a relationship* between helper and helpee (John 6:63; 16:7-13;
> 1 John 4:6).

> *Exploring the problems,* trying to clarify issues and determine what has
> been done in the past to tackle the problem (Rom 8:26).

> *Deciding on a course of action.* There may be several possible alterna-
> tives which could be tried one at a time (John 14:26; 1 Cor 2:13).

> *Stimulating action* which helper and helpee evaluate together. When
> something does not work, they should try again (John 16:13; Acts 10:
> 19-20; 16:6).

> *Terminating the counseling relationship* and encouraging the helpee to
> apply what he has learned as he launches out on his own (Rom 8:14).

THE WHEN AND WHERE OF SUCCESSFUL ADOLESCENT COUNSELING

Many years ago the medical profession recognized that the best way to
treat disease is to prevent it before it starts. This has now become a widely
accepted conclusion among counselors. Helping young people with their
problems is an important part of their work, but of equal importance is
the anticipation and prevention of teenage problems.

While using different terminology, some of the other chapters in this
book focus on the prevention of problems. When adults train youth in
personal Bible study, or prepare them for marriage, or give them vocational counseling, they are helping youth avoid problems which might
otherwise develop.

Prevention has two parts. First, there is the avoiding of a problem altogether and second, there is the stopping of a slowly developing problem
before it gets worse. A youth retreat in which the leader discusses dating,
for example, might help some people to avoid problems that accompany
adolescent overinvolvement with the opposite sex. Others, who are already involved heavily, might be alerted to the dangers so that they can
be helped to change their behavior before more serious dating problems
develop.

All of this suggests that adolescent counseling is not restricted to those

3. Gary R. Collins, *How to Be a People Helper* (Santa Ana, Calif.: Vision House,
1976), p. 52.

occasions when a counselor and a counselee talk over a problem. Counseling in its broadest sense is an ongoing relationship in which youth meetings, Bible studies, retreats, parties, sports events, and every other aspect of the youth program is designed with both the spiritual and psychological maturation and well-being of the young people in mind.

When problems do arise, it is well to remember that counseling need not take place in an office or other formal setting. Sometimes such situations are threatening, especially for a young person who might prefer the informality of a living room or coffee shop. While not very conducive to good counseling skills (and not very orthodox), young people sometimes feel even more comfortable if they can talk while working on a car, shooting baskets, or engaging in some other activity. These can be relationship-building experiences and when rapport and trust have been developed, the counselor often can move to a more formal kind of face-to-face counseling. Sometimes a casual but caring contact earlier pays rich dividends when the young person returns for more in-depth counseling later.

The main thing to remember in these informal counseling situations is the need for confidentiality. It can be relaxing to counsel in a coffee shop, but there also can be numerous interruptions, and it is difficult to discuss personal issues when surrounded by other people. In all counseling, efforts should be made to insure confidentiality; the counselor who wants to have a continuing ministry in this area should learn to keep quiet about his counseling sessions.

Counseling is hard work. It often results in failure, and this can be very discouraging when one has worked long and hard with a person. There are times, however, when improvement is seen, and on rare occasions it comes dramatically. If the adult leader is a committed follower of Jesus Christ, is open to the Holy Spirit's guidance, and is willing to work on developing and improving counseling skills,[4] he will find himself more frequently involved in the exciting experience of being God's instrument through which He touches and changes young lives.

When Jesus gave the Great Commission shortly before His ascent into heaven, He instructed His disciples to make other disciples—by winning people to Christ and teaching them what Christ had taught. One of the teachings of Jesus was the importance of showing compassion. Paul expressed this beautifully when he wrote that believers should rejoice with those who rejoice, weep with those who weep, and bear one another's burdens in a spirit of Christian love (Rom 12:15; Gal 6:2). Counseling, there-

4. The author has developed a self-contained training program for the development of counseling skills in church leaders. For more information on the People Helper program, write Vision House Publishers, 1507 East McFadden Avenue, Santa Ana, California, 92705.

fore, is not a secondary part of the youth leader's ministry. It is a core part of his work, especially when he realizes that the prevention of problems is as important as the treatment. Helping people to anticipate and deal with the difficulties of life, and moving young people beyond their problems and toward spiritual maturity is implied in the Great Commission. It can be one of the most challenging, frustrating, and rewarding aspects of the youth program in the church.

FOR FURTHER READING

Blees, Robert A., and the staff of First Community Church. *Counseling with Teen-Agers.* Englewood Cliffs, N.J.: Prentice-Hall, 1965.

Brammer, Lawrence M. *The Helping Relationship.* Englewood Cliffs, N.J.: Prentice-Hall, 1973.

Clinebell, Howard J., Jr. *Basic Types of Pastoral Counseling.* Nashville: Abingdon, 1966.

Collins, Gary R. *Effective Counseling.* Carol Stream, Ill.: Creation House, 1972.

———. *How to Be a People Helper.* Santa Ana, Calif.: Vision House, 1976.

Crabb, Lawrence. *Basic Principles of Biblical Counseling.* Grand Rapids: Zondervan, 1975.

Drakeford, John B. *The Awesome Power of the Listening Ear.* Waco, Tex.: Word, 1967.

Frellick, Francis I. *Helping Youth in Conflict.* Englewood Cliffs, N.J.: Prentice-Hall, 1965.

Howe, Reuel L. *The Miracle of Dialogue.* New York: Seabury, 1963.

Morris, Paul D. *Love Therapy.* Wheaton: Tyndale, 1974.

Narramore, Clyde M. *Counseling with Youth.* Grand Rapids: Zondervan, 1966.

Patterson, C. H. *Relationship Counseling and Psychotherapy.* New York: Harper & Row, 1974.

Schneiders, Alexander A., ed. *Counseling the Adolescent.* San Francisco: Chandler, 1967.

Skoglund, Elizabeth. *Can I Talk to You?* Glendale, Calif.: Regal, 1977.

———. *Where Do I Go to Buy Happiness?* Downers Grove, Ill.: InterVarsity, 1972.

Ward, Waylon O. *The Bible in Counseling.* Chicago: Moody, 1977.

31

Preparing Youth for Marriage

H. Norman Wright

ONE OF THE SAFEST STATEMENTS that can be made with any degree of certainty today is that the vast majority of young people will marry. How many of them will remain married or discover any degree of happiness is an unanswerable question. Voices of concern are heard from laymen to professional family life educators, from the secular field to the evangelical church. The National Alliance for Family Life survey of 2,500 professional family-life educators revealed the following facts: (1) Ninety-eight percent of them stated there is a definite need for strengthening family life in this nation. (2) When asked the question "Are churches doing an adequate job of promoting and maintaining family life as a contemporary concept?" 66 percent said no. (3) Another question which relates to this chapter was, "Do you feel that young people are receiving adequate preparation for marriage from their parents?" Only 3 percent said definitely yes whereas 93 percent said no.[1] If parents are not doing the job, who is? In most cases churches have made just token ventures into this field, although it is gratifying to see some of the strides which are currently being made. Most Christian colleges do not have a required course in family life or marriage preparation and numerous Christian schools do not even have such an elective course in their curriculum.

Youthful marriages are of deepening concern, because the younger the ages of the couples the greater is the possibility of the bride being pregnant and the higher is the risk of this union ending in divorce. Several states have acted to curtail youthful marriages and also to provide some preparation and guidance. In California, for example, a person under the age of eighteen must have not only parental permission in order to marry but also a court order. Usually the court order carries with it the stipula-

1. National Alliance for Family Life survey, 1972.

H. NORMAN WRIGHT, M.R.E., M.A., is Associate Professor of Psychology, Biola College, La Mirada, California.

tion of premarital counseling. Some judges are also flatly refusing to grant court orders to couples under fifteen.

The church has one of the most advantageous positions for marriage preparation of any group. Youth, parents, and, in fact, the entire family can be educated by the church for better marriage preparation. A total marriage preparation program must include instruction for parents of children and youth of all ages and direct teaching to the youth within the church. Herbert Otto has stated that those in the best position to do marriage enrichment are churches and ministers.[2] If this is true for marriage enrichment, it is equally true for marriage preparation.

The proper place for marriage preparation is the home. Youth need a model of a healthy Christian marriage with healthy patterns of communication, problem-solving skills, creative resolving of disagreements, and demonstration of love and appropriate male-female behavior.

However, because many homes will not be changed and because many youth come from non-Christian homes, churches must fill the gap where families are inadequate.

QUESTIONS YOUTH ASK ABOUT DATING AND MARRIAGE

Young people face numerous questions about marriage: Who is the right partner for me and how will I know? How can I be sure that it will work out? What if I don't find someone before I get out of college?

Unfortunately, a person's level of insecurity or self-image strongly influences his dating pattern and behavior and his choice of a future mate. Many young people seek to bolster their low self-image by dating or marrying indiscriminately, with almost anyone who will date or marry them. The questions that junior high and high school youth are asking about sexuality today are questions that in years past were asked by college-age youth.

Assisting youth in establishing proper dating patterns is an initial step in building standards for mate selection. Dating has marriage as its ultimate purpose. Therefore, certain guidelines must be followed: (a) a Christian young person should not date a non-Christian; (b) a Christian should not date a Christian who is spiritually immature; (c) a Christian teen should not date an emotionally immature person.

QUALITIES ESSENTIAL IN MARRIAGE PARTNERS

Miles has pointed out that experience and extensive sociological research have led to a rather clear picture of qualities in marriage partners

---

2. Herbert Otto, *Marriage and Family Enrichment* (Nashville: Abingdon, 1975).

essential for a successful marriage. These qualities should, he suggests, also be considered in selecting a dating partner:

1. Belief in God
2. Self-confidence, with positive determination to face and work through life's problems
3. Self-discipline and self-control, including reasonable control over bodily appetites, thoughts, temper, and personal relationships.
4. Ambition and purpose, including positive short-range and long-range life goals, and experience in responsible work
5. Willingness to admit mistakes, take responsibility for them, and profit by them
6. Mature ideas about how to handle money and things
7. Love, respect, and appreciation for one's home and family
8. Respect and appreciation of personal and individual rights, dignity, and freedom of others with the ability to look beyond their weaknesses to their strong qualities
9. A sense of humor, including the ability to laugh at oneself
10. A balanced view of sex, being neither ascetic nor hedonistic
11. Contentment and happiness

Miles adds the excellent observation that any young person looking for these qualities in a marriage companion should work diligently to develop these qualities in himself or herself.[3]

Finding a marriage partner is not so much finding the right person as it is becoming the right person. Both individuals can lose in the game of marriage, but it is just as possible for both to win!

FACTORS INFLUENCING MARRIAGE CHOICES

What is involved in the process of selecting a mate? What factors, conscious or unconscious, move people toward one another? Several reasons, apart from "being in love," account for marriage.

Pregnancy is still a reason that couples marry. In fact, about one-fourth of all marriages are consummated when the bride is pregnant. It is also probable that many of these marriages would have never occurred had the woman not been pregnant. Research on these marriages shows a relationship between a premarital pregnancy and unhappiness in marriage.[4] These marriages need not end in divorce nor unhappiness; the forgiveness of Jesus Christ can affect this situation as well as any of the others.

Rebound is another reason for some marriages. After a dating couple

3. Herbert Miles, *The Dating Game* (Grand Rapids: Zondervan, 1975), pp. 56-57.
4. Adapted from David Knox, *Marriage: Who, When, Why* (Englewood Cliffs, N.J.: Prentice Hall, 1975), pp. 136-42.

"break up," one of the partners sometimes soon finds another person to marry. In a sense, this is a frantic attempt to establish desirability in the eyes of the person who terminated the dating relationship. Marriage on the rebound is questionable because the marriage occurs in reference to the previous man or woman and not in reference to the person being married.

Rebellion is another reason some young people marry. If a teen's parents do not approve of their young person's dating partner, that teen may get married anyway in order to demonstrate his control over his own life. Unfortunately, such a young person is then using his marriage partner to get back at his parents.

Some people marry as an attempt to *escape* from an unhappy home environment. Fighting, alcohol, and abuse, are some of the reasons given. This kind of marriage is risky because it often does not include genuine feelings of mutual trust, respect, and mature love.

Loneliness is another motive for marriage. Some cannot bear the thought of remaining alone for the rest of their days, and yet they fail to realize that a person can be married and still feel terribly lonely. Instantaneous intimacy does not occur at the altar but must be developed over months and years of sharing and involvement. This reason may also place a strain on the relationship, because one partner may be saying, "I'm so lonely. Be with me all of the time and make me happy." The problems stemming from this attitude are apparent.

Physical appearance is a factor that possibly influences everyone to one degree or another. Our society is highly influenced by the cult of youth and beauty. Often, standards for physical appearance in the other partner are not so much to satisfy one's needs but simply to gain the approval and admiration of others. Some build their self-concept on their partner's physical attributes.

Social pressure may be a direct or indirect motive, and may come from several sources. Friends, parents, churches, and schools convey the message, "It is normal to be married, and therefore you should 'get with it.' " On some college campuses a malady known as "senior panic" occurs during the final year of college, especially among unmarried women. For some young people, engagement and marriage is a means of gaining status.

Guilt and pity are reasons for some marriages. A person may marry someone out of feeling sorry for his partner's physical defects or illness. However, having a poor lot in life does not guarantee a stable marital relationship.[5]

5. Adapted from J. Richard Udry, *The Social Context of Marriage*, paper ed., (Philadelphia: Lippincott, 1974), pp. 157ff.

Part of the ministry to youth involves helping them become aware of the reasons people choose a marital partner. One needs to choose a marriage partner out of strength and not out of weakness. Helping youth develop a strong self-concept is basic in helping them achieve healthy marital relationships.

SESSIONS ON MARRIAGE PREPARATION

The following three-point outline has been the basis for many marriage preparation sessions for young people and could be adopted for similar programs.

I. A Christian Standard for Sexual Behavior

    A. Adultery and fornication are condemned in Scripture.

        1. Adultery is expressly prohibited in the Ten Commandments (Exod 20:14) and is condemned in many other passages in the Old Testament (e.g., Gen 20:3; Prov 6:32-33; Jer 5:7-8).

        2. Jesus repeated the commandment prohibiting adultery (Mark 10:19) and even added that looking on a woman to lust after her amounts to committing adultery with her in one's heart (Matt 5:27-28). He condemned both adultery and fornication (Mark 7:20-23; also see Mark 10:11-12).

        3. One of the few "essentials" that the apostles at the Jerusalem Council felt necessary to mention in their letter to the Antioch Christians was that they abstain from fornication (Acts 15:28-29).

        4. Paul speaks out strongly against sex outside of marriage in many of his letters. For example:

        a. 1 Corinthians 6:9-20 (NASB). Paul warns that those who continue to practice fornication or adultery "shall not inherit the kingdom of God" (v. 9). He adds that our bodies are "not for immorality, but for the Lord" (v. 13). In fact, believers' bodies are "members of Christ" (v. 15), and "temples of the Holy Spirit" who indwells them (v. 19). Accordingly, they are to glorify God in their bodies (v. 20) by fleeing immorality (v. 18).

        b. Galatians 5:19-21 (NASB). Sexual immorality, impurity, sensuality, and carousing are all included in Paul's list of the "deeds of the flesh," the doers of which will not inherit the kingdom of God. Christians are to display the fruit of the Holy Spirit, which includes love, patience, goodness, and self-control (vv. 22-23).

c. Ephesians 5:3-12 (NASB). Paul urges the Ephesian Christians not to let sexual sins of immorality or impurity "even be named" among them (v. 3). Moreover, they were told not to participate in the "deeds of darkness," for the light will expose and reprove them (v. 13). See also Romans 13:9; 1 Corinthians 5:9-11; 10:8; 2 Corinthians 12:21; Colossians 3:5-7; 1 Thessalonians 4:3-7; 2 Timothy 2:22.

5. Other New Testament authors were equally emphatic in their condemnation of sex outside of marriage. See Hebrews 13:4; James 2:11; 2 Peter 2:9-16; Jude 7; and Revelation 2:20-22; 9:21.

B. An example of a biblical figure who fled from sexual immorality is Joseph (Gen 39:7-12, NASB). His master's wife asked him repeatedly, day after day, to lie with her, but Joseph refused each time: "How then could I do this great evil, and sin against God?" (v. 9). One day when he was doing his work around the house, she caught him by his garment and asked him again. Understanding the seriousness of the temptation, Joseph "left his garment in her hand and fled, and went outside" (v. 12).

II. Benefits of Waiting until Marriage

A. *No guilt.* God's design for sex is that it be a part of marriage (Heb 13:4). Not waiting for marriage creates guilt that hampers one's relationships with Him, with one's partner, and with many others.

B. *No fear.* Waiting insures that one will never need be afraid—not even to the extent of one fleeting thought—of having to build a marriage on an unexpected pregnancy.

C. *No comparison.* Waiting insures that a spouse will never fall into the devastating trap of comparing his spouse's sexual performance with that of a previous sexual partner.

D. *Spiritual growth.* Positively, waiting will help one subject physical drives to the lordship of Christ, and thereby develop self-control, an important aspect of the fruit of the Holy Spirit. Also, if those marriage partners are later separated temporarily (e.g., for a business trip), then this discipline early in their relationship will give them confidence and trust in each other during that time of separation.

E. *Greater joy.* Waiting insures that there will be something saved for the marriage relationship, for that first night and for the many nights thereafter. The anticipation of the fulfillment of their relationship in sexual union is exciting, and should not be spoiled by a premarital relationship.

III. How Far Shall We Go before Marriage?

    A. A general principle which may be applied to all unmarried partners is this: That which has its natural end in sexual intercourse should be held to your wedding night. This means that the unmarried should not engage in any physical activity which will build up the other person's sexual drives to the point of no return. In the context of a different problem—whether to eat certain types of food—Paul exhorts Christians not to do anything that may cause a brother (or sister) to stumble (Rom 14:13, 21). Thus both persons must be sensitive to each other and must place the other's spiritual health ahead of his own desire for physical fulfillment. When in doubt, don't! For "whatever is not from faith is sin" (Rom 14:23, NASB). Couples should pray alone and together about their physical relationship. If a couple cannot visualize Jesus Christ smiling at the two of them, the Holy Spirit may be urging them to "pull back the reins" a little, for the sake of their love for the Lord and for each other.

    B. These suggestions do not mean that an engaged couple are not to relate to each other physically before marriage through kisses and caresses, but it does mean that the two of them will make Jesus Christ the Lord of their sexual life, and that they should wait till marriage for the physical expressions that lead to complete sexual fulfillment.

PREMARITAL COUNSELING IN A GROUP SETTING

Traditionally, premarital counseling has included just the minister and the couple who plan to be married. In theory and in practice the one-couple setting is perhaps the best method.

However, group premarital counseling can be used to complement the one-couple approach and assist college-age young people in their selection of a future mate. Many engaged couples involved in premarital counseling have commented that they wish they had known earlier in life what they are now learning about marriage.

For the past years several local church college departments have regularly included group premarital counseling in their Sunday morning or evening activities. As a result of these six- to eight-week study programs, attitudes and changes of behavior have been observed. Young people have indicated that some of the mystique and veneer that envelope marriage had been removed, giving them a more objective and knowledgeable approach to the marriage relationship.

The following material outlines a series of resources designed to prepare college-age young people for the marriage relationship. (These can also be used with high school groups.)

Resource 1: The Agree-Disagree Sheet. During the first meeting with the collegians or high school students, give each student a duplicated copy of the following agree-disagree statements. Ask the students to read each statement to themselves, decide whether they agree or disagree with it, and write a check mark in the appropriate blank. After the students have completed the sheets, ask how many agree with the first statement and then how many disagree with the first statement. Proceed accordingly with each of the other sentences. (They are to indicate their agreement or disagreement by raising their hands.) Usually there is a mixture of agreement and disagreement on most of the statements.

Spend the rest of the session in small groups discussing the statements, with each person sharing why he answered as he did. During the next few weeks the group instructor may wish to discuss one, two, or three of the statements at each session and draw some conclusions. He should have studied the pros and cons of each statement and be able to lead the students to sound conclusions.[6]

Agree   Disagree

_____ _____   1. In looking forward to marriage, mutual interests are more important than physical attraction.

_____ _____   2. A person who has some feelings of insecurity would do well to get married because marriage would solve these feelings or problems.

_____ _____   3. Persons who get married should not attempt to change each other. Each spouse should fully accept the other the way he is and trust that he, in return, will be accepted.

_____ _____   4. The statement "opposites attract" has been linked to marriage. Most authorities feel that opposites get along quite well.

_____ _____   5. Sex, in actuality, is the main reason people marry.

_____ _____   6. If you are engaged to someone and some things in that person's life bother you, it is best to try to change him before you marry.

6. For additional information on using the agree-disagree sheet, see H. Norman Wright, *Ways To Help Them Learn: Adults* (Glendale, Calif.: Regal, 1971).

_____ _____ 7. After a Christian couple is engaged, they can have more freedom in their sexual expression with one another than before.

_____ _____ 8. If a person has complete sexual relations with another, he should go ahead and marry that person because of what the Scriptures teach about the sexual relationship.

_____ _____ 9. If a person has any kind of emotional difficulties, he should get these resolved before he gets married.

_____ _____ 10. In some instances it is all right for a Christian to marry a non-Christian.

_____ _____ 11. In God's plan there is a person chosen or selected by Him to be your future wife or husband. (Could there be a second or even a third choice?)

_____ _____ 12. When love hits, you know it.

_____ _____ 13. If you are going to love a person, you will "know" after a short time.

_____ _____ 14. Love is more of a feeling than a relationship.

Resource 2: Discussion Questions. Ask the students to give their views on the following questions:

1. When is a person ready for marriage?
2. Do you think everyone should marry? Why or why not?
3. Why do people marry? Which reasons are sound and which ones are not, and why?

Resource 3: Sentence Completion. The following sentence-completion activity can be used by itself or with the agree-disagree sheet. Ask the students to complete the statements one at a time, writing down the first words that come to their minds. Each of the first seven statements should be completed with as few words as possible.

1. Marriage is ___ ___ ___
2. Men are ___ ___ ___
3. Women are ___ ___ ___
4. Sex is ___ ___ ___
5. My attitudes toward marriage have been shaped by ___ ___ ___
6. In marriage a man is ___ ___ ___
7. In marriage a woman is ___ ___ ___
8. If someone said to me, "Marriage is a contract," I would ___ ___ ___
   (Indicate if you would agree or disagree.)

When everyone has completed the statements, discuss statements 1-7. This usually brings out the varying attitudes people hold toward marriage and sex. Center the discussion around proper and improper attitudes toward marriage and the ways improper attitudes can be changed.

Then discuss statement 8. Most students believe that marriage is a contract. The present writer believes that it is not. Most contracts contain "if" clauses and "escape" clauses. Marriage is *more* than a contract. In this connection read and discuss these two definitions of marriage:

1. "Is marriage a private action of two persons in love, or a public act of two pledging a contract? Neither; it is something other. Very much other! Basically, the Christian view of marriage is not that it is primarily or essentially a binding legal and social contract. The Christian understands marriage as a covenant made under God and in the presence of fellow members of the Christian family. Such a pledge endures, not because of the force of law or the fear of its sanctions, but because an unconditional covenant has been made. A covenant more solemn, more binding, more permanent than any legal contract."[7]
2. "Marriage is a total commitment of the total person for total life."

Resource 4: Film and Discussion. Ask each student to describe in writing the man or woman he would like to marry (i.e., to answer the question, "What qualities are you looking for in a life mate?") Then have them share what they wrote. Show the film, *We do! We do!* (Teleketics Productions, 1227 South Santee Street, Los Angeles, Calif. 90015). This ten-minute film—partly humorous, partly serious—shows the attitudes and influences facing a young couple about to be married. An excellent discussion guide accompanies the film. Allow as much time as possible for discussion. Actually, several sessions could be spent discussing this film and it could be shown more than once. At the end of the session conclude with this statement:

"Earlier we heard many of your descriptions of the person you want to marry. Most of you seem to have high standards for your mate and are looking for someone with specific qualities. My question to you at this point is this: If you met this person, what would there be about you that would make the person fall in love with you? What good and bad qualities do you have? Do you have the same qualities you expect to find in your mate? Perhaps instead of being so concerned about finding the right person, we should work on becoming the right person and the other will work out."

7. David Augsburger, *Cherishable: Love and Marriage* (Scottdale, Pa.: Herald, 1971), p. 16.

Resource 5: Basic Questions about Marriage. Discuss these questions about marriage:

1. What is the difference between love and infatuation? How can you be sure?
2. What kind of love is necessary for marriage?
3. Is it possible to love two people at the same time?
4. In what areas must two people agree before they marry?
5. In light of present low moral standards and the problem of overpopulation, should a Christian couple bring more children into the world?
6. If you could give a young couple only three Scripture verses to guide them in their marriage, what verses would you select?

Resource 6: Tapes. Several tapes are available that provide valuable information for class discussions. One excellent tape is "Christian Principles of Selecting a Mate," by David Seamands (available from Tape Ministries, P. O. Box 3389, Pasadena, Calif. 91100).

OTHER MEANS OF MARRIAGE PREPARATION

In planning ways to impart scriptural concepts about dating and marriage, church leaders may consider these additional activities:

1. A series of sermons by the pastor or other specialists
2. A weekend retreat or seminar on the subject
3. Private counseling sessions
4. Messages and discussions at camp
5. Church library[8]

FOR FURTHER READING

Banowsky, William S. *It's a Playboy World.* Old Tappan, N.J.: Revell, 1969.
Bird, Lewis P., and Reilly, Christopher T. *Learning to Love: A Guide to Sex Education through the Church.* Waco, Tex.: Word, 1971.
Duvall, Evelyn Millis. *Why Wait till Marriage?* New York: Association, 1965.
Feucht, Oscar E., ed. *Helping Families through the Church.* Rev. ed. St. Louis: Concordia, 1971.
———. *Sex and the Church.* St. Louis: Concordia, 1961.
Honsey, Paul G. et al. *Engagement and Marriage.* St. Louis: Concordia, 1959.
Knox, David. *Marriage: Why, When, Why.* Englewood Cliffs, N.J.: Prentice-Hall, 1975.
Mace, David. *Getting Ready for Marriage.* Nashville: Abingdon, 1972.
Miles, Herbert. *The Dating Game.* Grand Rapids: Zondervan, 1975.
———. *Sexual Understanding before Marriage.* Grand Rapids: Zondervan, 1971.
dervan, 1971.

8. See the books listed under "For Further Reading."

Moser, Leslie E., and Moser, Ruth Small. *Guiding Your Son or Daughter toward Successful Marriage*. Grand Rapids: Baker, 1967.

Peale, Norman Vincent. *Sin, Sex, and Self-Control*. New York: Doubleday, 1965.

Ridenour, Fritz. *It All Depends*. Glendale, Calif.: Regal, 1969.

Scanzoni, Letha. *Sex Is a Parent Affair*. Glendale, Calif.: Regal, 1973.

Shedd, Charles. *Letters to Karen: On Keeping Love in Marriage*. Waco, Tex.: Word, 1965.

———. *Letters to Philip: On How to Treat a Woman*. Waco, Tex.: Word, 1968.

———. *Smart Dads I Know*. Kansas City: Sheed & Ward, 1975.

White, John. *Eros Defiled: The Christian and Sexual Sin*. Downers Grove, Ill.: InterVarsity, 1977.

Wright, H. Norman. *Premarital Counseling*. Chicago: Moody, 1977.

32

Vocational Counseling

Kenneth O. Gangel

"FROM SPRINGTIME TO SUMMER" is the title of a chapter in Paul Tournier's book, *The Seasons of Life*. This chapter deals with the stage in life's "seasons" in which a person passes from childhood to adulthood. Tournier, in an amazing attempt to integrate the views of the apostle Paul, Freud, and Jung, concludes, "There is therefore a striking parallel today between the views of science and of faith. Both see man as being drawn through a continuous changing, which, from one step to another, leads him to some destination. This implies meaning to his evolving existence."[1]

Borrowing that imagery for the purposes of this chapter, it might be said that vocational interest on the part of a teenager and the corresponding vocational counseling on the part of his adult leaders are like the buds and twigs which signal the presence of springtime and the imminence of summer. Perhaps no other subject apart from dating and marriage so occupies the mind and conversation of later adolescence as does his life-work and preparation for that work.

Consequently, if Christian leaders would be God's husbandmen, His nurturing gardeners in the vineyard of life, they dare not minimize the importance of vocational guidance in the lives of teenagers both in their homes and churches. An interesting relationship exists between the way psychotherapist Carl Rogers describes the behavior of progress in clients as they proceed from sickness to health and the growth of teenagers in the maturing process of adolescence.

> To be what he truly is, this is the path of life which he appears to value most highly, when he is free to move in any direction. It is not simply an intellectual value choice, but seems to be the best description of the grop-

1. Paul Tournier, *The Seasons of Life* (Richmond, Va.: Knox, 1963), p. 24.

KENNETH O. GANGEL, Ph.D., is President of Miami Christian College, Miami, Florida.

ing, tentative, uncertain behaviors by which he moves exploringly toward what he wants to be.[2]

But work in the garden of growth is not always easy for the caretakers. Watering, fertilizing, aerating the soil, pruning the vines, are hard work. And Christian leaders who would help young people in this crucial area of vocational guidance must be prepared to assist them in at least four areas: building biblical foundations; understanding contemporary vocation; providing adequate preparation; and developing spiritual maturation.

BUILDING BIBLICAL FOUNDATIONS

The term *vocation* appears in the King James Version only in Ephesians 4:1. The Greek word is *klēsis* from the verb *kalein* which means "to call." Actually, therefore, the noun form should be rendered "calling," which is the way it is translated most of the other times it appears. Many Christians have relegated the concept of "calling" to two rather limited and mutually exclusive ideas, neither of which is adequate in dealing with biblical material. One view is to relegate the calling to only Christian service, emphasizing a person's "call to the mission field" or "call to preach." The other view, which is a reversal of the first, is the purely secular understanding of a "calling" as a job, occupation, or profession.

VOCATION AS A THEOLOGICAL CONCEPT

In the Old Testament the concept of calling is both individual and national. Israel is called collectively into a covenant relationship to be God's people in a pagan world. But Abraham is called specifically to participate in God's purposes and plans. In like manner God called Moses, David, the prophets, and others to their specific tasks throughout the centuries of Old Testament history. It is interesting to notice that David's "vocation" would be considered secular today. He was a politician. Isaiah, on the other hand, would be viewed as having a uniquely "religious vocation" as preacher, teacher, and Bible writer. Yet, there is no difference in God's view regarding their calling or their participation in His magnificent plan for Israel and the world.

In the New Testament the concept of calling centered in the word *kalein* and its cognates, which appear almost two hundred times in the gospels and epistles, though a theological thrust appears in only about seventy of these instances. God's truth regarding a Christian understand-

2. Carl R. Rogers, *A Therapist's View of Personal Goals* (Wallingford, Pa.: Pendle Hill, 1960), p. 19.

ing of vocation comes largely through the work of the apostle Paul. Several key passages must be examined in order to understand some of the basic principles.

1. Becoming a Christian does not necessarily involve a change of "vocation." "You were bought at a price; do not become slaves of men. Brothers, each man, as responsible to God, should remain in the situation God called him to" (1 Cor 7:23-24, NIV).

2. Christian vocation is inseparably connected with a "worthy life." "As a prisoner for the Lord, then, I urge you to live a life worthy of the calling you have received. Be completely humble and gentle; be patient, bearing with one another in love. Make every effort to keep the unity of the Spirit through the bond of peace. There is one body and one Spirit—just as you were called to one hope when you were called—one Lord, one faith, one baptism; one God and Father of all, who is over all and through all and in all" (Eph 4:1-6, NIV).

3. Whatever his vocation, a Christian is ultimately "employed" by God Himself. "Whatever you do, work at it with all your heart, as working for the Lord, not for men, since you know that you will receive an inheritance from the Lord as a reward. It is the Lord Christ you are serving. Anyone who does wrong will be repaid for his wrong, and there is no favoritism" (Col 3:23-25, NIV). Therefore, whether banking or the pastorate, carpentry or missions—one must know the will of God regarding one's vocation.

4. God's calling carries with it a distinct and noble purpose declaring His praises in all that one does. "But you are a chosen people, a royal priesthood, a holy nation, a people belonging to God, that you may declare the praises of him who called you out of darkness into his wonderful light. Once you were not a people, but now you are the people of God; once you had not received mercy, but now you have received mercy" (1 Pet 2:9-10, NIV).

So the subject is vast and the Christian leader who would handle this holy task of vocational counseling in an adequate fashion must study the Scriptures carefully to build first his own biblical foundation in order that he may assist young people in their responsibility to approach vocational questions biblically. Barnette has written, "An examination of the doctrine of calling in the Bible is the first step toward a recovery of its true meaning and significance for the Christian today. Christian calling roots in the Old Testament and comes to full fruition in the New."[3]

3. Henlee H. Barnette, *Christian Calling and Vocation* (Grand Rapids: Baker, 1965), p. 16.

GOD'S CALL AND GOD'S GIFTS

Balance is a key word in the Christian life. And among the many things that must be balanced is our understanding of the relationship between spiritual gifts and God's call. Though the subject of spiritual gifts is controversial, most evangelicals conclude that one's ministry in the church (and conceivably also his lifetime employment) is related to a proper understanding of what his spiritual gift (s) may be.

It is not the writer's purpose here to deal with an enumeration of the spiritual gifts, how spiritual gifts differ from abilities, or how one can understand what is spiritual. That has been done in a separate volume.[4]

What *is* important here is that an understanding of one's spiritual gift will not give a Christian young person all the information he needs by which to make an intelligent choice regarding life vocation. For example, even if he ascertains he has the gift of teaching, he would not thereby know whether God wants him to use that gift in a Christian college, on the mission field, in the local church, or in a secular university.

Consequently, the Bible speaks of a *call*. God gives believers spiritual gifts, and He through the Holy Spirit (who is also the instrument of the giving of the gifts) calls them to use those gifts in certain places at certain times. Strommen, who has done extensive research with young people between the ages of fifteen and twenty-three, suggests, "The second major imperative in youth work is to help youth into a feeling of mission, of being sent—of being sent for a purpose and a task. It is to know the sense of purposefulness that grips the person who has responded to God's love."[5]

It has been commonly recognized in counseling Christian young people that choosing a vocation is probably the third most important decision they will ever make, following the decision to trust Jesus Christ as Saviour, and the selection of a life partner. Obviously, these desisions are not necessarily made in that order, but the third-place position in the lineup of importance certainly ranks vocational counseling high among the priority tasks of the person who works with youth. But how does a young person understand God's call for his life? There is, of course, no simple answer. Indeed, this entire chapter is only the beginning of an answer. Nevertheless, an attempt is made here to offer basic principles in answer to that question.

GOD'S POWER IN THE LIVES OF HIS PEOPLE

Christian young people need to take into consideration not only what they want to be (which is important) but also what God wants them to be.

4. Kenneth O. Gangel, *You and Your Spiritual Gifts* (Chicago: Moody, 1975).
5. Merton P. Strommen, *Bridging the Gap* (Minneapolis: Augsburg, 1973), p. 88.

Quite obviously, these would not necessarily have to be in conflict, though in the self-centered life governed by fleshly desires, it is quite possible that they will be. The motto, "God's commands are God's enablings" is more than the words for a plaque. What a frightening thing for a teenager who doubts his own abilities, and struggles with a constant identity crisis, to face the understanding of God's gifts and calling for his life. But what a comforting thing to know that God stands ready to produce as well as predict. The key to success in Christian living is the power of the Holy Spirit producing the righteousness of Christ in believers as they come to a genuinely biblical understanding of Christian "vocation." Lloyd Ahlem speaks encouraging words:

> I know of no other grounds for reworking so completely one's self-identity. It will positively change life. Eventually, personal feelings of inferiority and worthlessness will vanish. Fear and a sense of inadequacy will disappear, for it is virtually impossible to hang on to them when one lives continually with a God-given assumption of righteousness![6]

So in vocational counseling as in everything else in the Christian life, one must begin with biblical foundations. One dare not try to short-circuit the process. Nor should youth workers try to be the Holy Spirit in the lives of their teens. No Christian young person should choose a life-work or a life-style purely on the basis of "adequate information." Instead, his choice should begin with an understanding of how the Spirit makes the Word vibrant and practical in the lives of God's people.

UNDERSTANDING CONTEMPORARY VOCATION

The subject of vocational counseling cannot be discussed intelligently with young people without helping them understand the kind of societal context in which they will be exercising their vocations. Contemporary vocation, for example, in North American culture must cope with the deficient philosophies of materialism, humanism, and nihilism.

Many people among the "haves" and the "have-nots" still live for "things." Augsburger describes this problem well:

> Somehow we must break the endless, vicious circle of overwork. This circle is that: *We want things, and things cost money, and money costs work, and work costs time.* Of course, in the time left over we use the things that cost money. . . . Can we break this circle of slavery?
>
> No! But Christ can if we let Him master our time, money, and work.
>
> Because our problem is a problem of priorities. It's a matter of our basic

---

6. Lloyd H. Ahlem, *Do I Have to Be Me?* (Glendale, Calif.: Regal(1973), p. 157.

values being out of skew, and it takes more than just will power to get one's value system back in line to establish the right priorities.[7]

Others live and work for "mankind," but in a vacuum of values that refuses to recognize God and finds the measure of all things in man himself. Then others have given up; they are the nihilists whose futile concept of society leads them to the contemplation of everything from thievery to suicide.

THE BROADENING CONCEPT OF "MINISTRY"

Quite obviously, the Bible declares that a Christian can and must serve God in any vocation. Indeed, he should not enter a vocation in which he cannot serve God, for that kind of vocation would be sinful in its very essence. But there was a time when evangelicals considered *ministry* to be only pastoral service and missionary work.

But their horizons have been lifted and their understandings lengthened. To be sure, there are specific church-related vocations and these will be discussed later. But is it not possible to serve Christ in the *ministry* of education? Or in the *ministry* of social service? Or in the *ministry* of nursing? Or in the *ministry* of mass communications, such as Christian radio or television? In a helpful though outdated book entitled *Careers for Christian Youth*, a number of authors provide information on how the Christian can serve His Lord in such varied areas as medicine, science, law, government, business, labor unions and labor management, librarianship, and television.[8]

CHURCH-RELATED VOCATIONS

The great twelfth chapter of First Corinthians deals with two major New Testament themes: spiritual gifts, and the unity-in-diversity which can be demonstrated in both the human physical body and the divine spiritual body, the church. Early in the chapter Paul writes, "There are different kinds of spiritual gifts, but the same Spirit. There are different kinds of service, but the same Lord. There are different kinds of working, but the same God works all of them in all men" (1 Cor 12:4-6, NIV).

The last quarter of the twentieth century is experiencing a revival of interest in the local church. There is also a commensurate revival in the ministries of the church in their new-found variety discussed earlier. It has always been possible for a young man to become a pastor, but only in the last few decades have young men specifically trained to become "ministers of education." There may be nothing new about being a missionary,

7. David Augsburger, *Man, Am I Uptight!* (Chicago: Moody, 1970), p. 52.
8. John W. Sigsworth, ed., *Careers for Christian Youth* (Chicago: Moody, 1956).

but only the present era of history has seen missionary pilots who perform fantastic aeronautical feats in the name of Jesus Christ! More young men and women are going to evangelical seminaries now than ever before in the history of the church.

This is a great time in history to counsel young people toward church-related vocations! The opportunities are available, the interest is growing, and the training is better than it has ever been before. Southard wrote about a great Christian leader from the past who speaks to the question of the variety and verification of ministry for the Lord:

> Martin Luther presented the same idea [as that which appears in 1 Corinthians 12] in his *treatise on good works*. He protested against the Roman practice of considering daily work on a lower moral level than working in a convent, singing, playing the organ, saying the Mass, or going to Rome. He wrote, "All works, let their name be what it may, become great only when they flow from faith, the first, greatest, and noblest of works."[9]

Providing Adequate Preparation

Youth leaders cannot adequately counsel young people for a Christian understanding of vocation unless youth are reminded that no vocation can be either personally satisfying or of use to God and man unless one has adequate preparation for it. Donald Gray Barnhouse said, "If I had only three years to serve Christ, I would spend two of them studying."

Readers may differ on what constitutes "adequate" preparation. But all should agree that there are at least four areas in which preparation for vocation takes place: the family, the church, the school, and the college. Certainly, a fifth area, seminary or graduate school, could be discussed, but that is here included as a part of "college."

PREPARATION IN THE FAMILY

Vocational values, like all other values, begin at home. What young boy growing up in a parsonage will "desire the office of an overseer" if he has agonized with his parents through many hours of bitter statements of how difficult and harrowing the pastoral ministry is; if he has seen his father abused by people in several congregations; if he has had to spend most of his childhood and youth alone while his father has been too busy ministering to other people and to other people's children? On the other hand, how encouraging it is to see a child from a missionary home want to return to the same field in which his parents have served four or five terms among a people of different culture and language with whom he grew up!

9. Samuel Southard, *Counseling for Church Vocations* (Nashville: Broadman, 1957), p. 49.

Not only do the values of vocation begin in the home, but also positive modeling and motivation for a proper attitude toward work in general, and Christian work in particular. Harvard educational philosopher Jerome S. Bruner reminds us that "the relative absence of identification figures probably throws the young today more onto each other's resources and creates an isolated peer culture, which in turn cuts down contact with adult model figures the more."[10] Somehow the Christian parent must break through the societal barriers and provide the positive model for a Christian philosophy of vocation as early as possible in the home.

PREPARATION IN THE CHURCH

Building on the values, models, and motivation of the Christian home, the church adds three more components to the preparational process: perspective, programs, and personnel. The *perspective* emerges because the church is a family of families. It is something larger than just mom, dad, and the kids, and even larger than the extended family including close relatives. Here the emerging Christian adolescent is able to talk to Christians who are active in a number of different vocations, yet who put Jesus Christ at the head of their lives. Here he sees people making a living by serving Christ "full-time."

In various programs such as the youth group or the Sunday school class, he is introduced on an even wider basis to an examination of the important biblical foundations for vocation. Through professionally prepared curriculum literature, paperback books from evangelical publishers, and perhaps even uniquely designed "Christian career days," he is confronted regularly with programs designed not only to help him grow in his spiritual life but also consider how that life will be spent.

Of greatest importance is the contact with people. Church-renewal expert Larry Richards writes:

> Growth toward maturity, and the healing that often must take place in persons before they are free to grow, comes essentially through involvement with others in the processes of ministry—particularly through Body relationships and Scripture. The church of the New Testament is a transforming *community*, and transformation is a community transaction, not primarily a transaction between two persons—especially when they are cast as *counselor and counselee*.[11]

10. Jerome S. Bruner, "The Uses of Immaturity" in *Social Change and Human Behavior*, ed. George V. Coelho and Eli A. Rubenstein (Rockville, Md.: National Inst. of Mental Health, 1972), p. 18.
11. Lawrence O. Richards, *Youth Ministry: Its Renewal in the Local Church* (Grand Rapids: Zondervan, 1972), p. 153.

PREPARATION IN THE SCHOOL

After spending those first crucial five years at home, a young child enters twelve years of required socialization called "formal education." The greatest contribution of school in general is to force the child and adolescent into an enormous variety of experiences related to dealing with other people in constantly changing settings. Initially, the individual tends to relive his primary family experiences in any other group to which he belongs. Then, peer group pressure and the influence of professional educators mix with the influence of the home to form a changing attitude toward self and everything outside of self.

One could make an argument here for the Christian school, but that is not the purpose of this chapter. Quite obviously, Christian teachers in a Christian setting will be able to offer a more biblical view of what vocation is and how the Christian prepares for it than will teachers whose total orientation to life is secular or even pagan.

PREPARATION IN THE COLLEGE

Writing as a college educator, this author brings his own prejudices to this subject but must hasten to say that post-secondary education is not essential for adequate service in all vocations. Nevertheless, the viewpoint of James F. Gregory is noteworthy:

> With the goals of life briefly defined, observe next that he who feels himself the steward of his years and potentialities will not stop short of the best preparation possible for life. It may be confidently urged that education *through the college level should be the experience of every Christian capable of such training.* . . . Furthermore, college-trained Christian leadership is imperative if the moral values essential to human survival are to leaven society.[12]

One volume essential to the Christian leader's ministry and vocational counseling with young people is Robert Webber's *How to Choose a Christian College.* He urges young people to "prepare short-term goals in your long range plan" and then tells them, "First, you should decide what kind of schooling you want beyond high school. Then you must determine where you will go to obtain this education."[13] Though written with a Christian liberal arts college bias (Webber teaches at Wheaton College, Wheaton, Ill.), the book is unique in its presentation of the various aspects of decision-making facing the young person contemplating graduation from high school and the entering of college.

12. Cited in John W. Sigsworth, ed., *Careers for Christian Youth* (Chicago: Moody, 1956), pp. 8-9.
13. Robert Webber, *How to Choose a Christian College* (Carol Stream, Ill.: Creation House, 1973), p. 26.

Developing Spiritual Maturation

In the final analysis, vocational counseling has to do with spiritual growth. It is always a process and not an event. One cannot simply sit down with a teenager for fifteen minutes or even two hours and accomplish "vocational counseling." The process is an ongoing alertness to the training programs of home and church which make up almost two decades from the time the child is able to speak until the time he graduates from college. During that time young people can be helped in knowing and applying the following four ingredients of spiritual maturation.

GOD'S WILL FOR THEIR LIVES

In a monograph dealing with the subject of how to help teenagers find God's will for their lives, the author indicated four component factors: (1) the better a Christian knows God's Word the more accurately he can discern God's will; (2) sensitivity to the inner witness of the Holy Spirit is necessary; (3) providential circumstances often reveal God's plan; and (4) God gives us guidance through other people.[14]

GOD'S WILL THROUGH THEIR LIVES

Augsburger identifies seven characteristics of spiritual maturity:

A rich and reflective faith
A dynamic quality concerning the structure of faith
A consistency of moral behavior
The development of ability to use constructively both authority and
  freedom
A faith that is comprehensive, unified, and integrated
An ability to enter into meaningful relationships with other persons
A continual desire for perfection[15]

As adults help lead young people through the maturing process, those leaders want the promise of wisdom to which they so often turn (James 1:5) to be reflected in the teens' lives as well. Growth in wisdom is a part of general spiritual growth.

GOD'S SPIRIT IN THEIR LIVES

The Spirit of God lives within Christian young people just as He does in Christian adults. When it comes to the matter of "God's call" and

14. Kenneth O. Gangel, *Guiding Teens Regarding Their Future*, Christian Education Monographs: Youth Workers Series, no. 7 (Glen Ellyn, Ill.: Scripture Press Ministries, 1971).
15. A. Don Augsburger, *Creating Christian Personality* (Scottdale, Pa.: Herald, 1966), pp. 110-11.

"God's will," there is no substitute for helping them understand how to be sensitive to the Holy Spirit's leading in their lives. The apostle Paul reminds believers, "We have not received the spirit of the world, but the Spirit who is from God, that we may understand what God has freely given us" (1 Cor 2:12, NIV). Soderholm correctly noted that God guides young people through their own minds and that "this avenue of guidance includes three factors: (*a*) the young person's own sanctified sense of doing the right thing, (*b*) his desires, and (*c*) his peace of mind."[16]

It should be clear that youth workers cannot assist a teen in understanding how the Spirit works in his life unless they first understand how He works in their lives. And this includes not only understanding the process, but also being continually sensitive to how He enables them to be the kind of counselors who can help young people toward a Christian understanding of vocation.

GOD'S WORK FOR THEIR LIVES

Soderholm suggests ten helpful questions which can be used with teenagers in leading them to evaluate their own vocational interests:

1. How can I best honor the Lord with my talents and abilities?
2. How can my life be used in causing others to know God and to love Him?
3. How can I be used to teach others the Word of God?
4. Will this occupation bring honor to me or to the Lord?
5. Am I really interested in this occupation?
6. Do my grades show that I have the abilities necessary for this occupation?
7. Will my associations with people in this occupation give me opportunity to reach them for Christ? Or are they more likely to lead me astray?
8. Do I have complete peace about going into this occupation?
9. Can I enter into every aspect of this occupation in such a way that I can do it as unto the Lord?
10. Will the occupation leave me enough time to do direct Christian work—to have personal Bible studies with others, to use my home for the purpose of reaching others for Christ? Or will I become so engrossed in the work or in the advancement that I will forget my ministry to people who need to know God?[17]

It is important to remember that in any aspect of counseling teenagers one must be a genuine communicator. And communication is more than

16. Marjorie E. Soderholm, "Counseling Youth for Their Future" in *Youth and the Church*, ed. Roy G. Irving and Roy B. Zuck (Chicago: Moody, 1968), p. 417.
17. Ibid., pp. 419-20.

just articulation; it is also getting close to young people by listening and making them feel comfortable in the presence of their adult leaders.

It takes time, it takes effort, and there are disappointing moments. But having spent almost twenty years in working with young people in the local church and the Christian college and seminary, this writer can testify that the rewards are frequent and immensely positive. Many pastors, missionaries, Christian teachers, and Christ-centered leaders in dozens of other occupations have been helped to a Christian understanding of biblical vocation because of scores of faithful youth leaders who have given of themselves in ministry to youth.

For Further Reading

Ahlem, Lloyd H. *Do I Have to Be Me?* Glendale, Calif.: Regal, 1973.

Barnette, Henlee H. *Christian Calling and Vocation.* Grand Rapids: Baker, 1965.

Bruner, Jerome S. *Social Change in Human Behavior.* Rockville, Md.: Nat. Inst. of Mental Health, 1972.

Richards, Lawrence O. *Youth Ministry: Its Renewal in the Local Church.* Grand Rapids: Zondervan, 1972.

Sigsworth, John W. *Careers for Christian Youth.* Chicago: Moody, 1956.

Southard, Samuel. *Counseling for Church Vocations.* Nashville: Broadman, 1957.

Strommen, Merton P. *Bridging the Gap.* Minneapolis: Augsburg, 1973.

Tournier, Paul. *The Seasons of Life.* Richmond, Va.: Knox, 1963.

Vocational Guidance Series. Nashville: S. S. Board, Southern Baptist Convention.

Vocational Series. Fort Worth, Tex.: Radio and Television Commission, Southern Baptist Convention.

Webber, Robert. *How to Choose a Christian College.* Carol Stream, Ill.: Creation House, n.d.

33

Working with Parents of Youth

Jay Kesler

THE ROLE OF THE YOUTH WORKER

AFTER TWENTY-FIVE years of working with young people, Youth For Christ International wanted a more precise picture of the American teenager. YFC wanted to know hard facts about his values and about the people in his life who most influence those values. Through an affiliation with the Institute for Research in Human Learning, of Michigan State University, such a study was conducted, employing the most sophisticated research techniques available. The study was essentially a questionnaire survey conducted on a coast-to-coast basis, involving nearly forty thousand subjects and well over one hundred field investigators. The instrument was well refined through extensive field trials and therefore provided a highly accurate representation of modern teen outlook and influence.

Some of the results (many of which are not germane to this book) were surprising, but most of the data were confirmations of "hunches" that had never before been proven.[1] There was a strong confirmation, for instance, of the rather large influence that parents exert on the outlook of their children.

It has always been known that peers had a strong, even predominant influence, but parents showed a surprising strength in the overall picture. Professionals, interestingly enough, exerted significant influence only in their field of training. For example, religious leaders had been most influential in matters of technical religious knowledge but had almost negligible influence on the moral attitude of teens. Peers and parents were more influential than professional youth workers.

1. The data on reliability and validity of the instrument, as well as the technical aspects of the design and research, can be obtained from the Institute for Research in Human Learning, Michigan State University, 202 Ericson Hall, East Lansing, Michigan 48823.

JAY KESLER, D.D., is President of Youth For Christ International, Wheaton, Illinois.

Two conclusions seem obvious:

1. The serious youth worker must recognize that working with youth necessarily means working with adults. He must decide to structure his ministry to reflect the strong influence that parents are exerting on their children. He probably already believes that peer pressure is significant, but he may not have guessed that, regardless of modern social trends, children are still largely the product of their homes.
2. In order to be most effective with youth, the role of the youth worker should not be that of a "religious leader" but that of a caring friend, an adult peer, an interpreter of youth to parents and of parents to youth.

THE LIMITATIONS OF THE MINISTRY

At the outset, the youth worker must realize that the ministry of working with youth carries with it some unavoidable limitations. Every youth worker, prospective and active, would do well to give serious consideration to the following facts.

1. *The fact of his own limited experience.* Since he is more than likely adolescent or post-adolescent himself, much of what he knows about life and about this job of working with teens, he has read in a textbook somewhere. He is the victim of a high theory-practice ratio, which makes him vulnerable to the habit of approaching specific, unique problems with general, often irrelevant material. If he is married and has small children, he begins to see that, for example, if he cannot effectively control his own two-year-old, he may have to think twice about someone else's teenager.

2. *The fact that he has only a limited exposure to the young people he works with.* Young people are like icebergs. A typical youth worker sees only the tip of the iceberg and perhaps only one side of it. Parents, however, see many facets. They are involved with their teen in the problems of education and of social adjustment in and out of the home. They see his moods, his strengths, his weaknesses. Because of normal family intimacies, a parent is often far more beneath the young persons' surface than either of them realize. The youth worker must understand this.

Modern, responsible youth work that emphasizes relational orientation in the use of, say, stress situations as a part of the total program, tends to uncover more facets of the teen than did previous methods. This is good, but a weekend stress-hike and two or three long talks simply cannot reveal what a young person's parents have learned about him over the space of years.

3. *The fact that he will make only a limited contribution.* Obviously, most of the people in the world have grown up without the help of a re-

ligious youth worker, so apparently this function, like most functions, is not indispensable.

Then, too, there are many other youth workers in a teen's life, many other influences on his character and development. The schoolteacher, the guidance counselor, the coach—these are additional people who work at the edge of the family and have their own unique input. The Christian youth worker needs to understand that his will be a fractional contribution.

The point of bringing these considerations to mind is to instill perspective, not pessimism. The wise youth worker will want to strive for achievable, realistic goals. Disappointments will be experienced in this ministry, but some of it can be avoided simply by recognizing these basic limitations. Then, the worker will be better prepared to take on the challenges of youth ministry with an informed confidence.

UNDERSTANDING THE PROBLEMS

The youth worker is problem-oriented. All young people have problems of some sort. Many of them experience problems at home, difficulties with parents.

This is hardly a new or modern problem. It is as old as Romeo and Juliet: two unreasonable parents were more interested in a social feud than in the love affair growing between their children. It is as old as the prodigal son: a young man woke up one morning and decided that the restraints of home had suddenly become intolerable. These stories are timeless; they deal with problems common to all humanity, not just American teenagers.

One of the basic tensions that has always developed within the family structure is the parent's responsibility to impose restraints on the child, and the child's desire to be free of these restraints. Part of the problem is that both parent and child are essentially right.

The child is born into the home completely dependent on his parents. Obviously, an infant cannot live more than a few days without the affection and care of his mother. The parent is responsible, however, to help the child gradually gain independence as he matures physically, emotionally, mentally, and spiritually. Many parents fight against this and many refuse to believe that this is their responsibility. They receive certain emotional and psychological supports from their position of dominance, so that their feeling of self-worth decreases with the independence of the child.

As time passes, tensions build. The rate at which a parent is willing to grant independence is often too slow for the child. At times, a parent is justified in his restraint; sometimes he is not.

THE ADOLESCENCE PHENOMENON

An added twist to the problem is the teenage phenomenon. This period of adolescence is more than a chronological time span. It is also a cultural phenomenon that is relatively modern.

In earlier primitive days, when the demands of a young person were to till the soil or tend sheep, a young person could reach his capacity to be independently productive at fourteen or fifteen years of age. That is why, for instance, the Bible does not refer to "teenage" problems as such. In Bible times there were no such persons as "teens." An individual was either a child or an adult. Many Bible students believe that Mary, the mother of Christ, may have been as young as fifteen or not much older than sixteen when she gave birth to Jesus. (It is intriguing to consider that Mary, the author of the eloquent magnificat in Luke 1:46-55, was about the age of the average high school cheerleader.) This provides a little perspective on the modernity of the problem.

In early times, when a girl reached physical maturity, she married; a boy lived under his father's roof until he was ready to take on a trade and support himself. Even then, he usually followed in his father's footsteps and became a kind of apprentice to him, growing up under his tutelage. The society was simple and homogeneous. Only a few vocational options were open to young men and none to young women. Hence, young people experienced relatively little of the kind of social and economic pressure to "advance" that college students face today. Whereas their culture was characterized by stability and simplicity, our is defined by mobility and complexity.

One's capacity to compete in our technological society probably implies finishing high school and, in many cases, college. This period called "adolescence," the period between puberty and college graduation, is a period of lag, a period of frustration. Graham Blaine calls it "the time of necessary rebellion."[2] It is frustrating because while the adolescent's body is strong and capable of doing a man's work or fulfilling a man's sexual role, society does not allow him to do either. The perceptive adolescent will understand that such things as school athletics and the dating syndrome are partly substitutes—delay activities—for adult labor and family productivity.

Then there is the problem of the adolescent's mind. His parents and his teachers constantly remind him that he knows so much more than they did at his age, but at the same time they remind him, "When I was your age, I was out making a living, supporting myself and sending money

2. Graham B. Blaine, Jr., *Youth and the Hazards of Affluence* (New York: Harper & Row, 1966), p. 6.

home to the folks." The message that comes across is that high school and college youth have about the same status as calisthenics—after a point, the only value of doing pushups is the ability to do more pushups. And so we have the problem of the "professional student" or the college dropout. Both of them have had, perhaps, a little more than average insight into what education is doing and what society ("reality") is doing.

In this time between the young person's physical-mental maturation and his social productivity, his parents and his mentors are trying to discourage many natural, normal commitments and attachments. This is where the tension begins to build. But I think it is important to identify the problem here. The problem is not the parent or the child or the school. The problem is this synthetic phenomenon called "adolescence." It has to be understood and accepted as a fact of modern life. It has to be reckoned with. And the youth worker must take it as one of his roles to be a communicator of these facts to both parents and youth.

OVERCOMING PARENT-TEEN TENSION

This tension between parent and teen is much like playing a fish that has just been hooked. If a person has a very small fish on a line with a fifteen-pound test, there is no problem. He can be arbitrary with the fish; he can lock the reel, lean back, and pull. It's easy. Many parents start out with their children much like that. They are entrusted with this little fish who isn't putting up much of a fight. They learn to be pretty arbitrary. And it works, for a while.

At the outset, child discipline is almost exclusively external. If a baby crawls in the wrong direction, his parents pick him up and point him in the other direction. If the baby picks up a family heirloom, the parents "explain," perhaps with a spank, that it is not to be touched, and the matter is settled. This kind of discipline which is almost entirely on the external level, is an appropriate and effective means of controlling an infant.

But it is neither an appropriate nor an effective means of controlling a teenager. He may still insist on going the wrong direction—he wants to stay out later than his parents want him to stay out; he wants to be with people his parents don't want him to be with. He may insist on picking up the wrong things—he wants to buy things, go places, and do things that his parents feel would be injurious. The problem is, the teenager is a bigger "fish."

Now, the parents can continue to lock the reel and lean back, but in the attempt to pull him up, the teenager may break all the tackle and be gone. On the other hand, a good fisherman can land a thirty-pound fish with a fifteen-pound line if he knows how to work with him. It is another way of talking about permissive or sensitive discipline.

The story of the prodigal son is a good illustration. Parents must realize the possibility that one day in response to harsh, arbitrary discipline on their part, or by just plain rebellion on his part, their boy may wake up to the fact that he does not have to do what he has been told to do. He may suddenly realize that he is quite capable of resisting his father if he tries to interfere with his plans any longer. And so there is a standoff. It is the parents' will against his. They said no, and he says yes. And if he is of legal age, they can do little or nothing to keep him from walking out the door.

After the door slams, the parents have time to reflect on the principle that the effectiveness of arbitrary, external discipline is inversely proportional to the maturity and intelligence (or just plain strength) of the child or teen. Herein lies the beauty of the parable that Jesus told: Many teens will go to a "far country." But no matter how far away that country is, they can be bound to their parents by a cord of love, a cord of such strength and resilience that it can pull an embarrassed, disappointed, and broken child back to a father's open arms.

Apparently the prodigal's father did the right thing. Instead of locking the reel, he let out the line. In losing his boy he saved him. He came back with a better perspective on his father's restrictions. He realized that the rules of the house were much like the rules of God—on the surface they appear arbitrary and oppressive, but in reality, they are designed to protect us from the hog pen of a dissolute life. He came to see that his father's estimation of his maturity was slightly more accurate than his own.

This is the goal of parenthood—to develop independence in the child, the kind of independence that is based on an understanding and respect which makes the young person want to keep coming home, not because he is dependent on the parent and cannot get along without him, but because he respects him and wants to come back to gain what he passed up when he was younger.

The wise youth worker will strive to help parents understand the important principle that there is far more strength in intelligent love than in arbitrary law. And he will appeal to his teenagers to learn to appreciate and respect the role of parents, to understand that, in the great majority of cases, genuine concern for their children is their chief motivation.

WORKING WITH PARENTS AND YOUTH: WEDGE OR BRIDGE?

The youth worker is very often in a strategic place between parents and youth. In that "in-between" position, he can become a wedge or a bridge. He can draw them closer together and help them solve some of their problems, or he can drive them apart and contribute to their problems. Every youth worker should be aware of the following crucial areas.

1. *Begin to build equity with parents.* Working with parents is like putting money in a bank: the investment will give a substantial return. If a youth worker establishes a solid relationship with a teen's parents, then later on, when he needs advice and support for the youth program or help in dealing with their teen, that fund of respect and mutual trust will be there to draw on.

2. *Do not take sides.* A youth worker can demonstrate his concern for the unity of the family by building mature friendships with teens and by showing them his respect for parents.

The wise youth worker holds regular meetings, formal and informal, in which parents can talk freely. Formal meetings have great value in getting all the parents from the youth group together at one time to voice problems and share concerns. It usually becomes evident in these meetings that teens have sought to use the youth worker against their parents. They have learned the old "divide and conquer" trick and one of the most effective counters is this sort of large meeting.

Informal meetings, with a few or even one set of parents, can be invaluable for getting at specific problems that adults are often unwilling to share in larger groups. In addition, the youth worker can benefit from meetings with teens and parents together. The youth worker should observe the teens with their own parents and with the parents of other young people.

3. *Make use of adult models.* The proper use of adult models is essential to the balance and success of a youth worker's program. The job is too big for one person, regardless of how bright he is. Many youth workers may react negatively to this concept, because they tend to think that using adult assistants will cramp their "lone ranger" style with the teens. Well, in the opinion of this writer, that kind of style needs some cramping.

The fact is that young people have a spectrum of needs that no youth worker can meet alone. Adolescents need good examples from peers, examples they can respect and rely on. But they also need good examples of adults. They do not want "examples of adults trying to be like kids. Adulthood is in style for adults. Teens want adults, not competition, for parents and counselors. They want adulthood as something to look forward to."[3] Parents who understand this principle and are willing to sub-

3. Jay Kesler, *Let's Succeed with Our Teenagers* (Elgin, Ill.: David C. Cook, 1973), p. 20.

mit to the rigors of a vital youth program can be invaluable to a well-rounded ministry.

A set of parents working with the youth group can often explain parents to teens better than a youth worker can. A teen might say, for instance, "My folks don't love me. They hassle me if I come in too late." An adult working with the youth group, who has rapport with this young person, can probably interpret his parents' goals and motivations to him better than anyone else. Because he is a parent himself, he can honestly relate the frustrations and problems that parents confront in disciplining teens.

The youth leader needs to work closely with his adult assistants, helping them, for one thing, to understand the young people from the leader's perspective. They may need to learn, for example, about communicating to a group of restless teens.

Many adults tend to confuse deportment with attention. The fact that everyone is sitting in rows and staring at a speaker does not necessarily mean they are listening. By contrast, teens who are lying around on the floor, leaning against the walls, with ho-hum looks on their faces, are sometimes listening very well. A certain level of feedback and jabbering in a room is not necessarily bad. The youth leader must decide what the limits are to be. To some parents, this will be an entirely new thing, and its value may have to be explained to them.

This is another way to remove a wedge that is often driven between parents and their youth by a well-meaning but incompetent youth worker. It involves a lot more work, but in view of long-range benefits, it is well worth it.

4. *Turn a crisis into an opportunity.* One of the best ways to build a bridge between parents and teens is by being available to mediate a family crisis. Suppose, for instance, John's father has overdisciplined him, really overdone it, and John comes to the youth worker with a plan to leave home. Here the youth worker has a choice to make. He could say, "Yes, it looks like he's really done a number on you; you're stuck with a very unreasonable dad." Or he could say, "Well, John, we have a tough situation here; let's see if we can get with your dad and work it out."

The youth worker can then telephone John's father and interpret John to him, telling him how his boy feels about the discipline. And he can try to explain the father to his son, helping him see that even adults make mistakes, but like everyone else they should have a chance to make it right. Hence, out of a crisis situation the youth worker can create a positive learning experience in repentance and forgiveness.

5. *Recognize that parents are different too.* A youth worker knows from experience that every young person is different. Because so many backgrounds and attitudes are reflected in his group, he uses different techniques with each one. Parents are different, too. The effectiveness of a leader's relationships with them will depend on his keeping this in mind.

Parents of non-Christian youth may have fears and suspicions about the youth leader and his work. They may have a stereotyped concept of all religious young people, which pictures the youth worker either a "spacey" guru or a fanatical Jesus freak who is trying to steal their teens and force them to live in a commune. A clear statement of goals—exactly what the church is trying to accomplish with their youth—will help clear the air.

On the other hand, some Christian parents will expect the youth worker to bring the young people around to their conception of what the Christian life is all about. Those parents consider the adult leader with youth a failure if he is not preaching at them, harping about their clothes, their manners, their spiritual lives, and their relations with the opposite sex. Those parents tend to presume the worker to be unusually strict. Again, a statement of goals will establish the church's position and perhaps eliminate some pressure. Then the worker will have a foundation for further discussions with them.

The vast majority of parents, though, will be glad for the help available from youth workers, glad to help accomplish valid, worthy goals with their children.

Then, too, every good youth worker will want to follow certain rules in order to establish good relationships with all parents. For example, he should respect the parents' desire for curfew time for their teens. If a teenager is out late, beyond his normal time for bed, parents resent it, even if the teen has been at a religious meeting.

6. *Affirm, encourage, and support.* Because the present period of history is particularly difficult for parents, what they need most today is affirmation, encouragement, and support. At another point in history they might have needed exhortation to discipline their teens, or reminders to protect their children from any number of social evils. Today, however, many parents are mesmerized by social evils. They are frightened by them, fearing that effective parenting is impossible. Schools have taken the education of their children, churches have taken the Christian education of their teens, and now many parents are abdicating their role altogether by saying, "Let the professionals do it."

This trend must be strongly opposed, and especially by the youth worker because he will be pegged by the teens' parents as merely one more professional who has come on the scene to deal with their youth. The youth worker must be sensitive to this. He must be careful not to undermine respect for parents' opinions nor to usurp parental authority. The principle of using parents in the youth program is a sure way of communicating to the parents and to the teens that adults can contribute to the success of a youth ministry because of their experience, maturity, and foresight.

A worker should never attempt to establish rapport with youth at the expense of parental respect and authority. Apparently, some youth workers have thought that this is justified if in doing so they can communicate some "spiritual truth." That, however, is wrong. No "spiritual truth" is that important; God does not honor that approach. And since parents probably have more to do with inculcating spiritual truths than the youth worker, cooperation with parents is extremely important.

"Honor your father and mother" (Eph 6:2, NASB). "Do not provoke your children to anger" (6:4). These are two biblical principles that cannot be separated. They exist side by side in the mind of God, and the youth worker must see that a great part of his job is to get young people and parents to hear what God is saying and what pertains to them. The youth worker is a bridge; he stands between these verses as a sort of hyphen, attempting to do his part to balance the parent-teen relationship.

The rewards of this kind of ministry are far-reaching and long-lasting. Long after the youth worker has gone to another town or another church, his contribution will continue to bear fruit.

A ministry with young people, then, involves a ministry with adults. The successful youth worker will work competently with both. If anyone should ask who he is and what he is doing, he could summarize his ministry by saying, "I'm a bridge. I look for gaps between the generations and then do my best, with God's help, to span them."

FOR FURTHER READING

Bronfenbrenner, Urie. "The Origins of Alienation." *Scientific American,* August 1974, pp. 53-57, 60.
Dobson, James. *Dare to Discipline.* Wheaton, Ill.: Tyndale, 1970.
———. *Hide or Seek.* Old Tappan, N.J.: Revell, 1971.
Dreikurs, Rudolf. *Children: The Challenge.* New York: Duell, Sloan & Pearce, 1964.
———. *The Challenge of Parenthood.* New York: Hawthorn, 1958.
Gangel, Kenneth O. *The Family First.* Minneapolis: His International Service, 1972.
Ginott, Haim G. *Between Parent and Teenager.* New York: Macmillan, 1969.
———. *Between Parent and Child.* New York: Macmillan, 1965.
Harris, Thomas A. *I'm O.K.—You're O.K.* New York: Harper & Row, 1969.

Kesler, Jay. *Let's Succeed with Our Teenagers.* Elgin, Ill.: David C. Cook, 1973.

MacDonald, Gordon. *The Effective Father.* Wheaton, Ill.: Tyndale, 1977.

McLean, Gordon. *God Help Me—I'm A Parent!* Carol Stream, Ill.: Creation House, 1972.

Myra, Harold. *Is There a Place I Can Scream?* Garden City, N.Y.: Doubleday, 1975.

Narramore, Bruce. *Help—I'm A Parent!* Grand Rapids: Zondervan, 1972.

Narramore, Bruce, and Counts, Bill. *Guilt and Freedom.* Santa Ana, Calif.: Vision House, 1974.

Powell, John. *The Secret of Staying in Love.* Niles, Ill.: Argus, 1974.

——. *Why Am I Afraid to Tell You Who I Am?* Niles, Ill.: Argus, 1969.

Schaeffer, Edith. *What Is a Family?* Old Tappan, N.J.: Revell, 1975.

Wakefield, Norman. *You Can Have a Happier Family.* Glendale, Calif.: Regal, 1977.

White, Burton L. *The First Three Years of Life.* Englewood Cliffs, N.J.: Prentice-Hall, 1975.

Wright, H. Norman. *Communication: Key to Your Marriage.* Glendale, Calif.: Regal, 1974.

Moody Press, a ministry of the Moody Bible Institute, is designed for education, evangelization, and edification. If we may assist you in knowing more about Christ and the Christian life, please write us without obligation: Moody Press, c/o MLM, Chicago, Illinois 60610.